The Ancient Maya of Mexico

Approaches to Anthropological Archaeology
Series Editor: Thomas E. Levy, University of California, San Diego

Editorial Board
Guillermo Algaze, University of California, San Diego
Geoffrey E. Braswell (University of California, San Diego)
Paul S. Goldstein, University of California, San Diego
Joyce Marcus, University of Michigan

This series recognizes the fundamental role that anthropology now plays in archaeology and also integrates the strengths of various research paradigms that characterize archaeology on the world scene today. Some of these different approaches include 'New' or 'Processual' archaeology, 'Post-Processual', evolutionist, cognitive, symbolic, Marxist, and historical archaeologies. Anthropological archaeology accomplishes its goals by taking into account the cultural and, when possible, historical context of the material remains being studied. This involves the development of models concerning the formative role of cognition, symbolism, and ideology in human societies to explain the more material and economic dimensions of human culture that are the natural purview of archaeological data. It also involves an understanding of the cultural ecology of the societies being studied, and of the limitations and opportunities that the environment (both natural and cultural) imposes on the evolution or devolution of human societies. Based on the assumption that cultures never develop in isolation, Anthropological Archaeology takes a regional approach to tackling fundamental issues concerning past cultural evolution anywhere in the world.

Published

Archaeology, Anthropology and Cult: The Sanctuary at Gilat, Israel
Edited by Thomas E. Levy

Connectivity in Antiquity: Globalization as a Long Term Historical Process
Edited by Øystein LaBinaca and Sandra Arnold Scham

Israel's Ethnogenesis: Settlement, Interaction, Expansion and Resistance
Avraham Faust

Axe Age: Acheulian Tool-making from Quarry to Discard
Edited by Naama Goren-Inbar and Gonen Sharon

New Approaches to Old Stones: Recent Studies of Ground Stone Artifacts
Edited by Yorke M. Rowan and Jennie R. Ebeling

Prehistoric Societies on the Northern Frontiers of China: Archaeological Perspectives on Identity Formation and Economic Change during the First Millennium BCE
Gideon Shelach

Dawn of the Metal Age: Technology and Society during the Levantine Chalcolithic
Jonathan M. Golden

Metal, Nomads and Culture Contact: The Middle East and North Africa
Nils Anfinset

Animal Husbandry in Ancient Israel—A Zoo-archaeological Perspective: Herd Management, Economic Strategies and Animal Exploitation
Aharon Sassoon

Ultimate Devotion: The Historical Impact and Archaeological Expression of Intense Religious Movements
Yoav Arbel

Structured Worlds: The Archaeology of Hunter-Gatherer Thought and Action
Edited by Aubrey Cannon

Early Bronze Age Goods Exchange in the Southern Levant: A Marxist Perspective
Ianir Milevski

Agency and Identity in the Ancient Near East: New Paths Forward
Edited by Sharon R. Steadman and Jennifer C. Ross

The Technology of Maya Civilization: Political Economy and Beyond in Lithic Studies
Edited by Zachary X. Hruby, Geoffrey E. Braswell, and Oswaldo Chinchilla Mazariegos

The Ancient Maya of Mexico

Reinterpreting the Past of the Northern Maya Lowlands

Edited by

Geoffrey E. Braswell

Published by Equinox Publishing Ltd

UK: Unit S3, Kelham House, 3 Lancaster Street, Sheffield, S3 8AF
USA: ISD, 70 Enterprise Drive, Bristol, CT 06010

www.equinoxpub.com

First published 2012

© Editorial matter and selection, Geoffrey E. Braswell 2012. Individual contributions, the contributors.

All rights reserved. No part of this publication may be reproduced or transmitted in any form or by any means, electronic or mechanical, including photocopying, recording or any information storage or retrieval system, without prior permission in writing from the publishers.

ISBN: 978-1-908049-31-5 (hardback)

British Library Cataloguing-in-Publication Data
A catalogue record for this book is available from the British Library.

Library of Congress Cataloguing-in-Publication Data
The ancient Maya of Mexico : reinterpreting the past of the Northern Maya lowlands / edited by Geoffrey E. Braswell.
    p. cm. -- (Approaches to anthropological archaeology)
  Includes bibliographical references and index.
  ISBN 978-1-908049-31-5 (hb)
 1. Mayas--Mexico--Yucatán (State)--Antiquities. 2. Mayas--Mexico--Yucatán (State)--Social life and customs. 3. Mayas--Mexico--Yucatán (State)--Politics and government. 4. Social archaeology--Mexico--Yucatán (State) 5. Yucatán (Mexico : State)--Antiquities. 6. Yucatán (Mexico : State)--History. I. Braswell, Geoffrey E.
  F1435.1.Y89A63 2011
  972'.65--dc22
                                2011011031

Typeset and copyedited by Forthcoming Publications Ltd
www.forthcomingpublications.com

Printed and bound by CPI Group (UK) Ltd, Croydon

To E. Wyllys Andrews V,
archaeologist, teacher, colleague,
friend, and inspiration

Contents

Contributors   ix
List of Figures   xi
List of Tables   xiv

1. **The Ancient Maya of Mexico:
   Reinterpreting the Past of the Northern Maya Lowlands**
   Geoffrey E. Braswell   1

Part I
THE PRECLASSIC PERIOD

2. **The Origins of the Mesoamerican Ballgame:
   A New Perspective from the Northern Maya Lowlands**
   David S. Anderson   43

3. **The Architecture of Power and Sociopolitical Complexity in
   Northwestern Yucatan during the Preclassic Period**
   Nancy Peniche May   65

4. **Maya Political Cycling and the Story of the Kaan Polity**
   Joyce Marcus   88

Part II
THE EARLY AND LATE CLASSIC PERIODS

5. **Urbanism, Architecture, and Internationalism in the
   Northern Lowlands during the Early Classic**
   Scott R. Hutson   119

6. **The Political and Economic Organization of Late Classic States
   in the Peninsular Gulf Coast: The View from Champoton, Campeche**
   Jerald Ek   143

7. **5,000 Sites and Counting:
   The Inspiration of Maya Settlement Studies**
   Walter R. T. Witschey and Clifford T. Brown   170

Part III
THE TERMINAL CLASSIC AND
EARLY POSTCLASSIC PERIODS

8. **The Nunnery Quadrangle of Uxmal**
   William M. Ringle — 191

9. **In the Shadow of the Pyramid:**
   Excavations of the Great Platform of Chichen Itza
   Geoffrey E. Braswell and Nancy Peniche May — 229

10. **Divide and Rule: Interpreting Site Perimeter Walls**
    in the Northern Maya Lowlands and Beyond
    Lauren D. Hahn and Geoffrey E. Braswell — 264

Part IV
THE LATE POSTCLASSIC TO HISTORICAL PERIODS

11. **Rain and Fertility Rituals in Postclassic Yucatan**
    Featuring Chaak and Chak Chel
    Gabrielle Vail and Christine Hernández — 285

12. **Poor Mayapan**
    Clifford T. Brown, April A. Watson, Ashley Gravlin-Beman
    and Larry S. Liebovitch — 306

13. **Maya Collapse or Resilience? Lessons from the**
    Spanish Conquest and the Caste War of Yucatan
    Rani T. Alexander — 325

Part V
CONCLUSIONS

14. **Yucatan at the Crossroads**
    Joyce Marcus — 349

Index — 373

Contributors

Rani T. Alexander is Professor of Anthropology at New Mexico State University. She specializes in the Late Postclassic and historic period archaeology of the Yucatan peninsula and has worked extensively in southwestern Campeche and central Yucatan.
E-mail: raalexan@nmsu.edu

David S. Anderson received his Ph.D. from Tulane University in 2010 and is the director of the Xtobo Archaeological Project. His research focuses on the Preclassic period in Mesoamerica, specializing in the study of the northern Maya lowlands.
E-mail: danders3@tulane.edu

Geoffrey E. Braswell is an Associate Professor of Anthropology at the University of California, San Diego, and director of the Toledo Regional Interaction Project, Belize.
E-mail: gbraswell@ucsd.edu

Clifford T. Brown is an Associate Professor of Anthropology at Florida Atlantic University in Boca Raton, Florida. He has worked extensively in the northern Maya lowlands and is currently investigating the prehistory of northeast Nicaragua.
E-mail: ctbrown@fau.edu

Jerald Ek is a Ph.D. student at the State University of New York at Albany, a research associate of the Autonomous University of Campeche, and is the director of the Champoton Regional Settlement Survey.
E-mail: jerryek@hotmail.com

Ashley Gravlin-Beman recently graduated with a B.A. in Anthropology (summa cum laude) from Florida Atlantic University.
E-mail: ashleycgravlin@yahoo.com

Lauren D. Hahn is a Ph.D. student at the University of California, San Diego. She has conducted archaeological fieldwork in Mexico and Belize.
E-mail: ldhahn@ucsd.edu

Christine Hernández is a research fellow of the Middle American Research Institute of Tulane University, adjunct instructor, archaeologist, and independent scholar. She is best known for research in Michoacan archaeology and studies of highland Mexican and Maya codices.
E-mail: chernand@tulane.edu

Scott R. Hutson is an Associate Professor of Anthropology at the University of Kentucky and is currently directing archaeological research along the ancient causeway connecting Uci and Cansahcab, Yucatan.
E-mail: scotthutson@uky.edu

Larry S. Liebovitch is Dean of the Division of Mathematics and Natural Sciences and Professor of Physics at Queens College, City University of New York. He earned a Ph.D. in Astronomy from Harvard University and uses complex systems such as fractals, chaos, neural networks, and other nonlinear methods to study molecular, cellular, and psychological systems.
E-mail: larry.liebovitch@qc.cuny.edu

Joyce Marcus is the Robert L. Carneiro Distinguished University Professor of Social Evolution and the Curator of Latin American Archaeology at the Museum of Anthropology, University of Michigan.
E-mail: joymar@umich.edu

Nancy Peniche May is a Ph.D. student at the University of California, San Diego, and a graduate of the Faculty of Anthropological Sciences of the Autonomous University of Yucatan. She has conducted archaeological fieldwork and laboratory work in Mexico and is currently working in Belize.
E-mail: npeniche@ucsd.edu

William M. Ringle is Professor of Anthropology at Davidson College. He is currently co-director of the Bolonchen Regional Archaeological Project and prior to that, was co-director of the Ek Balam Project.
E-mail: biringle@davidson.edu

Gabrielle Vail is a research scholar at New College of Florida and the director of the Florida Institute for Hieroglyphic Research. She is best known for her work on the Maya codices (www.mayacodices.org).
E-mail: gvail@ncf.edu

April A. Watson is a M.A. candidate at the Department of Anthropology, Florida Atlantic University, and has recently completed a thesis on the predictive modeling of archaeological site locations in eastern Cuba.
E-mail: awatso21@fau.edu

Walter R. T. Witschey is Professor of Anthropology and Science Education at Longwood University, a Research Fellow of the Middle American Research Institute, Tulane University, and co-principal investigator of the Electronic Atlas of Ancient Maya Sites.
E-Mail: witscheywr@longwood.edu

List of Figures

1.1	Archaeological sites of the northern Maya lowlands	6
1.2	Late Preclassic structures at Komchen	7
1.3	The massive Middle Preclassic platform at Xocnaceh	8
1.4	Ake Structure 1, an example of megalithic style architecture	11
1.5	Acanceh Structure 1, a Peten-style pyramid	11
1.6	Architecture incorporating Maya variants of the *talud-tablero*	14
1.7	Exterior façade of the tomb of U K'it Kan Le'k Tok', Ek Balam	17
1.8	Stacked monster masks found on the corners of Maya structures	18
2.1	Preclassic sites documented by the Proyecto Costa Maya	45
2.2	The nine principal features of ballcourt architecture	46
2.3	Profile of the eastern structure of the ballcourt at Pitaya	49
2.4	Profile of the ballcourt at Na On	49
2.5	Plan of the ballcourt at Xanila	50
2.6	La Union	51
2.7	Ulila	54
2.8	Sinantoh	54
2.9	San Jeronimo I	55
2.10	Map of Xtobo	55
3.1	Architectural core of Xaman Susula	74
3.2	Plan of Structure 1714-Asub	76
3.3	Structure 1714-Asub, viewed from the south	76
3.4	Celts made of green igneous stone	78
4.1	Eight examples of the Snake Head Emblem Glyph	89
4.2	Key sites of northern Guatemala and southern Campeche	93
4.3	Area administered by Snake Head Polity during seventh century A.D.	94
4.4	Stela 1, Nakbe	95
4.5	Dzibanche prisoner steps	98
4.6	Dzibanche prisoner steps	99
4.7	Phrase of four hieroglyphs from Naranjo	100
4.8	Two examples of the expression "Lord of Chiik Nahb"	100
4.9	Examples of the Bat Polity	101
4.10	Structure II at Calakmul	102
4.11	Names of nine rulers of the *Kaan* Polity	103
4.12	Structure of the *Kaan* Polity emblem glyph	105
4.13	Calakmul Stela 114	106
4.14	Calakmul Stela 43	107
4.15	Photographs of Calakmul Stelae 28 and 29	110
4.16	Drawings of Calakmul Stelae 28 and 29	110
4.17	Photograph of El Peru Stela 34	111
4.18	Drawing of El Peru Stela 34	111

5.1	Map of Izamal	121
5.2	Ruins of Chunchumil	123
5.3	Structure 38s14 of the 21 de Abril site	128
5.4	Structure 27b of Santa Teresa	129
5.5	Supports from cylindrical tripod vases	136
6.1	Location of Champoton	146
6.2	Project study area, Champoton	147
6.3	Demographic trends in Champoton region	149
6.4	Map of Ulumal	150
6.5	Map of the central zone of San Dimas	151
6.6	Types within the Champoton 4 ceramic complex	154
6.7	The spatial distribution of the Canbalam ceramic sphere	154
6.8	Types within the Champoton 5 ceramic complex	155
6.9	Types within the Champoton 6 ceramic complex	156
6.10	Fishing weights from midden deposits at coastal sites	160
7.1	Early explorers of the Maya area	172
7.2	The M.A.R.I. map of Maya sites	173
7.3	The Electronic Atlas of Ancient Maya Sites	174
7.4	Site map of the Electronic Atlas of Ancient Maya Sites	178
7.5	Chicxulub crater and higher elevation at center of the peninsula	179
7.6	Location of Tikal on the continental divide	180
7.7	Settlement area studied using fractal model and survey	181
7.8	K'inich Kakmo' pyramid, Izamal, Yucatan	185
8.1	The Nunnery Quadrangle, Uxmal	192
8.2	Quadrangle to the south of Structure 1B2, Kabah	193
8.3	Central Uxmal	194
8.4	*Mapa Quinatzin*	194
8.5	Moteuczoma's palace, *Codex Mendoza*	196
8.6	Uxmal Stela 17	201
8.7	Augustus Le Plongeon in the Nunnery Quadrangle	202
8.8	House of the Governor and the north wing of the Nunnery	204
8.9	Front (west) façade, east wing, Nunnery Quadrangle	206
8.10	Mosaic heads from the east wing façade	207
8.11	Front (east) façade and plan, west wing, Nunnery Quadrangle	209
8.12	Mask stacks of the west wing façade	210
8.13	Feathered serpents	211
8.14	Canopies and stone huts, west wing, Nunnery Quadrangle	212
8.15	Front (north) façade, south wing, Nunnery Quadrangle	215
8.16	Structures compared with the Nunnery Quadrangle	216
8.17	Front (south) façade, north wing, Nunnery Quadrangle	218
8.18	Comparison of north wing mask stacks	218
8.19	Fathered serpents on the façade of the Uxmal ballcourt	220
9.1	Carved lintel, Akab' Tz'ib'	230
9.2	Great Platform of Chichen Itza	231
9.3	"Old Chichen" and "New Chichen"	232
9.4	Profile and floors of the Great Platform	234
9.5	Plan of Operation AC	239
9.6	Operation AC, excavations east of the Castillo	240

9.7	Platform Feature AC16, as well as later floors	241
9.8	Stage I of construction	242
9.9	Platform Feature AC3, Stage IIA	243
9.10	Stage II of construction	244
9.11	Platform Feature AC10	245
9.12	Profile of east side of platform Feature AC10	246
9.13	Stage III of construction	247
9.14	Stair Feature AC19 on platform Feature AC10	247
9.15	Stage IV of construction	248
9.16	Plan of patio-gallery structure Feature AC8	249
9.17	Patio-gallery structure Feature AC8	249
9.18	Stage V, VI, and VIII floors	251
9.19	Construction sequence of the Great Platform	253
10.1	Mural, Upper Temple of the Jaguars, Chichen Itza	270
10.2	Hypothetical reconstruction of Str. 2C12, Chichen Itza	272
10.3	Northern excavated section of the wall	273
10.4	Sections of the wall	274
10.5	Profiles of the wall	275
10.6	Pieces of architectural sculpture incorporated into the buttress wall	278
11.1	A plan of the Balankanche Cave complex	287
11.2	Group I artifacts *in situ* in Balankanche Cave	288
11.3	Group III artifacts *in situ* in Balankanche Cave	289
11.4	The almanac on page 30a of the Madrid Codex	290
11.5	Chaak and Chak Chel, Dresden page 42b	291
11.6	Reconstruction of Mural 2 of Tulum Structure 16	292
11.7	Detail from Mural 2 in Tulum Structure 16	293
11.8	Elderly female deities in the Maya codices	294
11.9	Representations of highland Mexican goddesses	295
11.10	Aspects of Chak Chel likened to Mexican goddesses	296
11.11	Center panel from Madrid pages 75-76	297
11.12	Yearbearer ceremonies on Dresden pages 25-28	297
11.13	Carved stone censers portraying figures wearing flayed skins	301
11.14	Painted Tlaloc effigy vessels from Balankanche Cave	301
12.1	Detail from map of Mayapan	307
12.2	"Mayapan House Type"	314
12.3	Detail of map of Palenque	315
12.4	Detail of the Demetrio sheet of the map of Sayil	316
12.5	Pareto distribution of house sizes	317
13.1	The Stages of the Adaptive Cycle	327
13.2	Map of nineteenth-century Yucatan	330
13.3	The church in Yaxcaba	337
13.4	The *palacio municipal* of Ebtun	337
13.5	The *casa principal* of Hacienda Cetelac	338
13.6	The *comisaria municipal* of Xanla	339
13.7	Shrine with dressed cross at Tzaab	339
14.1	Will Andrews and Joyce Marcus at Copan	361

List of Tables

2.1	Preclassic ballcourts of northwest Yucatan	49
2.2	Pottery collected from ballcourt sites in northwest Yucatan	53
4.1	A summary of the history of the *Kaan* Polity	108
6.1	Ceramic chronology of the Champoton Regional Settlement Survey	148
8.1	Radiocarbon dates from the Nunnery Quadrangle	200
11.1	Number of artifacts recovered from offering assemblages in Groups I-VI at Balankanche Cave grouped according to artifact type	287
12.1	Descriptive statistics for houses at Mayapan, Palenque, and Sayil	318
13.1	Adaptive cycles in Historic period Yucatan	331
13.2	Distribution of population in the Ebtun Region	335

1 The Ancient Maya of Mexico

Reinterpreting the Past of the Northern Maya Lowlands

Geoffrey E. Braswell

The three modern Mexican states of Campeche, Yucatan, and Quintana Roo compose roughly half of the Maya area. The northern Maya lowlands, whose southern boundary runs east–west through south central Quintana Roo and Campeche at approximately 19 degrees north latitude, is—with the exception of the Puuc hills—a generally flat plain characterized by low scrub forest, moderate to low rainfall, little surface water, a subtropical climate, and many of the most spectacular cities ever built in the New World. For this reason, the archaeological sites of the Yucatan peninsula, including Chichen Itza, Tulum, Uxmal, and Coba, are among the most visited anywhere in the Americas.

The northern lowlands have long been the focus of Mexican archaeologists studying the Maya. Most of the projects of the past 30 years have been directed by investigators at the Instituto Nacional de Antropología e Historia (INAH) center in Merida, or by investigators at newer INAH centers in Campeche and Chetumal. Other important projects have been conducted by faculty and students at Mexican universities, by foreign scholars, and, recently, by a small group of independent Mexican archaeologists (see Bey 2006:14-15 for a partial publication list of many of these projects). Results of archaeological research in the northern Maya lowlands are regularly presented at meetings held in Mexico, Guatemala, the United States, and Europe. Publications concerning the archaeology, epigraphy, and art history of the region appear with growing frequency not only in Spanish and English, but also in German and French. Despite this, outside of Mexico the ancient past of the northern Maya lowlands remains less known and captures the eye of the public less frequently than does that of the tropical rainforests of the southern and central lowlands of Guatemala, Belize, Honduras, and Chiapas, Mexico. Major textbooks and popular works published in English tend either to omit the northern lowlands (Demarest 2004) or to concentrate coverage on the Terminal Classic to Postclassic periods (e.g., Coe 2011; Schele and Freidel 1990; Schele and Mathews 1999; Sharer with Traxler 2006). George Bey (2006:16) quips that "[u]nfortunately, many authors think that it is not until the Terminal Classic period that the north is worth examining."

Long considered to be a passive periphery by many who do not work in the area, the northern Maya lowlands has been depicted as a region where: (1) political and economic complexity began quite late and was derived from elsewhere; (2) the culture was largely illiterate and did not produce important works of art or architecture before about A.D. 800; (3) the pottery is dull and uninteresting compared to the vivid polychromes of the south; and (4) after a relatively brief but magnificent florescence, society slipped backwards into "decadence" and the region again became a passive backwater. Insofar as the northern lowlands experienced cultural elaboration, it was generally thought to have been the result of interaction first with the Maya of Guatemalan lowlands and with the Teotihuacanos of central Mexico, and later with the Toltecs and Aztecs.

Aims of the Ancient Maya of Mexico: Reinterpreting the Past of the Northern Maya Lowlands

The past 20 years have seen a revolution in our interpretations of social and political process in the northern Maya lowlands, but the great advances made by archaeologists to our understanding of this half of the Maya area are still under-represented in both scholarly and popular Anglophone literature (cf. Kowalski and Kristan-Graham 2007; Mathews and Morrison 2006; Shaw and Mathews 2005). One goal of this volume, therefore, is to present the results of new and important archaeological, epigraphic, and art historical research in the Mexican states of Yucatan, Campeche, and Quintana Roo. Except for this introduction and a broadly synthetic concluding essay that reviews what we have learned and seeks to define new goals and directions for the future of archaeology in the northern lowlands (Chapter 14), this volume presents original research. The organization of the volume is chronological (from the Middle Preclassic to colonial and modern periods), so that readers will understand how new data and interpretations have changed the whole of our understanding of Maya history.

A second goal of this volume is to pay tribute to E. Wyllys Andrews V, who has been in the vanguard of northern lowland archaeology for forty years. Earlier versions of many of our chapters were presented at the first of two sessions held in Will's honor at the 75th Annual Meeting of the Society for American Archaeology in Saint Louis, Missouri. The hundreds of people present at both sessions—as well as at a party held in his honor—testify to Will's continuing contributions to the archaeology of the northern Maya lowlands. His special roles as teacher, mentor, colleague, and friend during his many years as Director of the Middle American Research Institute at Tulane University have been formative and inspirational, and mean a great deal to us all.

The New Paradigm

In a recent essay, Fernando Robles Castellanos (n.d.) has summarized what he calls the "new paradigm" regarding recent developments in our understanding of the Middle Preclassic period in northwest Yucatan. That work—to which Robles, Anthony Andrews, Tomás Gallareta Negrón, and scholars working at INAH (Chapter 3), Tulane University (Chapter 2), and other institutions have made great contributions—builds on research directed by Will Andrews at Komchen. For me, the many important changes to our general view of the prehistory of the northern lowlands that have emerged and coalesced during the past two decades can also be called a new paradigm, albeit in a metaphorical rather than literal sense. Using this phrase particularly acknowledges the role that these scholars and their many colleagues in Merida and beyond have played in forming this new perspective. Nonetheless, any historical summary is subject to bias, and my choice here is to draw attention to and emphasize the importance of contributions made by Will Andrews to our new and evolving perspective.

Rather than summarize each chapter in this volume, I hope to show how they are embedded within this new paradigm. Will's impact has been felt most strongly in discussions of the origins of Preclassic society and the transition from the Classic to the Postclassic period, that is, to questions concerning the rise and fall of hierarchy and complexity. These are themes that he has also pursued in his work at Quelepa, El Salvador (Andrews 1976), and at Copan, Honduras (Andrews and Fash 1992; Fash et al. 2004). In the northern Maya lowlands, however, it is difficult to identify any era after the Palaeoindian period or any processual question to which Will has not made important contributions.

Recent research in the northern Maya lowlands has revealed temporal parallels with emerging complexity in other parts of Mesoamerica, and even precocious developments that occurred first in the northern Maya lowlands. Two archaeological projects have discovered hundreds of Middle Preclassic sites in northwest Yucatan and dozens of some of the earliest ballcourts known in Mesoamerica (Chapter 2). Scholars working outside of the modern city of Merida have found the earliest "throne room" in the Americas, implying that a complex chiefdom evolved in Yucatan by the late Middle Preclassic (Chapter 3). A particularly complex example of early "dynamic cycling" is demonstrated for Calakmul (a central lowland site in far southern Campeche) that grew eventually to be one of the largest cities in the Classic Maya world (Chapter 4). Work in north central Yucatan (Chapter 5) and Campeche (Chapter 6) has challenged our views about the transitions from the Preclassic to the Classic, and the Classic to the Postclassic. A new mapping project, which can trace its roots back to Frans Blom's work at the Middle American Research Institute, reveals that the density of known sites in the northern Maya lowlands is greater than anywhere else in the Maya area (Chapter 7). The art and architectural planning of Uxmal, one of the most famous of all Maya sites in Mexico, demonstrates that it was one of the ancient "Tollans," a great pilgrimage city on par with the Toltec capital of Tula (Chapter 8). Recent research at Chichen Itza reveals that the "International" style of the site center developed slowly over time and was not introduced by invaders from central Mexico or elsewhere (Chapter 9), and that a wall surrounding the center of the city first served to define sacred space and only later came to have a defensive function (Chapter 10). Analyses of Maya codices, murals, and cave assemblages suggest that appeasement of both local and foreign rain deities, and also of fertility deities linked to agriculture, became very important at the end of the Terminal Classic period (Chapter 11). This lends tangential support to the notion that the demographic decline of Chichen Itza and Uxmal might have been stimulated by poor agricultural conditions and drought. Most importantly, these rituals of renewal and regeneration continued throughout the Postclassic period, demonstrating great continuity. Although Mayapan, the last capital of the northern Maya lowlands, has often been depicted as culturally "decadent," there have been few satisfactory explanations for its condition. Household archaeology reveals that, compared to earlier sites, Mayapan was relatively impoverished (Chapter 12). Finally, although it is often argued that the Spanish conquest is a boundary that clouds comparison between the prehispanic past and historical periods, archaeological and historical evidence demonstrates that during both periods, communities employed similar resilience strategies that often buffered society from the effects of periodic catastrophe and "dynamic cycling" (Chapter 13).

Four themes run consistently throughout our volume and this new paradigm. First, the northern Maya lowlands have their own incredibly rich history and fascinating in situ story to tell. Second, it is not even possible to understand the central and southern lowlands without considering the northern Maya lowlands. All three areas were integrated, and their histories are interlaced. Third, interaction and competition—at the site level, from a regional perspective, and even when considering the Maya area as a whole—are important forces that drove many cycles of rising and falling sociopolitical complexity. Finally, Will Andrews' many intellectual contributions provide a solid foundation for much of this new research.

Palaeoindian Period (Ca. 13,500–8000 B.C.)

Palaeoindian discoveries are rather rare in the Maya area (Lohse et al. 2006). For the most part, with the exception of cave sites in the Guatemalan highlands (Gruhn and Bryan 1977), they consist of tools or bones recovered without context. Earlier claims for a Palaeoindian presence at Loltun Cave, Yucatan (Velázquez Valádez 1980), now seem unsupported. One of the most recent and exciting developments in the new paradigm has been the discovery of human remains and artifacts in submerged cave systems in Quintana Roo (Barclay 2008; González González et al. 2008, 2010; Than 2010; Universal 2010). To date, five sets of human remains—called the Woman of Hoyo Negro (*Artdaily* 2012; Rissolo 2012), the "Eve" of Naharon, the Woman of Las Palmas, the Man of El Templo, and the Young Man of Hol Chan—have been reported. The last of these sets of remains was found in an articulated position suggesting that it was deliberately placed in the cave (Than 2010). Also found in such submerged caves are hearths, chipped stone tools, and faunal remains, including examples from extinct Pleistocene species, such as a gomphothere (*Artdaily* 2012). Water-filled caves are extremely dynamic systems, and understanding site formation processes can be daunting. Dating the remains has also proven somewhat controversial. Nonetheless, the presence of stalactites and stalagmites in these caves indicate that they once were largely dry, and formed at a time before sea levels rose 15 meters or more at the end of the last Ice Age.

Archaeologists and biological anthropologists who have conducted preliminary studies of these human remains argue that they share more physical traits in common with inhabitants from South Asia and Indonesia than they do with people from northern Asia (González González et al. 2008; see also Barclay 2008; Than 2010; Universal 2010). For these scholars, the implication is that there were multiple migrations across the Bering Straits, that these new finds pertain to a pre-Clovis migration, and that subsistence patterns probably did not rely on Pleistocene megafauna. Such claims, no doubt, will continue to be controversial until many more examples are known. What is clear is that as similar research becomes more difficult to conduct elsewhere in North America, remains such as these found in Quintana Roo will become central to any understanding of the peopling of the New World.

Reconstructions of the climate and ecology of Yucatan ca. 15,000–10,000 years ago suggest that it was dominated by dry savanna, grassland, and perhaps even desert. Like today, surface water would have been scarce, and caves where rainwater collected—after percolating through the limestone—would have been important places for early inhabitants of the new landscape to find water. Although we cannot directly connect these early inhabitants to the Maya who have lived in Yucatan for at least the last 2,800 years, it may be that the importance of caves as ritual places where water was abundant dates back to these early times.

Archaic and Early Preclassic Periods (Ca. 8000–1100 B.C.)

We know little about the Palaeoindian period in Yucatan, but the Archaic and Early Formative are complete lacunae. It is even possible that the Early Preclassic (ca. 2000 B.C.-1100 B.C.)—by which I mean a developmental, cultural, or adaptive stage, rather than a chronological period—did not exist in Yucatan.

With the exception of northern Belize (Pohl et al. 1996) and the Chantuto zone of Chiapas (Voorhies 2004), very few Archaic sites are known in the Maya region (see Lohse 2010). Despite the lack of physical sites, a complex picture of the emergence of settled village life and agriculture has developed in those regions where we have sediment and soil cores. In several areas, maize pollen, charcoal, and other evidence demonstrate that the landscape was cleared and burned and that cultigens were known by 3000 B.C., even though we do not have direct evidence of habitation sites (e.g., Neff et al. 2006; Pohl et al. 1996; Robinson et al. 2002). Nonetheless, the adoption of permanent sedentism, a subsistence strategy based solely on agriculture, and the use of ceramics did not begin to occur in the Maya lowlands until roughly 1100 B.C. (uncalibrated 930 b.c.). It is probable that gourds, nets, baskets, and other perishable tools were used instead of pottery until this time. We do not know why the transition to a Preclassic lifestyle was so late. Some areas may not yet have been inhabited, population levels were undoubtedly low, and it might also be that environmental uncertainty made foraging and hunting supplemented by horticulture a more viable adaptation than agriculture.

In sum, with the exceptions of the Pacific Coast and Piedmont, the Salama Valley of Baja Verapaz, western Honduras, and perhaps Kaminaljuyu, there is to this day no evidence in the Maya area of an Early Preclassic lifestyle parallel to that known for other parts of Mesoamerica during the second millennium B.C. Most sites dating to this time period might be best called culturally "Preceramic," "Aceramic," or even "Terminal Archaic," rather than Early Preclassic, even though they date to a time that is traditionally known by that name. To me, it seems most likely that settled village life was introduced into the Maya lowlands—including the northern lowlands—at the inception of the Middle Preclassic period (Andrews 1990, 2003; Andrews et al. 2008). The Early Preclassic—as a stage characterized by the beginnings of village life, agriculture, and pottery—has so far proven to be as elusive as Basketmaker I has been for the U.S. Southwest.

Nevertheless, it is still possible that someday we may find Early Preclassic pottery and evidence of settled village life dating to before 1100 B.C. in the Maya lowlands (Chapter 14; see Stanton 2000). For two reasons, such evidence may prove even harder to find in the northern lowlands than in the south. First, swamps, ponds, and lakes where sediments accumulate are rare or nonexistent in much of the region, especially northwestern Yucatan where our most vibrant evidence for a subsequent Middle Preclassic occupation is found. For this reason, soil coring of the sort that has been useful elsewhere to document late Archaic occupations and landscape modification is neither particularly feasible nor efficacious. Second, the northern Maya lowlands are characterized by very shallow soils. Deeply buried and well-preserved contexts are the exception rather than the norm in Yucatan. Moreover, architecture dating to later periods was often built directly on bedrock. If there were any Early Preclassic villages in Yucatan, many were probably destroyed either by natural processes or by scraping the palimpsest of earlier settlements in order to build new ones.

Middle Preclassic Period (1100/800 B.C.–400/300 B.C.)

It is not known, therefore, if there was a substantial population in the northern Maya lowlands before the Middle Preclassic period. The lack of strong evidence for a permanent occupation could be taken as implying that the region was uninhabited during the first portion of the Middle Preclassic, ca. 1100–800 B.C. (Ball 1977). Alternatively, foragers and horticulturalists—or even early agriculturalists such as those who lived in western Belize and other parts of the Maya region—could have been present and their remains are too ephemeral or nondescript to identify. There are now tantalizing ceramic clues that perhaps such an initial Middle Preclassic occupation exists.

Pottery of the Early Middle Preclassic

Three ceramic spheres dating to the initial Middle Preclassic have been identified in the central Maya lowlands. These are Xe/Real Xe (identified in the western Peten, and perhaps associated with Mixe-Zoquean speakers rather than with early Maya), Eb/Cunil/Kanocha[1] (identified principally in the eastern Peten and documented most fully in the Belize Valley), and Swasey (localized in northern Belize).

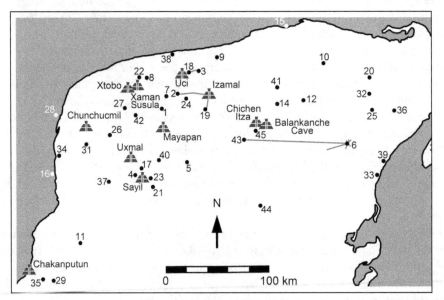

Figure 1.1. Archaeological sites of the northern Maya lowlands. Pyramid symbols with text names represent sites that are the major foci of the chapters in this volume, numbered dots mark sites that are discussed in less detail, and lines represent *sacbeob*. These symbols do not indicate the relative size or importance of sites. 1=Acanceh, 2=Ake, 3=Cansahcab, 4=Chac II, 5=Chacchob, 6=Coba, 7=Cuca, 8=Dzibilchaltun, 9=Dzilam, 10=Dzonot Ake, 11=Edzna, 12=Ek Balam, 13=El Meco, 14=Ichmul de Morley, 15=Isla Cerritos, 16=Jaina, 17=Kabah, 18=Kancab, 19=Kantunil, 20=Kantunilkin, 21=Kiuic, 22=Komchen, 23=Labna, 24=Muna, 25=Naranjal, 26=Oxkintok, 27=Poxila, 28=Punta Canbalam, 29=San Dimas, 30=San Gervasio, 31=Siho, 32=Tres Lagunas, 33=Tulum, 34=Uaymil, 35=Ulumal, 36=Victoria, 37=Xcalumkin, 38=Xcambo, 39=Xelha, 40=Xocnaceh, 41=Xuenkal, 42=Yaxcopoil, 43=Yaxuna, 44=Yo'okop, 45=Yula.

Figure 1.2. Late Preclassic structures at Komchen, excavated and consolidated by E. Wyllys Andrews V and William M. Ringle. April 2009.

According to Will Andrews et al. (2008), sherds with incised decorations resembling Eb/Cunil/Canocha pottery have been found at Komchen and Kiuic (Figures 1.1 and 1.2). At Komchen, the Ek phase, to which this material belongs, has been re-dated and is now considered to predate and be antecedent to Early Nabanche. More recently, Will Andrews (in Andrews and Bey 2011) has argued that the "Cunil-like" pottery at Komchen is more closely related to western Belize pottery dating to the early facet of the Jenney Creek phase, which post-dates Cunil/Kanocha and which began ca. 850 B.C. That is, Ek-phase pottery at Komchen dates to sometime before—but perhaps not long before—about 800 B.C., and is an antecedent to Early Nabanche pottery (Andrews and Bey 2011; cf. Ceballos Gallareta and Robles Castellanos n.d.). At Kiuic, George Bey has found that some Bah-phase pottery contains the same pan-Mesoamerican incised decorations incorporated into pottery with clear Early Nabanche pastes (Andrews and Bey 2011; Andrews et al. 2008). Kiuic is a Puuc site. It astounds me to think that just ten years ago, there was little evidence demonstrating a clear occupation in the Puuc region before the Early Classic period. The discovery of Middle Formative contexts at Kiuic, Paso del Macho, and Xocnaceh has extended our knowledge of the occupation of the Puuc back in time more than 1,200 years.

The recognition of design elements also found on early Middle Preclassic Jenney Creek pottery in the northern Maya lowlands is important because it pushes back the beginning of pottery production in northwest Yucatan to the ninth century B.C., at least a hundred years earlier than previously demonstrated. Nonetheless, this probably should not be construed as implying the arrival of pottery-using inhabitants who migrated from the eastern Peten or western Belize. Later Middle Preclassic pottery from the area shares much in common with ceramics known from the southwest Peten and even Chiapas (Andrews 1990, 2003), suggesting a more complex picture of multiple waves of ideas—and perhaps of some people—coming from different places at different times. Moreover, if there were foragers or horticulturalists living in Yucatan before about 900 B.C., then the adoption of pottery and settled village life might represent a complex fusion of local and introduced culture. This might explain why northern variations of southern pottery are different (Stanton 2000). Simple migration models do not appear supported because the pottery of the northern lowlands, even from its earliest beginnings, is not identical to types known elsewhere.

Complexity and Monumentality during the Late Middle Preclassic Period

By about 600 B.C., the picture begins to clear. It is amazing now to consider that as recently as the turn of this century, just three Middle Preclassic sites (including Komchen) were known in northwest Yucatan, and—although Middle Preclassic pottery was first identified a long time ago (Brainerd 1958)—only a few more Middle Preclassic structures were known across all of the northern Maya lowlands.

In the last 20 years, late Middle Formative ceramics and even architecture have been found at a wide variety of sites across the northern Maya lowlands, and research at these places has been central to the emergence of the new paradigm (Anderson 2003, 2010; Andrews and Robles Castellanos 2004; Gallareta Negrón and Ringle 2004; Gallareta Negrón et al. 2005; Medina Castillo 2003, 2005; Peniche May 2010; Robles Castellanos n.d.).

Several sites in northwest Yucatan—including Xocaneh, Poxila, and Xtobo—contain massive stone platforms (Figure 1.3), and smaller public buildings such as ballcourts (Chapter 2), *sacbes* (raised causeways), temple pyramids, and even what might be called a "throne room" (Chapter 3). Many of these early northwestern sites are built with very large or even massive stones, in what can be construed as a precursor to the megalithic style (Chapter 5) of the Late Preclassic and Early Classic periods.

Similar developments are seen at the Mamom-sphere site of Yaxuna (Ardren and Johnstone 1996; Stanton and Ardren 2005), and—of course—at more distant sites in the central Maya lowlands such as Calakmul (Chapter 4). Such monumentality was thought until recently to be limited to that last region, but we now know that it emerged in some parts of the northern Maya lowlands at about the same time as large structures were built at Nakbe and other late Middle Preclassic sites located in the El Mirador basin.

Figure 1.3. The massive Middle Preclassic platform at Xocnaceh, excavated and consolidated by Tomás Gallareta Negrón. April 2009.

In northwest Yucatan, settlement density reached a level not known elsewhere in the Maya region (Chapter 2). This does not seem to be merely a result of survey coverage or the visibility of sites. It has long been known that during the Late Classic period, this corner of Yucatan was one of the most densely settled regions anywhere in the Maya world (see Figure 7.4). It appears as though the same factors that promoted rapid growth during the Late Classic may also have stimulated early settlement in northwest Yucatan. Just as importantly, there is evidence in this region that a three-tiered settlement hierarchy developed during the late Middle Preclassic, and it is reasonable to expect that such elaborate hierarchies will be found elsewhere in the north dating to this time period.

Such settlement hierarchies, massive public architecture equal in size to anything known at contemporary sites in the central and southern Maya lowlands, and the presence of imported prestige goods (Robles Castellanos n.d.) together imply complex political organization. Such precocious late Middle Preclassic polities could have been complex chiefdoms (Chapter 3) or archaic states, or have cycled between different levels of complexity (Chapter 4). For the moment, I prefer to think of late Middle Preclassic and Late Preclassic polities in the northern lowlands as chiefdoms with various and changing degrees of hierarchical and heterarchical organization, but by the end of the Late Preclassic I have little doubt that archaic states characterized the peaks of such cycles in the northern Maya lowlands, as they did further south (Chapter 4).

Trade with the Olmecs

Excavations at Xocnaceh, Poxila, Xaman Susulha, and other sites have discovered significant quantities of celts made of green igneous stone (Chapter 3; Gallareta Negrón and Ringle 2004; Robles Castellanos n.d.). The exact geological source of these imported objects is not yet known, but they could have been made in the Tuxtla region of southern Veracruz, located in the Olmec heartland. Other evidence of direct or indirect trade with this region includes Olmec-style or, more accurately, Middle Formative carved jade and greenstone. The most famous of these jade artifacts were found at Chacsinkin (Andrews 1986). Since then, more jade and greenstone artifacts have been found in unambiguous Middle Preclassic contexts at Poxila and Tipikal (Robles Castellanos n.d.; Peraza Lope et al. 2002).

We also have evidence that Olmecs imported goods from the northern Maya lowlands. Although no Gulf coast pottery has been recovered in Yucatan, Middle Preclassic Early Nabanche ceramics have been found at La Venta, Tres Zapotes, and San Andres in southern Veracruz and western Tabasco (Andrews 1986; Von Nagy et al. 2002). It should be no surprise that exchange between the Olmec heartland and the northern Maya lowlands was reciprocal, and that ideas and goods did not simply flow from the Olmec to the Maya.

The implication of this wealth of new information on the Middle Preclassic of the northern lowlands is that we cannot now consider the region to be a cultural, political, or economic backwater (Bey 2006). The first large towns containing massive public stone structures were built by paramount rulers in the Peten, the Valley of Oaxaca, the Valley of Mexico, and the northern Maya lowlands at roughly the same time: the late Middle Preclassic.

Late Preclassic Period (400/300 B.C.–A.D. 250/400)

The late Middle Preclassic pottery of Komchen is called the Early Nabanche complex. Since he first defined it, Andrews (1988) has emphasized the strong similarities between that complex and Mamom pottery found in the central and southern Maya lowlands. Both, for example, contain the ubiquitous Joventud and Chunhinta ceramic groups. For Andrews (1990), the Middle Preclassic is the period during which the greatest similarity is seen in Maya pottery over the entire Maya lowlands.

Of course, Joventud Red from Komchen is not quite the same as Joventud Red from, for example, Tikal. Moreover, there are ceramic groups at sites in the north that do not appear in the south or appear in greatly different concentrations, and the reverse is also true. For this reason, other scholars—most notably Joseph Ball (in Ball and Taschek 2007; Rissolo et al. 2005) and Fernando Robles Castellanos (n.d.; Ceballos Gallareta and Castellanos Robles n.d.)—prefer to define Nabanche as a sphere distinct from Mamom/Chicanel, despite these strong similarities. If the validity of these distinct spheres is accepted—and plenty of sites in the north seem to have both Mamom/Chicanel and Nabanche pottery—then an interesting pattern emerges. Ball and Taschek (2007) have noted that sites where Nabanche (both early and late) pottery is dominant, megalithic style architecture dating to the Late Preclassic and Early Classic is found (Figure 1.4; Chapter 5; Mathews and Maldonado Cárdenas 2006). Conversely, sites where Mamom/Chicanel pottery is dominant tend—during the Late Preclassic and following Early Classic—to have Peten-style pyramids with stucco masks set on either side of central staircases (Figure 1.5). Some northern lowland sites, such as Yaxuna, even built triadic groups like those found at Calakmul and elsewhere in the central Maya lowlands. Nonetheless, this pattern is not perfect. Xtobo is a Nabanche sphere site that contains a double triadic structure.

The point is that relatively small regional differences in material culture seen in the late Middle Preclassic period continued and even amplified during the Late Preclassic period. These differences are immediately obvious in architecture. Scott Hutson (Chapter 5) emphasizes that there are two "clusters" of sites with megalithic-style architecture: the plains east and north of Merida (sites including Izamal, Ake, Uci) and the Yalahau region of northern Quintana Roo (sites such as El Naranjo, San Angel, and Tres Lagunas). Nonetheless, the pattern is not particularly strong (see Mathews and Maldonado Cárdenas 2006:Figure 5.2), and there are other examples of megalithic architecture from the Puuc region and as far away as Champoton (Chapter 6). As Hutson contends, it is probably incorrect to assume that the distribution of megalithic architecture can be used to find the boundaries of Late Preclassic and Early Classic polities (cf. Stanton 2000:568, who argues that the presence of a megalithic platform at Yaxuna suggests political and economic domination of that site by Izamal). Mathews and Maldonado Cárdenas (2006) prefer to see the distribution of megalithic architecture as indicating a Late Preclassic to Early Classic interaction sphere.

Recently, scholars have argued that transitional Late Preclassic/Early Classic ceramics of the northern Maya lowlands should be divided into five distinct spheres (Ceballos Gallareta and Jiménez Álvarez 2005; Glover and Stanton 2010). Without doubting this or questioning the assertion that ceramic regionalism increased towards the end of the Late Preclassic, it seems equally important to stress how much was still shared across the whole of the Maya lowlands during this period. By emphasizing the growing differences in the trees, we may lose sight of the fact that in the Late Preclassic, we are all still in the same forest. In no later period do we see ceramic groups or systems so widely shared as in Late Preclassic times, but it is not yet clear what this implies. It was during the late Early Classic period that the pottery of the northern Maya lowlands and central/southern Maya lowlands became dramatically different.

Figure 1.4. Ake Structure 1, an example of megalithic style architecture, excavated and consolidated by Rubén Maldonado Cárdenas. April 2009.

Figure 1.5. Acanceh Structure 1, a Peten-style pyramid with stucco masks flanking a central stair, excavated and consolidated by Beatriz Quintal Suaste. January 2003 (top) and May 2009 (bottom).

Models of Increasing Complexity

Increasing regionalism—albeit with the important caveat that much was still shared over great distances—is therefore considered a hallmark of the Late Preclassic in the northern Maya lowlands. Populations grew, settlement density increased in many areas such as the Puuc, the Yalahau region, and—most especially—within a distance of 50 kilometers from the coast. In the southwest, Edzna grew to be an important Peten-related center during the Late Preclassic Baluartes phase (Forsyth 1983). Several models explaining the further elaboration of political complexity during this period have been proposed and are summarized by Bey (2006:28-30). Factors such as environmental and social circumscription, the presence of commercially exploitable salt along the north and northwest coasts, regional competition, and ceremonialism have all been cited as contributing to this growth (Ball 1977; Dunning 1992; Ringle 1999). What these models share is that they do not presuppose that political complexity was the result of interference by or the emulation of neighbors in the southern and central Maya lowlands. Instead, they emphasize local and regional factors. This focus on the northern lowlands as a source of its own change is characteristic of the new paradigm. In situ evolution is key.

It may be time to reconsider certain aspects of these models. To begin with, we now know that political complexity and population growth began not in the Late Preclassic but during the Middle Preclassic. Moreover, Komchen no longer stands out as the unique example of a Middle Preclassic site in the northern Maya lowlands, and we now know that there were other large and even more complex sites at that early time. The roots of elaboration and complexity, therefore, go deeper than the Late Preclassic period, so we should not focus solely on that period when seeking to explain process. Second, such isolationist models do not seem viable given how much material culture was still shared across the entire Maya lowlands during the Late Preclassic period. The northern lowlands certainly were not peripheral to changes happening elsewhere in the Maya region at that time, nor were the inhabitants of the region passive victims of that change. Instead, I look forward to reading soon about new models that portray the northern Maya lowlands as actively engaged in the processes that transformed the *entire* Maya world during the Late Preclassic.

Early Classic Period (A.D. 250/400–600)

For decades, our understanding of the southern Maya lowlands was dominated by our knowledge of Tikal. We tended to view the entire region through a Tikal-centric lens, so the "Middle Classic hiatus" of that site was once thought to have been a widespread phenomenon (e.g., Willey 1974). Similarly, a great deal of what we know about the Early Classic northern lowlands was derived from Middle American Research Institute research directed by Bill and Will Andrews at Dzibilchaltun and Komchen. These two sites experienced significant population loss during the transition to the Early Classic period (Andrews 1981, 1988; Andrews and Andrews 1980). It is therefore not surprising that other archaeologists extrapolated this local pattern of demographic decline to much of the northern Maya lowlands, and did not consider population levels to rise again until the Late Classic period (Dunning 1992:65; Lincoln 1985:55, both cited by Bey 2006:31). In fact, demographic loss during the long and poorly understood transition between the Late Preclassic and Early Classic period has been documented at other sites and other areas, including the Peten-related site of Edzna (Forsyth 1983), Yaxuna, and the Yalahau region (Glover and Amador 2005; Glover and Stanton 2010).[2]

Nevertheless, the pattern of demographic decline during the Early Classic period was not universal in the northern Maya lowlands. Large Early Classic centers and even cities have long been known. These include Acanceh (Hagar 1914; Seler 1911), Ake (Roys and Shook 1966), Uci (Maldonado Cárdenas 1979), Oxkintok (Shook 1940), Coba (Andrews 1938; Thompson et al. 1932; Villa Rojas 1934), and—of course—Izamal (Stephens 1868).

That the monumental architecture surrounding the great plaza of Izamal is among the most massive ever built by the Maya is not a new discovery (Figure 7.8). That the area of the city itself grew to be 53 square-kilometers—nearly half that of Tikal at its maximum Late Classic extent—is a surprising new observation (Chapter 5; Burgos Villanueva et al. 2004). We can conservatively argue that the borders of the Izamal polity were defined by the length of its longest *sacbes*, 29.7 and 14.2 kilometers, implying that it encompassed an area of at least 1,320 square-kilometers. But the Izamal polity might have been much larger, and probably included more distant sites such as Xcambo, located on the north coast some 51 kilometers from Izamal (Sierra Sosa 1999). Thus, the large city of Izamal was clearly the capital of an important regional state during the Early Classic period (Chapter 5; see especially Millet Cámara 1999; Maldonado Cárdenas 1995).

Despite its size, Izamal is all too frequently overlooked by archaeologists who work outside the northern lowlands. This is because the site lacks hieroglyphic texts, because it has no currently visible artwork (although the stucco mask on the Kabul structure illustrated by Catherwood is an icon of Maya archaeology), because much of the ancient city was destroyed long ago by the growth of the colonial and modern town, because dating its architecture has proven somewhat difficult, because it is known from the books of *Chilam Balam* as a Postclassic center, and simply because it is not located in the central or southern Maya lowlands.

The Early Classic period in the northern lowlands is marked not only by the emergence of large cities and states like Izamal, but also by greatly increased international trade, the emergence of partially commercialized market economies, and—by the late Early Classic—a ceramic tradition that would distinguish the northern lowlands from the south for the remainder of the prehispanic period.

International Trade and Teotihuacan "Influence"

The two sites that have contributed the most in recent years to our knowledge of international trade during the Early Classic are Xcambo and Chunchucmil. Excavation of the first, a small coastal settlement with megalithic architecture, has revealed important trade connections with coastal Campeche, Tabasco, and Belize. Most notably, polychrome pottery at Xcambo likely was imported from the Peten (Sierra Sosa 1999, 2001). In addition to being an important trade center almost certainly linked to Izamal, Xcambo was—and still is—a salt-producing community.

Chunchucmil (Chapter 5) is unique in several respects. First, the population density of this Early Classic city of 31,000 to 43,000 inhabitants is greater than that of many other Maya cities such as Tikal, Izamal, and Calakmul. Second, it is located in an especially infertile area, suggesting that food was imported and some activity other than farming supported the local population. Third, the public architecture of the city is small and modest in comparison to that of other major Maya cities. For these and other reasons, Bruce Dahlin and his colleagues have argued that Chunchucmil was an important gateway community and market city that supported itself through trade (e.g., Dahlin and Ardren 2002; Dahlin et al. 2007; Hutson et al. 2006, 2010).

Figure 1.6. Architecture from northwest Yucatan incorporating Maya variants of the *talud-tablero* form, best known from Teotihuacan. Top: Structure MA1, Oxkintok excavated and consolidated by Manuel Rivera Dorado, April 2009; Bottom: Temple of the Seven Dolls, Dzibilchaltun, excavated and consolidated by E. Wyllys Andrews IV, January 2003.

Despite their involvement in international trade, Chunchucmil and Xcambo exhibit only the weakest of ties with the great central Mexican city of Teotihuacan. To me, this seems to be the general rule for the northern lowlands. Teotihuacan inspired *talud-tablero* architecture has been found at several sites in the region (Andrews 1979b), but always in an eclectic style combining Maya, central Mexican, and even Gulf coast elements (Figure 1.6). For Oxkintok, one of the few late Early Classic sites in the northern Maya lowlands that displays a somewhat wider range of foreign cultural traits, Carmen Varela Torrecilla and I (2003) have argued that interaction reflects participation in a pan-Mesoamerican exchange system that included not only Teotihuacan, but also—and more importantly from the perspective of Oxkintok—sites in the Maya highlands and central lowlands.

As the power of Teotihuacan waned, followed about 150 years later by the decline of central lowland cities such as Calakmul and Tikal, Oxkintok and other cities in the north continued to strengthen and broaden their international ties. Most importantly, we stress that the rather limited evidence for indirect exchange with Teotihuacan does not imply that such interaction somehow stimulated the rise of Oxkintok. Instead, we see growing internationalism as a *natural consequence* of the emergence of Oxkintok as the capital of a regional state during the late Early Classic period. This general argument can be extended to many important northern lowland cities of the period, including those that exhibit neither direct nor indirect ties with Teotihuacan.

Michael Smyth and his colleagues who work at the nearby and much smaller Puuc site called Chac II have argued for a very different interpretation of Teotihuacan interaction (Smyth and Ortegón Zapata 2006; Smyth and Rogart 2004). They cite foreign-style residential architecture, ceramics, artwork, and burial practices as implying that Teotihuacanos or their surrogates married into the local population and lived at Chac II. Most importantly, they see this interaction with central Mexico as stimulating the rise of urbanism in the region. It is beyond the scope of this introduction to address their hypothesis in detail, but I concur strongly with Stanton (2005) and do not see most of what is presented as evidence from Chac II of interaction with Teotihuacan as indicating the presence of foreign colonists. Moreover, I cannot imagine a viable reason why Teotihuacan would establish a trading post or enclave at this small site, and yet ignore already existing, large, and nearby market centers such as Chunchucmil. The ideological importance of the Gruta de Chac (Smyth and Ortegón Zapata 2006:139), a local cave containing water, surely is insufficient; there are many other caves with water in them that are closer to Teotihuacan. If there were foreigners at Chac II, they must have been in hiding during the Early Classic period.

Early Classic Ceramics of the Northern Lowlands

One of the defining characteristics of the Early Classic period throughout the lowlands is the appearance of the first polychrome pottery. Polychrome ceramics dating to both the Early and Late Classic period are found at northern Maya lowland sites, but—with the exception of some coastal trading communities—the quantities decline dramatically the farther one moves to the north and the further forward one moves in time. By the late Early Classic period, ceramic production and decoration techniques in the northern Maya lowlands became quite distinct from those of the southern and central Maya lowlands, reflecting a weakening of interaction between the two areas.

Varela Torrecilla (1998; Varela Torrecilla and Braswell 2003) has argued that three important changes in ceramic manufacturing occurred at the Puuc site of Oxkintok during the period of A.D. 500/550–600. First, there was a complete cessation of the local production of polychrome pottery at the site at this time. Second, improvements in firing technology led to the development of the hard-paste ceramics that are so diagnostic of the Late and Terminal Classic periods. Third, production became highly standardized, likely because of direct control by elites. Although there is debate as to whether or not the Oxkintok Regional Phase constitutes a distinct ceramic phase or is a facet of a larger phase (Robles Castellanos 2000), what is clear is that in the late sixth century A.D., the earliest pottery related to Slate ware was produced in the Puuc region.

Late Classic Period (A.D. 600–780)

The Late Classic period saw great population growth, cultural florescence, and political expansion. Although some polychromes were produced at a wide range of northern lowland sites during the Early Classic, there were only two important production zones of polychrome pottery in the north during the Late Classic: the Rio Bec-Calakmul region and northeast Campeche, specifically an area containing Edzna and the Chenes zone (Ball 1975; Boucher and

Palomo 1995; Forsyth 1983; Matheny 1970; Nelson 1973:136; Williams-Beck 1999). In contrast, the well-fired but relatively plain pottery of the Cehpech sphere—which had its beginnings at the end of the Early Classic in the Puuc region—became widespread across the peninsula at this time. By A.D. 700 or 750, in fact, Edzna ceased to produce or consume polychrome pottery and became a Cehpech-sphere site. Thus, the divergence between the ceramics of the northern Maya lowlands and the southern and central Maya lowlands that characterized the Early Classic period continued and increased during Late Classic times.

By A.D. 730, population levels in the Puuc region rose to new heights, and many sites flourished. At this time, the building technique of core-veneer masonry, which had its roots in the sixth century, became the dominant construction method of the region. During the course of the Late and Terminal Classic periods, Puuc masonry would reach levels of elaboration and elegance unknown elsewhere in the Maya area (Chapter 8). Variants of Puuc-style masonry, sometimes incorporating load-bearing walls, eventually spread across the northern Maya lowlands from Edzna to Ek Balam.

During the Late Classic period, Dzibilchaltun became a massive and densely populated city (Andrews 1981). Population densities in northwest Yucatan grew to their greatest extent, a level, as mentioned above, not seen anywhere else in the Maya lowlands. Late Classic pottery of Dzibilchaltun included large amounts of Muna Slate, a diagnostic kind of pottery within the Cehpech complex. Very small quantities of polychromes were imported from the southern and central Maya lowlands at the onset of Late Classic, but later in the period all imported polychromes came from either the Chenes region or the Rio Bec zone. After about A.D. 750, virtually no polychromes were traded to Dzibilchaltun (Andrews 1975:245).

Izamal continued to thrive during the Late Classic period. Other large northern sites that reached their greatest extent during the Late Classic period include Edzna, Sayil, Coba, and Ek Balam. Two major projects at Ek Balam have contributed greatly to our understanding of that site (Bey et al. 1997, 1998; Houk 2006; Lacadena García-Gallo 2005; Ringle and Bey 2001; Ringle et al. 2004; Vargas de la Peña and Castillo Borges 1999, 2005). The first, directed by Will Andrews' former Tulane graduate students, mapped the city, conducted settlement and environmental studies, excavated in habitation zones outside of the epicenter, and developed a detailed ceramic typology and chronology. The second project, directed by scholars based at the INAH regional center in Merida, excavated and consolidated the grandest structures in the epicenter of Ek Balam and studied the texts and monuments of the site. Data generated by both projects complement each other, and demonstrate that site-center, urban, and rural hinterland studies are all necessary to understand the history of an ancient Maya city.

Ek Balam at the End of the Late Classic Period

Occupation of Ek Balam extends from the Middle Preclassic into the colonial period, but the site was at its peak during the Late Classic and Terminal Classic periods. During the Late Classic period, Ek Balam belonged to the Cehpech sphere, but the ceramics of the site more closely resemble materials from Dzibilchaltun and the Puuc region than eastern Cehpech pottery from nearby Coba (Bey et al. 1998:114). Some architecture at Ek Balam contains features of the Puuc style, strengthening this association.

Although Ek Balam was settled long before the end of the Late Classic period, we now know that it was a dynastic capital with an emblem glyph for only a short period of time beginning at the very end of the Late Classic and extending a few generations into the early Terminal Classic period. U K'it Kan Le'k Tok', the dynastic founder of Ek Balam who built much of the visible architecture in the epicenter of the site, ruled from A.D. 770 to 801 (Chapter 14). The excavation of his tomb on Structure 1 by the INAH team was one of the most spectacular discoveries of the 1990s (Figure 1.7). The decorated façade outside the tomb is rightly said to evoke the Chenes architectural style. The doorway is a large monster mouth that is surrounded by teeth, and up above are eyes and a nose. To enter the building, one must climb over the teeth and walk across the lower jaw. Although Chenes-style buildings are known in the Puuc, this example is very far afield from the Chenes region.

Perhaps more striking than the overall design of the structure are its details. In many respects, the three-dimensional sculpture on the façade has more in common with Late Classic sculpture from Copan, Honduras—the site where Will Andrews directed his most recent fieldwork—than with sculpture found at any other site in the northern lowlands. Carved skulls on the lower molding of this structure resemble similar skulls on Structure 10L-22 of Copan, built in A.D. 705.[3] The doorway on the exterior façade of Structure 10L-22 also can be said to be Chenes in style, despite the great distance between Copan and the northern Maya lowlands.

Figure 1.7. Exterior façade of the tomb of U K'it Kan Le'k Tok', Ek Balam, excavated by Leticia Vargas de la Peña and Víctor Castillo Borges. Top: May 2003, before the consolidated pillar supporting the nose above the doorway was removed. Bottom: March 2008.

More remarkable ties with Structure 10L-22 of Copan can be seen in many examples of Late to Terminal Classic Rio Bec and Chenes architecture, as well as in Terminal Classic Puuc architecture. One of the hallmarks of all these styles is stacked monster masks (Chapter 8). Monster masks of the sort that are commonly called "Chaaks," but most of which appear to be variants of the Wits' earth monster, begin to adorn the corners of structures built in the northern lowlands in the late eighth century. In the Puuc region, they are *de rigueur* on Classic Puuc Mosaic style structures dating to A.D. 830–900/950 (Figure 1.8 left). The earliest currently visible example, however, of such stacked monster masks is found on Structure 10L-22 of Copan, built in A.D. 715 to commemorate the earlier inauguration of the ruler Waxaklajuun Ub'aj K'awiil (Figure 1.8 right). A still earlier example of stacked Wits' corner masks was found deeply buried within the Copan Acropolis (Robert J. Sharer, personal communication 2011). The chronological placements of the tomb of U K'it Kan Le'k Tok', the northern lowland monster mask stacks, and the examples at Copan imply that the flow of the direction of these architectural and sculptural ideas must have been from south to north (see Sharer 1994:638). But it must also be that ideas from the northern lowlands flowed southwards during the Late Classic period, as people had for some time (Sharer 2003). Terminal Classic architecture at Nakum, Guatemala, for example, is reminiscent of core-veneer Puuc-style architecture.

Figure 1.8. Stacked monster masks found on the corners of Maya structures. Left: Palace of the Governor, Uxmal (September 2008). Right: Structure 10L-22, Copan (May 1991). The Copan mask stack predates all known examples from the northern Maya lowlands.

Terminal Classic (A.D. 780–900/950) and Early Postclassic (A.D. 900/950–1200) Periods

In the northern Maya lowlands, the Terminal Classic and Early Postclassic periods are characterized by the rise of great cities, dramatic demographic surges, the apex of regional art and architectural styles, and great increases in mercantilism, long-distance trade, marketing behavior, and participation in a world religion (Braswell 2010; Braswell and Glascock 2007; Ringle et al. 1998). These two periods are also characterized by the collapse of all these things. Such collapse took place in most of the northern lowlands during the Terminal Classic, and somewhat later at Chichen Itza in the Early Postclassic period.

Terminal Classic Highs and Lows

During the Terminal Classic period, the great city of Uxmal emerged as the most powerful political capital in the Puuc region (Chapter 8), and Chichen Itza quickly grew—virtually *de novo*—to be the largest and most powerful city in west-central Yucatan (Chapters 9–11). As in the southern and central Maya lowlands, some sites and regions experienced political and demographic collapse during the Terminal Classic period. These include the Rio Bec region just south of the southern fringe of the northern lowlands. In Quintana Roo, Coba ceased to be a great city relatively early in the Terminal Classic period, as did the major metropolis of Calakmul in the central Maya lowlands of southeastern Campeche (Chapter 4; Braswell et al. 2004). At Ek Balam, there are no hieroglyphic texts that unambiguously postdate A.D. 841 (Lacadena García-Gallo 2002), suggesting that the decline of dynastic rule at that site might have occurred during the middle of the ninth century. By about A.D. 900, sites relatively close to the emerging Chichen Itza—such as Yaxuna and Ek Balam—suffered significant depopulation and near-to-total abandonment. To the west, large quantities of ceramics and exotic Mexican obsidian dating to the Terminal Classic period demonstrate that the city of Izamal continued to flourish during this period, but probably suffered significant decline sometime after A.D. 1000. In northwest Yucatan, Dzibilchaltun certainly saw significant political upheaval during the Terminal Classic period (Andrews and Andrews 1980), but some structures were built then and incorporate stylistic elements from the Puuc region and Chichen Itza (Andrews 1979a). Nonetheless, Dzibilchaltun was virtually abandoned by the beginning of the Early Postclassic period. To the southeast, construction activity at Edzna continued into the Terminal Classic period, and both ceramics and architecture dating to this time are closely tied to the Puuc region (Forsyth 1983). Edzna collapsed at roughly the same time as Puuc polities to the northeast.

The pattern of decline grew as the Terminal Classic progressed and transitioned into the Early Postclassic period. Although the beginning of the tenth century saw the absolute height of art and architecture at Uxmal, there is little evidence that Puuc-style constructions were built at that site—or anywhere else in the region—after about A.D. 925 (Chapter 8). We cannot precisely date the collapse of Uxmal, but it seems to have occurred within 20 to 50 years of its peak. At roughly the same time, the entire Puuc region suffered a demographic decline from which it never recovered. Small C-shaped and L-shaped structures were built in plazas and in front of palaces and temples at Uxmal (Huchím Herrera and García Ayala 2000), and at other Puuc sites during or shortly after the demographic collapse. In fact, these enigmatic structures are found at many other northern and even central lowland Maya sites dating to the late

Terminal Classic/Early Postclassic (Bey et al. 1997). It is tempting to link them to a political takeover or re-occupation by people from Chichen Itza, but the cultural affiliation of these structures is insecure. At Xkipche—a relatively modest Puuc site not far from Uxmal—such buildings are associated with late Cehpech ceramics (Hanns Prem, cited in Braswell et al. 2011), suggesting that they probably do not represent an invasion from outside the Puuc. Moreover, these kinds of structures are not known at Chichen Itza itself (E. Wyllys Andrews V, personal communication 2011).

Thus, by A.D. 900/950, the end of the Terminal Classic period as defined for this volume, most of the cities of the northern Maya lowlands were either abandoned or were occupied by small, remnant populations. I have chosen to use this date to divide the Terminal Classic and Early Postclassic because it marks both the end of the Puuc florescence and the construction of the Castillo, the first great International style structure on the Great Platform of Chichen Itza (Chapter 9). By the end of the Terminal Classic period, population levels dropped across the peninsula, and—for the most part—became concentrated in coastal communities (Chapter 6; Andrews and Sabloff 1986; Benavides Castillo 1981; Eaton and Ball 1978; Robles Castellanos and Andrews 2000). The great exception to this general pattern is Chichen Itza, which flourished for the first 100 to 150 years of the Early Postclassic period.

It has been suggested that the decline of Coba (Andrews and Robles Castellanos 1985), Dzibilchaltun, and the Puuc region (Andrews and Sabloff 1986) might have been caused by the military expansion of Chichen Itza. Perhaps this was the case for fortified Ek Balam and Yaxuna (Freidel 2007; Ringle et al. 2004). But in the new paradigm, Chichen Itza expansion models are not as popular as they once were, in part because there does not seem to be a time period when Chichen Itza-style ceramics dominated the peninsula as a "horizon." The regional state of Chichen Itza—although certainly significant in size—was much smaller than we once thought, and its great influence might best be conceived in terms of religious and economic authority rather than direct political dominance or military control.

The North and South during the Terminal Classic Drought

Recently, Andrews et al. (2003) have made an important contribution to our understanding of the relevant factors and timing of the end of Classic civilization in the northern Maya lowlands. They argue that demographic and political declines in the north at the end of the Terminal Classic should be linked to the great "Classic Maya Collapse" that occurred somewhat earlier in the southern and central lowlands (Culbert 1973; Demarest et al. 2004). They assert that considered together, the collapse of the south and the north constituted a chain of events that took place over a 200–250-year period.

The political and demographic processes of collapse began in the south, perhaps with endemic warfare in the Petexbatun region (Demarest 2004), with the defeat of Calakmul by Tikal and of Copan by Quirigua (Braswell et al. 2004), and—most importantly—with a long-term and harsh drought (Curtis et al. 1996; Haug et al. 2003; Hodell et al. 2001). The effects of these events—which probably led to the displacement of large numbers of people within the context of ever-declining climatic conditions—radiated outward in waves from the central and southern lowlands, culminating in the collapse of the Puuc and much of the north during the first half of the tenth century A.D. Demographic shifts to the coastal margins of the peninsula during the Terminal Classic period (Chapter 6) not only indicate greater participation in international, sea-based trade routes, but also should be interpreted as an adaptation to an environment that could no longer reliably support large, inland populations of farmers. Among the many remaining questions is how and why Chichen Itza managed to survive—and actually thrive—throughout the tenth and well into the eleventh century A.D. (Chapters 9–10). Sacred offerings in nearby Balankanche Cave are consistent with calling for rain and fertility (one might speculate to end a drought), but careful analysis shows that they were made within the broader and periodic context of scheduled renewal rituals (Chapter 11). Moreover, these rituals of creation, renewal, and regeneration continued at least until the Spanish conquest—that is, after the Terminal Classic drought—and involved performers of both genders.

The Cehpech-Sotuta Problem

The argument put forward by Andrews et al. (2003) relies on two related and important changes to our understanding of the chronology of the northern Maya lowlands that are central to the new paradigm. The first change concerns absolute dates. We now know that there was very little or no monumental construction in the Puuc region after about A.D. 925 (Chapter 8). Moreover, we know that the traditional chronological placement of Chichen Itza (A.D. 1000–1200) is too late. We still do not know precisely when the last building was raised at Chichen Itza, but most of the structures currently visible in the northern (and slightly later) portion of the site center were built during the interval A.D. 900/950–1050 (Chapter 9), at the end of the Terminal Classic and at the beginning of the Early Postclassic periods.

The second and related chronological issue centers on the resolution of an old debate concerning the ceramics of the Puuc region, Dzibilchaltun, Coba, and many other sites with Late and Terminal Classic components. Although the specific ceramic complexes of these sites differ, and distinct—but closely related—ceramic spheres can be drawn, they all can be called "Cehpech." The Cehpech sphere was first defined by Robert E. Smith (1971:144-169) and—if we expand its original definition to include ceramic groups from both the northwestern and northeastern peninsula—consists of pottery belonging to the Chum Unslipped, Muna Slate, Ticul Thin Slate, Teabo Red, Altar Fine Orange, Balancan Fine Orange, Holactun Cream, Achote, Zupulche, Vista Alegre, and Maquina Red ceramic groups (Smith 1971; Robles Castellanos 1990, 2005). Smith dated the Cehpech sphere to the Terminal Classic period, ca. A.D. 800–1000. According to Smith, Cehpech pottery dominated the entire northern lowlands during this period and was subsequently replaced by ceramics of the Sotuta sphere centered at Chichen Itza. Sotuta ceramic groups include Sisal Unslipped, Dzitas Slate, Dzibiac Red, Tinum, Silho Fine Orange, Tohil Plumbate, and small quantities of other imports. Smith (1971) argued that the Sotuta sphere came to dominate the northern Maya lowlands, replacing Cehpech during the interval of A.D. 1000–1200.

It is important to note that many of the differences between the Cehpech and Sotuta complexes seem rather small to an outsider: they both contain hard-fired slate wares, analogous red utilitarian wares, rather similar unslipped pottery, and different sorts of Fine Orange. Both complexes are clearly related—but certainly not identical—in terms of technology and decoration. The distinctions between them are most obvious in diagnostic forms (particularly in the Sotuta complex) and in the different local resources used to build the pottery. With these important exceptions, the Cehpech and Sotuta complexes look more like variations on a set of similar themes rather than pottery belonging to dramatically different ceramic traditions. There certainly is no good reason to consider Cehpech ceramics as "Maya" and Sotuta pottery as "Toltec-Maya."

By the late 1970s, Smith's replacement scenario was widely questioned (Ball 1977, 1979; Lincoln 1986, 1990; Ringle et al. 1998; Robles Castellanos 2005). Alternative partial and complete "overlap" models were proposed. Unlike Smith, who assumed that the differences between Cehpech and Sotuta were entirely chronological, the overlap models suggest that a great deal of the variation is spatial or regional in character. Moreover, we now know that the Sotuta sphere did not come to encompass all—or even most—of the northern lowlands. Although some Sotuta pottery is found at quite a lot of sites dating to the Terminal Classic and Early Postclassic periods, the sphere itself is limited to the region around Chichen Itza, sites between there and the north coast, and a few east coast sites. Most scholars now favor a partial overlap model, where the hard-fired ceramics of the Cehpech complex began to be produced during the sixth century A.D., and the widest distribution of the sphere (or spheres) is roughly A.D. 730–900/950 (Robles Castellanos 2005). In contrast, Sotuta pottery began to be produced in the area immediately surrounding Chichen Itza at about A.D. 800/850 (Pérez de Heredia Puente 2008), spread to its maximum distribution during the period A.D. 900/950–1050, and then continued to be produced at some Early Postclassic coastal sites that outlived Chichen Itza itself.

International Trade of Ceramics and Obsidian during the Terminal Classic

Throughout the Maya lowlands, the Terminal Classic period is characterized by increasing international trade. In some cases, this seems to reflect collapse. At Copan, Honduras, for example, locally produced fine-line incised and carved vessels and polychrome pottery imported from the Peten were replaced by polychromes produced in non-Maya northern and central Honduras (Bill 1997). At Calakmul, locally and regionally produced polychromes were replaced by imported Slate ware and local imitations (Braswell et al. 2004). Throughout much of the lowlands, imported Fine Orange ware and locally made vessels in similar forms with similar carved designs began to appear about A.D. 830. The sense I have is that remnant local elites who no longer had access to—or knowledge of how to make—Late Classic polychromes reached out to more distant trading partners for status-endowing ceramics. This is not the case for the northern lowlands, where many important pottery-producing centers thrived during the Terminal Classic period. Thus, imported Fine Orange and Tohil Plumbate were added to locally and regionally produced "elite" wares. Northern elites searched further afield for goods such as Mexican obsidian and turquoise. These materials came to supplement or even replace obsidian and jade from the Maya highlands, which became harder to acquire after the collapse of polities in the southern and central lowlands.

Throughout most of the Classic period, consumers in the northern Maya lowlands received the bulk of their obsidian from the El Chayal source area, located approximately 25 kilometers northeast of Kaminaljuyu. This remained the case for most sites in the northern lowlands during the Terminal Classic period, suggesting that consumers relied on attenuating connections with the south and, importantly, the recycling of old and discarded artifacts to meet their needs for obsidian (Braswell and Glascock 2011). In comparison, even in the earliest architectural contexts of Chichen Itza that date to before about A.D. 800/850, a significant proportion of the obsidian comes from source areas in central and west Mexico. In declining order of frequency, these Mexican sources are Ucareo (Michoacan), Pachuca (Hidalgo), Zaragoza (Puebla), Paredon (Puebla), Pico de Orizaba (Veracruz), Zacualtipan (Hidalgo), and Otumba (Estado de Mexico; Braswell and Glascock 2007:Figura 6; Braswell et al. 2011:Table 2). By the end of the Terminal Classic and throughout the Early Postclassic period, roughly 70 percent of all obsidian consumed at Chichen Itza would come from these sources. Similar consumption patterns are seen at Isla Cerritos, a northern port of Chichen Itza (Andrews et al.

1989). A strong correlation emerges: those sites with lots of Sotuta ceramics tended to have access to exotic obsidian from Mexico. In contrast, those sites with little or no Sotuta material (i.e., Cehpech sites) relied almost exclusively on the El Chayal source. Finally, sites with significant quantities of pottery belonging to both complexes—such as Xuenkal and Ichmul de Morley—exhibit a mixed pattern of obsidian procurement (Braswell, unpublished data on Xuenkal 2008; Braswell and Glascock 2007:Figuras 3-7; Smith et al. 2006:164-166). At some sites, this third pattern may reflect temporal distinctions between periods before and during the era of Itza economic dominance.

Only four northern lowland sites dating to the Terminal Classic that are outside of the Chichen Itza realm show great reliance on Mexican obsidian. These are Izamal (where Sotuta ceramics are quite common, and which may have been politically or economically tied to Chichen Itza), Siho, Uaymil, and Oxkintok (Braswell and Glascock 2007). Siho is, for the most part, a Late Classic period site with limited Terminal Classic pottery (Fernández Souza et al. 2003). It appears likely that the Mexican obsidian at this site (33 percent of the entire sample) dates to the end of occupation ca. A.D. 800–850. Uaymil is a Late to Terminal Classic site that could have served as the port for Uxmal (Cobos Palma 2004; Cobos Palma et al. 2005; Inurreta Díaz and Cobos Palma 2003) or perhaps for some other Puuc site, such as Oxkintok. The sample of obsidian from Uaymil is small, but procurement patterns there seem to mirror those of Siho (Braswell and Glascock 2007:Figura 3). In two ways, obsidian procurement patterns at Oxkintok are quite different from those of any other Puuc site I have studied. First, fully 53 percent of the obsidian recovered from the site comes from central Mexico. Unique for any site in the northern lowlands dating to any time period, most of the Mexican obsidian is green and comes from the Pachuca, Hidalgo source (Braswell and Glascock 2007:Figura 4). I stress that the green obsidian I have studied was not associated with "Middle Classic" contexts dating to the Oxkintok Regional phase, and hence, cannot be attributed to earlier trade with Teotihuacan (Varela Torrecilla and Braswell 2003). Chichen Itza, via its port at Isla Cerritos, therefore, was not the only Terminal Classic site with access to obsidian from central Mexico. Some seems to have entered the northern lowlands from the west, and Oxkintok may have had its own highly distinct exchange relations.

Market Economy during the Terminal Classic and Early Postclassic

Michael D. Glascock and I have argued that obsidian procurement patterns in the northern Maya lowlands imply: (1) that Chichen Itza had widespread exchange connections—direct or indirect—with a variety of sites in central Mexico; (2) that the Toltec site of Tula is but one of these sites; (3) that a fully commercialized and competitive market system emerged in Mesoamerica by the Epiclassic/Terminal Classic period; and (4) that first Chichen Itza (ca. A.D. 800) and later Uxmal (ca. A.D. 900–950) participated in this system (Braswell 2003, 2010; Braswell and Glascock 2003, 2007). Maya involvement in this pan-Mesoamerican market system, however, did not survive the collapse of Chichen Itza. In later periods, Maya economies seem to have been organized as simpler, partially commercialized markets, or even as redistributive systems (Braswell 2010).

Chichen Itza and the Toltecs during the Early Postclassic Period

The most enduring question about Chichen Itza—and to a lesser degree, Uxmal—has been the nature of interaction with the Toltecs of Tula. The traditional perspective, most completely formulated by Tozzer (1957), is that there were two periods of occupation at Chichen Itza

(Chapter 9). At first, the site was occupied by Maya who built structures in a local variation of the Puuc style. The "Chichen Maya" period was followed by a "Toltec-Maya" occupation, when structures and art exhibiting strong similarities with examples at Tula were built. For Tozzer—among many other scholars since Charnay (1887)—the explanation was invasion; the Toltec legendary hero Ce Acatl Topiltzin Quetzalcoatl came to Yucatan, established a new militaristic political order, and built a new version of Tula—albeit on a much grander scale (see Gillespie 2007 for an explanation of how this perspective developed).

By the late 1970s, many scholars came to challenge this scenario, noting that there was little evidence at Chichen Itza for distinct "Chichen Maya" and "Toltec-Maya" occupations (the Cehpech-Sotuta chronological debate, in part, is related to this issue; see also Lincoln 1986:152), and that dates for the site were too early and did not accord well with the legendary chronology of Quetzalcoatl of Tula (see Andrews 1979a:Table 1). Other versions of the invasion scenario proposed that it was not precisely Toltecs from Tula who came to Yucatan, but instead successive waves of "Mexicanized" Chontal-speaking Maya from the Gulf Coast called the Putun. Complex migration routes for Putun groups—including the Itza—have been proposed (Thompson 1970; Schele and Freidel 1990:497, 350; Schele and Mathews 1999). Problems of chronology and the literal accuracy of Aztec ethnohistorical documents can be resolved by appealing to different versions of the Putun model, but it, too, has come under close scrutiny. Although the books of *Chilam Balam* certainly discuss quite a lot of migration myths, it is uncertain that the Putun—as some kind of distinct ethnic group that included the Itza—existed outside of the mind of J. Eric S. Thompson (Kremer 1994:303). One wonders as well why the Itza language is so closely related to Yucatec rather than to Chontal.

A key aspect of the new paradigm was proposed by William M. Ringle, Tomás Gallareta Negrón, and George J. Bey (1998). They argue that the most visible manifestations of internationalism during the late Terminal Classic and Early Postclassic periods were caused by the participation of Uxmal and Chichen Itza in a world religion focused on the feathered serpent deity called Kukulcan[4] by the Maya and Quetzalcoatl by Nahuatl speakers. They suggest that Chichen Itza and—for a brief period in the early tenth century—Uxmal were cathedral cities in a web of centers dedicated to the cult of the Feathered Serpent, which may have had its ultimate origin at Early Classic Teotihuacan (Ringle 2004). Other important nodes in the network included the great city of Cholula (McCafferty 2007), Xochicalco, El Tajin, and—of course—Tula.

For Ringle (Chapter 8), the term "Toltec" can be applied to all participants in this religion regardless of the polity to which they belonged, and all cities involved in the network are "Tollans." Thus, the cult of Quetzalcoatl/Kukulcan was an international phenomenon that transcended political boundaries. Similarities between Chichen Itza and Tula developed because of the international character of the religion. Both cities, as well as others in the network, were important pilgrimage centers, so for this reason art and architectural styles developed that were understandable—"readable"—by elite pilgrims who belonged to distinct cultures and who spoke different languages. Nonetheless, the International style of each city is somewhat different, reflecting an eclectic mixture of local and pan-Mesoamerican ideas. Trade, of course, follows the *hajj*. The presence at Chichen Itza of significant quantities of imported central Mexican obsidian and smaller amounts of turquoise from even farther away reflects participation in this international network. It is likely, in fact, that increased trade acted as a stimulus for further integration within the pan-Mesoamerican cult.

According to Ringle (2004, 2009), a key aspect of the cult of Quetzalcoatl/Kukulcan was political investiture, especially in conjunction with military roles. Important public architecture at cities such as Chichen Itza and Uxmal were theaters/stages where such investiture ceremonies took place. Although it is somewhat unlikely that the ballgame was ever played in the Great Ballcourt of Chichen Itza, it is highly probable that it saw the coronation of rulers from various communities. The importance of Chichen Itza as the regional center of this elite investiture cult might help explain why it continued to be occupied long after the collapse of Uxmal and many other sites in the northern lowlands. In fact, it seems as though the great city of Chichen Itza, like Monte Alban in the Valley of Oaxaca, was never totally abandoned. During the Early Postclassic, leaders of demographically reduced and fractured polities still depended on the authority of Chichen Itza as the sole regional center that could legitimize rulership. Such small, client polities, many of which were located near the coast, may have supported Chichen Itza. What is now clear is that during the chaos of the Early Postclassic period, Chichen Itza was not the capital of a peninsular empire. Instead, its ritual suzerainty far exceeded the bounds of its political sovereignty. Its survival—for a time—might be attributable to this fact.

Political Structure of Chichen Itza

Another important focus of research in the new paradigm is the political structure of Chichen Itza. Archaeologists, art historians, and epigraphers have long been perplexed by the apparent lack of royal graves, acropolis-type palaces,[5] images showing divine kings, and historical king lists at Chichen Itza. Such evidence is not common in the northern Maya lowlands, although there are important dynastic monuments at Coba, Edzna, and—to a somewhat limited degree—Ek Balam, Chichen Itza, Uxmal, Xcalumkin, Dzibilchaltun, Sayil, and a few other sites.

Most texts from Chichen Itza date to a very narrow time period during the reign of K'ak'upakal, who "stands out as the most prominent figure, accompanied by his brother K'inil Kopol, who oversaw many building activities. And yet, K'inil Kopol certainly was of lesser rank..." (Grube and Krochock 2007:229). Before the 1990s, no clear royal tomb had been excavated in the northern lowlands; now we have examples from Yaxuna, Oxkintok, and—most spectacularly—Ek Balam. But none have been excavated so far at Chichen Itza, with the possible exception of the looted "High Priest's Grave" in the Osario pyramid (Thompson and Thompson 1938).

The apparent lack of the "cult of kings" so common in the southern and central lowlands has led some to suggest that the nature of rulership in the north, and especially at Chichen Itza, was significantly different. David Stuart wrote an important and widely circulated letter in 1988 in which he proposed that the glyph *yitaaj*, used to link two individuals in Classic Maya texts, should be glossed as "sibling of." He further suggested that references in Landa (Tozzer 1941) to Chichen Itza being founded by three brothers might imply a system of joint rulership, known in later periods as *multepal*, at that site. This idea was quite popular during the 1990s (Krochock and Freidel 1994; Schele and Freidel 1990), but became discredited when the provisional gloss of *yitaaj* fell through (Grube and Krochock 2007:229). Some scholars have argued that Chichen Itza had a strongly centralized government headed by a divine king or a pair of kings (Cobos Palma 2007; Lincoln 1990). Ringle (2004), however, envisions distinct and dual estates of secular/military and priestly roles, each advised by councils. We still have a long way to go before we arrive at a consensus regarding how Chichen Itza was ruled.

The End of the Early Postclassic Period

The last century of the Early Postclassic, ca. A.D. 1100–1200, was a dark age. The demographic collapse that began during the Terminal Classic period continued, and, after the collapse of Chichen Itza, very few significant settlements were located in inland regions. Just as the ceramic complexes of the Terminal Classic period have been subject to chronological re-evaluation, so too has Smith's (1971) succeeding Hocaba ceramic complex.

According to Smith, the Hocaba "phase" dates to A.D. 1200–1250/1300, and marks the transition into the Late Postclassic of Mayapan. It now seems more likely that Hocaba pottery dates to the period A.D. 1000/1050–1200/1250, and it should be stressed that—compared to pottery dating to earlier and later periods in the northern lowlands—it is uncommon to rare, supporting the notion that the eleventh and twelfth centuries saw a population nadir in the north.

Many of the ceramic groups that Smith (1971) included in the Hocaba "complex" are also present in and diagnostic of the ensuing, and better understood, Tases complex. For this reason, Ringle et al. (1998:189-191) argue that Hocaba does not constitute a complete ceramic complex. Instead at Mayapan, Hocaba-Tases represents early settlement before the full Tases complex. Hocaba pottery such as Peto Cream ware appears at Chichen Itza, in Balankanche Cave, and at Isla Cerritos in contexts that also have Sotuta pottery, implying that the Hocaba "complex" also overlaps with Sotuta (Andrews 1970; Andrews and Andrews 1980; Andrews et al. 1988; Gallareta Negrón et al. 1989; Brainerd 1958:57; Ringle et al. 1998). At Chichen Itza, Hocaba pottery is found mixed with Sotuta material in exclusively post-construction contexts. That is, it dates to the eleventh and perhaps early twelfth century A.D. at that city, and marks its decline.

Discoveries of small quantities of Terminal Classic pottery at Mayapan, but no standing architecture, imply that a small settlement existed there before the collapse of Chichen Itza (Peraza Lope et al. 2006:153-155; Pollock et al. 1962:6, 92). The earliest known sub-Castillo temple at Mayapan dates to some time during the eleventh or twelfth centuries (Peraza Lope et al. 2006). This, along with the presence of Sotuta-Hocaba pottery in post-construction contexts at Chichen Itza and of Hocaba-Tases and even trace amounts of Sotuta and Cehpech pottery at Mayapan, links the chronologies of the two cities together. Although there is no single period when both can be said to have been large cities, Chichen Itza and Mayapan were partially contemporary. Mayapan may be said to have "profited in the aftermath of Chichen Itza, rising in the twelfth century, following Chichen's fall, and peaking from the thirteenth to early fifteenth centuries A.D." (Peraza Lope et al. 2006:172).

Late Postclassic Period (A.D. 1200–1540)

With the foundation of Mayapan, ethnohistorical accounts begin to provide historical as well as anthropological insights into the prehispanic northern Maya lowlands. Nonetheless, the chronologies of documents such as the books of *Chilam Balam* seem "telescoped," sometimes flattening events from different periods into one, and at other times seeming to imply that the life of particular individuals extended over vast periods of time (Chapter 10). Despite many attempts to align *k'atun* chronologies with western concepts of time (e.g., Edmonson 1982, 1986; Milbrath and Peraza Lope 2003; Roys 1967), such documents reflect Maya conceptions about how time ought to be cyclically organized. For this reason, we probably not should take literally the dates given for different events, or to make emic chronology fit archaeological data. Even more importantly, we should not try to force our growing archaeological knowledge of Mayapan to fit into *k'atun* cycles.

Recent archaeological projects at Mayapan have contributed greatly to our understanding of this city (Chapter 12; Brown 1999, 2005, 2006; Masson and Peraza Lope 2005; Milbrath and Peraza Lope 2003; Peraza Lope et al. 2001, 2006). Although there is evidence for a limited Terminal Classic occupation, the power of Mayapan began to coalesce during the twelfth century, near the end of the Early Postclassic period. The books of *Chilam Balam* discuss attacks against Chichen Itza, and it is conceivable that Mayapan may have played some role in the final destruction of what must have been already a very depleted place (Chapter 10). Perhaps such people from Mayapan belonged to the Xiu group, which the *Chilam Balam of Mani* states founded the city. Alternatively, the founders of Mayapan may have been Cocom elite coming from Chichen Itza (Ringle et al. 1998:190-191, 225).

The great period of Mayapan does not seem to have begun much before about A.D. 1200 (Peraza Lope et al. 2006), and ended—according to both chronicles and radiocarbon dates— about A.D. 1440. Mayapan, therefore, represents a "peak" between the twin valleys of the twelfth century and the last century before the Spanish conquest of Yucatan (Chapter 4). Two periods of major construction seem to have occurred at Mayapan during the thirteenth and fourteenth centuries (Peraza Lope et al. 2006). It is tempting to link one of these surges in construction activity to activities by the Cocoms and the other to the Xius.

Structures Q-87a and Q-88a, two halls in the Round Temple group located in the site center, were burned sometime in the fourteenth century, as was Str. Y-45a, an outlying elite house (Peraza Lope et al. 2006:165, 173). Also, two mass graves or "bone beds" were excavated at Structure Q-79/79a and in the Itzmal Chen group. These date to the thirteenth or fourteenth centuries (Peraza Lope et al. 2006:162, 173, Figure 7). Thus, it might very well be that Mayapan saw internal conflict during its apogee, perhaps even between the two groups— the Cocoms and Xius—that historical chronicles say dominated the politics of the city.

Mayapan, of course, is not the only Late Postclassic site in the northern lowlands. But it certainly was the largest inland site during most of that period. Demographic trends that began in the Terminal Classic period—with many of the largest settlements located on the coast— continued in the Late Postclassic period. One area with particularly dense settlement is the eastern coast of central Quintana Roo. There, Late Postclassic sites are so closely packed together that they form an almost continuous—but very narrow—strip (Andrews 1985, 1986). In recent decades, INAH investigators and Anthony Andrews have conducted important research at sites such as El Meco (Andrews and Robles Castellanos 1986), Xelha (Peraza Lope and Toscano 1983), San Gervasio (Peraza Lope 1993, 2005; Sierra Sosa 1994; Sierra Sosa and Robles Castellanos 1988), among many others (for an account of this work, see Con Uribe 2005).

Long-Distance Interaction during the Late Postclassic Period

Mayapan maintained or renewed economic ties with central Mexico. Many noble and affluent commoner families seem to have had access to imported goods, but there is no unambiguous evidence of a resident barrio of foreigners at the site (Masson and Peraza Lope 2010). The most visible evidence of long-distance interaction is seen in the International style (or "Mixteca-Puebla" style) murals found at the site and also painted at other important Late Postclassic communities in the northern lowlands such as Ruinas de San Angel, Coba, Tulum-Tancah, Xelha, and Sant Rita Corozal (Boone and Smith 2003; Gallareta Negrón and Taube 2005; Miller 1982, 1986; Taube 2010).

A curious shift between the Terminal Classic/Early Postclassic and Late Postclassic periods is that very little obsidian from central Mexican sources reached Yucatan during the Late Postclassic period. At Mayapan itself, virtually all obsidian comes from the Ixtepeque, Guatemala source, with small quantities also brought in from El Chayal. In contrast, only trace quantities of Mexican obsidian are found (Escamilla Ojeda 2004). This shift from a reliance on El Chayal and Mexican obsidian to material from Ixtepeque typifies most of the Maya lowlands during this time period. Late Postclassic contexts at sites such as Xelha and San Gervasio on the east coast, and in the Champoton region on the west coast, are dominated by obsidian from the Ixtepeque source (Braswell and Glascock 2007; unpublished data from the Champoton Regional Settlement Survey collected by Braswell, 2009), although earlier contexts from these same sites and regions exhibit different procurement patterns.

Two of the most fascinating aspects concerning obsidian at Mayapan are its abundance and distribution. The quantity of obsidian recovered by the *Proyecto Mayapán*, directed by Carlos Peraza Lope and studied by Bárbara Escamilla Ojeda (2004)—more than 14,000 pieces—is greater than that recovered by all other archaeological projects in Yucatan during the last 20 years *combined*. Excavations conducted by that project at Mayapan focused on the epicenter of the site, but work elsewhere suggests that commoner households had very limited access to obsidian (Brown 1999). I have argued that this distribution pattern implies that, during the Late Postclassic period, obsidian was not distributed at Mayapan through a competitive market (Braswell 2010). Instead, its availability is more consistent with an administered market or, even more likely, polyadic redistribution. Nonetheless, we need more quantified data from outlying structures to be sure of this conclusion.

Late Postclassic "Decadence"

Since the 1950s, when the Carnegie Institute of Washington conducted research at Mayapan, its art and architecture have all too frequently been labeled as "decadent," a pejorative also applied to Late Postclassic sites on the east coast of Quintana Roo (Chapter 12; Freidel and Sabloff 1984). The term was originally adopted because of perceived parallels between the artifice of late nineteenth-century European art and literature of the Decadent movement and Postclassic Maya architecture, pottery, and painting. Various reasons have been proposed for this "decadence" (e.g., Rathje 1975), and others have tried to dismiss the apparent poverty of the city. Clifford Brown et al. (Chapter 12), however, contend that Mayapan *was* impoverished. Their perspective, argued from measures of both absolute wealth and its distribution, suggests that increased trade may not always create prosperity and can skew distributions of what wealth is generated. This message should resonate during the NAFTA era.

Colonial Period and Beyond (A.D. 1540–Present)

The Maya of course, did not disappear with the Spanish conquest. Since the publication of Anthony Andrews' (1981) article "Historical Archaeology in Yucatan: A Preliminary Framework," colonial, independence, and Caste War archaeology have flourished in the northern Maya lowlands. In our volume, Rani Alexander (Chapter 13) considers both the Spanish conquest and the Caste War as yet two more examples of "collapses" that were experienced by the Maya. Rather than employing Joyce Marcus' Dynamic Model (Chapter 4), Alexander interprets collapse and reorganization in terms of resilience theory and Panarchy (Holling and Gunderson 2002; Redman 2005).

Alexander stresses three points. First, the collapse of the tenth through twelfth centuries was by no means the most severe demographic contraction experienced by the Maya of the northern lowlands. Those of the conquest and Caste War were arguably worse. Second, the effects of these historical collapses were not uniform, but tended to affect smaller settlements more than larger ones. Large communities with a sense of place or historical memory tended not to be completely abandoned. Third, different groups—including the Xiu and Cocom—adopted very different strategies to maintain autonomy. In both the conquest and the Caste War, the western Xiu accommodated to new political and economic conditions, while the eastern Cocom rose up in armed resistance.

Alexander's analysis suggests that the Maya of the northern lowlands today are in a period of conservation before yet another episode of release or collapse. State-sponsored resource extraction, the appropriation of community land for tourism and other purposes, the end of the *ejido* system, and a way of life that promotes migration to large cities rather than traditional agricultural practices are accelerating. We do not know yet how the Maya of our new century will react to these changes, but Alexander argues that they may come up with new strategies to improve resilience.

E. Wyllys Andrews V: An Archaeological Appreciation

Will Andrews' contributions have been central to the development of this new paradigm for the archaeology of the northern Maya lowlands. His ceramic analyses have identified the two earliest complexes known in the northern lowlands: Ek and Early Nabanche. He has also identified Early Nabanche pottery in the Olmec region and Middle Formative jades in the northern lowlands, suggestig that interaction between the Maya and the Olmec was bidirectional. Andrews' fieldwork at Komchen (conducted, of course, with his student Bill Ringle) provided the first clear picture of village life during the Middle Preclassic period in northwest Yucatan. His studies of architecture led to important conclusions concerning the distribution of hybrid Teotihuacan-Maya architectural traits in the northern Maya lowlands, as well as the spread of Puuc-style architecture beyond that region during the Late and Terminal Classic period. His interests in the Classic Maya Collapse, the chronologies of Chichen Itza and the Puuc region, and evidence for an extended period of drought have allowed us to consider the decline of many Terminal Classic cities of the northern lowlands as an extension of similar processes to the south, and afforded us an important understanding of the transition into the Postclassic period.

Will's many contributions can be seen not only in his publications, but also in the many archaeologists he has inspired. These include at least three "professional generations" of scholars. The first contains the many friends and colleagues that he has made over the years, including Joyce Marcus, who contributed two chapters to our volume. The second professional generation is comprised of the many graduate students Will taught at Tulane. Among these are Bill Ringle, David Anderson, Walter Witschey, Cliff Brown, Gabrielle Vail, Christine Hernández, Rani Alexander, and me. The impact of a third professional generation, who consider Will to be their "grandadvisor," is also beginning to be felt. In our collection, this group is represented by Nancy Peniche, Lauren Hahn, April Watson, and Ashley Gravlin-Beman. Even wider still is the vast network of archaeologists in the northern lowlands who have never been Will's students and who have not worked with him in the field, but who, nonetheless, are directly and indirectly inspired by his work. Among these scholars are Jerry Ek and Scott Hutson. But of course, all four of these groups contain many, many more people—in the United States, Mexico, Canada, Honduras, Spain, Germany, and other countries—who could easily fill a shelf with volumes in Will's honor.

Will, we dedicate this book to you in thanks for being our teacher, our friend, and an inspiration for the work we do. We hope you find merit in our work that depends so much on your solid foundation.

Acknowledgments

This introduction obviously borrows quite liberally the idea of a "new paradigm" from Robles Castellanos' (n.d.) summary of advances that he and others have made to our understanding of the Middle Preclassic. It owes even more to Bey's (2006) masterful précis in *Lifeways in the Northern Maya Lowlands*. Where that chapter leaves off, the end of the Early Classic, I have had to forge ahead without George's expert guidance. To do this, I have relied on numerous colleagues and experts including the authors of the chapters in our volume, Robert Sharer, Dorie Reents-Budet, Traci Ardren, Ron Bishop, and—more than anyone else—Will Andrews himself. For this reason, I happily attribute the many factual and interpretive errors in this chapter to Will. I also gratefully acknowledge the participation in our original session of Aline Magnoni, Tomás Gallareta Negrón, Anthony Andrews, and Jeremy Sabloff, who, for various reasons, could not contribute to this volume. A special thanks is due to an anonymous reviewer who carefully read an earlier version of our manuscript and made very important and helpful comments. This work has benefitted greatly from these comments. Finally, I wish to thank all the contributors for their patience with my editing and many questions.

Notes

1. Cunil pottery from western Belize is now being called "Early Formative" or "Early Preclassic" because it has design motifs that elsewhere date to that period. Nonetheless, radiocarbon dates place Cunil at the transition between the Early and Middle Preclassic periods. It may be that Cunil pottery eventually will be pushed back in time or that a predecessor dating only to the Early Preclassic/Formative will be found in the Maya lowlands.

2. Ceramicists working in the northern Maya lowlands and western Belize—among other areas—have found it somewhat difficult to distinguish between pottery dating to roughly A.D. 100–250 and A.D. 250–400/430. This is because important Late Preclassic types, including members of the Sierra group, persisted in these regions long after the Early Classic Tzakol sphere emerged in the central Peten. Juan Pedro Laporte (1995) has used the expression "Peripheral Chicanel" to describe this phenomenon in the southeast Peten. The situation is further complicated by so-called "Protoclassic" modes (Brady et al. 1998). Thus, Glover and Stanton (2010), for example, fold both Laporte's "Peripheral Chicanel" and the "Protoclassic" into a period they call the Terminal Preclassic, dating from 75 B.C. to A.D. 400. The decline of the Yalahau region is therefore said to take place at the end of the Terminal Preclassic period, which is chronologically equivalent to the first half of the Early Classic period at Tikal, that is, ca. A.D. 250–400.

3. Moving far into the realm of speculation, I wonder if Altar L at Copan might possibly depict Ruler 16 engaging in a legitimization rite with U K'it Kan Le'k Tok' as ruler of Ek Balam. The figure on the right side of the altar sits on the name U K'it Tok'. The calendar round date of 3 Chicchan 3 Uo is generally thought to correspond with 8 February, A.D. 822 (a time when the king of Copan was likely dead), but it could also correspond to 21 February, A.D. 770. The accession of U K'it Kan Le'k Tok' as the dynastic founder of Ek Balam is not precisely known, but two candidates for this event are 9 April and 26 May A.D. 770 (Lacadena García-Gallo 2002; see Chapter 14). I admit that there is much to argue

against this interpretation, but it is not inconceivable that the time between February and April A.D. 770 represents the movement of the Ek Balam lord from Copan to the northern city.

4. An alternate spelling for this name is K'uk'ulkan. The proper way to spell Mayan words using Roman letters is a matter of continuing discussion. Guatemalan Mayan languages are now properly written according to a single official orthography adopted by Maya leaders and passed into law by the Guatemalan congress. Nonetheless, Yucatec (or Yukatek) Mayan of the northern lowlands has a much longer and continuous history as a written language than do most of the Mayan languages of Guatemala, and it has its own well-established orthography. Given that the use of either orthography implies a political decision, I have opted in this volume to let the authors themselves choose which set of conventions to employ. Like many, I tend to prefer the "new" orthography for words and names translated from Classic Maya texts, but employ the "traditional" orthography for the names of well-known sites and historical figures in the northern Maya lowlands.

5. Chichen Itza lacks acropolis-style palaces, but has an over abundance of palace structures built in other styles. The Monjas complex and Akab' Tz'ib', south of the Great Platform, are palaces. So too are the Initial Series Group (Osorio León 2004, 2005; Schmidt 2007) and the immense Bovedas Group southeast of the Great Platform.

References

Anderson, David. 2003. El asentamiento preclásico en la región noroeste de Yucatán, translated by Fernando Robles. In Andrews and Castellanos 2003:46-61.
— 2010. *Xtobo, Yucatan, Mexico: The Study of a Preclassic Maya Community*. Ph.D. dissertation, Department of Anthropology, Tulane University. University Microfilms, Ann Arbor.
Andrews, Anthony P. 1981. Historical Archaeology in Yucatan: A Preliminary Framework. *Historical Archaeology* 15:1-18.
— 1985. The Archaeology and History of Northern Quintana Roo. In *Geology and Hydrogeology of the Yucatan and Quaternary Geology of Northeastern Yucatan Peninsula*, edited by W. C. Ward, A. E. Weidie, and W. Back, pp. 127-143. New Orleans Geological Society, New Orleans.
— 1986. Reconocimiento arqueológico de Can Cún a Playa del Carmen, Quintana Roo. *Boletín de la Escuela de Ciencias Antropológicas de la Universidad de Yucatán* 13(78):3-19.
Andrews, Anthony P., E. Wyllys Andrews V, and J. Fernando Robles Castellanos. 2003. The Northern Maya Collapse and its Aftermath. *Ancient Mesoamerica* 14:151-156.
Andrews, Anthony P., Frank Asaro, Helen V. Michels, Fred H. Stross, and Pura Cervera Rivero. 1989. The Obsidian Trade at Isla Cerritos, Yucatan, Mexico. *Journal of Field Archaeology* 16:355-363.
Andrews, Anthony P., Tomás Gallareta Negrón, J. Fernando Robles Castellanos, Rafael Cobos Palma, and Pura Cervera Rivero. 1988. Isla Cerritos: An Itza Trading Port on the North Coast of Yucatan, Mexico. *National Geographic Research* 4:196-207.
Andrews, Anthony P., and J. Fernando Robles Castellanos. 1985. Chichén Itzá and Cobá: An Itzá–Maya Standoff in Early Postclassic Yucatán. In *The Lowland Maya Postclassic*, edited by Arlen F. Chase and Prudence M. Rice, pp. 62-72. University of Texas, Austin.
— 1986. *Excavaciones arqueológicas en El Meco, Quintana Roo, 1977*. Colección Cientifica 158. Instituto Nacional de Antropología e Historia, Mexico City.
— 2004. An Archaeological Survey of Northwest Yucatan, Mexico. *Mexicon* 26:7-14.
Andrews, E. Wyllys, IV. 1938. Some New Material from Coba, Quintana Roo, Mexico. *Ethnos* 3(2-3):33-46.
— 1970. *Balankanche, Throne of the Jaguar Priest*. Publication No. 32. Middle American Research Institute, Tulane University, New Orleans.
Andrews, E. Wyllys, IV, and E. Wyllys Andrews V. 1980. *Excavations at Dzibilchaltún, Yucatán, Mexico*. Publication No. 48. Middle American Research Institute, Tulane University, New Orleans.
Andrews, E. Wyllys, V. 1975. Archaeological Context and Significance of the Polychrome Pottery. In *The Polychrome Pottery of Dzibilchaltun, Yucatan, Mexico: Typology and Archaeological Context*, by

Joseph W. Ball and E. Wyllys Andrews V, pp. 234-246. Publication No. 31. Middle American Research Institute, Tulane University, New Orleans.
— 1976. *The Archaeology of Quelepa, El Salvador.* Publication No. 42. Middle American Research Institute, Tulane University, New Orleans.
— 1979a. Some Comments on Puuc Architecture of the Northern Yucatan Peninsula. In Mills 1979:1-17.
— 1979b. Early Central Mexican Architectural Traits at Dzibilchaltun, Yucatan. *Proceedings of the 42nd International Congress of Americanists* 8:237-249. Paris.
— 1981. Dzibilchaltun. In *Supplement to the Handbook of Middle American Indians*, vol. 1, edited by Jeremy A. Sabloff, pp. 313-341. University of Texas, Austin.
— 1986. Olmec Jades from Chacsinkin, Yucatan and Maya Ceramics from La Venta, Tabasco. In *Research and Reflections in Archaeology and History: Essays in Honor of Doris Stone*, edited by E. Wyllys Andrews V, pp. 11-49. Publication No. 57. Middle American Research Institute, Tulane University, New Orleans.
— 1988. Ceramic Units from Komchen, Yucatan, Mexico. *Cerámica de cultura maya* 15:51-64.
— 1990. The Early Ceramic History of the Lowland Maya. In *Vision and Revision in Maya Studies*, edited by Flora S. Clancy and Peter D. Harrison, pp. 1-19. University of New Mexico, Albuquerque.
— 2003. New Thoughts on Komchen and the Late Middle Preclassic. Paper presented at the Second Annual Tulane Maya Symposium, New Orleans.
Andrews, E. Wyllys, V, and George J. Bey III. 2011. The Earliest Ceramics of the Northern Maya Lowlands. Paper presented at the VIIIth Tulane Maya Symposium, New Orleans.
Andrews, E. Wyllys, V, George J. Bey III, and Christopher Gunn. 2008. Rethinking the Early Ceramic History of the Northern Maya Lowlands: New Evidence and Interpretations. Paper presented at the 73rd Annual Meeting of the Society for American Archaeology, Vancouver.
Andrews, E. Wyllys, V, and Barbara Fash. 1992. Continuity and Change in a Royal Maya Residential Complex at Copan. *Ancient Mesoamerica* 3:63-88.
Andrews V, E. Wyllys, and Jeremy A. Sabloff. 1986. Classic to Postclassic: A Summary Discussion. In Sabloff and Andrews V 1986:433-456.
Ardren, Traci A., and Dave Johnstone. 1996. A Middle Preclassic Ceremonial Structure from Yaxuná, Yucatán, Mexico. Paper presented at the 61st Annual Meeting of the Society for American Archaeology, New Orleans.
Artdaily. 2012. Archaeologists from INAH Conduct Research at Hoyo Negro Flooded Cave in Quintana Roo. Online: www.artdaily.org/index.asp?int_sec=2&int_new=45564.
Ball, Joseph W. 1975. Ceramic Typology. In *The Polychrome Pottery of Dzibilchaltun, Yucatan, Mexico: Typology and Archaeological Context*, by Joseph W. Ball and E. Wyllys Andrews V, pp. 231-233. Publication No. 31. Middle American Research Institute, Tulane University, New Orleans.
— 1977. The Rise of the Northern Maya Chiefdoms: A Socio-processual Analysis, Part 1. In *The Origins of Maya Civilization*, edited by Richard E. W. Adams, pp. 101-132. University of New Mexico, Albuquerque.
— 1979. Ceramics, Culture History, and the Puuc Tradition: Some Alternative Possibilities. In Mills 1979:18-35.
Ball, Joseph W., and Jennifer T. Taschek. 2007. "Mixed Deposits," Composite Complexes," or "Hybrid Assemblages?" A Fresh Reexamination of Middle Preclassic (Formative) Ceramics and Ceramic Assemblages from the Northern Maya Lowlands. In *Archaeology, Art, and Ethnogenesis in Mesoamerican Prehistory: Papers in Honor of Gareth W. Lowe*, edited by Lynneth S. Lowe and Mary E. Pye, pp. 173-191. Papers of the New World Archaeological Foundation 68, Brigham Young University, Provo.
Barclay, Eliza. 2008. Oldest Skeleton in Americas Found in Underwater Cave? *National Geographic News*, 8 September, 2008. Online: http://news.nationalgeographic.com/news/2008/09/080903-oldest-skeletons.html.

Benavides Castillo, Antonio. 1981. Cobá y Tulum: Adaptación al medio ambiente y control del medio social. *Estudios de Cultura Maya* 13:205-222.

Bey, George J., III. 2006. Changing Archaeological Perspectives on the Northern Maya Lowlands. In Mathews and Morrison 2006:13-37.

Bey III, George J., Tara M. Bond, William M. Ringle, Craig A. Hanson, Charles W. Houck, and Carlos Peraza Lope. 1998. The Ceramic Chronology of Ek Balam, Yucatan, Mexico. *Ancient Mesoamerica* 9:101-120.

Bey, George J., III, Craig A. Hanson, and William M. Ringle. 1997. Classic to Postclassic at Ek Balam, Yucatán: Architectural and Ceramic Evidence for Defining the Transition. *Latin American Antiquity* 8:237-254.

Bill, Cassandra R. 1997. *Patterns of Variation and Change in Dynastic Period Ceramics and Ceramic Production at Copan, Honduras.* Ph.D. dissertation, Department of Anthropology, Tulane University. University Microfilms, An Arbor.

Boone, Elizabeth H., and Michael E. Smith. 2003. Postclassic International Styles and Symbol Sets. In Smith and Berdan 2003:186-193.

Boucher, Sylviane, and Yoly Palomo. 1995. El grupo K'inich Naranja: Un sistema cerámico del Clásico Tardío en el noroeste de la península de Yucatán. In *Memorias del Segundo Congreso Internacional de Mayistas*, pp. 239-274. Universidad Nacional Autónoma de México, Mexico City.

Brady, James E., Joseph W. Ball, Ronald L. Bishop, Duncan C. Pring, Norman Hammond, and Rupert A. Housley. 1998. The Lowland Maya "Protoclassic": A Reconsideration of its Nature and Significance. *Ancient Mesoamerica* 9:17-38.

Brainerd, George W. 1958. *The Archaeological Ceramics of Yucatán.* Anthropological Records 19. University of California, Berkeley.

Braswell, Geoffrey E. 2003. Obsidian Exchange Spheres of Postclassic Mesoamerica. In Smith and Berdan 2003:131-158.

— 2010. The Rise and Fall of Market Exchange: A Dynamic Approach to Ancient Maya Economy. In *Archaeological Approaches to Market Exchange in Pre-Capitalist Societies*, edited by Christopher P. Garraty and Barbara L. Stark, pp. 127-140. University of Utah, Salt Lake City.

Braswell, Geoffrey E. (editor). 2003. *The Maya and Teotihuacan: Reinterpreting Early Classic Interaction.* University of Texas, Austin.

Braswell, Geoffrey E., and Michael D. Glascock. 2003. The Emergence of Market Economies in the Ancient Maya World: Obsidian Exchange in Terminal Classic Yucatán, Mexico. In *Geochemical Evidence for Long Distance Exchange*, edited by Michael D. Glascock, pp. 33-52. Bergin & Garvey, Westport, CT.

— 2007. El intercambio de la obsidiana y el desarrollo de las economías de tipo mercado en la región maya. In *XX simposio de investigaciones arqueológicas en Guatemala, 2006*, edited by Juan Pedro Laporte, Bárbara Arroyo, and Héctor Mejía, pp. 13-26. Museo Nacional de Arqueología y Etnología, Guatemala.

— 2011. Procurement and Production of Obsidian Artifacts at Calakmul. In *The Technology of Maya Civilization: Political Economy and Beyond*, edited by Zachary X. Hruby, Geoffrey E. Braswell, and Oswaldo Chinchilla Mazariegos, pp. 119-129. Equinox Publishing, London.

Braswell, Geoffrey E., Joel D. Gunn María del Rosario Domínguez Carrasco, William J. Folan, Laraine Fletcher, Abel Morales López, and Michael D. Glascock. 2004. Defining the Terminal Classic at Calakmul, Campeche. In Demarest, Rice, and Rice 2004:162-194.

Braswell, Geoffrey E., Iken Paap, and Michael D. Glascock. 2011. The Obsidian and Ceramics of the Puuc Region: Chronology, Lithic Procurement, and Production. *Ancient Mesoamerica* 22:135-154.

Brown, Clifford T. 1999. *Mayapán Society and Ancient Maya Social Organization.* Ph.D. dissertation, Department of Anthropology, Tulane University. University Microfilms, Ann Arbor.

— 2005. Caves, Karst, and Settlement at Mayapán, Yucatán. In *In the Maw of the Earth Monster: Mesoamerican Ritual Cave Use*, edited by James E. Brady and Keith M. Prufer, pp. 373-402. University of Texas, Austin.

— 2006. Water Sources at Mayapán, Yucatán, México. In *Precolumbian Water Management: Ideology, Ritual, and Power*, edited by Lisa Lucero and Barbara Fash, pp 171-188. University of Arizona, Tucson.

Burgos Villanueva, Rafael, Miguel Covarrubias Reyna, and Jorge Estrada Faisal. 2004. Estudios sobre la periferia de Izamal, Yucatan. *Los Investigadores de la Cultura Maya* 12(1):249-256. Universidad Autonóma de Campeche, Campeche.

Carrión, Beatriz Leonor Merino, and Ángel García Cook (editors). 2005. In *La producción alfarera en el México Antiguo*, vol. 1. Instituto Nacional de Antropologia e Historia, Mexico City.

Ceballos Gallareta, Teresa, and Fernando Robles Castellanos. n.d. Las etapas más tempranas de la alfarería maya en el noroeste de la península de Yucatán. *Ancient Mesoamerica*. Manuscript in review.

Ceballos Gallareta, Teresa, and Socorro Jiménez Álvarez. 2005. Las esferas cerámicas del horizonte Cochuah del clasico temprano (c. 250–600 d.C.) en el norte de la peninsula de Yucatán. In Carrión and Cook 2005:561-580.

Charnay, Désiré. 1887. *Ancient Cities of the New World: Being Voyages and Explorations in Mexico and Central America from 1857–1882*. Harper & Brothers, New York.

Cobos Palma, Rafael. 2004. Entre la costa y el interior: Reconocimiento de una región del occidente de Yucatán. En *XVII Simposio de investigaciones arqueológicas en Guatemala, 2003*, edited by Juan Pedro Laporte, Bárbara Arroyo, Héctor L. Escobedo, and Héctor Mejía, pp. 61-66. Museo Nacional de Arqueología y Etnología, Guatemala City.

— 2007. Multepal or Centralized Kingship? New Evidence on Governmental Organization at Chichén Itzá. In Kowalski and Kristan-Graham 2007:315-343.

Cobos Palma, Rafael, Lilia Fernández Souza, and Nancy Peniche May. 2005. Las columnatas de Uaymil: su función durante el clásico terminal. In *Los investigadores de la cultura maya* 13(1):245-252. Universidad Autónoma de Campeche, Campeche.

Coe, Michael D. 2011. *The Maya*. 8th edn. Thames & Hudson, London and New York.

Con Uribe, María José. 2005. The East Coast of Quintana Roo: A Brief Account of Archaeological Work. In Shaw and Mathews 2005:15-29.

Culbert, T. Patrick. 1973. *The Classic Maya Collapse*. University of New Mexico, Albuquerque.

Curtis, Jason H., David A. Hodell, and Mark Brenner. 1996. Climate Variability on the Yucatan Peninsula (Mexico) during the Past 3500 Years, and Implications for Maya Cultural Evolution. *Quaternary Research* 46:37-47.

Dahlin, Bruce H., and Traci Ardren. 2002. Modes of Exchange and Regional Patterns: Chunchucmil, Yucatan, Mexico. In *Ancient Maya Political Economies*, edited by Marilyn Masson, and David A. Freidel, pp. 249-284. Altamira, Walnut Creek.

Dahlin, Bruce H., Christopher T. Jensen, Richard E. Terry, David R. Wright, and Timothy Beach. 2007. In Search of an Ancient Maya Market. *Latin American Antiquity* 18:363-384.

Demarest, Arthur A. 2004. After the Maelstrom: Collapse of the Classic Maya Kingdoms and the Terminal Classic in Western Peten. In Demarest, Rice, and Rice 2004:102-124.

Demarest, Arthur A., Prudence M. Rice, and Don S. Rice (editors). 2004. *The Terminal Classic in the Maya Lowlands*. University Press of Colorado, Boulder.

Dunning, Nicholas P. 1992. *Lords of the Hills: Ancient Maya Settlement in the Puuc Region, Yucatan, Mexico*. Monographs in World Archaeology 15. Prehistory, Madison.

Eaton, Jack D., and Joseph W. Ball (editors). 1978. *Studies of the Archaeology of Coastal Campeche, México*. Publication No. 46. Middle American Research Institute, Tulane University, New Orleans.

Edmonson, Munro S. 1982. *The Ancient Future of the Itza: The Book of Chilam Balam of Tizimin*. University of Texas, Austin.

— 1986. *Heaven Born Merida and its Destiny: The Book of Chilam Balam of Chumayel*. University of Texas, Austin.

Escamilla Ojeda, Bárbara. 2004. *Los artefactos de obsidiana de Mayapan*. Licenciatura thesis, Facultad de Ciencias Antropológicas, Universidad Autónoma de Yucatán, Merida.

Fash, William L., E. Wyllys Andrews V, and T. Kam Manahan. 2004. Political Decentralization, Dynastic Collapse, and the Early Postclassic in the Urban Center of Copán, Honduras. In Demarest, Rice, and Rice 2004:260-287.

Fernández Souza, Lilia, Rafael Cobos, and María Luisa Vázquez de Ágredos. 2003. Análisis de una estructura de tipo palacio en Siho, Yucatán. In Laporte et al. 2003:1016-1022.

Forsyth, Donald W. 1983. *Investigations at Edzná, Campeche, Mexico. Volume 2: Ceramics*. Papers of the New World Archaeological Foundation 46, Brigham Young University, Provo.

Freidel, David A. 2007. War and Statecraft in the Northern Maya Lowlands: Yaxuna and Chichén Itzá. In Kowalski and Kristan-Graham 2007:345-375.

Freidel, David A., and Jeremy A. Sabloff. 1984. *Cozumel: Late Maya Settlement Patterns*. Academic, New York.

Gallareta Negrón, Tomás, and Karl A. Taube. 2005. Late Postclassic Occupation in the Ruinas de San Angel Region. In Mathews and Morrison 2006:87-111.

Gallareta Negrón, Tomás, and William M. Ringle. 2004. *The Earliest Occupation of the Puuc Region, Yucatan, Mexico: New Perspectives from Xocnaceh and Paso del Macho*. Paper presented at the 103rd Annual Meeting of the American Anthropological Association, Atlanta.

Gallareta Negrón, Tomás, William M. Ringle, Rossana May Ciau, Julieta Ramos Pacheco, and Ramón Carrillo Sánchez. 2005. Evidencias de ocupación durante el período preclásico en el Puuc: Xocnaceh y Paso del Macho. Paper presented at the Segundo Congreso Internacional de Cultural Maya, Merida.

Gallareta Negrón, Tomás, Fernando Robles Castellanos, Anthony P. Andrews, Rafael Cobos, and Pura Cervera Rivero. 1989. Isla Cerritos: Un puerto maya prehispánico de la costa norte de Yucatán, México. *Memorias del segundo Coloquio Internacional de Mayistas* 1:311-332. Universidad Autónoma de Yucatán, Merida.

Gillespie, Susan D. 2007. Toltecs, Tula, and Chichén Itzá: The Development of an Archaeological Myth. In Kowalski and Kristan-Graham 2007:85-127.

Glover, Jeffrey B., and Fabio E. Amador. 2005. Recent Research in the Yalahau Region: Methodological Concerns and Preliminary Results of a Regional Survey. In Shaw and Mathews 2005:51-65.

Glover, Jeffrey B., and Travis W. Stanton. 2010. Assessing the Role of Preclassic Traditions in the Formation of Early Classic Yucatec Cultures, Mexico. *Journal of Field Archaeology* 35:58-77.

González González, Arturo H., Carmen Rojas Sandoval, Alejandro Terrazas Mata, Martha Benavente Sanvicente, Wolfgang Stinnesbeck, Jeronimo Aviles O., Magdalena de los Ríos, and Eugenio Acevez. 2008. The Arrival of Humans on the Yucatan Peninsula: Evidence from Submerged Caves in the State of Quintana Roo, Mexico. *Current Research in the Pleistocene* 25:1-24.

González González, Arturo H., Alejandro Terrazas M., Martha Benavente, Jerónimo Avilés, Eugenio Aceves, and Wolfgang Stinnesbeck. 2010. La arqueología subacuática y el poblamiento de América. *Arqueología Mexicana* 18(105):53-57.

Grube, Nikolai, and Ruth J. Krochock. 2007. Reading between the Lines: Hieroglyphic Texts from Chichén Itzá and its Neighbors. In Kowalski and Kristan-Graham 2007:205-249.

Gruhn, Ruth, and Alan L. Bryan. 1977. Los Tapiales: A Paleo-Indian Campsite in the Guatemalan Highlands. *Proceedings of the American Philosophical Society* 121(3):235-273.

Gunderson, Lance H., and C. S. Holling (editors). 2002. *Panarchy: Understanding Transformations in Human and Natural Systems*. Island Press, Washington.

Hagar, Stansbury. 1914. Maya Zodiac of Acanceh. *American Anthropologist* 16:88-95.

Haug, Gerald H., Detlef Günther, Larry C. Peterson, Daniel M. Sigman, Konrad A. Hughen, and Beat Aeschlimann. 2003. Climate and the Collapse of Maya Civilization. *Science* 299 (5613):1731-1735.

Hodell, David A., Mark Brenner, Jason H. Curtis, and Thomas Guilderson. 2001. Solar Forcing of Drought Frequency in the Maya Lowlands. *Science* 292(5520):1367-1370.

Holling, C. S., and Lance H. Gunderson. 2002. Resilience and Adaptive Cycles. In Gunderson and Holling 2002:25-62.

Houk, Charles W. 2006. Cenotes, Wetlands, and Hinterland Settlement. In Mathews and Morrison 2006:56-76.

Huchím Herrera, José, and César García Ayala. 2000. La Arquitectura que denota una ocupacion tardia en Uxmal, Yucatán. *Los Investigadores de la Cultura Maya* 8(1):138-154. Universidad Autónoma de Campeche, Campeche.

Hutson, Scott R., Bruce H. Dahlin and Daniel E. Mazeau. 2010. Commerce and Cooperation among the Classic Maya: The Chunchucmil Case. In *Cooperation in Social and Economic Life*, edited by Robert C. Marshall, pp. 81-103. Altamira, Lanham.

Hutson, Scott R., Aline Magnoni, Daniel E. Mazeau, and Travis W. Stanton. 2006. The Archaeology of Urban Houselots at Chunchucmil, Yucatán. In Mathews and Morrison 2006:77-92.

Inurreta Díaz, Armando, and Rafael Cobos Palma. 2003. El intercambio marítimo durante el clásico terminal: Uaymil en la costa occidental de Yucatán. In Laporte et al. 2003:1023-1029.

Kowalski, Jeff Karl, and Cynthia Kristan-Graham (editors). 2007. *Twin Tollans: Chichén Itzá, Tula, and the Epiclassic to Early Postclassic Mesoamerican World*. Dumbarton Oaks, Washington, D.C.

Kremer, Jürgen. 1994. The Putun Hypothesis Reconsidered. In Prem 1994:289-307.

Krochock, Ruth J., and David A. Freidel. 1994. Ballcourts and the Evolution of Political Rhetoric at Chichén Itzá, Yucatán, Mexico. In Prem 1994:359-375.

Lacadena García-Gallo, Alfonso. 2002. The Glyphic Corpus from Ek' Balam, Yucatán, México. Report to the Foundation for the Advancement of Mesoamerican Research, Incorporated. Online: http://www.famsi.org/reports/01057/index.html

— 2005. Los jeroglíficos de Ek' Balam. *Arqueología mexicana* 13(76):64-69.

Laporte, Juan Pedro. 1995. Una actualización a la secuencia cerámica del área de Dolores, Petén. *Revista del Atlas Arqueológico de Guatemala* 3:40-68. Instituto de Antropología e Historia, Guatemala City.

Laporte, Juan Pedro, Bárbara Arroyo, Héctor L. Escobedo, and Héctor Mejía (editors). 2003. *XVI Simposio de Investigaciones Arqueológicas en Guatemala, 2002*. Museo Nacional de Arqueología y Etnología, Guatemala City.

Lincoln, Charles E. 1985. Ceramics and Ceramic Chronology. In *A Consideration of the Early Classic Period in the Maya Lowlands*, edited by Gordon R. Willey and Peter Mathews, pp. 55-94. Publication No. 10. Institute of MesoAmerican Studies. State University of New York, Albany.

— 1986. The Chronology of Chichen Itza: A Review of the Literature. In Sabloff and Andrews V 1986:141-195.

— 1990. *Ethnicity and Social Organization at Chichen Itza, Yucatan, Mexico*. Ph.D. dissertation, Department of Anthropology, Harvard University. University Microfilms, Ann Arbor.

Lohse, Jon C. 2010. Archaic Origins of the Lowland Maya. *Latin American Antiquity* 21:312-352.

Lohse, Jon C., Jaime Awe, Cameron Griffith, Robert M. Rosenswig, and Fred Valdez, Jr. 2006. Preceramic Occupations in Belize: Updating the Paleoindian and Archaic Record. *Latin American Antiquity* 17:209-226.

Maldonado Cárdenas, Rubén. 1979. Izamal-Ake y Uci-Cansahcab sistemas prehispanicos del norte de Yucatan. *Boletín de la escuela de ciencias antropológicas de la Universidad de Yucatán* 6(36):33-44.

— 1995. Los sistemas de caminos del norte de Yucatan. In *Seis ensayos sobre antiguos patrones de asentamiento en el área maya*, edited by Ernesto Vargas Pacheco, pp. 68-92. Universidad Nacional Autonoma de Mexico, Instituto de Investigaciones Antropologicas, Mexico, D.F.

Masson, Marilyn A., and Carlos Peraza Lope. 2005. Nuevas investigaciones en tres unidades residenciales fuera del area monumental de Mayapan. *Los Investigadores de la cultura maya*, 13(2):411–424. Universidad Autónoma de Campeche, Campeche.

— 2010. Evidence for Maya-Mexican Interaction in the Archaeological Record of Mayapán. In Vail and Hernández 2010:77-113.

Matheny, Ray T. 1970. *The Ceramics of Aguacatal*, Campeche, Mexico. Papers of the New World Archaeological Foundation 27, Brigham Young University, Provo.

Mathews, Jennifer P., and Rubén Maldonado Cárdenas. 2006. Late Formative and Early Classic Interaction Spheres Reflected in the Megalithic Style. In Mathews and Morrison 2006:95-118.

Mathews, Jennifer P., and Bethany A. Morrison (editors). 2006. *Lifeways in the Northern Maya Lowlands: New Approaches to Archaeology in the Yucatán Peninsula*. University of Arizona, Tucson.

Medina Castillo, Edgar. 2003. Los Juegos de Pelota de la región noroeste de Yucatán. In Andrews and Castellanos 2003:62-87.

— 2005. *El juego de pelota del preclásico medio en el noroeste de Yucatán, México*. Licenciatura thesis, Facultad de Ciencias Antropológicas, Universidad Autónoma de Yucatán, Merida.

McCafferty, Geoffrey G. 2007. So What Else Is New? A Cholulacentric Perspective on Lowland/Highland Interaction During the Classic/Postclassic Transition. In Kowalski and Kristan-Graham 2007:449-479.

Milbrath, Susan, and Carlos Peraza Lope. 2003. Revisiting Mayapan: Mexico's Last Maya Capital. *Ancient Mesoamerica* 13:1-46.

Miller, Arthur G. 1982. *On the Edge of the Sea: Mural Painting at Tancah-Tulum, Quintana Roo, Mexico*. Dumbarton Oaks, Washington, D.C.

— 1986. From the Maya Margins: Images of Postclassic Politics. In Sabloff and Andrews V 1986:199-223.

Millet Cámara, Luís. 1999. Los mayas de Yucatán: Entre las colinas y el estero. *Arqueología mexicana* 7(37):4-13.

Mills, Lawrence (editor). 1979. *The Puuc: New Perspectives*. Scholarly Studies in the Liberal Arts Publication 1. Central College, Pella, Iowa.

Neff, Hector, Deborah M. Pearsall, John G. Jones, Barbara Arroyo, Shawn K. Collins, and Dorothy E. Freidel. 2006. Early Maya Adaptive Patterns: Mid-Late Holocene Paleoenvironmental Evidence from Pacific Guatemala. *Latin American Antiquity* 17:287-315.

Nelson, Fred W. 1973. *Archaeological Investigations at Dzibilnocac, Campeche, Mexico*. Papers of the New World Archaeological Foundation 33, Brigham Young University, Provo.

Osorio León, José F. 2004. *La Estructura 5C4 (Templo de la Serie Inicial): Un edificio clave para la cronología de Chichén Itzá*. Licenciatura thesis, Facultad de Antropología, Universidad de Yucatán, Merida.

— 2005. La Sub-estructura de los Estucos (5C-4-I): Un ejemplo de arquitectura temprana en Chichen Itza. In Laporte, Arroyo, and Mejía 2005:836-846.

Peniche May, Nancy. 2010. *The Architecture of Power and Sociopolitical Complexity in Northwestern Yucatan during the Preclassic Period*. Unpublished M.A. thesis, Department of Anthropology University of California, San Diego.

Peraza Lope, Carlos. 1993. Estudio y secuencia del material cerámico de San Gervasio, Cozumel. Licenciatura thesis, Facultad de Ciencias Antropológicas, Universidad Autónoma de Yucatán, Merida.

— 2005. Ceramic Analyses and Sequence from San Gervasio, Cozumel. In Shaw and Mathews 2005:77-86.

Peraza Lope, Carlos, Pedro Delgado Kú, and Bárbara Escamilla Ojeda. 2001. Descubrimientos recientes en Mayapán, Yucatán. *Los investigadores de la cultura maya* 9(1):285–293.

—2002. Investigaciones de un edifico del preclásico medio en Tipikal, Yucatán. *Los investigadores de la cultura maya* 10(1):263-276.

Peraza Lope, Carlos, Marilyn A. Masson, Timothy S. Hare, and Pedro Candelario Delgado Kú. 2006. The Chronology of Mayapán: New Radiocarbon Evidence. *Ancient Mesoamerica* 17:153-175.

Peraza Lope, Carlos, and Lourdes Toscano. 1983. Investigaciones recientes en el sitio de Xelhá, Quintana Roo. Paper presented at the XVIII Mesa Redonda de la Sociedad Mexicana de Antropología, Taxco.

Pérez de Heredia Puente, Eduardo. 2008. Chen K'u: The Ceramic of the Sacred Cenote at Chichén Itzá: Study of the Ceramic Fragments of the Explorations Conducted in the 60s. Report to the Foundation for the Advancement of Mesoamerican Research, Incorporated. Online: http://www.famsi.org/reports/97061/index.html.

Pohl, Mary D., Kevin O. Pope, John G. Jones, John S. Jacob, Dolores R. Piperno, Susan D. de France, David L. Lentz, John A. Gifford, Marie E. Danforth, and J. Kathryn Josserand. 1996. Early Agriculture in the Maya Lowlands. *Latin American Antiquity* 7:355-372.

Pollock, Harry E. D., Ralph L. Roys, Tatiana Proskouriakoff, and A. Ledyard Smith. 1962. *Mayapan, Yucatan, Mexico*. Publication 619, Carnegie Institution of Washington, Washington, D.C.

Prem, Hanns J. (editor). 1994. *Hidden among the Hills: Maya Archaeology of the Northwest Yucatan Peninsula*. Acta Mesoamericana 7. Von Flemming, Möckmühl.

Rathje, William L. 1975. The Last Tango in Mayapán: A Tentative Trajectory of Production-Distribution Systems. In *Ancient Civilization and Trade*, edited by Jeremy A. Sabloff and Carl C. Lamberg-Karlovsky, pp. 409-448. University of New Mexico, Albuquerque.

Redman, Charles L. 2005. Resilience Theory in Archaeology. *American Anthropologist* 107:70-77.

Ringle, William M. 1999. Pre-Classic Cityscapes: Ritual Politics among the Early Lowland Maya. In *Social Patterns in Pre-Classic Mesoamerica*, edited by David C. Grove and Rosemary A. Joyce, pp. 183-223. Dumbarton Oaks, Washington, D.C.

— 2004. On the Political Organization of Chichen Itza. *Ancient Mesoamerica* 15:167-218.

— 2009. The Art of War: Imagery of the Upper Temple of the Jaguars, Chichen Itza. *Ancient Mesoamerica* 20:15-44.

Ringle, William M., and George J. Bey III. 2001. Post-Classic and Terminal Classic Courts of the Northern Maya Lowlands. In *Royal Courts of the Ancient Maya: Volume 2, Data and Case Studies*, edited by Takeshi Inomata and Stephen D. Houston, pp. 266–307. Westview Press, Boulder.

Ringle, William M., George J. Bey III, Tara M. Bond-Freeman, Craig A. Hanson, Charles W. Houk, and J. Gregory Smith. 2004. The Decline of the East: The Classic to Postclassic Transition at Ek Balam, Yucatán. In Demarest, Rice, and Rice 2004:485-516.

Ringle, William, Tomás Gallereta Negrón, and George J. Bey III. 1998. The Return of Quetzalcoatl: Evidence for the Spread of a World Religion during the Epiclassic Period. *Ancient Mesoamerica* 9:183-232.

Rissolo, Dominique. 2012. Hoyo Negro Completes Project to Safeguard Site. Online: www.archaeologist.org/news/currentprojects/7628.

Rissolo, Dominique, José Manuel Ochoa Rodríguez, and Joseph W. Ball. 2005. A Reassessment of the Midle Preclassic in Northern Quintana Roo. In Shaw and Mathews 2005:66-76.

Robinson, Eugenia J., Pat M. Farrell, Kitty F. Emery, Dorothy E. Freidel, and Geoffrey E. Braswell. 2002. Preclassic Settlements and Geomorphology in the Highlands of Guatemala: Excavations at Urias, Valley of Antigua. In *Incidents of Archaeology in Central America and Yucatán*, edited by Michael Love, Héctor Escobedo, and Marion Popenoe de Hatch, pp. 251-276. University Press of the Americas, Lanham.

Robles Castellanos, J. Fernando. 1990. *La secuencia cerámica de la región de Cobá, Quintana Roo*. Serie Arqueología 184. Instituto Nacional de Antropología e Historia, Mexico City.

— 2000. Review of *El clásico medio en el noroccidente de Yucatán: La fase Oxkintok Regional en Oxkintok (Yucatán) como paradigma* by Carmen Varela Torrecilla. *Latin American Antiquity* 11:206-207.

— 2005. Las esferas cerámicas Cehpech y Sotuta del apogeo del Clásico Tardío (c. 730–900 d.c.) en el norte de la Península de Yucatán. In Carrión and Cook 2005:281-344.

— n.d. El Nuevo paradigma de la cronología e índole de la genesis de la civilización maya en el norte de la Península de Yucatán. In *Pathways to Complexity*, edited by Kathryn Brown and George J. Bey III. In preparation.

Robles Castellanos, J. Fernando, and Anthony P. Andrews (editors). 2000. *Proyecto Costa Maya: Reporte interino, Temporada 2000: Reconocimiento arqueológico de la esquina noroeste de la peninsula de Yucatán*. Instituto Nacional de Antropología e Historia, Merida.

Roys, Ralph L. 1967. *The Book of Chilam Balam of Chumayel*. University of Oklahoma, Norman.

Roys, Lawrence, and Edwin M. Shook. 1966. Preliminary Report on the Ruins of Ake, Yucatan. *Memoirs of the Society for American Archaeology*, No. 20. Salt Lake City, Utah.

Sabloff, Jeremy A., and E. Wyllys Andrews V (editors). 1986. *Late Lowland Maya Civilization*. School of American Research and University of New Mexico, Albuquerque.

Schele, Linda, and David Freidel. 1990. *A Forest of Kings: Untold Stories of the Ancient Maya*. William Morrow, New York.

Schele, Linda, and Peter Mathews. 1999. *The Code of Kings: The Language of Seven Sacred Maya Temples and Tombs*. Scribner, New York.

Schmidt, Peter J. 2007. Birds, Ceramics, and Cacao: New Excavations at Chichén Itzá, Yucatan. In Kowalski and Kristan-Graham 2007:151-203.

Seler, Eduard. 1911. Die Stuckfassade von Acanceh in Yukatan. *Sitzungsberichter der Königlichen Preußischen Akademie der Wissenschaften* 47:1011-1025.

Sharer, Robert J. 1994. *The Ancient Maya*. 5th edn. Stanford University, Stanford.

— 2003. Founding Events and Teotihuacan Connections at Copan, Honduras. In Braswell 2003:143-165.

Sharer, Robert J., with Loa Traxler. 2006. *The Ancient Maya*. 6th edn. Stanford University, Stanford.

Shaw, Justine M., and Jennifer P. Mathews (editors). 2005. *Quintana Roo Archaeology*. University of Arizona, Tucson.

Shook, Edwin M. 1940. Exploration in the Ruins of Oxkintok, Yucatan. *Revista mexicana de estudios antropológicos* 4:165-171.

Sierra Sosa, Thelma Noemí. 1994. *Contribución al estudio de los asentamientos de San Gervasio, Isla de Cozumel*. Serie Arqueología 279. Instituto Nacional de Antropología e Historia, Mexico City.

— 1999. Xcambó: Codiciado enclave económico del Clásico Maya. *Arqueología mexicana* 7(37):40-47.

— 2001. Xcambó. *Mexicon* 23:27.

Sierra Sosa, Thelma Noemí, and J. Fernando Robles Castellanos. 1998. Investigaciones arqueológicas en San Gervasio, Isla de Cozumel. In *Cozumel. Un encuentro en la historia*, edited by Eva Saavedra and Jorge Sobrino, pp. 1-16. Fondo de Publicaciones y Ediciones de Quintana Roo, Mexico City.

Smith, J. Gregory, William M. Ringle, and Tara M. Bond-Freeman. 2006. Ichmul de Morley and Northern Maya Political Dynamics. In Mathews and Morrison 2006:155-172.

Smith, Michael E., and Frances F. Berdan (editors). 2003. *The Postclassic Mesoamerican World*. University of Utah, Salt Lake City.

Smith, Robert E. 1971. *The Pottery of Mayapan: Including Studies of Ceramic Material from Uxmal, Kabah, and Chichen Itza*. 2 vols. Papers of the Peabody Museum of Archaeology and Ethnology 66. Harvard University, Cambridge, Mass.

Smyth, Michael P., and David Ortegón Zapata. 2006. Foreign Lords and Early Classic Interaction at Chac II. In Mathews and Morrison 2006:119-141.

Smyth, Michael P., and Daniel Rogart. 2004. A Teotihuacan Presence at Chac II, Yucatan, Mexico. *Ancient Mesoamerica* 15:17-47.

Stanton, Travis W. 2000. *Heterarchy, Hierarchy, and the Emergence of the Northern Lowland Maya: A Study of Complexity at Yaxuna, Yucatan, Mexico (400 B.C.–A.D. 600)*. Ph.D. dissertation, Department of Anthropology, Southern Methodist University. University Microfilms, Ann Arbor.

— 2005. Taluds, Tripods, and Teotihuacanos: A Critique of Central Mexican Influence in Classic Period Yucatan. *Mayab* 18:17-35.

Stanton, Travis W. and Traci Ardren. 2005. The Middle Formative of Yucatan in Context: The View from Yaxuna. *Ancient Mesoamerica* 16:213-228.

Stephens, John L. 1868. *Incidents of Travel in Yucatan*. 2 vols. Harper & Brothers, New York.

Taube, Karl A. 2010. At Dawn's Edge: Tulúm, Santa Rita and Floral Symbolism in the International Style of Late Postclassic Mesoamerica. In Vail and Hernández 2010:145-191.

Than, Ker. 2010. Undersea Cave Yields One of Oldest Skeletons in Americas. *National Geographic Daily News*, 14 September 2010. Online: http://news.nationalgeographic.com/news/2010/09/100915-oldest-skeleton-underwater-cave-science/.

Thompson, Edward H., and J. Eric S. Thompson. 1938. *The High Priest's Grave, Chichen Itza, Yucatan, Mexico*. Anthropological Series 27(1), Field Museum of Natural History, Chicago.

Thompson, J. Eric S. 1970. *Maya History and Religion*. University of Oklahoma, Norman.
Thompson, J. Eric S., Harry E. D. Pollock, and Jean Charlot. 1932. *A Preliminary Study of the Ruins of Coba, Quintana Roo, Mexico*. Publication 424, Carnegie Institution of Washington, Washington, D.C.
Tozzer, Alfred M. 1941. *Landa's Relación de las Cosas de Yucatán: A Translation*. Papers of the Peabody Museum of American Archaeology and Ethnology 18. Harvard University, Cambridge, Mass.
— 1957. *Chichén Itzá and Its Cenote of Sacrifice*. Memoirs of the Peabody Museum of Archaeology and Ethnology 11 and 12. Harvard University, Cambridge, Mass.
Universal, El. 2010. INAH reconstruye fisionomía de mujer de Era del Hielo. *El Universal*, 23 July 2010. Online: http://www.eluniversal.com.mx/articulos/59770.html.
Vail, Gabrielle, and Christine Hernández (editors). 2010. *Astronomers, Scribes, and Priests: International Interchange between the Northern Maya Lowlands and Central Mexico during the Late Postclassic Period*. Dumbarton Oaks, Washington, D.C.
Varela Torrecilla, Carmen. 1998. *El clásico medio en el noroccidente de Yucatán: La fase Oxkintok Regional en Oxkintok (Yucatán) como paradigma*. BAR International Series 739. British Archaeological Reports, Oxford.
Varela Torrecilla, Carmen, and Geoffrey E. Braswell. 2003. Teotihuacan and Oxkintok: New Perspectives from Yucatán. In Braswell 2003:249-271.
Vargas de la Peña, Leticia, and Víctor Castillo Borges. 1999. Ek' Balam: Ciudad que empieza a revelar sus secretos. *Arqueología Mexicana* 7(37):24-31.
— 2005. Hallazgos Recientes en Ek' Balam. *Arqueología Mexicana* 13(76):56-63.
Velázquez Valádez, Ricardo. 1980. Recent Discoveries in the Caves of Loltun, Yucatán, Mexico. *Mexicon* 2:53-55.
Villa Rojas, Alfonso. 1934. The Yaxuna-Coba Causeway. *Contributions to American Archaeology* 2(9):187-208. Publication 436, Carnegie Institute of Washington, Washington, D.C.
Von Nagy, Christopher L., Mary D. Pohl, and Kevin O. Pope. 2002. Ceramic Chronology of the La Venta Polity: The View from San Andres, Tabasco. Paper presented at the 67th Annual Meeting of the Society for American Archaeology, Denver.
Voorhies, Barbara. 2004. *Coastal Collectors in the Holocene: The Chantuto People of Southwest Mexico*. University of Florida, Gainsville.
Williams-Beck, Lorraine A. 1999. *Tiempo en trozos: Cerámica de la region de los Chenes, Campeche, México*. Gobierno del Estado de Campeche et al., Campeche.
Willey, Gordon R. 1974. The Classic Maya Hiatus: A Rehearsal for the Collapse? In *Mesoamerican Archaeology: New Approaches*, edited by Norman Hammond, pp. 417-444. University of Texas, Austin.

Part I

THE PRECLASSIC PERIOD

2 The Origins of the Mesoamerican Ballgame

A New Perspective from the Northern Maya Lowlands

David S. Anderson

Abstract

The Mesoamerican ballgame is a subject that has received a great deal of attention from scholars. This attention has largely focused on the political and societal implications of the game for Classic and Postclassic period Mesoamerican cultures. Discussions of the antiquity of the ballgame often focus simply on the oldest known Preclassic examples of ballcourt architecture, and assume that these earliest courts played a similar role to their later counterparts. Recent discoveries of more than 20 examples of Middle Preclassic ballcourts at Maya sites in northwest Yucatan provide a new source of data on the early Mesoamerican ballgame and a new perspective on its societal role.

> It was a game of much recreation to them and enjoyment specially for those who took it as pastime and entertainment... They were so clever both those of one side and those of the other in not allowing the ball to stop that it was marvelous—for if to see those of our country (Spain) play ball with their hands gives us such pleasure and surprise, then seeing skill and speed with which some of them play, how much more must we praise those who with such skill and dexterity and elegance play it with buttocks and with knees (Duran, quoted by Blom 1932:491-492).

The ballgame described by the Spanish chronicler Diego Duran is one of the most widely known cultural traits of ancient Mesoamerica, and it has been the subject of numerous studies, commentaries, conferences, and dissertations (e.g., Blom 1932; Fox 1994, 1996; Hill and Clark 2001; Leyenaar 1978; Medina Castillo 2005; Oliveros 1988; Scarborough and Wilcox 1991; Taladoire 1981, 2003; Uriarte 1992; van Bussel et al. 1991; Whalen and Minnis 1996; Whittington 2001). The majority of these studies have focused on the ballgame as a political or ritual institution of the ruling classes during the Classic and Postclassic periods of Mesoamerica rather than as a sport or game. As a result, we most readily associate the ballgame with politics, ritual, cosmology, and other aspects of elite culture. In publications where Preclassic versions of the game come under discussion, they tend to be interpreted through this pre-established paradigm. For example, in describing an Olmec rubber ballgame, Richard Diehl (2004:105) states that "the game was primarily a religious observance in which players representing supernatural and culture heroes played out predetermined scenarios that often ended in the sacrificial death of at least one protagonist." The majority of this statement is based on data that postdate the Olmec culture by several centuries or more. A further example can be found in the announcement by Warren D. Hill, Michael Blake, and John E. Clark (1998) of the discovery of an Early Preclassic ballcourt at the site of Paso de la Amada in Chiapas, Mexico. The presence of a ballcourt at the site is taken to indicate the development of a complex sociopolitical system, and while discussing the possibility of additional contemporary ballcourts, the authors propose that "the earliest ball courts should be located in sites with evidence of status differences among community members" (Hill et al. 1998). In a later publication, Hill and Clark (2001:331) further propose that "the ballgame played a notable role in the origins of the first formal community governments in Mesoamerica."

The extent to which we can apply known cultural traditions from later periods to earlier periods needs to be carefully considered. Should we expect that a game employed in political and ritual activities began as such, or should we perhaps expect that it began as a game that was later co-opted for other purposes? Recently, 24 previously unreported Middle Preclassic ballcourts (Figure 2.1) have been recorded in northwest Yucatan during surveys of the region by the Proyecto Costa Maya (PCM) (Andrews and Robles Castellanos 2004; Medina Castillo 2003, 2005; Robles Castellanos and Andrews 2000, 2001, 2003) and the Proyecto Salvamento Arqueológico Ciudad Caucel (PSACC) (Robles Castellanos and Ligorred Perramon 2008). Almost all of the ballcourts encountered were found at sites that lacked signs of significant social stratification; one site consisted of no more than the ballcourt and two apsidal house foundations. These data seemed to contradict the prediction made by Hill et al. (1998) and are difficult to interpret within the traditional paradigm of the ballgame as an elite political or ritual activity. If we reconsider, however, the quote by Diego Duran that opens this chapter, it is clear that at the time of contact the ballgame was also a recreational activity, something that people participated in for the sake of enjoyment and fun. This aspect of the Mesoamerican ballgame has only occasionally been addressed in reference to earlier versions of the game, but would have been a part of this athletic contest during all periods. In light of the new data from northwest Yucatan, and through a reexamination of previously published evidence, I contend that the earliest forms of the ballgame in Mesoamerica represent a communal tradition of sport that was only later adopted by the sociopolitical elite to use for political ends.

The distinction between elite and common cultural traditions is central to the discussion of the ballgames origins. Building on a long tradition of the study of social stratification within sociocultural anthropology (e.g., Earle 1997; Marcus 1983; Wason 1994) and Mesoamerican studies (e.g., Chase and Chase 1992; Lohse and Valdez 2004), we can define the elite as those individuals who had access to institutionalized political, social, economic, or religious power. Commoners are then, in turn, those people who cannot access these sources of power freely. Although this is, admittedly, a simple dichotomy, it is useful for this discussion. In order to evaluate the central premise of this chapter, we must identify whether the early ballgame was part of an institution of symbolic power with restricted access, or if it was a tradition more freely accessible to everyone within the society.

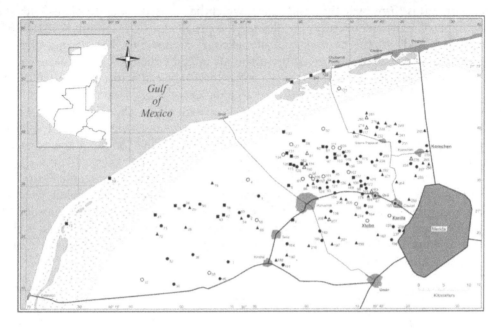

Figure 2.1. Preclassic sites documented by the Proyecto Costa Maya (Robles Castellanos and Andrews 2003). Sites denoted by triangles were occupied in the Middle Preclassic, squares were occupied in the Late Preclassic, and circles were occupied in both periods. Hollow symbols represent sites with ballcourts.

Categories of Evidence for the Mesoamerican Ballgame

Before moving to the principal topic, I wish first to address the categories of archaeological evidence that can be used to identify ballgame activity. The study of the ballgame represents a classic archaeological problem in that we are attempting to address a social activity through its limited associated material remains. Like many such archaeological problems, scholars have relied on different sorts of data and applied varying standards to identify the presence of ballgame activity. In this chapter, three types of evidence are used to argue for the presence of ballgame activity. They include ballcourt architecture, artistic or iconographic depictions of the ballgame or ballplayers, and the few examples of prehispanic rubber balls that survive today. Each of these forms of evidence presents its own strengths and weaknesses, which are discussed below.

Ballcourts

Ballcourts have long served as the primary form of evidence used to demonstrate the existence of the ballgame (e.g., Blom 1932). Our foundation for identifying what constitutes a ballcourt derives from the initial ethnohistoric accounts that describe the courts that native Mesoamericans used to play the ballgame (e.g., Blom 1932; Taladoire 1991). These base descriptions have been reinforced through iconographic and archaeological studies (e.g., Cohodas 1991; Nicholson and Quiñones Keber 1991; Taladoire 1981, 2001). As a result, we have a wide variety of sources confirming the general form of a ballcourt as an I-shaped space created principally by two long parallel structures. There is, however, a significant amount of variability within this form over time and space, which has caused some problems with the identification of ballcourt architecture. To alleviate this problem, Eric Taladoire (1981, 2001) made a detailed study of the components of ballcourt architecture identifying what he considers to be nine principal features of the form: (1) lateral structures; (2) upper wall; (3) aprons; (4) benches; (5) bench walls; (6) the playing field; (7) the end fields; (8) back walls; and (9) end walls (Figure 2.2). In addition to these architectural features, we may also add two decorative features that have been recorded in association with many ballcourts: ballcourt rings and marker stones (Scarborough 2001:70). Ballcourt rings are stone rings embedded in the upper walls of a ballcourt, and ballcourt marker stones are typically round, altar-like carved stones found along the centerline of the playing field.

Given that these features are amassed from a sample of ballcourts spanning the entirety of Mesoamerica and nearly 2000 years of development, we must expect that most ballcourts will not exhibit all of these features. For example, end fields and back walls show considerable variation over space and time (Taladoire 2001:Figure 115). There is, nevertheless, a clear continuity in architectural form from the ballcourts the Spanish observed at the time of contact to Preclassic examples recorded by archaeologists.

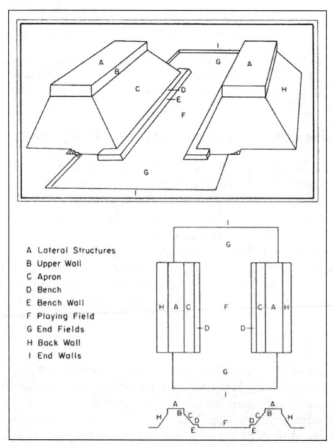

Figure 2.2. The nine principal features of ballcourt architecture proposed by Eric Taladoire (2001:Figure 113).

One complication involved with using ballcourts to identify ballgame activity is the presumption that these spaces were used exclusively for playing a ballgame. Defined public spaces often served multiple functions. The ballcourts and playing fields of our own contemporary cultures are used for everything from school graduation ceremonies to hosting carnivals, not to mention the original games they were created for (David Grove, personal communication 1998). In his study of the Maya ballgame, John G. Fox (1996:491-493) assembled evidence from across the Maya region for ballcourts used as the location of ritual feasts and other activities. The presence of a ballcourt, therefore, may not always imply that it was used principally for playing the ballgame. Furthermore, some of the more elaborate ballcourts in Mesoamerica may have been intended as symbolic structures rather than as actual playing spaces. The Great Ballcourt at Chichen Itza in Yucatan, Mexico, for example, is two to three times the size of most other ballcourts in Mesoamerica and includes elaborate architectural details and carvings (Coggins 2001:129; Ringle 2004:170). At the very least, the mammoth proportions of this ballcourt would require a very different style of play (Taladoire 2001:100), if it ever was used for such a purpose. It is also important to keep in mind that formal ballcourts are not necessary for playing many forms of the ballgame. Ethnographic sources describe games played in open fields with no architecture involved (Leyenaar 2001). As a result, the extent of ballgame activity could be considerably wider than is indicated by the distribution of ballcourts. For example, to date, no ballcourt has been found at Teotihuacan, but a mural found at the site clearly depicts people playing a form of the ballgame (Taladoire 2003).

Iconographic Depictions

Many studies of the Mesoamerican ballgame have focused on iconography depicting the ballgame or its players (e.g., Chinchilla Mazariegos 1992; Cohodas 1991; Ekholm 1991; Uriarte 2001). These images provide an excellent emic view into the ballgame in that they depict how Mesoamericans who sponsored artistic production imagined the game. The most useful examples have been those in which individuals are shown in the act of playing the game. Such images are frequently found on Classic period Maya codex style vases (Cohodas 1991; Zender 2004), as well as in sculptures (Cohodas 1991) and ceramic figurines (Ekholm 1991). Working from these images, scholars have identified typical elements of ballplayer attire and regalia, such as waist belts and kneepads, as well as poses or postures associated with the ballgame (Cohodas 1991; Day 2001; Scott 2001). This has in turn allowed for the identification of figures dressed as ballplayers that are not shown in the act of playing the ballgame.

The weakness of an iconographic approach is that it presumes we are correctly viewing and interpreting the iconography of another culture. Although some examples seem patently clear, others are more difficult to interpret. For example, Karl Taube (2004:15) has proposed that the figures in La Venta Stela 2 are holding implements associated with a version of the game where players strike the ball with a stick instead of with their hips (see Taladoire 2003). While Taube's interpretation may be correct, other scholars have interpreted the objects held by the individuals on Stela 2 as ceremonial bars associated with rulership (Pool 2007:167), resembling the ceremonial bars held by later Mesoamerican rulers (e.g., Schele and Miller 1986: 72-73). These implements could also be weapons. Perhaps most frustratingly of all, all three interpretations could be correct if ceremonial bars developed from ballgame sticks that were also used in war.

The famous Olmec colossal heads provide another example of problematic interpretation. Some scholars have held that the headdresses depicted on the sculptures represent ballgame helmets (Coe 1968:110; Hill and Clark 2001:334), while others argue that there is little basis for this interpretation (Diehl 2004:105; Taladoire 2001:107). For these reasons, my bias in this chapter is to rely only on the imagery most explicitly associated with the ballgame. This may lead to under-identification of ballgame iconography, but that result is likely to be less damaging than over-identification.

Rubber Balls

On rare occasions, actual prehispanic rubber balls have been found in excavations (Ortiz and Del Carmen Rodríguez 2000). Although these instances represent remarkable moments of preservation, assumptions that the balls are necessarily associated with the ballgame need to be considered carefully. Rubber was also widely used in Mesoamerica for incense and other ritual purposes (Filoy Nadal 2001). We know relatively little about prehispanic manufacturing techniques for rubber, but ethnohistorical and historical sources document indigenous methods. In order to manufacture rubber, one must collect latex sap from rubber-producing trees, such as *Castilla elastica*. This sap must be combined with other ingredients and boiled to "accelerate the coagulation process, while at the same time increasing the plasticity and elasticity of the rubber" (Filoy Nadal 2001:26). This process results in the production of elastic threads, which are best preserved by being rolled into balls. Thus, the discovery of rubber fragments, or even rubber balls, cannot be considered an automatic indication of ballgame activity.

The Middle Preclassic Ballcourts of Northwest Yucatan

The 24 Middle Preclassic ballcourts found in northwest Yucatan (Table 2.1) offer a large new set of data from which to investigate the role of the ballgame in Preclassic Mesoamerica. The first 23 of these ballcourts were recorded during a survey of the region carried out by the PCM between 1999 and 2002 (Andrews and Robles Castellanos 2004; Robles Castellanos and Andrews 2000, 2001, 2003).[1] The final Middle Preclassic ballcourt was located at the site of Xanila in 2007 by the PSACC during a survey carried out in advance of a new housing development (Robles Castellanos and Ligorred Perramon 2008).

Due to the rarity of Middle Preclassic ballcourts and the unusual context of these examples, special care was taken in both identifying these structures and in establishing their associated period of occupation. As they stand today, all of the ballcourts found in northwest Yucatan exhibit at least five of Taladoire's (1981, 2001) nine features of ballcourt architecture. In most cases, it is probable that excavations would reveal additional features. When viewed as a group, all nine of Taladoire's features are represented. One of the best preserved examples comes from the site of Pitaya where, without excavation, we can still identify the upper wall, the apron, and four more of Taladoire's features (Figure 2.3). Test excavations carried out by the PCM within the ballcourts documented the existence of benches and aprons at four more sites and upper walls at two sites (Figure 2.4), further confirming the characteristic ballcourt profile. The horizontal excavation of the eastern structure of the Xanila ballcourt also revealed a bench and apron, but no upper wall. The most notable addition from the excavation at Xanila was the discovery of a ballcourt marker in the center of the playing field (Figure 2.5). Unlike later Classic period markers, the Xanila marker was made up of multiple rough-cut pieces of limestone arranged in a circle.

Table 2.1. The Preclassic ballcourts of northwest Yucatan.

Site Name	Site No.	Playing Field Length	Width	Orientation
Benatunas	4	20m	7m	25°
Chayil-Regina	207	20m	5m	6°
Choko K'at	55	24m	6m	25°
Chuk'te	32	18m	6m	25°
Chun Bohom	81	16m	5m	8°
Chunche Chen	109	21m	5m	10°
Cubano	160	20m	7m	345°
Halal 2	134	18m	7m	25°
Kaniste 2	91	20m	6m	8°
Kanseb	279	20m	7m	0°
Lázero Cárdenas	305	14m	4m	5°
Loreto	183	14m	5m	2°
Na On	127	15m	8m	10°
Pitaya	92	15m	7m	354°
San Jeronimo 1	156	20m	8m	350°
Sin Nombre	275	21m	6m	5°
Sinab	98	25m	8m	350°
Sinantoh	58	25m	6m	25°
Uaya	168	24m	7m	8°
Ulilá 1	107	22m	7m	10°
Unión	101	22m	4m	10°
Xanila	-	25m	7m	15°
Xkitinche	111	23m	7m	0°
Xtobo	166	14m	5m	0°

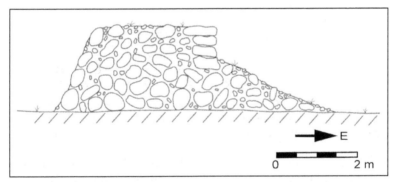

Figure 2.3. East–west profile of the eastern structure of the ballcourt at Pitaya (CY-92), Yucatan. Drawing by Fernando Robles Castellanos.

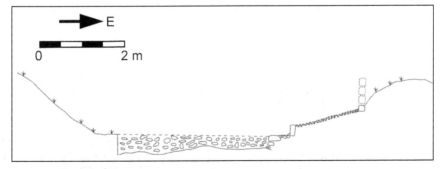

Figure 2.4. Profile of the ballcourt at Na On (CY-127), Yucatan. Drawing by the author and A. Cantero.

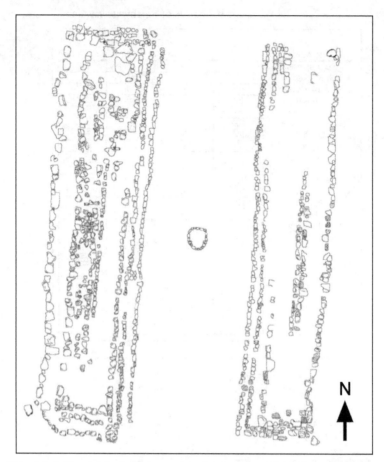

Figure 2.5. Plan of the ballcourt at Xanila, Yucatan. The ballcourt measures 25 m North–South. Drawing by Donato España and Edgar Medina.

Looking more broadly at the form of these ballcourts, there is notable variability. The length of the parallel structures ranges from 14 to 25 meters, and the distance between the parallel structures ranges from three to ten meters. The orientation of all the lateral structures is roughly north–south, but the specific bearing deviates as much as 25 degrees. The height of the lateral structures also varies from approximately half a meter up to two meters. As is common in much of Mesoamerica, the end walls of these ballcourts are defined by separate platforms referred to as closing structures. Some of the northwest Yucatan ballcourts include a closing structure at both the north and south ends, but most of the ballcourts had only one closing structure found on either the northern or southern end of the playing field. These variations in form and dimension are not unusual in ballcourts, and, given the repeated presence of more diagnostic ballcourt features, should not dissuade us from identifying these structures as ballcourts.

Regular patterns in associated architecture support the notion that the ballcourts of northwest Yucatan belong to a unified regional tradition. At 17 of the 24 ballcourt sites, complex platforms are located in close proximity to the ballcourt. These complex platforms consist of an approximately one-meter-tall basal platform with multiple superplatforms built on top. Typically, one of the superplatforms is noticeably taller and larger than the others. A good example of such a platform is at the site of Union (Figure 2.6). The specific shape of these complex platforms varies widely making it difficult to provide a more precise definition, but platforms matching this description were habitually found in association with ballcourts and rarely seen at other sites. Over the course of the PCM, such structures came to be known as *chan* (little) acropoli. The regular presence of *chan* acropoli with ballcourts suggests that these complexes were part of a contemporaneous tradition, but the most important evidence for contemporaneity comes from the pottery sherds found in association with the ballcourts.

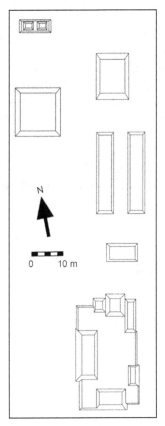

Figure 2.6. La Union (CY-101), Yucatan.
Drawing by Crorey Lawton and K. Sumrow.

Ceramics Associated with the Ballcourts

Surface collections of pottery were made at each ballcourt site, and whenever possible targeted surface collections were made from the ballcourts themselves. Additional pottery sherds were recovered from the seven test pits excavated by the PCM at a sample of the ballcourt sites, as well as from the horizontal excavations of the eastern lateral structure at Xanila carried out by the PSACC. Regrettably, these excavations did not yield charcoal for radiocarbon dating, and contexts were not sealed beneath preserved floors. Thus, comparative ceramic seriation was the primary means used to identify the period in which the ballcourts were built and used. The recovered pottery sherds were classified to the group level in the Type-Variety classification system (Smith et al. 1960) by the PCM and PSACC ceramicists (Ceballos Gallareta et al. 2008; Robles Castellanos and Ceballos Gallareta 2003). The pottery groups identified in the collections can be associated with the Preclassic, Classic, and Postclassic periods, but the only time period found to be represented at all of the ballcourt sites was the Preclassic (Table 2.2). In addition, one of the ballcourt sites, Lazero Cardenas, included only Preclassic pottery groups, therefore making any other period of occupation at the site unlikely.

The two most common pottery groups, in terms of both percentage and distribution, were Dzudzuquil and Tipikal/Unto. Together they make up almost half of the pottery collection, and examples of each group were found at 22 of the 24 sites with ballcourts. Dzudzuquil is a characteristic pottery group of the Middle Preclassic period in the northern Maya lowlands, and is considered to be a part of the Mamom horizon (Andrews 1988, 1989; Hernández Hernández 2005). The Tipikal/Unto group is primarily considered to be a Late Preclassic pottery group associated with the Chicanel horizon (Andrews 1988, 1989; Hernández Hernández 2005; Smith 1971; cf. Ball 1978:110, 1979 who separates these into two distinct groups). Recent excavations have shown that the group can date to as early as the Middle Preclassic (Ceballos Gallareta 2005; Ceballos Gallareta et al. 2008; Robles Castellanos 1997; Robles Castellanos and Ceballos Gallareta 2003). The next two most common pottery groups recovered from ballcourt sites are Joventud and Chunhinta, both of which are traditional members of the Mamom horizon and associated with the Middle Preclassic period (Andrews 1988, 1989; Smith 1971). Neither Joventud nor Chunhinta pottery was found with as great a frequency as Dzudzuquil or Tipikal/Unto, but they were recovered from 17 and 18 of the ballcourt sites, respectively. Although this evidence is not incontrovertible, the ballcourt sites are more closely associated with the Middle Preclassic period than any other time period.

Regional Settlement Pattern and Ballcourt Sites

To reiterate, the early date of these ballcourts is not their only unusual characteristic. The majority are found at relatively small sites. In addition to the ballcourt sites themselves, the PCM documented a dense regional Preclassic occupation (Figure 2.1). Within the survey zone of the project, a total of 140 Preclassic sites were recorded. These include 116 sites with Middle Preclassic and 92 sites with Late Preclassic occupations (Anderson 2003). This large collection of sites is particularly remarkable considering that prior to the survey, only eight Preclassic sites were known in the region (Andrews and Andrews 1980:16; Eaton 1978: 34-37; Shook 1955: 291-292). The Preclassic sites encountered by the PCM were arranged in a three-tiered regional hierarchy of small, medium, and large sites (Anderson 2010; Anderson et al. 2011). Only two sites were confirmed as belonging to the top tier of settlements. They are Komchen, which was the focus of a project led by E. Wyllys Andrews V (Andrews 1988; Andrews et al. 1980; Ringle 1985; Ringle and Andrews 1990), and Xtobo, which was first reported by the PCM and was the subject of my own dissertation research (Anderson 2003, 2010, n.d.). It is uncertain when these sites emerged as regional centers, but some time between the late Middle Preclassic and early Late Preclassic, the sites of Komchen and Xtobo significantly expanded in size and gained notable influence within the region. All of the ballcourts in far northwest Yucatan—with the single exception of the ballcourt at Xtobo—are found at second-tier or even third-tier settlements.

The site of Ulila is a typical ballcourt site with a *chan* acropolis and a handful of small platforms and structures (Figure 2.7). Sinantoh is another good example of this pattern (Figure 2.8). Some ballcourt sites include larger structures, such as the site of Sinab, which has two

Table 2.2. Group classification of the pottery collected from ballcourt sites in northwest Yucatan, Mexico.

Sites	Colonial	Nabulá	Sihó	Muna	Ticul	Teabo	Ich Cansihó	Chum	Chuhumá	Chablekal	Balancan/Altar	Koxolac	Baca	Batres	Oxil	Maxcanú	Balanza	Aguila	Timucuy	Shangurro	Dzilam	Xanabá	Sierra	Polvero	Sapote	Flor	Sabán/Achiotes	Tipikal/Unto	Chuhinta	Dzudzuquil	Pital	Juventud	Total
Benautnas	28	3		25	1			48						1									11			54				2			145
Chun Bohom																														3			3
Chayil-Regina				4				6					1		2	3											3	8	1	2		2	29
Chokokat				2	2			16			1																	8	1	8			42
Chukté				1				1	1				2	1	5	14						11	3					17	1	13		11	66
Chunché Chén				4		1		1	1			1	1	5	2	6							8				15	30	12	43			136
Cubano				3											9								1					15	4			9	46
Halal 2																						3						9					12
Kanisté 2	26		1	2		1		1						1	11	17							1				23	13	5	31		13	147
Kanseb																					1		1					20	8	20		17	67
L. Cárdenas																												8	15	16	2	4	45
Loreto	2			1												3							4						4	14		1	32
Na Om															2	1			1			4					3	44	20	150		60	282
Pitaya															12	3						4					21	12	12	71		40	163
S. Jerónimo 1				6								1			8	2						10						8	4	2			35
Sin Nombre		2										2		2	2	4	1		1	3		16		2			6	20	4	4		9	65
Sinab			1	8	1	2							2	19	6	8			1	1			6				6	61	18	198		51	384
Sinantoh			3	10				17					3		8	4							1					58		8			136
Uaya						2																4	6					17	13	53	2	24	136
Ulilá				1																			1					6	7	7		2	25
Unión																							1					19	8	34		8	70
Xanila															3	3						1					2	4	6	8		5	32
Xkitinche		1		100		8		32	1					9	94	60						8					15	153	52	162	9	79	787
Xtobo				3			10			4					24	12		3	4	1		3	2		4		2	17	17	79		53	217
Total:	28	6	5	170	4	12	10	122	2	4	1	3	9	38	164	140	1	3	7	5	1	64	49	2	4	54	96	562	207	928	13	388	3102
Percentage:	0.9	0.2	0.2	5.5	0.1	0.4	0.3	3.9	0.1	0.1	0.0	0.1	0.3	1.2	5.3	4.5	0.0	0.1	0.2	0.2	0.0	2.1	1.6	0.1	0.1	1.7	3.1	18.1	6.7	29.9	0.4	12.5	

platforms over three meters tall, but such sites are in the minority. It is likely that in addition to the stone architecture currently visible, each of these sites contained multiple perishable structures. The presence of *chan* acropoli at many of the ballcourt sites and of large structures at Sinantoh implies that some high-status construction activity occurred within these communities. Nevertheless most of these sites represent small village settlements with minimal signs of sociopolitical stratification. Two atypical examples of ballcourt sites in the region are San Jeronimo 1 and Xtobo. San Jeronimo I is the smallest site recorded with a ballcourt, and contains few other structures (Figure 2.9). Due to its very small size, San Jeronimo I clearly belongs in the third tier of the regional settlement pattern. Xtobo, in contrast, is the largest settlement with a ballcourt. This site covers approximately one square kilometer and includes 384 visible structures (Figure 2.10). Investigations at Xtobo identified signs of significant social stratification in the form of pyramids, a plaza, elite residential architecture, and foreign trade goods (Anderson 2010, n.d.).

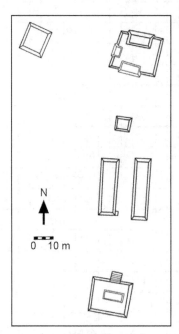

Figure 2.7. Ulila (CY-107), Yucatan. Drawing by Crorey Lawton and Edgar Medina.

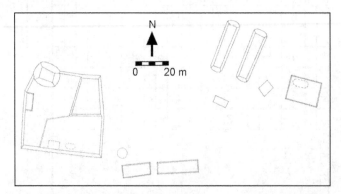

Figure 2.8. Sinantoh (CY-58), Yucatan. Drawing by the author.

THE ORIGINS OF THE MESOAMERICAN BALLGAME 55

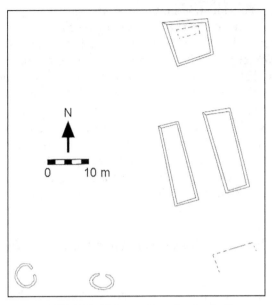

Figure 2.9. San Jeronimo I (CY-156), Yucatan. Drawing by A. Torres and Crorey Lawton.

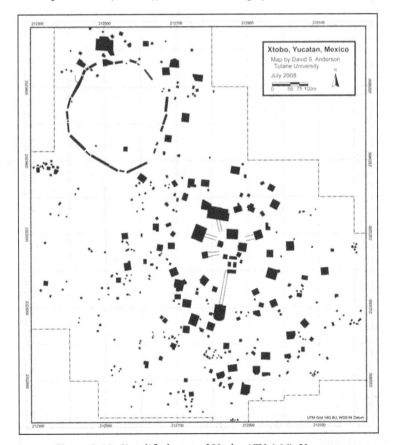

Figure 2.10. Simplified map of Xtobo (CY-166), Yucatan.

In summary, northwest Yucatan was home to a widespread regional ballcourt tradition during the Middle Preclassic period. Several of these sites continued to be occupied during the Late Preclassic period, but no ballcourts were found at Late Preclassic sites that lacked an earlier occupation. Even Komchen, the largest Late Preclassic settlement in the region, does not have a ballcourt. It seems likely that the ballcourt tradition waned in popularity by the Late Preclassic period, and might have been abandoned entirely by that time. During the Middle Preclassic, ballcourts were built at sites of all sizes, but they are most common at second-tier settlements that resemble small villages. It should be said that there is no direct evidence to prove that these ballcourts were used in actual ballgames, and if they were, it would have been necessary to import the rubber balls (Filoy Nadal 2001:Figure 8). The architectural traits of these structures, however, are clearly related to the ballcourts of later periods, and it is likely that that the activities carried out in association with them were also related to those activities carried out in later ballcourts.

Evidence for the Middle Preclassic Ballgame beyond Northwest Yucatan

Relatively few other examples of Middle Preclassic ballcourts are known in other parts of Mesoamerica, and they are quite rare outside the Maya area. Elsewhere in the Maya region, Middle Preclassic ballcourts have been reported at Tak'alik Ab'aj in southeastern Guatemala (Schieber de Lavarreda 1994), Nakbe in northern Guatemala, and Paso del Macho in the Puuc hills of Yucatan (Gallareta Negrón et al. 2005). Middle Preclassic ballcourts are also known in the Grijalva River Valley of Chiapas at Finca Acapulco, El Vergel, and San Mateo, and also at the site of La Libertad in southern Chiapas (Agrinier 1991). One more possible Middle Preclassic ballcourt has been described for Campanillo in western Mexico, but the dating of this structure is questionable (Weigand 1991).

With the exception of Paso del Macho, which is similar in scale to the ballcourt sites documented by the PCM, all of these other examples are found at relatively prominent regional centers and therefore fit the traditional paradigm. In his study of ballcourts in southern Chiapas, however, Pierre Agrinier (1991:Table 10.6) lists an additional 28 sites in the Upper Grijalva River Valley with ballcourts that may date to the Middle Preclassic. These ballcourts were recorded during regional surveys and their specific dates of construction have not been ascertained (de Montmollin 1995; Lowe 1959; Rivero Torres 1990). They are found at relatively small settlements and, if they do date to the Middle Preclassic, they could represent another example of the pattern seen in northwest Yucatan.

There are several other Middle Preclassic structures that have been proposed as ballcourts, but which are questionable examples for various reasons. Structures at the Olmec centers of San Lorenzo (Coe and Diehl 1980:29, 62) and La Venta (Wyshak et al. 1971) have been proposed as ballcourts, but they exhibit very few of Taladorie's ballcourt features. Ballcourts have also been proposed for the sites of Teopantecuanitlan (Martínez Donjuan 1995) and El Macayal (Ortiz and Del Carmen Rodríguez 1992; see also Hill and Clark 2001), but published data about these structures is too limited to assess their forms. And finally, excavations at the site of Chalcatzingo in Morelos, Mexico, encountered a portion of a structure that resembled a ballcourt, but too little of the structure was exposed to be certain (Grove and Cyphers Guillén 1987:26). If these structures are ultimately demonstrated to be Middle Preclassic ballcourts, then they would significantly expand our knowledge of the distribution of the tradition.

Aside from ballcourts, there is limited additional evidence for a Middle Preclassic ballgame. To my knowledge, no examples of rubber dating to the Middle Preclassic have been documented, and there are relatively few iconographic representations of ballgame activity that date to the period. The catalog published in conjunction with the *Sport of Life and Death* museum exhibit (Whittington 2001) includes several figurines that are listed as Middle Preclassic ballplayers. Nonetheless, the provenience and dating of many of these examples are questionable. One example (Whittington 2001:154) is listed as from Chalcatzingo, but the artifact was not published in David C. Grove's (1984, 1987) monographs on the site. Grove (personal communication 2010) confirms that the figurine was not recovered by any excavation known to him. In addition, some of these figurines may not depict ballplayers. The jade figurine pictured in Plate 11 clearly depicts a human figure, but it does not exhibit traditional ballplayer attributes. Instead it appears to have been included due to its unusual headdress. As mentioned above, Karl Taube (2004:15) has proposed that the figures on La Venta Stela 2 hold ballgame sticks. To reiterate, the distinction between a ballgame stick and other similar objects is difficult to demonstrate for this image. There are no other potential examples of Middle Preclassic ballgame iconography known to me.

Even if we accept that these examples represent Middle Preclassic depictions of the ballgame, it is clear that such imagery was uncommon during this time period. This is particularly remarkable when we consider the otherwise prolific nature of Middle Preclassic artists (Lesure 2004).

Evidence for an Early Preclassic Ballgame

Multiple forms of evidence suggest the existence of the ballgame during the Early Preclassic period and, as during the Middle Preclassic period, it appears to have been widely dispersed throughout Mesoamerica. As mentioned above, the site of Paso de la Amada, Chiapas, includes an Early Preclassic ballcourt (Hill et al. 1998; Hill and Clark 2001). This is generally accepted as the oldest known ballcourt in Mesoamerica (Diehl 2004:135; Flannery and Marcus 2000:8; Taladoire 2001:107). To date, no other Early Preclassic ballcourts have been identified. Excavations in these structures revealed benches attached to the interior side of the lateral structures (Hill et al. 1998:84). Although there are no aprons connecting the benches to the lateral structures, the profile resembles that of a ballcourt (Hill and Clark 2001:Figure 5).

In comparison to the later Middle Preclassic examples, the ballcourt at Paso de la Amada is unusually large. It is composed of two lateral structures that form a playing field approximately 80 meters long and seven meters wide. The majority of the known Middle Preclassic ballcourts have lengths similar to those seen in northwest Yucatan (i.e., between 14 and 25 meters). The ballcourt at the site of Campanillo in West Mexico is an exception measuring about 40 meters long, yet still the Paso de la Amada ballcourt is twice that length. Construction of the Paso de la Amada ballcourt appears to have taken place between 1400 and 1250 B.C. (Hill et al. 1998:878), making it five to six hundred years older than the known Middle Preclassic ballcourts. If the ballgame and the construction of ballcourts were central to the emergence of government and complex cultural institutions in Mesoamerica, as argued by Hill and Clark (2001), there is a long gap without ballcourt construction that needs to be explained.

Iconographic depictions of ballgame activity dating to the Early Preclassic are largely confined to portable figurines. The figurines are both more numerous and more reliably identified as related to the ballgame than their Middle Preclassic counterparts. One of the better known examples is a group of ten ceramic figurines recovered from an early West Mexican shaft tomb at the site of El Opeño (Oliveros 1988). Several of the figurines are dressed in protective gear and molded into different athletic poses, while other figurines lack gear and are posed in reclining positions. It is thought that together the figurines would have been arranged to create a ballgame scene complete with players and spectators (Oliveros 1988:192). Other examples of Early Preclassic ballplayer figurines have been reported from burials at the sites of Tlatilco and Tlapacoya in central Mexico (Bradley 2001). Some of these figurines are particularly clear examples depicting individuals both dressed as ballplayers and holding balls. In addition, ballplayer figurines have been reported from the site of San Lorenzo (Coe and Diehl 1980) in the Gulf coast region. Some Early Preclassic monumental sculptures may depict ballplayers, but the number of examples is limited and subject to some controversy. The most probable example is San Lorenzo Monument 34, which depicts a kneeling male figure wearing a wide belt reminiscent of later ballgame belts and yolks (Coe 1968:83). Some scholars still suggest that the Olmec colossal heads depict ballplayers (Clark 2007:30; Hill and Clark 2001:334), but most scholars no longer accept this interpretation (Diehl 2004:105; Taladoire 2001:107).

Perhaps the most famous piece of evidence used to argue for the existence of an Early Preclassic ballgame are the rubber balls excavated from the anaerobic soils of El Manati, Veracruz (Ortíz Ceballos and Rodríguez 1999). A total of twelve rubber balls have been recovered from the site, although five of these were found by locals and thus lack a precise context. The balls range from eight to 20 centimeters in diameter and two are notably oblong. The presence of manufactured rubber balls clearly demonstrates the possibility of an Early Preclassic ballgame. Nevertheless, the fact that rubber was used as incense and in offerings should make us somewhat cautious in accepting this interpretation.

Conclusions

What do we know about the Mesoamerican ballgame in the Middle to Early Preclassic period? The evidence is widespread, but shows some distinct patterns. Almost all of the ballcourts known from these periods are found in the Maya region or the neighboring highlands near the Isthmus of Tehuantepec. These two regions also share additional architectural forms during the Preclassic period, most notably the "E-Groups" (Clark and Hansen 2001). If the Campanillo ballcourt in West Mexico does in fact date to the Middle Preclassic period, then it would appear that the ballcourt form was already known throughout Mesoamerica at this time, but for now it exists as a significant outlier to the distribution. In contrast to the ballcourts, all examples of ballplayer figurines from this period are found west of the Isthmus. Also, all examples of Early to Middle Preclassic monumental sculpture that have been associated with the ballgame are found at the Olmec centers of San Lorenzo and La Venta, but these examples are questionable. The rubber balls found at El Manati are the strongest evidence for a version of the ballgame in the Gulf coast region.

The variability in the distribution of the evidence for an Early and Middle Preclassic ballgame may suggest variability in the ways in which the game was played and the role it held within local cultures. All too often we consider the ballgame to be a single entity, but evidence supports significant variation in practice. Eric Taladoire (2003) makes a strong argument for the existence of at least three versions of the ballgame during the prehispanic period. The evidence presented here may imply that these variations in ballgame practice began as early as the Early Preclassic period.

Returning to the initial premise of this chapter, we must ask if the evidence demonstrates that the Early and Middle Preclassic ballgame was an institution of symbolic power with restricted access, or if it was a tradition freely accessible to everyone within the society. The reality is likely too complex for this simple dichotomy; nonetheless, the evidence does suggest that in many cases the ballgame was not controlled by elites. If we include the recently discovered examples in northwest Yucatan, the majority of currently known Middle Preclassic ballcourts are found at relatively small sites lacking overt signs of sociopolitical stratification. Scholars have often thought of ballcourts as elite construction projects due to their large scale and central position at many later Classic sites, but the Middle Preclassic ballcourts are quite modest in scale. The ballcourts of northwest Yucatan are no larger than many of the habitation platforms found at the same sites, and if we expect platforms to be built by family groups, the same could be said of the ballcourts. Given the distribution of ballcourts at sites of all sizes in northwest Yucatan, it would seem that any community that wanted to build a ballcourt could do so. In this case, therefore, the ballgame cannot be said to be associated exclusively with institutionalized power or control, nor was it restricted to any single segment of society.

There is, however, clear elite involvement in the ballgame during these early periods, even in northwest Yucatan. The ballcourt at Xtobo strongly suggests that the elites of an important regional center took part in the ballgame. The fine quality of Early Preclassic ballplayer figurines found elsewhere in Mesoamerica further suggests elite involvement in the tradition, but involvement does not have to be understood as influence or control. In Middle Preclassic northwest Yucatan, the ballgame was clearly a popular tradition. The widespread nature of the courts, and the presence of courts at small sites, suggest that everyone who could played the game. Throughout the history of the world, elites have often adopted the customs of the people they sought to control, not to take control of those customs, but rather to build a connection with the people. Early Mesoamerican elites may very well have adopted the ballgame for similar motives; not to create an elaborate ritual or political institution, but rather to curry favor by adopting a popular tradition.

Acknowledgments

The data presented in this chapter are the result of the work of many people who are all owed thanks. The Proyecto Costa Maya was directed by Tony Andrews and Fernando Robles, and the Proyecto Salvamento Archaeológico de Ciudad Caucel was directed by Fernando Robles and Josep Ligored. I owe personal thanks to these scholars for including me in their projects and granting me access to the resulting data. These projects were made possible through funding from the National Geographic Society, the Instituto Nacional de Antropológia e Historia de México, and the Middle American Research Institute of Tulane University, New Orleans. Finally, I wish to thank Will Andrews for his council and support throughout my education and fieldwork. Maya archaeology would not be what it is today without his tireless efforts.

Notes

1. Two additional ballcourts were also found during the course of the PCM survey. One at the site of Tzikul (Site 123) was dated to the Early Classic period, and one at an unnamed site (Site 212) could not be dated.

2. The Tipikal/Unto group is treated by some scholars as a single ceramic group, traditionally called the Tipikal group (Andrews 1988,1989; Smith 1971). Others separate Tipikal and Unto into two separate groups (e.g., Ball 1978:110, 1979).

References

Agrinier, Pierre. 1991. Ballcourts of Southern Chiapas, Mexico. In Scarborough and Wilcox 1991:175-194.

Anderson, David S. 2003. El asentamiento preclásico en la región noroeste de Yucatán, translated by Fernando Robles. In Robles Castellanos and Andrews 2003:46-61.

— 2010. *Xtobo, Yucatan, Mexico: The Study of a Preclassic Maya Community*. Ph.D. dissertation, Department of Anthropology, Tulane University. University Microfilms, Ann Arbor.

— 2011. Xtobo, Yucatán, México, and the Emergent Preclassic of the Northern Maya Lowlands. *Ancient Mesoamerica* 22:201-322.

Anderson, David S., Fernando Robles Castellanos, and Anthony P. Andrews. n.d. The Preclassic Settlement of Northwest Yucatán: Recharting the Pathway to Complexity. In *Pathways to Complexity in the Maya Lowlands: The Preclassic Development*, edited by George J. Bey III and Kathryn Brown. Volume in preparation.

Andrews, Anthony P., and Fernando Robles Castellanos. 2004. An Archaeological Survey of Northwest Yucatan, Mexico. *Mexicon* 26:7-14.

Andrews IV, E. Wyllys, and E. Wyllys Andrews V. 1980. *Excavations at Dzibilchaltun, Yucatan, Mexico*. Middle American Research Institute Publication 48. Tulane University, New Orleans.

Andrews V, E. Wyllys. 1988. Ceramic Units from Komchen, Yucatan, Mexico. *Ceramica de Cultura Maya* 15:51-64.

— 1989. Ceramics of Komchen, Yucatán México. Unpublished manuscript on file at the Middle American Research Institute, Tulane University, New Orleans.

Andrews V, E. Wyllys, Noberto Gonzalez Crespo, and William M. Ringle. 1980. *Map of the Ruins of Komchen, Yucatan, Mexico*. Limited distribution. On file at Middle American Research Institute, Tulane University, New Orleans.

Ball, Joseph W. 1978. Archaeological Pottery of the Yucatan–Campeche Coast. In Eaton and Ball 1978:69-146.

— 1979. Dzibilchaltun Formative Ceramics. Unpublished manuscript on file at the Middle American Research Institute, Tulane University, New Orleans.

Blom, Frans. 1932. The Maya Ball-game *Pok-ta-pok* (Called *Tlachtli* by the Aztec). In *Middle American Papers*, edited by Frans Blom and Maurice Ries, pp. 486-527. Middle American Research Institute, Publication 4. Tulane University, New Orleans.

Bradley, Douglas E. 2001. Gender, Power, and Fertility in the Olmec Ritual Ballgame. In Whittington 2001:33-39.

Ceballos Gallareta, Teresa. 2005. *Informe del análisis preliminar de la cerámica del sitio arqueológico 16Qd (7) 152, Fracc. "Villa Magna del Sur" en la Col. Serapio Rendón del Municipio de Mérida*. Instituto Nacional de Antropología e Historia, Merida.

Ceballos Gallareta, Teresa, Fernando Robles Castellanos, and Nereyda Quiñones Loría. 2008. La secuencia cerámica preliminar de los sitios de la reserva territorial de Caucel, municipio de Mérida. In *Informe del proyecto salvamento arqueológico en áreas de crecimiento urbano de la ciudad de Mérida, Yucatán, etapa Ciudad Caucel (2004–2006)*, edited by Fernando Robles Castellanos and Josep

Ligorred Perramon, pp. 3328-3351. Instituto Nacional de Antropología e Historia Centro and the Departamento de Patrimonio Arqueológico y Ecológico Municipal, Merida.

Chase, Arlen F., and Diane Z. Chase (editors). 1992. *Mesoamerican Elites: An Archaeological Assessment*. University of Oklahoma, Norman.

Chinchilla Mazariegos, Oswaldo. 1992. El juego de pelota en la escritura y el arte maya clásico: intrepretaciones recientes In *El juego de pelota en Mesoamérica: Raíces y supervivencia*, edited by María Teresa Uriarte, pp. 157-167. Colección América Nuestra 39. Siglo XXI, Mexico City.

Clark, John E. 2007. Mesoamerica's First State. In *The Political Economy of Ancient Mesoamerica: Transformations during the Formative and Classic Periods*, edited by Vernon L. Scarborough and John E. Clark, pp. 11-46. University of New Mexico, Albuquerque.

Clark, John E., and Richard D. Hansen. 2001. The Architecture of Early Kingship: Comparative Perspectives on the Origins of the Maya Royal Court. In *Royal Courts of the Ancient Maya, Volume 2: Data and Case Studies*, edited by Takeshi Inomata and Stephen D. Houston, pp. 1-45. Westview, Boulder.

Coe, Michael D. 1968. *America's First Civilization: Discovering the Olmec*. American Heritage, New York.

Coe, Michael D., and Richard A. Diehl. 1980. *In the Land of the Olmec: The Archaeology of San Lorenzo Tenochtitlán*, vol. 1. University of Texas, Austin.

Coggins, Clemency Chase. 2001. Chichén Itzá (Yucatán, México). In Evans and Webster 2001:127-133.

Cohodas, Marvin. 1991. Ballgame Imagery of the Maya Lowlands: History and Iconography. In Scarborough and Wilcox 1991:251-288.

Day, Jane Stevenson. 2001. Performing on the Court. In Whittington 2001:64-77.

de Montmollin, Olivier. 1995. *Settlement and Politics in Three Classic Maya Polities*. Monographs in World Archaeology 24. Prehistory Press, Madison.

Diehl, Richard A. 2004. *The Olmecs: America's First Civilization*. Thames & Hudson, London.

Earle, Timothy. 1997. *How Chiefs Come to Power: The Political Economy in Prehistory*. Stanford University, Stanford.

Eaton, Jack D. 1978. Archaeological Survey of the Yucatan–Campeche Coast. In Eaton and Ball 1978:1-67.

Eaton, Jack D., and Joseph W. Ball (editors). 1978. *Studies in the Archaeology of Coastal Yucatan and Campeche, Mexico*. Middle American Research Institute, Publication 46. Tulane University, New Orleans.

Ekholm, Susanna M. 1991. Ceramic Figurines and the Mesoamerican Ballgame. In Scarborough and Wilcox 1991:241-250.

Evans, Susan T., and David L. Webster (editors). 2001. *Archaeology of Ancient Mexico and Central America: An Encyclopedia*. Garland, New York.

Filoy Nadal, Laura. 2001. Rubber and Rubber Balls in Mesoamerica. In Whittington 2001:21-31.

Flannery, Kent V., and Joyce Marcus. 2000. Formative Mexican Chiefdoms and the Myth of the "Mother Culture." *Journal of Anthropological Archaeology* 19:1-37.

Fox, John Gerald. 1994. *Putting the Heart Back in the Court: Ballcourts and Ritual Action in Mesoamerica*. Ph.D. dissertation, Department of Anthropology, Harvard University. University Microfilms, Ann Arbor.

— 1996. Playing with Power: Ballcourts and Political Ritual in Southern Mesoamerica. *Current Anthropology* 37:483-509.

Gallareta Negrón, Tomás, William M. Ringle, Rossana May Ciau, Juluieta Ramos Pacheco, and Ramón Carrillo Sánchez. 2005. Evidencias de ocupación durante el período preclásico en el Puuc: Xocnaceh y Paso del Macho. Paper presented at the Segundo Congreso Internacional de Cultural Maya, Merida.

Grove, David C. 1984. *Chalcatzingo: Excavations on the Olmec Frontier*. New Aspects of Antiquity. Thames & Hudson, London.

Grove, David C. (editor). 1987. *Ancient Chalcatzingo*. University of Texas, Austin.

Grove, David C., and Ann Cyphers Guillén. 1987. The Excavations. In Grove 1987:21-55.
Hernández Hernández, Concepción. 2005. La cerámica del periodo preclásico tardío (300 a.C.–350 d.C.) en el norte de la península de Yucatán. In *La producción alfarera en el México antiguo, Volumen I*, edited by Beatriz L. Merino Carrión and Ángel García Cook, pp. 753-779. Serie arqueología 484. Instituto Nacional de Antropología e Historia, Mexico City.
Hill, Warren D., Michael Blake, and John E. Clark. 1998. Ball Court Design Dates Back 3,400 years. *Nature* 392:878-879.
Hill, Warren D., and John E. Clark. 2001. Sports, Gambling, and Government: America's First Social Compact? *American Anthropologist* 103:331-345.
Lesure, Richard G. 2004. Shared Art Styles and Long-Distance Contact in Early Mesoamerica. In *Mesoamerican Archaeology: Theory and Practice*, edited by Julia A. Hendon and Rosemary A. Joyce, pp. 73-96. Blackwell Publishing, Malden.
Leyenaar, Ted J. J. 1978. *Ulama: The Perpetuation in Mexico of the Pre-Spanish Ball Game Ullamaliztli*, translated by I. Seeger. Mededelingen van het Rijksmuseum voor Volkenkunde 23. E.J. Brill, Leiden.
— 2001. The Modern Ballgames of Sinaloa: A Survival of the Aztec Ullamaliztli. In Whittington 2001:122-129.
Lohse, Jon C., and Fred Valdez (editors). 2004. *Ancient Maya Commoners*. University of Texas, Austin.
Lowe, Gareth W. 1959. *Archaeological Exploration of the Upper Gijalva River, Chiapas, Mexico*. New World Archaeological Foundation Publication 2. Brigham Young University, Provo.
Marcus, George E. (editor). 1983. *Elites: Ethnographic Issues*. University of New Mexico, Albuquerque.
Martínez Donjuan, Guadalupe. 1995. Teopantecuanitlán: sitio olmeca en Guerrero. *Arqueología Mexicana* 2(12):58-62.
Medina Castillo, Edgar. 2003. Los Juegos de Pelota de la región noroeste de Yucatán. In Robles Castellanos and Andrews 2003:62-87.
— 2005. *El juego de pelota del preclásico medio en el noroeste de Yucatán, México*. Licensiatura thesis, Facultad de Ciencias Antropológicas, Universidad Autónoma de Yucatán, Merida.
Nicholson, Henry B., and Eloise Quiñones Keber. 1991. Ballcourt Images in Central Mexican Native Tradition Pictorial Manuscripts. In van Bussel, van Dongen, and Leyenaar 1991:119-133.
Oliveros, José Arturo. 1988. Juego de pelota entre las ofrendas del Opeño, Michoacan. In *Ensayos de Alfarería Prehispánica e Histórica de Mesoamérica: Homenaje a Eduardo Noguera Auza*, edited by Mari Carmen Serra Puche and Carlos Navarrete Cáceres, pp. 187-204. Universidad Nacional Autonoma de México, Mexico City.
Ortíz Ceballos, Ponciano, and María del Carmen Rodríguez. 1999. Olmec Ritual Behavior at El Manatí: A Sacred Space. In *Social Patterns in Pre-Classic Mesoamerica*, edited by David C. Grove and Rosemary A. Joyce, pp. 225-254. Dumbarton Oaks, Washington, D.C.
Ortiz, Ponciano, and María del Carmen Rodríguez. 1992. Las ofrendas de El Manatí y su posible asociación con el juego de pelota: Un yugo a destiempo. In Uriarte 1992:55-67.
— 2000. The Sacred Hill of El Manatí: A Preliminary Discussion of the Site's Ritual Paraphernalia. In *Olmec Art and Archaeology in Mesoamerica*, edited by John E. Clark and Mary E. Pye, pp. 75-94. Studies in the History of Art 58. National Gallery of Art, Washington, D.C.
Pool, Christopher A. 2007. *Olmec Archaeology and Early Mesoamerica*. Cambridge University, Cambridge.
Ringle, William M. 1985. *The Settlement Patterns of Komchen, Yucatan, Mexico*. Ph.D. dissertation, Department of Anthropology, Tulane University. University Microfilms, Ann Arbor.
— 2004. On the Political Organization of Chichen Itza. *Ancient Mesoamerica* 15:167-218.
Ringle, William M., and E. Wyllys Andrews V. 1990. The Demography of Komchen, an Early Maya Town in Northern Yucatan. In *Precolumbian Population History in the Maya Lowlands*, edited by T. Patrick Culbert and Don S. Rice, pp. 215-243. University of New Mexico, Albuquerque.
Rivero Torres, Sonia E. 1990. *Patrón de asentamiento rural en la región de San Gregorio, Chiapas, para el Clásico Tardío*. Instituto Nacional de Antropología e Historia, Mexico City.

Robles Castellanos, Fernando. 1997. Tipología de la cerámica de la gruta Loltún, Yucatán, que se encuentra en el Museo Peabody de la Universidad de Harvard. In *Homenaje al profesor César A. Sáenz*, edited by Ángel García Cook, Alba Guadalupe Mastache, Beatriz L. Merino Carrión, and Sonia Rivero Torres, pp. 251-317. Instituto Nacional de Antropología e Historia, Mexico City.

Robles Castellanos, Fernando, and Anthony P. Andrews (editors). 2000. *Proyecto Costa Maya: Reporte interino, Temporada 2000: Reconocimiento arqueológico de la esquina noroeste de la peninsula de Yucatán*. Instituto Nacional de Antropología e Historia, Merida.

— 2001. *Proyecto Costa Maya: Reporte interino, Temporada 2001: Reconocimiento arqueológico de la esquina noroeste de la peninsula de Yucatán*. Instituto Nacional de Antropología e Historia, Merida.

— 2003. *Proyecto Costa Maya: Reporte interino, Temporada 2002: Reconocimiento arqueológico de la esquina noroeste de la peninsula de Yucatán*. Instituto Nacional de Antropología e Historia, Merida.

Robles Castellanos, Fernando, and Teresa Ceballos Gallareta. 2003. La cronología cerámica preliminar del noroeste de la península de Yucatán. In Robles Castellanos and Andrews 2003:38-45.

Robles Castellanos, Fernando, and Josep Ligorred Perramon. 2008. Salvamento arqueológico en áreas de crecimiento urbano de la ciudad de Mérida, Yucatán, etapa Ciudad Caucel. In *Informe del proyecto salvamento arqueológico en áreas de crecimiento urbano de la ciudad de Mérida, Yucatán, etapa Ciudad Caucel (2004–2006)*, edited by Fernando Robles Castellanos and Josep Ligorred Perramon. Instituto Nacional de Antropología e Historia and the Departamento de Patrimonio Arqueológico y Ecológico Municipal, Merida.

Scarborough, Vernon L. 2001. Ball Game. In Evans and Webster 2001:67-71.

Scarborough, Vernon L., and David R. Wilcox (editors). 1991. *The Mesoamerican Ballgame*. University of Arizona, Tucson.

Schele, Linda, and Mary Ellen Miller. 1986. *The Blood of Kings: Dynasty and Ritual in Maya Art*. George Braziller, New York.

Schieber de Lavarreda, Christa. 1994. A Middle Preclassic Clay Ball Court at Abaj Takalik, Guatemala. *Mexicon* 16:77-84.

Scott, John F. 2001. Dressed to Kill: Stone Regalia of the Mesoamerican Ballgame. In Whittington 2001:50-63.

Shook, Edwin M. 1955. Yucatan and Chiapas. *Carnegie Institution of Washington Yearbook* 54:289-295.

Smith, Robert E. 1971. *The Pottery of Mayapan: Including Studies of Ceramic Material from Uxmal, Kabah, and Chichen Itza*. 2 vols. Papers of the Peabody Museum of Archaeology and Ethnology 66. Harvard University, Cambridge, Mass.

Smith, Robert E., Gordon R. Willey, and James C. Gifford. 1960. The Type-Variety Concept as a Basis for the Analysis of Maya Pottery. *American Antiquity* 25:330-340.

Taladoire, Eric. 1981. *Les terrains de jeu de balle (Mésoamérique et Sud-ouest des Etats-Unis)*. Etudes Mesoamericaines, Serie II 4. Mission Archeologique et Ethnologique Française au Mexique, Mexico City.

— 1991. Le codex de Xalapa: Mapa del juego de pelota. In van Bussel, van Dongen, and Leyenaar 1991:111-118.

— 2001. The Architectural Background of the Pre-Hispanic Ballgame: An Evolutionary Perspective. In Whittington 2001:97-115.

— 2003. Could We Speak of the Super Bowl at Flushing Meadows? La Pelota Mixteca, a Third Pre-Hispanic Ballgame, and its Possible Architectural Context. *Ancient Mesoamerica* 14:319-342.

Taube, Karl A. 2004. *Olmec Art at Dumbarton Oaks*. Pre-Columbian Art at Dumbarton Oaks 2. Dumbarton Oaks, Washington, D.C.

Uriarte, María Teresa (editor). 1992. *El juego de pelota en Mesoamérica: Raíces y supervivencia*. Colección América Nuestra 39. Siglo XXI, Mexico City.

— 2001. Unity in Duality: The Practice and Symbols of the Mesoamerican Ballgame. In Whittington 2001:40-49.

van Bussel, Gerard W., Paul L.F. van Dongen, and Ted J.J. Leyenaar (editors). 1991. *The Mesoamerican Ballgame: Papers Presented at the International Colloquium "The Mesoamerican Ballgame 2000 BC–AD 2000"*. Rijksmuseum voor Volkenkunde, Leiden.

Wason, Paul K. 1994. *The Archaeology of Rank*. Cambridge University, Cambridge.

Weigand, Phil C. 1991. The Western Mesoamerican Tlachco: A Two-Thousand-Year Perspective. In Scarborough and Wilcox 1991:73-86.

Whalen, Michael E., and Paul E. Minnis. 1996. Ball Courts and Political Centralization in the Casas Grandes Region. *American Antiquity* 61:732-746.

Whittington, E. Michael (editor). 2001. *The Sport of Life and Death: The Mesoamerican Ballgame*. Thames & Hudson, London.

Wyshak, Lillian W., Rainer Berger, John A. Graham, and Robert F. Heizer. 1971. A Possible Ball Court at La Venta, Mexico. *Nature* 232:650-651.

Zender, Marc. 2004. Sport, Spectacle and Political Theater: New Views of the Classic Maya Ballgame. *PARI Journal* 4(4):10-12.

3 The Architecture of Power and Sociopolitical Complexity in Northwestern Yucatan during the Preclassic Period

Nancy Peniche May

Abstract

Recent archaeological explorations in the northern Maya lowlands demonstrate that social complexity emerged as early as the second half of the Middle Preclassic period. This has required us to discard models that consider the northern lowlands as a peripheral region where sociopolitical elaboration occurred at a later time and as the result of external influence. Current debate focuses on the nature and level of sociopolitical organization during the late Middle Preclassic, specifically whether northern polities should be considered as chiefdoms or as states. This chapter approaches the question by analyzing a specific public building, one that is considered as embodying and expressing asymmetrical social relations.

Structure 1714 is located at Xaman Susula, a middle-rank site in the three-tiered settlement pattern hierarchy of northwestern Yucatan. The structure is the largest and most impressive one at the site. It is characterized by the presence of the earliest throne reported in the entire Maya lowlands. The analysis of Structure 1714, in conjunction with aspects of site planning and regional settlement pattern, indicate that Xaman Susula was organized at the level of chiefdom. Most importantly, it is argued that this society is best understood as an individualizing chiefdom that employed an exclusionary or network strategy of political integration.

The Preclassic period is a time of great interest in the history of the northern Maya lowlands, as well as elsewhere in Mesoamerica, because it witnessed the emergence and consolidation of social and political complexity. Nonetheless, the scale and nature of organization during this period are still topics of debate. There are several means through which we can approach these subjects, among them the analysis of the architecture of power. Here I follow principles proposed by Moore (1996) in his study of the architecture of power in the Andes. As Moore (1996) points out, we can understand the political organization of an ancient society because architecture embodies and expresses asymmetrical social relations. This is because one expression of power is the organization of the social effort needed to build this type of architecture.

As relations of power change, the architecture of power might change as well. Hence architecture of power is a useful tool in understanding the scale and nature of the political organization of ancient societies.

Moore's discussion is relevant to the case of the northern Maya lowlands of southeastern Mexico. Recent explorations in this area have provided evidence that social and political complexity first appeared in the Puuc Region during the Middle Preclassic period (1000–400/300 B.C.). Regional centers such as Poxila and Xocnaceh emerged during the late Middle Preclassic and were abandoned before the end of this period (Robles Castellanos and Ceballos Gallareta n.d.). At the end of the Middle Preclassic period, Xtobo emerged as the regional center of northwestern Yucatan, and its peak florescence might have occurred during the early Late Preclassic (Ceballos Gallareta and Robles Castellanos n.d.). Although we now know that complex polities existed in the northern lowlands in these early periods, the scale and nature of political organization are still topics of debate. Specifically, the debate among Maya archaeologists centers on the question of whether these precocious polities are best described as chiefdoms (Anderson 2005) or states (Robles Castellanos and Ceballos Gallareta n.d.).

Explorations at the small site of Xaman Susula (Figure 1.1), outside of Merida, Yucatan, have provided information that may be useful in examining the models of political organization proposed for the transitional period between the Middle Preclassic and Late Preclassic. These excavations revealed an early Late Preclassic building, Structure 1714-Asub, whose unique architectural and functional features are helpful in resolving this debate. Through the analysis of Structure 1714-Asub, I propose that polities in the northwestern Maya lowlands were organized at the chiefdom level during the Middle Preclassic to Late Preclassic transition. Most importantly, I argue that this society was an individualizing chiefdom that employed an exclusionary or network strategy of political integration (Blanton et al. 1996; Renfrew 1974).

The Architecture of Power and its Relation to Complexity

Throughout the anthropological and archaeological literature, architecture or "built forms" have been used as a means to study several aspects of ancient societies (Kolb 1994; Lawrence and Low 1990). Such studies are based on the principle that man-made constructions, as part of the built environment, can reflect a variety of cultural behaviors. Current approaches consider that architecture also has an active part in this relation because built forms also shape cultural behavior (Lawrence and Low 1990; Moore 1996). That is, the relation between architecture and human behavior is interactive.

Among the multiple aspects of ancient societies that we can reach through the study of structures, I am interested in the ways that architecture reproduces the development of different forms of social organization, particularly social relations associated with power. This research is based on the idea that built forms and the meanings associated with them are manipulated by elites to communicate values in relation to social and political change (Lawrence and Low 1990:469; see also Kolb 1994). Both public and residential structures are useful in the study of sociopolitical organization, although information about the nature of relations of power that we can obtain differs according to the type of architecture.

Residences are ideal symbols of status and power. Because of this, residential structures may serve as evidence of asymmetrical social relations because they represent the social status of their individual occupants. Furthermore, residences collectively express the social structure of the community of which they are part and change in recognizable ways as society changes

(Cliff 1988, after Watson 1994:136). Residences as architecture of power include chiefs' houses in chiefdom-level societies and palaces in state-level societies. In the latter case, we must remember that palaces combine both residential and public functions. They exist, therefore, between private and public architecture.

Like residences, the architecture and spatial arrangement of structures that had specialized, non-domestic functions (or "public buildings") can also provide specific information about the nature of the community of which they are part (see Blanton et al. 1996; Renfrew 1974). I follow the principle that attributes of public buildings change in recognizable ways as society changes (Kolb 1994; Watson 1994). Such change in public buildings could be a response related to the set of activities performed in the public buildings. Moore (1996) argues that public buildings provide evidence of different public orders. This is because the different social entities representing different levels of social complexity vary in relation to their reliance on consent and coercion, which are the twin foundations of power. Additionally, if one expression of power is the direction of social effort, public constructions may reflect the exercise of power in concrete form (Moore 1996).

Public buildings are defined as structures that had specialized, non-domestic functions. The identification of public buildings therefore requires a clear understanding of what constitutes domestic activities, which may vary considerably over time and among different societies. In Mesoamerica, Marcus and Flannery (1996:91) have proposed some attributes that can help identify public buildings. According to them, public buildings are usually built on the highest places and subfloor dedicatory offerings are a common feature. Marcus and Flannery (1996) have also pointed out that it is not unusual for these kinds of structures to be rebuilt several times in the same place. These criteria are also some of the formal attributes that have been proposed to identify buildings with some type of ceremonial or ritual function (Brown and Sheets 2000; Lesure 1999), reflecting the problem that for Mesoamerica, "public building" is often used as a synonym for "ceremonial" or "ritual structure." Yet the range of public activities performed in ancient Mesoamerica includes more than ceremonies and ritual activities.

For this reason, we should expect to find a variety of public buildings at Mesoamerican sites. Moreover, the architectural attributes of these buildings should vary according to their function. In order to identify public buildings correctly it is important to know the variety of activities that may have been performed in them. This identification is crucial when studying complexity because some types of buildings are diagnostic of specific social structures. The goal of the following sections is to present the characteristics of those buildings that provide evidence regarding political structure. Because I argue that particular traits of architecture of power depend on the characteristics of a given society, I focus my discussion on the Maya area and Mesoamerica.

As a cautionary note, it is important to remember that the argument that "form follows function" can be circular and cause us to lose sight of the diverse roles that a structure might play within various contexts. Nonetheless, I think that architectural features do suggest the range of functions that a structure could have performed. In order to confirm any hypothesis regarding the activities conducted in or near a structure, it is of course necessary to analyze artifacts associated with that structure.

Architecture of Power in State-Level Societies: Palaces as Elite Residences and Public Spaces

The term "palace" is often poorly defined in archaeological literature about the Maya. The attributes that define palaces have not been clearly identified because formal and functional characteristics are often both described together. The term "palace" must be functional and not related to the particular architectural characteristics of structures (Ball and Taschek 2001:165). I consider the best definition of palace to be that of Webster and Inomata:

> Palaces are the residences of individuals of wealth or high social rank, along with their families and retinues, and they include facilities appropriate to the ritual, political, recreational, and economic functions of elite households and individuals as foci of social power (Webster and Inomata 2004:149).

From Webster and Inomata, we see that a palace must consist of two main parts—a private residence and a public place—both of which are essential. Palaces are also always related to elite activities and are an essential trait of complex stratified societies (Christie 2006:3; Flannery 1998:21). According to Flannery (1998:21), the reason for this is that only state-level societies were able to organize labor to build these kinds of structures, a point I return to below. Furthermore, palaces may be possessed not only by the ruler, but also by other nobles. This is because despite a tendency toward centralization in archaic states, significant administrative and judiciary functions are carried out by elites other than the ruler (Inomata and Houston 2001:13).

Despite the fact that palaces can have a great variety of architectural manifestations, certain features consistently appear in all palaces that correspond to their particular functions. In the Maya area, private and public spaces are usually separated although not always in a sharp manner. Therefore, palaces tend to be multi-room buildings, each room having a specific residential or public function. As residences of the highest authorities of a state-level society, palaces should have evidence of domestic life. Consequently we should be able to identify spaces where domestic activities, such as food production, eating, and craft or artistic production, were carried out. *Metates*, fire hearths, and food refuse are good indicators of domestic spaces. Craft production facilities also may be present. Additionally, features such as burials of individuals of all ages and sexes, caches, private shrines, and long sleeping benches may indicate permanent residence (Harrison and Andrews 2004:114; Webster 2001:154).

Because palaces fulfilled administrative, judicial, ceremonial, diplomatic, and other public functions, they include facilities and features designed for political, economic, and ritual use. In that sense, the architecture of palaces should reflect, to a greater or lesser degree, activities including: feasts, alliance formation, rituals witnessed by visitors and locals, elite ancestor worship, conjuring, visions, the presentation of captives, formal audiences, witnessing of processions, the creation of status-reinforcing social distance for the royal household and court, and the claiming of access to or control of special resources or activities (Demarest 2006:119-120).

In the Maya area, open spaces such as courtyards and plazas have been identified as palace features associated with public or semipublic rituals and exchanges (Pillsbury and Evans 1998:2). Another architectural feature that has been used to identify political, ritual, and economic administration is a particular kind of bench labeled as a "throne." A bench can be designated as a throne when it is built in the main chamber of a building in front of the central access door to the edifice and placed against the back wall of the room (Valdés 2001:150).

Rulers or other high officials sat on this particular kind of bench in order to fulfill the political, economic, and ritual administration of the court (Harrison 2003:113). In fact, based on the representations on polychrome vessels from the Late Classic period, we can affirm that structures with thrones were the scenes of many different activities. In structures of this type, lords presided over visiting delegations, presentations of tribute or gifts, and public or semi-public ritual performances such as divination rituals and the displays of prisoners (Harrison 2003:113; Reents-Budet 2001:203). Nonetheless, the main function of thrones and throne rooms was to serve as the literal and symbolic seat of political power. House E in the palace at Palenque is one of many examples of such a throne room.

Thrones are usually found in rooms in larger buildings that served multiple public and private functions, which allows them to be labeled as palaces. Throne rooms are usually located in the center of such architectural complexes. Throne rooms have also been called "scenic palaces" or "presentation palaces" (Valdés 2001:151), because they have wide central doorways that open toward a courtyard or plaza. Sometimes *sacbes* or causeways are associated with scenic palaces (Valdés 2001:151). Palaces 32 and 33 of Tamarindito Group B and structures M7-22 and M7-32 at the Palace Group of Aguateca are examples of this kind of structure. These buildings have been interpreted as being non-residential because their doors are too wide to allow privacy within the structure (Valdés 2001:151; see also Valdés 1997). Lords seated on these thrones would have observed what was happening outside, and people congregated outside would have witnessed events inside the room.

Harrison (2001) proposed the term "throne structure," an architectural type that includes separate single-room buildings with thrones. These buildings are adjoined to residential buildings (i.e., Structure 5D-59 at Tikal; see Harrison 2001:91) or special-function structures (Structure 5D-123 at Tikal; see Harrison 2001:92). Their main characteristic is that access to throne structures is limited and restricted. The construction of separate and multiple throne structures implies that palace functions were spread over different buildings and were not centralized in a single structure or complex. Throne structures might have been associated with other kinds of events that did not require the presence of a large number of people, such as certain rituals, political meetings, or less formal events (Valdés 2001:156; see Harrison 2001). Whatever their functions were, throne structures were strictly public buildings and because of that they cannot on their own be categorized as palaces.

It is important to mention that there are some thrones that were built outside of buildings. Some were attached to an exterior wall, such as Structure M7-32 at Aguateca (Valdés 2001:156). Other thrones were built on low platforms without evidence of walls or constructions around them (see Chapter 9 for a discussion of outside thrones at Uxmal). These probably were once covered with a roof made of perishable materials or a canopy of cotton. An example of this latter style is the throne found in the Lost World Group at Tikal (Valdés 2001:154). It is difficult to infer whether such outside thrones had the same function as the thrones found inside structures, or if they fulfilled very special functions. A polychrome vase discovered in the Lost World Group is important to this question. This vessel depicts a jaguar cub being offered to the Tikal ruler seated on an outside throne (Valdés 2001:156). From this, it might be inferred that thrones on platforms could have had an administrative function. In fact, Demarest et al. (2003) think that these outside thrones functioned in the same manner as "presentation palaces."

Architecture of Power in Chiefdom-Level Societies: Chiefly Residences and Public Buildings

In the archaeological literature on Mesoamerica there is a great discrepancy in the attention paid to the palaces of states versus the architecture of chiefdom-level societies. Because of this, the attributes that define the architecture of chiefdoms—especially the architecture of power, meaning chiefly houses and public buildings—are not very well established. Nonetheless, it is possible to identify some of the key attributes of chiefdom-level architecture through a review of the anthropological and archaeological literature.

First of all, the main trait that characterizes chiefdoms, architecturally speaking, is the fact that there is a marked separation between private or domestic spaces and public spaces. That is to say, no structure combines both private and public functions. Thus, in contrast to the state societies where palaces were built as both private residences and public spaces, chiefdoms lack structures that exhibit this kind of dual functionality. The reason for the lack of integration of public and private spaces into a single building complex could be related to the nature of political organization. Chiefs do not have enough power to centralize all functions into a single space (Flannery 1998). Strategies of control or integration may also serve to segregate space. For example, in some chiefly societies, chiefs attain and maintain their power through control of ritual. They might be more interested in investing labor in public buildings than in their houses. Whatever the explanation is, the fact is that chiefdom societies lack palaces. Instead, they have public buildings and separate private residences where commoners and chiefs live. Two important questions are: (1) How can we differentiate between the houses of elites and commoners in a chiefdom?; and (2) What are the defining characteristics of a public building in a chiefdom-level society?

Flannery (1998:21) has argued that in chiefdom-level societies it is not possible to distinguish between elite and commoner houses because chiefs do not have enough power to organize labor to build their residences. For this reason, elite and non-elite houses have the same characteristics. In contrast, Blake (1991:28) has stated that many documented examples of chiefdoms demonstrate that the dwellings of chief are usually more sumptuous than the residences of commoners. A cross-cultural ethnographic and ethnohistorical study of 51 prestate societies in the Americas carried out by Feinman and Neitzel (1984) supports Blake. According to this research, chiefly houses can be recognized based on size, form (decoration, construction materials, and style), location, and interior furniture (Feinman and Neitzel 1984:57). Feinman and Neitzel (1984) note great variation in the residential architecture of leaders, from Carib chiefs whose houses were only slightly larger than those of commoners, to the enormous and elaborately ornamented houses built on high mounds that belonged to Natchez leaders. I argue that three variables—size, form, and location of chiefly houses—depended on the specific nature of the chiefdoms.

It is well known that chiefdoms are not a monolithic category (e.g., Feinman and Neitzel 1984; Flannery 1999a). The concept of "chiefdom" has been used to describe a wide range of societies that share the notion of inherited social differentiation. There are, therefore, a wide variety of *kinds* of chiefdoms. Flannery (1999), for example, distinguishes between Mesoamerican and Near East chiefdoms based on the manner used by elites to express rank and status. In Mesoamerica, chiefs depended on the "flamboyant use of sumptuary goods and their use of chiefly warfare to create multivillage polities" (Flannery 1999:44). In contrast, in the Near East, leaders relied more on face-to face alliance building with competitors, and on religious purity, piety, and knowledge. In chiefdoms in the Near East, competition was always present (Flannery 1999:44).

These data support Renfrew's (1974) assertion that some chiefdoms are individualizing and some are group-oriented. Both types of chiefdoms are relatively similar in overall sociopolitical complexity, but are organized in markedly different ways. In this sense, Renfrew's (1974) model is analogous to the dual-processual model of political integration proposed by Blanton et al. (1996; see also Feinman 2001). According to Blanton et al. (1996), political actors make use of different strategies that can be understood in terms of two strategies of power (exclusionary and corporate) and two sources of that power (objective and symbolic). These organizational modes are not exclusive to state-level and chiefdom-level societies.

Individualizing chiefdoms. Individualizing chiefdoms use an exclusionary or network strategy in which specific actors work to develop a political system built around their monopolistic control of objective sources of power. These include wealth and factors related to production (Blanton et al. 1996). Political actors in individualizing chiefdoms forge connections with their counterparts in other autonomous polities, and engage in the trade of prestige goods, war, and strategic marriages (Blanton et al. 1996). In this type of chiefdom there is a great emphasis on the individual, and differences in rank and privilege can be great. This may be manifest in the use of sumptuary or luxury goods, special housing, and the construction of elaborate burial monuments (Feinman 2001:160; Renfrew 1974). Most importantly, we should find a marked differentiation among elite and non-elite houses. Chiefly houses are larger and different in form (material of construction, style, ornamentation, or shape of the building) than the houses lived in by commoners. Moreover, they are few in number compared to commoner houses (Blake et al. 2006:194). Such houses also may be located near public buildings, but communal ritual and public constructions are generally not as important as chiefly houses (Renfrew 1974).

Group-oriented chiefdoms. In contrast to individualized chiefdoms, group-oriented chiefdoms rely on corporate strategies of political integration. Group definition is important because power is shared across different sectors of society. The distribution of power is structured, determined, legitimated, and controlled (Blanton et al. 1996). Elite residences and burials are not very different from the rest of the population because these polities deemphasize differences in access to personal wealth (Feinman 1991). That is, individuals are anonymous in the archaeological record (Feinman 2001). This means that all the houses—even the houses of chiefs—have the same basic form, although there may be some differences in size. Chiefly houses may also be identified by their locations, often near public buildings. Instead of individual wealth and power, communal activities and group rituals are of great importance to chiefdoms of this kind. As a result, collective labor is used to build monumental public architecture dedicated to communal ritual and other activities rather than chiefly houses (Feinman 2001; Renfrew 1974).

Feinman (2001) argues that both corporate and exclusionary strategies may be used within the same polity. Thus, chiefdoms should exhibit continuous variation along a dimension of corporate/exclusionary political strategies. Such variation may be seen cross-culturally or within a single region over time.

Residences and public buildings. Excavations of elite residences, whether in individualizing or group-oriented societies, should provide evidence of the same range of household activities practiced in lower-status houses. This means we should be able to demonstrate that such buildings were residences where men, women, and children conducted domestic activities. In contrast, excavations of public buildings should provide evidence of specialized activities that were not conducted in houses. Marcus and Flannery (1996:91) have proposed attributes that can help to identify public buildings in Mesoamerica. Public buildings are usually built on the highest sites in a community. Subfloor dedicatory offerings are common. Additionally, public buildings were often rebuilt several times in the same place and with the same orientation. Nonetheless, the main architectural characteristics of a public building depend on its specific functions (Blake 1991:30). These, in turn, are related to the activities performed in the structure by chiefs and other elites.

According to Feinman and Neitzel (1984:50), the leaders of pre-state societies carried out a variety of functions that can be classified as related to redistribution (collecting, storing, and allocating tribute and other goods, as well as organizing feasts), ideology (sponsoring ceremonies and guarding public morality), administration (leading public meetings, appointing officials, and supervising community tasks), judicial functions (resolving disputes, punishing offenders), subsistence, inter-village activities (controlling trade, declaring war, building alliances, and hosting guests), and the storage of information (maintaining territorial boundaries and genealogical histories). Some of these activities could have been performed in public structures and open spaces (Blake et al. 2006:193). In Mesoamerica, temples, men's houses, ballcourts, and dance platforms are among the public buildings identified for chiefdoms, although none of these are uniquely associated with this level of social complexity.

Men's houses. Communal men's houses were built by cooperative groups for religious rituals, periodic feasting, and large public gatherings. According to Blake (1991), men's houses tend to be larger than average residences because they must accommodate large numbers of people. They may not differ structurally from ordinary residences. The activities—all male-focused—that are conducted in a men's house differ considerably from those carried out in residences. Although men's houses are found in chiefdom-level societies, they are considered the remnants of a previous stage of sociopolitical complexity. In fact, communal men's houses are typical of segmentary societies (Blake 1991; Flannery and Marcus 2005). That is, they began as public buildings in egalitarian societies that were led by adult men who passed through multiple rituals on their way to achieving high status (Flannery and Marcus 2005).

Temples. According to Flannery and Marcus (2005), the first temples built in the Valley of Oaxaca appeared as political complexity coalesced. Specifically, Flannery and Marcus (2005) associate the construction of temples with the emergence of complex chiefdoms. Architectural attributes of temples may vary according to region or site. Mesoamerican archaeologists have developed formal criteria for recognizing temples and other ceremonial buildings in the archaeological record (Becker 1971; Brown and Sheets 2000; Leventhal 1983; Marcus 1978; Marcus and Flannery 1996). Ceremonial buildings have a special location—for the Classic Maya, they were often positioned on the eastern side of the plaza or located at the highest point at a site (Becker 1971; Brown and Sheets 2000). They also have a formalized building plan, which consists of an open antechamber with restricted access to the innermost rooms (Marcus 1978). Ceremonial structures also tend to be rebuilt several times in the same place following the same orientation (Marcus and Flannery 1996). Additionally, ceremonial buildings tend to be built on higher platforms with less usable surface area than those that support domestic structures (Becker 1971). Ceremonial structures are also characterized by increasing floor elevations, that is, the height of the floor tends to increase as one proceeds from the antechamber deeper inside the structure (Marcus 1978). In some cases, an elaborate construction technique can be used for inferring ritual function (Leventhal 1983). As a final point, ceremonial buildings are frequently characterized by the presence of subfloor caches and burials (Marcus and Flannery 1996).

Ballcourts and performance structures. Mesoamerican, and particularly Maya sites often have other, special types of religious and ceremonial buildings. The ballgame was part of a complex political, ritual, and perhaps economic system. The meaning, importance, morphology, and iconography of the ballcourt varied across space and time. Nonetheless, ballcourts all share certain characteristics related to the techniques of the game (see Taladoire 2000:23-24). All ballcourts contain two long, parallel, and narrow range structures separated by a long, narrow flat space (see Chapter 2). Each range structure is composed of a sloping wall topped by a vertical body. The sloping walls, which face each other between the two range structures, end either directly on the court or on a low bench (Taladoire 2000:24). Performance structures are another specialized kind of ceremonial building. These platforms are round or keyhole in shape, and found mainly in Belize (Aimers et al. 2000; Hendon 1999, 2000). Hendon (1999, 2000) points out that these keyhole-shaped structures are usually associated with domestic areas and argues that the ceremonial activity conducted on the platforms was usually conducted by emerging elite who were vying for power. It is possible that dances were performed on them.

Two points to consider are that the architecture of chiefdoms must contain at least some public buildings, and there should be at least some differentiation between elite and commoner houses. But we cannot infer the presence of chiefdom-level sociopolitical organization solely from the presence of public buildings, because such structures were also built by both egalitarian and state-level societies. Nonetheless, the public buildings of chiefdoms are often more elaborate than those of egalitarian societies, and some have more specialized functions.

Architectural features alone are often insufficient for supporting the hypothesis that a particular society was organized as a chiefdom. We also must consider regional settlement patterns. Simple chiefdoms have two levels of settlement, consisting of the village of the chief and other, smaller settlements. Complex chiefdoms exhibit three levels of settlement hierarchy, implying two levels in the decision-making hierarchy. In the case of state-level societies, public buildings may be more specialized and more elaborate than those of chiefdom-level societies. Moreover, they are often associated with palaces. Finally, states have settlement hierarchies with at least four levels (Earle 2002:54; see Wright 1984).

In summary, architecture of power is used as a means to express asymmetrical social relations. As the nature of power changes, the characteristics of such architecture change. Through the study of architecture of power, we can obtain information about political complexity (see Feinman 1991). The study of architecture of power holds great potential for understanding political complexity in northwestern Yucatan during the Middle Preclassic to Late Preclassic transition. Some archaeologists (Anderson 2005; Gallareta Negrón et al. 2005) have argued that data from several sites suggest that the polity centered at Xtobo was organized as a chiefdom. In contrast, other scholars argue that Xtobo was the capital of a coercive and centralized archaic state (Robles Castellanos and Ceballos Gallareta n.d.).

Explorations of Xaman Susula, a small site near Merida, Yucatan, have provided data that are useful for examining political organization. During explorations of this site, we excavated a peculiar building, Structure 1714 A-sub, whose unique architectural and functional characteristics allow us to classify it as a public building. This structure is ideal for testing models of political organization proposed for the Middle Preclassic to Late Preclassic transition in northwestern Yucatan.

Xamán Susula

The archaeological site of Xamán Susula is located west of Merida, Yucatan, in an area known as Ciudad Caucel. Occupation of the site began during the late Middle Preclassic period (ca. 800–400/300 B.C.), reached its peak during the early Late Preclassic (ca. 400/300 B.C.–A.D. 250) and continued into the Early Classic period (A.D. 250–550) when the site was almost completely abandoned. There is also evidence of a limited reoccupation during the Late and Terminal Classic period (A.D. 550–1050). Uriarte Torres (2007) states that today the entire site is six hectares in area and consists of 105 structures. Nonetheless, Xamán Susula once could have been larger because a modern limestone quarry, which might have destroyed many structures, is located immediately south of the architectural site core.

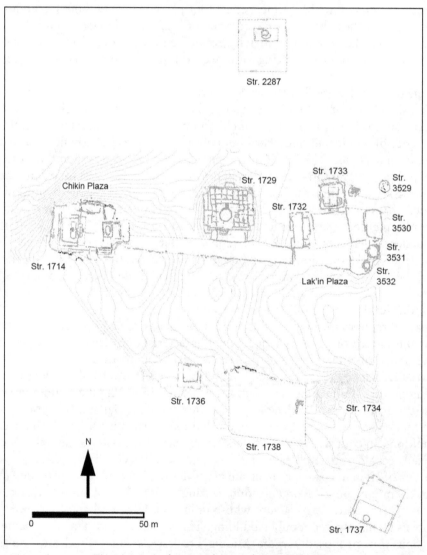

Figure 3.1. Architectural core of Xamán Susula.

Based on the architectural features and extent of the site core, as well as the regional settlement pattern, it is likely that Xaman Susula was a second-rank site in a three-tiered settlement hierarchy (Anderson 2005). It possibly functioned as an administrative center for the surrounding villages during the early Late Preclassic (Uriarte Torres 2007). Xaman Susula may have been under the power of Xtobo, the largest regional center of northwestern Yucatan at this time.

The architectural arrangement of Xaman Susula during the early Late Preclassic was very special and it represents a unique case in northwestern Yucatan (Figure 3.1). The public area of Xaman Susula consisted of the Chikin Plaza to the west and the Lak'in Plaza to the east. During this time, the Chikin Plaza consisted solely of the basal platform supporting Structure 1714-Asub, a room holding a throne-like bench. The Lak'in Plaza underwent a series of construction phases. In its first manifestation, the Lak'in Plaza contained a T-shaped platform (Structure 1732) that defined the western edge of the plaza, and also a basal platform with a superstructure (Structure 1733) to the east. In later consecutive construction phases, the ancient inhabitants of Xaman Susula built: (1) a rectangular platform (Structure 3530); (2) a small circular foundation (3529) and a rectangular platform with inside corners (Structure 3531); (3) a circular structure (Structure 3532); and (4) the second architectural phase of Structure 1732. Structure 1729-Sub, a key-hole shape structure, was also part of the architectural core. A 74-meter long and 7.5-meter wide *sacbe* was built to join the two plazas and integrate the architectural core. Importantly, the *sacbe*, the throne of Structure 1714-Asub, and Structure 3532 of the Lak'in Plaza are aligned with each other. The *sacbe* also functioned to separate public and domestic areas. Structures 1736 and 1738 are located south of the *sacbe* and were built during this same period. Structure 1738 had a domestic function. It is possible that Structures 1737 and 1734 also date to the beginning of the Late Preclassic, but these structures have not yet been explored. More domestic platforms are located north of the architectural core.

Structure 1714-Asub

Excavations conducted during 2006 and 2008 revealed that Structure 1714 was built in at least five major stages, with several additional and minor construction episodes (Peniche 2010; Peniche and Rodríguez n.d.). During the late Middle Preclassic period, the structure consisted of two independent units, a basal platform that first supported two (and then later three) eastern structures, as well as a possible altar to the west (construction Stages I–III). At the beginning of the Late Preclassic period, these were integrated into a single basal platform supporting a room with a throne-like bench (Stage IV). During the Early Classic, the structure underwent another major modification whose characteristics are not clear because of looting (Stage V).

The Stage IV platform is rectangular, has rounded corners, and was covered with stucco. It is 28 meters long, 23.5 meters wide, and stands 20 to 100 cm above the irregular ground. Access to the top of the platform was not restricted. The basal platform supports a building, Structure 1714-Asub, which stands in the middle of the platform (Figure 3.2).

Structure 1714-Asub consists of a room with a door on the east side. The interior space is only 6.8 meters by 1.8 meters. The interior walls, as well as the exterior eastern wall, were built with shaped stones. The most interesting aspect of the construction is that the interior walls of Structure 1714-Asub were built in the shape of a *talud* of stepped blocks. Seven postholes imply that beams supported a perishable roof. The floor and interior surface of the room were plastered. There are no indications of other decorative features.

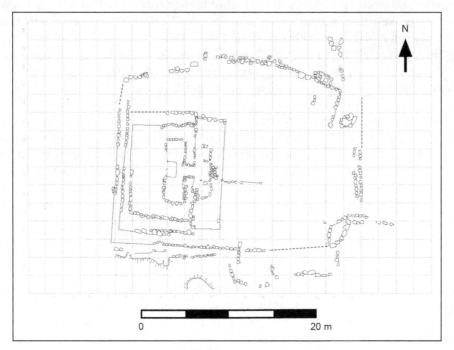

Figure 3.2. Plan of Structure 1714-Asub.

Figure 3.3. Structure 1714-Asub, viewed from the south.

The most interesting architectural feature of Structure 1714-Asub is a well-preserved stucco bench (Figure 3.3). The bench is rectangular in shape with rounded corners and measures 1.7 meters long by 1.1 meters wide by 24 centimeters high. It is located in the center of the room and faces the door. Because of its characteristics, I consider it to be a throne (see Valdés 2001). Other Late Preclassic Maya thrones have been reported at Kaminaljuyu and Abaj Takalik. In the Maya lowlands, thrones were built in the latter half of the Early Classic period at Uaxactun (Valdés 2001:153). The throne of Xaman Susula, which dates to the beginning of the Late Preclassic period, is the oldest known example in Yucatan and perhaps all of the Maya lowlands.

Structure 1714-Asub underwent three minor remodeling phases. The first consisted of the construction of fours stone alignments on the platform outside Structure 1714-Asub. The function of these alignments is unclear. During the second phase of remodeling, an exterior bench was attached to the eastern wall of Structure 1714-Asub. Somewhat later, the northern and southern walls of Structure 1714-Asub were modified.

At some point during the Late Preclassic period, Structure 1714-Asub was burned. We found burned gray soil on the stucco floor, as well as wood charcoal. Elsewhere on the platform, but outside of the room, we also found burned gray soil. Stones dating to the third remodeling phase are discolored by heat, implying that the fire took place after these modifications were made. The back or western wall and the stepped tiers associated with the throne were completely dismantled after the fire. The interior of the room was filled with stones and the entrance was completely blocked off. We recovered large ceramic sherds from the floor as well as two "plaster smoothers" with traces of cinnabar from the top of the throne. All this evidence suggests that Structure 1714-Asub may have been ritually terminated. I argue that this event was probably linked to the fall of Xtobo and concomitant changes in political power that occurred in the middle of the Late Preclassic period.

Artifacts Recovered from Structure 1714-Asub

During excavation of Structure 1714-Asub, we recovered pottery belonging to the Early Nabanche complex (Saban, Chunhinta, Joventud, Dzudzuquil, Tipikal, and Tamanche groups) as well as limited quantities of pottery assigned to the Xanaba ceramic group. Ceballos Gallareta and Robles Castellanos (n.d.) argue that production of Xanaba group ceramics began at the end of the Middle Preclassic period and became widespread during the Late Nabanche phase. A single radiocarbon date (INAH-XA, no laboratory number) of 2,202 + 20 years B.P. (two sigma) was determined from charcoal recovered from on top of the stucco floor of the room (Ceballos Gallareta and Robles Castellanos n.d.). This is equivalent to a calibrated date of 362 (269, 265) 201 B.C. The charcoal is interpreted as coming from a wooden post that supported the roof (Peniche May et al. 2009). Based on the low percentage of Xanaba ceramics along with the calibrated radiocarbon date, we date the construction of Structure 1714-Asub to the transition between the Middle and Late Preclassic periods.

An offering was found beneath the floor of the basal platform, deposited during the construction of Structure 1714-Asub and covering an earlier feature. The offering was placed beneath where the access to Structure 1714-Asub would be built. It consists of the body of an *olla* assigned to the Saban ceramic group and the neck of another *olla* belonging to the Joventud ceramic group. These pieces were found articulated together as if they were the same vessel. Another possible offering, a fragment of a grinding stone, was encountered in the fill of the northeast wall of Structure 1714-Asub.

Small celts made of a green igneous stone were recovered from the fill of Structure 1714-Asub. Similar artifacts have been found at the Middle Preclassic sites of Poxila and Xocnaceh. At Ciudad Caucel, celts of green igneous stone were unearthed in special structures, such as the Xanila ballcourt, where five celts were found in the ballcourt marker as an offering. We do not know where the material used to make these celts comes from, but they were obtained through interregional exchange (Figure 3.4).

Other lithic artifacts made of chert and obsidian were recovered during the excavation. These include 84 chert artifacts, 72 of which were chunks. Other chert artifacts include six percussion flakes, two thinning flakes, a macroblade fragment, a bifacial point, and a unifacial scraper. Five prismatic blades made of obsidian were also recovered.

Figure 3.4. Celts made of green igneous stone recovered from Structure 1714-Asub.

Discussion

How was the early Late Preclassic polity—of which Xaman Susula was a part—organized? Structure 1714-Asub provides important clues. Given the architectural features of this structure, the arrangement and kinds of buildings at Xaman Susula, and the larger regional settlement pattern, I propose two hypotheses.

The first hypothesis is based on the fact that, superficially, the architectural and spatial characteristics of Structure 1714-Asub are similar to Classic period palaces such as Palaces 32 and 33 of Group B, Tamarindito (Valdés 1997) and structures M7-22 and M7-32 of the Palace Group of Aguateca (Inomata 1997). The throne in Structure 1714-Asub is located on the center line of the structure, is clearly visible from the large open space outside the door, and is aligned with and located at the end of an important *sacbe*. As stated above, throughout the archaeological literature, palaces are considered one indicator of state-level social organization. But if Structure 1714-Asub was a palace structure, we should also be able to identify spaces dedicated to domestic activities as well as public facilities related to political, economic, and ritual activities. We should expect to find domestic features along with public open spaces and a room with a throne.

The data do not support the hypothesis that Structure 1714-Asub was a palace. This is because there is no evidence that it served as a residence. No residential features such as sleeping benches, hearths, grinding stones, or craft-production facilities were found during excavation. In fact, there are no signs of activities related to the production or consumption of food, the main indicators of domestic space. Moreover, the interior space of the structure is insufficient. The area of Structure 1714-Asub is just 12.2 square meters. If we subtract the area of the bench, the area is only 10.4 square meters. Maya archaeologists consider that buildings with a residential function should have an area of at least 20 square meters (Manzanilla 1986). If Structure 1714-Asub did not serve any residential function, then we should not call it a palace.

Following Marcus and Flannery (1996), the evidence from Structure 1714-Asub does affirm that it was a public building. Structure 1714-Asub is located at the highest point within the site, a typical setting for important public buildings. From this spot it is possible to observe the entire architectural core and the residential platforms located near the core, and also to be seen by people in these areas. The presence of an offering beneath the floor of the throne room and a series of rebuilding episodes are characteristics associated with public buildings rather than with residences in early Mesoamerica. Finally, the fact that Structure 1714-Asub experienced a fire supports the hypothesis that it was a public building that was intentionally destroyed and terminated.

The identification of Structure 1714-Asub as a public building but not as a residence implies that it was neither a "scenic palace" nor a "presentation palace" (Valdés 2001). Structure 1714-Asub consists of one single room and is not part of a multi-room structure, which is one of the characteristics of the "presentation palaces." Even though it has a throne, Structure 1714-Asub also cannot be categorized as a "throne structure" because it is neither adjoined to any domestic building nor does it have a restricted access as such buildings have at Tikal (Harrison 2001).

Although Structure 1714-Asub cannot be classified as a palace or throne structure—architectural types that are associated with state-level complexity—its throne and associated open space, as well as the way in which it is related to the *sacbe* and other structures at the site, all suggest that its function may have been somewhat similar to that of "scenic palaces," even though it cannot strictly be classified as such (Peniche May et al. 2009). Based on this, I propose that Structure 1714-Asub provided a public space where administrative, judicial, ritual, or inter-village activities took place.

My second hypothesis is that Structure 1714-Asub was a public structure—one not yet identified elsewhere in Mesoamerica—belonging to a chiefdom-level society. It is important to stress that Xaman Susula is a second-rank site within a three-tiered settlement hierarchy. A palace could have been present at the paramount site, Xtobo. Nonetheless, the fact that the regional settlement hierarchy has just three levels and, therefore, there were only two levels of political decision-making, suggests a chiefdom-level society (Anderson 2005; Feinman and Neitzel 1984; Wright 1984). I suggest that the arrangement of public and private spaces at Xaman Susula supports this hypothesis.

The architecture of chiefdoms is characterized by a separation between public and private spaces (Flannery 1998). At Xaman Susula, residential platforms are located south and north of the public area, and no residences are located in the public space immediately surrounding the architectural center. Moreover, no structures had both a public and a private function. We can classify the domestic platforms in two categories. At least four domestic platforms at the site are considerably larger than the others, although we could not affirm that they are otherwise different from other smaller domestic platforms at the site periphery. Two of these large platforms, Structures 1737 and 1738, are the closest to the public area. The largest platforms were probably the residences of the elite of Xaman Susula. The segregation of public and private spaces at Xaman Susula and the identification of possible elite residences are two elements that are also present in several sites of the Soconusco Region, such as Locona phase Paso de la Amada (Rosenswig 2000). Therefore, the arrangement of public and private spaces supports the hypothesis that this was a chiefdom-level society. At Xaman Susula, political and economic centralization were manifested in the concentration of power or wealth in a few individuals or lineages (see Feinman 2001).

Classification of Structure 1714-Asub

How should we classify Structure 1714-Asub? It is clear that it was not a chief's house like Mound 6 at Paso de la Amada (Blake 1991; Rosenswig 2000). Mound 6 consists of a series of apsidal structures. A construction sequence of at least six superimposed floors has been identified as dating to the Locona phase. All the floors were between 11 to 22 meters long and five to ten meters wide. During each construction episode, the structure increased in size and quality. This has been interpreted as indicating a change in the social and political status of its residents. Although Structure 1714-Asub and Mound 6 are comparable because of their setting and their multiple construction phases, Structure 1714-Asub is not a residence and therefore it cannot be labeled as the home of a chief.

Preclassic public buildings have often been classified as communal men's houses, temples, or performance platforms. Communal men's houses are a type of public building that is typical of segmentary societies. Men's houses were the space where political decision-making took place. This type of public building has been reported at San Jose Mogote in the Valley of Oaxaca during the Tierra Largas phase (1400–1100 B.C.). At San Jose Mogote, the men's house consists of a sequence of eight one-room buildings whose dimensions were four meters by six meters. These structures were apsidal in shape with wattle-and-daub walls and lime-plastered floors. Each structure was periodically razed and a new one was built in virtually the same place. Because of their small area, these structures are thought to have been restricted to a subgroup of the men in the village, those who passed through a series of rituals to attain high status (Marcus and Flannery 1996:87). These rituals do not necessarily imply the presence of status differentiation or decision-making specialization to the extent present in complex societies (Feinman 1991:241).

Structure 1714-Asub does not appear to be a men's house because the interior space of the room is too small—just 12.2 square meters—to allow more than a very few people to congregate. Moreover, the plan of Structure 1714-Asub is such that only one person could have sat on the throne at a time. This is different from the concept of a communal men's house. Most importantly, the fact that it is not a communal building supports the hypothesis of the existence of chiefdom-level complexity in Yucatan.

It is also clear that Structure 1714-Asub is not a performance platform. Architecturally, these structures are very well defined as circular platforms with a keyhole shape. But there is such a platform at Xaman Susula: Structure 1729-sub. The small circular platform called Structure 3532 that is aligned to the *sacbe* and Structure 1714-Asub might also have performed this function. Keyhole-shaped platforms have been reported at several Preclassic sites in Belize and are considered to be places where public ritual was performed by emergent or consolidating elites (Hendon 1999, 2000).

It is likely that most important ceremonial activities at Xaman Susula were conducted on these two performance platforms and in the Lak'in Plaza, which I argue was the ceremonial compound of the architectural core. Although some ritual activities might have been performed in Structure 1714-Asub, the main function of this structure does not appear related to ceremonial activities, which were likely conducted in these other locations. Structure 1714-Asub, therefore, cannot be considered to be a temple or other building dedicated primarily to ceremony, and it does not resemble Mesoamerican ceremonial buildings. In contrast, the structures of the Lak'in Plaza, particularly Structure 1733, do seem to be ceremonial buildings.

The arrangement of Structure 1714-Asub and the setting of the throne would have allowed a clear view toward the open space of the platform. Similarly, people in the open space would have had an unobstructed view of an individual seated on the throne within the structure. A seated noble could have led people gathered together on the platform, and witnessed the processions on the *sacbe*. Later Classic period polychrome vessels show such scenes (Harrison 2001:77; Reents-Budet 2001). Structure 1714-Asub, therefore, was a public building that symbolized the power of specific political actors. Thus, Structure 1714-Asub is an example of architecture of power focused on individuals.

Xaman Susula as Part of an Individualizing Chiefdom

The role of Structure 1714-Asub as symbol of power is supported by the recovery of elegant or elite ceramics similar to those reported from the Middle Preclassic sites of Xocnaceh and Poxila, two sites with complex and large acropoli (Peniche May et al. 2009). Ceramics of these types were not reported for any other structure of the architectural core of Xaman Susula. Moreover, the possibility that Structure 1714-Asub was the target of a ritual termination reinforces the possibility of the role that could have played during the early Late Preclassic period (Stanton et al. 2008). It has been proposed that the ritual destruction of structures that are symbols of power, such as structures with thrones, could have been the result of political defeat (Ambrosino 2003; Demarest et al. 2003). Perhaps this termination event may correspond with the fall of Xtobo and changes in political power in the northwestern Yucatan during the Late Preclassic period.

I argue that Xaman Susula was part of an individualizing chiefdom that utilized exclusionary or network strategies of political integration (Blanton et al. 1996; Feinman 2001; Renfrew 1974). I base this claim on several lines of evidence, including the characteristics of the domestic structures, the layout of Structure 1714-Asub, and the participation of the site in an exchange network that obtained exotic goods.

In individualizing chiefdoms, dominant political actors display differences of rank by building special domestic structures. Such residences can be recognized by size, shape, and location (Renfrew 1974; Rosenswig 2000). At Xaman Susula, there are two size categories of residential platforms. Two of the four large residential platforms, Structures 1737 and 1738, are located very close to public space in the site center. It is likely that these platforms supported the residences of political actors with concentrated power. The rest of the dwellings were built on small platforms located north and west of the architectural core. The presence of two marked types of domestic structures recalls Locona-phase Paso de la Amada, another example of an individualizing chiefdom (Rosenswig 2000).

Xaman Susula is a middle-ranked site in a three-tiered settlement hierarchy. It is unlikely, therefore, that the large platforms at Xaman Susula supported the houses of chiefs. All the characteristics that define the type of chiefdom to which Xaman Susula belonged, including more elaborate residences, are more likely to be found at Xtobo, the first-rank site that controlled Xaman Susula.

At Xaman Susula, I suspect that power was concentrated in four households. Among them, one political actor was predominant and he used Structure 1714-Asub for public activities. It is possible that the house of this political actor was built on top of Structure 1738, which had preferential access to the architecture of the public core.

Artifact assemblages recovered at Xaman Susula, mainly at Structure 1714-Asub, suggest that the political actors of Xaman Susula participated in a network strategy similar to those of other individualizing chiefdoms. According to Blanton et al.'s model (1996), political actors participated in exchange networks in order to gain prestige and power within both regional and local contexts. Status was obtained through the manipulation of social relationships beyond the local group, which were created and maintained through acts of gift giving, exchange, and payment. Such events could include the exchange of marriage partners, exotic goods, wealth, or knowledge.

Xaman Susula participated in interregional as well as local exchange networks. Xaman Susula was a middle-rank site in the regional settlement hierarchy, so it is likely that participation was indirect and that interregional exchange was mediated by higher-ranking elites at Xtobo. Through either direct or indirect participation in these networks, actors at Xaman Susula obtained igneous green stone used to make celts, elegant ceramics, and other prestige goods. It is interesting that igneous green stone and prestige ceramics were found exclusively in Structure 1714, which may suggest that such goods were limited to the political actors who used the throne room. Thus elite individuals from Xaman Susula might have participated in the exchange network in order to gain differential access to prestige goods, which translated into leadership within the local group. The throne room might have been used as a staging area where gift giving and other exchange events took place.

The presence of the throne inside Structure 1714-Asub supports the hypothesis that sociopolitical power was concentrated in a specific political actor at this site. This is because only one person at a time could have sat on it and from that vantage point witness events occurring inside or outside the room. The configuration of the core is such that the individual seated on the throne could have been observed from any spot in the public space. Hence, Structure 1714-Asub is a public building that emphasized an individual. In fact, even though there are other buildings that had ceremonial functions in the center of the site, the entire architectural arrangement of the core is focused on the throne room.

Preclassic individualizing chiefdoms are not exclusive to northwestern Yucatan. The sites of Paso de la Amada, San Lorenzo Tenochtitlan, La Venta, and Chalcatzingo are other potential examples. Nevertheless, corporate strategies were also employed during the Early and Middle Preclassic (Blanton et al. 1996). In the Valley of Oaxaca and the Basin of Mexico, collective labor was used to construct public spaces for communal ritual. In these areas, differences in rank were not strongly expressed in elaborate houses and burials (Feinman 2001; Rosenswing 2000).

If Xaman Susula was part of an individualizing chiefdom that participated in exclusionary and network strategies, then we might speculate about the collapse of the settlement. Leadership in such societies tends to be volatile and there is great potential for conflict

(Blanton et al. 1996:4). In these societies, any individual or household may attempt to establish network ties, which can lead to great internal competition for power. Moreover, individual military, training, and social skills are often important components of political success or failure. As a consequence, individualizing chiefdoms tend to be unstable and cycle on a generational scale. The termination of Structure 1714-Asub—the only structure in the entire site where we found evidence of such destruction—may have been the result of the collapse of network ties or the emergence of competitors. Because the throne room symbolized the power of dominant political actors, its destruction symbolized the defeat of those political actors.

Conclusions

New discoveries in the northern Maya lowlands require that we reformulate our understanding of political organization and complexity during the Preclassic period. It is now clear that by the second half of the Middle Preclassic period, complex polities began to coalesce in the Puuc region. Such complexity spread to northwestern Yucatan during the Middle to Late Preclassic transition. Nonetheless, scholars still debate if these polities were chiefdoms or states. Excavations and survey conducted at Xaman Susula, a middle-rank site in the three-tiered settlement hierarchy of northwestern Yucatan, have provided the means to test models concerning political organization during the early Late Preclassic.

The architectural features of the most impressive building of the site, Structure 1714-Asub, as well as material evidence obtained during its excavation, suggest that this building had a non-domestic function. It cannot be classified as either a palace or the house of a chief. It is certain that Structure 1714-Asub was a public building, but the features of the structure do not permit it to be classified as any of the previously established public building types known for the Preclassic period. It was not a men's house, a dancing platform, or a temple. The presence and location of the bench within the building, as well as the location and alignment of the structure in regard to others at the site, suggest that it may have served some of the functions of the scenic palaces typical of Classic-period sites.

Public buildings have been documented in egalitarian societies, chiefdom-level societies, and state-level societies. The elaborate nature of Structure 1714-Asub and the architectural core of the site imply that Xaman Susula was not organized at the tribal level. Likewise, the absence of a palace in the architectural core suggests that Xaman Susula was not the capital of a state, although we must wonder if a palace was present at the largest site in the region, Xtobo. In order to demonstrate that Xaman Susula was part of a chiefdom, the architectural features of its public building, the characteristics of domestic structures, the arrangement of the site, and regional settlement patterns must all be taken into account.

I argue that during the early Late Preclassic period, Xaman Susula was part of a chiefdom. My conclusion is based on four lines of evidence: (1) the presence of Structure 1714-Asub as a symbol of power of the chief (who lived in Xtobo) or of a local sub-chief who lived in one of the larger residences at Xaman Susula; (2) the identification of two categories of domestic structures, elite and non-elite, based on the location and size of residential architecture; (3) the segregation of public structures and the residences; and (4) the three-tiered hierarchy of the regional settlement pattern. Further explorations at the site of Xtobo could assist in corroborating this hypothesis.

I also argue that Xaman Susula was part of an individualizing chiefdom that employed exclusionary and network strategies. I base my argument on the presence of two marked types of domestic platforms, as well as the participation of actors at Xaman Susula in an exchange network from which they obtained prestige goods. Structure 1714-Asub, a unique building at the site, supports this hypothesis. Only one individual could be seated on the throne within the building. From this position, he could receive a few people in the room, lead activities on the platform, or witness events occurring in the architectural core.

Structure 1714-Asub, the throne room of Xaman Susula, represents a new type of building that has not been previously described for a Mesoamerican chiefdom. This building probably had administrative, judicial, ideological, and diplomatic functions. The construction of Structure 1714-Asub during the Middle to Late Preclassic transition witnesses the beginning of the institutionalization of those activities. This structure, including its throne, was used as a visual symbol through which the dominance and power of the regional chief or local subchief was reinforced. The throne room of Xaman Susula must be considered the precursor of the palaces that were built throughout the Maya area during later periods.

So little is known about Preclassic architecture in the northern Maya lowlands that it is very difficult to make regional comparisons. The lack of data from first- and third-rank sites in the regional settlement hierarchy—as well as from other second-rank sites—limits our ability to test hypotheses concerning regional political organization. Future explorations of public and residential buildings dating to the Preclassic period will improve our understanding of emergent complex polities in the northern Maya lowlands.

Acknowledgments

The research on which this chapter is based comes from two projects, *Proyecto de Salvamento Arqueológico Ciudad Caucel* directed by Dr. Fernando Robles Castellanos (INAH-Yucatan) and Josep Ligorred, and the *Proyecto Arqueológico Xamán Susulá*, directed by Dr. Fernando Robles Castellanos. Both projects were supported by the Gobierno del Estado de Yucatán. I wish to express my gratitude to Dr. Fernando Robles Castellanos for allowing me to participate in the projects and for his permission to study data from the excavations. Thanks also to each and every person who worked on both projects, especially those directly involved with the exploration of Xaman Susula: Teresa Ceballos Gallareta, Mauricio Germon Roche, Ana María Padilla Dorantes, María Luisa Parra Sánchez, Nereyda Quiñones Loria, and Mónica Rodríguez Pérez. I am also very grateful to Geoffrey E. Braswell and Sarah I. Baitzel of the University of California, San Diego for their comments on this chapter.

References

Aimers, James J., Terry G. Powis, and Jaime I. Awe. 2000. Preclassic Round Structures of the Upper Belize River Valley. *Latin American Antiquity* 11:71-86.

Ambrosino, James. 2003. The Function of a Maya Palace at Yaxuna: A Contextual Approach. In Christie 2003:253-273

Anderson, David S. 2005. Preclassic Settlement Patterns in Northwest Yucatan. *Mono y Conejo* 3:13-22. University of Texas, Austin.

Ball, Joseph, and Jennifer Taschek. 2001. The Buenavista-Cahal Pech Royal Court: Multi-palace Court Mobility and Usage in a Petty Lowland Maya Kingdom. In Inomata and Houston 2001b:165-200.

Becker, Marshall. 1971. *The Identification of a Second Plaza at Tikal, Guatemala and its Implications for Maya Social Complexity*. Ph.D. dissertation, Department of Anthropology, University of Pennsylvania. University Microfilms, Ann Arbor.

Blake, Michael T. 1991. An Emerging Early Formative Chiefdom at Paso de la Amada, Chiapas, Mexico. In *The Formation of Complex Society in Southern Mesoamerica*, edited by William R. Fowler, Jr., pp. 27-45. CRC, Boca Raton.

Blake, Michael T., Richard G. Lesure, Warren D. Hill, Luis Barba, and John E. Clark. 2006. The Residence of Power at Paso de la Amada, Mexico. In Christie and Sarro 2006:191-210.

Blanton, Richard, Gary M. Feinman, Stephen A. Kowalewski, and Peter N. Peregrine. 1996. A Dual-Processual Theory for the Evolution of Mesoamerican Civilization. *Current Anthropology* 37:1-14.

Brown, Linda, and Payson Sheets. 2000. Distinguishing Domestic from Ceremonial Structures in Southern Mesoamerica: Suggestions from Cerén, El Salvador. *Mayab* 13:11-21.

Ceballos Gallareta, Teresa, and Fernando Robles Castellanos. n.d. Las etapas más tempranas de la alfarería maya en el noroeste de la península de Yucatán. *Ancient Mesoamerica*. In press.

Christie, Jessica J. 2006. Introduction. In Christie and Sarro 2006:1-20.

Christie, Jessica J. (editor). 2003. *Maya Palaces and Elite Residences: An Interdisciplinary Approach*. University of Texas, Austin.

Christie, Jessica J., and Patricia J. Sarro (editors). 2006. *Palaces and Power in the Americas: From Peru to the Northwest Coast*. University of Texas, Austin.

Demarest, Arthur A. 2006. Sacred and Profane Mountains of the Pasion: Contrasting Architectural Paths to Power. In Christie and Sarro 2006:117-140.

Demarest, Arthur, Kim Morgan, Claudia Wolley, and Héctor Escobedo. 2003. The Political Acquisition of Sacred Geography: The Murciélagos Complex at Dos Pilas. In Christie 2003:120-153.

Earle, Timothy. 2002. *Bronze Age Economics: The Beginnings of Political Economies*. Westview, Boulder.

Evans, Susan T., and Joanne Pillsbury (editors). 2004. *Palaces of the Ancient New World*. Dumbarton Oaks, Washington, D.C.

Feinman, Gary M. 1991. Demography, Surplus, and Inequality: Early Political Formations in Highland Mesoamerica. In *Chiefdoms: Power, Economy and Ideology*, edited by Timothy Earle, pp. 229-262. Cambridge University, Cambridge.

— 2001. Mesoamerican Political Complexity: The Corporate-Network Dimension. In *From Leaders to Rulers*, edited by Jonathan Haas, pp. 151-175. Kluwer Academic/Plenum, New York.

Feinman, Gary M., and Jill Neitzel. 1984. Too Many Types: An Overview of Sedentary Prestate Societies in the Americas. *Advances in Archaeological Method and Theory* 7:39-102.

Flannery, Kent. 1998. The Ground Plans of Archaic States. In *Archaic States*, edited by Gary. M. Feinman and Joyce Marcus, pp. 15-58. School of American Research, Santa Fe.

— 1999. Chiefdoms in the Early Near East: Why It's so Hard to Identify Them. In *The Iranian World: Essays on Iranian Art and Archaeology*, edited by Abbas Alizadeh, Yousef Majidzadeh, and Sadegh M. Shahmirzadi, pp. 44-63. Iran University, Tehran.

Flannery, Kent V., and Joyce Marcus. 2005. *Excavations at San José Mogote 1: The Household Archaeology*. Memoirs of the Museum of Anthropology 40. University of Michigan, Ann Arbor.

Gallareta Negrón, Tomás, William M. Ringle, Rossana May Ciau, Julieta Ramos Pacheco, and Ramón Carillo Sánchez. 2005. Evidencias de ocupación durante el período Preclásico en el Puuc: Xocnaceh y Paso del Macho. Paper presented at the Segundo Congreso Internacional de Cultura Maya, Merida.

Harrison, Peter. 2001. Thrones and Throne Structures in the Central Acropolis of Tikal as an Expression of the Royal Court. In Inomata and Houston 2001b:74-101.

— 2003. Palaces of the Royal Court at Tikal. In Christie 2003:98-119.

Harrison, Peter, and E. Wyllys Andrews V. 2004. Palaces of Tikal and Copán. In Evans and Pillsbury 2004:113-148.

Hendon, Julia. 1999. The Pre-Classic Maya Compound as the Focus of Social Identity. In *Social Patterns in Pre-Classic Mesoamerica*, edited by David C. Grove and Rosemary Joyce, pp. 97-125. Dumbarton Oaks, Washington, D.C.

— 2000. Round Structures, Household Identity, and Public Performance in Preclassic Maya Society. *Latin American Antiquity* 11:299-301.

Inomata, Takeshi. 1997. The Last Days of a Fortified Classic Maya Center: Archaeological Investigations at Aguateca, Guatemala. *Ancient Mesoamerica* 8:337-351.

Inomata, Takeshi, and Stephen Houston. 2001. Opening the Royal Maya Court. In Inomata and Houston 2001a:3-23.

Inomata, Takeshi, and Stephen Houston (editors). 2001a. *Royal Courts of the Ancient Maya*, vol. 1. Westview, Boulder.

— 2001b. *Royal Courts of the Ancient Maya*, vol. 2. Westview, Boulder.

Kolb, Michael J. 1994. Monumentality and the Rise of Religious Authority in Precontact Hawai'i. *Current Anthropology* 35:521-547.

Lawrence, Denisse, and Setha Low. 1990. The Built Environment and the Spatial Form. *Annual Reviews in Anthropology* 19:453-505.

Lesure, Richard G. 1999. Platform Architecture and Activity Patterns in an Early Mesoamerican Village in Chiapas, Mexico. *Journal of Field Archaeology* 26:391-406.

Leventhal, Richard M. 1983. Household Groups and Classic Maya Religion. In *Prehistoric Settlement Patterns: Essays in Honor of Gordon Willey*, edited by Evan Z. Vogt and Richard M. Leventhal, pp. 55-76. University of New Mexico and Peabody Museum of Archaeology and Ethnology. Harvard University, Cambridge.

Manzanilla, Linda. 1986. Introducción. In *Unidades habitacionales Mesoamericanas y sus Áreas de Actividad*, edited by Linda Manzanilla, pp. 9-18. Universidad Nacional Autonoma de Mexico, Mexico.

Marcus, Joyce. 1978. Archaeology and Religion: A Comparison of the Zapotec and Maya. *World Archaeology* 10:172-191.

Marcus, Joyce, and Kent V. Flannery. 1996. *Zapotec Civilization: How Urban Society Evolved in Mexico's Oaxaca Valley*. Thames & Hudson, London.

Moore, Jerry. 1996. *Architecture and Power in the Ancient Andes: The Archaeology of Public Buildings*. Cambridge University, Cambridge.

Peniche May, Nancy. 2010. *The Architecture of Power and Sociopolitical Complexity in Northwestern Yucatan during the Preclassic Period*. Unpublished M.A. thesis, Department of Anthropology University of California, San Diego.

Peniche May, Nancy, and Mónica Rodríguez Pérez. n.d. Estructura 1714. *Proyecto arqueológico Xamán Susulá. Informe de las temporadas de campo 2006 y 2008*, edited by Fernando Robles Castellanos. Report to the Instituto Nacional de Antropología e Historia, Mexico.

Peniche May, Nancy, Mónica Rodríguez Pérez, and Teresa Ceballos Gallareta. 2009. La función de un edificio preclásico: La estructura 1714 de Xamán Susulá. *Los Investigadores de la Cultura Maya* 18:253-264. Universidad Autónoma de Campeche, Campeche.

Pillsbury, Joanne, and Susan T. Evans. 1998. Palaces of the Ancient New World: An Introduction. In Evans and Pillsbury 2004:1-5.

Reents-Budet, Dorie. 2001. Classic Maya Concepts of the Royal Court: An Analysis of Rendering on Pictorial Ceramics. In Inomata and Houston 2001a:195-236.

Renfrew, Colin. 1974. Beyond a Subsistence Economy: The Evolution of Social Organization in Prehistoric Europe. In *Reconstructing Complex Societies: An Archaeological Colloquium*, edited by Charlotte B. Moore, pp. 69-95. Supplement to the Bulletin of the American Schools of Oriental Research 20. Henry N. Sawyer, Charlestown.

Robles Castellanos, Fernando, and Teresa Ceballos Gallareta. n.d. Revalidando la génesis precoz de la complejidad político-cultural maya en el noroeste de la Península de Yucatán. In *Pathways to Complexity*, edited by M. Kathryn Brown and George J. Bey III. Manuscript in preparation.

Rosenswig, Robert M. 2000. Some Political Processes of Ranked Societies. *Journal of Anthropological Archaeology* 19:413-460.

Stanton, Travis, Kathryn Brown, and Jonathan Pagliaro. 2008. Garbage of the Gods? Squatters, Refuse Disposal, and Termination Rituals among the Ancient Maya. *Latin America Antiquity* 19:227-247.

Taladoire, Eric. 2000. El juego de pelota mesoamericano. Origen y desarrollo. *Arqueología Mexicana* 44:19-27.

Uriarte Torres, Alejandro. 2007. Aproximación al estudio de los patrones de asentamiento preclásicos de Caucel, Yucatán. Paper presented at the Séptimo Congreso Internacional de Mayistas, Merida.

Valdés, Juan Antonio. 1997. Tamarindito: Archaeology and Regional Politics in the Petexbatun Region. *Ancient Mesoamerica* 8:321-335.

— 2001. Palaces and Thrones Tied to the Destiny of the Royal Courts in the Maya Lowlands. In Inomata and Houston 2001b:138-166.

Watson, Paul K. 1994. *The Archaeology of Rank*. Cambridge University, Cambridge.

Webster, David. 2001. Spatial Dimensions of Maya Courtly Life: Problems and Issues. In Inomata and Houston 2001a:130-167.

Webster, David, and Takeshi Inomata. 2004. Identifying Subroyal Elite Palaces at Copán and Aguateca. In Evans and Pillsbury 2004:149-180.

Wright, Henry T. 1984. Prestate Political Formations. In *On the Evolution of Complex Societies: Essays in Honor of Harry Hoijer*, edited by Timothy Earle, pp. 41-78. Undena, Lancaster, Calif.

4 Maya Political Cycling and the Story of the *Kaan* Polity

Joyce Marcus

Abstract

By combining two frameworks (the Dynamic Model and that of political cycling), I use both textual and archaeological evidence to document the origins of the Maya state. The geographic focus is the base of the Yucatan Peninsula, focusing special attention on sites in Quintana Roo, Campeche, and the Mirador Basin. I examine several eras that witnessed a series of major oscillations, with huge centers taking their turn at the top of the administrative hierarchy. I document the shift from flamboyant rank society to initial state, a shift back to flamboyant rank society, and then the rise of a much larger expansionist Maya state.

In this paper I seek both to honor the career of E. Wyllys Andrews and to address a long-standing archaeological question. The question is one that I began asking myself before the ink was dry on my doctoral dissertation: "If the Snake Head refers to Calakmul, why does that emblem glyph appear so late in the archaeological sequence, especially since Calakmul was an important place even during the Middle and Late Preclassic?" Only after I began utilizing a framework that combined both the Dynamic Model (Marcus 1992, 1993) and the notion of political cycling (Anderson 1990; Wright 1984) did I see some of the ways that one might explain the distribution of the *Kaan*, or Snake Head, emblem glyph (Figure 4.1).

Addressing a question of Preclassic political organization seems particularly appropriate as a way to honor Andrews, because so much of his research has been focused on that period (Andrews 1981, 1990; Ringle and Andrews 1988, 1990). "Digging a Preclassic site like Komchen," he once said at the Atlanta SAA meetings, "has been truly rewarding" but "understanding the Preclassic will be possible only after long-term excavation is conducted at many sites."

Using Andrews' statements as a point of departure, I will examine political cycling during the Middle and Late Preclassic (800 B.C.–A.D. 250) in the Mirador Basin (Figure 4.2), an area that extends from the base of the Yucatan Peninsula of Mexico south into Guatemala (Benavides 2005; Carrasco 2000; Carrasco and Colón 2005; Dahlin 1984; Folan, Šprajc, et al. 2005; Forsyth 1989, 1993; García Cruz 1993; Grube 2005; Hansen 1990, 1994, 1998, 2002; Marcus 2004b; Matheny 1980; Robichaux and Pruett 2005; Ruppert and Denison 1943; Šprajc 2004, 2008; Šprajc, Folan, and González H. 2005; Šprajc, Morales A., and Hansen 2009).

The Mirador Basin is an appropriate laboratory for the study of political cycling because it witnessed a series of major oscillations, with huge Preclassic centers taking their turn at the top of the administrative hierarchy. This pattern of shifting political centers seems to differ from that of other Maya regions, such as the polity administered by Tikal, which used the same emblem glyph from A.D. 292 to 869 (Berlin 1958; Jones 1977; Jones and Satterthwaite 1982; Marcus 1976; Martin 2003; Martin and Grube 2008; Schele and Freidel 1990).

In the Mirador Basin we seem to see the shift from flamboyant rank society to initial state, a shift back to flamboyant rank society, and then the rise of a much larger expansionist state that lasted until A.D. 695. By studying the distribution of the Snake Head emblem glyph, we can suggest fairly precise dates for some of the political rises and falls of key centers. Extensive excavations, however, will be necessary to establish what happened at the many key centers that lack hieroglyphs and associated dates.

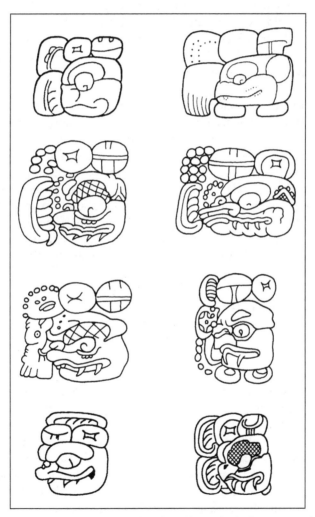

Figure 4.1. Eight examples of the Snake Head Emblem Glyph designating the Kaan Polity (redrawn from Marcus 1987:Figure 65 g, h, i, j; Marcus 2004b:Figure 14 c, f, h; Velásquez García 2004:Figure 14).

Documenting Shifts in Political Control and the Loss of Autonomy

Societies with hereditary rank represent the first moment in Maya history during which village autonomy was transcended, allowing higher-order centers to control lower-order centers. Once we can demonstrate that lower-order centers have lost their independence, we are on our way to identifying multisite polities (Carneiro 1970, 1981; Grinin et al. 2004; Marcus 1976, 2004a, 2008; Wright 1977, 1984).

Although differences in site size have often been used to suggest the presence of an administrative hierarchy, size is not enough. Real evidence for the loss of autonomy is needed—for example, showing that lower-order centers were required to deliver goods and labor service to higher-order centers (Marcus and Flannery 1996:108-110, 198-199). Leaders at higher-order centers could exact tribute, command men to build large public works, or conscript men from subordinate villages to defend them whenever enemies attacked. If we can demonstrate that Preclassic Maya hereditary chiefs controlled labor and goods from smaller sites, we will be closer to demonstrating administrative control by larger centers (e.g., Marcus 2004b, 2008).

At present we can show that Preclassic centers varied in size, monumentality, and pace of development, but have limited evidence for tribute and labor demands (Chase and Chase 1995; Folan et al. 1995; Hansen 1998; Matheny 1980, 1986, 1987; Sharer and Traxler 2006). We also need a finer-grained chronology, especially if the ability to maintain control of lower-order centers was short-lived and fluctuating. Some administrative hierarchies may have oscillated between two levels and three levels every 25 years. Such short-term oscillations would be impossible to detect, given ceramic phases that span several hundred years. We cannot as yet establish the hierarchical position of each site during 25-year periods, even with hieroglyphs.

Before looking at sites in the Mirador Basin, it would be useful to examine some well-documented cases of cycling. For this we can turn to the chiefly societies of Panama and the Southeastern United States.

Rank Societies in Sixteenth-Century Panama

According to Spanish eyewitnesses, dozens of Panamanian societies showed evidence of chiefly competition as well as marital and trading alliances (Anghera 1912; Fernández de Oviedo y Valdés 1959; Linares 1977; Lothrop 1937; Sauer 1966).

Hereditary Panamanian chiefs, or *quevís,* were the highest ranking members of society. Below them were subchiefs, or *sacos,* some of whom were brothers of the chief. Then came the *çabras,* honored commoners who had gained status through military prowess. Some of these *çabras* were given land, women, slaves, and even the opportunity to administer subordinate villages. Sons of *çabras* were allowed to inherit titles from their fathers only if they, too, became professional warriors (Helms 1979:13). Captives and war prisoners (*pacos*) served as litter bearers and burden carriers for the chief (Fernández de Oviedo y Valdés 1959; Lothrop 1937). The tattoos on the faces of *pacos* designated the lord to whom they belonged.

We know important details about a few of these Panamanian chiefs and their subchiefs. One well-known chief, Natá, was served by 11 subchiefs, each of whom oversaw his own district. Another chief, Parita, came to control a large territory (or "chiefdom") by conquering 12 other chiefs and incorporating their realms, some of which lay three to four days' walk from Parita's village (Andagoya 1865; Espinosa 1873:32-33; Lothrop 1937:10).

Parita conquered Chicacotra, Suema, Guararé, Sangana, and eight other chiefs (Lothrop 1937:10 n. 2) after having attracted many fighting men. The Spanish soldier Pascual de Andagoya (1865:30) noted that the *queví* of Escoria had fewer fighting men than Parita. This shortage of warriors meant that Escoria's men had to fight continuously, while Parita had the luxury of rotating his men. In one of the many fierce battles between Parita and the *queví* of Escoria, however, Parita lost (Lothrop 1937:10). Following this victory, the *queví* of Escoria married a close relative of Parita's (Fernández de Oviedo y Valdés 1853, Book 29, Chapter 10, pp. 47-48), and it was this marriage alliance that brought about temporary peace.

Establishing military prowess, competitive advantages, and marital alliances were three of the strategies employed by the chiefly societies of Panama. Their chiefly territories were continually in flux, expanding and contracting over time and creating shifts in the administrative hierarchy.

Rank Societies of the Southeastern United States

Native American rank societies of the southeastern United States also expanded, collapsed, and reorganized themselves. When one chiefly polity collapsed some of its population either voluntarily joined, or was forcibly absorbed into, another polity. For example, a number of Savannah River sites were abandoned by A.D. 1450, and sites on the Oconee River experienced a huge population increase (Kowalewski and Hatch 1991; Rudolph and Blanton 1981). Other powerful Mississippian societies also occurred in the Santee-Wateree drainage; still later, during the middle of the sixteenth century, the provinces of Ocute and Cofitachequi emerged (Anderson 1996:190).

There is evidence that chiefly cycling could occur at intervals of one hundred years or less. This is a period of time significantly shorter than most ceramic periods (which can last 300–500 years), suggesting that the rise and fall of some rank societies could go undetected simply by being embedded within a long ceramic phase. If similar cycles took place within the Maya Middle and Late Preclassic—a period of almost a thousand years—many cycles could go undetected.

David Hally (1996) has shown that most Mississippian rank societies in northern Georgia lasted less than one hundred years. When one of these chiefly societies declined, a second often developed 100–200 years later virtually in the same place. Hally (1996:115) suggests that many rank societies: (1) lost their independence and ended up being incorporated into other polities; and (2) collapsed and disappeared entirely along with their supporting populations; or (3) lost one level of their sociopolitical hierarchy and no longer qualified as rank societies.

Hally argues that mound construction at one site ceased when another site took it over politically. Site abandonment could also occur when there was a gap in chiefly succession, when there was endemic raiding, or when laborers in satellite villages fled or were absorbed into another polity. Similar scenarios may well fit the Preclassic Maya sequence of the Mirador Basin.

From Autonomous Village to Rank Society

The shift from mobile hunter-gatherers to fully sedentary villagers was a gradual process that occurred at different times throughout Mesoamerica. It was complete by 1600–1500 B.C. on the Pacific coast, but probably not until 1000 B.C. in the Mirador Basin. We do not know why it took longer in some regions than others.

Despite these variations in timing, the Preclassic was a crucial era all over Mesoamerica. Among the noteworthy developments were an increased reliance on domesticated plants, a newly increased range of ritual and burial practices, increasing evidence for hereditary inequality, an escalation of interregional trade in prestige goods, and (at least in some areas) an explosion of inter-village raiding and monumental public building.

By 1000 B.C. the Maya were living in autonomous villages, with little or no evidence that any community controlled another. As our sample of early villages increases, we are becoming increasingly aware of regional as well as local differences. Apsidal houses, for example, were typical of New River sites, while circular houses were typical of Belize River sites. Villagers along the Belize River used figurines, while some New River villagers did not. At the Maya site of K'axob (McAnany 2004) we see burials like those in the early Valley of Oaxaca (Marcus and Flannery 1996), in which differences in prestige were shown by burying some men in a seated position. These seated men had been bundled, suggesting that their burial treatment was protracted, and that they may have been important ancestors who had been kept around and venerated before reburial. As true rank developed, some emerging Maya elites placed marine shells and jade beads in the graves of their children.

The earliest villages in the Mirador Basin may still be deeply buried under sites like Tintal, Xulnal, La Florida, Calakmul, Naachtun, El Mirador, Porvenir, Pacaya, La Muralla, Nakbe, Tintal, and Wakna. Of these, Nakbe, El Mirador, and Calakmul were among the largest, with their size manifested both in the extent of the site and in the monumentality of individual structures. For example, by Late Preclassic times both Structure II of Calakmul and the El Tigre pyramid of El Mirador reached 55 meters in height (Folan et al. 1995:316). Such use of labor suggests that leaders could attract large numbers of followers and command them to build immense structures.

Late Preclassic Maya sites varied greatly in their concern with display and monumentality, with those in Belize usually lacking monumental constructions, while those in the Mirador Basin were committed to creating truly impressive pyramids. While El Mirador had the largest pyramids, some structures at Tikal or Lamanai could be as tall as 20 or 33 meters, respectively (Laporte and Fialko 1995; Pendergast 1981).

Some early rank societies of the Mirador Basin at this time not only invested in monumentality, but also seem to have had administrative hierarchies of between two and three levels. When three levels existed, the chief presumably lived at the largest and most defensible site or paramount center. Sites at the second level of the hierarchy may have been under subchiefs who (based on what we know of the later Maya) were relatives or in-laws of the chief. Conflict probably occurred between chiefs at different paramount centers, as well as between chiefs and their ambitious subchiefs. Given available Late Preclassic data, we could make the case that two-level hierarchies characterized parts of Belize and three-level hierarchies characterized the Mirador Basin.

Late Preclassic Maya societies witnessed increasing evidence for construction of triadic temples, intra-community causeways linking plaza groups, and inter-site roads linking major centers to their satellite communities. These roads serve as proxies for the hierarchical relations among sites. We also see increased evidence for conflict, including mass graves of young males, the construction of defensive walls and palisades, the burning of temples, and the stripping of stucco masks from temple and platform façades. The assumption of an earlier generation of archaeologists that this was a peaceful era had to be scrapped when evidence emerged to show that Late Preclassic leaders could be intensely competitive, and that some communities burned the buildings of their rivals (Brown and Garber 2003).

Nakbe

One of the earliest paramount centers in the Mirador Basin was Nakbe, located to the southeast of El Mirador (Figures 4.2 and 4.3). Nakbe had an east–west layout, with a causeway linking its West Group to its East Group. This east–west layout with intra-site causeways can also be seen at El Mirador, Pol Box, and other sites.

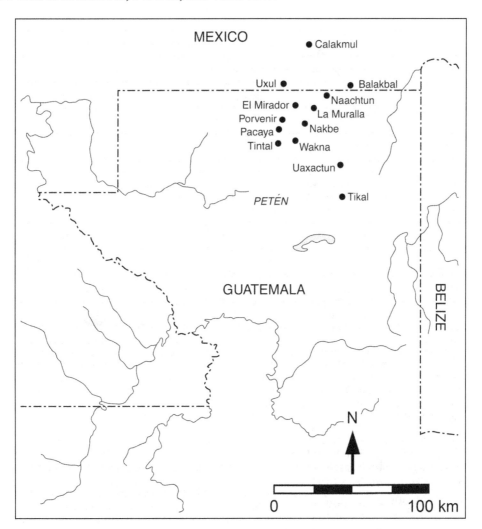

Figure 4.2. Key sites of northern Guatemala and southern Campeche, Mexico (redrawn from Hansen 1998:Figure 2 and Marcus 2004b:Figure 3).

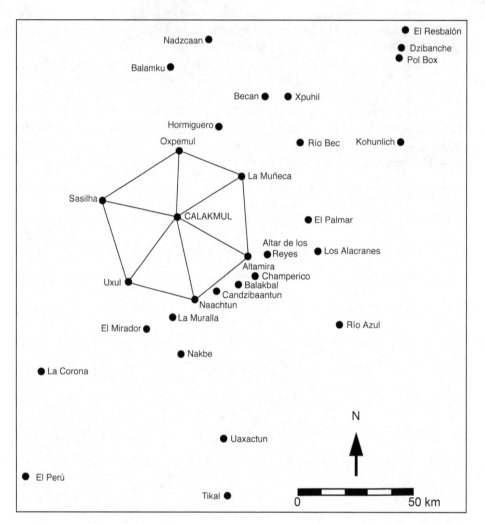

Figure 4.3. During the seventh century A.D., when the Snake Head Polity had its capital at Calakmul, it administered three zones: (1) an innermost zone that lay within the hexagon; (2) a zone that extended from Campeche and Quintana Roo into Guatemala; and (3) an outer political sphere that included far-flung allies like Caracol, Naranjo, Dos Pilas, and Quirigua (adapted from Marcus 2004b:Figure 1).

The earliest constructions (1000–800 B.C.) at Nakbe consisted of simple earth floors with postholes intruding into bedrock (Hansen 1998). By 800 B.C. Nakbe covered 50 hectares, with three-meter-high stone platforms that evidently supported perishable structures. Thick plaster floors appeared by 600 B.C. Sometime between 600 and 400 B.C., major platforms reached eight meters in height and the first ballcourt was constructed. In the East Group, some structures reached more than 16 meters in height and both intra-site and inter-site causeways made their appearance.

Intensified agriculture accompanied the rise of Nakbe. Artificial garden plots delimited by stone walls were filled with rich soils taken from bajos or depressions. This soil was laboriously transported from low-lying areas. Water storage facilities were also constructed at this time, since these garden plots (as well as the very large population) would need water during the long dry season. These investments in intensive agricultural features, together with the development of monumental architecture, imply new strategies for organizing labor. Symbols of rulership used by later Maya kings—the headband and mat motifs—are already present on Middle Preclassic figurines at Nakbe, suggesting that some symbols and elements of political authority were already in use.

By Late Preclassic times, an inter-site causeway was built to link the Western Group of Nakbe to El Mirador. Stela 1 of Nakbe, found in the main plaza of the Western Group, bears no hieroglyphs but does shows two Maya lords facing each other, one of them pointing to the floating head of an ancestor (Figure 4.4). Similar stelae, depicting ancestors floating above the head of the current ruler (and probably legitimizing him) have been found at Kaminaljuyu, Tikal, and El Baul (Marcus 1976).

Figure 4.4. Stela 1, Nakbe, shows two lords that face each other. The lord (at left) points at his ancestor, a theme that occurs on Cycle 8 and Cycle 10 monuments (redrawn from Sharer and Traxler 2006:Figure 5.17).

Another innovation at Nakbe was the so-called E Group, an architectural complex named for its resemblance to Group E at Uaxactun (Chase and Chase 1995; Hansen 1998; Ricketson and Ricketson 1937). Such an E Group consists of a large pyramid on the west side of a plaza, facing a long platform that supports three smaller structures on the east side of the plaza. On the east side of an E group plaza, the sun rises directly behind the middle temple (E-II at Uaxactun) on the vernal equinox, when day and night are of equal length. It rises behind the north temple (E-I) on the summer solstice or longest day; behind the middle temple again during the autumnal equinox; and finally, behind the south temple (E-III) on the winter solstice or shortest day of the year. E Group plazas are known from several sites, including Nakbe, El Mirador, Calakmul, Uaxactun, Caracol, Cenote, and Wakna (Chase and Chase 1995; Folan et al. 1995; Hansen 1998).

Because of its early date, it is fair to say that Nakbe was the prototype for later Maya cities with its causeways, stelae and altars, plazas, ballcourt, and impressive stone platforms. At some point, however, Nakbe cycled down, becoming less important and losing much of its population. Soon other sites like El Mirador and Calakmul became huge, ultimately replacing Nakbe as major centers.

El Mirador

The massive site of El Mirador also had a series of roads radiating out from it. This road system can be interpreted as evidence that El Mirador needed access to, and presumably controlled, a series of satellite communities. One road leads southeast to Nakbe, while another leads north to Calakmul (Folan, Marcus, and Miller 1995:Figures 3, 4).

El Mirador came to be the largest Late Preclassic site in the southern Maya lowlands. Its monumental architecture demonstrates that its leaders were able to attract more laborers than did rival communities; El Mirador used that labor force to construct roads, plazas, and temples on a huge scale (Folan et al. 1995; Hansen 1998; Matheny 1980, 1986).

Like Nakbe, El Mirador was laid out east–west. The Western Group at El Mirador, linked by a causeway to the Eastern or La Danta Group, was built on a natural hill. Key to understanding El Mirador is a series of public buildings, including one that has been called a Late Preclassic palace. If this structure proves to be a palace, it would be the oldest known so far from the Maya region.

Another innovation at El Mirador was the so-called triadic temple complex, composed of one large temple flanked by two smaller ones. The Western Group of El Mirador was dominated by the triadic temple complex known as El Tigre, while a smaller triad with stucco masks can be seen on Structure 34 (Hansen 1984, 1990, 1998; Matheny 1980). El Tigre alone covers an area six times greater than the largest Late Classic building at Tikal.

An unanswered question, therefore, is this: Was El Mirador the flamboyant paramount center of a powerful rank society, or did it briefly become the capital of a state at A.D. 100, only to collapse around A.D. 150?

Evaluating the El Mirador Case

Based on what we know about early states elsewhere (e.g., Claessen and van de Velde 1991; Grinin et al. 2004; Marcus 1992, 1998; Marcus and Feinman 1998; Marcus and Flannery 1996; Spencer 2010; Spencer and Redmond 2004), here are some important questions whose answers may help resolve the status of El Mirador:

1. Do settlement patterns in the Mirador Basin show a shift from a three-level to a four-level hierarchy?
2. Is the building in the Western Group truly a palace?
3. Are the handmade figurines used in family ritual gradually replaced by paraphernalia used by fulltime priests?
4. Are secondary centers linked to El Mirador by well-made roads?
5. Do hieroglyphic texts mention dynastic founders?
6. Do secondary centers mention the emblem glyphs of the primary centers?
7. Are there institutions and personnel at El Mirador that do not occur at lower-order centers?

At the moment, we have positive answers for less than half of these questions concerning El Mirador.

Whether or not El Mirador achieved the status of a state, any such status was short-lived. What El Mirador may show us is that the formation of the first Maya states took place in an atmosphere of competition, with centers frustrating the attempts of their rivals to consolidate political power in the Mirador Basin for several centuries.

Balakbal, Candzibaantun, and Dzibanche

It has not been possible to establish the ancient names for Nakbe and El Mirador. We are therefore left to wonder when and how the Snake Head glyph became attached to a specific capital and ruling dynasty. When the government of Nakbe collapsed, its competitor El Mirador gained the upper hand, a position that the latter site enjoyed until A.D. 150.

El Mirador, too, had many competitors (perhaps including Calakmul, Kinichna, and Dzibanche) and when El Mirador collapsed, the political void was filled by Dzibanche, Calakmul, and at least a few other sites to the east of Calakmul. One of these was Balakbal, a site first explored in 1934 (Ruppert and Denison 1943). Balakbal erected an early stela (Stela 5) that records the accession of a king to the throne in A.D. 386. Contemporaneous monuments were set up at Candzibaantun, a site located just a few kilometers north of the Guatemalan border (Šprajc 2004, 2008).

Several sites, including Calakmul, Dzibanche, Balakbal, and Candzibaantun, were part of an interacting network. The polity to which they belonged may have been called the Bat Polity from A.D. 400–500 and the Snake Head Polity beginning around A.D. 500 (Martin 2005). We have unanswered questions, nevertheless, about where the capital and royal palace of the polity were located during each decade. Did the Bat Polity (ca. A.D. 400–500) or the *Kaan* Polity (ca. A.D. 500–900) have one capital at a time or several? Did each ruler have palaces at several different sites? How did the seat of power shift through time? Answering these questions will be difficult because no one site offers us a full and continuous record of well-preserved and legible texts, and the excavation of all the relevant palaces will take years to accomplish.

Dzibanche has the distinction of being the first Maya site to mention a ruler associated with the Snake Head glyph (Figures 4.5 and 4.6). That fact has led some scholars to suggest (1) that he was the ruler of Dzibanche and (2) that Dzibanche was the capital of the *Kaan* Polity at A.D. 500 (Grube 2004; Martin 2004; Nalda 2004a, 2004b; Velásquez García 2004). This *Kaan* Polity ruler, as well as his successor, are alleged to have conducted war in the Dzibanche and El Resbalon region and to have taken prisoners who are depicted on the risers of steps in prisoner staircases.

Figure 4.5. Dzibanche prisoner steps (drawn by Kay Clahassey from Velásquez García 2004:Figures 2, 3, 5). Velásquez García reads the text on Monument 5 as: "On 11 Ok he entered the town of Xook Ucha'…, the prisoner of Yuknoom Ch'een, divine lord of Kaan" [The expression "he entered the town" has been interpreted as "he defeated" or "he conquered."]. The text on Monument 6 text can be read: "On 18 K'ayab' he entered the town of Ch'en…Lord of." The incompletely preserved text on Monument 7b features one clear bat glyph.

Whether Dzibanche was the capital of the *Kaan* Polity at this time or merely a secondary center acting at the behest of the *Kaan* king (whose capital was located elsewhere) is not yet clear (Esparza Olguín and Pérez Gutiérrez 2009; Grube 2004; Martin 2004). Whatever the case, the Dzibanche staircase depicts the captives taken by a *Kaan* Polity ruler, reinforcing our suspicion that Maya state formation took place in the context of military competition.

The fact that the Snake Head emblem appears in texts at Dzibanche, El Resbalon, and Pol Box before it appears at Calakmul may reveal one of two things: either (1) the capital shifted as one set of rulers took over from another, or (2) the lords at secondary centers could use the glyph when acting on behalf of the primary center. Grube (2005) and Martin (2005) now argue that the Snake Head emblem was used by Calakmul, but only for one hundred years from A.D. 636 to 736. Before A.D. 636, and again after A.D. 736, they suggest that Calakmul used the bat as its polity name. If future research continues to uphold the following sequence—use of the Bat emblem, then the Snake Head emblem, and then re-use of the Bat emblem—we will have an amazing case of political cycling that will be difficult to match with data from other Maya regions.

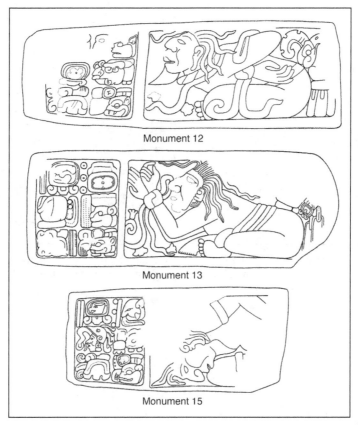

Figure 4.6. Dzibanche prisoner steps (drawn by Kay Clahassey from Velásquez García 2004:Figures 13, 14, 16). Monument 12, as read by Velásquez García, says: "On...Sootz [he entered the town of]..., prisoner of the divine lord of Kaan." Monument 13 can be read: "On 5 Chikchan 3 Yaxkin [August 8, A.D. 490]...B'ahlam, the prisoner of the divine lord of Kaan, was captured." Monument 15 can be read: "On 10 Ajaw 8 Xul [July 25, A.D. 484] he entered the town of...Kaanal, prisoner of the divine lord of Kaan." [The expression "he entered the town" has been interpreted as "he defeated" or "he conquered."]

It is frustrating that so many Calakmul stelae, even most of those carved between A.D. 650 and 900, lack emblem glyphs altogether (Marcus 1987:171-177). The rarity of emblem glyphs is unusual, and contrasts with their frequent use on the stelae at other cities. Perhaps the eroded state of so many Calakmul monuments is a contributing factor. The result, which is ironic, is that Calakmul's actions are best known from its subordinate sites and far-flung allies (Marcus 2004b).

The Calakmul Story

The history of Calakmul (Table 4.1) began in the Middle Preclassic, although we do not know how large it was at that time, nor are we sure what name referred to Calakmul itself or to the larger polity in which it resided (Folan et al. 1995). Based on the earliest texts at Calakmul, the site may have been called "Three Stones" or *Uxte'tuun* (Figure 4.7). The area near the huge body of water adjacent to the site, the Bajo Laberinto, may have been called "Coatimundi Aguada" or *Chiik Nahb* (Figures 4.7 and 4.8). The polity as a whole, encompassing chunks of southern Campeche and Quintana Roo, may have been known for a time as the Chatan Polity, the Bat Polity (Figure 4.9), or both.

Figure 4.7. This phrase of four hieroglyphs from Naranjo can be interpreted as "Yuknoom Head of the Snake Head Polity at the Place of Three Stones, Lord of Chiik Nahb" (redrawn from Marcus 2004b:Figure 2v-y).

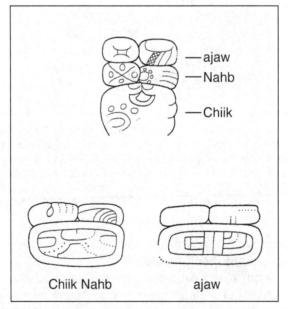

Figure 4.8. Two examples of the expression "Lord of Chiik Nahb," a title that may refer to the settlement adjacent to Bajo El Laberinto at Calakmul (top, from Monument 6 at Calakmul; bottom, from Stela 114 at Calakmul).

Figure 4.9. Examples of the Bat Polity. All the examples in the first row are from Calakmul (Stelae 114, 59, and 62). The second row has examples from other sites—Oxpemul (Stela 2) and Naachtun (Stela 23).

The Snake Head emblem glyph did not appear at Calakmul until A.D. 636. I originally attributed the absence of this glyph from the earliest texts of Calakmul either to (1) the scarcity of monuments at Calakmul from A.D. 300–500 (although two monuments are now known, the second monument was not discovered until 1994); (2) the extremely poor quality of the limestone used for such monuments, which contributed to their badly eroded condition; or (3) the possibility that some of the early stelae of Calakmul were intentionally incorporated into the fill of later buildings (Marcus 1987; Marcus and Folan 1994; Pincemin et al. 1998:319-323). It is possible that future excavations at Calakmul will expose more stelae buried inside later buildings. I say this because the two earliest stelae at Calakmul were reused during a late refurbishment of Structure II, the largest temple platform (Figure 4.10).

Even though we do not know the name for Calakmul during Late Preclassic times, we can infer that it attracted many followers and controlled a lot of manpower. Its public buildings were some of the biggest the Maya ever built (Folan et al. 1995). Another indication of the large labor force of Calakmul is the road system that connected Calakmul, El Mirador, and other sites (Folan, Marcus, and Miller 1995). The Calakmul–Mirador road may have been originally created during El Mirador's rise, but when Calakmul seized the upper hand after A.D. 150 it invested in huge pyramids.

Once El Mirador began to decline, Calakmul linked itself to a series of equidistantly spaced sites like Naachtun, Oxpemul, Balakbal, and Uxul (Marcus 1973, 2004b; Robichaux and Pruett 2005; Ruppert and Denison 1943; Šprajc 2008). There appears to be a good fit between the actual location of this inner core of subordinate centers and the predictions I made earlier based on Central Place Theory (Marcus 1973, 1976). This theory posits that the most efficient way to administer subordinate sites on an unbounded level plain is to space them equidistantly from each other and from the capital. Most efficient is an arrangement in which subordinate centers are spaced one day's travel from the capital, which appears to have been 30–35 kilometers in the Calakmul case (Figure 4.3).

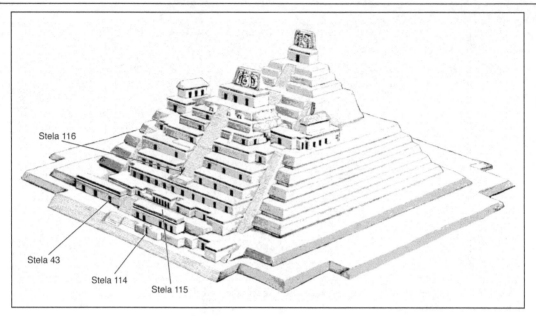

Figure 4.10. Structure II at Calakmul, showing how the oldest stelae at the site were re-set on the platform (drawn by Kay Clahassey from a drawing by Ernesto Tamay Segovia and a photo by Eldon Leiter).

El Mirador and Calakmul battled for supremacy in the Mirador Basin, and it would appear that at some point they reversed roles: Calakmul went from being a secondary center under El Mirador to a primary center above El Mirador. One of the lessons we learn from their struggle is that some cycles of consolidation and collapse were shorter than a typical phase defined by pottery style. Here is where dated monuments can provide a more detailed chronology of events. A second lesson is that multiple competitive cycles among several sites were needed to create new hierarchies.

Learning from the demise of El Mirador and avoiding a similar collapse, Calakmul succeeded in creating an enduring state by incorporating even more satellites than El Mirador and holding on to them. The oldest monument at Calakmul (Stela 114), which mentions the dates A.D. 431 and 435, refers to one ruler as the Lord of Chiik Nahb, and to another as King of the Bat Polity (Pincemin et al. 1998:Figures 6–8). At this date, however, there is no mention of the Snake Head Polity on this monument or anywhere else in the Mirador Basin. The next stela at Calakmul (Stela 43), which dates to A.D. 514, associates a ruler with the phrase *k'uhul chatan winik*, a title possibly meaning "Divine Man of Chatan."

Until we have more texts, it is difficult to say more about the place names or polity names associated with the rulers of Calakmul between A.D. 200 and 500. We can say that Calakmul continued to develop, reaching its peak between A.D. 500 and 695. At this point it had more than 6,250 buildings scattered throughout an area of more than 30 square kilometers, with a population estimated at 50,000 (Folan et al. 1995).

Although Calakmul produced the most stelae of any Maya site (117), all but two were commissioned by rulers who lived and ruled after A.D. 500. The first use of the Snake Head emblem occurs between A.D. 500 and 600, on a series of monuments at three sites. Those monuments suggest that the rulers of the Snake Head Polity were attempting to consolidate the core of their territory by force. All three sites, Dzibanche, El Resbalon, and Pol Box, were located to the northeast of Calakmul (Figure 4.3). One Snake Head king named Yuknoom Ch'een I reigned from A.D. 500 to 520 (Figure 4.11); he is mentioned on the prisoner stairway at Dzibanche (Figures 4.5 and 4.6). Another Snake Head king, K'altuun Hix (A.D. 520–546), may have been responsible for taking the prisoners depicted on the steps at El Resbalon (Carrasco and Boucher 1987; Velásquez García 2004). K'altuun Hix is also known to have presided over the A.D. 546 inauguration of a Naranjo ruler named Aj Wosal (Schele and Freidel 1990:175-177). The next Snake Head king (Sky Witness) installed a ruler in A.D. 561 at Los Alacranes; in A.D. 562 he was victorious in a battle that led to his control of Caracol and to the sacrifice of the former ally of that site, the Tikal ruler. Such a defeat might explain why Tikal did not set up any carved stones for the next 130 years.

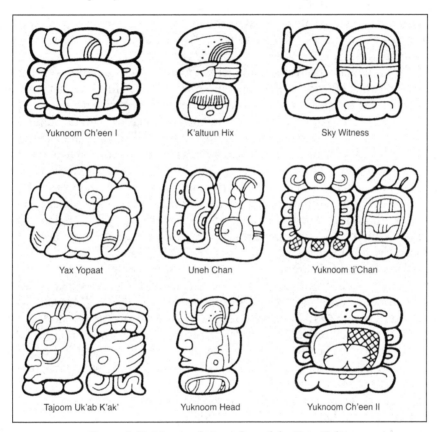

Figure 4.11. Names of nine rulers of the *Kaan* Polity
(adapted from Marcus 2004b; Martin and Grube 2008).

Since both Dzibanche and El Resbalon created prisoner staircases that commemorated the military deeds of the divine lords of the Snake Head Polity, scholars have interpreted the carved steps in various ways: either (1) the Snake Head Polity had its capital at Dzibanche from A.D. 500–600 and these steps commemorate the victorious ruler of Dzibanche; (2) the Snake Head king was the conqueror of Dzibanche and his capital was at Calakmul; or (3) the secondary center of Dzibanche was allowed to use the Snake Head emblem when acting at the behest of the Snake Head king, whose capital was located elsewhere (Grube 2004; Martin 2004; Nalda 2004a; Velásquez García 2004, 2005).

During the entire century from A.D. 500 to 600, the rulers of the Snake Head Polity were using conquest to extend the radius of their state. They ultimately came to control a large part of Campeche, Quintana Roo, and the Peten, and maintained a network of far-flung allies well beyond those zones (Marcus and Folan 1994). With El Mirador now out of the picture, and with the governmental structures of several other sites collapsing, Calakmul, Dzibanche, or other Snake Head dynastic seats were establishing networks of allies that would enable them to fill the political vacuum.

In A.D. 579 a ruler named Uneh Chan assumed the throne of the Snake Head Polity (Figure 4.11). He led one attack on Palenque in April of A.D. 599, and a second attack twelve years later in April of A.D. 611. These attacks against Palenque, which reveal the ambition of the Snake Head Polity to extend its territory to the west, are mentioned on monuments commissioned by a much later Palenque ruler, the legendary Pacal. Perhaps Pacal sought to show that earlier Palenque rulers had lost to Uneh Chan and the Snake Head Polity, but it would not happen to him (Schele 1994).

By A.D. 636, we can finally point to monuments showing that Calakmul was the capital of the *Kaan* Polity. The Snake Head emblem may have been used before this date at Calakmul, but demonstrating that will depend on recovering hieroglyphic evidence from A.D. 300 to 631. The seventh and eighth centuries A.D. saw Calakmul maintaining ties with far-flung allies while successfully holding on to many of its neighboring subjects. The Calakmul network was a mosaic of allies rather than a continuous bloc, and its rulers seem not to have concerned themselves about the intervening gaps (Marcus and Folan 1994). So extensive were these alliances that the Snake Head emblem was mentioned more widely than the Tikal emblem glyph. This wide distribution, combined with the contexts in which so many subordinate centers mentioned the Snake Head emblem, was what originally led me to suggest that Calakmul might be one of the most important Maya capitals, administering a state with a multi-tiered hierarchy of sublords (e.g., Marcus 1973, 1987, 1993).

The principal strategy of Calakmul was to expand its domain by military conquest. At the same time, it seemed also to want to convert the friends of Tikal into enemies of that site. These strategies worked during the period from A.D. 562 until 695 (Marcus 1993, 1998, 2004b; Marcus and Folan 1994; Martin 2003, 2005; Martin and Grube 2008; Schele and Freidel 1990). We can assume that two results were that some former subjects (1) stopped paying tribute and labor service to Tikal and (2) provided tribute and military service to Calakmul instead. A more complete history of the Snake Head Polity would help us develop a more detailed model for Maya statecraft.

Many of the strategies employed by the Snake Head Polity were shared with early states elsewhere in the ancient world (Marcus 1992, 1998). Included were the incorporation of sites by military force, the installation of loyal rulers at subordinate sites, sending out Calakmul princesses to marry subordinate lords, and requiring rulers of subordinate sites to attend the inaugurations of Calakmul rulers.

Solving the Mystery of the Snake Head Emblem Glyph

When I originally proposed that the Snake Head was the emblem glyph of Calakmul (Marcus 1973), I was puzzled by its late appearance at Calakmul itself. I considered it possible, however, that earlier examples of the Snake Head emblem would appear at Calakmul once extensive excavations were undertaken. Since that time, of course, several events have altered our perspective. First, Maya epigraphers (e.g., Grube 2004; Helmke and Awe 2008; Marcus

1993; Martin and Grube 2008; Mathews 1991; Stuart and Houston 1994) now see emblem glyphs as titles that can be roughly translated "Divine Lord of Polity X" (Figure 4.12). And while cities could not move around, kings and royal families could.

A second event was the discovery in 1994 of the oldest known monument at Calakmul—Stela 114, carved in A.D. 435 (Marcus and Folan 1994). This monument (Figure 4.13) did not mention the Snake Head emblem glyph, but did bear a Bat emblem and a title that can be read Lord of Chiik Nahb (Figure 4.8, lower row). The latter title contains a place name that endured as a reference to Calakmul (Marcus and Folan 1994; Martin and Grube 2008; Pincemin et al. 1998).

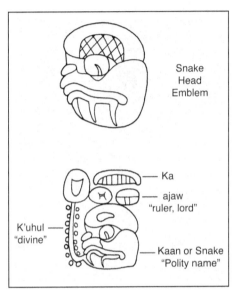

Figure 4.12. Structure of the *Kaan* Polity emblem glyph, "Divine Lord of the Snake Polity" (from Marcus 1987:Figure 65e).

A third event was the discovery of king lists for the Snake Head Polity, recorded on a dozen polychrome "Dynastic Vases" (Martin 1997; Martin and Grube 2008). These vessels, believed to have been painted in the Mirador Basin, provide a list of 19 legendary or semi-legendary rulers who trace their ancestry back to a mythical dynastic founder dubbed Skyraiser, who is shown holding the sky over his head. This retrospective king list was probably painted between A.D. 650 and 750, and may have been commissioned to establish both time depth and continuity for the rulers of the Snake Head Polity. Unfortunately, we have not been able to link most of the specific names and dates in that king list to the dates and names of rulers recorded on stone monuments.

Codex-style vessels (Hansen et al. 1991), once thought to have been painted at Nakbe, are also known from Calakmul itself. While excavating on the south side of Structure XX at Calakmul, a huge palace complex measuring 336 meters by 344 meters and featuring 17 courtyards and an estimated 80 buildings, Kai Delvendahl (2004) recovered more than 600 codex-style ceramic fragments, many of which seem to date from A.D. 650 to 750. Among the fragments was one that featured the Snake Emblem glyph; other fragments give the title *k'uhul chatan winik* ("Divine Man of Chatan"), a title that goes back to A.D. 514 at Calakmul on Stela 43.

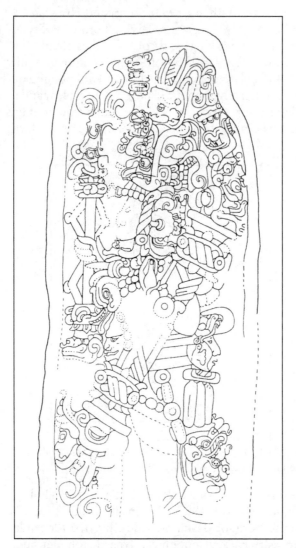

Figure 4.13. Stela 114, carved in A.D. 435, was re-set in front of Structure II at Calakmul (redrawn from Pincemin et al. 1998:Figure 6).

What these three events lead us to believe is that the Maya of the Mirador Basin conceived of a *Kaan* Polity that periodically moved its seat of power, as first Nakbe, then El Mirador, then perhaps Dzibanche, and finally Calakmul achieved supremacy. Such cycling is not without precedent in the Maya lowlands. For example, Braswell (personal communication 2009; Braswell et al. 2005) reports that in southern Belize, the site of Uxbenka was the seat of power between A.D. 300 and 500; Uxbenka was then supplanted by Pusilha; then Pusilha was supplanted by Uxbenka and Nimli Punit, and finally by Lubaantun.

Figure 4.14. Stela 43, carved in A.D. 514, was re-set in front of Structure II at Calakmul (drawn by Kay Clahassey).

In the case of the Mirador Basin, at least two alternative scenarios are possible. In one scenario, the dominant dynasty of the Snake Head Polity formed at Nakbe, moved its seat of power to El Mirador when that site took over from Nakbe, and finally wound up at Calakmul when El Mirador collapsed. In the second scenario, the Snake Head dynasty formed at Calakmul after supplanting the Bat dynasty, and sought to legitimize itself by commissioning king lists on polychrome vessels (and perhaps by alleging that its origins could be traced back to Nakbe and El Mirador). Other scenarios involving Kinichna, Dzibanche, and other sites are certainly possible, since competition and jockeying for power among multiple players were required to create a new hierarchical level.

The Process of Cycling Up and Cycling Down

Anthropological archaeologists often search for patterns and processes common to more than one geographic region. Several regions of Mesoamerica have shown us that competition among rival sites could serve as the driving force that created larger and more spectacular polities. Over and over again, we find that without the presence of multiple competing agents, many regions might not have developed centralized government at all. Competition from rivals drove some rulers to achieve things they would not otherwise have achieved.

It now appears that the process of state formation in the Mirador Basin was similar to that proposed for the Zapotec (Marcus and Flannery 1996; Spencer and Redmond 2001, 2004) and the Mixtec (Balkansky 1998; Balkansky et al. 2004). The leaders of rival Preclassic societies used political centralization and military force to avoid being taken over by their rivals. Once their autonomy was assured, they expanded preemptively against weaker neighbors. This expansion succeeded because many groups could not defend themselves against new political strategies and larger bodies of warriors.

Some Maya cities, like Tikal, seem to have retained one emblem glyph throughout their history. The situation in the Mirador Basin was too dynamic for that. As Nakbe, then El Mirador, then Dzibanche, then finally Calakmul rose to power, there were inevitable changes in royal houses and their capital cities. Whether or not the Bat Polity was embedded within the Snake Head Polity, or supplanted by it, is not clear. What is clear is that much still remains to be learned about the competitive relations between centers of Campeche and Quintana Roo, and the extent to which the Dynamic Model can establish their rise and fall.

Perhaps the most intriguing unanswered question is how the Mirador Basin managed to achieve such a headstart on monumentality and political complexity, compared to other lowland Maya regions. Did it have something to do with the unusual density of sites and the close proximity of rival cities? Might some of the competing actors have been junior and senior lineages from the same noble families? What was the relationship between Bat rulers and Snake Head rulers? What revisionist history were the codex-style painted vessels designed to establish? The story of the *Kaan* Polity, if we ever come to know it fully, may place the Mirador Basin front and center in our efforts to understand how the earliest Maya states formed.

Table 4.1. A Summary of the History of the *Kaan* Polity.

A.D. 430–435	The accession of a ruler in A.D. 411 is mentioned on Stela 114 at Calakmul, a monument set up in front of Structure II (Figure 4.10). Although there is no mention of the Snake Head emblem, a Bat emblem (Figure 4.9, upper row, far left) and Chiik Nahb (Figure 8, lower row), one of the ancient names of Calakmul, do occur.
A.D. 514	Another ruler is depicted on Stela 43 at Calakmul (Figure 4.14). Neither the Snake or Bat emblem is given, but another title—"Divine Man of Chatan" or *k'uhul chatan winik*—does appear.
A.D. 500–520	The first mention of the Snake Head Polity occurs at the site of Dzibanche in association with a ruler named Yuknoom Ch'een I, who is said to be the "Holy Lord of the Snake Head Polity" (Figure 4.1, top row, at right; Figures 4.5 and 4.6) He is said to have taken the prisoners that are depicted on the risers of stone steps at Dzibanche (Figures 4.5 and 4.6). Because the Snake Head emblem glyph is not attested at Calakmul itself at this time, one possibility is that the Snake Head capital at A.D. 500 was at Dzibanche or other site.

A.D. 535–546	Another ruler, K'altuun Hix (Figure 4.11), is associated with the Snake Head Polity; he is said to have overseen the inauguration of the ruler at Naranjo (Aj Wosal) in A.D. 546 (Schele and Freidel 1990:177).
A.D. 561–572	Sky Witness (Figure 4.11), the ruler of the Snake Head Polity, is reported to have done two key things: (1) in A.D. 561 he is said to have placed a ruler on the throne of Los Alacranes; and (2) in A.D. 562 he is said to have allied with Caracol to defeat Tikal.
A.D. 572–579	Yax Yopaat (Figure 4.11), ruler of the Snake Head Polity, is mentioned at Dzibanche in A.D. 573 (apparently as participant in the celebration of a *k'atun* ending (end of a 20-year period) and at Pol Box, a site not far south (Esparza Olguín and Pérez Gutiérrez 2009; Martin and Grube 2008).
A.D. 579–611	Uneh Chan (Figure 4.11), ruler of the Snake Head Polity, celebrated victories over Palenque in April, 599 and April, 611 (Marcus 2004b:Figure 13).
A.D. 619	Yuknoom ti'Chan (Figure 4.11), ruler of the Snake Head Polity, reinforced the earlier alliance between Calakmul and Caracol by attending an event with the ruler of Caracol.
A.D. 622–630	Tajoom Uk'ab K'ak' (Figure 4.11), ruler of the Snake Head Polity, is mentioned on a monument at Caracol. Although Stelae 28 and 29 (Figures 4.15, 4.16) at Calakmul commemorate a royal marital pair on two eroded stones, no preserved Snake Head emblem glyph can be discerned.
A.D. 630–636	Yuknoom Head (Figures 4.7 and 4.11)—ruler of the Snake Head Polity at Three Stones, Lord of Chiik Nahb—conquered Naranjo in A.D. 631. As emphasized by Martin and Grube (2008:106), Yuknoom Head is described as the Snake Head king "at Three Stones" (*ta uxte'tuun*), the ancient name of Calakmul; they suggest that "this unique phrasing could well seek to differentiate him [Yuknoom Head] from other Snake kings and their capitals—a further hint that some significant change had occurred."
A.D. 636–686	During the 50-year reign of Yuknoom Ch'een II (Figure 4.11) we see a Calakmul ruler clearly designated as king of the capital of the Snake Head Polity. This ruler is famous for interacting with many far-flung allies.
A.D. 686–695	The Calakmul ruler named Yuknoom Yich'aak K'ahk' arranged the marriage of his sister (Ix K'ab'el) to Kinich Bahlam, the ruler of El Peru (a site now called Waka'). Ix K'ab'el has the high-ranking title of *ix kaloomte'* (Figures 4.17 and 4.18). (Although her stela at El Peru once stood next to that of her husband [Marcus 1987:Figures 49 and 50] her monument now resides in Cleveland, Ohio, while that of her husband is in Fort Worth, Texas!) Yuknoom Yich'aak K'ahk's strategy of creating loyal allies by marrying off his sister is one favored by several rulers. Furthermore, the act of commissioning paired stelae to depict a husband and wife is typical of Calakmul (Marcus 1987:136) and some of its subordinate centers.
A.D. 686–750	Retrospective King Lists (19 rulers in a dynasty) were commissioned by one or more rulers of the Snake Head Polity. Although these King Lists are recorded on Dynastic Vases thought to have been painted at Nakbe, we do not know who commissioned them or where they were manufactured.

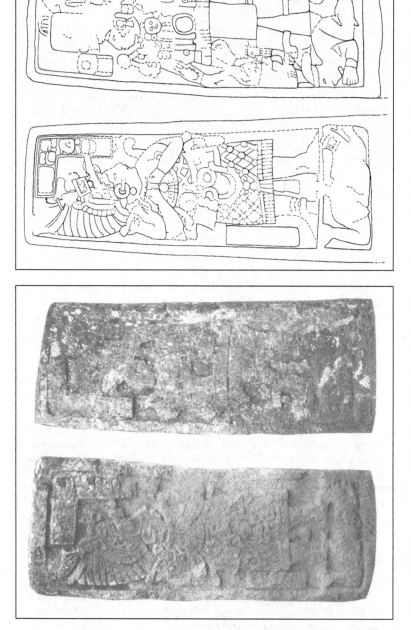

Figure 4.16. Stelae 28 and 29 from Calakmul (adapted from Ruppert and Denison 1943:Plates 49c and 49d; Marcus 1987:Figure 48).

Figure 4.15. Photographs of Stelae 28 and 29, showing the ruler and his wife at Calakmul in A.D. 623. Both the ruler (at right) and his wife (at left) stand on the backs of prisoners.

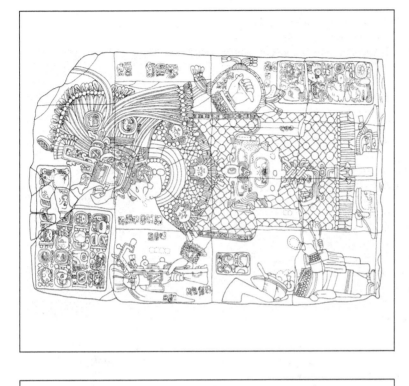

Figure 4.17. Stela 34, El Peru (now called Waka') depicts a woman from Calakmul named Ix K'ab'el. Like the paired stelae at Calakmul that depict married couples, this monument was set up next to that of her husband. Both stelae were dedicated on March 16, A.D. 692 (Marcus 1976: Frontispiece; Marcus 1987: Figure 61).

Figure 4.18. Stela 34, El Peru (now called Waka') showing the royal princess from Calakmul whose name glyphs (Ix K'ab'el) appear in her headdress as well as in the main text (redrawn from Miller 1974: Figure 2 and Marcus 1987: Figure 50).

References

Andagoya, Pascual de. 1865. *Narrative of the Proceedings of Pedrarias Davila*, translated and edited by Clements R. Markham. Hakluyt Society, London.

Anderson, David G. 1990. *Political Evolution in Chiefdom Societies: Cycling in the Late Prehistoric Southeastern United States*. Ph.D. dissertation, Department of Anthropology, University of Michigan. University Microfilms, Ann Arbor.

— 1996. Chiefly Cycling and Large-scale Abandonments as Viewed from the Savannah River Basin. In Scarry 1996:150-191.

Andrews, E. Wyllys, V. 1981. Dzibilchaltun. In *Supplement to the Handbook of Middle American Indians: Volume 1, Archaeology*, edited by Jeremy A. Sabloff, pp. 313-341. University of Texas, Austin.

— 1990. The Early Ceramic History of the Lowland Maya. In *Vision and Revision in Maya Studies*, edited by Flora S. Clancy and Peter D. Harrison, pp. 1-19. University of New Mexico, Albuquerque.

Anghera, Peter Martyr d'. 1912. *De Orbe Novo: The Eight Decades of Peter Martyr D'Anghera*. 2 vols. G. P. Putnam's Sons, New York.

Balkansky, Andrew K. 1998. Urbanism and Early State Formation in the Huamelulpan Valley of Southern Mexico. *Latin American Antiquity* 9:37-67.

Balkansky, Andrew K., Verónica Pérez Rodríguez, and Stephen A. Kowalewski. 2004. Monte Negro and the Urban Revolution in Oaxaca, Mexico. *Latin American Antiquity* 15:33-60.

Benavides C., Antonio. 2005. Campeche Archaeology at the Turn of the Century. *Anthropological Notebooks* 11:13-30.

Berlin, Heinrich. 1958. El glifo "emblema" en las inscripciones mayas. *Journal de la Société des Américanistes* 47:111-119.

Braswell, Geoffrey E., Christian M. Prager, and Cassandra R. Bill. 2005. The Kingdom of the Avocado: Recent Investigations at Pusilhá, a Classic Maya City of Southern Belize. *Anthropological Notebooks* 11:59-86. Slovene Anthropological Society, Ljubljana.

Brown, M. Kathryn, and James F. Garber. 2003. Evidence of Conflict During the Middle Formative in the Maya Lowlands: A View from Blackman Eddy, Belize. In *Ancient Mesoamerican Warfare*, edited by M. Kathryn Brown and Travis W. Stanton, pp. 91-108. AltaMira Press, Walnut Creek.

Carneiro, Robert L. 1970. A Theory of the Origin of the State. *Science* 169:733-738.

— 1981. The Chiefdom: Precursor of the State. In *The Transition to Statehood in the New World*, edited by Grant D. Jones and Robert Kautz, pp. 37-79. Cambridge University, Cambridge.

Carrasco Vargas, Ramón. 2000. El *cuchcabal* de la Cabeza de Serpiente. *Arqueología Mexicana* 7(42):12-19.

Carrasco Vargas, Ramón, and Marinés Colón González. 2005. El reino de Kaan y la antigua ciudad maya de Calakmul. *Arqueología Mexicana* 13(75):40-47.

Carrasco Vargas, Ramón, and Sylviane Boucher. 1987. Las escaleras jeroglíficas del Resbalón, Quintana Roo. In *Primer Simposio Mundial sobre Epigrafía Maya 1986*, pp. 1-21. Ministerio de Cultura y Deportes, Instituto de Antropología e Historia y Asociación Tikal, Guatemala.

Chase, Arlen, and Diane Z. Chase. 1995. External Impetus, Internal Synthesis, and Standardization: Group Assemblages and the Crystallization of Classic Maya Society in the Southern Lowlands. In *The Emergence of Lowland Maya Civilization: The Transition from the Preclassic to the Early Classic*, edited by Nikolai Grube, pp. 87-101. Acta Mesoamericana 8. Verlag Anton Saurwein, Möckmühl.

Claessen, Henri J. M., and P. van de Velde (editors). 1991. *Early State Economics*. Transaction Publishers, New Brunswick.

Dahlin, Bruce H. 1984. A Colossus in Guatemala: The Preclassic City of El Mirador. *Archaeology* 37(5):18-25.

Delvendahl, Kai. 2004. Codex-style Fragments from Structure XX, Calakmul. Online: www.mayavase.com/essays/.

Esparza Olguín, Octavio Q., and Vania E. Pérez Gutiérrez. 2009. Archaeological and Epigraphic Studies in Pol Box, Quintana Roo. *The PARI Journal* 9(3):1-16.

Espinosa, Gaspar de. 1873. Relacion e proceso quel Licenciado Gaspar Despinosa, Alcalde mayor, hizo en el viaje que por mandado del muy magnifico Señor Pedrarias de Avila... In *Colección de documentos inéditos relativos al descubrimiento, conquista y organización de las antiguas posesiones españolas de América y Oceanía*, vol. 20, pp. 5-119. Madrid.

Feinman, Gary M., and Joyce Marcus (editors). 1998. *Archaic States*. SAR, Santa Fe.

Fernández de Oviedo y Valdés, Gonzalo. 1959. *Natural History of the West Indies*, translated and edited by Sterling A. Stoudemire. University of North Carolina, Chapel Hill.

Folan, William J., Joyce Marcus, and W. Frank Miller. 1995. Verification of a Maya Settlement Model through Remote Sensing. *Cambridge Archaeological Journal* 5:277-283.

Folan, William J., J. Marcus, S. Pincemin, M. del R. Domínguez Carrasco, L. Fletcher, and A. Morales López. 1995. Calakmul: New Data from an Ancient Maya Capital in Campeche, Mexico. *Latin American Antiquity* 6:310-334.

Folan, William J., Ivan Šprajc, Raymundo González, Hubert Robichaux, María del Rosario Domínguez Carrasco, Abel Morales López, Candace Pruett, and Joel D. Gunn. 2005. Las ruinas de Oxpemul, Campeche, México: una corte real fortificada en la frontera norte entre el estado regional de Calakmul y Río Bec. In *Los Investigadores de la Cultura Maya* 13(2):476-486. Universidad Autónoma de Campeche, Campeche.

Forsyth, Donald W. 1989. *The Ceramics of El Mirador, Petén, Guatemala*. El Mirador Series, Part 4. Papers of the New World Archaeological Foundation 63. Brigham Young University, Provo.

— 1993. The Ceramic Sequence at Nakbé. *Ancient Mesoamerica* 4:31-53.

García Cruz, F. 1993. Nadzcaan: un nuevo sitio al sur de Campeche. *Mexicon* 15:95-97.

Grinin, L. E., R. L. Carneiro, D. M. Bondarenko, N. N. Kradin, and A.V. Korotayev (editors). 2004. *The Early State: Its Alternatives and Analogues*. Uchitel, Volgograd.

Grube, Nikolai. 2004. El origen de la dinastía Kaan. In Nalda 2004a:114-131.

— 2005. Toponyms, Emblem Glyphs, and the Political Geography of Southern Campeche. *Anthropological Notebooks* 11:89-102.

Hally, David J. 1996. Platform-Mound Construction and the Instability of Mississippian Chiefdoms. In Scarry 1996:92-127.

Hansen, Richard D. 1984. *Excavations on Structure 34 and the Tigre Area, El Mirador, El Petén, Guatemala: A New Look at the Preclassic Lowland Maya*. M.A. thesis, Department of Anthropology, Brigham Young University, Provo.

—1990. *Excavations in the Tigre Complex, El Mirador, Petén, Guatemala*. El Mirador Series, Part 3. Papers of the New World Archaeological Foundation 62. Brigham Young University, Provo.

— 1994. Investigaciones arqueológicas en el norte del Petén, Guatemala: una mirada diacrónica de los orígenes mayas. In *Campeche Maya Colonial*, edited by William J. Folan, pp. 14-54. Universidad Autónoma de Campeche, Campeche.

— 1998. Continuity and Disjunction: The Pre-Classic Antecedents of Classic Maya Architecture. In *Function and Meaning in Classic Maya Architecture*, edited by Stephen D. Houston, pp. 49-122. Dumbarton Oaks, Washington, D.C.

— 2002. The Architectural Development of an Early Maya Structure at Nakbé, Petén, Guatemala. Report to the Foundation for the Advancement of Mesoamerican Studies, Inc. Online: www.famsi.org.

Hansen, Richard D., Ronald L. Bishop, and Federico Fahsen. 1991. Notes on Maya Codex-Style Ceramics from Nakbe, Peten, Guatemala. *Ancient Mesoamerica* 2:225-243.

Helmke, Christophe, and Jaime Awe. 2008. Organización territorial de los antiguos mayas de Belice Central: confluencia de datos arqueológicos y epigráficos. *Mayab* 20:65-91.

Helms, Mary W. 1979. *Ancient Panama: Chiefs in Search of Power*. University of Texas, Austin.

Jones, Christopher. 1977. Inauguration Dates of Three Late Classic Rulers of Tikal, Guatemala. *American Antiquity* 42:28-60.

Jones, Christopher, and Linton Satterthwaite. 1982. *The Monuments and Inscriptions of Tikal: The Carved Monuments*. Tikal Reports 33, Part A. University Museum, University of Pennsylvania, Philadelphia.

Kowalewski, Stephen A., and James W. Hatch. 1991. The Sixteenth-Century Expansion of Settlement in the Upper Oconee Watershed, Georgia. *Southeastern Archaeology* 10:1-17.

Laporte, Juan Pedro, and Vilma Fialko. 1995. Un reencuentro con Mundo Perdido, Tikal, Guatemala. *Ancient Mesoamerica* 6:41-94.

Linares, Olga F. 1977. *Ecology and the Arts in Ancient Panama*. Studies in Pre-Columbian Art and Archaeology 17. Dumbarton Oaks, Washington, D.C.

Lothrop, Samuel K. 1937. *Coclé: An Archaeological Study of Central Panama*, Part I. Peabody Museum of Archaeology and Ethnology, Memoir 7. Harvard University, Cambridge.

Marcus, Joyce. 1973. Territorial Organization of the Lowland Classic Maya. *Science* 180:911-916.

— 1976. *Emblem and State in the Classic Maya Lowlands*. Dumbarton Oaks, Washington, D.C.

— 1987. *The Inscriptions of Calakmul: Royal Marriage at a Maya City in Campeche, Mexico*. Technical Report 21, Museum of Anthropology, University of Michigan, Ann Arbor.

— 1992. Dynamic Cycles of Mesoamerican States. *National Geographic Research & Exploration* 8:392-411.

— 1993. Ancient Maya Political Organization. In *Lowland Maya Civilization in the Eighth Century A.D.*, edited by Jeremy A. Sabloff and John S. Henderson, pp. 111-183. Dumbarton Oaks, Washington, D.C.

— 1998. The Peaks and Valleys of Ancient States: An Extension of the Dynamic Model. In Feinman and Marcus 1998:59-94.

— 2004a. Primary and Secondary State Formation in Southern Mesoamerica. In *Understanding Early Classic Copan*, edited by Ellen E. Bell, Marcello A. Canuto, and Robert J. Sharer, pp. 357-373. University Museum Press, University of Pennsylvania, Philadelphia.

—2004b. Calakmul y su papel en el origen del estado maya. *Los Investigadores de la Cultura Maya* 12(1):14-31. Universidad Autónoma de Campeche, Campeche.

— 2008. The Archaeological Evidence for Social Evolution. *Annual Review of Anthropology* 37:251-266.

Marcus, Joyce, and Gary M. Feinman. 1998. Introduction. In Feinman and Marcus 1998:3-13.

Marcus, Joyce, and Kent V. Flannery. 1996. *Zapotec Civilization*. Thames & Hudson, London and New York.

Marcus, Joyce, and William J. Folan. 1994. Una estela más del siglo V y nueva información sobre Pata de Jaguar, gobernante de Calakmul, Campeche en el siglo VII. *Gaceta Universitaria* IV(15–16):21-26.

Martin, Simon. 1997. The Painted King List: A Commentary on Codex-Style Dynastic Vases. In *The Maya Vase Book: Volume 5, A Corpus of Roll-out Photographs*, by Justin Kerr, pp. 846-863. Kerr Associates, New York.

— 2003. In Line of the Founder: A View of Dynastic Politics at Tikal. In *Tikal: Dynasties, Foreigners, & Affairs of State,* edited by Jeremy A. Sabloff, pp. 3-45. SAR, Santa Fe.

— 2004. Preguntas epigráficas acerca de los escalones de Dzibanché. In Nalda 2004a:104-115.

— 2005. Of Snakes and Bats: Shifting Identities at Calakmul. *The PARI Journal* 6(2):5-15.

Martin, Simon, and Nikolai Grube. 2008. *Chronicle of the Maya Kings and Queens: Deciphering the Dynasties of the Ancient Maya*. 2nd edition. Thames & Hudson, London.

Matheny, Raymond T. 1980. *El Mirador, Petén, Guatemala, An Interim Report*. Papers of the New World Archaeological Foundation 45. Brigham Young University, Provo.

— 1986. Investigations at El Mirador, Petén, Guatemala. *National Geographic Research* 2:332-353.

— 1987. Early States in the Maya Lowlands during the Late Preclassic Period: Edzna and El Mirador. In *City States of the Maya: Art and Architecture*, edited by Elizabeth P. Benson, pp. 1-44. Rocky Mountain Institute for Pre-Columbian Studies, Denver.

Mathews, Peter. 1991. Classic Maya Emblem Glyphs. In *Classic Maya Political History*, edited by T. Patrick Culbert, pp. 19-29. Cambridge University, Cambridge.

McAnany, Patricia A. (editor). 2004. *K'axob*. Cotsen Institute of Archaeology, University of California at Los Angeles.

Miller, Jeffrey H. 1974. Notes on a Stelae Pair Probably from Calakmul, Campeche, Mexico. In *Primera Mesa Redonda de Palenque, Part I*, edited by Merle Greene Roberston, pp. 149-161. Robert Louis Stevenson School, Pebble Beach, California.

Nalda, Enrique (editor). 2004a. *Los Cautivos de Dzibanché*. Instituto Nacional de Antropología e Historia, Mexico.

Nalda, Enrique. 2004b. Dzibanché: El contexto de los cautivos. In Nalda 2004a:14-55.

Pendergast, David M. 1981. Lamanai, Belize: Summary of Excavation Results, 1974–1980. *Journal of Field Archaeology* 8:29-53.

Pincemin, Sophia, J. Marcus, L. Florey Folan, W. J. Folan, M. del R. Domínguez Carrasco, and A. Morales López. 1998. Extending the Calakmul Dynasty Back in Time: A New Stela from a Maya Capital in Campeche, Mexico. *Latin American Antiquity* 9:310-327.

Ricketson, Oliver G., Jr., and Edith Bayles Ricketson. 1937. *Uaxactun, Guatemala, Group E, 1926–1931*. Publication 477, Carnegie Institution of Washington, Washington, D.C.

Ringle, William M., and E. Wyllys Andrews V. 1988. Formative Residences at Komchen, Yucatan, Mexico. In *Household and Community in the Mesoamerican Past*, edited by Richard R. Wilk and Wendy Ashmore pp. 171-197. University of New Mexico Press, Albuquerque.

— 1990. The Demography of Komchen, An Early Maya Town in Northern Yucatan. In *Precolumbian Population History in the Maya Lowlands*, edited by T. Patrick Culbert and Don S. Rice, pp. 215-243. University of New Mexico Press, Albuquerque.

Robichaux, Hubert R., and Candace Pruett. 2005. Las Inscripciones de Oxpemul. In *Los Investigadores de la Cultura Maya* 13(1):29-43. Universidad Autónoma de Campeche, Campeche.

Rudolph, James L., and Dennis B. Blanton. 1981. A Discussion of Mississippian Settlement in the Georgia Piedmont. *Early Georgia* 8:14-37.

Ruppert, Karl and John H. Denison, Jr. 1943. *Archaeological Reconnaissance in Campeche, Quintana Roo, and Peten*. Publication 543, Carnegie Institution of Washington, Washington, D.C.

Sauer, Carl. 1966. *The Early Spanish Main*. University of California, Berkeley.

Scarry, John F. (editor). 1996. *Political Structure and Change in the Prehistoric Southeastern United States*. University Press of Florida, Gainesville.

Schele, Linda. 1994. Some Thoughts on the Inscriptions of House C. In *Seventh Palenque Round Table, 1989*, vol. 9, edited by Merle G. Robertson and Virginia M. Fields, pp. 1-10. The Pre-Columbian Art Research Institute, San Francisco.

Schele, Linda, and David Freidel. 1990. *A Forest of Kings*. William Morrow, New York.

Sharer, Robert J., with Loa P. Traxler. 2006. *The Ancient Maya*. 6th edition. Stanford University Press, Stanford.

Spencer, Charles S. 2010. Territorial Expansion and Primary State Formation. *Proceedings of the National Academy of Sciences* 107(16):7119-7126.

Spencer, Charles S., and Elsa M. Redmond. 2001. Multilevel Selection and Political Evolution in the Valley of Oaxaca, 500–100 BC. *Journal of Anthropological Archaeology* 20:195-229.

— 2004. Primary State Formation in Mesoamerica. *Annual Review of Anthropology* 33:173-199.

Šprajc, Ivan. 2004. Maya Sites and Monuments in SE Campeche, Mexico. *Journal of Field Archaeology* 29:385-407.

— 2008. *Reconocimiento arqueológico en el sureste del estado de Campeche, México: 1996–2005*. BAR International Series 1742. Paris Monographs in American Archaeology 19. British Archaeological Reports, Oxford.

Šprajc, Ivan, William J. Folan, and Raymundo González Heredia. 2005. Las Ruinas de Oxpemul, Campeche: su redescubrimiento después de 70 años de olvido. In *Los Investigadores de la Cultura Maya* 13(1):19-27. Universidad Autónoma de Campeche, Campeche, Mexico.

Šprajc, Ivan, Carlos Morales-Aguilar, and Richard D. Hansen. 2009. Early Maya Astronomy and Urban Planning at El Mirador, Peten, Guatemala. *Anthropological Notebooks* 15(3):79-101.

Stuart, David, and Stephen D. Houston. 1994. *Classic Maya Place Names*. Studies in Pre-Columbian Art and Archaeology 33. Dumbarton Oaks, Washington, D.C.

Velásquez García, Erik. 2004. Los escalones jeroglíficos de Dzibanché. In Nalda 2004a:79-103.

— 2005. The Captives of Dzibanche. *The PARI Journal 6(2)*:1-4.
Wright, Henry T. 1977. Recent Research on the Origin of the State. *Annual Review of Anthropology* 6:379-397.
— 1984. Prestate Political Formations. *On the Evolution of Complex Societies: Essays in Honor of Harry Hoijer*, edited by Timothy K. Earle, pp. 41-78. Undena, Malibu.

Part II

THE EARLY AND LATE CLASSIC PERIODS

5 Urbanism, Architecture, and Internationalism in the Northern Lowlands during the Early Classic

Scott R. Hutson

Abstract

Scholars have long recognized the Late and Terminal Classic periods in northern Yucatan as times of dynamism and cultural florescence. Meanwhile, recent research on the Preclassic reveals that this era witnessed a surprising degree of social complexity. Bracketed by these two exceptional chapters in Yucatecan prehistory, the Early Classic period can come across as a lull, with declines in settlement reported for some areas. Nonetheless, a growing body of data shows that the Early Classic saw a number of exciting developments, such as the appearance of the first urban centers and the intensification of interregional interaction. This paper discusses examples of these integrations as seen especially from the perspective of Chunchucmil, Izamal, and Uci.

> "The Early Classic Maya in the north were not country bumpkins living in the backwaters of the Maya world" (Bey 2006:36).

The Late and Terminal Classic periods in the northern Maya lowlands have long attracted the attention of both scholars and tourists because of the growth of massive cities, the florescence of a regional architectural style, and an embrace of international contacts extending to central Mexico and beyond. This was not the first time, however, that the peninsula experienced such developments. In this chapter I discuss urbanism, distinctive regional architecture, and internationalization in one of the least known periods in Yucatan, the Early Classic (Glover and Stanton 2010:60). In demonstrating these remarkable developments, I draw heavily on data from two projects with which I have been affiliated—the Pakbeh Regional Economy Program (PREP) at Chunchucmil and the Uci/Cansahcab Regional Integration Project (UCRIP).

With regard to urbanism, I will discuss Chunchucmil, which had a greater density of structures and population than any earlier northern lowland city, and Izamal, which was larger than any preceding northern lowland site. Of the two cities, Chunchucmil is less like Classic Maya metropolises in the southern and central lowlands. I provide systematic evidence for a market economy at Chunchucmil and suggest that such an economy helps explain the peculiarly dense form of urbanism at that site.

With regard to architecture, the inhabitants of ancient Yucatan developed what is called the "megalithic style." Recent research shows that they used this style not only to build monumental structures, but also to construct modest domestic platforms. New data on the distribution of megalithic architecture across the peninsula allow us to make propositions about politics and interaction.

With regard to internationalization, interregional and long-distance contacts were intense during the Early Classic. Excavations in a representative sample of households support the conclusion that Chunchucmil played a role in these contacts by acting as a gateway for long-distance trade. These data illuminate international contacts at other Early Classic northern lowland sites such as Oxkintok, Xcambo, and Chac II. Leaders at these and other sites engaged in different kinds of relations, most of them indirect, with the largest Mesoamerican center of the time, Teotihuacan. Such leaders did not use hieroglyphic literacy to the same degree as their counterparts in the southern lowlands. Nevertheless, with their extraordinary cities, their architectural achievements, and their cosmopolitan contacts, the leaders of the northern Maya lowlands were certainly not "country bumpkins" (Bey 2006:36).

Urbanism

In the last decade, settlement-pattern studies at Chunchucmil and Izamal have shown that these two sites were the largest in Yucatan during the Early Classic period (Figure 1.1). This research provides fresh contributions to our understanding of ancient cites in the Maya world. I begin by describing results of recent investigations at the two sites and conclude by comparing Chunchucmil and Izamal with other Maya cities.

Settlement Patterns at Izamal

Settlement research at Izamal began at the site core (Burgos Villanueva et al. 2003) and then moved to the site periphery as part of an attempt to define the boundaries of the site. Rafael Burgos Villanueva, Miguel Covarrubias Reyna, and Jorge Estrada Faisal (2004) established the boundaries of the site by analyzing aerial photographs. This same team continued to survey beyond Izamal as part of the Ah Kin Chel project, which focuses on a 6,200 square-kilometer area that roughly corresponds with the boundaries of the Postclassic Ah Kin Chel province (Burgos Villanueva et al. 2005, 2006). Data on the hinterland of Izamal come from salvage projects along the roads from Izamal to Hoctun, Kantunil, and Tepakan, as well as from a new research project at Dzilam Gonzalez, initiated by Covarrubias Reyna and Burgos Villanueva in 2010.

Izamal is most famous for the Kinich Kak Moo pyramid. With a base measuring 185 meters to a side and 17 meters high (Millet Cámara and Burgos Villanueva 2006), the Kinich Kak Moo trails only the Danta complex at El Mirador as the most voluminous building in the Maya world. Perhaps even more astonishing than the volume of the Kinich Kak Moo is the surface area of the city as a whole. Burgos Villanueva et al. (2004) estimate that the city covered 53 square kilometers, equivalent to a circle with a radius of over four kilometers (Figure 5.1). This supersedes previous estimates of a two- to three-kilometer radius (Lincoln 1980). Following a method adapted from the survey of Teotihuacan (Millon 1973), Burgos Villanueva et al. define the boundaries of Izamal as being located in places where there is at least a 300-meter gap between structures.

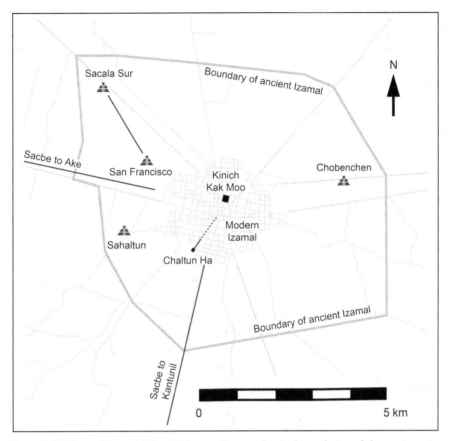

Figure 5.1. Map of Izamal. The thick grey line marks the boundaries of the ancient site, black lines represent *sacbes*.

Given the lack of an excavation sampling-program across the 53 square kilometers of settlement, the chronology of this settlement is uncertain. Eight seasons (between 1992 and 2001) of excavation and architectural restoration at the site core (Millet Cámara and Burgos Villanueva 2006; Quiñones Cetina 2003:31) and surface collections across the Ah Kin Chel region (Burgos Villanueva et al. 2006:184) show that Terminal Classic pottery is more common than pottery from any other time period. Nonetheless, the abundance of durable Late and Terminal Classic slatewares may have more to do with taphonomy and the organization of ceramic production in those periods than with chronology and demography. Other evidence suggests that Izamal became urban in the Early Classic. Millet Cámara and Burgos Villanueva date the construction of the megalithic Kinich Kak Moo to the Protoclassic (150 B.C.–A.D. 250) and the Early Classic (A.D. 250–600). This agrees with the first- through fifth-century A.D. range for AMS dates from megalithic structures in Quintana Roo (Mathews 2001). Although Middle and Late Preclassic ceramics were also found while restoring the sides of the Kinich Kak Moo, these sherds make up only one percent of the pottery from excavations (Quiñones Cetina 2003:31). Intensive ceramic analysis was also conducted on the Itzamatul structure (on the east side of the main plaza) and the Habuc structure (southeast of the main plaza). Combined with architectural studies, the ceramic analysis suggests that both were built in the Early Classic (Millet Cámara and Burgos Villanueva 2006; Quiñones Cetina 2003:268). Thus, the main plaza of Izamal took shape in the Early Classic, leading Millet Cámara (1999) to conclude that this was when Izamal consolidated its control over labor and other sites. Maldonado Cárdenas (1979, 1995) claims a late Early Classic date for the consolidation of control by Izamal. In sum, Izamal became a city in the Early Classic, though we do not yet know what portion of the 53 square kilometers was occupied at this time.

Three findings stand out for a comparative discussion of urbanism. First, the site appears to be a garden city in the sense that there are many open spaces within the 53-square-kilometer polygon (Burgos Villanueva et al. 2005:436-437; cf. Dunning 1992). Second, the causeway system of the site is more complex than once thought. It has long been known that Izamal has inter-site causeways connecting it to Ake (29.7 kilometers to the west) and Kantunil (14.2 kilometers to the south). Izamal also has an intra-site causeway connecting the site center to the Chaltun Ha monumental group, located 1.5 kilometers southwest of the Kinich Kak Moo, and a causeway that runs for 2.5 kilometers northwest from the San Francisco barrio (located 2 kilometers west of the Kinich Kak Moo) to the satellite site of Sacala Sur. The exact chronology of these intrasite causeways is not certain. Thus, because Izamal possesses both inter- and intra-site causeways, it resembles Coba. Although fewer intra-site *sacbes* (elevated causeways or roads) have been documented at Izamal than at Coba, destruction brought about by continuous occupation since the sixteenth century has likely obliterated other causeways connected to the site core. Third, the growth of Izamal appears to have led to the absorption of sites that once existed apart from the city (Burgos Villanueva et al. 2005:428). Some of these "satellite sites," such as Sahaltun and Chobenchen, have their own monumental architecture and their own internal *sacbes* connecting large mound complexes. Publication of systematic mapping transects between satellite sites and the edges of modern Izamal will address the question of how closely these sites were connected to the core.

Settlement Patterns at Chunchucmil

In many ways, Chunchucmil (Figure 5.2) contrasts sharply with Izamal. Edward Kurjack and colleagues (Kurjack and Garza Tarazona de González 1981; Vlcek et al. 1978) recognized the urban nature of Chunchucmil over 30 years ago. Nevertheless, it took a dozen field seasons, initiated by Bruce Dahlin in the 1990s and completed in 2006, to gain clear knowledge of the scale, density, form, function, and chronology of this ancient city. Dahlin's PREP mapped a total of 11.77 square kilometers and dug test pits in 162 different architectural contexts. These efforts revealed that Chunchucmil was more densely populated than the great Classic period Maya metropolises of Tikal, Calakmul, Dzibilchaltun, Caracol, and Coba (Magnoni 2007). Moreover, the site presents a detailed record of spatial organization, preserved in the form of dozens of kilometers of houselot boundary walls and alleys. Although the site had small occupations in the Preclassic and the Late to Terminal Classic periods, the vast majority of the city dates to the latter part of the Early Classic.

PREP archaeologists recognize three settlement zones at Chunchucmil (see Hutson et al. 2008). The innermost zone contains the site center, consisting of a one square-kilometer cluster of temple complexes, streets, causeways, a single ballcourt, and a marketplace. A second zone, the residential core, surrounds the site center and consists of densely packed houselots ringed by stone walls or *albarradas*. The density of the residential core, which covers about 7.5 square kilometers, is 950 structures per square kilometer. The third zone, the residential periphery, rings the residential core and differs from it in two ways: (1) settlement density drops to 350 structures per square kilometer; and (2) small pockets of unclaimed space, not encircled by *albarradas*, can be found. The residential periphery covers about 8.5 square kilometers. Beyond the residential periphery, we find what others call "intersite" settlement (Rice and Rice 1990), characterized by a density of about 50 structures per square kilometer, and also linear strips of settlement that my coauthors and I call "fingers" (Hutson et al. 2008). These fingers have a density of 120 structures per square kilometer and connect to other sites. The three concentric zones of Chunchucmil and its fingers cover 20 to 25 square kilometers and held an estimated population of 31,000 to 43,000 (Magnoni 2007).

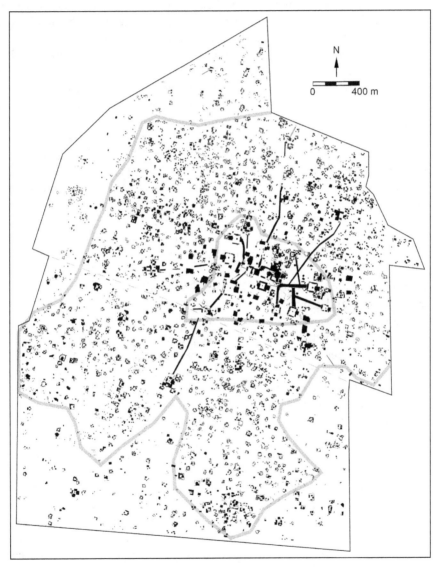

Figure 5.2. Ruins of Chunchumil showing 9.4 square kilometers of the site. The site center zone lies within the inner gray polygon. The residential core zone lies within the outer gray polygon, although some of the residential core extends to the northeast beyond the bounds of the map. The rest of what is visible on this map pertains to the residential periphery.

Comparing Urbanism at Izamal, Chunchucmil, and other Classic Maya Sites

Because Izamal lacks the same intensity of settlement research, comparisons between Izamal and Chunchucmil cannot progress far. Nonetheless, Chunchucmil contrasts with Izamal in many ways. First, Chunchucmil has no focal pyramid. This suggests that Chunchucmil had a form of political organization based not on a single holy lord but rather on sharing power among multiple factions. Second, Chunchucmil lacks inter-site causeways. Following Kurjack and Andrews' (1976) interpretation of such causeways, this could mean that Chunchucmil lacked territorial ambitions. Third, the settlement of Chunchucmil is more densely packed than that of Izamal, where open spaces appear to have been larger and more common in that garden city. We do, however, have evidence of gardening within the tight spaces of Chunchucmil houselots (Hutson et al. 2007). Finally, the growth of Chunchucmil did not engulf preexisting sites as was the case at Izamal. Rather than expanding far from the site center, residents at Chunchucmil packed themselves in tightly.

Comparing Chunchucmil and Izamal with other extensively mapped Late Classic Maya urban centers (specifically Coba, Tikal, Caracol, Dzibilchaltun, and La Milpa) brings into sharp relief the different kinds of urbanism that exist in the Maya area. The three concentric zones of Chunchucmil (center, residential core, and residential periphery) resemble the three concentric zones of Tikal (epicenter, center, and periphery; Puleston 1983:24-25; cf. Webster et al. 2007), but are much more dense and compact. Dzibilchaltun also exhibits three concentric zones when vaulted structures are considered (Kurjack 1979). Yet if we also consider non-vaulted buildings, the middle zone disappears, leaving only the site core and a series of about 30 settlement clusters. As Kurjack (1974:89) notes, this pattern is "not consistent with the general notion of what a nucleated community should be like." This is quite different from Chunchucmil, where nucleation takes the form of concentric density gradients within the city, but is potentially similar to Izamal insofar as Burgos Villanueva et al. (2005) note the presence of open spaces within the boundaries of that site. Caracol exhibits a concentric plan consisting of an epicenter of palaces and temples surrounded by the houses of a nutritionally deficient supporting population. These are in turn surrounded by residential groups with contiguous agricultural plots, many of which are terraced (Chase and Chase 2004:142). With about 2.5 hectares of land each, such residential groups are rather dispersed, creating a sprawl of more than one hundred square kilometers. The low density of settlement at Caracol confounds the distinction between rural and urban. Such sprawl incorporates minor centers in a way that recalls the alleged incorporation of satellite sites at Izamal. La Milpa (Tourtellot et al. 2003) also resembles Caracol and Izamal in the sense of a low-density sprawl sprinkled here and there with minor centers.

In sum, Izamal appears to resemble the low-density cities of Tikal, Caracol, and La Milpa more so than does Chunchucmil. This is notable in light of observations that northern lowland settlement is generally denser than southern lowland settlement (Drennan 1988). Since Izamal does not fit this observed pattern, geographical differences between the northern and central lowlands do not provide sufficient explanation for differences in settlement density. Dzibilchaltun is denser than the central lowland sites, but is not a close match to Chunchucmil because Dzibilchaltun does not exhibit similar nucleation. Chunchucmil most closely resembles Coba, which has high settlement density as well as the kind of intra-site density thresholds (concentric density gradients akin to the threshold at Chunchucmil between the residential core and residential periphery) that attest to residential nucleation (Folan et al. 1983).

Two factors help account for the differences in urbanism observed between Chunchucmil and most other sites. First, cities like Caracol and La Milpa were less nucleated because most of their residents were farmers whose labor-intensive terraced agricultural plots were adjacent to their houses. These plots were not mere gardens that supplemented larger yields from outfields beyond the city. Rather, these plots constituted the principal farmlands of the site. If such sprawling sites are to be considered cities, they are not so much garden cities as farming cities. Although people at Chunchucmil did maintain kitchen gardens, most of its residents were not farmers (Dahlin et al. 2005). This brings me to the second factor that may account for the many differences observed in the settlement patterns of Chunchucmil: marketing.

Market Behavior at Chunchucmil

The presence of markets is a key ingredient of classical definitions of urbanism. Markets encourage the occupational specialization that is a trademark of cities. Just as importantly, economically interdependent social units *require* markets in order to ensure the efficient circulation of goods. Such marketing probably existed alongside the vestiges of traditional mechanisms such as reciprocity and redistribution. Hirth (1998) isolates three approaches to identifying marketplace exchange: contextual, configurational, and distributional. The contextual approach infers marketing "from the presence of cultural features believed to require the provisioning and distribution functions of the market to exist, for example, large cities and full-time craft specialists" (Hirth 1998:453). The status of Chunchucmil as a large city is beyond doubt. Full-time craft specialization at Chunchucmil has been harder to identify, due in part to the perishable nature of evidence. The configurational approach focuses on the physical identification of actual market places. Dahlin et al. (2007) have pursued this approach at Chunchucmil by marshalling architectural, locational, and soil-chemistry evidence that identify a broad space at the center of the city as a marketplace (see also Dahlin and Ardren 2002). Finally, the distributional approach infers marketing by showing that the distribution of goods across a site conforms to the expectations of marketplace exchange. A systematic test-pitting program that targeted a representative sample of architectural contexts across Chunchucmil permits a distributional approach, which I explore here using data on obsidian blades.

The test-pitting program revealed that blade-production debris was found in only a small number of household contexts, yet finished blades were found in many. Some mechanism, therefore, must have functioned to distribute blades from the few producers to the multiple consumers. We have tested three models to account for the pattern in blade distribution at Chunchucmil: marketing, redistribution, and reciprocity (Hutson et al. 2010). If blades were distributed by marketing, we would expect them to be spread relatively evenly across the site because marketplaces provide equal access to commodities for all consuming units (Hirth 1998:455). Redistributive systems have spheres of distribution smaller than that of the market because they are not as efficient in moving large volumes of goods (Hirth 1998:454). In particular, redistribution reproduces status hierarchies (see also Clark 1987) insofar as the most powerful actors, those charged with redistributing obsidian, keep a large portion of obsidian for themselves. In other words, with redistribution, we would expect more obsidian in higher status contexts. Reciprocity is even more inefficient than redistribution and would therefore result in a very limited spatial distribution of obsidian across the site.

The test-pitting program at Chunchucmil allows a rather clear discrimination between marketing, redistribution, and reciprocity. PREP archaeologists excavated a 13 percent representative sample of the 1,250 architectural contexts found while mapping the site. Excavation samples of this scale at sites this large are rare for the Maya area. The excavation program included 841 test pits distributed in 162 architectural contexts. Most of these architectural contexts are patio groups, consisting of at least three or four buildings facing onto one or more patios. To arrive at the sample of 162 contexts, we stratified the 1,250 architectural contexts into types based on the number of buildings per context, size of architecture, and the presence or absence of features such as *sascaberas* (limestone quarries) and houselot walls. We further stratified the 1,250 contexts by location, creating a stratum for each square-kilometer block on our map. Random numbers were used to select contexts within each block and type. For example, all twenty of the Type 8 architectural contexts (patio groups with five or fewer structures) found within the Pollo block (located immediately northwest of the site center datum) were given numbers. Six of these numbers were selected at random, and those six contexts were subject to up to eight test pits each. Excavations in 21 of the 162 sampled contexts yielded very few artifacts and were dropped from the sample. We dropped 11 more contexts because they did not date to the Early Classic.

To test distributional models, we grouped the 130 remaining contexts into four categories that we thought would best represent different social statuses. The highest status category included architectural groups with massive pyramids. Although the large temples in these groups suggest ritual activities serving larger sections of the population, excavations indicate that these groups also contained residences (Blackmore and Ardren 2001). The next three categories of architectural contexts consist of large residential groups with 11 or more stone platforms (N=13), medium-sized residential groups with six to ten stone platforms (N=38), and small residential groups with five or fewer stone platforms (N=64). All but 11 of the groups in these three categories are encircled by low stone walls. We refer to such encircled groups as houselots. We initially thought that the division of patio groups into large, medium, and small categories would correspond roughly to social status. This is because patio groups with more buildings tend to have more residents, implying greater wealth (Netting 1982), and also tend to have larger buildings, implying greater control of labor and resources (cf. Hendon 1992). Nonetheless, we cannot be certain that we have captured status differences with these four categories of architectural contexts.

We found that obsidian was distributed relatively evenly across the four categories of architectural groups, therefore supporting the marketing model of distribution (Hutson et al. 2010). The small residential groups had the most obsidian (expressed as a ratio with ceramic counts), followed by the medium-sized residential groups, the large residential groups, and, finally, the monumental groups. Nonetheless, differences in the relative quantities of obsidian tend to be quite small. The only statistically significant difference is that observed between small residential groups and groups with large pyramids ($t = -2.77$, $p = 0.002$, $df = 77$). Insofar as our four categories mark status distinctions, this finding challenges the notion of obsidian as a good denoting wealth.

Thus, we have configurational, contextual, and distributional evidence that Chunchucmil was a market center. Although other large Maya sites also may have had markets, the people of Chunchucmil committed themselves to commerce more than to farming. This helps explain the exceptional form that urbanism took at Chunchucmil: high settlement density and residential nucleation in the form of concentric density gradients within the city. Current research by Bruce Dahlin and Richard Terry at Coba, the only other heavily nucleated Classic Maya metropolis, may also suggest marketing at that site.

Megalithic Architecture

Scholars have known about megalithic buildings at Izamal, Dzilam, and Ake since the nineteenth century explorations of John L. Stephens (1843), Etienne Brasseur de Bourbourg (1865), and Desiré Charnay (1863). Stephens' description of Structure 1 at Ake conveys the impression that the ancient buildings made on the explorers:

> The ascent is on the south side, by an immense staircase, forming an approach of rude grandeur, perhaps equal to any that ever existed in the country. Each step is four feet five inches long, and one foot five inches in height… It was a new and extraordinary feature, entirely different from any we had seen, and at the very end of our journey, when we supposed ourselves familiar with the character of American ruins, threw over them a new air of mystery (Stephens 1843:304).

I follow Mathews and Maldonado Cárdenas (2006) in using the word "style" to refer to the salient characteristics of megalithic buildings. Ceramics from many sites and accelerator mass spectrometry dates from charcoal inclusions in mortar from El Naranjal (Mathews 2001) show that these buildings were constructed at the end of the Late Preclassic (first centuries A.D.) and during the Early Classic periods.

Many authors have described the style; Taube (1995) and Mathews (1998) provide systematic descriptions of it. The megalithic style is characterized by platforms with retaining walls that contain large, dressed facing stones (usually a meter or more in length). These large stones have rounded corners, giving them a pillow shape and distinguishing them from other massive, horizontally laid stones at sites such as Dzibilchaltun. The ancient Maya often built apron corbels with these megaliths and gave both the sub-apron wall and the projecting apron a slant, or *talud*. Many large megalithic buildings have rounded corners, a trait also found in non-monumental buildings. Of course, the style did not develop in the northern lowlands in a vacuum. Megalithic traits such as buildings with rounded corners and apron moldings suggest traffic in ideas with the central lowlands. Perhaps the closest architectural analog to the northern lowland megalithic style is found in the El Mirador basin, where late Middle Preclassic buildings often have tenoned apron moldings, *taluds*, and stone blocks measuring up to one meter long (Hansen 1998). At the beginning of the Late Preclassic, however, large stones in the El Mirador basin ceased to be used and smaller ones were employed in such constructions. This is intriguing because if megalithic buildings date only to the late Middle Preclassic in the El Mirador basin, but appear in the latter part of the Late Preclassic in northern Yucatan, then there is no chronological overlap. This chronological gap suggests that connections between the megalithic styles of these two regions are at best indirect.

The Distribution of Megalithic Architecture

New research has clarified the geographic distribution of megalithic architecture and confirmed its widespread use in domestic, non-monumental contexts. Whereas it was once thought that megalithic constructions were confined to the vicinity of Izamal, archaeologists working in the Yalahau region in Northern Quintana Roo have revealed many sites with megalithic architecture (Glover 2006; Mathews 2003; Mathews and Maldonado Cárdenas 2006). The two largest sites in the region are Kantunilkin to the north and El Naranjal to the south (Glover 2006). At El Naranjal, 16 of 25 monumental structures exhibit megalithic stonework (Mathews and Maldonado Cárdenas 2006). The megalithic style also appears in the monumental structures of the two second-tier sites near El Naranjal—Tres Lagunas and Victoria—and is present at four third-tier sites near El Naranjal (Glover and Stanton 2010). There is some debate as to whether Kantunilkin has megalithic architecture (Glover and Stanton 2010:70), however, sites near Kantunilkin lack megalithic architecture. This has led Glover (2006) to propose the existence of a "megalithic polity" centered at El Naranjal and a "non-megalithic polity" centered at Kantunilkin.

We can talk, therefore, of two areas of megalithic architecture in the northern lowlands: a western core centered at Izamal and an eastern core centered at El Naranjal. Archaeologists have found megalithic architecture beyond these cores, but a rough distinction must be made between sites where megalithic architecture predominates (in the sense that most of the major buildings are megalithic) and sites that have only a few megalithic buildings. Only in the two core areas do we find sites (e.g., Izamal, Ake, El Naranjal, Victoria) where megalithic architecture predominates.

Some researchers theorize that the appearance of megalithic architecture at sites beyond the two core areas indicates political influence emanating from those cores (Burgos Villanueva et al. 2006:177; Stanton 2000:568). If this is the case, the spotty distribution of megalithic architecture beyond the cores implies complexly drawn, geographically discontinuous spheres of political influence. I take the case of Oxkintok and Izamal as an example. Mathews and Maldonado Cárdenas (2006) report the megalithic construction style at Structures MA-7, DZ-7, and the Tzat Tun Tzat at Oxkintok. In the area between Oxkintok and Izamal, several important contemporary sites—Acanceh and Yaxcopoil, for instance—have no megalithic architecture (Burgos Villanueva et al. 2006). It is as if Izamal influence leapfrogged over unaffected areas to reach Oxkintok. Regardless of what kind of relation existed between Oxkintok and Izamal, the lack of geographic continuity between the spaces where megalithic construction appears suggests a complex landscape of geopolitical relations that cannot be reduced to maps with clear, unbroken lines encompassing the influence of any one center (Smith 2003:133).

Figure 5.3. Structure 38s14 of the 21 de Abril site, an example of a domestic megalithic platform.

Figure 5.4. Structure 27b of Santa Teresa (16d-d[5]:71), an example of a domestic megalithic platform.

Although the areas around Izamal and El Naranjal may both have formed cores of the style, the distribution of megalithic architecture around Izamal differs sharply from that around El Naranjal. The most important difference is that the smallest sites in the El Naranjal polity lack megalithic buildings whereas megalithic construction is common at the smallest sites near Izamal. The Ah Kin Chel project, which has mapped Izamal and conducted multiple surveys beyond Izamal, has reported many such sites (Burgos Villanueva et al. 2006). The Uci-Cansahcab Regional Integration Project (UCRIP, directed by the author) also has discovered and mapped small sites with megalithic architecture. These include Ticopo-2, located three kilometers west of Uci, and 21 de Abril, located five kilometers east of Uci. At these sites, which lack both monumental and public architecture, megalithic constructions consist of low, domestic platforms (Figures 5.3 and 5.4). Joseph Stair (2010) is currently completing a study of domestic megalithic architecture in this area, focusing on variations in the megaliths themselves and how these correlate with aspects of the buildings of which they are a part.

The characteristics of domestic megalithic architecture include platform retaining walls with horizontally laid large stones with smooth corners. These platforms are generally quadrangular and often have rounded corners, much like their monumental counterparts. Most of these platforms are rather broad, covering an area greater than 200 square meters. It is common to see a megalithic platform grouped with smaller, non-megalithic, roughly circular structures made of limestone cobble fill (*chi'ich*). The diameter of these structures is usually less than six meters. In most megalithic buildings, only one course of megalithic stones is visible on the surface, and the platforms are generally less than one meter high. Although there are no domestic megalithic buildings at the smallest sites in the El Naranjal core, some are found at third-tier sites such as Chan Pich, San Lorenzo, and San Roman (Glover and Stanton 2010:70). At these sites, however, megalithic buildings usually have several stacked courses of megaliths, giving the platforms more height.

The Adoption of the Megalithic Style: Emulation, Coercion, or Folk Style?

The fact that the megalithic style is seen at all levels of the settlement hierarchy around Izamal but only in the upper three levels around El Naranjal could suggest that the style spread from the western core to the eastern core. This argument is based on the assumption that the style is indigenous to the area where it is found in domestic platforms of the smallest sites, and was adopted by elites in the area where it is found only in higher status contexts. This adoption of the megalithic style, perhaps by the mechanism of interaction spheres suggested by Mathews (1998), would have been a means by which elites created social distinctions (à la Bourdieu 1984), before the style had the time to trickle down to the bottom of the settlement hierarchy.

We should be cautious, however, about insisting upon the directionality of the spread of the style from the western core to the eastern core because we are not yet certain of how the style developed and spread within the western core itself. Several explanations could account for the fact that farmers at the smallest sites and leaders at the largest sites (as well as many in between) built their buildings in the megalithic style. One possibility is that it was deployed first by the leaders at Izamal, and then emulated by smaller and smaller sites. At Uci and in its hinterland, we have found that domestic megalithic platforms tend to be larger than non-megalithic platforms (Hutson 2010a). Insofar as platform size relates to the command of resources, and because status emulation requires a baseline of expendable resources to begin with, the fact that better endowed households were the ones that built megalithic platforms could be construed as weakly supporting the notion that the megalithic style spread to the lowest rungs of the settlement hierarchy via emulation.

Instead of emulation, people lower down in the settlement hierarchy may have been pressured into adopting the megalithic style. This appears to have been the case with wall trenches in and around Cahokia, in the Mississippi Valley. At A.D. 1050, house construction at Cahokia abruptly shifted from single-set-post walls to wall-trenches. Rural farmers on the edges of the Mississippi Bottom adopted the wall trenches more slowly, while some dug postholes disguised as wall-trenches or built wall trenches for just a portion of their houses. Pauketat and Alt (2005) argue that these feigned wall trenches and hybrids show a grudging and sometimes only partial acceptance of a top-down imposition from Cahokia. Closer in time and space, at Teotihuacan, the standard 15.5-degree building orientation was imposed upon all apartment compounds within the city. If the megalithic style were imposed from the top down, we would expect nearly all buildings in the sphere of influence of Izamal to exhibit this style. At Uci and nearby sites investigated by the UCRIP, not all of the broad domestic platforms are megalithic. But non-megalithic buildings may date to later time periods and therefore have no bearing on the question of the spread of the megalithic style. Due to a surprising shortage of diagnostic ceramics in and around Uci, it has been difficult to assign platforms to specific periods. Nevertheless, within our very small, unrepresentative sample, non-megalithic platforms date to the Late and Terminal Classic periods (Hutson 2010b). Some megalithic platforms have both Early Classic and Late Classic ceramics. One domestic megalithic platform had exclusively Late Classic ceramics, suggesting that it may be an architectural anachronism.

Thus, investigations of domestic megalithic architecture have not progressed to a degree where they can address the question of whether the style was imposed from above. Observations of monumental buildings at Uci and Kancab (located eight kilometers east of Uci along the causeway to Cansahcab) can be helpful. Monumental buildings at Uci and Kancab are different from their counterparts at Izamal. First, the megaliths at Uci and Kancab are much smaller than those found at Izamal. Second, Uci and Kancab lack the wide (greater than 30 meters) megalithic stairways found, for example, at the Kinich Kak Moo pyramid of Izamal and Structure 1 of Ake. These data suggest that the builders of monuments at Uci and Kancab selectively emulated some aspects of the megalithic style at Izamal and Ake and chose not to incorporate other aspects of the style. That is, megalithic architecture was not imposed upon them lock, stock, and barrel.

Rather than the megalithic style originating from leaders at the top of the settlement hierarchy, either through un-coerced emulation or forced adoption, it may be that people first developed aspects of the megalithic style in domestic contexts, creating a folk architecture, and leaders later gave the style its grandest expression in monumental constructions. In other words, leaders may have appropriated a vernacular style and adapted it to their own purposes, as has been proposed for later Puuc-style architecture where elements of thatched roof houses were copied in the stone palaces of the elites. Doing so would have made the monumental constructions of leaders intelligible to commoners because they were essentially grounding their monuments in conventions to which everyone could easily relate. Alternatively, builders of domestic platforms and monumental pyramids may have contributed equally to the development of the style.

Other fruitful themes for future research extend beyond evaluating different scenarios for the development and spread of the megalithic style. For instance, looking at variations—from one building to the next—in megalithic construction at the domestic level could be a profitable way of getting at differences in how people literally made and remade their worlds (Pauketat and Alt 2005). Understanding the degree to which people were committed to traditions of practice requires the close study of the most basic ways in which they built their worlds, stone by stone. In a different vein, megalithic stones have recently played a pivotal role in new thinking about the vitality of material, the physicality of the natural world, and the way that it interferes with and shapes human projects (Scarre 2004; Tilley 2004). In the northern lowlands, megalithic stones constitute a visually and emotionally striking component of the built environment of the Maya and a consideration of their materiality may contribute to conversations about agency (Olsen 2003; Webmoor and Witmore 2008).

In summary, observations of the distribution of the megalithic style both horizontally across the peninsula and vertically in settlement hierarchies within the same micro-region permit tentative conclusions about politics and interaction. Megalithic architecture predominates in two cores: Izamal in the west and El Naranjal in the east. Despite sharing an architectural style, the next section makes clear that these two areas were part of different ceramic spheres. The fact that megalithic architecture was used for modest house platforms at all levels of the settlement hierarchy around Izamal, but was used only by elites at the large sites around El

Naranjal, suggests that the architectural style originated around Izamal. The spread of megalithic architecture beyond these cores was light and uneven, suggesting the complexity and unpredictability of regional interaction.

Internationalism

During the Early Classic, the Maya of the highlands, southern lowlands, and central lowlands participated in extensive long-distance exchanges of people, ideas, and objects that integrated the Mesoamerican world (Braswell 2003). Recent fieldwork at four sites with significant Early Classic occupations—Xcambo, Chac II, Oxkintok, and Chunchucmil (Figure 1.1)—shows that this network of integration did not bypass the northern lowlands.

Xcambo, located on the North Coast of Yucatan, was a port site and salt shipping center with megalithic stairways on the three largest temples of its main plaza, Plaza 1. Sierra Sosa (1999) argues that Izamal, located 51 kilometers inland and to the southeast, controlled Xcambo. It had an abundance of Peten-style polychromes, attesting to its role in linking Izamal with providers of jade and obsidian far to the south. Xcambo does not appear to have strong connections to Teotihuacan. Fully 98.6 percent of the 1,078 obsidian artifacts recovered from Xcambo come from sources in highland Guatemala, while less than 0.4 percent is green obsidian from the Pachuca, Hidalgo, source that is so common at Teotihuacan (Braswell and Glascock 2007:Figura 5).

Chac II and Oxkintok are both sites in the Puuc hills, and both have material culture with Teotihuacan influence. Based on excavations at Chac II, Smyth (Smyth and Ortegon 2006; Smyth and Rogart 2004) has argued that Teotihuacan had a direct influence on the rise of urban centers in the Puuc region (cf. Chapter 15; Stanton 2005). From the perspective of Oxkintok, Varela Torrecilla and Braswell (2003) argue that international contacts also stimulated the genesis and development of the Puuc region. Nevertheless, the accounts of Smyth on the one hand and Varela Torrecilla and Braswell on the other differ in an important way. Smyth argues for the presence of an enclave of Teotihuacanos who were attracted to the cave near Chac II and an alleged overland trade route. At Oxkintok, the data argue against an enclave of foreigners. Rather than merely duplicating foreign styles, potters combined local innovations with elements from Maya sites to the south as well as Teotihuacan ceramic traits, perhaps filtered through southern Maya lenses. Varela Torrecilla and Braswell (2003) argue that local leaders used these creative, hybrid styles to reformulate existing political and economic systems.

Obsidian Procurement at Chunchucmil

Data from Chunchucmil provide a valuable perspective on the nature of internationalism at these sites because fieldwork has focused systematically on the livelihoods of the non-royal segment of the population. At Chunchucmil we can assess the degree to which common people were involved in interregional interaction using data from the representative sample of the 1,250 architectural contexts described above. In my discussion of urbanism, the distribution of obsidian within Chunchucmil corroborated other lines of evidence for the presence of market exchange. The overall quantities of obsidian, which I now discuss, suggest that, in addition to marketing within the site, the people of Chunchucmil took part in significant interregional commerce. Visual sourcing and X-ray fluorescence show that the vast majority (96 percent) of the obsidian at Chunchucmil comes from the El Chayal source in highland Guatemala.

At Chunchucmil a sample of excavations from the Early Classic yielded 597.4 grams of obsidian (858 artifacts) and 603.38 kilograms of ceramics, yielding an obsidian-to-pottery mass ratio of 9.9×10^{-4}. At Chac II, Smyth's excavations in Early and Middle Classic contexts yielded 110.4 grams of obsidian (79 artifacts, 81 percent of which come from El Chayal) and 377.51 kilograms of pottery (Michael Smyth, personal communication, 2008). The ratio of obsidian mass to ceramic mass is therefore just 2.9×10^{-4}. At Edzna, Nelson et al. (1977, 1983) report 96 obsidian artifacts from NWAF excavations, though only nine of these come from Early Classic contexts. Excavations of approximately 133 cubic meters in residential contexts in the northwest portion of the site yielded six obsidian blades from contexts where Early Classic ceramics dominated or made up a large portion of the ceramic debris (Matheny et al. 1983). Quantification of obsidian as a ratio with ceramics is difficult for Edzna because ceramic weights are not given. Furthermore, not all excavations were screened. Nonetheless, assuming a modest average of 10 grams per sherd, the ratio of obsidian mass to sherd mass at Edzna is 1.5×10^{-4} versus 9.9×10^{-4} for Chunchucmil. Put another way, the ratio of obsidian to volume of excavation at Edzna was approximately 0.14 grams of obsidian per cubic meter, as opposed to 2.20 grams of obsidian per cubic meter at Chunchucmil. Intensive and extensive excavations under the direction of David Friedel at Yaxuna, which had a substantial Early Classic occupation, recovered a total of only 180 obsidian artifacts (Braswell and Glascock 2007). Although excavations at Yaxuna focused more on monumental architecture than at Chunchucmil, this is still a small amount of obsidian compared to the nearly 3,000 obsidian artifacts recovered during excavations at Chunchucmil.

Thus, Chunchucmil had access to an abundance of obsidian compared to other northern lowland sites dating to the Early Classic period. Although explanations that consider craft specialization and the local availability of other lithic materials may account for part of this abundance, the explanation that best fits other lines of data is that Chunchucmil was a gateway community (Hirth 1978), from which obsidian arriving by sea along the Gulf Coast was distributed to sites further inland. Models of directional trade in long-distance or interregional goods (e.g., Renfrew 1977) would predict less obsidian at Chunchucmil than at important inland sites if obsidian had arrived at Chunchucmil via an overland route, perhaps passing through sites such as Chac II. Instead, the data suggest that obsidian first passed through Chunchucmil on its way to these other sites. The involvement of Chunchucmil in interregional trade makes sense because its population was too large to be supported by local agriculture.

Chunchucmil as a Gateway Community

The conclusion that Chunchucmil was involved in coastal trade has interesting ramifications for long distance contacts at Xcambo, Oxkintok, and Chac II. Izamal merchants operating out of Xcambo and Chunchucmil merchants operating out of Punta Canbalam (Dahlin et al. 1998) or another site would have used the same trade route along the west coast of Yucatan (in the Late Classic, Xcambo was also trading along the east coast of Yucatan; Sierra Sosa 1999). Nonetheless, contacts between Izamal and Chunchucmil did not result in an interchange of architectural styles. The monumental buildings of Chunchucmil show no evidence of the megalithic style. Additionally, the Early Classic domestic architecture of the site takes the form of central lowland-style patio groups (often with shrines on the east side; e.g., Becker 1991) as opposed to the broad platforms seen at Izamal and its megalithic neighbors. Thus, Izamal, the site with the most impressive monumental architecture, and hence, power, did not dominate international contacts in the northern lowlands during the Early Classic period. On the other hand, the leaders of Izamal may have been in decline by the time Chunchucmil was at its peak at the end of the Early Classic.

As Chunchucmil was booming in the fifth and sixth centuries A.D., Oxkintok, located only 27 kilometers to the east, also became more prosperous, gaining access to goods from the Guatemalan highlands (Varela Torrecilla and Braswell 2003). Chunchucmil was most likely the portal through which Oxkintok received jade, cinnabar, and obsidian. At Oxkintok, the best evidence for participation in the international system comes from monumental architecture and elite tombs. Although research at Chunchucmil did not focus on monumental architecture and elite tombs, other lines of evidence, such as ceramics and domestic architecture, indicate a very close connection between Oxkintok and Chunchucmil. Ceramics at Chunchucmil during its sixth century apex are nearly identical to ceramics at Oxkintok: assemblages from both sites are part of the Oxkintok Regional complex (Varela Torrecilla 1998). Both sites also share Proto-Puuc architecture during this period. The presence of hieroglyphic stone carvings at Oxkintok and their absence at Chunchucmil could be taken to suggest that Oxkintok was the innovator of cultural styles and Chunchucmil merely the receiver. Several points contest this notion. First, since no monumental architecture has been excavated at Chunchucmil, it is premature to declare that Chunchucmil lacks the kind of hieroglyphic lintels found at Oxkintok. Second, in demographic terms, Chunchucmil dwarfed Oxkintok by a factor of at least ten during the Early Classic. Settlement maps of Oxkintok reveal that the area of the site during the fifth and sixth centuries was between one and two square kilometers. Chunchucmil covered at least twenty square kilometers at this time. The great population of Chunchucmil during the Early Classic period implies that the site was too big to be a vassal of any of its neighbors, regardless of whether or not it had stone carvings. Velázquez Morlet and de la Rosa (1995) are most likely correct in delimiting the bounds of the Oxkintok polity in such a way that it excludes Chunchucmil.

The role of Chunchucmil as a trade center also speaks to developments at Chac II. Stanton (2005) argues that data posited for an enclave of foreigners at Chac II are inexact and notes that the alleged residences of these foreigners date to after A.D. 550, a time when Teotihuacan was already in decline. Data from Chunchucmil cannot address the notion of an enclave at Chac II, but can illuminate Smyth's suggestion that Teotihuacanos were interested in Chac II in part because of its position along a potential long-distance trade route. When compared to obsidian data from Chac II, similar data from Chunchucmil suggest that the major trade route in northwestern Yucatan followed the coast as opposed to passing overland (see also Hutson et al. 2010).

Open-Work Ceramic Supports in the Maya area and Central Mexico

At Chunchucmil, connections to Teotihuacan are rare, but excavations of monumental architecture at Chunchucmil may someday change this perspective. Obsidian from Pachuca, Hidalgo, and other sources in Central Mexico is very scant. As noted above, 96 percent of the obsidian collected at Chunchucmil comes from the El Chayal, Guatemala source. Furthermore, none of the ceramics recovered from the 841 test pits at Chunchucmil manifest an association with Teotihuacan. There are no Thin Orange sherds, *candeleros*, *floreros*, or direct-rim cylindrical tripods in the sample from the test pits. Nevertheless, block excavations in residential groups revealed a single building with a *talud-tablero* façade (discussed at length by Ardren and Lowry [2011]) and a pottery form that is often associated with central Mexico: direct-rim cylinder tripod vessels with open-work supports.

Ortíz Ceballos and Santley (1998) have closely analyzed open-work supports from Matacapan and compared these with open-work supports from Teotihuacan and the Maya area. My own inspection of open-work supports adds additional Maya data to the picture and suggests a spatial pattern, but I do not intend this analysis to be comprehensive. At Teotihuacan, open-work hollow rectangular supports are standard on vases with plano-relief incision. Such incisions were executed on locally made, polished ware cylindrical vases dating to the Early and Late Xolalpan phases (Rattray 2001:223, 255). Open-work hollow rectangular supports continued to be made during the Metepec phase (Rattray 2001:283). Rattray (2001:221) believes that polished ware, plano-relief vessels made in Teotihuacan were inspired by similar vessels from the coast of Veracruz. Ortíz Ceballos and Santley (1998:413) agree with the similarities pointed out by Rattray, but believe that it is just as likely that Teotihuacan plano-relief vessels inspired those at Matacapan.

Ortíz Ceballos and Santley (1998) present six types of open-work supports. In the Maya area, open-work supports most often fall into Ortíz Ceballos and Santley's Type E (Figure 5.5a, b), which is distinguished by a set of three triangular windows. Ortíz Ceballos and Santley's Type E predominates at Copan, where six of the eight vessels with open-work supports in the Hunal and Margarita tombs, pertaining to the dynastic founder and his wife, respectively (Reents-Budet et al. 2004), are of Type E (Figure 5.5c). At Kaminaljuyu, gashes into solid slab feet are more common than the open-work technique, but the most common design style (8 of a total of 16 vessels with decorated supports from the Carnegie excavations) conforms to Type E (Figure 5.5d, e; Kidder et al. 1946:Figures 171-179). In contrast, Type E open-work supports beyond the Maya area are far less common. At Matacapan, the most common design on open-work supports consists of "two intertwined incised elements set in a panel" (Type A) "often situated above a carved sloping talud" (Type B; Santley et al. 1987:89). At Teotihuacan, examples of Type E supports are extremely rare. Rattray reports a single example but this vessel, of San Martin Thin Orange, was probably imported from Puebla. Vessels with Type E open-work supports were displayed in the *Teotihuacan: Art from the City of the Gods* exhibit in San Francisco (Berrin and Pasztory 1993), but since they lacked provenience, we cannot be sure where they were actually found. Thus, in spatial terms, Type E supports are most common in the Maya area, and are less and less common as one moves westward beyond the Maya area.

In the northern lowlands, open-work supports reported for Oxkintok (Varela 1998: 68, 83) and Yaxuna (Stanton 2005) conform to Type E (Figure 5.5f, g). Open-work supports at Xcambo and Chunchucmil, however, do not clearly conform to Type E. Of the four fragments of vessels with open-work hollow rectangular supports at Chunchucmil, one clearly conforms to Ortíz Ceballos and Santley's Type D, a common style of support at Teotihuacan which is also the design found on the Dazzler, a post-fire painted cylindrical tripod found in the Margarita tomb at Copan (Figure 5.5h-k; see also Ardren and Lowry 2011). Two do not conform to any of the types presented by Ortíz Ceballos and Santley, although the fourth has a vague resemblance to Type E (Figure 5.5l-n).

Since Type E open-work supports are much more common in the Maya area than elsewhere, the connection of pottery with this kind of support to Teotihuacan must be fairly indirect. Varela Torrecilla and Braswell (2003; see also Stanton 2005) make this same point with regard to direct-rim cylindrical tripod vessels in general. Such vessels found in the northern lowlands lack the plano-relief incisions and painted stucco decorations common on vessels more directly associated with Teotihuacan. Along these lines, two examples of vessels with open-work supports found at Oxkintok are not even cylindrical vases (e.g., Varela Torrecilla 1998:Figure 3.16). Although Type D open-work supports have a more direct connection to Teotihuacan, the vessel on which these supports appear at Chunchucmil is intensely Maya in its other attributes (Ardren and Lowry 2011).

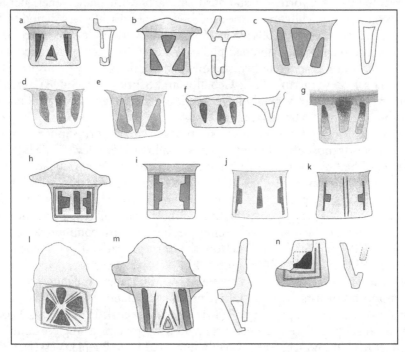

Figure 5.5. Supports from cylindrical tripod vases: (a-b) Examples of type E from Matacapan (adapted from Ortíz Ceballos and Santley 1998:408); (c) Type E from Copan (adapted from Reents-Budet et al. 2004:Figure 9.9c); (d-e) Type E from Kaminaljuyu (adapted from Kidder 1947: 171); (f) Type E from Oxkintok (adapted from Varela Torrecilla 1998:Figura 3.29); (g) Type from Yaxuna (adapted from Stanton 2005:Figure 4); (h-i) Examples of type D from Matacapan (adapted from Ortíz Ceballos and Santley 1998:408); (j) Type D in the "Dazzler" vessel, Copan (adapted from Bell et al. 2004:Plate 7a); (k) Type D from Chunchucmil (adapted from photograph by Traci Ardren, used with permission); (l) Type D from Xcambo (adapted from Ceballos Gallareta 2003:Figura 42j); (m-n) Type D from Chunchucmil.

Conclusion

In his recent review of the state of the field, Bey expressed excitement about "the growing understanding of the nature and scale of Early Classic Maya society in the north" (2006:36). The current paper both adds details and synthesizes some of the themes of this growing understanding. As presented in the first section, the scale of the two largest Early Classic sites in the northern lowlands, Izamal and Chunchucmil, was startling. Our understanding of the nature of these two sites benefits from comparing them with other large, well-mapped Classic centers. Whereas Izamal exhibits similarities to low-density farming cities like Caracol, La Milpa, and Tikal, Chunchucmil is very different; it is dense and heavily nucleated but without a dominant ceremonial complex in its nucleus. The best explanation most likely draws on the status of Chunchucmil as a market center. My colleagues and I invested an inordinate amount of resources acquiring distributional evidence for marketing at Chunchucmil. Archaeologists rarely put the distributional approach into practice at such large sites because it requires a representative sample of architectural contexts. For a site the size of Chunchucmil, this required over 800 test pits. Numbingly unglamorous as it may seem, the distributional approach is the only way to determine whether markets actually served a significant part of a populace. We were able to conclude with confidence that the markets of Chunchucmil succeeded in distributing obsidian almost evenly to the 31,000 to 43,000 occupants of the site. A causal relation between marketing and settlement density has not been demonstrated, but these two aspects of urbanism are found together at Chunchucmil in a way not seen at other Classic Maya sites.

This chapter also presented new findings on megalithic architecture, a celebrated regional style. The style predominated in monumental buildings in two parts of the northern lowlands: in the west around Izamal and in the east around Naranjal. In the western core area, people built megalithic structures at all levels of the settlement hierarchy, in both domestic and monumental contexts. This did not happen in the eastern core area. Despite its popularity in both the east and west, the megalithic style never achieved the status of a horizon style. Ceramic evidence reiterates this lack of cultural unification in the north: there were five ceramic spheres in the northern lowlands during the Early Classic period (Ceballos Gallareta and Jiménez Álvarez 2005). Yet there were important interactions between people from these different spheres. Megalithic builders around Izamal shared an architectural style with megalithic builders around Naranjal, yet they used different pottery. In other words, architectural style overlapped only partially with ceramic style. If the distribution of megalithic architecture permits a sketch of the outlines of a political system, this system consisted of multiple, complex, and only partially overlapping coalitions.

Evidence for internationalism helps to flesh out this outline of Early Classic political and economic organization. Xcambo, Chunchucmil, Oxkintok, and Chac II all maintained connections with other Maya regions and the broader Mesoamerican world. Yet the sites did so in different ways. For example, both Chunchucmil and Izamal (via the Xcambo port) used the Gulf Coast as an interregional and long-distance trade route. Nevertheless, the architecture of Chunchucmil shows no influence from Izamal. Although the domestic architecture of Chunchucmil is more Peten-like than that of Izamal, Xcambo—the port site of Izamal—has more Peten pottery than does Chunchucmil. Data presented here suggest that Chunchucmil was the gateway through which Early Classic centers further inland—especially Oxkintok and Chac II— received obsidian. Despite the tentative conclusion that Chunchucmil was "bladerunning" (Jackson and Love 1991) for Oxkintok and Chac II, the three sites appear to have been independent of each other. I mean this not just in political terms, but also in the kinds of political strategies they used. Both Chac II and Oxkintok have features associated with Teotihuacan, but the nature of foreign influence seen at Oxkintok is different from that expressed at Chac II. Oxkintok and Chunchucmil interpreted Teotihuacan similarly: they took Teotihuacano templates, such as the direct-rim cylindrical tripod vase, and hybridized them along both broadly Maya and intensely local lines, which we see in the specific decorative attributes of tripod supports. Far from being a backwater, such cultural creativity, not to mention the presence of thriving urban centers with architectural innovations, situates the Early Classic northern lowlands as a compelling case study for anthropological research on complex societies.

Acknowledgments

I dedicate this paper to Bruce Dahlin, without whom none of it would have been possible. The Consejo de Arqueología, INAH, provided permits for PREP and UCRIP projects. Funding for PREP and UCRIP research cited in this paper came from NSF and the Wenner Gren Foundation, respectively. I thank Shannon Plank for helpful comments. I thank Teresa Ceballos Gallareta for letting me use information from her *licenciatura* thesis and Traci Ardren for granting me access to unpublished data from Chunchucmil. Jacob Welch helped prepare Figure 5.5. Finally, I thank Will Andrews for encouraging generations of scientific work in the northern lowlands.

References

Ardren, Traci, and Justin Lowry. 2011. Chunchucmil, Teotihuacan, y el Grupo Lool. Paper presented at the Tercer Simposio Internacional de Mayistas. Merida.

Becker, Marshall. 1991. Plaza Plans at Tikal, Guatemala and at Other Lowland Maya Sites: Evidence for Patterns of Culture Change. *Cuadernos de Arquitectura Mesoamericana* 14:11-26.

Bell, Ellen, Marcello Canuto, and Robert J. Sharer (editors). 2004. *Understanding Early Classic Copan*. University of Pennsylvania Museum of Archaeology and Anthropology, Philadelphia.

Berrin, Kathleen, and Esther Pasztory (editors). 1993. *Art from the City of the Gods*. Thames & Hudson, New York.

Bey, George J. 2006. Changing Archaeological Perspectives on the Northern Maya Lowlands. In Mathews and Morrison 2006:13-37.

Blackmore, Chelsea, and Traci Ardren. 2001. Excavations at the Pich Group. In *Pakbeh Regional Economy Program: Report of the 2001 Field Season*, edited by Bruce H. Dahlin and Daniel E. Mazeau, pp. 58-68. Report submitted to Consejo de Arqueología, Instituto Nacional de Antropología e Historia, Mexico City.

Bourdieu, Pierre. 1984. *Distinction: A Social Critique of the Judgment of Taste*, translated by Richard Nice. Harvard University, Cambridge, Mass.

Brasseur de Bourbourg, Charles-Etienne. 1865. Rapport sur les ruines de Mayapan et d'Uxmal au Yucatan (Mexique). In *Archives de la Commission Scientifique du Méxique*, vol. 2, pp. 234-288. Imprimerie Impériale, Paris.

Braswell, Geoffrey E. (editor). 2003. *The Maya and Teotihuacan: Reinterpreting Early Classic Interaction*. University of Texas, Austin.

Braswell, Geoffrey E., and Michael D. Glascock. 2007. El Intercambio de la obsidiana y el desarrollo de las economías de tipo mercado en la región Maya. In *XX Simposio de investigaciones arqueológicas en Guatemala, 2006*, edited by Juan Pedro Laporte, Bárbara Arroyo, and Hector Mejia, pp. 13-26. Museo Nacional de Arqueología y Etnología, Guatemala City.

Burgos Villanueva, Rafael, Jorge Estrada Faisal, and Juan G. Targa. 2003. Una aproximación al patrón de asentamiento del sitio de Izamal, Yucatán. *Los Investigadores de la Cultura Maya* 11:312-324. Universidad Autonóma de Campeche, Campeche.

Burgos Villanueva, Rafael, Miguel Covarrubias Reyna, and Jorge Estrada Faisal. 2004. Estudios sobre la periferia de Izamal, Yucatan. *Los Investigadores de la Cultura Maya* 12:249-256. Universidad Autonóma de Campeche, Campeche.

— 2005. Estudios en la periferia de Izamal: El área de transición entre una zona de producción agricola y una zona limítrofe de ocupación humana al poniente del área urbana. *Los Investigadores de la Cultura Maya* 13:425-444. Universidad Autonóma de Campeche, Campeche.

Burgos Villanueva, Rafael, Miguel Covarrubias Reyna, and Sara Dzul Góngora. 2006. Estudios en la región de Ah Kin Chel desde la perspectiva de Izamal, Yucatán. *Los Investigadores de la Cultura Maya* 14:170-184. Universidad Autonóma de Campeche, Campeche.

Ceballos Gallareta, Teresa. 2003. *La cronología cerámica del puerto maya de Xcambó, costa norte de Yucatán: Complejo Xtampú*. Licenciatura thesis, Facultad de Ciencias Antropológicas, Universidad Autónoma de Yucatán, Merida.

Ceballos Gallareta, Teresa, and Socorro Jiménez Álvarez. 2005. Las esferas cerámicas del horizonte Cochuah del Clásico Temprano (c. 250–600 d.C.) en el norte de la península de Yucatán. In *La producción alfarera en el México Antiguo II*, edited by Beatriz Leonor Merino Carrión and Ángel García Cook, pp. 561-580. Instituto Nacional de Antropologia e Historia, Mexico City.

Charnay, Désiré, and Eugène Emmanuel Viollet-le-Duc. 1863. *Cités et Ruines Américaines: Mitla, Palenque, Izamal, Chichen Itza, Uxmal*. Gide, Paris.

Chase, Diane Z., and Arlen F. Chase. 2004. Archaeological perspectives on Classic Maya Social Organization from Caracol, Belize. *Ancient Mesoamerica* 15:139-147.

Clark, John E. 1987. Politics, Prismatic Blades, and Mesoamerican Civilization. In *The Organization of Core Technology*, edited by Jay K. Johnson and C. A. Morrow, pp. 259-284. Westview, Boulder.

Dahlin, Bruce H., Anthony P. Andrews, Timothy Beach, Clara Bezanilla, Patricia Farrell, Sheryl Luzzader-Beach, and Valerie McCormick. 1998. Punta Canbalam in Context: A Peripatetic Coastal Site in Northwest Campeche, Mexico. *Ancient Mesoamerica* 9:1-15.

Dahlin, Bruce H., and Traci Ardren. 2002. Modes of Exchange and Regional Patterns: Chunchucmil, Yucatan, Mexico. In *Ancient Maya Political Economies*, edited by Marilyn Masson and David Freidel, pp. 249-284. Altamira, Walnut Creek.

Dahlin, Bruce H., Timothy Beach, Sheryl Luzzadder-Beach, David Hixson, Scott R. Hutson, Aline Magnoni, Eugenia B. Mansell, and Daniel Mazeau. 2005. Reconstructing Agricultural Self-Sufficiency at Chunchucmil, Yucatan, Mexico. *Ancient Mesoamerica* 16:229-247.

Dahlin, Bruce H., Christopher T. Jensen, Richard E. Terry, David R. Wright, and Timothy Beach. 2007. In Search of an Ancient Maya Market. *Latin American Antiquity* 18:363-384.

Drennan, Robert D. 1988. Household Location and Compact Versus Dispersed Settlement in Prehispanic Mesoamerica. In *Household and Community in the Mesoamerican Past*, edited by Richard Wilk and Wendy Ashmore, pp. 273-293. University of New Mexico, Albuquerque.

Dunning, Nicholas P. 1992. *Lords of the Hills: Ancient Maya Settlement in the Puuc Region, Yucatan, Mexico*. Monographs in World Archaeology 15. Prehistory, Madison.

Folan, William J., Ellen R. Kintz, and Laraine A. Fletcher. 1983. *Coba: A Classic Maya Metropolis*. Academic, New York.

Glover, Jeffrey B. 2006. *The Yalahau Regional Settlement Pattern Survey: A Study of Ancient Maya Social Organization in Northern Quintana Roo, Mexico*. Ph.D. dissertation, Department of Anthropology, University of California, Riverside. University Microfilms, Ann Arbor.

Glover, Jeffrey B., and Travis Stanton. 2010. Assessing the Role of Preclassic Traditions in the Formation of Early Classic Yucatec Cultures, Mexico. *Journal of Field Archaeology* 35:58-77.

Hansen, Richard D. 1998. Continuity and Disjunction: The Pre-Classic Antecedents of Classic Maya Architecture. In *Function and Meaning in Classic Maya Architecture*, edited by Stephen D. Houston, pp. 49-122. Dumbarton Oaks, Washington, D.C.

Hendon, Julia A. 1992. The Interpretation of Survey Data: Two Case Studies from the Maya Area. *Latin American Antiquity* 3:22-42.

Hirth, Kenneth G. 1978. Interregional Trade and the Formation of Gateway Cities. *American Antiquity* 43:35-45.

— 1998. The Distributional Approach: A New Way to Identify Marketplace Exchange in the Archaeological Record. *Current Anthropology* 39:451-476.

Hutson, Scott R. 2010a. *Proyecto Arqueológico Sacbe de Ucí-Cansahcab: Informe de la temporada de campo 2009*. Report submitted to Consejo de Arqueología, Instituto Nacional de Antropología e Historia, Mexico City.

— 2010b. *Proyecto Arqueológico Sacbe de Ucí-Cansahcab: Informe de la temporada de campo 2010*. Report submitted to Consejo de Arqueología, Instituto Nacional de Antropología e Historia, Mexico City.

Hutson, Scott R., Bruce H. Dahlin, and Daniel E. Mazeau. 2010. Commerce and Cooperation among the Classic Maya: The Chunchucmil Case. In *Cooperation in Social and Economic Life*, edited by Robert C. Marshall, pp. 81-103. Altamira, Lanham.

Hutson, Scott R., David Hixson, Aline Magnoni, Daniel E. Mazeau, and Bruce H. Dahlin. 2008. Site and Community at Chunchucmil and Ancient Maya Urban Centers. *Journal of Field Archaeology* 33:19-40.

Hutson, Scott R., Travis W. Stanton, Aline Magnoni, Richard E. Terry, and Jason Craner. 2007. Beyond the Buildings: Formation Processes of Ancient Maya Houselots and Methods for the Study of Non-architectural Space. *Journal of Anthropological Archaeology* 26:442-473.

Jackson, Thomas L., and Michael W. Love. 1991. Blade Running: Middle Preclassic Obsidian Exchange and the Introduction of Prismatic Blades at La Blanca, Guatemala. *Ancient Mesoamerica* 2:47-59.

Kidder, Alfred V. 1947. *The Artifacts of Uaxactun Guatemala*. Publication 576. Carnegie Institution of Washington, Washington, D.C.

Kidder, Alfred V., Jesse D. Jennings, and Edwin M. Shook. 1946. *Excavations at Kaminaljuyu, Guatemala*. Publication 561, Carnegie Institute of Washington, Washington, D.C.

Kurjack, Edward B. 1974. *Prehistoric Lowland Maya Community and Social Organization: A Case Study at Dzibilchaltun, Yucatan, Mexico*. Publication 38. Middle American Research Institute, New Orleans.

— 1979. Introduction to the Map of the Ruins of Dzibilchaltun. In *Map of the Ruins of Dzibilchaltun, Yucatan, Mexico*, edited by George Stuart, John C. Scheffler, Edward B. Kurjack, and John W. Cottier, pp. 1-16. Publication 47. Middle American Research Institute, New Orleans.

Kurjack, Edward B., and E. Wyllys Andrews V. 1976. Early Boundary Maintenance in Northwest Yucatan, Mexico. *American Antiquity* 41:318-325.

Kurjack, Edward B., and Silvia Garza Tarazona de González. 1981. Pre-Colombian Community Form and Distribution in the Northern Maya Area. In *Lowland Maya Settlement Patterns*, edited by Wendy Ashmore, pp. 287-309. University of New Mexico, Albuquerque.

Lincoln, Charles E. 1980. *A Preliminary Assessment of Izamal, Yucatan, Mexico*. Unpublished B.A. Honors Thesis, Department of Anthropology, Tulane University, New Orleans.

Magnoni, Aline. 2007. Population Estimates at the Ancient Maya City of Chunchucmil, Yucatán, Mexico. In *Digital Discovery: Exploring New Frontiers in Human Heritage. Computer Applications and Quantitative Methods in Archaeology, CAA 2006, Proceedings of the 34th Conference, Fargo, United States, April 2006*, edited by Jeffrey T. Clark and Emily M. Hagemeister, pp. 175-182. Archaeolingua, Budapest.

Maldonado Cárdenas, Rubén. 1979. Izamal-Ake y Uci-Cansahcab sistemas prehispanicos del norte de Yucatan. *Boletín de la escuela de ciencias antropológicas de la Universidad de Yucatán* 6(36):33-44.

— 1995. Los sistemas de caminos del norte de Yucatan. In Pacheco 1995:68-92.

Matheny, Raymond T., Deanne Gurr, Donald W. Forsyth, and Forest R. Hauck. 1983. *Investigations at Edzna, Campeche, Mexico: Volume 1, Part 1, The Hydraulic System*. Papers of the New World Archaeological Foundation 46. Brigham Young University, Provo.

Mathews, Jennifer P. 1998. *The Ties that Bind: The Ancient Maya Interaction Spheres of the Late PreClassic and Early Classic Periods in the Northern Yucatan Peninsula*. Ph.D. dissertation, Department of Anthropology, University of California at Riverside. University Microfilms, Ann Arbor.

— 2001. Radiocarbon Dating of Mortar and Charcoal Inclusions in Architectural Mortar: A Case Study in the Maya Region, Quintana Roo, Mexico. *Journal of Field Archaeology* 28:395-400.

— 2003. Megalithic Architecture at the Site of Victoria, Quintana Roo. *Mexicon* 25:74-77.

Mathews, Jennifer P., and Rubén Maldonado Cárdenas. 2006. Late Formative and Early Classic Interaction Spheres Reflected in the Megalithic Style. In Mathews and Morrison 2006:95-118.

Mathews, Jennifer P., and Bethany A. Morrison (editors). 2006. *Lifeways in the Northern Lowlands: New Approaches to Maya Archaeology*. University of Arizona, Tucson.

Millet Cámara, L. 1999. Los mayas de Yucatán: Entre las colinas y el estero. *Arqueología mexicana* 7(37):4-13.

Millet Cámara, Luís, and Rafael Burgos Villanueva. 2006. Izamal: Una Aproximación a su arquitectura. In *Los mayas de ayer y hoy: Memorias del Primer Congreso Internacional de Cultura Maya*, edited by Alfredo Barrera Rubio and Ruth Gubler, pp. 132-155. Solar Servicio Editoriales, Merida.

Millon, Rene. 1973. *Urbanization at Teotihuacan, Mexico: Volume 1, The Teotihuacan Map: Part 1, Text*. University of Texas, Austin.

Nelson, Fred. W., Kirk K. Nielsen, Nolan F. Mangelson, Max W. Hill, and Raymond T. Matheny. 1977. Preliminary Studies of the Trace Element Composition of Obsidian Artifacts from Northern Campeche Mexico. *American Antiquity* 42:209-225.

Nelson, Fred W., David A. Phillips, and Alfredo Barrera Rubio. 1983. Trace Element Analysis of Obsidian Artifacts from the Northern Maya Lowlands. In *Investigations at Edzna, Campeche, Mexico, Appendix A*, edited by Raymond T. Matheny, pp. 204-219. New World Archaeological Foundation, Provo.

Netting, Robert McC. 1982. Some Home Truths on Household Size and Wealth. *American Behavioral Scientist* 2:641-661.

Olsen, Bjørnar. 2003. Material Culture after Text: Re-Membering Things. *Norwegian Archaeological Review* 36:87-104.

Ortíz Ceballos, Ponciano, and Robert S. Santley. 1998. Matacapan, un ejemplo de enclave teotihuacano en la costa del golfo. In *Los Ritmos de cambio en Teotihuacan: Reflexiones y discusiones de su cronología*, edited by Rosa Brambila Paz and Rubén Cabrera Castro, pp. 377-460. Instituto Nacional de Antropología e Historia, Mexico City.

Pacheco, Ernesto Vargas (editor). 1995. *Seis ensayos sobre antiguos patrones de asentamiento en el área maya*. Universidad Nacional Autonoma de Mexico, Instituto de Investigaciones Antropologicas, Mexico, D.F.

Pauketat, Timothy R., and Susan M. Alt. 2005. Agency in a Postmold? Physicality and the Archaeology of Culture-Making. *Journal of Archaeological Method and Theory* 12:257-281.

Puleston, Dennis. 1983. *The Settlement Survey of Tikal*. The Tikal Reports 13. The University Museum, University of Pennsylvania, Philadelphia.

Quiñones Cetina, Lucía Guadalupe. 2003. *Del preclásico medio al clásico temprano: Una propuesta de fechamiento para el área de nuclear de Izamal, Yucatán*, Licenciatura thesis, Facultad de Ciencias Antropológicas, Universidad Autonoma de Yucatán, Merida.

Rattray, Evelyn C. 2001. *Teotihuacan: Ceramics, Chronology and Cultural Trends*—Teotihuacan: Cerámica, Cronología y Tendencias Culturales. INAH/University of Pittsburgh, Mexico City.

Reents-Budet, Dorie, Ellen E. Bell, Loa P. Traxler, and Ronald L. Bishop. 2004. Early Classic Ceramic Offerings at Copan: A Comparison of the Hunal, Margarita and Sub-Jaguar Tombs. In *Understanding Early Classic Copan*, edited by Ellen E. Bell, Marcello Canuto and Robert J. Sharer, pp. 159-190. University of Pennsylvania Press, Philadelphia.

Renfrew, Colin. 1977. Alternative Models for Exchange and Spatial Distribution. In *Exchange Systems in Prehistory*, edited by Timothy K. Earle and Jon E. Ericson, pp. 71-90. Academic, New York.

Rice, Don S., and Prudence M. Rice. 1990. Population Size and Population Change in the Central Peten Lakes Region, Guatemala. In *Pre-Colombian Population History in the Maya Lowlands*, edited by T. Patrick Culbert and Don S. Rice, pp. 123-148. University of New Mexico, Albuquerque.

Santley, Robert, Clare Yarborough, and Barbara Hall. 1987. Enclaves, Ethnicity, and the Archaeological Record at Matacapan. In *Ethnicity and Culture: Proceedings of the Eighteenth Annual Conference of the Archaeological Association of the University of Calgary*, edited by Réginald Auger, pp. 85-100. Calgary Archaeological Association, Calgary.

Scarre, Christopher. 2004. Displaying the Stones: The Materiality of Megalithic Monuments. In *Rethinking Materiality: The Engagements of Mind with the Material World*, edited by Elizabeth DeMarrais, Chris Gosden, and Colin Renfrew, pp. 141-152. McDonald Institute Monographs, Cambridge.

Sierra Sosa, Thelma N. 1999. Xcambó: Codiciado enclave conómico del Clásico Maya. *Arqueología Mexicana* 7(37):40-47.

Smith, Adam T. 2003. *The Political Landscape: Constellations of Authority in Early Complex Polities*. University of California, Berkeley.

Smyth, Michael P., and Davíd Ortegón Zapata. 2006. Foreign Lords and Early Classic Interaction at Chac II, Yucatan. In Mathews and Morrison 2006:119-141.

Smyth, Michael P., and Daniel Rogart. 2004. A Teotihuacan Presence at Chac II, Yucatan, Mexico. *Ancient Mesoamerica* 15:17-47.

Stair, Joseph. 2010. Diversity in Domestic Architecture at Ucí: An Analysis of Megalithic Stones. Paper presented at the 75th Annual Meeting of the Society for American Archaeology, St. Louis.

Stanton, Travis W. 2000. *Heterarchy, Hierarchy, and the Emergence of the Northern Lowland Maya: A Study of Complexity at Yaxuna, Yucatan, Mexico*. Ph.D. dissertation, Department of Anthropology, Southern Methodist University. University Microfilms, Ann Arbor.

— 2005. Taluds, Tripods, and Teotihuacanos: A Critique of Central Mexican Influence in Classic Period Yucatan. *Mayab* 18:17-35.

Stephens, John L. 1843. *Incidents of Travel in Yucatan*. Harper & Brothers, New York.

Taube, Karl A. 1995. The Monumental Architecture of the Yalahau Region and the Megalithic Style of the Northern Maya Lowlands. In *The View from Yalahau: 1993 Archaelogical Investigations in Northern Quintana Roo, Mexico*, edited by Scott Fedick and Karl A. Taube, pp. 79-87. Latin American Studies Program, Field Report Series 2. Latin American Studies Program, University of California at Riverside.

Tilley, Christopher. 2004. *The Materiality of Stone: Explorations in Landscape Phenomenology*. Berg, Oxford.

Tourtellot, Gair, Gloria Everson, and Norman Hammond. 2003. Late Classic Maya Heterarchy, Hierarchy, and Landscape at La Milpa, Belize. In *Heterarchy, Political Economy, and the Ancient Maya: The Three Rivers Region of the East-Central Yucatan Peninsula*, edited by Vernon L. Scarborough, Fred J. Valdez, and Nicholas Dunning, pp. 37-51. University of Arizona, Tucson.

Webmoor, Timothy, and Chris L. Witmore. 2008. Things are Us. *Norwegian Archaeology Review* 41(1):53-66.

Webster, David, Timothy Murtha, Kirk D. Straight, Jay Silverstein, Horacio Martinez, Richard E. Terry, and Richard Burnett. 2007. The Great Tikal Earthwork Revisited. *Journal of Field Archaeology* 32:41-64.

Varela Torrecilla, Carmen. 1998. *El Clásico Medio en el noroccidente de Yucatán*. Paris Monographs in American Archaeology 2, BAR International Series 739. British Archaeological Review, Oxford.

Varela Torrecilla, Carmen, and Geoffrey E. Braswell. 2003. Teotihuacan and Oxkintok: New Perspectives from Northern Yucatan. In *The Maya and Teotihuacan: Reinterpreting Early Classic Interaction*, edited by Geoffrey E. Braswell, pp. 249-271. University of Texas, Austin.

Velázquez Morlet, Adriana, and Edmundo López de la Rosa. 1995. La región y la ciudad [Oxkintok]: Dinámica de los patrones de asentamiento en el occidente de Yucatán. In Pacheco 1995:93 122.

Vlcck, David, Silvia Garza Tarazona de González, and Edward B. Kurjack. 1978. Contemporary Maya Farming and Ancient Settlements: Some Disconcerting Evidence. In *Prehispanic Maya Agriculture*, edited by Peter D. Harrison and B. L. Turner, pp. 211-223. University of New Mexico, Albuquerque.

6 The Political and Economic Organization of Late Classic States in the Peninsular Gulf Coast

The View from Champoton, Campeche

Jerald Ek

Abstract

Research surrounding the modern city of Champoton has focused primarily on the importance of the prehispanic polity of Chakanputun during the Postclassic period. Nevertheless, recent investigations have documented substantial evidence of much earlier cultural developments. This new research within the Rio Champoton drainage has provided important information about the political and economic organization of polities along the central Campeche coast during earlier phases of the prehispanic era. This chapter examines patterns of economic and political change that took place during the Late and Terminal Classic periods, focusing specifically on shifting patterns of political affiliation, settlement patterns, and the changing role of Gulf Coast groups in interregional exchange networks.

The Rio Champoton basin of Campeche, Mexico, was the territory of the ancient Maya province of Chakanputun,[1] a late Maya polity well documented in Spanish ethnohistorical sources (Figure 1.1; Ruz Lhuillier 1969; Scholes and Roys 1968; Vargas Pacheco 1994, 2001). Chakanputun was one of several important yet poorly understood states located along the Gulf Coast periphery of the Maya area that rose to prominence late in the prehispanic era. Data from recent investigations by the Champoton Regional Settlement Survey (CRSS) at several sites within the surrounding region reflect a disjunction between inland and coastal zones during the latter part of the Late Classic and into the Terminal Classic, with demographic expansion along the coastal margin. This shift was associated with changes in ceramic sphere affiliation and increasing participation in coastal trade networks.

I begin this chapter with a review of the archaeology of the Gulf Coast periphery of the Maya lowlands, and discuss influential theories about the role of local groups in larger-scale cultural dynamics. Next, I outline recent research undertaken by the CRSS along the central

Campeche coast. Data from settlement survey, ceramic analysis, and household test-excavations reflect major changes in the regional political landscape, in subsistence systems, and in long-distance trade networks. These data are examined within the context of broader cultural developments associated with the collapse of the inland polities of the southern Maya lowlands and the subsequent reorganization of economic and political systems during the Terminal Classic period. The sequence of events that unfolded in the Rio Champoton drainage provides insights regarding the nature of broader pan-Mesoamerican trends. These changes in regional economic systems were part of a general trend towards increasing long-distance trade and interaction that became fully manifested in the highly integrated and international economies of the Terminal Classic and Postclassic periods.

The Chontal Maya of the Gulf Coast

The ancient city of Chakanputun was located on the central coast of Campeche, near the northwestern periphery of the Maya area. This region, referred to here as the Peninsular Gulf Coast, includes the west coast of the Yucatan peninsula and the river deltas of coastal Tabasco. This area corresponds to the approximate geographic extent of the Chontal Maya language (Scholes and Roys 1968; Vargas Pacheco 2001), encompassing the coastal margin from central Campeche to the Rio Copilco, near the site of Comalcalco, and extending an unknown distance inland (Figures 6.7 and 7.4). Communities of the Peninsular Gulf Coast were strategically positioned near the major maritime trade route linking the Maya area with coastal Veracruz and highland Mexico. Several large rivers drain into the Gulf Coast between southern Campeche and Tabasco, and connected Gulf Coast polities with centers in the western Maya lowlands, the Maya highlands, the Peten, the edge of the Puuc region, and across the base of the Yucatan peninsula to the Caribbean. During the Postclassic and contact periods, mercantile cities such as Chakanputun, Potonchan, Xicalango, and Itzamkanac facilitated the movement of goods in a trans-isthmian network focused on the Gulf Coast maritime trade route (Ruz Lhuillier 1969; Scholes and Roys 1968; Vargas Pacheco 2001).

The ancient polities of the Peninsular Gulf Coast have long been portrayed as active agents in the collapse of large city-states in the southern Maya lowlands and the introduction of foreign and new material culture in the Terminal Classic and Postclassic periods (Adams 1973; Ball and Taschek 1989; Graham 1973; Ochoa and Vargas Pacheco 1980; Sabloff and Willey 1967; Thompson 1970). Gulf Coast peoples have been correlated with ethnic groups including the Putun (Thompson 1970), Itza (Andrews et al. 1988; Ball 1986; Kowalski 1989), and Chontal Maya (Fox 1987; Ochoa and Vargas Pacheco 1980; Scholes and Roys 1968; Vargas Pacheco 2001). These peoples have in turn been associated with the introduction of Mexican cultural traits into the Maya area, with purported roles ranging from outright military conquest (Adams 1973; Sabloff and Willey 1967; Thompson 1970) to opportunistic domination of maritime trade networks (Andrews et al. 1988; Freidel and Scarborough 1982; Kepecs et al. 1994). Such models have typically focused on the effects of militant coastal traders on economic systems in the central Maya lowlands and other regions outside their Gulf Coast homeland (see Ball and Taschek 1989; Fox 1987; McVicker 1985; Sabloff and Willey 1967; Thompson 1970).

Critics of these hypotheses have explained the emergence of foreign or new material culture styles as indigenous developments (Schele and Mathews 1998; Tourtellot and González 2004) or have highlighted contradictory ethnohistorical information (Kaplan 1998; Kremer 1994).

Although many older models are no longer widely accepted, the role played by Gulf Coast groups in the events of the Classic to Postclassic transition remains a topic of disciplinary interest. There is a general consensus that the frontier region between the Maya lowlands and central Mexico—including coastal zones of Campeche, Tabasco, and Veracruz—took on much greater pan-Mesoamerican significance during the Terminal Classic/Epiclassic period (Arnold III 1997; Ball 1977; Berlin 1956; Borenstein 2005; Curet et al. 1993; Ek and Rosado Ramírez 2005; Ensor 2003; Gallegos Gómora and Armijo Torres 2001; Inurreta Diaz 2004; Sisson 1976).

The Ancient Maya Polity of Chakanputun

The ancient city of Chakanputun is located beneath the modern city of Champoton, Campeche, at the mouth of the Rio Champoton. The Rio Champoton is the northernmost of the large rivers that drain into the Gulf Coast, and the only navigable waterway providing access into this portion of the Yucatan peninsula. This strategic geographical location provided opportunities for the control of both coastal trade and inland commercial traffic via the river and across the peninsula to the Caribbean. The physical landscape around Champoton also provides opportunities for a variety of subsistence strategies. The region includes highly productive maritime resource extraction zones along the coastal margin and adjacent estuary zones in the Rio Champoton (Collier 1964; Eaton 1978:26).

Prior to research conducted in the past decade, archaeological investigations in the Rio Champoton drainage were limited to coastal surveys. Ruz's (1969) study of the Campeche coast included surface collections and limited test pits near the modern city. A later reconnaissance of the entire north and west coasts of the Yucatan peninsula by Eaton (1978) revealed a pattern of coastal settlement in the Preclassic and Postclassic periods, with sparse Classic period occupation of the coastal margin (Ball 1978). Both of these studies documented a Postclassic—but no earlier—occupation at Champoton. Although these projects helped to elucidate general patterns of coastal settlement, there has been little ensuing research that builds upon these investigations. The focus on the coastal fringe, with limited inland research, perpetuated the view of Champoton as an exclusively Postclassic center.

More recent research along the central coast of Campeche has included salvage projects undertaken for the construction of the highway between Campeche and Champoton (Benavides Castillo 2003; Zapata 1997) and a large hotel complex south of Champoton (Anaya C. et al. 2009). These projects have documented a greater range of site types and occupational periods than the initial coastal surveys, with the densest occupations dating to the Preclassic and Classic periods. Nevertheless, the area between the city of Campeche and the Isthmus of Tehuantepec remains among the most poorly understood parts of Mesoamerica.

Recent investigations by the Proyecto Champoton, undertaken by William Folan and colleagues from the Universidad Autónoma de Campeche, have substantially refined our understanding of the prehispanic history of this ancient polity (see Folan et al. 2002; Folan et al. 2004; Forsyth and Jordan 2003). Folan's research consisted of excavations in several architectural complexes in the northern section of the modern city of Champoton, documenting occupations extending from the Middle Preclassic through the Late Postclassic periods. Investigation of the distribution of column drums and reutilized stones by members of Folan's project suggests that the monumental center of the ancient city of Chakanputun was located in the Barrio Pozo Monte, in the northeastern corner of the modern city (Folan et al.

2003). Of particular importance was the documentation of a large Late Preclassic platform, built in a unique megalithic architectural style (Chapter 5), which was extensively modified during the Postclassic period (see Folan et al. 2002; Folan et al. 2004; Forsyth and Jordan 2003).

The Champoton Regional Settlement Survey

Recent archaeological research in the Rio Champoton drainage by the CRSS has radically altered previous models of regional demographic, political, and economic processes (Ek 2006b, 2008, 2009a, 2009b, n.d.; Ek and Cruz Alvarado 2010; Ek and Rosado Ramírez 2004, 2005). The CRSS was initiated in collaboration with the Proyecto Champoton to provide a regional perspective complementing excavations in the modern city of Champoton. The CRSS was regional in scope, incorporating reconnaissance, intensive settlement survey, and test excavations. The first stage of the project consisted of reconnaissance of known sites within the municipio of Champoton and neighboring areas. The reconnaissance identified subordinate centers within the Champoton regional state that are known from ethnohistorical sources (Arnabar Gunam 2001; Molina Solís 1943, 1973), and located sites using information from local informants and aerial photographs. In total, thirteen prehispanic centers were located, investigated, and registered (Figure 6.1). Over the course of the reconnaissance, preliminary maps were produced for the central zones of each site, and surface collections were recovered allowing the construction of a rough regional chronology for the area.

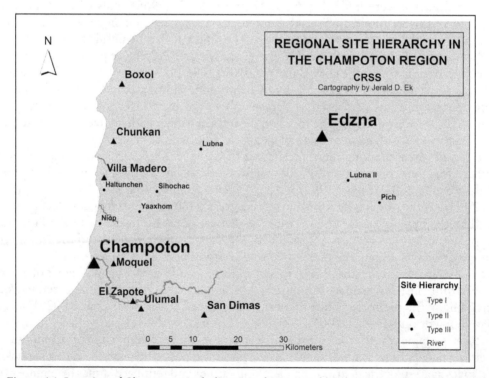

Figure 6.1. Location of Champoton including sites documented by this project during the initial regional reconnaissance and subsequent settlement survey within the Rio Champoton basin.

THE POLITICAL AND ECONOMIC ORGANIZATION OF LATE CLASSIC STATES

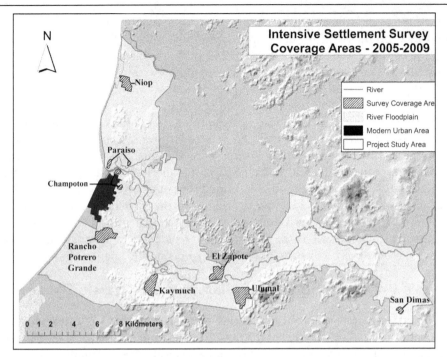

Figure 6.2. Project study area for the intensive settlement survey and testing phases of the project, including survey coverage for the seven zones selected for focused research.

The second phase of the project consisted of intensive settlement survey at seven sites identified in the regional reconnaissance. The project study area was restricted to the Rio Champoton drainage and the adjacent coastal margin. The seven sites selected for more intensive investigations included various intact parts of Chakanputun (surrounding modern Champoton and the town of Paraiso), Niop, Rancho Potrero Grande, Kaymuch, El Zapote, Ulumal, and San Dimas (Figure 6.1). These seven loci were selected for intensive mapping and testing because preliminary ceramic data indicated that their site chronologies spanned the Classic to Postclassic transition. Furthermore, these seven zones provide a good sample of the geographic and environmental diversity within the study area. The sample included peripheral settlement surrounding the ancient city of Chakanputun, two areas of dispersed settlement on the coastal margin (Rancho Potrero Grande and Niop), two large Late Classic centers located inland along the Rio Champoton (Ulumal and San Dimas), a small agrarian hamlet dating to the Postclassic period (Kaymuch), and a medium sized center dating to the Early Postclassic period (El Zapote).

Settlement survey consisted of full coverage mapping within large, contiguous zones, each measuring approximately one square kilometer in area (Figure 6.2). Mapping was undertaken using transits and survey-grade GPS equipment, and recorded all architecture, topography, and relevant cultural features within each of the seven sites. Exceptions to this method included San Dimas (where tape-and-compass mapping were more feasible because of dense vegetation and time constraints) and the area surrounding Champoton (where extensive destruction caused by modern construction allowed mapping in just four localized patches of relatively undisturbed terrain). Over the course of the project, a total of 7.2 square kilometers was intensively mapped within these seven survey zones. To complement data recovered during the regional reconnaissance and to provide a broader picture of occupational histories at each site, concentrations of artifacts on the surface were mapped with GPS units and surface collections were taken during the course of the survey. A total of 261 such collections were recovered, providing important information about occupational chronologies within different portions of each site.

The final phase of the CRSS project consisted of test excavations in residential contexts. The goal of these excavations was to locate and sample midden deposits located adjacent to residential structures. Individual structures were selected for testing using a two-step sampling method. First, large clusters of residential groups were identified from the maps of the seven areas subjected to intensive settlement survey. A random sample of these clusters was drawn to select areas for test excavations. Second, a stratified random sample (based on architectural volume) was drawn to select individual structures for testing. This ensured a representative sample of the status continuum at each of the seven sites. Excavation units consisted of one- by two-meter units, typically located on the peripheries of residential complexes. Data from these excavations were crucial for reconstructing patterns of economic change.

Demographic Processes during the Classic to Postclassic Transition

The results of the regional reconnaissance and settlement survey revealed evidence for demographic shifts and radical changes in the political landscape over two millennia of human occupation (Table 6.1). The earliest occupation in the region, called Champoton 1a, dates to the early Middle Preclassic period. Although the exact chronological placement of the Champoton 1a occupation is still under investigation, similarities in ceramic types with documented early complexes at other sites suggest that it was contemporary with some of the earliest sedentary communities currently known in the Maya Lowland (Ek n.d.). Population expansion took place during the late Middle Preclassic (Champoton 1b) and Late Preclassic (Champoton 2) periods. Ceramics dating to Champoton 1b belong to the Mamom sphere, and those dating to the Champoton 2 times are assigned to the Chicanel sphere. Populations within the region peaked during the Late Preclassic period, when nearly every site in the study area shows some evidence of occupation.

Table 6.1. Preliminary regional ceramic chronology developed during the course of the Champoton Regional Settlement Survey. Final designation of ceramic complexes will follow the chronological framework being developed by Donald Forsyth based on his analysis of ceramic materials excavated by the *Proyecto Champotón*.

Preliminary Complex	Period	Approximate Date
Champoton 8	Protohistoric	A.D. 1400–1550
Champoton 7b	Late Postclassic	A.D. 1250–1400
Champoton 7a	Early Postclassic	A.D. 1000–1250
Champoton 6	Terminal Classic	A.D. 800–1000
Champoton 5	Late Classic – Canbalam	A.D. 700–900
Champoton 4	Late Classic – Agua Potable	A.D. 550–750
Champoton 3	Early Classic	A.D. 250–550
Champoton 2	Late Preclassic	300 B.C.–A.D. 250
Champoton 1b	Late Middle Preclassic	600–300 B.C.
Champoton 1a	Early Middle Preclassic	1000/800–600 B.C.

THE POLITICAL AND ECONOMIC ORGANIZATION OF LATE CLASSIC STATES   149

Following a hiatus in construction at most sites during the Early Classic period (Champoton 3), a complex pattern of fluorescence, decline, and political reorganization characterized the Late Classic to Postclassic periods. Also characteristic of these centuries are rapidly shifting patterns of ceramic sphere affiliation, changes in regional economic systems, and changes in settlement patterns and political organization (Ek 2008, 2009a; Ek and Cruz Alvarado 2010; Ek and Rosado Ramírez 2005).

The Late Classic Period

Following a demographic boom in both coastal and inland areas during the Late Preclassic period (Champoton 2), occupation of the coastal margin declined dramatically (Figure 6.3). During the early part of the Late Classic period, settlement within the region was concentrated around the two inland centers of Ulumal and San Dimas. These centers differ from Preclassic sites in having clearly demarcated central zones with public architecture.

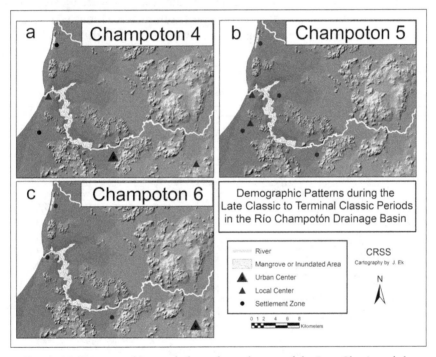

Figure 6.3. Demographic trends from the early part of the Late Classic and the Terminal Classic period (including the Champoton 4 to 6 ceramic complexes).

Ulumal is a medium-sized center located approximately 15 kilometers inland from the coast (Figure 6.4). The site center consists of three public plazas with an internal *sacbe* linking the central precinct to an elite residential group. The largest buildings at the site are built on a 2.5-meter high platform in the northern portion of the epicenter. This zone is characterized by restricted access, and includes the two largest temples and a large elite residential group. The south plaza area abuts the northern platform and includes a ballcourt and several range-type structures. A *sacbe* from the south plaza connects the site center with a smaller elite residential complex to the south. Settlement survey at Ulumal encompassed a total area of 1.7 square kilometers. Based on reconnaissance to the west and north of the site center, the mapped area represents approximately ten percent of the entire urban zone. Although initial development at Ulumal dates to the Late Preclassic period, our data suggest that the majority of construction seems to pertain to the early facet of the Late Classic Period (Champoton 4).

San Dimas is located near the south bank of the Rio Champoton, 35 kilometers inland from coast. Although mapping at San Dimas was limited to the central precinct, our data suggest that the site is larger than Ulumal in both population and scale of monumental architecture (Figure 6.5). The site center consists of two principal public groups connected by a *sacbe* or ramp. The main public plaza consists of several temples and range structures. A second public plaza is located on what is likely a heavily modified natural hill. Construction of this plaza included expansion of the natural slope of the hill into a truncated pyramid that supported ten superstructures. The slope of the hilltop plaza is terraced, and is connected to the lower plaza by a very large *sacbe* that extends up the hill. This may include a monumental staircase near the upper part of the plaza. Several substantial elite residential complexes are located to the south and west of the two principal plazas. Although excavations at San Dimas were more limited than at Ulumal, data from surface collections and excavations suggest that initial development of the site center started in the late Middle Preclassic period (Champoton 1b), and that the apogee of the site dates to the latter part of the Late Classic and Terminal Classic (Champoton 6).

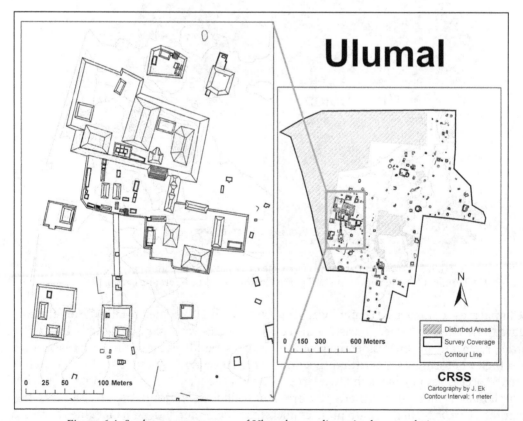

Figure 6.4. Settlement survey map of Ulumal, a medium-sized center dating to the early facet of the Late Classic period.

Figure 6.5. Preliminary map of the central zone of the site of San Dimas, located approximately 30 kilometers inland from the mouth of the Rio Champoton. San Dimas is the largest civic-ceremonial center documented during the course of the Champoton Regional Settlement Survey.

In comparison to the decentralized, dispersed settlement that characterized Late Preclassic settlement patterns, the Late Classic political landscape of the Rio Champoton basin was clearly much more centralized (Figure 6.3). Both Ulumal and San Dimas had large, concentrated populations. With the exception of two small settlements at Champoton and Niop, the widespread, dispersed settlement pattern in coastal zones that characterized the Preclassic period is absent during the Late Classic. The precise nature of the political hierarchy during the Classic period is still far from clear. Important unresolved questions concern the relationship between the two cities of Ulumal and San Dimas. Ceramic evidence suggests that the sites overlap chronologically, although San Dimas shows stronger ceramic links with sites in the Chenes region that date to the Terminal Classic period. Ceramics, particularly during the Champoton 4 phase, reflect strong similarities with the larger polity of Edzna, perhaps indicating the area was subsumed beneath the political hegemony of that center. The nature of links between Ulumal and San Dimas with more distant centers—especially with Edzna—is an important topic for future research.

The Terminal Classic Period

During the Terminal Classic period, Ulumal fell into decline and was abandoned. In contrast, San Dimas reoriented itself politically and economically with the Chenes region to the east. Terminal Classic occupations of coastal zones expanded greatly, and many Preclassic mounds at Niop, Rancho Potrero Grande, Moquel, and Champoton were reoccupied. Nevertheless, as in the Late Preclassic period, the pattern of coastal settlement was highly dispersed.

Two possible Terminal Classic seats of power along the coast are near the city of Champoton and at the site of Moquel. Unfortunately, historical and modern construction has largely erased evidence of Classic occupation in Champoton. Nevertheless, excavations by the Proyecto Champoton and the CRSS have documented substantial evidence of Terminal Classic materials near the northeastern limits of the modern city, including a few substantial intact mounds (Ek 2006a, 2008, 2009a; Folan et al. 2002; Folan et al. 2004; Forsyth and Jordan 2003).

A similar pattern has been documented at the site of Moquel, located along the northern banks of the Rio Champoton. As at Champoton, modern construction has greatly impacted the prehispanic architecture at Moquel. A large structure in the central part of the modern town of Moquel has a chronology similar to that of Champoton, with substantial Preclassic occupation and later reoccupation dating to the Terminal Classic (Folan et al. 2003; Forsyth and Jordan 2003). It is possible that Moquel and Champoton were seats of power during the Terminal Classic period, prior to the centralization of populations and political power at Chakanputun during the ensuing Postclassic period (Ek 2008, 2009a; Ek and Rosado Ramírez 2005). In fact, it is likely that Champoton began its ascent to regional dominance at this time, a trend that would continue into the Postclassic period.

Beyond Champoton and Moquel, settlement is extensive and dispersed, mirroring the settlement pattern that existed during the Late Preclassic period. Near the site of Niop, located along the coastal margin north of Champoton, there is evidence of a large zone with relatively dispersed settlement. The area seems to lack a notable center. Instead, settlement consists of multiple clusters of residential groups, often surrounding larger residential platforms and a few small, possibly public complexes. Settlement survey at Niop covered a total area of 85 hectares adjacent to the hacienda. Reconnaissance beyond the surveyed zone revealed continuous occupation over a zone of at least three square kilometers.

The same pattern was identified at Rancho Potrero Grande, located south of Champoton between the coastal margin and the floodplain of the Rio Champoton. As at Niop, there is evidence that Preclassic platforms were reoccupied during the Terminal Classic period. A total area of 1.47 square kilometers was intensively surveyed at Rancho Potrero Grande. Architecture ranged from very low platforms to some buildings up to three meters high. Some structures were grouped into small clusters, with four groups consisting of more elaborate and possibly public architecture. Like Niop, Rancho Potrero Grande lacks a central precinct and any large monumental public architecture.

The settlement pattern discussed here is consistent with other data gathered during regional reconnaissance. To the north of Champoton, centers such as Villa Madero and Chuncan rose to political power in the Terminal Classic period (Ek and Rosado Ramírez 2004). This shift was accompanied by a general reorientation of settlement patterns along coastal zones (see also Benavides Castillo 2003; Zapata 1997). As in the Late Preclassic, both settlement patterns and artifact assemblages reflect heavy reliance on marine food resources.

The following sections examine in greater detail the complex patterns of ceramic sphere affiliation observed for different sites in the CRSS project area, and discuss what they imply regarding political and economic systems.

Late to Terminal Classic Ceramic Chronology and Sphere Affiliation

Ceramic collections from 13 sites studied by the CRSS have been analyzed and categorized according to the Type-Variety system. Studied materials were recovered from 261 surface collections and 99 test excavations. The framework for this preliminary analysis is derived from the more comprehensive ceramic chronology developed by Donald Forsyth of Brigham Young University for materials excavated by the Proyecto Champoton (Forsyth 2004, 2008; Forsyth and Jordan 2003). Final classification of types, varieties, phases, and spheres will follow conclusions yet to be published in Forsyth's ceramic chronology of Champoton. Nevertheless, currently available data provide valuable information about Terminal Classic economic and social processes in the region.

Provisional phase designations have been created over the course of ceramic analysis to provide preliminary chronological units for the study of diachronic processes (Table 6.1). Ceramics dating to the Late and Terminal Classic periods in Champoton have been subdivided into three spatio-temporal categories, termed Champoton 4, Champoton 5, and Champoton 6 (Ek and Cruz Alvarado 2010). Their precise chronological placement and degree of overlap are complicated and a subject of continuing research.

Champoton 4

The Champoton 4 ceramic complex demonstrates strong similarities with the contemporary Agua Potable complex from the site of Edzna (Forsyth 1983). The primary ceramic components in this complex are the Charote, Tonanche, Carpizo, and Cambio groups, and several polychrome types also are common (Figure 6.6). Both typological and modal similarities link Champoton 4 and Agua Potable ceramics with contemporary assemblages in the Chenes and Peten regions of southeastern Campeche and further east into the central Maya lowlands (Forsyth 1983). Although we have no radiometric dates for the complex at Champoton, the closely related Agua Potable complex at Edzna has been dated by Forsyth (1983) to the relatively restricted time period of A.D. 600–700.

Champoton 4 materials form a major component of the ceramics recovered from Ulumal and San Dimas. Unmixed Champoton 4 deposits were also identified in some excavations at Niop, although in much lower frequencies than at the inland sites. Similarities in the ceramic inventories of Ulumal, San Dimas, and Edzna are most likely the result of trade and interaction focused on the riverine route along the Rio Champoton extending from the coast into the interior.

Champoton 5

The Champoton 5 complex represents a dramatic break in ceramic links with inland areas. This complex is part of the coastal Canbalam ceramic sphere, which was first proposed by Joseph Ball (1978:134) and refined considerably by Socorro Jiménez Álvarez at Xcambo (Jiménez Álvarez et al. 2006; Jiménez Álvarez 2002; Jiménez et al. 2000). At that site, the Xcambo complex—dating to A.D. 550–700—contains both Canbalam-sphere and Cehpech-sphere ceramic types. The spatial distribution of the Canbalam sphere is geographically restricted to

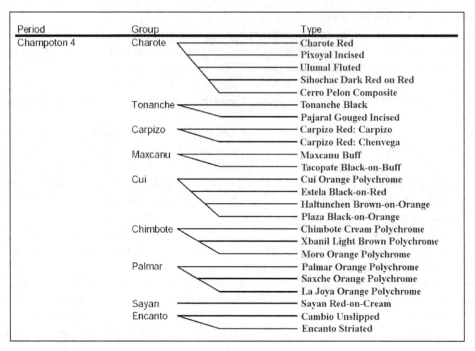

Figure 6.6. Component types within the Champoton 4 ceramic complex.

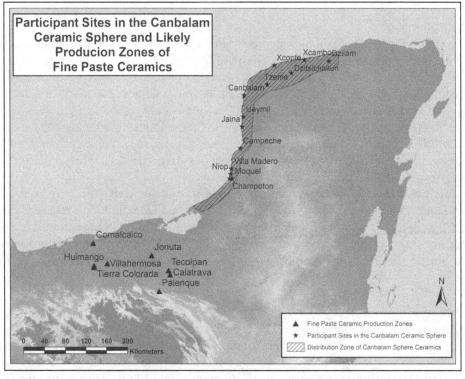

Figure 6.7. The spatial distribution of the Canbalam ceramic sphere and identified loci of production of fine paste wares. Note the coastal distribution of the Canbalam sphere, centered on the Gulf Coast maritime trade route.

the western and northwestern coasts of the Yucatan peninsula, extending along the Peninsular Gulf Coast from Laguna de Terminos to Bocas de Dzilam, Yucatan (Figure 6.7; Ball 1978; Jiménez Álvarez et al. 2006; Jiménez Álvarez 2002; Jiménez et al. 2000; Robles Castellanos and Andrews 2000).

Important components of the Champoton 5 complex include the Nimun, Baca, Tenabo, Chablekal, and Dzitbalche groups (Figure 6.8). Fine paste wares make their first appearance in the Champoton ceramic assemblage at this time, including an early variety of Chablekal Fine Grey (Jiménez Álvarez et al. 2006), Dzitbalche/Isla Fina Fine Buff, Balancan/Altar Fine Orange, Tsicul Fine Black, and Huimanguillo Fine Brown. Several types within the Champoton 5 complex share strong modal similarities—including vessel forms and decorative motifs—with ceramics manufactured in the plains of Tabasco and along the Rio Coatzacoalcos in Veracruz (Coe and Diehl 1980:Figures 195 and 196; Jiménez Álvarez et al. 2006:504-505). Furthermore, the Dzitbalche/Isla Fina group likely represents an important import ware produced in Veracruz (Jiménez Álvarez et al. 2006).

The spatial distribution of Champoton 5 ceramics within the project study areas is restricted largely to the coastal margin. Sites with substantial quantities of Champoton 5 materials include Champoton and Niop. The appearance of Champoton 5 ceramics is associated with the demographic movement to the coast, which consisted of the re-occupation of many Preclassic mounds at Niop, Rancho Potrero Grande, Moquel, and Champoton. In contrast to the coast, Canbalam sphere ceramics are uncommon to rare at inland sites. At Ulumal, the few areas within the site that had materials pertaining to post-Champoton 4 phases had only modest quantities of Canbalam ceramics. Canbalam ceramics are almost entirely absent at San Dimas. These data reflect a clear distance decay pattern, with Champoton 5 materials becoming less frequent as one moves inland from the coast.

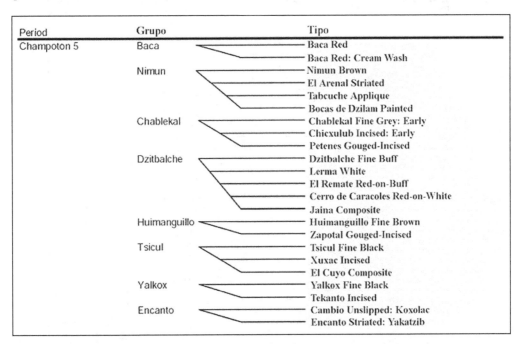

Figure 6.8. Component types within the Champoton 5 ceramic complex.

In general, the Champoton 5 phase reflects a radical reorientation to the Gulf Coast in terms of demography, direction of cultural influence, norms of ceramic production, trade networks, and economic organization (Ek 2009a; Ek and Cruz Alvarado 2010). Ceramic links with Edzna and other inland centers reduced dramatically, evidenced particularly in the rarity of Cehpech sphere ceramics common in eastern Campeche, the Puuc hills, and the northern plains of Yucatan. Furthermore, non-local trade wares, particularly fine paste ceramics, became a major component of the ceramic assemblage for the first time during this period. Fine paste groups produced in the lower Usumacinta region of Tabasco and as far as southern Veracruz are found in high frequencies and within a wide range of contexts, indicating increasing long-distance exchange of ceramics. The quantity of fine past wares in the serving vessel sub-assemblage at Champoton continued to increase through the Terminal Classic and into the Postclassic period (Bishop et al. 2006; Ek and Cruz Alvarado 2010; Forsyth 2004).

Champoton 6

In contrast to Champoton 5, the Champoton 6 ceramic complex reflects continuity in links between sites in the Rio Champoton drainage, Edzna, and the Chenes region. Champoton 6 shares many types with the Muralla complex of Edzna (Figure 6.9). Component ceramic groups in this complex include Ticul Thin Slate, Chablekal Fine Grey, Hontun Grey, Acapulquito Unslipped, and unnamed slate and red ware groups with strong modal similarities with materials from the Chenes region. This range of ceramic groups reflects at least peripheral participation in the Cehpech sphere, with closest modal similarities to western Cehpech materials (Ek and Cruz Alvarado 2010).

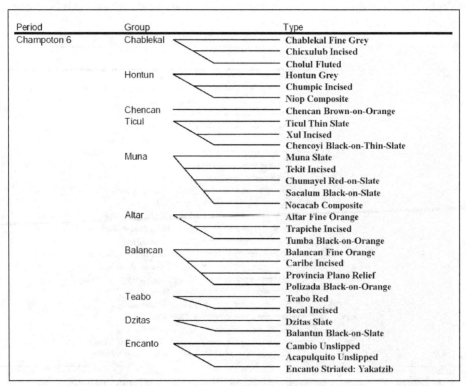

Figure 6.9. Component types within the Champoton 6 ceramic complex.

The main departure from the contemporary Muralla complex at Edzna is the relative rarity of slate and red wares pertaining to the Muna and Teabo groups. The only exception to this is Ticul Thin Slate, which appears to be a trade ware within the Champoton 6 complex. Local versions of slate and red wares appear in relatively low frequencies. These materials likely pertain to previously undefined ceramic groups, and share some similarities with types documented in the Chenes region. In other areas of the Champoton region, fine paste ceramics seem to fill the niche of favored serving wares beginning in the Terminal Classic period. Indeed, as Forsyth (2004) has pointed out, the prevalence of fine paste wares (instead of monochrome redwares) in the serving ware sub-assemblage is one of the defining characteristics of late ceramic assemblages in the Champoton region through the Postclassic period.

Champoton 6 ceramics are found in significant quantities at San Dimas. Beyond this site, the overall frequency of such materials is low. At coastal sites such as Champoton and Niop, I often found Champoton 6 materials mixed with Champoton 5 ceramics, making it difficult to define two distinct temporal phases. These mixed contexts could represent a late facet of the Terminal Classic period when Canbalam sphere ceramics were still in use. At inland sites, Champoton 6 is more prevent and easily defined. An important distinction between Champoton 5 and 6, assuming some degree of chronological overlap, is the marked absence of significant quantities of Fine Orange wares, later forms of Chablekal Fine Grey, and Isla Fina Fine Buff in Champoton 6 assemblages. These trade wares were moved along the Gulf Coast trade route during the Terminal Classic period (Jiménez Álvarez et al. 2006; Jiménez et al. 2000; Robles Castellanos and Andrews 2000). The ceramic assemblage from San Dimas demonstrates that this site was clearly excluded from such a coastal network where these kinds of pottery were exchanged.

Chronological Overlap

Understanding the degree of temporal overlap between the Champoton 4, 5, and 6 complexes has been complicated by a variety of factors. At Niop, contexts with high frequencies of Canbalam sphere materials were found intermixed with Champoton 6 ceramics pertaining to the Cehpech sphere in later levels, and with Champoton 4 types in earlier deposits (Ek and Cruz Alvarado 2010). The degree of chronological overlap is far less notable at inland sites, such as Ulumal and San Dimas, where Canbalam sphere materials are less frequent. Nevertheless, we found Champoton 4 and Champoton 6 materials in mixed contexts, mirroring a pattern documented in the contemporary transition between the Agua Potable and Muralla complexes at Edzna (Forsyth 1983).

The long span of most ceramic phases established in the Maya area and the lack of radiometric dates for pertinent archaeological contexts at Champoton have complicated attempts to understand the exact period of use of Canbalam types or the degree of overlap with earlier and later complexes. Canbalam sphere ceramics at Xcambo are restricted to the early Late Classic Xcambo complex (Jiménez Álvarez 2002). This overlaps with the Agua Potable complex of Edzna (Forsyth 1983:220). Sites along the northwest corner of the Yucatan peninsula investigated by the Proyecto Costa Maya have Canbalam sphere ceramics that are tentatively dated to the period between A.D. 600–900 (Andrews and Robles Castellanos 2004; Robles Castellanos and Andrews 2000, 2004; Robles Castellanos and Ceballos Gallareta 2002), which overlaps with both the Agua Potable and Muralla complexes at Edzna (Forsyth 1983:220).

Although we do not have chronometric dates for the best stratigraphic sequences relevant to the issue of the chronological placement of Champoton 4, 5, and 6, contextual data from coastal sites provide clues about the temporal ordering of the three complexes. It is possible that the appearance of Canbalam pottery was quite limited in time. Thus, Champoton 5 could represent a transitional facet between Champoton 4 and 6. To reiterate, one of the most important aspects of the appearance of Canbalam ceramics is not chronological but is spatial in character—Champoton 5 pottery has a limited distribution focused along the coastal margin.

Ceramics, Political Boundaries, and Economic Systems

The spatial distribution of Canbalam ceramics has clear implications for understanding the nature of coastal trade routes dating to the latter part of the Late Classic period. Champoton 5 marks a notable break with earlier ceramic traditions in the region, which were characterized by strong links to Edzna and the interior Maya lowlands. The decrease in Canbalam sphere ceramics with distance from the coast, and the ceramic links between San Dimas and the Chenes region during the Terminal Classic could reflect the establishment of a political boundary somewhere between the middle and upper reaches of the Rio Champoton. Clearly, economic systems linking inland and coastal zones were not as integrated as during earlier periods. This is quite striking, because the Rio Champoton would have provided an excellent avenue for the movement of canoe-borne commercial traffic extending inland as far as Edzna. Instead, the distribution of Canbalam ceramics suggests that imported pottery—and even shared norms of ceramic production—did not penetrate far inland during this time.

Ceramic groups—particularly those within the serving vessel sub-assemblages of the Champoton 4, 5, and 6 complexes—also are important for understanding the fundamental changes in production and distribution of status-linked pottery during the Late and Terminal Classic periods. The most elaborate serving vessels in the Champoton 4 complex consist of painted polychrome vessels of the Palmar, Saxche, Cui, and Chimbote groups. During the beginning of the Late Classic, polychrome ceramics had a restricted distribution reflecting elite control of production and distribution. Thus, the specialized skill and esoteric knowledge materialized within locally produced polychrome pottery imbued these items with social value.

During Champoton 5 times, fine paste wares replaced polychrome ceramics as the dominant serving ware sub-assemblage. The replacement of polychromes with fine paste wares represents a fundamental change in the characteristics by which consumers assigned social value to status-linked pottery. The exclusivity of fine paste ceramics was embedded in their unmistakably non-local origins. Compositional analyses of fine paste ceramics from Champoton and other sites in and beyond the Maya area have allowed the identification of production zones for fine paste wares in the lower Usumacinta, Laguna de Terminos, coastal Tabasco, and Veracruz regions (Bishop 2003; Bishop et al. 2008; Bishop et al. 2006; Forsyth 2004). Because of the unique properties and limited distribution of clays used in the production of fine paste ceramics, such pottery would have been clearly recognizable to consumers as exotic items. Thus, the shift from the locally produced polychrome pottery of Champoton 4 to the imported fine paste wares of the Canbalam sphere reflects a change in the procurement of status-linked ceramics. During Champoton 4 times, such pottery was made by specialists attached to local elites, but during Champoton 5 times status-linked pottery used in coastal zones was obtained through international trade.

Evidence from lithic debitage and tools also reflects the important role of interregional trade in local economic systems during the Late and Terminal Classic periods (Ek and Ferguson

2011). Tool assemblages at most sites demonstrate extensive recycling, indicating the scarcity of lithic resources within the local region. Coarse-grained chert tools were produced at San Dimas, but at all other sites both tools and debitage consist predominantly of fine-grained cherts and chalcedonies. Debitage at these other sites includes very low quantities of primary and secondary reduction flakes. Instead, final stage reduction, resharpening, and recycling flakes are more common. These data demonstrate an extreme degree of concern among consumers to conserve material to the greatest degree possible, with a high degree of efficiency evident in consumption patterns. This is most likely the result of a lack of local chert resources and reliance on interregional trade networks for the acquisition of lithic tools (Ek and Ferguson 2011).

There is a clear correlation between the demographic shifts outlined in this chapter and changes in the direction and nature of interregional exchange networks. During the early part of the Late Classic period (Champoton 4), trade was largely regional in scope and focused on the Rio Champoton. There were strong ceramic similarities between the small coastal settlement of Niop, Ulumal, San Dimas, and the large city of Edzna. In contrast, evidence for long-distance trade dating to this period is not abundant.

With the demographic movement to coastal settlement and the introduction of Canbalam sphere ceramics, exchange systems expanded in scale and shifted to long-distance networks focused on coastal trade routes. Evidence of long-distance exchange increased dramatically at coastal sites such as Champoton and Niop, with imported ceramics and increased quantities of obsidian reflecting increased access to exotic goods. These various sources of data reflect a shift to increasing mercantilism and participation in long-distance coastal trade that would grow even more during the Postclassic period.

These changes in interregional exchange networks immediately preceded the rise of Chakanputun as the dominant urban center in the region. Although how this center rose to regional supremacy is not currently clear, it seems likely that centralization of populations near the modern city of Champoton began during the Terminal Classic and continued in the Early Postclassic period. By the Late Postclassic, after the decline and abandonment of the site of El Zapote, Chakanputun dominated the political landscape in the Champoton drainage basin (Ek 2008, 2011). Throughout the Postclassic period, long-distance trade played an important role in the local economy.

Subsistence Economy

The series of transformations that took place between Champoton 4 and Champoton 6 are also correlated with fundamental changes in the subsistence economy. These changes include a shift from agricultural staples to a reliance on marine resources. This process is apparent in lithic tools, settlement patterns, and shell and faunal collections from household middens (Ek 2009a; Ek and Ferguson 2011).

The demographic patterns outlined here provide some evidence of how the locations of sites were chosen. Ulumal and San Dimas are both located in inland areas near large expansive low-lying areas. Both sites are situated on ecotones, in both cases at the boundary between low-lying terrain near the river floodplain and hilly upland areas. Such areas would be highly favorable for agriculture.

In contrast, sites with Champoton 5 occupations are located adjacent to the coastal margin. Soils in this area are generally thin and poorly suited for agriculture. Nonetheless, communities like Niop and Champoton were strategically located adjacent to the productive marine extraction zones of the coastal margin and estuary of the Rio Champoton. Because of shallow waters and nutrient enrichment from river discharge into the Gulf, the coastal margin provides abundant opportunities for food production (Collier 1964; Ek 2008, 2009a; Lange 1971).

Artifact assemblages from inland and coastal sites reflect these different food-production strategies. At the site of Niop, test excavations adjacent to 23 residential structures indicate intensive marine resource exploitation during all periods of occupation. Middens at Niop yielded large quantities of marine shell, with many platforms seeming to specialize in specific species (Ek 2009a). These dense sheet middens likely represent the remains of the specialized gathering and processing of food for local exchange. Areas adjacent to the Rio Champoton—particularly at Champoton, Paraiso, and Rancho Potrero Grande—yielded high frequencies of riverine food resources, especially oysters. Although it is likely that agriculture also provided a significant contribution to the local subsistence economy, it is clear that marine and riverine food resources were major staples in coastal areas. In contrast, even though Ulumal and San Dimas are both located close to the upper reaches of the Rio Champoton, shell and fish bones are very rare in midden deposits at these two sites.

Stone tools also indicate major differences in food-production practices. Lithic tool assemblages at Ulumal and San Dimas reflect a subsistence strategy focused on agricultural food production. The most common tool types at these two centers include oval and general utility bifaces, both of which are associated with agricultural tasks (Ek and Ferguson 2011). Far fewer of these tool types are encountered at sites located on the coast (Ek 2009a; Ek and Ferguson 2011).

Coastal lithic tool assemblages include very few tools overall, with modest numbers of thin bifaces, stemmed blades, prismatic blades, and projectile points (Ek and Ferguson 2011). However, artifact assemblages from coastal sites include high frequencies of net weights. Two types of net weights are ubiquitous in Late and Terminal Classic deposits. The more common form is a notched ceramic sherd likely used with fishing lines (Figure 6.10; Ek 2009a; Ek and Ferguson 2011). Larger and heavier groundstone weights, most likely used to submerge nets, also are common. These important differences in tool assemblages between coastal and inland zones are consistent with the settlement pattern data outlined above, reflecting very different subsistence strategies. Inland communities focused primarily on the production of agricultural staples, while coastal communities focused predominantly on marine and riverine food resources.

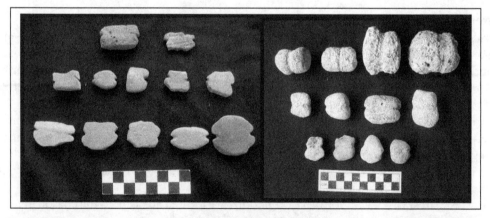

Figure 6.10. Examples of two types of fishing weights commonly encountered in midden deposits at coastal sites. It is likely that the larger, pecked limestone weights were used to sink nets, while the smaller notched ceramic sherds were used to weight fishing lines.

Conclusions

The demographic, political, and economic processes that took place in the Rio Champoton drainage provide a case study for understanding the broader cultural dynamics that characterized the Classic to Postclassic transition. While the large Late Classic cities located in the Central Maya lowlands fell into political decline and abandonment, Gulf Coast states flourished within the new economic systems of the Terminal Classic period. The mechanisms through which the ancient peoples of Champoton weathered political and economic turmoil include reorganizations of settlement, subsistence systems, trade networks, and political hierarchy.

The demographic shift from large inland centers like Ulumal and San Dimas to coastal sites that began at the end of the Late Classic period was part of a radical change in settlement ecology. This process is associated with a notable change in food production, that is, a shift from agriculture to a greater reliance on marine and riverine resources. This process is reflected in settlement patterns, tool assemblages, and midden deposits from household contexts.

It is important to note that these shifts occurred during a period of climatic change and increasing drought that has been documented by a growing body of research undertaken in the past decades. Paleoclimatic studies have found evidence of a shift to dryer and warmer conditions, with increasing frequencies of one- to two-year droughts starting during the eighth century A.D. (Brenner et al. 2001; Curtis et al. 1996; Curtis et al. 1998; Folan et al. 1983; Gunn and Adams 1981; Hodell et al. 1995, 2001; Leyden et al. 1996; Whitmore et al. 1996). Such unpredictable droughts would have had negative effects on food-production systems based on traditional Maya agriculture.

In the Champoton region, an important response to climatic change appears to have been the diversification of subsistence and an increased reliance on marine resources. It is clear that marine resources were a dietary mainstay among coastal groups at Spanish contact, and the increased settlement density in these zones could reflect the spread of coastal communities that adopted this subsistence strategy during the Terminal Classic period.

The shift to coastal zones evident at Champoton is part of a generalized demographic pattern in western Yucatan and the Gulf Coast periphery, extending beyond the Maya lowlands. Dramatic population increases occurred in southern Veracruz between A.D. 700 and 1000, and populations shifted from inland settlements to coastal areas (Borenstein 2005; Killion and Urcid 2001:19). There also was an influx of peoples to coastal zones in the Chontalpa of Tabasco (Berlin 1953, 1956; Ensor 2003; Gallegos Gómora and Armijo Torres 2001; Peniche Rivero 1973) and the Laguna de Terminos region (Jiménez Valdez 1987; Matheny 1970; Ruz Lhuillier 1969). A similar pattern has been noted along the Peninsular Gulf Coast at Uaymil (Cobos et al. 2006; Inurreta Diaz 2004), Jaina (Benavides Castillo 2002; Pina Chan 1968; Ruz Lhuillier 1969), and the central Campeche coast (Eaton and Ball 1978; Ek 2006a, 2008, 2009a; Rivera et al. 1982; Robles Castellanos and Andrews 2000; Zapata 1997). Increases in coastal populations also occurred at this time in northwestern and northern Yucatan (Andrews et al. 1988; Gallareta Negrón et al. 1989; Jiménez Álvarez et al. 2006; Jiménez et al. 2000; Kepecs 1999, 2003), and even as far as the Caribbean coast (Joyce 1991; Masson 2000, 2003; McKillop 1996). Beyond coastal zones, research along the Candelaria River (Vargas Pacheco 1994, 1998, 2001) and across the base of the Yucatan peninsula indicates that location on inland trade routes, particularly along rivers, became a major factor determining settlement

(Alexander 2000; Alexander and Canché Manzanero 2005; Chase and Chase 1982; Hammond 1983).

This demographic movement to the coast was associated with fundamental alterations in the direction, nature, and extent of interregional and long-distance exchange networks. Late Classic trade in the Champoton region appears to have been largely regional in scale and focused on the Rio Champoton. Canal systems documented at Edzna (Andrews 1984; Benavides Castillo 1994, 1997, 2003; Matheny 1986) likely linked the city with the upper reaches of the Rio Champoton, facilitating the movement of both goods and people between Edzna and the Gulf of Mexico via San Dimas and Ulumal. Strong ceramic similarities between Late Classic materials at Ulumal and the contemporary Agua Potable complex at Edzna (Forsyth 1983) reflect this interaction (see Ek 2009a, 2010; Ek and Cruz Alvarado 2010). Evidence of long-distance trade at this time is limited. Instead, we have documented the movement of goods and limited trade in polychrome pottery within a regional interaction network. This small-scale, river-focused trade network is consistent with a bounded solar market system administered through the city of Edzna (Smith 1976).

During the Terminal Classic period, exchange systems expanded in scale and shifted to long-distance networks focused on coastal trade routes (Ek 2009a). Evidence of long-distance exchange increased dramatically at sites on the coast such as Niop and Champoton, reflecting increased access to exotic goods. Ceramic links with Edzna greatly diminished, and types belonging to the coastal Canbalam ceramic sphere came to replace regionally produced high-status pottery. These include imported fine paste ceramics produced in the middle and lower Usumacinta region, Tabasco, and Veracruz (Bishop et al. 2006; Ek 2009a, 2009b). Access to obsidian and other exotic goods also increased during this period. These data demonstrate a shift to increasing mercantilism and participation in long-distance coastal trade that would continue during the Postclassic period.

Changes seen in the ceramics of the Champoton region are common at coastal trade centers dating to the Terminal Classic. Sites that participated in the Canbalam ceramic sphere—between Bocas de Dzilam and Laguna de Terminos—show a dramatic increase in connections with distant areas (Jiménez Álvarez 2002; Jiménez Álvarez et al. 2006; Robles Castellanos and Andrews 2000, 2004). These links extended across coastal zones in the Maya area to coastal Veracruz and are just now being examined in detail (Jiménez Álvarez 2002; Jiménez Álvarez et al., 2000, 2006). Among the most striking aspects of the Canbalam phenomenon is the increase in ceramic diversity found at participating polities.

During the Terminal Classic/Epiclassic period and across Mesoamerica, there was a shift from the exchange of low-bulk, high-value items to the movement of bulk goods via maritime trade routes (Andrews 1983, 1990; Berdan et al. 2003; Dahlin and Ardren 2002; Kepecs et al. 1994; West 2002). This, in turn, reflected a general pan-Mesoamerican pattern of increasing commercialism, interregional exchange, and the strengthening of ties among previously disparate parts of Mesoamerica (see Andrews and Sabloff 1986; Berlo and Diehl 1989; Braswell 2003; Freidel and Sabloff 1984; Masson 2000; Masson et al. 2006; Milbrath and Peraza Lope 2003; Sabloff and Rathje 1975; Smith and Berdan 2003). The data from the Champoton region are consistent with broader evidence for increasing interaction during this fascinating period in Mesoamerican history.

Acknowledgments

I would like to thank the Consejo de Arqueología of the Instituto Nacional de Antropología e Historia, the Centro INAH Campeche, William Folan, Lynda Florey Folan, Marilyn Masson, Donald Forsyth, Josalyn Ferguson, José Antonio Hernández Trujeque, Geoff Braswell, Roberto Rosado Ramírez, Michael E. Smith, Tomas Arnabar Gunam, Felix Arcoha Gómez, Elizabeth Graham, and the Centro de Investigaciones Históricas y Sociales of the Universidad Autónoma de Campeche for assistance and support during the various phases of the Champoton Regional Settlement Survey. I would like to thank William Folan, Lynda Florey Folan, and José Antonio Hernández Trujeque for their assistance and support while undertaking fieldwork in Champoton. Without their help, this project would not have been possible. Finally, I would like to thank Marilyn Masson for her guidance and feedback during all phases of this project. The Champoton Regional Settlement Survey was funded by grants from SUNY Albany, the Foundation for the Advancement of Mesoamerican Studies, the IIE Fulbright Program, the Institute for Mesoamerican Studies, and the National Science Foundation.

Note

1. The term "Chakanputun," as employed in this paper, refers to both the contact period city and the area subject to it as documented by several Spanish chroniclers during the sixteenth century. The seat of the Chakanputun polity is widely believed to correspond to the modern city of Champoton, located on the central Campeche coast at the mouth of the Rio Champoton (Arnabar Gunam 2001; Eaton and Ball 1978; Folan et al. 2002, 2004; Roys 1957; Ruz Lhuillier 1969). The ancient city of Chakanputun has been largely destroyed by continuous occupation from colonial times to the present. Given the degree of destruction of the ancient capital city and the various accounts of prehispanic migrations associated with Chakanputun that are outlined in the books of Chilam Balam, it is difficult to know if this polity existed before the Postclassic period. Thus, in this chapter, Chakanputun refers specifically to the Postclassic polity.

References

Adams, Richard E. W. 1973. Maya Collapse: Transformation and Termination in the Ceramic Sequence at Altar de Sacrificios. In Culbert 1973:133-163.

Alexander, Rani T. 2000. Patrones de asentamiento agregados en el sudoeste de Campeche: Una visión desde la Isla Cilvituk. *Mesoámerica* 39:359-391.

Alexander, Rani T., and Elena Canché Manzanero. 2005. Isla Cilvituk y las redes de comercio en el suroeste de Campeche. In *Memorias del Primer Congreso Internacional de Cultura Maya: En honor de Alfredo Barrera Vásquez y George Andrews*, edited by Alfredo Barrera Rubio and Ruth Gubler, pp. 617-637. Centro INAH Yucatan, Merida.

Anaya C., Augustín, Heber Ojeda M., David Salazar A., Adriana Sánchez L., and Vicente Suarez Aguilar. 2009. Características de los Sitios Costeros Periféricos de Champotón, Campeche. In *XXII Simposio de Investigaciones Arqueológicas en Guatemala, 2008*, vol. 2, edited by Juan Pedro Laporte, Bárbara Arroyo, and Héctor E. Mejía, pp. 755-771. Museo Nacional de Arqueología e Etnologia, Guatemala City.

Andrews, Anthony P. 1983. *Maya Salt Production and Trade*. University of Arizona, Tucson.

— 1990. The Role of Trading Ports in Maya Civilization. In *Vision and Revision in Maya Studies*, edited by Flora S. Clancy and Peter D. Harrison, pp. 159-167. University of New Mexico, Albuquerque.

Andrews, Anthony P., Tomas Gallareta Negron, Fernando Robles Castellanos, Rafael Cobos, and Pura Cervera R. 1988. Isla Cerritos: An Itzá Trading Port on the North Coast of Yucatan, Mexico. *National Geographic Research* 4:196-207.

Andrews, Anthony P., and Fernando Robles Castellanos. 2004. An Archaeological Survey of Northwest Yucatan, Mexico. *Mexicon* 26:7-14.

Andrews, George F. 1984. *Edzna, Campeche, Mexico: Settlement Patterns and Monumental Architecture.* Foundation for Latin American Anthropological Research, Culver City.

Andrews V, E. Wyllys, and Jeremy A. Sabloff. 1986. Classic to Postclassic: A Summary Discussion. In Sabloff and Andrews V 1986:433-456.

Arnabar Gunam, Tomás. 2001. El cacicazgo de Champotón en el siglo XVI. *Los investigadores de la cultura Maya* 9:368-380.

Arnold III, Phillip J. 1997. Introduction to Part 2. In *Olmec to Aztec: Settlement Patterns in the Ancient Gulf Lowlands*, edited by Barbara L. Stark and Phillip J. Arnold III, pp. 139-143. University of Arizona, Tucson.

Ball, Joseph W. 1977. An Hypothetical Outline of Costal Maya Prehistory: 300 B.C.–A.D. 1200. In *Social Process in Maya Prehistory*, edited by Norman Hammond, pp. 167-196. Academic, London.

— 1978. Archaeological Pottery of the Yucatan–Campeche Coast. In Eaton and Ball 1978:69-146.

— 1986. Campeche, the Itza, and the Postclassic: A Study of Ethnohistorical Archaeology. In Sabloff and Andrews V 1986:379-408.

Ball, Joseph W., and Jennifer T. Taschek. 1989. Teotihuacan's Fall and the Rise of the Itza: Realignments and Role Changes in the Terminal Classic Maya Lowlands. In Berlo and Diehl 1989:187-200.

Benavides Castillo, Antonio. 1994. Edzná y el suroeste de la región del Puuc. In Prem 1994:121-132.

— 1997. *Edzna: A Pre-Columbian City in Campeche.* INAH/University of Pittsburgh, Pittsburgh.

— 2002. Principales hallazgos de la temporada 2000 en Jaina. *Los unvestigadores de la cultura maya* 10:88-101.

— 2003. Edzná y la región occidental del Puuc. *Estudios de cultura maya* 23:163-188.

Berdan, Frances F., Marilyn A. Masson, Janine Gasco, and Michael E. Smith. 2003. An International Economy. In Smith and Berdan 2003:96-108.

Berlin, Heinrich. 1953. Archaeological Reconnaissance in Tabasco. In *Current Reports*, vol. 1, pp. 101-130. Carnegie Institution of Washington, Washington, D.C.

— 1956. *Late Pottery Horizons of Tabasco, Mexico.* Contributions of American Anthropology and History Publication 606. Carnegie Institution of Washington, Washington, D.C.

Berlo, Janet C., and Richard A. Diehl (editors). 1989. *Mesoamerica after the Decline of Teotihuacan.* Dumbarton Oaks, Washington, D.C.

Bishop, Ronald L. 2003. Five Decades of Maya Fine Orange Ceramic Investigation by INAA. In *Patterns and Process: A Festschrift in Honor of Dr. Edward V. Sayre*, edited by Lambertus van Zelst, pp. 81-91. Smithsonian Center for Materials Research and Education, Suitland.

Bishop, Ronald L., M. James. Blackman, Antonio Benavides Castillo, Socorro del Pilar Jiménez Álvarez, Robert L. Rands, and Erin L. Sears. 2008. Naturaleza material y evolución en el norte y noroeste de las tierras bajas mayas. *Los investigadores de la cultura maya* 16:13-30. Universidad Autónoma de Campeche, Campeche.

Bishop, Ronald L., M. James Blackman, Erin L. Sears, William J. Folan, and Donald W. Forsyth. 2006. Observaciones iniciales sobre el consumo de la cerámica de Champotón. *Los investigadores de la cultura maya* 14:137-145. Universidad Autónoma de Campeche, Campeche.

Borenstein, Joshua A. 2005. Epiclassic Political Organization in Southern Veracruz, Mexico: Segmentary versus Centralized Integration. *Ancient Mesoamerica* 16:11-21.

Braswell, Geoffrey E. 2003. Postclassic Mesoamerican Obsidian Exchange Spheres. In Smith and Berdan 2003:131-158.

Brenner, Mark, David A. Hoddel, Jason H. Curtis, Michael Rosenmeier, Michael Binford, and Mark Abbott. 2001. Abrupt Climate Change and Pre-Columbian Cultural Collapse. In *Interhemispheric Climate Linkages*, edited by Vera Markgraf, pp. 87-103. Academic, New York.

Chase, Diane Z., and Arlen F. Chase. 1982. Yucatec Influence in Terminal Classic Northern Belize. *American Antiquity* 47:596-614.

Cobos, Rafael, Lilia Fernández Souza, Nancy Peniche May, Rodolfo Canto Carrillo, María Luisa Vázquez de Agredos, Socorro Jiménez Álvarez, Maricruz Góngora Aguilar, Russel Rosado Quijano and Vera Tiesler Blos. 2006. *El surgimiento de la civilización en el occidente de Yucatán: Los orígenes de la complejidad social en Sihó. Informe de la Temporada de Campo 2004*. Report to the Consejo de Arqueología, Instituto Nacional de Antropología e Historia, Mexico City.

Coe, Michael D., and Richard A. Diehl. 1980. *The Archaeology of San Lorenzo Tenochtitlan, Vol. 1: In the Land of the Olmec*. University of Texas, Austin.

Collier, A. 1964. The American Mediterranean. In *Handbook of the Middle American Indians*, vol. 1, edited by G. R. Willey, pp. 122-142. University of Texas, Austin

Crespo, Norberto Gonzalez, and Ángel García Cook (editors). 2000. *La producción alfarera en el México antiguo*. Instituto Nacional de Antropología e Historía, Mexico City.

Culbert, T. Patrick (editor). 1943. *The Classic Maya Collapse*. School of American Research, University of New Mexico, Albuquerque.

Curet, Luís Antonio, Barbara L. Stark, and S. Vasquez Z. 1993. Postclassic Change in South-Central Veracruz, Mexico. *Ancient Mesoamerica* 5:13-32.

Curtis, Jason H., Mark Brenner, David A. Hodell, Richard A. Balser, Gerald A. Islebe, and Henry Hooghiemstra. 1998. A Multi-Proxy Study of Holocene Environmental Change in the Maya Lowlands of Peten, Guatemala. *Journal of Paleoliminology* 19:139-159.

Curtis, Jason H., David A. Hodell, and Mark Brenner. 1996. Climate Variability on the Yucatán Peninsula (Mexico) during the Past 3500 Years, and Implication for Maya Cultural Evolution. *Quaternary Research* 46:37-47.

Dahlin, Bruce H., and Traci Ardren. 2002. Modes of Exchange and Regional Patterns: Chunchucmil, Yucatan. In Masson and Freidel 2002:249-285.

Eaton, Jack D. 1978. Archaeological Survey of the Yucatan–Campeche Coast. In Eaton and Ball 1978:v-67.

Eaton, Jack D., and Joseph W. Ball (editors). 1978. *Studies of the Archaeology of Coastal Campeche, México*. Middle American Research Institute Publication 46. Tulane University, New Orleans.

Ek, Jerald D. 2006a. *The Champoton Regional Settlement Survey: Results from the 2005 Field Season*. Report to the Foundation for the Advancement of Mesoamerican Studies, Inc. Online: www.famsi.org.

— 2006b. *Reconocimiento del asentamiento y excavaciones arqueológicos de la región de Champotón: Resultados de la temporada de campo 2005*. Report Submitted to the Instituto Nacional de Antropología e Historia, Campeche.

— 2008. Patrones demográficos y transformaciones económicas en Champotón, Campeche. *Los investigadores de la cultura maya* 16:135-148.

— 2009a. Cambios en los sistemas de subsistencia y intercambio interregional en Champotón, Campeche. *Los investigadores de la cultura maya* 17:177-191.

— 2009b. *Investigaciones regionales en Champotón, Campeche: Resultados de la temporada de Campo 2007*. Report Submitted to the Consejo de Arqueología del Instituto Nacional de Antropología e Historia, Mexico City.

— 2010. Changing Patterns of Ceramic Sphere Affiliation in the Rio Champoton Drainage, Campeche Mexico. Paper presented at the Paper presented at the 75th Annual Meeting of the Society for American Archaeology, St. Louis.

— 2011. Political Intrigue in the Realm of Chakanputun: Warfare and Political Centralization during the Postclassic Period in Champoton, Campeche. Paper presented at the 2011 Annual Meeting of the Society for American Archaeology, Sacramento.

— n.d. Patrones de asentamiento y cronología: Cerámica del periodo formativo en la cuenca del Rio Champoton, Campeche. In *La costa de Campeche en los tiempos prehispanicos: Una visión 50 años despues*, edited by Rafael Cobos Palma. Universidad Nacional Autónoma de México, Mexico D.F. In press.

Ek, Jerald D., and Wilberth Cruz Alvarado. 2010. Cambios en patrones de afiliación de esferas cerámicas en el drenaje del Río Champotón, Campeche. *Los investigadores de la cultura maya* 18:203-218.

Ek, Jerald D., and Josalyn M. Ferguson. 2011. Producción de herramientas líticas en el drenaje del Río Champotón, Campeche, México. *Los investigadores de la cultura maya* 19. In press.

Ek, Jerald D., and Roberto Rosado Ramírez. 2004. *Reconocimiento del asentamiento arqueológico de la región de Champotón: Resultados de la temporada de campo 2003*. Report Submitted to the Instituto Nacional de Antropología e Historia, Campeche.

— 2005. Transformaciones políticas, económicas, y ambientales en Champotón, Campeche. *Los investigadores de la cultura maya* 13:276-290.

Ensor, Bradley E. 2003. Islas de los Cerros: A Coastal Site Complex near Comalcalco, Tabasco, Mexico. *Mexicon* 23:106-111.

Folan, William J., Lynda Florey Folan, Abel Morales, Raymundo Gonzalez, Vera Tiesler Blos, David Bolles, Roberto Ruiz, and Joel D. Gunn. 2003. Champotón, Campeche: Su presencia en el desarrollo cultural del Golfo de México y su corredor eco-arqueológico. *Los investigadores de la cultura maya* 11:64-71.

Folan, William J., Joel D. Gunn, Jack D. Eaton, and Robert W. Patch. 1983. Paleoclimatological Patterning in Southern Mesoamerica. *Journal of Field Archaeology* 10:453-468.

Folan, William J., Abel Morales, Rosario Dominguez, Roberto Ruiz, Raymundo Gonzalez, Joel D. Gunn, Lynda Florey, M. Barredo, José Antonio Hernandez, and David Bolles. 2002. La ciudad y puerto de Champotón, Campeche: Una encrucijada del Gulfo de México y su corredor Eco-Arqueológico. *Los investigadores de la cultura maya* 10:8-16.

Folan, William J., Abel Morales López, José Antonio Hernández Trujeque, Raymundo González Heredia, Lynda Florey Folan, David Bolles, and Joel D. Gunn. 2004. Recientes excavaciones en el barrio de Pozo Monte en la ciudad y puerto de Champotón (Chakan Putun) Campeche: Un lugar central del preclásico medio a posclásico en la costa oeste de la Península de Yucatán. *Los investigadores de la cultura maya* 12:38-53.

Forsyth, Donald W. 1983. *Investigations at Edzna, Campeche, Mexico: Ceramics*. Papers of the New World Archaeological Foundation 46, Part II. Brigham Young University, Provo.

— 2004. Reflexiones sobre la ocupación postclásica en Champotón a través de la cerámica. *Los investigadores de la cultura maya* 12:32-38.

— 2008. El preclásico superior en la costa y tierra adentro del suroeste de Campeche. *Los investigadores de la cultura maya* 16:213-218.

Forsyth, Donald W., and Aaron Jordan. 2003. La secuencia cerámica de Champotón, Campeche: Un ensayo preliminar. *Los investigadores de la cultura maya* 11:56-63.

Fox, John W. 1987. *Maya Postclassic State Formation*. Cambridge University, Cambridge.

Freidel, David A., and Jeremy A. Sabloff. 1984. *Cozumel: Late Maya Settlement Patterns*. Academic, New York.

Freidel, David A., and Vernon Scarborough. 1982. Subsistence, Trade, and Development of the Coastal Maya. In *Spaniards and Indians in Southeastern Mesoamerica: Essays on the History of Ethnic Relations*, edited by Murdo J. Macleod and Robert Wasserstrom, pp. 40-63. University of Nebraska, Lincoln.

Gallareta Negrón, Tomás, Fernando Robles Castellanos, Anthony P. Andrews, Rafael Cobos, and Pura Cervera Rivero. 1989. Isla Cerritos: Un puerto maya prehispánico de la costa norte de Yucatán, México. *Memorias del segundo Coloquio Internacional de Mayistas* 1:311-332. Universidad Autónoma de Yucatán, Merida.

Gallegos Gómora, Judith, and Ricardo Armijo Torres. 2001. La cerámica de Tabasco durante el clásico. In Crespo and Cook 2000:505-560.

Graham, John A. 1973. Aspects of Non-Classic Presences in the Inscriptions and Sculptural Art of Seibal. In Culbert 1973:207-217.

Gunn, Joel D., and Richard E. W. Adams. 1981. Climatic Change, Culture, and Civilizations in North America. *World Archaeology* 13:87-100.

Hammond, Norman. 1983. Nohmul, Belize: 1982 Excavations. *Journal of Field Archaeology* 10:245-254.

Hodell, David A., Mark Brenner, Jason H. Curtis, and Thomas Guilderson. 2001. Solar Forcing of Drought Frequency in the Maya Lowlands. *Science* 292(5520):1367-1370.

Hodell, David A., Jason H. Curtis, and Mark Brenner. 1995. Possible Role of Climate in the Collapse of the Classic Maya Civilization. *Nature* 375(6530):391-394.

Inurreta Diaz, Armando Franscisco. 2004. *Uaymil: Un puerto de transbordo en la costa norte de Campeche*. Universidad Autónoma de Campeche, Campeche.

Jiménez Álvarez, Socorro, Roberto Belmar, Thelma Sierra, and Heajoo Chung. 2006. Estudio tecnológico de la cerámica de pasta fina "Chablekal Temprano e Isla Fina" del sitio costero de Xcambó, Yucatán. *Los investigadores de la cultura maya* 14:502-515.

Jiménez Álvarez, Socorro del Pilar. 2002. *La cronología cerámica del puerto maya de Xcambó, costa norte de Yucatán: Complejo cerámico Xcambó y complejo cerámico Cayalac*. Licenciatura thesis, Facultad de Ciencias Antropológicas, Universidad Autónoma de Yucatán, Merida.

Jiménez, Socorro, Teresa Ceballos, and Thelma Sierra Sosa. 2000. Las insólitas cerámicas del litoral noroeste de la península de Yucatán en el clásico tardío: La Esfera cerámica Canbalam. In Crespo and Cook 2000:345-371.

Jiménez Valdez, Gloria Martha. 1987. Algunas consideraciones arqueológicas sobre la península de Xicalango, Campeche. *Anales de antropología* 24:115-126.

Joyce, Rosemary. 1991. *Cerro Palenque: Power and Identity on the Maya Periphery*. University of Texas, Austin.

Kaplan, Jonathan. 1998. Un habeas corpus en el caso de los Putun. Clásico terminal, epiclásico o postclasico? In *XI simposio de investigaciones arqueológicas en Guatemala, 1997*, edited by Juan Pedro Laporte and Héctor L. Escobedo, vol. 2, pp. 807-815. Museo Nacional de Arqueología y Etnología, Guatemala City.

Kepecs, Susan. 1999. *The Political Economy of Chikinchel, Yucatán, Mexico: A Diachronic Analysis from the Prehispanic Era through the Age of Spanish Administration*. Ph.D. dissertation, Department of Anthropology, University of Wisconsin-Madison. University Microfilms, Ann Arbor.

— 2003. Chikinchel. In Smith and Berdan 2003:259-268.

Kepecs, Susan, Gary Feinman, and Sylviane Boucher. 1994. Chichen Itza and Its Hinterland: A World Systems Approach. *Ancient Mesoamerica* 5:141-158.

Killion, Thomas W., and Javier Urcid. 2001. The Olmec Legacy: Cultural Continuity on Mexico's Southern Gulf Coast. *Journal of Field Archaeology* 28:3-25.

Kowalski, Jeff K. 1989. Who Am I among the Itza? Links Between Northern Yucatan and the Western Maya Lowlands and Highlands. In Berlo and Diehl 1989:173-186.

Kremer, Jürgen. 1994. The Putun Hypothesis Reconsidered. In Prem 1994:289-307.

Lange, Frederick W. 1971. Marine Resources: A Viable Subsistence Alternative for the Prehistoric Lowland Maya. *American Anthropologist* 73:619-639.

Leyden, Barbara W., Mark Brenner, Tom Whitmore, Jason H. Curtis, Dolores R. Piperno, and Bruce H. Dahlin. 1996. A Record of Long- and Short-Term Climatic Variation from Northwest Yucatan: Cenote San José Chalchacá. In *The Managed Mosaic: Ancient Maya Agriculture and Resource Use*, edited by Scott L. Fedick, pp. 30-50. University of New Mexico, Albuquerque.

Masson, Marilyn A. 2000. *In the Realm of Nachan Kan: Postclassic Maya Archaeology at Laguna de On, Belize*. University of Colorado, Boulder.

— 2003. Economic Patterns in Northern Belize. In Smith and Berdan 2003:269-281.

Masson, Marilyn A., and David Freidel (editors). 2002. *Ancient Maya Political Economies*. Alta Mira, New York.

Masson, Marilyn A., Timothy S. Hare, and Carlos Peraza Lope. 2006. Late Postclassic Economic Transformations at Mayapán. In *After Collapse: The Regeneration of Complex Societies*, edited by Glenn M. Schwartz and John J. Nichols, pp. 188-207. University of Arizona, Tucson.

Matheny, Ray T. 1970. *The Ceramics of Aguacatal, Campeche, Mexico*. Papers of the New World Archaeological Foundation 27. Brigham Young University, Provo.

— 1986. Early States in the Maya Lowlands during the Late Preclassic Period: Edzna and El Mirador. In *City-States of the Maya: Art and Architecture*, edited by Elizabeth P. Benson, pp. 1-44. Rock Mountain Insititute for Pre-Columbian Studies, Denver.

McKillop, Heather. 1996. Ancient Maya Trading Ports and the Integration of Long-Distance and Regional Economies: Wild Cane Cay in South-Coastal Belize. *Ancient Mesoamerica* 7:49-62.

McVicker, Donald. 1985. The "Mayanized" Mexicans. *American Antiquity* 50:82-101.

Milbrath, Susan, and Carlos Peraza Lope. 2003. Revisiting Mayapan: Mexico's Last Maya Capital. *Ancient Mesoamerica* 14:1-46.

Molina Solís, Juan Franscisco. 1943. *Historia del Descubrimiento y Conquista de Yucatán*. Ediciones Mayab, Merida.

— 1973. *História de Yucatán*. Ediciones Mensaje, Merida.

Ochoa, Lorenzo, and Ernesto Vargas Pacheco. 1980. El Colapso Maya, Los Chontales y Xicalango. *Estudios de Cultura Maya* 22:61-91.

Peniche Rivero, Piedad de Carmen. 1973. *Comalcalco, Tabasco: Su cerámica, artefactos y enterramientos*. Licenciatura thesis, Facultad de Ciencias Antropológicas, Universidad Autónoma de Yucatán.

Pina Chan, Róman. 1968. *Jaina: La casa en el Agua*. Instituto Nacional de Antropología e Historia, Mexico City.

Prem, Hanns J. (editor). 1994. *Hidden Among the Hills: Maya Archaeology of the Northwest Yucatan Peninsula*. Acta Mesoamericana 7. Von Flemming, Möckmühl.

Rivera, Miguel, José Luis de Rojas, and Emma Sanchez. 1982. Exploraciones Arqueológicas en Haltunchén, Campeche. *Revista española de antropología americana* 12:9-110.

Robles Castellanos, Fernando, and Anthony P. Andrews. 2000. *Proyecto Costa Maya: Interacción coast-interior entre los mayas. Reporte interino, temporada 2000: Reconocimiento arqueológico de la esquina noroeste de la península de Yucatán*. Report submitted to the Consejo de Arqueología, Instituto Nacional de Antropología e Historía, Mexico City.

— 2004. Proyecto Costa Maya: Reconocimiento arqueológico de la esquina noroeste de la península de Yucatán. In *XVII simposio de investigaciones arqueológicas en Guatemala, 2003*, edited by Juan Pedro Laporte, Bárbara Arroyo, Héctor L. Escobedo and Héctor E. Mejía, vol. 1, pp. 47-66. Museo Nacional de Arqueología y Etnología, Guatemala City.

Robles Castellanos, Fernando, and Teresa Ceballos Gallareta. 2002. La cronología cerámica preliminar del noroeste de la península de Yucatán. In *Proyecto Costa Maya: Reconocimiento arqueológico en el noroeste de Yucatán, México: Reporte interino, temporada 2002*, edited by Fernando Robles Castellanos and Anthony P. Andrews. Report submitted to the Consejo de Arqueología, Instituto Nacional de Antropología e Historía, Mexico City.

Roys, Ralph L. 1957. *The Political Geography of the Yucatan Maya*. Publication 613. Carnegie Instition of Washington, Washington, D.C.

Ruz Lhuillier, Alberto. 1969. *La costa de Campeche en los tiempos prehispánicos*. Instituto Nacional de Antropología e Historía, Mexico City.

Sabloff, Jeremy A., and E. Wyllys Andrews V (editors). 1986. *Late Lowland Maya Civilization: Classic to Postclassic*. University of New Mexico, Albuquerque.

Sabloff, Jeremy A., and William L. Rathje. 1975. *A Study of Changing Pre-Columbian Commercial Systems: The 1972–1973 Seasons at Cozumel, Mexico*. Peabody Museum Monographs 3. Harvard University, Cambridge, Mass.

Sabloff, Jeremy A., and Gordon R. Willey. 1967. The Collapse of Maya Civilization in the Southern Lowlands: A Consideration of History and Process. *Southwest Journal of Anthropology* 23:311-336.

Schele, Linda, and Peter Mathews. 1998. *The Code of Kings: The Language of Seven Sacred Maya Temples and Tombs*. Scribner, New York.

Scholes, France V., and Ralph L. Roys. 1968. *The Maya Chontal Indians of Acalan-Tixchel*. University of Oklahoma, Norman.

Sisson, Edward B. 1976. *Settlement Patterns and Land Use in the Northwestern Chontalpa*. Unpublished PhD dissertation, Harvard University, Cambridge, Mass.

Smith, Carol A. 1976. Exchange Systems and the Spatial Distribution of Elites: The Organization of Stratification in Agrarian Societies. In *Regional Analysis, Volume 2, Social Systems*, edited by Carol A. Smith, pp. 309-374. Academic, New York.

Smith, Michael E., and Frances F. Berdan (editors). 2003. *The Postclassic Mesoamerican World*. University of Utah, Salt Lake City.

Thompson, J. Eric S. 1970. *Maya History and Religion*. University of Oklahoma, Norman.

Tourtellot, Gair, and Jason J. González. 2004. The Last Hurrah: Continuity and Transformation at Seibal. In *The Terminal Classic in the Maya Lowlands: Collapse, Transition, and Transformation*, edited by Arthur A. Demarest, Prudence M. Rice, and Don S. Rice, pp. 60-82. University Press of Colorado, Boulder.

Vargas Pacheco, Ernesto. 1994. Sintesis de la historia prehispánica de los mayas chontales de Tabasco-Campeche. *América indígena, historia prehispánica* 1-2:15-61.

— 1998. El dominio de las rutas fluviales en la región chontal. Acalan: El lugar de las canoas. In *Rutas de intercambio en mesoamérica*, edited by Evelyn C. Rattray, pp. 259-276. Instituto de Investigaciones Antropológicas-Universida Nacional Autónoma de México, Mexico City.

— 2001. *Itzamkanac y Acalan: Tiempos de crisis anticipando el futuro*. Instituto de Investigaciones Antropológicas, Universidad Nacional Autónoma de México, Mexico City.

West, Georgia. 2002. Ceramic Exchange in the Late Classic and Postclassic Maya Lowlands: A Diachronic Approach. In Masson and Freidel 2002:140-196.

Whitmore, Tom, Mark Brenner, Jason H. Curtis, Bruce H. Dahlin, and Barbara Leyden. 1996. Holocene Climatic and Human Influences on Lakes of the Yucatán Peninsula, Mexico: An Interdisciplinary, Paleolimnological Approach. *The Holocene* 6:273-287.

Zapata, Renée Lorelei. 1997. Arqueologia de Algunos Sitios de La Costa Central de Campeche. *Los investigadores de la cultura maya* 5(2):406-411.

7 5,000 Sites and Counting

The Inspiration of Maya Settlement Studies

Walter R. T. Witschey and Clifford T. Brown

Abstract

This chapter describes a long-term mapping project designed to create a database of all known Maya sites, inspired originally by E. Wyllys Andrews V. To date, more than 5,000 Maya archaeological sites have been located and positioned on a master map, and data suitable for GIS analysis have been recorded in a public-access website. Data have been used by a wide range of scholars, by graduate and undergraduate students, and by primary and secondary school students and their teachers.

One of our early Will Andrews-inspired projects was computer-based—bringing LANDSAT data, first available in 1978, to the PC level for further analysis. We were interested then in a project that fascinated many others, including Tom Sever and Charles Duller: recognition of Maya sites from remote sense data. Over the last 18 years, that interest has evolved into a long-lasting project. The project is the Electronic Atlas of Ancient Maya Sites (EAAMS; Brown and Witschey 2000, 2001, 2002, 2010; Witschey and Brown 2001, 2002). It is a compendium of site-location data and other information about published Maya sites. Details of the organization of the site data, our earlier research, and data in a form for use with Google Earth may all be found on our project website (http://MayaGIS.smv.org).

Archaeological research on the ancient Maya has traditionally focused on the site as the unit of study and analysis. Most projects focus on mapping and excavating a single site and, furthermore, they often devote most of their efforts to studying monumental ceremonial and public buildings. The late 1950s and early 1960s witnessed archaeological projects that began to correct the disproportionate attention given to the temples, tombs, and palaces.

The Carnegie Institution mapped almost all of Mayapan, in Yucatan (Jones 1950, 1952, 1957). E. Wyllys Andrews IV and the Middle American Research Institute mapped Dzibilchaltun and beyond (Stuart et al. 1979). Members of the University of Pennsylvania Tikal Project mapped much of that site (Carr and Hazard 1961), and eventually extended their survey to sample the outskirts of the city (Puleston 1974, 1983).

Later in the 1960s and 1970s, interest developed in rural settlement, which turned out to be surprisingly dense (Thomas 1981). None of this work, although extremely valuable in its own right, helped us understand the overall pattern of Maya settlement during a particular period.

To achieve that goal, regional surveys were needed and they were few, indeed. The Carnegie Institution did sponsor some regional work early on, such as Pollock's (1970, 1980) surveys of the Puuc and Chenes regions, but the results were not published for many years and, more significantly, Carnegie researchers were not as interested in patterns of settlement as they were in studying architectural monuments and their history. Ruppert and Denison's (1943) survey of southern Campeche and Heinrich Berlin's (1953) survey of Tabasco fall into a similar category. William Bullard (1960), however, probably deserves credit for pioneering the study of the regional patterning of Maya settlement in his reconnaissance of the northwest Peten.

In the last 30 years, however, regional surveys have become too numerous to mention (e.g., Andrews 1983, 1986; Andrew et al. 1989; Borgstede 2002, 2004, 2005; Borgstede and Mathieu 2007; Glover and Amador 2005; Góngora Salas 2000; Johnstone and Shaw 2006; Kepecs 1999; Robles Castellanos and Andrews 2003; Sisson 1976; Šprajc 2004; Šprajc et al. 2001; West et al. 1969; Williams-Beck 1998). These surveys have varied in scope from small areas to large regions measuring thousands of square kilometers. The intensity of survey has also widely varied, usually inversely to the area that is covered.

Recent areal surveys can be divided into three categories. First are those that are carried out just because an area is unknown and seems potentially interesting. This is essentially survey for its own sake. More often, survey is performed with the ulterior motive of locating sites for future evaluation (usually of a sample) with the ultimate goal of setting up camp at the coolest one for a long-term excavation. In a few cases, the survey is an add-on to a site-based project, to "put the site in its regional context." All these approaches are perfectly legitimate and have their place in the arsenal of archaeological methods. But the result has been a shocking menagerie of data sets that often are incomparable.

The truth is that after a tremendous amount of work by thousands of dedicated archaeologists under the most onerous conditions, and the expenditure of many millions of dollars, we still do not have a strong grasp of the overall pattern of Maya settlement.

The governments of Mexico and Guatemala in particular have made significant efforts, over a long period of time, to document known archaeological sites within their territories. Their goals have been legal and administrative as well as scientific. The result has been a series of maps and atlases of great importance and utility (e.g., Departamento de Monumentos Prehispánicos y Coloniales 1991; Garza Tarazona de González and Kurjack 1980; Müller 1959, 1960; Piña Chan 1967).

Having collated and mapped the vast majority of available data, however, we can state without fear of contradiction that there are major patterns in the distribution of archaeological sites that cannot be explained with the information now available. For example, the two largest concentrations of sites in our atlas appear in the Maya highlands (including Chiapas) and in the northwest corner of the Yucatan Peninsula (including the Puuc region). We all, of course, think rightly or wrongly of the Peten as the Maya heartland. Are the concentrations of sites in the south and the northwest then simply an artifact of the survey conditions and intensity in those regions? Compared to the southern lowlands, the northwest and the highlands are much easier to survey; they have much better visibility, are much more densely populated, and are much more accessible. It seems plausible if not inevitable, therefore, that more sites would be known in those areas. On the other hand, the density of sites in northwest Yucatan has long been a subject of comment, and seems to be more than a function of survey conditions (see Chapters 1 to 3). Certainly, major differences in the overall archaeological sequences exist between the northern, central, and southern Maya regions, but do these explain the differences in the spatial distribution of sites we can observe? We believe that the only way to resolve this type of question will be to conduct more intensive and more highly standardized surveys in carefully selected areas to sample the distributions of settlement for statistical testing of hypotheses. The Electronic Atlas of Ancient Maya Sites is one step along this path.

Such compendia begin in the modern era with Stephens and Catherwood (Stephens 1969[1841], 1843), who mention about 250 places (Figure 7.1a,b), but visited far fewer ruins in their travels. From 1924 through 1940 at Harvard and later at Tulane, Frans Blom (Figure 7.1c) and his colleagues compiled the Middle American Research Institute (M.A.R.I.) map, which by 1940 had grown to include 1,717 archaeological sites and 838 towns in Middle America (Figure 7.2). Approximately 1,500 of those sites are in the Maya region.

Figure 7.1. Early explorers of the Maya area: (a) John L. Stephens; (b) map of archaeological sites in southern Mexico and Central America compiled by Stephens (1969); (c) Frans Blom (photograph reproduced with permission of the Middle American Research Institute, Tulane University).

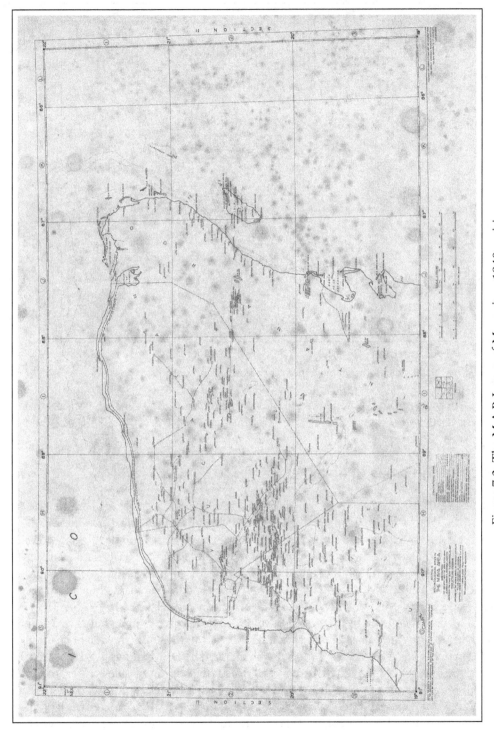

Figure 7.2. The M.A.R.I. map of Maya sites, 1940 revision (reproduced with permission of the Middle American Research Institute, Tulane University).

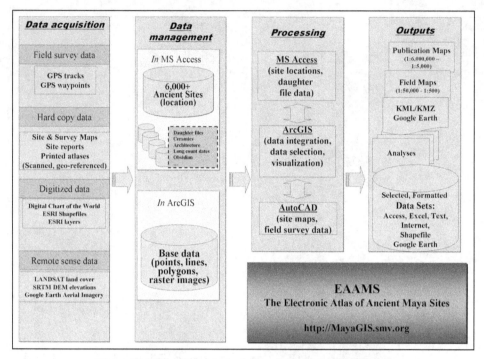

Figure 7.3. The Electronic Atlas of Ancient Maya Sites: data acquisition, management, processing, and outputs.

Today, as an Andrews-inspired extension of earlier M.A.R.I. work, the EAAMS consists of a modern database used with Geographic Information Systems software (ArcGIS 9.3.1) and other software tools (Figure 7.3).

Methodology of the Atlas Project

Data Sources: Base Map

We have taken the data for the base map of the EAAMS from various sources. One of the problems inherent in our large-scale approach has been the difficulty of developing data sources that are consistent across the five nations included in the map. One basic data source is the Digital Chart of the World (DCW), originally developed for air navigation by the United States military (Danko 1992; DMA 1992; ESRI 1993). Our topographic data come from the Shuttle Radar Topography Mission (SRTM) digital elevation model (DEM) (NASA 1999, 2011). The SRTM data, acquired by STS-99 (Space Transportation System, that is, a Space Shuttle flight) in 2000, provide consistent elevation data across all the countries at a horizontal resolution of 90 meters and a vertical resolution of one meter. The DEM allows us to represent elevation in various ways. Rather than using traditional hypsography, we prefer tinted hypsometry, hill slope shading, or both. We also have incorporated land-use data from LANDSAT; NASA provides three-band false color land use images at 14.25-meter horizontal resolution derived from LANDSAT imagery (Earth Satellite Corporation 2004; Tucker et al. 2004; <https://zulu.ssc.nasa.gov/mrsid/>).

Data Sources: Archaeology

The archaeological data come from many sources, too many to list individually, so here we provide only a brief indication. The site location data are obviously critical and, predictably, have required much effort to compile. We convert x-y coordinate data to decimal degrees of latitude and longitude registered to the WGS84 spheroid and datum.

Our collection of data from multiple sources, some quite old, often results in our converting both spheroid and datum. A spheroid is an ideal model of the surface of the earth based on a rotated ellipse. For example, data collected before the latter part of the twentieth century frequently used the Clark 1866 spheroid. A datum is a localized modification to an ellipsoid, designed to better account for variations in elevation. A frequently used older datum for maps in the Maya area is the North American 1927 datum (NAD27), based upon the Clarke 1866 ellipsoid. All points in the Atlas are initially recorded in their original basis (such as NAD 1927 Clarke 1866) and then transformed mathematically into latitudes and longitudes based upon the World Geodetic System (WGS) 1984 spheroid (ellipsoid) and the WGS 1984 datum.

Note also that data are usually available in projected form either directly on paper maps or in projected coordinate systems (such as Universal Transverse Mercator, or UTM). In the GIS, however, we maintain the data in latitude-longitude, in decimal degree format. Latitude-longitude, of course, is a spherical, geographic coordinate system. Changing the data from projected formats to latitude-longitude requires algorithms that de-project the datasets. We generally use the algorithms supplied by Environmental Research Systems, Inc., the publisher of the software.

We started compiling data with the finest archaeological atlas of the Maya area, Garza Tarazona de González and Kurjack's (1980) *Atlas Arqueológico del Estado de Yucatán*. We supplemented those data with the site locations and refinements published by Dunning (1992:Table 5-1). We also added the extensive data from Andrews' surveys between Chichen Itza and the north coast (Andrews et al. 1989); between Chichen Itza and Ek Balam (Smith 2000), Kepecs' (1999) survey of the Chikinchel province, a survey in the northwest corner of the Peninsula (Robles Castellanos and Andrews 2003); and a study of the northeast part of the peninsula (Góngora Salas 2000).

Then we added the data from the other three archaeological atlases from the Mexican portion of the Maya area: Florencia Müller's (1959, 1960) atlases of Campeche and Quintana Roo, and Piña Chan's (1967) atlas of Chiapas. Unfortunately, the maps in Müller's pioneering early work are rather imprecise and the accompanying documentation rather exiguous. We have added to or refined the Campeche data with data from Williams-Beck's (1988) survey of northern Campeche, Šprajc's (2004; Šprajc et al. 2001) survey of southern Campeche, Ruppert and Denison's (1943) old Carnegie survey (the greater part of which fell within Campeche), and Jerry Ek's recent work around Champoton (Chapter 6). We checked some of Lorraine Williams-Beck's data points from northern Campeche (including Xk'ombec and Xcalumkin) with our own GPS points, and they turned out to be extremely accurate, after we determined which datum was used.

In Quintana Roo, we have included the data from the Yalahau project in the north (Glover and Amador 2005), Harrison and Fry's survey of the south-central portion of the state, and Fernando Cortés de Brásdefer's (1984) GPS points from the southern part of the state. For the coast of Quintana Roo, we extracted data from Anthony Andrews' surveys (1983, 1986), and we also incorporated GPS points taken by Witschey. In southern Yucatan and central Quintana Roo, we have included data from the Yo'okop-Ichmul survey (Johnstone and Shaw 2006). Piña

Chan's (1967) atlas of Chiapas has provided a strong dataset for Chiapas. It includes 609 sites that appear to be mapped with some precision, although unfortunately he does not provide clear indications of site size or rank.

In Tabasco, we have included the data from Heinrich Berlin's (1953) survey for the Carnegie Institution, Robert West's geographical studies (West et al. 1969), and Chris Von Nagy's survey (2003) and Ed Sisson's (1976) Harvard dissertation describing his work in the Chontalpa.

For Guatemala, we began with Morley's famous and monumental *Inscriptions of Peten* (1938), which contains surprisingly accurate maps. Then we digitized the 806 site locations and supplementary data from the 1:500,000 scale archaeological map sheets of Guatemala published by the Departamento de Monumentos Prehispánicos y Coloniales (1991). We added data from Laporte's recent survey of the southeastern Petén and Borgstede's (2004) survey of the western Maya highlands.

For Belize, we have included the results of Sidrys' (1983) survey in the north, Anabel Ford's work (2005) in the west-central part of the country, and Elizabeth Graham's (1994) work in the south. For the entire region, we also include, as mentioned earlier, the data from the Tulane M.A.R.I. map of 1940 (Blom et al. 1940).

As noted earlier, these are only the major sources incorporated into the database. We also have National Geographic's site data from their famous map of the Maya area, courtesy of Anabel Ford. We also have been fortunate to receive site locations through personal communications from Karl Herbert Meyer, Anthony Andrews, Payson Sheets, Joyce Kelly, and David Hixson, among many others. We are profoundly grateful for these contributions to the project. We continue to add data regularly and expect that the final data set will be very comprehensive.

Precision, Accuracy, and Completeness

We wish to be extremely forthright about the precision, accuracy, and completeness of the EAAMS. It is not difficult to find ambiguities or questionable locations among the data, but these are not the result of sloppy work. We conducted our work with great precision, but the EAAMS accuracy fundamentally depends on the accuracy of the original data sources.

In this regard, the sources vary widely. Some site locations are extremely accurate. But some older works were created when accurate maps of the region were rare or nonexistent. Even some of the newer work created with the assistance of GPS is less accurate than we desire, in part because of the "selective availability" of the GPS system. This refers to the random errors incorporated into GPS signals by the U.S. military for national security reasons. Selective availability has now been shut off, but its prior existence still affects some older data sources. In addition, we must remember that early GPS receivers were cumbersome and finicky.

To increase the accuracy of our data, we generally attempt to confirm site locations using small-scale topographic maps, Google Earth, SRTM elevations, LANDSAT images, or other data sources. In many cases, this has been impossible, particularly with smaller sites, but we have often succeeded with major sites. We also note that for many sites we have multiple coordinate sets from different sources. Choosing among the coordinates for a site requires an evaluation of the reliability of the sources. As a matter of policy, we have generally preferred GPS points over locations determined by traditional orienteering. But we have also found that not all GPS points are accurate. Sadly, some people publish GPS points without providing full information about the settings of the instrument, for example, the mapping datum used.

Others have furnished points obviously in error due to failure to read or utilize the GPS receiver properly. A notable exception is Karl Herbert Mayer, who regularly collects and publishes site location data in *Mexicon*, derived from personal GPS readings. These data have been supplied in tabular form to the EAAMS project.

The use of projected map data has also introduced errors into our maps. Recall that site locations are maintained in decimal degrees of latitude and longitude. When necessary, published data are converted to this format. Converting projected data from, for example, Universal Transverse Mercator (UTM) coordinates to latitude and longitude necessarily incorporates some proportion of the error or distortion inherent in the projection process, and the error increases with distance from the lines of tangency of the UTM zone.

The EAAMS is also necessarily incomplete, in more than one way. First, most sites are represented by points, not polygons. Of course, many Maya sites are large and therefore representing them as points is an incomplete representation. On a regional scale, the difference is minor. The alternative, drawing polygons for sites, would be easy when the data are available, but they are rarely available, that is, few sites have been completely mapped. Defining the boundaries of Maya sites is notoriously difficult because the edges of the urban zone usually blend imperceptibly into the rural settlement pattern; Dzibilchaltun is a good example. Only a few Maya sites—most notably the walled city of Mayapan—have relatively clear boundaries. In a few cases, we have marked sites with polygons, but normally we choose to eschew this set of complications, at least for now, by using size-scaled symbols at specific points to mark sites. The ultimate solution to this problem would be to include maps of all structures (and features) at all sites. Although this we have the technology to do this, it is currently impractical.

Second, the problem of defining sites extends out into the hinterland. In rural, agricultural areas, is every structure a site? Is every farmstead? Is every pyramidal structure? What about artifact scatters that lack visible architecture? There is no consensus on an answer to what constitutes a site, but it is probably fair to say that the site concept does not apply to individual structures within larger groups. The fairest and most realistic way to represent these data is to mark every structure, but we have not reached that level of detail. It would also be possible to shade or hatch survey transects in such a manner that the symbology reflects the density or character of the settlement, and we have considered doing this, but it not clear how useful the information would be.

Third, the EAAMS does not include all sites. Not all sites are known. Many areas have not been surveyed. Some known sites are not correctly mapped or located. Our research has not been truly exhaustive. We have searched extensively for data, and we have supplemented the major sources with regional sources, such as local and regional surveys. We have checked some individual site reports for site locations, but we have not yet reviewed every site report. The most important sources we have not been able to consult are government site files. The regional centers of INAH in Mexico as well as the national institutes of the other national governments of the Maya area all have site files as well as archives of unpublished reports that contain many site locations. These data are usually held in confidence, for understandable reasons, and we have not been able to obtain access to them.

Finally, given the problems of site definition and the destruction of sites over the years by both natural and cultural forces, we find it difficult to envisage exactly what "complete" would really mean. So, although our atlas is the most complete one ever produced, it is still significantly incomplete. We continue to add data and to improve the accuracy of the current dataset, but it is unlikely to become "complete" any time in the foreseeable future.

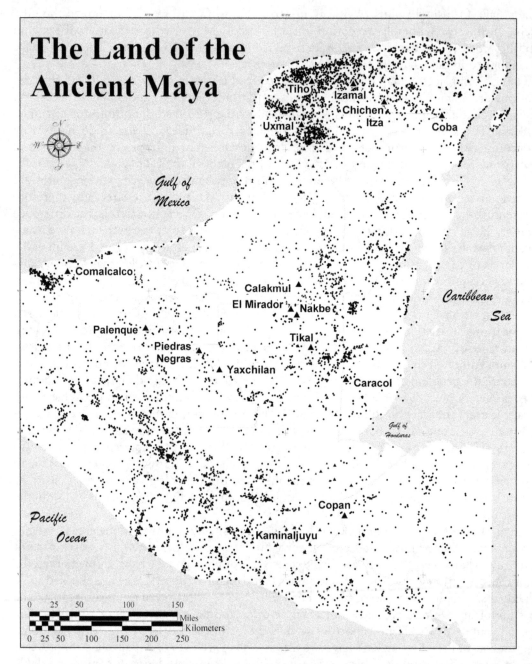

Figure 7.4. Site map of the Electronic Atlas of Ancient Maya Sites.

Figure 7.5. Chicxulub crater and higher elevation at center of the peninsula, as revealed by the Shuttle Radar Topography Mission Digital Elevation Model.

The EAAMS, as of April 2010, contains location information for 6,111 archaeological sites, more than 5,000 of which are in the Maya area, and useful rank-size information for most of these sites (Figure 7.4). It also carries consistent elevation data. Much other data is there as well.

This view of the Maya area has revealed the landform in new ways, highlighting for us the rim of the Chicxulub crater relative to the *cenote* zone, the curving line of higher elevation in the center of the peninsula (Figure 7.5), and the continental divide between Gulf and Caribbean, with Tikal sitting astride the divide (Figure 7.6).

In the time since our work on the EAAMS began, and with Will Andrews' encouragement, we have made a small number of interesting research contributions based on it, including the review of several settlement pattern theories. We have demonstrated, for several areas, that Maya settlements are fractally distributed, as is much other archaeological data in "our broken past" (Brown and Witschey 2003; Brown et al. 2005). We have also used our fractal findings to estimate the number of sites in a poorly surveyed region, subsequently examined the region, and recorded new sites (Figure 7.7; Brown and Peraza Lope 2006).

The most rewarding part of our work is the topic of the rest of our chapter: the inspiration that others draw from the project to build and maintain an electronic atlas of site location data.

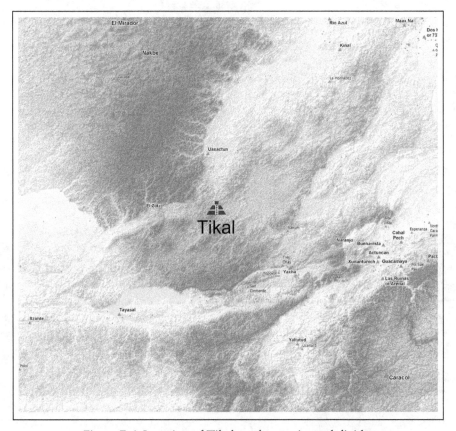

Figure 7.6. Location of Tikal on the continental divide,
as revealed by the Shuttle Radar Topography Mission Digital Elevation Model.

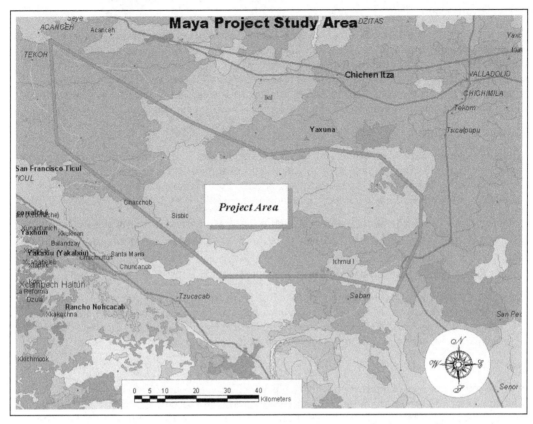

Figure 7.7. Settlement area studied first using fractal model and subsequently surveyed.

Use of the Electronic Atlas of Archaeological Maya Sites by University Scholars

The publication of the Electronic Atlas in three forms—maps, computer datasets and Google Earth files—has led to a steady interaction and interchange between us, other researchers, and students engaged in both Maya research and Geographic Information Systems studies. The information exchange is of two primary forms: (1) the supply of information to Brown and me about new sites, new publications, political boundary changes, and other data; and (2) the supply of information by us, in usable computer files, to those doing their own research, analysis, and mapping.

We hope that just as Will Andrews' encouragement has been an inspiration to us, the availability of site location data has been an inspiration to a number of students and researchers. Here is a small sample of examples from dating to 2009 and 2010.

Caleb Gallemore (personal communication 2010), a graduate student at Ohio State University, is "…working on a class GIS project intended to become part of my dissertation involving mapping the changing extent of control of the Mayan city-states over time." For him, we supplied a data set of 75 sites to pair with emblem glyph data.

Matthew Thomas said,

> I am currently a sophomore at Boston University. I am writing to you in regard to a course I am taking here called "Introduction to GIS," in which I would like to complete my final project using data that the professor has provided on Belize as well as additional data on Maya archaeological sites in the country. Your website is very helpful and it seems like you are very accommodating to those who request the data. I am willing to prepare whatever need be in order to most easily obtain the coordinates of all the sites in Belize (Mathew Thomas, personal communication 2010).

Andreas Fuls writes:

> I think that you already have most if not all of the [Maler] sites in your list, but I realized that some sites have alternative names (synonyms). For example, Dzula in your list is called Dsulachen with the synonyms Dsulaaktun, Dsula, Dzulá. For other sites like Seibal/El Ceibal the name changed (Andreas Fuls, personal communication 2010).

His comment points out the beauty of a searchable database with synonyms and orthographic alternatives. A quick search in EAAMS for "eibal" allows novices and professionals alike to retrieve data for Seibal and El Ceibal.

Patrick Rohrer was daunted at first about his research challenge:

> I'm a first semester graduate student at UCF taking a GIS Applications in Archaeology course and doing a project on the relationship between *cenotes* and ancient Maya settlements. I was thinking of focusing on the Yucatan, which I realize is still a large area, but any GIS data dealing with such topics would be greatly appreciated (Patrick Rohrer, personal communication 2010).

Witschey replied:

> May we suggest an area of interest on which to focus?... You may wish to look at the rim of the Chicxulub Crater...whose rim appears as an artifact on the SRTM DEM from STS 99 (Shuttle Radar Topography Mission Digital Elevation Model flown by the 99th shuttle flight in approximately 2000).

Brown added:

> The water quality of the *cenotes* varies. It's not sea water, but it is low quality because of dissolved solids and accumulated salts due to high evaporation rates (the area is very dry and hot). Some is completely undrinkable but may be used for watering livestock. The Mexican government (INEGI) has published some water quality data on the *cenotes*, and I believe Sheryl Luzzader-Beach (from George Mason University) has also done some testing and analysis of the water in the *cenotes*. There seem to be relatively few archaeological sites in the *Cenote* Zone. Walter and I once carried out a small survey to see if the gap in settlement around the *Cenote* Zone was a real gap or due to lack of survey. We did find some more sites, but did not really resolve the question entirely.

Rohrer seemed to catch the spark, and replied,

> You read my mind! I've just been looking into the "*Cenote* Zone" left behind by the Chicxulub Crater on a wikimap someone threw together which was fun to mess around with. I believe that will be my focus for this project. I'd like to make it as detailed as possible, and where possible include information in the dataset like size, depth, and/or quality of the water (at least whether it is saltwater or drinkable, etc.) in some of the more "relevant" (associated with major sites) *cenotes*. I realize I may have to piece together much of this information myself and add it to GIS, and that it may only be available for certain spots. Perhaps one day in the not too distant future I can dive down there and help compile this data and map underwater caves as well (Patrick Rohrer, personal communication, 2009)!

Hubert Smith reported:

> I will be in Yucatan in March and have been trying to locate San Isidro Buleb. No luck. Just a map which places it well South of Kinil and South of Tixmeauc. But the map also mis-places Xaya, Chican, and Kinil (Hubert Smith, personal communication 2010).

Brown and Witschey were able to reply,

> Please see our Atlas sites by going to http://MayaGIS.smv.org/MayaSites.KMZ. This is a KML file that you can open immediately in Google Earth, or download to your machine, and run in Google Earth. Sites are in three groups (rank 1, 2, and 3-5) and alphabetical within group. They have references in them for the source of the location information. I just pulled up San Isidro Buleb from that file, which shows it 3.8 km SSE of the village of Tixmehuac. I also looked up the Garza and Kurjack UTM coordinates (Garza Tarazona de González and Kurjack 1980), which also check with that location.

Requests come from far afield, including from Vyacheslav Babyshev in Russia, regarding flooded caves with archaeological features.

We received correspondence from Nicholas Carter:

> My M.A. thesis on GIS modeling of trends in Maya orthography is nearly complete, although the specific topics have shifted somewhat. I've been tracking the choice of prepositions, for instance, which I think may reveal some interesting correspondences to other spelling choices. My database having grown quite a bit this semester, I wonder if I could bother you for some more site coordinates, attached here in an Excel spreadsheet (Nicholas Carter, personal communication 2009).

Ultimately, we received a copy of his M.A. thesis (Carter 2009).

Carl Wendt of CSU Fullerton wrote,

> I am teaching a class on GIS and Archaeology this semester. As part of the requirements, I have my students making posters on their term research projects. I read your article in the SAA Record on the database you put together on Maya sites. I shared this with my students and one is interested in doing [a] project that looks at various environmental variables and site location. He wants to see how environment/ecology played into site location and settlement density, etc. You mentioned that you are willing to share your data, and we were wondering if you would consider this an appropriate use. If so, he is interested in looking at the entire Maya area to start with, and then maybe focusing on a smaller sub-region (Carl Wendt, personal communication 2009).

We transmitted GIS data to him for his students, and received analyses back from three students, Ryan DeStepheno, Amy Black, and Leaa Short.

Thus, it is clear that the EAAMS has been an inspiration to graduate and undergraduate researchers and their advisors. In addition, we find that the data compilation is of value to corporate and governmental agencies as well. Here are two examples.

Kenneth Gorton of ESRI (a GIS software company) reported:

> I recently returned from our Latin America User Conference in Bogotá where I used your data in one of my plenary session demos. I also used it during the plenary of our Central America UC in Guatemala in August and in some technical briefs and workshops. Needless to say, the Guatemalans were quite pleased and interested since it deals directly with their national heritage and pride. I thank you for the opportunity to use your data for this (Kenneth Gorton, personal communication 2009).

Cissy Montilla of CONACULTA in Mexico wrote to us:

> Soy la directora del Sistema de Información Cultural de México http://sic.conaculta.gob.mx, es un sistema de información geocodificado en que hemos venido trabajando desde hace un buen tiempo, ponemos a sus órdenes este desarrollo si acaso hubiera algo que les pueda ser de utilidad...También trabajamos un portal de portales http://www.ecultura.gob.mx con 3500 enlaces a páginas de cultura de México y del mundo.
>
> Queremos saber si tienen ustedes algún problema en que pongamos un enlace a su página en todos aquellos registros relacionados con el tema maya? Y también un enlace a su página en Ecultura...
>
> Si quisieran publicar en nuestro Centro de Documentación algún documento o texto o investigación estamos a la orden, lo único que tienen que hacer es enviármelo con la autorización por el mismo conducto, nosotros hacemos una breve reseña en español y ponemos el texto original en inglés. En total en los dos websites tenemos casi 20,000 visitas diarias además enviamos cada quince días un boletín de novedades a 33,000 suscriptores que se han inscrito voluntariamente.
>
> Mil gracias por este maravilloso trabajo, me despido a sus órdenes y quedo a la espera de sus comentarios (Cissy Montilla, personal communication 2009).

We provided data and replied:

> Dado que hemos colaborado por muchos años con el INAH, naturalmente estamos dispuestos a servirles de cualquiera manera que podamos. Siéntase libre de crear enlaces a nuestra páginas. Nuestro SIG es muy grande sin embargo sería un placer contribuir algo a las páginas de CONACULTA, tal vez mapas arqueológicos de la región maya, pero necesitamos advertirle que las coordenadas exactas de los sitios arqueológicos tienen que quedarse confidenciales (es decir, no se puede publicarlas).
>
> Puede usar http://MayaGIS.smv.org y además http://Muyil.smv.org. Si les podemos servir de cualquiera forma, solamente tiene que dejarnos saber.

This inspired flow of information is not strictly one way out from the EAAMS. There is also a steady flow of new information coming into the Atlas. In one week in April 2010, we received location data for two sites, suggestions leading to a new reference with twenty additional sites, and an email from Stephen Merk with GPS location data for Xtukil (Stephen Merk, personal communication 2010).

As an adjunct to traditional data-gathering techniques, we are now exploring the use of a web-crawling robot ("bot") to analyze online documents for geographic references to Maya sites.

Uses of the EAAMS in Primary and Secondary Education

Will Andrews' inspiration for the EAAMS is propagating through the primary and secondary education world in the U.S.A. We have recently begun forays into the world of building Google Earth files. Our first experiments and trials with constructing data sets that are directly usable in Google Earth began early in 2006. Work has progressed, and in February 2010, we posted the first complete data set of the sites in the EAAMS to the Google Earth Gallery and the general public. Our file is "altitude sensitive" in the sense that zooming in reveals more and more sites. As Google replaces its initial LANDSAT imagery with high-resolution aerials, more and more site detail is available, free, via the internet (Figure 7.8).

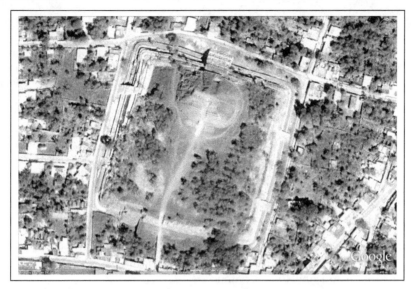

Figure 7.8. Google Earth image of K'inich Kakmo' pyramid, Izamal, Yucatan.

Our interest in support for the Google Earth platform is driven in part by the rapid adoption of Google Earth as a teaching tool in primary and secondary classrooms. In the first quarter of 2010, we conducted a small survey, a non-random sample of teachers in Virginia. Our hopes were to hear from 20 or 30 such teachers, and to our surprise, we had 250 respondents. Of those who responded, 55 percent claimed knowledge of Google Earth, and another 32 percent claimed some acquaintance. Over 55 percent of responders said they actively used Google Earth in lessons, especially in social studies, geography, and map study classes. Thirty percent of all respondents report active student use of Google Earth in their work.

Teacher comments include:

The students where excited to see that they could go to any place in the world by the use of Google Earth.

My students love this program and often choose it as a reward option.

I used Google Earth when we were talking about maps and map skills in Social Studies. The students really enjoyed seeing an actual map that was not a drawing.

I like Google Earth because the children are in awe when we use it…it captivates their attention and they learn to use it quickly.

Google Earth is great for showing locations of civilizations in relation to our own place on Earth. It is also nice to help students see the climate/habitat of locations being studied (terrain details).

We believe that the availability of accessible data for Google, capable of flying the student to more than 100 Maya sites now visible from the free aerial imagery in Google Earth, is part of inspiring the next generation of Mayanists…folks such as you and me who became interested, and then inspired by our mentors such as Will Andrews.

We can think of no more fitting way to honor Will Andrews than to contribute to inspiring the work of rising students of the magnificent Maya.

References

Andrews, Anthony P. 1983. Reconocimiento Arqueológico de Tulum a Punta Allen, Quintana Roo. *Boletín de la Escuela de Ciencias Antropológicas de la Universidad de Yucatán* 11(61):15-31.

—1986. Reconocimiento Arqueológico de Cancun a Playa del Carmen, Quintana Roo. *Boletín de la Escuela de Ciencias Antropológicas de la Universidad de Yucatán* 13(78):3-19.

Andrews, Anthony P., Tomás Gallareta Negrón, and Rafael Cobos Palma. 1989. *Preliminary Report of the Cupul Survey Project: An Archaeological Reconnaissance between Chichén Itzá and the North Coast of Yucatán, Mexico*. Report to the Centro Regional de Yucatán, Instituto Nacional de Antropología e Historia, Mexico.

Berlin, Heinrich. 1953. Archaeological Reconnaissance in Tabasco. *Current Reports* 7. Carnegie Institution of Washington, Washington, D.C.

Blom, Frans, Oliver G. Ricketson Jr., Erhardt Kramer, and S. K. Lowe. 1940. Index of Maya Sites for Use with the Map of Archaeological Sites in the Maya area (MARI Map 1940). Middle American Research Institute, Tulane University, New Orleans.

Borgstede, Greg. 2002. Settlement Patterns and Variation in the Western Highlands, Guatemala. Report to the Foundation for the Advancement of Mesoamerican Studies, Inc. Online: http://www.famsi.org/reports/00040/index.html.

— 2004. *Ethnicity and Archaeology in the Western Maya Highlands, Guatemala*. Ph.D. dissertation, Department of Anthropology, University of Pennsylvania. University Microfilms, Ann Arbor.

— 2005. Exploring the Western Highlands of Guatemala: New Perspectives on the Ancient Maya. *Expedition* 47(1):10.

Borgstede, Greg, and James R. Mathieu. 2007. Defensibility and Settlement Patterns in the Guatemalan Maya Highlands. *Latin American Antiquity* 18:191-211.

Brown, Clifford T., and Carlos Peraza Lope. 2006. *2005 Field Season*. Report to the Centro Regional de Yucatán, Instituto Nacional de Antropología e Historia, Mexico.

Brown, Clifford T., and Walter R. T. Witschey. 2000. Building a GIS System of Ancient Lowland Maya Settlement. Paper presented at the 65th Annual Meeting of the Society for American Archaeology, Philadelphia, Pennsylvania.

— 2001. The Geographic Analysis of Ancient Maya Settlement and Polity. Paper presented at the 2001 Pacific Neighborhood Consortium and Electronic Cultural Atlas Initiative, City University, Hong Kong.

— 2002. Results from the Electronic Atlas of Ancient Maya Sites. Paper presented at the 67th Annual Meeting of the Society for American Archaeology, Denver.

— 2003. The Fractal Geometry of Ancient Maya Settlement. *Journal of Archaeological Science* 30:1619-1632.

— 2010. Electronic Atlas of Ancient Maya Sites, available at http://MayaGIS.smv.org.

Brown, Clifford T., Walter R. T. Witschey, and Larry S. Liebovitch. 2005. The Broken Past: Fractals in Archaeology. *Journal of Archaeological Method and Theory* 12:37-78.

Bullard, William R. 1960. Maya Settlement Pattern in Northeastern Peten, Guatemala. *American Antiquity* 25:355-372.

Carr, Robert F., and James E. Hazard. 1961. *Map of the Ruins of Tikal, El Peten, Guatemala*. Tikal Report 11. University Museum, University of Pennsylvania, Philadelphia.

Carter, Nicholas P. 2009. *Paleographic Trends and Linguistic Processes in Classic Ch'olti'an: A Spaciotemporal Distributional Analysis*. M.A. thesis, Department of Anthropology, Brown University, Providence.

Cortés de Brásdefer, Fernando. 1984. El Registro de Sitios Arqueologicos en Quintana Roo. *Boletin de la Escuela de Ciencias Antropologicos de la Universidad Autonoma de Yucatan* 12(68):13-20. Merida.

Danko, David M. 1992. The Digital Chart of the World Project. *Photogrammetric Engineering & Remote Sensing* 58:1125-1128.

Departamento de Monumentos Prehispánicos y Coloniales. 1991. Mapa Arqueológico de la República de Guatemala. Instituto Geographico Militar, Ministerio de la Defensa Nacional y Departamento de Monumentos Prehispanicos y Coloniales, Instituto de Antropologia e Historia de Guatemala, Guatemala City.

DMA (Defense Mapping Agency). 1992. Military Specification for the Digital Chart of the World (DCW). Defense Mapping Agency. MIL-D-89009.

Dunning, Nicholas P. 1992. *Lords of the Hills: Ancient Maya Settlement in the Puuc Region, Yucatán, Mexico*. Prehistory Press, Madison.

Earth Satellite Corporation. 2004. Geocover Orthorectified LANDSAT Enhanced Thematic Mapper (ETM+). Compressed Mosaics, Earth Satellite Corporation.

ESRI [Environmental Systems Research Institute]. 1993. Digital Chart of the World for Use with ESRI Desktop Software 1:1000000 (CD-ROM). Environmental Systems Research Institute, Redlands.

Ford, Anabel. 2005. *El Pilar Reports*. Manuscript on file at ISBER/MesoAmerican Research Center University of California Santa Barbara.

Garza Tarazona de González, Silvia, and Edward B. Kurjack. 1980. *Atlas Arqueológico del Estado de Yucatán*. 2 vols. Instituto Nacional de Antropología e Historia, Mexico.

Glover, Jeffrey B., and Fabio E. Amador. 2005. Recent Research in the Yalahau Region: Methodological Concerns and Preliminary Results of a Regional Survey. In *Quintana Roo Archaeology*, edited by Justine M. Shaw and Jennifer P. Mathews, pp. 51-65. University of Arizona, Tucson.

Góngora Salas, Ángel. 2000. Northeastern Yucatán Project: Archaeological Survey in the Northeastern Corner of Yucatán, México. Report to the Foundation for the Advancement of Mesoamerican Studies, Inc. Online: http://www.famsi.org/reports/99040/index.html.

Graham, Elizabeth A. 1994. *The Highlands of the Lowlands: Environment and Archaeology in the Stann Creek District, Belize, Central America*. Monographs in World Archaeology 19. Prehistory Press, Madison.

Johnstone, Dave, and Justine M. Shaw. 2006. *Final Report of the Cochuah Regional Archaeological Survey's 2006 Analysis Season*. Online: http://online.redwoods.cc.ca.us/yookop/CRAS2006_report_text&figures.pdf.

Jones, Morris R. 1950. Survey and Base Map at Mayapan, Yucatan. In *Year Book No. 49 July 1, 1949–June 30, 1950*, pp. 194-197. Carnegie Institute of Washington, Washington, D.C.

— 1952. Topographic Map of the Ruins of Mayapan, Yucatan, Mexico. *Current Reports 1*. Department of Archaeology, Carnegie Institution of Washington, Washington, D.C.

— 1957. Topographic Map of the Ruins of Mayapan, Yucatan, Mexico. Carnegie Institution of Washington, Washington, D.C.

Kepecs, Susan. 1999. *The Political Economy of Chikinchel, Yucatan, Mexico: A Diachronic Analysis from the Prehispanic Era through the Age of Spanish Administration*. Ph.D. dissertation, Department of Anthropology, University of Wisconsin, Madison. University Microfilms, Ann Arbor.

Morley, Sylvanus Griswold. 1937–38. *Inscriptions of Peten*. 5 vols. Publication 437. Carnegie Institution of Washington, Washington, D.C.

Müller, Florencia. 1959. *Atlas arqueológico de la República Mexicana. 1, Quintana Roo*. Instituto Nacional de Antropología e Historia, Mexico.

— 1960. *Atlas arqueológico de la República Mexicana. 2, Campeche*. Instituto Nacional de Antropología e Historia, Mexico.

NASA. 1999. SRTM 90m Digital Elevation Model DEM. NASA Jet Propulsion Laboratory and the USGS EROS Data Center. Online: http://srtm.usgs.gov/, http://eros.usgs.gov/.

— 2011. Current LANDSAT Coverage circa 1990/2000. Available at: http://zulu.ssc.nasa.gov/mrsid/.

Piña Chan, Roman. 1967. *Atlas arqueológico de la República Mexicana. 3, Chiapas*. Instituto Nacional de Antropologia e História, Mexico.

Pollock, Harry E. D. 1970. Architectural Notes on Some Chenes Ruins. In *Monographs and Paper in Maya Archaeology*, edited by William R. Bullard, Jr., pp. 1-88. Papers of the Peabody Museum of Archaeology and Ethnology 61. Harvard University, Cambridge, Mass.

— 1980. *The Puuc: An Architectural Survey of the Hill Country of Yucatan and Northern Campeche, Mexico*. Memoirs of the Peabody Museum of Archaeology and Ethnology 19. Harvard University, Cambridge, Mass.

Puleston, Dennis E. 1974. Intersite Areas in the Vicinity of Tikal and Uaxactun. In *Mesoamerican Archaeology: New Approaches*, edited by Norman Hammond, pp. 303-311. University of Texas, Austin.

— 1983. *The Settlement Survey of Tikal*. Tikal Reports 13. University Museum, University of Pennsylvania, Philadelphia.

Robles Castellanos, Fernando, and Anthony P. Andrews. 2003. *Proyecto Costa Maya: reconocimiento arqueológico en el noroeste de Yucatán, México. Reporte Interino, Temporada 2002: Reconocimiento arqueológico de la esquina noroeste de la península de Yucatán y primeras aproximaciones a los temas de investigación. Informe para el Consejo Nacional de Arqueología de México*. Report on file at the Centro INAH Yucatan, National Geographic Society, and New College of Florida, Sarasota.

Ruppert, Karl, and John Hopkins Denison. 1943. *Archaeological reconnaissance in Campeche, Quintana Roo, and Peten*. Publication No. 543. Carnegie Institution of Washington, Washington, D.C.

Sidrys, Raymond V. 1983. *Archaeological Excavations in Northern Belize, Central America*. Monograph XVII, Institute of Archaeology, University of California, Los Angeles.

Sisson, Edward B. 1976. Archaeological Survey of the Chontalpa Region, Tabasco, Mexico. Ph.D. dissertation, Department of Anthropology, Harvard University, Cambridge. University Microfilms, Ann Arbor.

Smith, James Gregory. 2000. *The Chichén Itzá-Ek Balam Transect Project: An Intersite Perspective on the Political Organization of the Ancient Maya*. Ph.D. dissertation, Department of Anthropology, University of Pittsburgh. University Microfilms, Ann Arbor.

Šprajc, Ivan. 2004. Maya Sites and Monuments in SE Campeche. *Journal of Field Archaeology* 29(3/4):385-407.

Sprajc, Ivan, Tomaz Podobnikar, and Nikolai Grube. 2001. Archaeological Reconnaissance in Southeastern Campeche, Mexico: 2001 Field Season Report. Report to the Foundation for the Advancement of Mesoamerican Studies. Online: http://www.famsi.org/reports/00016/index.html.

Stephens, John L. 1969. *Incidents of Travel in Central America, Chiapas, and Yucatan* [1841]. Dover, Mineola. London.

— 1843. *Incidents of Travel in Yucatan*. Harper & Brothers, New York.

Stuart, Georg E., J. C. Scheffler, Edward B. Kurjack, and John W. Cottier. 1979. *Map of the Ruins of Dzibilchaltun, Yucatan, Mexico*. Publication 47. Middle American Research Institution, Tulane University, New Orleans.

Thomas, Prentice M. 1981. *Prehistoric Maya Settlement Patterns at Becan, Campeche, Mexico*. Publication 45. Middle American Research Institution, Tulane University, New Orleans.

Tucker, Compton J., Denelle M. Grant, and Jon D. Dykstra. 2004. NASA's Global Orthorectified LANDSAT Data Set. *Photogrammetric Engineering & Remote Sensing* 70(3):313-322.

Von Nagy, Christopher L. 2003. *Of Meandering Rivers and Shifting Towns: Landscape Evolution and Community within the Grijalva Delta*. Ph.D. dissertation, Department of Anthropology, Tulane University. University Microfilms, Ann Arbor.

West, Robert C., N. P. Psuty, and B. G. Thom. 1969. *The Tabasco Lowlands of Southeastern Mexico*. Coastal Studies Series 27. Louisiana State University, Baton Rouge.

Williams-Beck, Lorraine A. 1998. *El dominio de los batabob: El área Puuc occidental campechana*. Universidad Autónoma de Campeche, Campeche.

Witschey, Walter R. T., and Clifford T. Brown. 2001. Building a GIS System of Ancient Lowland Maya Settlement. Paper Presented at the 66th Annual Meetings of the Society for American Archaeology, New Orleans.

— 2002. The Electronic Atlas of Ancient Maya Sites. Paper Presented at the 67th Annual Meetings of the Society for American Archaeology, Denver.

Part III

THE TERMINAL CLASSIC AND EARLY POSTCLASSIC PERIODS

8 The Nunnery Quadrangle of Uxmal

William M. Ringle

Abstract

This chapter considers the function of the Nunnery Quadrangle of Uxmal, one of the most important examples of the Terminal Classic Puuc architectural style. Uxmal has several quadrangles, but the particular interest of the Nunnery is the manner in which a local architectural form, and most probably the social institutions that it housed, were modified by the incorporation of "Mexican" or "Toltec" iconography and architectural traits in the late ninth or early tenth centuries. These traits mark the emergence of Uxmal as another of the Epiclassic Tollans, as was Chichen Itza in eastern Yucatan.

The central argument of this chapter is that the Nunnery Quadrangle was the meeting place of the court of Uxmal and that each of its wings was dedicated to one of the four "estates" directing its governance. The four "estates" represented by the Nunnery Quadrangle are the king to the north, a priestly or noble council to the west, the military to the east, and the secondary clients subject to or allied with Uxmal to the south. The Nunnery, therefore, was the place where these four "estates" met to debate matters of state, make judgments, and carry out political rituals such as investiture. The prominence of the Nunnery and the elaboration of its architecture underscore the importance councils played in such polities, even though ultimate authority was vested in the king.

The proposition that the form and disposition of ancient buildings in some way reflect the ideologies of their occupants has been a fruitful one for the study of Maya urbanism (e.g., essays in Christie 2003; Evans and Pillsbury 2004; Houston 1998; Inomata and Houston 2001; Kowalski 1999). In most cases, emphasis has been on the cosmological, religious, or mythic underpinnings of architecture and site plans, but alternatively the sociopolitical relationships encoded in the built environment might be pursued. Although these are often halves of the same coin, a concentration on the former aspects often stops short of providing insight into the use of architectural complexes. Assumptions that architectural complexes exemplify standard Maya cosmological concepts may also obscure the particular cultural and historical circumstances that resulted in their genesis.

This contribution considers the function of the Nunnery Quadrangle of Uxmal (Figures 1.1 and 8.1), one of the emblematic structures of the Terminal Classic Puuc architectural style. George Bey and I suggested a few years ago that the Nunnery was the locus of the royal court of Uxmal (Ringle and Bey 2001:281), and in this chapter I shall enlarge upon subsequent comments amplifying this observation (Ringle 2003, 2004). The basic arrangement of the Nunnery is by no means unique. Quadrangles are among the earliest masonry complexes at many Puuc centers,[1] and the position of the large pyramid Structure 1B2 at Kabah and the quadrangle to the south of it is strikingly reminiscent of the Adivino-Pajaros complex relative to the Nunnery (Figure 8.2). Further north, Landa (1978:110) sketched a structure from Tiho that is very similar to the Nunnery, although he unfortunately provided no information on its function.

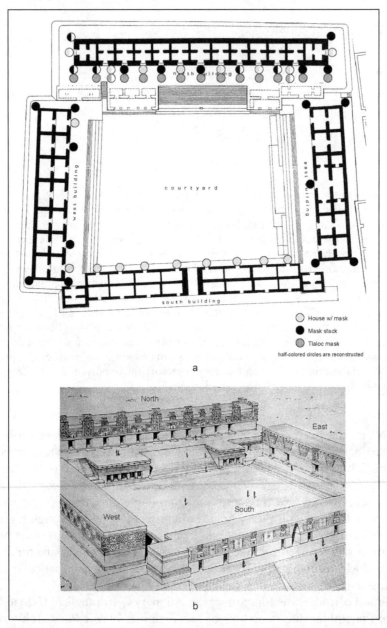

Figure 8.1. The Nunnery Quadrangle, Uxmal: (a) plan showing distribution of mask stacks, Tlaloc masks, and stone huts (Andrews 1995:219); (b) perspective view (http://academic.reed.edu/uxmal/).

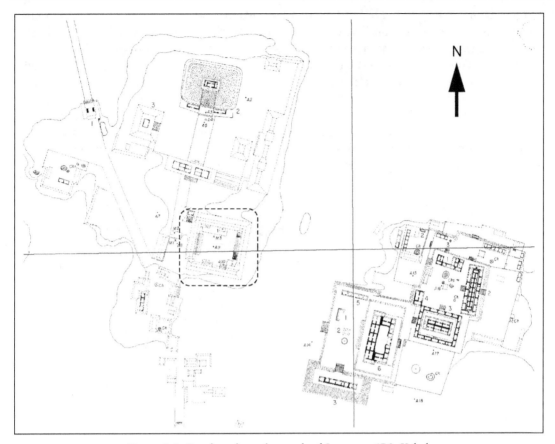

Figure 8.2. Quadrangle to the south of Structure 1B2, Kabah
(modified from Pollock 1980:Figure 281).

Uxmal itself has several quadrangles, but the particular interest of the Nunnery is the manner in which a local architectural form, and most probably the social institutions that it housed, were adapted to novel circumstances. Those circumstances are reflected in the adoption of "Mexican" iconography and architectural traits in the late ninth or early tenth centuries. My premise is that rather than being marks of conquest, these indicate Uxmal served as another of the Epiclassic Tollans, much as did Chichen Itza for eastern Yucatan.

The central argument of this paper is that each wing of the Nunnery Quadrangle represents a specific division within the political structure of Uxmal. These divisions are perhaps best characterized as akin to the estates of feudal Europe. That is, each wing belonged to a broad social division within the Uxmal polity, each of which had specific powers within the overall political structure. The four "estates" represented by the Nunnery Quadrangle are the king to the north, a priestly or noble council to the west, the military to the east, and the secondary clients subject to or allied with Uxmal to the south. The Nunnery, therefore, was the place where these four "estates" met to debate matters of state, make judgments, and carry out political rituals such as investiture. The prominence of the Nunnery and the elaboration of its architecture underscore the importance councils played in such polities, even though ultimate authority might be vested in the king.

Similar arrangements prevailed at Chichen Itza, Mitla, and in representations of Nahua "palaces" from Tenochtitlan and Texcoco. All of these cities had some claim to "Toltec" ancestry,[1] and this ancestry may have included aspects of their political organization. In this chapter, I use 'Toltec' to refer to the broader political ideology symbolized by the feathered serpent, rather than restricting it to the inhabitants of Tula, Hidalgo. The roots of this tradition were probably in Early Classic Teotihuacan, but during the Epiclassic period, several centers assumed the mantle of Tollan, including Uxmal and Chichen Itza. Shared symbols of political legitimation, such as the feathered serpent, may thus be reflections of deeper commonalities of governance among such groups. At Uxmal, these symbols are almost wholly confined to the Nunnery, House of the Governor, and the ballcourt between them (Figure 8.3).

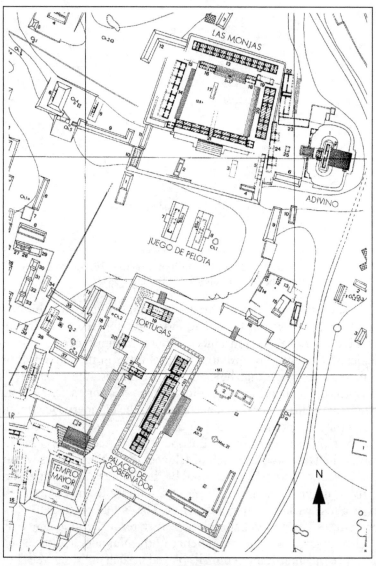

Figure 8.3. Central Uxmal, showing position of the Nunnery, ballcourt, and House of the Governor (modified from Graham 1992:4:83).

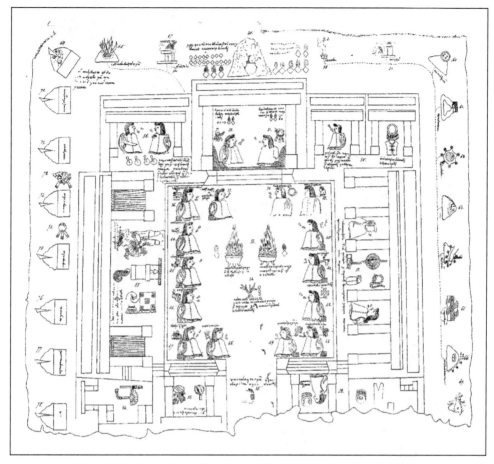

Figure 8.4. *Mapa Quinatzin*, second sheet (Mohar Betancourt 2004).

Nahua "palaces" had areas dedicated to political affairs that were distinct from the royal residential quarters (Evans 2004). As with the Nunnery, these consisted of halls arranged about an open quadrangle or patio, such as are depicted on the *Mapa Quinatzin* (Figure 8.4; Mohar Betancourt 2004) and in the *Codex Mendoza* (Figure 8.5; Berdan and Anawalt 1997:3:f. 69r), and as are discussed at length by Alva Ixtlilxochitl (1985:2:92-97). The use of such structures could have evolved through time. The fate of an earlier Texcocoan royal palace is particularly interesting in this respect:

> Built in the fourteenth century by Quinantzin, the [p]alace...was for many years the principal feature of Texcoco, housing the ruler and his court. Although over-shadowed by the buildings erected by Nezahualcoyotl and Nezahualpilli, it served as council hall for the lords of Texcoco up to the time of the Spanish conquest (Cline 1966:92–93, cited in Evans 2004).

Such shifts in the functions of entire complexes are evident elsewhere in the Puuc (Ringle et al. 2005), and it might be speculated that whatever the original form and function of the Nunnery Quadrangle, it was dramatically refurbished as a council hall as part of the decision to construct the House of the Governor as the main royal residence (for the latter, see Kowalski 1987:84-86).

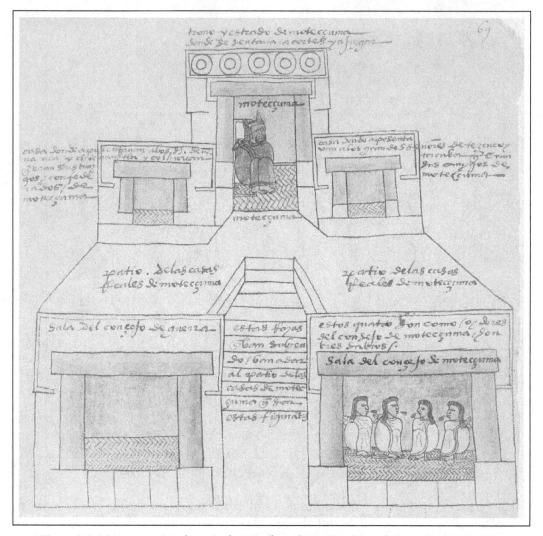

Figure 8.5. Moteuczoma's palace, *Codex Mendoza*, f. 69r (Berdan and Anawalt 1992:3:143).

Alternative Perspectives

The Nunnery has been most frequently interpreted through the lens of religious and ritual iconography. Jeff Kowalski (1990, 1994, 2007), the most prolific commentator on Uxmal, has suggested that the Nunnery Quadrangle reflects "an effort to replicate the well-documented quadripartite horizontal organization of the Maya cosmos, with east and west associated with the rising and setting sun and north and south corresponding to the upperworld and underworld" (Kowalski and Dunning 1999:280). Three lines of evidence are argued to support this position: (1) differences in the height of the four sides, with the north (upperworld) being the highest and the south (underworld) the lowest; (2) the number of doorways—13 to the north (argued to be the number of celestial heavens), nine to the south (the number of levels to the underworld), seven to the west (perhaps a seven-layered earth), and five to the east (supposedly relating to the five cardinal directions); and (3) the iconography of the sculpture on the building façades. Finally, Kowalski claims that the large *picota* found at the center of the Nunnery court represents the ceiba tree forming the Maya *axis mundi*.

Aside from doing little to explain its function, the evidence that the Nunnery Quadrangle was a Maya cosmogram is questionable. First of all, the layout of the Nunnery clearly is not rectangular, as might be expected of an idealized diagram of the cosmos. Much of the iconographic evidence marshaled in favor of this argument is equivocal and non-specific; nothing in the iconography suggests that particular layers of the cosmos are referenced, for instance. A more serious objection is that of Nielsen and Reunert (2009), who argue that the multi-level model of the Mesoamerican upper- and underworlds resulted from colonial borrowing of European concepts. They maintain that texts and imagery that are indisputably prehispanic in date document only a three-level system (underworld, upperworld, and this-world). Although numbers such as 13, nine, seven, and five were of undoubted prehispanic ritual importance, their connection to cosmic layers remains to be demonstrated. As for the *picota*, this type of marker is quite common at Puuc sites, although in smaller form. Smaller *picotas* are very often inverted frusta (truncated cones), and most are found in front of important buildings along their centerlines. All lack any sort of figural decoration that might identify them as ceibas, which have a distinctive spiny bark. These criticisms do not rule out Kowalski and Dunning's (1999) interpretation, because clearly some of the iconography is religious or mythological in nature, but do underline its tenuous basis. Left unanswered are the functions of the group as a whole and of its component structures. Similar criticisms can be directed at the most recent extended treatment of the Nunnery (Schele and Mathews 1998:257-289).

My own preference is to see the design of the Nunnery as an ingenious architectural solution to more pragmatic considerations. In my view, differences in heights of the buildings and their positions in the quadrangle are reflective of the relative prestige of the "estates" they represent. These estates are also the main subjects of the friezes above each building, as detailed below. As might be expected, the north wing, associated with the paramount, is the highest building, and is in fact the only structure with two stories. This difference is reinforced by stacks of four "Chak" masks topped by a Tlaloc panel, versus the three-mask stacks of the east and west wings. The east and west wings are of approximately equal height and distance from the north wing. Thus these two estates may have been of equal status, or at least were represented as such. This is in keeping with suggestions from other Tollans that both military and noble councils advised the king and account for the pervasive dualism of Toltec political symbolism. Finally, the south wing, which I argue housed clients of Uxmal, is the lowest and most distant from the king, and hence may be supposed to be of least status. Significantly, mask stacks are absent from this façade.

It may be supposed that each estate also varied in the number of high offices attached to it, and this, in my view, was the primary reason for differences in building plans, especially the number of rooms and doorways. The solution devised by the architects of the Nunnery for arranging four unequal branches of government about a courtyard is a particularly elegant one, but was not, in my view, ultimately based on cosmological concerns. Similarly, the differing number of façade motifs, especially of masks and houses, probably had more to do with political symbolism.

Dating the Nunnery Complex

Ceramics

The few organized excavations in the Nunnery Quadrangle have unfortunately been underreported, especially with regard to ceramics. None of Brainerd's units impinged on the Nunnery Quadrangle, and he found little or no admixture of what would now be called Sotuta ceramics in the 50,000 sherds collected from Uxmal (Brainerd 1958:31, Chart 1).[3] Smith (1971:1:259, Table 1b) had a similar experience. Cehpech ceramics formed the overwhelming majority of material from his trenches, with only four of more than 32,000 sherds belonging to the Sotuta complex. He did place two units outside the northeast and northwest corners of the Nunnery, but unfortunately did not include them in his analysis due to the paucity of ceramics from these trenches. The principal access stairway to the south of the Nunnery was cleared and consolidated in the 1980s, again without mention of Sotuta pottery, although no detailed tabulation of the ceramics is provided (Barrera Rubio and Huchím Herrera 1990:70-71).

In contrast, Ruz (1954:52) mentions finding sherds of Z Fine Orange and Plumbate (and perhaps Provincia Plano relief) on the surface of the Nunnery courtyard and in association with the later C-shaped structure at its center, although his ceramic data are not quantified. In the 1970s, the courtyard and adjacent basal platforms were trenched to house fixtures for the sound and light show. Although these excavations were never published, Anthony Andrews (personal communication 2010) reports that a substantial fraction of the recovered material belonged to the Sotuta sphere. Unfortunately, this collection was subsequently discarded. Konieczna and Mayer Guala (1976), who performed this work, did publish a short study of some ancillary excavations near the Nunnery, which also yielded sizeable quantities of Sotuta ceramics. Limited evidence thus indicates that Sotuta ceramics were present in the Nunnery in contrast to the overwhelming predominance of Cehpech materials elsewhere at the site.

A similar picture comes from the other buildings associated with the Nunnery. Consolidation of the ballcourt by Maldonado resulted in a small number of sherds from the Hocaba complex,[4] as well as a dedicatory cache containing a Z Fine Orange vessel (Kurjack et al. 1991:155-157). As for the House of the Governor, Brainerd (1958:31) reports that Ruz found a Fine Orange (variety indeterminate) dish in a cache buried in its basal platform. Smith (1971:1:259) excavated two trenches at the base of the basal platform supporting the structure, one of which had no identifiable material and the other only Cehpech types. Consolidation of the northern platform did yield some Sotuta material, however, including Silho Fine Orange and Tohil Plumbate (Barrera Rubio and Huchím Herrera 1990:34).

Architectural Stratigraphy

Stephens (1963:1:183) long ago observed that the original version of the north building of the Nunnery Quadrangle was encased within (but not buried by) a second outer façade. Erosa Peniche (1948:31) characterized the inner structure as "more primitive" than the final building, but Ruz's (1954, 1957) reports do not provide a detailed description of the buried façade. Ruz did show, however, that the pair of tandem rooms at either end of the North Wing was added as part of this later refurbishing of the exterior. In other words, the structure originally had only 11 doorways. The platform upon which it is built was also refurbished by covering the original vertical stepped faces of the sides with a single battered wall (*talud*), a Modified Florescent (Itza) architectural trait. Further evidence of earlier construction was found along the west side of the Nunnery:

Some years ago, a hole was dug in the rear platform of the western building, which clearly allowed us to see the upper part of an arch and some of the stones used to seal it. This hole was covered when the Light and Sound Show installations were put in. This tells us...that the western building was built over an existing structure (Zapata Alonzo 1983:42).

Of the buildings presently visible, Kowalski (1990) contends that the south structure was the first to be built, then the east and west structures, and finally the north structure, although he believes relatively little time elapsed between construction stages.

Absolute Dates

Five C-14 dates come from the Nunnery complex, although the fact that the first two samples were assayed during the early years of radiocarbon dating renders them somewhat suspect. The other three dates were recently collected by Hanns Prem and are reported in Vallo (2003). As can be seen in Table 8.1, the dates show little overall consistency, including two from the same beam that differ by over four centuries. The total range is more than six centuries. Sampling of the interiors of beams or reutilization of existing beams may have produced dates earlier than the actual construction of the Nunnery (Hanns Prem, personal communication 2010). Moreover, later dates may reflect the replacement of the original beams or contamination by modern pollutants.

Hieroglyphic texts offer a more precise construction date for the complex, although these too are not without their problems (Thompson 1941:106-108; Kowalski 1987:34-37). Schele and Mathews' (1998:286-287) analysis of the capstone texts from Building Y (a lower addition to the north structure), the east structure, and the south structure suggests that the final versions of the quadrangle date to the first decade of the tenth century A.D. Stela 17 (Figure 8.6), a seat-shaped monument resting on the stairs of the north building, is unfortunately very poorly preserved, but Morley believed he could detect "the day 12 Ahau perhaps preceded by a Tun 6 or a Tun 11" (quoted in Pollock 1980:274). Schele and Mathews (1998:288) argue that 12 Ajaw is in fact mentioned twice on the stone and Graham's (1992) drawing indicates a third may even be present (Figure 8.6:B5, C6, and F7). Because 12 Ajaw likely names the *k'atun* of the short count (reinforced by a possible preposition before B5), this would date events to between A.D. 889–909. As the drawing indicates, this date is less than secure, but does agree with the other hieroglyphic dates mentioned herein.

A final date that is possibly relevant comes from an unpublished photograph taken in the southeast corner of the Nunnery by (Alice?) Le Plongeon, presumably in the 1880s (Figure 8.7). The photograph shows Augustus Le Plongeon seated next to a pile of displaced architectural stones. He points dreamily toward a large stone phallus, beneath which is a stone, possibly an altar section, inscribed with the undoubted date 12 Ajaw. Beneath is another glyph with a coefficient of 12, a subfix of T116, *-ni*. To my eye, the central sign is the T528 *tun* sign. Although it is more common to have the *tun* sign precede the Ajaw date, this may be a reference to 10.3.12.0.0 (A.D. 901).

These dates also are in accord with interpretations of the hieroglyphic dates from the Uxmal ballcourt, relevant in being the only other structure at Uxmal bearing clear feathered-serpent iconography. Graham's (1992) drawing of the first ring indicates it bears the date * 17 Pop, 12th/17th *tun*, 12 Ajaw, while the second ring bears the date * Ix 16 Pop, 17th *tun* 12/13 Ajaw. Kelley (1982:15) argues that the two dates are 10.3.15.16.14 2 Ix 17 Pop (A.D. 905) and the other, less surely, a day later. Graña-Behrens (2002:444) argues for a somewhat earlier date of 10.3.11.15.14 11 Ix 17 Pop and the other one day later at 10.3.11.15.15 (12 Men) 18 Pop, A.D. 901, very close to the date that Morley believed he could read on Stela 17. Note that neither are Puuc-style dates.

Table 8.1. Radiocarbon dates and calibrations from the Nunnery Quadrangle.

SAMPLE	PROVENIENCE	AGE B.P.	CALIB 14 CALIBRATION	FAIRCHILD CALIBRATION (1 sigma)	VALLO (2003) (2 sigma)
IVIC-485	Nunnery addition	1210 ± 60	68.3 (1 sigma) cal AD 710–746 0.190 766–890 0.810 95.4 (2 sigma) cal AD 672–903 0.892 914–969 0.108	1133 BP ± 81 AD 817 ± 81	
GrN-613	North Wing beam	1065 ± 120	68.3 (1 sigma) cal AD 782–789 0.016 812–845 0.086 857–1048 0.767 1087–1122 0.101 1138–1150 0.030 95.4 (2 sigma) cal AD 692–749 0.050 764–1210 0.950	977 BP ± 124 AD 973 ± 124	
Erl-1316	North Wing, 2nd room from east, inner door	1565 ± 65	68.3 (1 sigma) cal AD 424–557 1.000 95.4 (2 sigma) cal AD 351–367 0.014 380–635 0.986	1448 BP ± 74 AD 502 ± 74	AD 390(513)636
Erl-1323	West Wing, 3rd room from north, inner door, eastern beam, core	1403 ± 34	68.3 (1 sigma) cal AD 618–658 1.000 95.4 (2 sigma) cal AD 586–671 1.000	1306 BP ± 19 AD 644 ± 19	AD 606(640)674
Erl-1317	Same, but outer part of beam	959 ± 35	68.3 (1 sigma) cal AD 1024–1050 0.324 1083–1125 0.503 1136–1151 0.172 95.4 (2 sigma) cal AD 1018–1159 1.000	885 BP ± 47 AD 1065 ± 47	AD 1019(1091)1163

Data for first two dates from Andrews (1979:Table 1). Last three dates from Vallo (2003: Table 3), with provenience information and comments kindly supplied by Hanns Prem (personal communication 2010)

THE NUNNERY QUADRANGLE OF UXMAL

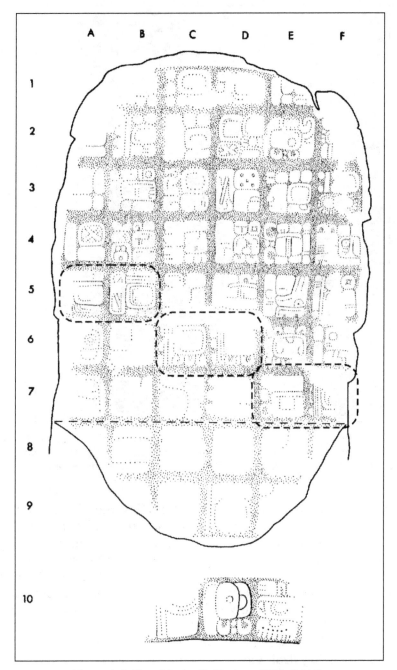

Figure 8.6. Uxmal Stela 17 (Graham 1992:4:111).

Figure 8.7. Augustus Le Plongeon in the southeast corner of the Nunnery Quadrangle with a miscellaneous sculpture. The dated monument is below the phallus. (Unpublished photograph, Le Plongeon photographic archive, George E. Stuart Collection, Wilson Library, UNC. Copy of original by Lawrence Desmond.)

No hieroglyphic dates survive from the House of the Governor, but Bricker and Bricker (1996) identify the topmost row of signs in the stacked serpent bands below the throne above the central doorway as a zodiac. On the assumption that this commemorates the sky at a maximum north or south Venus elongation, they argue for a date of either A.D. 910 or 912; Šprajc (quoted in Bricker and Bricker 1996:213) favors a date of A.D. 904. In any event, available evidence indicates that the final stages of the ballcourt, the Nunnery, and the House of the Governor were built at very nearly the same time, as part of a single architectural program, as Kowalski (1987:74) has long maintained.

These dates are among the latest from the Puuc region. Given that inscriptions in the north often commemorate building dedications, they support George Andrews' (1995:81-83) argument that the Late Uxmal Style is the last facet of the Puuc architectural sequence. With the exception of a single controversial date from the High Priest's Grave (Chapter 9), they also postdate the hieroglyphic dates from Chichen Itza. The conclusion must therefore be that the introduction of feathered serpent imagery appears later at Uxmal than at Chichen Itza and under different circumstances, given the near absence of dates from the Great Platform of that site. The scarcity of contemporary Puuc dates is also surely politically significant.

Description of the Nunnery Complex

The Nunnery was probably not a place of permanent residence, given the lack of *chultuns* for collecting and storing water. In our explorations of the Bolonchen District, we have likewise found that administrative units and putative "palaces" often lack *chultuns*. Interpretations of the buildings as meeting places also face the difficulty that no room of the Nunnery could have hosted more than a small number of people (Figure 8.1). None of the rooms are halls, and none of the rooms with access to the exterior communicate laterally. Thus general meetings of whoever occupied these buildings must have been held in the courtyard.

This is supported by the remains of an *adoratorio* that Ruz (1954:50) discovered while clearing the center of the courtyard. Only a few stones from the lowest course of its south and west sides remained, but enough to indicate a step on the west, in the direction of the west wing. He noted that previously a badly fragmented feline ("*tigre*") sculpture had been found in the rubble of this platform (illustrated in Kowalski 1990:Figure 9). The platform is thus probably the counterpart to the bicephalic jaguar seat found by Stephens on the radial shrine in front of the House of the Governor. In both cases, this was the point from which the ruler or initiate presided over larger gatherings.

The rooms facing onto the central patio of the Nunnery have no exterior egress. Although the corners of the quadrangle are open, the height of the basal platforms means that all traffic in and out of the Nunnery had to have been channeled through a small stairway between the north and east wings and, more formally, through the central open archway of the south building, which is fronted by a broad staircase. The only rooms opening to the exterior periphery are along the south side of the south building and at either end of the north building, none of which allows passage into the interior patio. Visibility of and access to the Nunnery court is thus highly restricted.

Although each of the wings has a different architectural program, subtle decorative patterns serve to integrate the whole. For instance, the north and west buildings are alike in having large paired *grecas* on their upper façades, S-shaped motifs that Schele and Mathews (1998:278) identify as cloud signs. The background mosaics of the west and north buildings are also alike and contrast with those employed on the south and east wings. The former pair employs what George Andrews (1995:333) refers to as complex latticework. By this he means a repeated diamond-shaped unit whose thick, serrated borders are strongly reminiscent of textile weaves such as are on Yaxchilan Lintel 24. The south and east wings of the Nunnery, in contrast, employ a simple pattern of X-shaped mosaic stones. Modifying Andrews' terminology slightly, this might be referred to as simple latticework. This is also the background used on the façade of the House of the Governor.

The use of mask stacks and imitation thatched huts on building façades also unifies the Nunnery architecturally, yet their distribution also signals important differences (Figure 8.1). For instance, the south building has only houses, the east building has only mask stacks. The west and north buildings have both, although the north has more of each. The north building is also unique in that only its mask stacks and huts are capped by Tlaloc masks, which are also absent from the House of the Governor and the ballcourt. On the façade of the west building, mask stacks and huts are displaced from the central doorways in favor of seated figures below canopies tied together by two interlaced feathered serpents. Across the way, on the east structure, masks are largely displaced by inverted "V"s formed of stacked serpent bars, although the central motif of the facade is a mask stack.

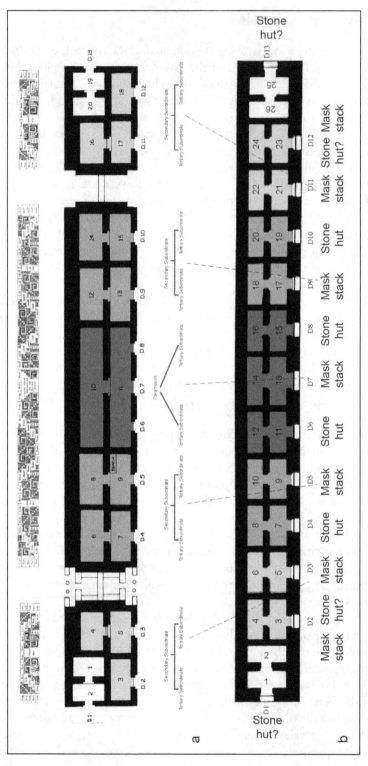

Figure 8.8. Comparative plans of the House of the Governor and the north wing of the Nunnery: (a) Plan and façade schematic of the House of the Governor; (b) plan of the north wing of the Nunnery (all from http://academic.reed.edu/uxmal/; originals in Andrews 1995:219 Kowalski 1987:Figure 41; Seler 1917:Figure 114).

Understanding the roles of mask stacks and stone huts is of crucial importance, but the masks in particular have proved remarkably resistant to interpretation. Looking at both symbols from the perspective of political organization, however, may provide a different approach. Some sense of their political role can be seen on the House of the Governor, whose façade is divided into five regions by elaborate trapezoids of stacked "Chaak" masks (Figure 8.8; Seler 1917). In the upper wall zone, each of the four exterior trapezoids encompasses exactly two doorways and two pairs of tandem rooms; the central trapezoid is larger and covers the central three doorways and two longer tandem rooms. Each of the four outer trapezoids bounds a central seated figure flanked by two smaller seated figures (Seler 1917; Kowalski 1987:181). The seated figure of the larger central trapezoid also has two attendants, but is much taller than any of the other figures and sits on an elaborate U-shaped throne; as mentioned, his is the only seat with the V-shaped serpent bar stack behind it. The masks therefore define a hierarchy of a paramount aided by four secondary nobles and ten tertiary officials, binding each to specific suites of palace rooms (the seated figures sit between the doorways bound by the trapezoids). These masks are identical, but those of the Nunnery are not, in my view because the latter refer to distinct offices.

The East Building

The east building, hypothesized to house the war council, has five doorways with mask stacks over the central doorway and at the corners (Figure 8.9). The remainder of the upper wall zone is filled with six V-shaped motifs each consisting of eight stacked bicephalic feathered serpent bars, increasing in length from bottom to top. Four of the V-shaped motifs are over the four exterior doors, and the other two flank the central doorway and its mask stack. A smaller version of just three bars lies over the central mask stack. Although Schele and Mathews (1998:268) suggest this was an image of a corncrib, this is highly unlikely because the same serpent bar stack is also found over the central door of the House of the Governor. This last stack also consists of eight bars except that the space between the bars is filled with a series of symbols, the top row of which Bricker and Bricker (1996) argue are zodiacal references. Since a seated ruler is immediately above this stack, the association instead seems to be with rulership.

Rather than a "house of magic" dedicated to Itzam Nah, as Schele and Mathews (1998:267) argue, various lines of evidence suggest that the east building housed the war council. Perhaps the strongest of Kowalski and Dunning's (1999:285) observations is that the east building "pertains to a Teotihuacan-related cult of war and sacrifice connected with Venus and the emergence of the sun from the Underworld," a point made earlier by Taube (1992: 60 n. 2). With this I would agree. For one thing, the building faces west, as do the serpent temples at Chichen Itza, many if not all of which can be associated with warrior activities.

The virtually identical medallions at the center of the serpent bar stacks are the clearest indicator of a military function (Figure 8.10). Each consists of the head and upper torso of a figure wearing a mosaic mask and a feathered headdress, behind which are two crossed spears or darts. This has been interpreted as the head of an owl, a bird with martial associations from Teotihuacan onward (Kowalski and Dunning 1999:286). Nevertheless, Teotihuacan owls, such as those from Tetitla, have a teardrop shaped pattern around the eyes and lack goggles, either around the eyes or above them. All the Teotihuacan examples are feathered, and none are sheathed in mosaics. In contrast, none of the Uxmal heads have feathers, their faces are covered with mosaic masks, and what appear to be mosaic tunics cover their upper torsos (mosaic tunics figure prominently in Toltec caches and in Toltec investiture rites elsewhere [Ringle 2004]). The ears of the Uxmal heads vary from round to pointed. The pointed examples closely resemble the convention for jaguar ears, and may refer to the jaguar god of the underworld, a god with clear martial associations.

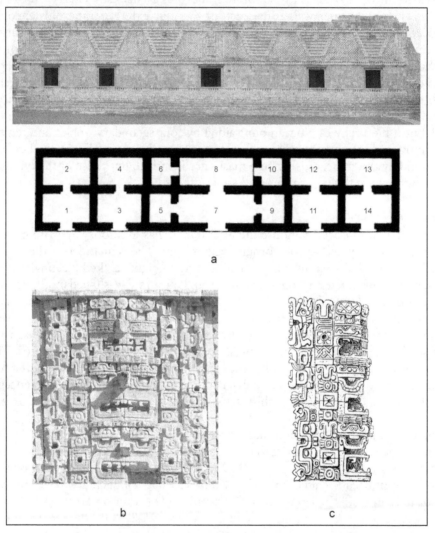

Figure 8.9. Front (west) façade, east wing, Nunnery Quadrangle (author photograph).

The mosaic goggles around the eyes of the Nunnery heads are very like those of mosaic mask heads from Teotihuacan. The same is true for the rings above the eyes, as an example of this head from the Uxmal ballcourt (Figure 8.10f) makes clear. In both cases these forehead rings are also occasionally feathered or have petals. For these reasons, Taube (1992: 60 n. 2) argues that the Uxmal heads are wearing a later version of the Teotihuacan war serpent mask. Double sets of goggle elements also characterize the main "effigy" of the Lower Temple of the Jaguars, Chichen Itza.

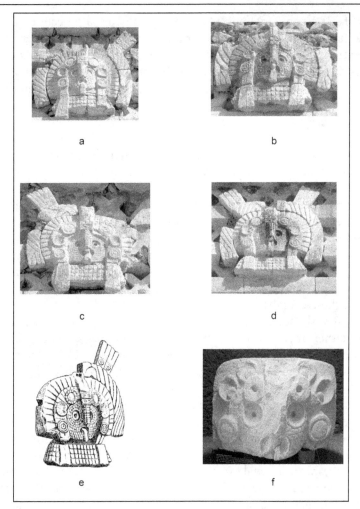

Figure 8.10. Mosaic heads from the east wing façade: (a-d) Rhyne 2008a; (e) Seler 1917: Figure 28; (f) author photograph (a–e from http://academic.reed.edu/uxmal/).

Most telling for the owl interpretation is the lack of a beak on the Uxmal heads. The mouths are badly damaged in some of the examples, but the figures seem to be extending their tongues. Instead of a beak, the nose and the center of the forehead are covered by a serrated element, above which are two knots fastening what might be a cluster of feathers or cloth strips. Knots are also diagnostic of Teotihuacan war serpents and warriors with war serpent headdresses (von Winning 1988:157, Figures 4a–c), where they are typically placed over the upper set of goggles. Here, however, the knots may serve to identify this central motif as a stingray spine perforator. Although tongue autosacrifice was more commonly practiced by females, penitential autosacrifice certainly characterized warrior rituals at Tenochtitlan, Tlaxcala, and Chichen Itza.

The mask stacks over the central doorway and the four corners of the east building also convey a consistent message (Figure 8.9). In each case, the bottom two of the three masks are identical with the exception of a few minor differences. However, in the extant cases the upper mask is distinguished by having supra-orbital plates marked with crossed bones and sub-orbital plates bearing T510f star/Venus emblems. (The T510f emblems also occur on the lower masks of the central stack, but not on the lower masks of the corners.) Both motifs are consistent with a military interpretation, the bones being another instance of the association of death imagery with warriors, and the T510 emblem relates to the feathered serpent/Venus dimension of Toltec warfare. With regard to the latter, Lamb (1980) argued some years ago that the number of Xs within the serpent bar stacks represents the synodical period of Venus. The heads at either end of the bands are also clearly feathered serpents and a few of the panels framing the mask stacks are as well, underscoring the relationship between Quetzalcoatl and militarism.

The V-shaped motifs suggest that six offices were housed in this structure (Figure 8.9).[5] The four outermost motifs lie directly above doorways fronting a pair of tandem rooms, and so may tie an office to each of the four pairs (Rooms 1–4, 11–14). As for the other two, Stephens (1963:1:185) noted that the east building is unusual in that the main door gave access to the only interior suite of chambers within the Nunnery (Rooms 5-10), two large rooms arranged in tandem fashion and connected by a central doorway, each in turn flanked on both ends by smaller compartments. The two innermost V-shaped motifs lie above the centerline of these flanking compartments, which only open internally. These internal doorways are distinctive in being ornamented with colonnettes, which are nearly always a façade element, and may suggest the formal nature of these chambers.

The two innermost V-shaped motifs (and the two offices they symbolize) may be linked to the interior suite in either of two ways. Each may have presided from one of the two central rooms (Rooms 7 and 8). The four flanking rooms (Rooms 5, 6, 9, 10) may have been occupied by four captains associated with the four pairs of outer rooms on occasions when all six captains conferred or were present for audiences. This may explain the placement of colonnettes above each of the interior room entrances as symbols of the four outer doorways of these captains. It may also suggest that the two central offices were more important than the outer four (hence the central mask stack), and that the six were divided into two symmetrical groups of three. Alternatively, the identity of the mosaic sculptures on the exterior may instead suggest that all six offices were equivalent, although again divided into two groups of three. In this arrangement, since each of the four outermost captains has a pair of rooms, the two innermost captains each may have been associated with two of the rooms flanking the two central tandem rooms (Rooms 5–6 and 9–10). The two central rooms, therefore, may have been reception or meeting rooms.

The absence of stone huts on the façade of the east building is significant. One possible explanation is that officials associated with stone huts on the other wings were landed nobility and heads of extended noble households. Military rank may have been based on other criteria. Among Nahua groups, commoners could ascend to relatively high rank through merit on the battlefield. Moreover, certain war councils had both commoner and noble members (precisely six in the case of Texcoco). War leaders at Uxmal may well have had multiple roles and in fact been household heads, but the emphasis on warfare on this wing made such symbolism irrelevant.

The West Building

The iconography of the upper wall zone of the west building is by far the most complex of the four wings. Some caution must be exerted, however, for much of the façade collapsed in the decade preceding Stephens' (1963:1:178-181) visit, leaving only the sections between Doors 2 and 3 and then above Door 6 intact. As reconstructed, the decoration of the upper wall zone consists of corner mask stacks, imitation huts surmounted by masks above Doors 1 and 7 and mask stacks above Doors 2 and 6. Three figures seated on thrones are each placed over Doors 3-5, with the seated figure over the central door (Door 5) being the most elaborate (Figure 8.11). The latter also has a mask above it on the upper molding above the frieze proper.

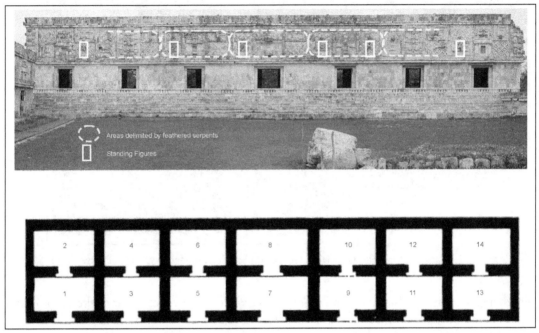

Figure 8.11. Front (east) façade and plan, west wing, Nunnery Quadrangle: (a) author composite photograph; (b) detail Andrews 1995:219 (from http://academic.reed.edu/uxmal/).

As with the east building, the masks of the façade and corners are quite similar with few distinctive decorative marks on their faces (Figure 8.12). The stacked masks of this side are distinguished by a frame of feathered serpent heads facing outwards with their tongues extended, perhaps symbolizing wind. The masks also wear a flowered headband, which Taube (2004: 85-87) argues identifies them as images of Flower Mountain, a celestial paradise. He notes similar masks are found at Chichen Itza and that flowered headbands appear as early as the Late Preclassic period at San Bartolo, Guatemala. The identification is an important one, but his brief discussion does not indicate why Flower Mountain might be prominent on this façade.

It is worthwhile noting that flowered headbands have a restricted spatial distribution within the Nunnery and are not invariant. On the west building, the masks of the stacks over Doors 2 and 6 all have a headband of repeated rosettes on what may be a feathered band, while the masks of the exterior stacks, and the masks over the huts and over the central doorway, have a central rosette with serpents (some feathered) extending to either side. One final detail distinguishes the exterior masks—each has a cruller-shaped motif between its brow plates. In a few cases the cruller is replaced by a flat circular motif, but these may have been added during restoration. In contrast, the masks of the central stack have circular button-like ornaments projecting from between their brow plates. Still other variants of the flower headband appear on the north building. Thus, there was no single "Flower Mountain" image on the Nunnery façades; on the west building the intention was clearly to distinguish the corner and doorway masks.

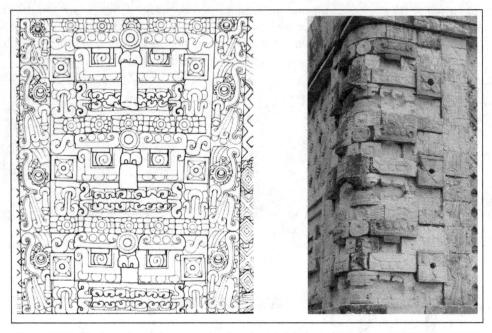

Figure 8.12. Mask stacks of the west wing façade: (a) Schele and Mathews 1998:Figure 7.36; (b) author photograph.

Feathered serpent heads also extend from the ends of the central element of the three-part upper and medial moldings. Puuc three-part moldings often represent bound or tied elements, and on the west building the serpents serve to bind the composition together, as they do on several structures at Chichen Itza. This is reinforced by the much more prominent twinned feathered serpents extending along the edges of the frieze proper, leaving only the two huts and the corner mask stacks outside of their coils. In four places the serpents intertwine to form vertical divisions that, together with their heads and tails, define five sections of the frieze (Figure 8.11). The flowered headband mask stacks and stone huts occupy the two outermost of the five sections and strictly speaking are not enclosed by the feathered serpents, although the head and tail of the feathered serpents pass behind the mask stacks to emerge on their far sides. The coils of the snake do, however, confine the three seated figures and their canopies in the second, third, and fourth divisions. The mask stacks and the feathered serpents thus function similarly to the trapezoidal mask stacks on the House of the Governor façade in bounding sculptures of particular offices.

Stephens (1963:1:179) was the first to note that the tails of the serpents bear "an ornament upon it like a turban, with a plume of feathers," but it remained for Schele and Mathews (1998:283-284) to connect this to the symbolism of the Feathered Serpent Pyramid at Teotihuacan (Figure 8.13). The latter is decorated with a series of undulating feathered serpents, on each of whose bodies lies a mosaic war serpent headdress (Sugiyama 1989; Taube 1992), essentially the same message conveyed by the headdress-on-feathered serpent of the west building of the Nunnery. Another variant can be found on the Pyramid of the Feathered Serpent at Xochicalco (Ringle et al. 1998), where the headdress is replaced by the full figure of a seated lord. Yet at Uxmal, the message of the plumed turban is unlikely to be warfare, since that theme is more directly associated with the east structure, a point to which I return below.

THE NUNNERY QUADRANGLE OF UXMAL **211**

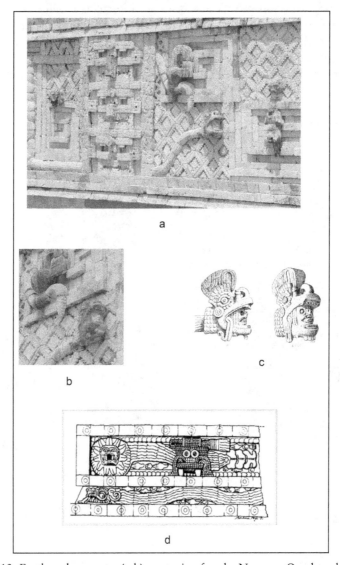

Figure 8.13. Feathered serpents: (a-b) west wing façade, Nunnery Quadrangle, Uxmal.

The façade above the central three rooms of this building is dominated by three multi-tiered feathered headdresses or canopies above what were probably seated figures, in my view indicating that this was the wing where investitures were carried out. The group performing these ceremonies was probably the feathered serpent priesthood, probably organized in dual fashion and housed in the end rooms of this building. Several pieces of evidence support this argument. First, the *adoratorio* at the center of the Nunnery patio faces the central doorway of the west building, not the more imposing north building. From this point, the sovereign could oversee rites such as investiture. Second is the headdress on the tail of the serpent. Headdresses were the costume element most freighted with political meaning, and the placement of the headdress was a peak moment in rites of investiture at sites such as Palenque. Third, the feathered serpent heads on the west building have small warriors emerging from their maws.

212 THE ANCIENT MAYA OF MEXICO

This is one of the more common motifs in Classic and Postclassic Mesoamerica, one of the most famous examples being the emergence of "Stripe Eye" from the maw of an Ehecatl serpent on ff. 36-38 of the *Codex Borgia* (Díaz and Rodgers 1993). I have argued that this represents the spiritual transformation undergone by an initiate in Toltec rites of investiture (Ringle 2004). It is interesting that in this case, the figure in the maw of the serpent appears to wear a mask similar to those over the doorways of the east building. Indeed, many of the figures depicted in the Nunnery Quadrangle are masked.

Figure 8.14. Canopies and stone huts, west wing, Nunnery Quadrangle, Uxmal: (a) central canopy (author photograph); (b) left and right flanking canopies (author photograph); (c) stone huts (from http://academic.reed.edu/uxmal/; Rhyne 2008a).

Fourth, the flowered headbands of the mask faces, whatever their religious or mythic referents, also mark lordship (the day Ajaw, after all, is cognate with "flower" in the central Mexican calendar). Schele (1998:500) pointed out that the façade of House E of Palenque was covered with images of blossoms. Although she concluded that "vision rites and contacting ancestors" characterized the area, the inscriptions and painted texts make clear that House E was the place of enthronement for several Palenque kings. At Chichen Itza, Taube's "Flower Mountain" head occupies the basal register of the piers of the Upper Temple of the Jaguars, another site arguably involved in investiture rites (Ringle 2004, 2009). At the Mercado, it even appears as a headband for some warriors (Taube 2004:Figure 15c). Variants of the flowered headband may therefore refer to particular ranks.

My final argument concerns the feathered objects over the three central doorways (Figure 8.14a). In my opinion they are not headdresses but feathered canopies whose elaborateness reflect the rank of the recipient. Several Guatemalan chronicles mention these as among the articles presented to initiates in "Tulan" by Nacxit (Quetzalcoatl). Such canopies were graded in size by rank. The *Título de Totonicapan*, for instance, states that "The lord Ajpop has four canopies over his throne, green feathers, a flute, and a drum. The Ajpop C'amja has three canopies over his. The Nima Rajpop Achij, two canopies, and the Ch'uti Rajpop Achij, only one" (Carmack and Mondloch 1983:183). Elaborate feathered backdrops lie behind all three of the canopies.

The central canopy, largest of the three, consists of three tiers surmounted by a top crown of upright feathers. Interestingly, this top crown is bound by a band to which three heads are attached; these I take to be variants of the three jade heads frequently attached to the headbands of Maya rulers. Also wrapped in feathered serpent coils, but separated by then from the central canopy, are two adjacent lesser canopies. These probably had two tiers, although only the lower tier remains in both examples; another fallen tier was found in the debris of the patio (Figure 8.7). The best-preserved example, over Door 3, has the lower torso of a seated figure in the niche below the canopy, as most probably did the other niches. Over the canopy is a head with round earspools and a distinctive hairstyle that frames the face in an arc rising to a prominent central ornament or topknot. Similar heads are seen on jades from the Great Cenote at Chichen Itza and in other offerings that might be construed as Toltec. The appearance of this head over what is clearly a secondary figure and canopy at Uxmal may indicate a reference to a secondary rank.

The headdresses on the tails of the two feathered serpents from the west building are clearly not cognates of the mosaic war serpent headdress on the façade of the Feathered Serpent Pyramid at Teotihuacan. The example from the Nunnery Quadrangle contains an upright crown of tall feathers, almost certainly from the quetzal. This then is very much like the headdress of the initiate at the center of the North Temple frieze at Chichen Itza and the *quetzalapanecayotl* headdress of the Aztecs (Ringle 2004:209-210). Thus, the offices being conferred were not those of war leaders, but political offices.

The façade is also decorated with a number of smaller figures, most in a very poor state of preservation. Six larger standing figures seem to be associated with each of the mosaic "cloud" *grecas*. The two outermost of these have what may be an animal head or headdress above them. They are naked except for a pectoral, and have serrated objects on their *penises* and upper thighs. These may be images of autosacrifice that complement those of the east building. The standing figure associated with the central doorway is unfortunately too damaged to analyze. The two associated with the smaller canopies wear capes or tunics. Most of the north figure is destroyed, but its pair to the south holds a large, thick stick, has a helmet, a cruller under the eyes, and a loincloth. No serrated motifs are found on this figure. The stick may be similar to the batons presented to Toltec initiates in the Guatemalan chronicles. Rex Koontz (2009:274-275) has also pointed out the significance of batons and capes in investiture imagery from Classic- and Epiclassic-period Veracruz.

To conclude discussion of this wing, I believe the stone hut and mask stack form a unit, as they also do on the façade of the north building. The two units here may be the offices of a pair of priests. As detailed in the *Relación de Cholula* (de Rojas 1927) and elsewhere, the Quetzalcoatl priesthood seems often to have been headed by a pair of priests. The serpent headbands of the masks above the two stone huts on the west building differ slightly; the north snake body has the markings of a serpent while the one to the south is feathered. Because the former had completely fallen from the building, this may be an error of restoration, but if not, the two may distinguish complementary officeholders (Figure 8.14b).

The South Building

The South Building has eight doorways, four on either side of the archway providing the main entry point to the quadrangle. Each door is surmounted by the sculpted image of a thatched hut, above which is an identical mask (Figure 8.15). The masks do not have a projecting long nose; the best preserved (Doors 1, 8, and 9) instead show a triangular or leaf-shaped nose with two nostrils. The supra-orbital plates are marked by parallel horizontal grooves, and large beaded volutes extend from the mouth, and the top and sides of the head. To maintain an approximately even spacing of the houses across the façade, the two doors nearest the central entrance are slightly off-center with respect to the rooms behind them and cluster closer to the arch. With due deference to Kowalski, this suggests that eight, rather than nine, was the operative number of offices associated with this wing, although this may have been an idealized number.

Schele and Mathews (1998:265) maintain that the small rosettes decorating the upper molding reference *itz*, "nectar" or "magic," thus in their opinion identifying this building as a "conjuring house." They identify the volutes as maize foliage, thus indicating the nature of this conjuring: "The South Building represents the house where the first people were made, and where their descendants remember First Father in his guise as a maize plant" (Schele and Mathews 1998:265). Kowalski and Dunning (1999:282) also identify this house with creation and the maize god. They agree that the volutes above the deity masks are maize leaves, linking them to images of the maize god emerging from a reptilian *witz* monster at Chichen Itza and elsewhere.

There are several difficulties with this interpretation. First, identical rosettes decorate the upper moldings of all but the north building, and so are not specific to the function of this building. Second, this interpretation does not explain why there are eight of these masks and huts. Third, the iconographic identifications are not convincing: nothing particularly characterizes the masks on this façade as being related to either *witz* or maize. In fact, these masks are notable for their extreme simplicity with respect to the other masks of the Nunnery: none have headbands, none have earspools, and the facial marks are spartan. Maya representations of maize foliage are also usually asymmetrical and less rigid than the volutes on these masks. These volutes are more probably examples of the types of wind symbolism discussed by Taube (2001).

THE NUNNERY QUADRANGLE OF UXMAL **215**

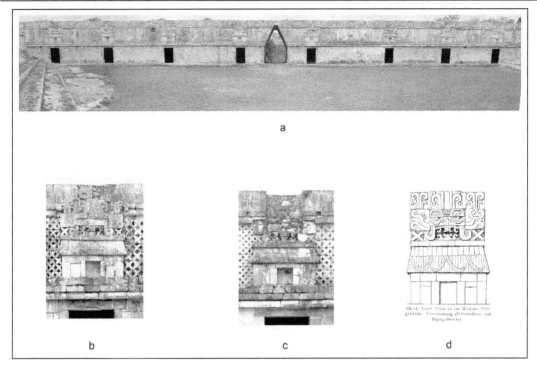

Figure 8.15. Front (north) façade, south wing, Nunnery Quadrangle: (a) panorama (author composite photograph); (b-d) stone huts (from http://academic.reed.edu/uxmal/; Rhyne 2008a; Seler 1917:Figure 17).

These explanations also ignore the fact that when Waldeck visited Uxmal, small, seated figures dressed in a loincloth and a feathered headdress occupied each of the hut doorways (Waldeck 1838:Plate 17). A more satisfying explanation is to identify each of these huts as lordly "houses" within the Uxmal polity. Their distance from the king in the north building, their lower elevation, and the unvarying simplicity of the façade masks suggest all these houses shared a lesser rank within the polity. The unique floor plan of this wing, which prevents internal communication between tandem rooms, may possibly be explained by suggesting that they housed the rulers of client towns and their retinues, but the latter were precluded from directly entering the privileged space of the central patio. The relatively low rank of these individuals is further indicated by the absence of mask stacks and feathered serpents in the roofs of the huts.

Similar spatial patterns hold at Chichen Itza. As I have noted, the lowest registers of the Lower Temple of the Jaguars and the North Temple all show rather motley processions of warriors in a variety of costumes who nevertheless participate in the important ceremonies depicted above them (Ringle 2004). In the Temple of the Chac Mool of Chichen Itza (Figure 8.16), whose columns and murals I believe reflect a layout similar to the Nunnery, the warriors on the piers in the outer portico also contrast with the more standard Toltec figures of the inner sanctum (Ringle 2004:201). On the *Mapa Quinatzin* (Figure 8.4), the communities who did not participate in the ruling councils are represented identically along the left edge by a mound and what may be a digging stick, in contrast to the higher ranking places, which have distinctive glyphs and place markers. Perhaps the treatment of the huts on the south building sprang from a similar impulse.

216 THE ANCIENT MAYA OF MEXICO

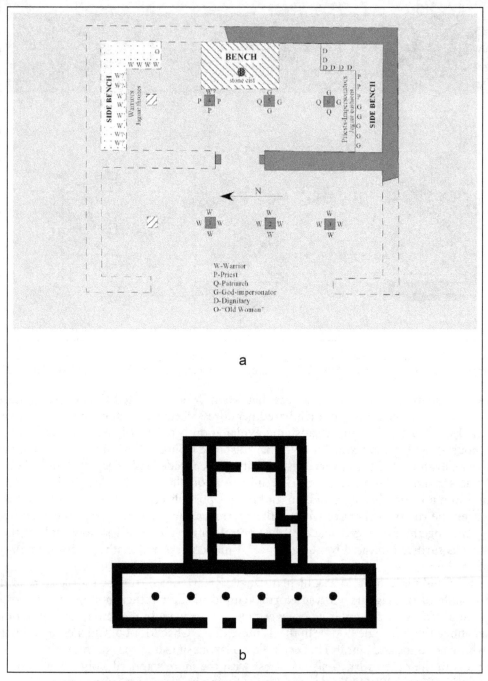

Figure 8.16. Structures compared with the Nunnery Quadrangle: (a) plan, Temple of the Chacmool, Chichen Itza (Ringle 2004:Figure 30); (b)Hall of the Columns, Mitla (redrawn after Marcus and Flannery 1983:Figure 8.30).

The North Building

As the tallest and largest of the structures, the north building is hypothesized to contain the royal reception rooms, although its façade suffered considerable collapse before it was first recorded. All that was left standing of the upper wall zone were the section between Doors 3 to 6 and the section from the mask stack to the east of Door 12 to the southeast corner mask stack. Nonetheless, the entire façade can be reconstructed on the assumption that the masks were arranged symmetrically about the midline of the structure, yielding seven mask stacks alternating with at least four stone huts across the upper wall zone, as well as mask stacks at each corner (Figure 8.17). Unfortunately, because only one mask survives from each hypothesized pair, this reconstruction remains only a strong likelihood. Because the north building is argued herein to be the reception quarters of the paramount residing in the House of the Governors, and since both structures have the same number of doors and a similar floor plan, it might be supposed that the former is a smaller version of the latter. The chief difficulty with this neat equation is that the upper wall zone of the House of the Governor represents the paramount flanked by four secondary nobles, in contrast to the seven offices that need to be accounted for on the façade of the north building—if it is accepted that mask stacks are in some way associated with offices.

The pairing of stone huts with mask stacks on the standing portion of the façade presents another problem of reconstruction. Two huts now survive and like most of the mask stacks, are directly over doorways. The exceptions are the outer two stacks, which are placed at the outer edges of (but not over) Doors 2 and 12, probably to avoid their being obscured by the east and west buildings, a natural concern if their symbolism was important. Unfortunately, the façade over Doors 2 and 12 collapsed long ago. It does not appear that sufficient room remained to accommodate another hut, but it is then puzzling why the outer mask stacks were not placed directly over these doors. Nevertheless, a single, rather wide, upright rectangular veneer stone to the left of the *greca* between Doors 2 and 3 is very likely from a hut that was also pushed closer to the centerline to help make the outer masks visible. (Thus, instead of an expected position over Door 2, it was located to the right of entrance.) If the central doorway was paired with huts on either side, the remainder of the façade may then have consisted of a mask stack paired with a stone hut. Huts also could have surmounted Doors 1 and 13 on either end of the building and have been paired with the outmost façade mask stacks, supporting the contention that the mask stack-stone hut combination was a fundamental symbolic unit at Uxmal. Unfortunately, a further impediment to proving this pattern is that the façades of both ends have fallen, leaving only the corner mask stacks on the east end and nothing whatsoever on the west end of the structure.

Despite problems posed by collapse, a possible interpretation of the north façade emerges from a close inspection of its surviving decoration, particularly the decorative scrolls framing the mask stacks (Figure 8.18). The central mask is bordered by a series of beaded dragon heads identical to inverted examples below each of the thrones on the House of the Governor façade. To my knowledge, these are the only masks so marked at Uxmal. This is also the only stack whose masks all wear a headband of some sort, although only the uppermost mask has the feather-and-flower headband. Two other masks in this stack have a continuous band of flowers and one has a band of crescent shaped elements. Given that this is the central room, with clear references to the House of the Governor (or at least to the zoomorph sustaining its thrones), this would seem to be the reception room of the paramount.

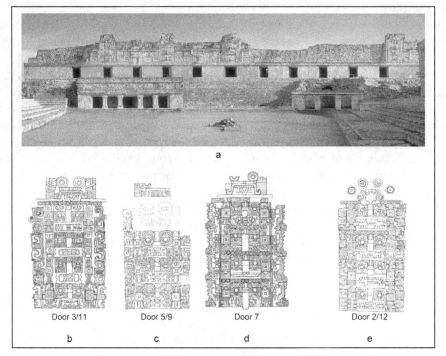

Figure 8.17. Front (south) façade, north wing, Nunnery Quadrangle: (a) panorama (from http://academic.reed.edu/uxmal/; Rhyne 2008a); (b–e) mask stacks (Schele and Mathews 1998:Figure 7.24).

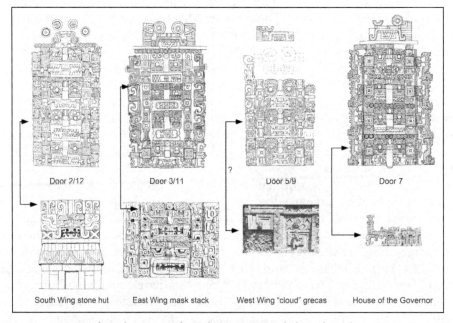

Figure 8.18. Comparison of north wing mask stacks (top row: Schele and Mathews 1998:Figure 7.24) with façade elements from other structures (bottom row: from http://academic.reed.edu/uxmal/; Seler 1917: Figures 17, 26, 117; third image from left is a photograph by the author).

In contrast, the crossed bones motif in the supra-orbital plates of two of the masks over Door 3 (and perhaps the collapsed Door 11) may reference identical motifs on the façade of the east building. Door 2 (and perhaps the absent Door 12), may then reference the south building, the two doors farthest from the center stack on the north façade corresponding to the Nunnery building farthest from the paramount. Confirmation comes from the framing scrolls of Door 1, beaded volutes, several of which directly replicate the patterns seen above and around the masks of the south building. This leaves only Door 5 and its fallen partner above Door 9. In this case, the lower two heads are framed by S-shaped "cloud" scrolls, suggesting a connection with the S-shaped *grecas* on the façade of the west building. Thus, the fact that the Nunnery has four wings, that the mask stacks of the north building are four high (rather than the usual three), and that three pairs of mask stacks flank the central mask of the north building all suggest that this façade attempts to unite all four estates in a single tableau.

The houses associated with mask stacks on the north façade may thus symbolize the noble houses related to each estate. The stone hut closest to the central mask stack is marked with a miniature pair of felines with intertwined tails in its doorway, undoubtedly a reference to the bicephalic jaguar thrones of the paramount. Unfortunately, the other surviving hut has no comparable details. The two extant houses both have three bicephalic serpents extending across the roof; along the top is a feathered serpent, below is a feathered serpent with a diamond-shaped body, and at the bottom is a pair of serpent heads emerging from the thatch. Kowalski and Dunning (1999:281) argue that these reflect the homophony of *kan*, "sky" and "serpent," in their view supporting identification of the north building with the upperworld. Yet the west building, which they claim symbolizes earth-sustaining powers, also has bicephalic serpents on the huts of its façade. The serpents are probably better understood as markers of Toltec political ideology, although I cannot as yet offer an explanation for why three different snakes are present. Each estate is thus represented by two houses, one on each side of the centerline. The paramount is flanked by a pair, and the other three estates are represented by two mask stack-stone hut dyads. These may have constituted a supreme council advising the paramount.

I conclude this section with a brief comment on the headbands of the north façade, which seem to be preferentially placed on the upper two masks of each mask stack. The upper two masks of Door 2 (and by extension, Door 12) have a headband of crescent or scalloped motifs, shared with the second mask of the central mask stack (Door 7). The masks uppermost above Doors 3 and 11 have a band consisting of a continuous series of rosettes, shared with the lower two masks of Door 7 and with the west building. Unfortunately, the uppermost masks of Doors 5 and 9 have not survived, but the uppermost mask of Door 7 has a band of feathers with rosettes placed at intervals, a headband not repeated elsewhere. Its placement suggests it was the headband of highest rank, and that the headbands of the masks below it replicated the arrangement of the headbands above the adjacent doors. This further supports the assertion that the north building housed a council composed of the other three estates.

The Ballcourt

Brief mention must be made of the ballcourt as the final member of the triumvirate of Late Uxmal-style structures that also includes the Nunnery and the Palace of the Governors (Andrews 1995:82). The ballcourt further illuminates the function of the Nunnery since, as noted by Kowalski and Dunning (1999:283), the centerline of the ballcourt extends directly through the central arch of the south building. Kowalski and Dunning (1999:283) interpret the ballcourt within a conventional lowland Maya framework, citing associations "with the underworld and with mythic cycles involving the death and resurrection of deities connected with astronomical bodies such as the sun, Venus, and the moon, and corresponding seasonal agricultural cycles." They also refer to the Hero Twins and solar macaws.

Overlooking for a moment the absence of any direct evidence for this interpretation (save for possible Venus imagery), it can also be faulted on historical grounds. The conventional lowland Maya ballgame might be expected to have arrived much earlier during the rise of Uxmal, yet the ballcourt is one of its latest monumental constructions, built when Uxmal was experiencing a wave of non-Maya influence.[6] The Uxmal ballcourt is, however, typically Maya in having a narrow alley, wide sloping benches, a northeast–southwest orientation, and most importantly, open end zones. In contrast, most courts at Chichen Itza and at contemporary central Mexican sites are I-shaped with end zones delimited by walls, and are oriented north–south. Yet it is glaringly obvious that the feathered serpent was the principal ornament along the benches of both the Uxmal and Chichen Itza courts. Two intertwined serpents were still visible along the sides of the ballcourt when seen by Stephens (1963:1:176), and although many sections fell before the first photographs were taken, Ruz's (1958:Figure 4) later excavations suggested two possibilities for their arrangement (Figure 8.19).

This suggests an alternative ballgame tradition should be sought. In my view, the role of the ballgame in Epiclassic and Postclassic rites of investiture provides a more historically grounded interpretive framework for the ballcourt and explains why it was built at the same time as the Nunnery. I have argued that the ballgame was central to investiture rituals at Chichen Itza and El Tajin, and similar cases can be made for Tula and Xochicalco (Ringle 2004, 2009). Recently, we (Ringle and Bey 2008) have also argued that most courts in northern Yucatan are late and associated with significant changes in political structure. These changes can be connected to the assumption of the role of "seating place" by cities such as Dzibilchaltun and Ek Balam along with new titles such as *kaloomte'*. Thus, the ballcourt at Uxmal may be a late manifestation of this wave of political change, except that there—as at Chichen Itza—new forms of Toltec legitimation were invoked.

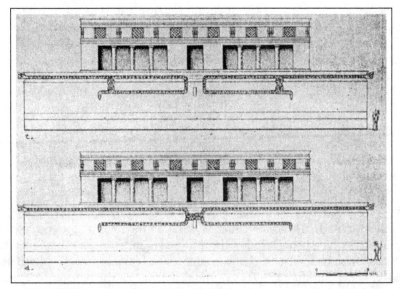

Figure 8.19. Reconstruction of the feathered serpents on the façade of the Uxmal ballcourt (Ruz 1958:Figure 4).

Ethnohistorical Parallels

As mentioned above, some descriptions and depictions of highland Mexican structures bear strong resemblances to the Nunnery Quadrangle. These parallels are not perfect, but do suggest a similar approach to governance. To begin, the figures painted on the benches and sculpted on the piers of the Temple of the Chacmool at Chichen Itza show a similar organization by estates (Ringle 2004:208). The figures located on the piers of the exterior portico of that structure are clothed in a variety of costumes, in my view corresponding to the lower tier of elites lodged in the south building of the Nunnery. The north building of the Nunnery, hypothesized to belong to the paramount, therefore corresponds to the central bench of the Temple of the Chacmool, placed against the back wall opposite the portico. Two rows of figures are painted on either side of this bench: to the north is a file of seated warriors in Toltec garb (therefore corresponding to the east building of the Nunnery), and to the south is a line of "priests," or more probably, noble councilors in non-military dress (Ringle 2004), whose affinities with the west building of the Nunnery completes the analogy.

Among the later highland Mexican groups, perhaps the most striking parallel is with the depiction of the palace of Nezahualcoyotl on the second sheet of the *Mapa Quinatzin*, an early (1542) colonial document from Texcoco (Evans 2004; Mohar Betancourt 2004). This sheet depicts only a portion of the palace, probably the patio (Alva Ixtlilxochitl 1985:2:93) described as "where the council rooms were." This was only one of a number of compounds comprising the palace; the royal residence proper was in another part of the complex.

At the head of the page is the royal dais or reception room. This building, like the north wing of the Nunnery, is shown as being somewhat taller than its neighbors and perhaps located on a raised basal platform, since it is fronted with a low staircase. At the center of the sheet, within the patio and below the rooms of the ruler, are the 14 seated dignitaries whom the commentary indicates comprised the ruling council (Alva Ixtlilxochitl 1985:2:94; Mohar Betancourt 2004:243-245). Alva Ixtlilxochitl's commentary notes that the hall in which these individuals met (not shown on the map) was divided into three parts. The first section was the room of the king. The second enclosed six high-ranking lords from principal towns within the kingdom, including Teotihuacan. Concerning the third group of eight lords, Alva Ixtlilxochitl (1985:2:94) states that "...this division was the outermost." That is, this group was at the furthest remove physically and politically from the throne of Texcoco, thus corresponding to the function of the south structure at Uxmal. Mohar Betancourt (2004:244-245) demonstrates that the seating of the counselors follows this hierarchy and the placement of client toponyms around the court with but a single exception. At the bottom of the page are three councilors not linked to toponyms (Tollantzinco, Cauachinanco, Xicotepec). Their toponyms may have been placed below the torn lower edge of the manuscript, but at any rate, these three towns are the farthest from Texcoco. Thus, the arrangement of the councilors on the map and their seating within the council hall shows a clear spatial order consistent with that hypothesized for the arrangement of the Nunnery Quadrangle.

Alva Ixtlilxochitl also mentions that a council house of war was adjacent to the north room across an entry passageway:

> ...following this was a passageway which led from this patio to another large [building] of the plaza, and on the other side of it was the large hall of the war council. Here at the head sat six natives of the city of Texcoco, three nobles and three citizens, and after them followed another

fifteen native captains of the principal cities and towns of the kingdom of Texcoco (Alva Ixtlilxochitl 1985:2:95).

This places the council of war on the opposite side of the plaza from the structure associated with the ruler, whereas the two are adjacent in the Nunnery. But the fact that there were six captains, like the six warriors on the façade of the east wing of the Nunnery, is striking. The other sides of the patio do not correspond to Uxmal; one was devoted to the arts and sciences (and not to the priesthood), and the opposite contained a series of rooms housing constables and treasury officials.

The depiction of Motecuhzoma's palace (*tecpancalli*) in the *Codex Mendoza* (Berdan and Anawalt 1992:f. 69r) also shows a series of buildings arranged around a central courtyard. Although Berdan and Anawalt (1992:2:222) identify this as an image of the *tlatocacalli*, the personal quarters of the emperor, because of the circular decorations above the doorway, this decoration was also present on other important noble buildings (Berdan and Anawalt 1992:2:224). My view is that this folio instead illustrates the royal reception and council halls, thus paralleling the *Mapa Quinatzin*. As with the Nunnery and the *Mapa Quinatzin*, the wing housing the ruler is highest and opposite the entrance to the courtyard; this is listed as a place where he held audiences and sat in judgment (Berdan and Anawalt 1992). The left wing of the quadrangle is listed as the council house of war and the right wing housed Motecuhzoma's council. In this last building, judges ruled on appeals from lower courts. The major difference is that no indication is made of a council of tributaries or noble houses, although there were guesthouses for the lords of the Triple Alliance (on the left) and for the lords of Tenayuca, Chiconauhtla, and Colhuacan (on the right) that flanked the royal dais room (Berdan and Anawalt 1992).

A final example is the Hall of Columns from Mitla. Kubler (1962:95-96, 148) argued that the architecture of Uxmal was strongly influenced by Oaxaca, and he drew a particular parallel between the Nunnery Quadrangle and the Columns Group quadrangle of Mitla. Current evidence dates the latter to the Late Postclassic, however, a position supported by the style of the paintings decorating the North Group (Flannery and Marcus 1983:296; Pohl 1999, 2002, 2005). Such similarities may therefore be the result of the involvement of Mitla in the later stages of the Mesoamerican Toltec tradition. Ethnohistorical descriptions describe Mitla as something like the "Vatican" of the Zapotec nobility (Flannery and Marcus 1983:297), a place where consultations and feasts were held and whose occupants functioned as oracles, functions similar to those played by other putative Tollans. More specifically, Pohl (1999) has demonstrated that the lintel paintings of the Church and Arroyo quadrangles depict three different creation epics—those of the Mixtecs, Tolteca-Chichimeca, and Zapotecs—indicating the involvement of Mitla in the Toltec tradition and its multiethnic domain.

The Hall of Columns of the North Group (Figure 8.16b) is mentioned as the "palace" and place of reception of the high priest or great seer (*uija-tào*; Burgoa 1989:2:Chapter 53; Marcus and Flannery 1983:297-298; Seler 1904). Note the similarity of its floor plan to the gallery-patio structures of Chichen Itza and the component sections of the Palacio Quemado at Tula. An important quotation of Burgoa describes the functions of each of the rooms of the Hall of Columns:

> One of the rooms above ground was the palace of the high priest, where he sat and slept, for the apartment offered room and opportunity for everything. The throne was like a high cushion, with a high back to lean against, all of tiger skin…

The second chamber above ground was that of the priests and the assistants of the high priests. The third was that of the king when he came. The fourth was that of the other chieftains and captains... Furthermore, there was no other administration of justice in this place than that of the high priest, to whose unlimited power all bowed (Burgoa 1674:2:124-125; translation in Seler 1904:251-252).

The arrangement of apartments by "estates" within the palace is quite close to that I propose for Uxmal, with the exception that one wing was devoted to the visiting overlord of Mitla (whose identity is not made clear). The overall function of this quadrangle as a reception place and council hall is also clear. Despite Burgoa's claims that the room of the high priest had "opportunity for everything," it seems likely that his actual residence was elsewhere.

Conclusions

This study attempts to demonstrate that the paramount of Uxmal was assisted by councils associated with three estates: the military, the priesthood, and representatives of the lesser noble houses of the polity. The leaders of both the military and priesthood used imagery associated with the feathered serpent, although more overtly in the latter case. I emphasize that careful attention to the details and disposition of the Nunnery masks provides one key to decoding the political structure of Uxmal. Past studies have usually concentrated on identifying these masks as one or another of the known codical deities, especially Itzam Nah, Chaak, or K'awil, but such blanket identifications founder when the true variety of the masks is confronted. Although masks probably do signal dynastic spirit generally, attention to the often minute differences between them provides a more satisfactory picture of their functions. Finally, attention to the numerology of floor plans, doorways, and façade elements may provide insight into the structure of offices associated with each estate. One problem remaining to be addressed is the relation of the council of the paramount depicted on the façade of the House of the Governor to the other councils of the Nunnery Quadrangle. Were they also the occupants of the north building, were only some of them present there, or were they a completely independent body?

There has been a lively debate concerning the political role of Uxmal at its early tenth-century peak (Dunning and Kowalski 1994; Kowalski and Dunning 1999; Kowalski 2003, 2007; Ringle 2004; Stanton and Gallareta Negrón 2001). According to one model, Uxmal reigned supreme as the political capital of the Puuc Hills due to the charismatic leadership and ambitious building projects of a Lord Chaak during the early tenth century. An alternative view attributes "Mexican" imagery at Uxmal to its conquest by Chichen Itza, and in general sees Uxmal as in rather desperate straits at this time. My own feeling is that evidence for an Itza presence at Uxmal is overstated. As Stanton and Gallareta Negrón (2001) acknowledge, the simple presence of Sotuta ceramics does not automatically reflect political relations, especially in the very small quantities present at Uxmal. It should not surprise us that small quantities of non-local ceramics might appear for a variety of reasons—feasting, gifting, exchange, and others—that in no way imply subjugation.

The ability of Uxmal to invest other nobles under Toltec auspices presumes either that it did so independently or under the direct watch of Chichen Itza. The way in which "Mexican-ness" is manifested at Uxmal, however, differs substantially from its expression at Chichen Itza. Although both sites have ballcourts marked by feathered serpents, these differ radically in their inspiration. In fact, few if any of the classic Toltec architectural forms at Chichen Itza were replicated at Uxmal, which has no serpent temples, no gallery-patio structures, and no colonnaded halls. If anything, Chichen Itza was on the receiving end of architectural influences from the Puuc realm (Andrews 1995). Uxmal also continued to pursue the "cult of personality" in erecting stelae dedicated to its paramounts, while at Chichen Itza a very different approach to depicting political relations is evident (Ringle 2004; Ringle and Bey 2009). Finally, the post-monumental phase at Uxmal seems to have involved the iconoclastic destruction of feathered serpent imagery, rather than its imposition as the conquest model would suggest. C-shaped structures on the broad terrace in front of the south building of the Nunnery incorporate segments of the feathered serpents that formerly adorned the ballcourt, indicating a collapse of the role of Uxmal as a Toltec center of investiture.

The regional capital model is perhaps more attractive, but with the caveat that Toltec investiture established relations of suzerainty rather than outright domination of the Puuc region, and that such ties may have been weak and short-lived. Feathered serpents simply do not appear elsewhere in the Puuc, but then the model suggested here argues that such traits would be associated with the persons invested and would most likely appear in grave lots. Unfortunately, not a single elite grave from a Puuc site dating to this time period has ever been reported.

The *Chilam Balam of Mani* states that Uxmal, together with Mayapan and Chichen Itza, comprised the League of Mayapan. Given that Mayapan derived ethnically and architecturally from the other two—in fact in some sources was a compromise between the powerful Xiu and Cupul families—lends the statement some credibility, but even 75 years ago it was clear that the three sites were not contemporaneous. If we understand all three centers to be Tollans, however, this can perhaps be understood as a retrospective attempt to establish the contours of Toltec sovereignty on the peninsula. Triple alliances were not unknown in prehispanic Mesoamerica. A triadic arrangement dominated the political landscape of central Mexico at the time of the conquest, of course, but less familiar are statements that this was but the latest of a series of similar arrangements (Davies 1977:297-302; Offner 1982:114; Zantwijk 1963:195). Chimalpahin (2003:1:81) states that Tula, Culhuacan, and Otompan ruled jointly for 191 years, and that following the collapse of Tula, power was shared between Culhuacan, Coatlichan, and Azcapotzalco. The mantles of these three cities were then inherited by Tenochtitlan, Texcoco, and Tlacopan respectively. We may thus see the League of Mayapan as exemplifying one way in which Toltec legitimacy was charted by Maya chroniclers of the Late Postclassic and early colonial periods. Whether or not these corresponded to political reality is difficult to judge. It is certainly possible that Chichen Itza and Uxmal commanded some ancestral ritual prestige during the period of the rise and florescence of Mayapan, although it is certainly unlikely that they commanded significant political authority at that time. But it does suggest that Uxmal was an independent player rather than a mere vassal of Chichen Itza.

Acknowledgments

I thank Tony Andrews for his comments on the Nunnery excavations during the 1970s and for several helpful bibliographic references. Hanns Prem kindly supplied information on his radiocarbon dates from the Nunnery, as well as several helpful comments. Karl Taube also provided useful suggestions. I have drawn heavily on the visual resources provided by Charles S. Rhyne's excellent website devoted to Uxmal, Kabah, Sayil, and Labna. Conversations over the years with colleagues Tomás Gallareta Negrón and George Bey have greatly stimulated my thoughts on Puuc archaeology. My deepest debt is to Will Andrews, who introduced me to Maya archaeology and has been the very model of a "real Mesoamerican archaeologist;" scholar, teacher, field man, and friend.

Notes

1. Fieldwork conducted by the Bolonchen Regional Archaeological Project, co-directed by Tomas Gallareta Negrón, George Bey, and me, has demonstrated the importance of quadrangles throughout the Classic-period occupation of the Puuc hills. Quadrangles are often the first types of public architecture at Puuc sites, and recent findings indicate that they were on occasion the last forms of civic architecture prior to abandonment.

2. Although the feathered serpent is not prominent at Mitla, Pohl (1999, 2002, 2005) has demonstrated that murals of the Arroyo group depict a Toltec cosmogony, as well as those of the Mixtecs and Zapotecs. Tenochtitlan claimed Toltec heritage through the first emperor, Chimalpahin, and his wife, residents of Culhuacan. Texcoco saw itself as the heir of the Toltec dynasty of Coatlichan.

3. Sotuta is the dominant ceramic complex at Chichen Itza and is often regarded as an indicator of interaction with that site. Sotuta ceramics tend to be very rare at most other sites in northern Yucatan that date to the Terminal Classic, where instead Cehpech complex ceramics are dominant. For many years it was thought that Cehpech predated Sotuta, but the current consensus is that there was considerable, if not complete, overlap between the two complexes.

4. Hocaba ceramics are generally viewed as the successor to the Sotuta complex and traditionally dated to A.D. 1200 and later. Considerable evidence, summarized in Ringle et al. (1998:189-192), now indicates that the complex appeared as early as A.D. 900–1000.

5. The V-shaped stack behind the central seated figure of the House of the Governor may therefore refer specifically to the role of the ruler as chief of the military.

6. It is no accident that the second Uxmal ballcourt is adjacent to a late round structure (Kowalski et al. 1996), further linking the Uxmal ballgame with "Mexican" influence and probably Quetzalcoatl.

References

Alva Ixtlilxochitl, Fernando de. 1985. *Obras Históricas*. 2 vols. Universidad Nacional Autónoma de México, Mexico City.

Andrews, E. Wyllys, V. 1979. Some Comments on Puuc Architecture of the Northern Yucatan Peninsula. In Mills 1979:1-17.

Andrews, George F. 1995. *Pyramids and Palaces, Monsters and Masks: The Golden Age of Maya Architecture: Volume 1, Architecture of the Puuc Region and the Northern Plains*. Labyrinthos, Lancaster.

Barrera Rubio, Alfredo, and José Huchím Herrera. 1990. *Architectural Restoration at Uxmal, 1986–1987*. Archaeology Reports 1. University of Pittsburgh, Pittsburgh.

Berdan, Frances F., and Patricia Rieff Anawalt. 1992. *The Codex Mendoza*. University of California, Berkeley.

Brainerd, George W. 1958. *The Archaeological Ceramics of Yucatan*. Anthropological Records 19. University of California, Berkeley.

Bricker, Harvey M., and Victoria R. Bricker. 1996. Astronomical References in the Throne Inscription of the Palace of the Governor at Uxmal. *Cambridge Archaeological Journal* 6:191-229.

Burgoa, Fray Francisco de. 1989. *Geográfica Descripción*. 2 vols. Biblioteca Porrua 97–98. Editorial Porrua, Mexico City.

Carmack, Robert M., and James L. Mondloch. 1983. *El título de Totonicapán: Texto, traducción y comentario*. Fuentes para el estudio de la cultura maya 3. Universidad Nacional Autónoma de México, Instituto de Investigaciones Filológicas, Centro de Estudios Mayas, Mexico City.

Chimalpahin, Domingo. 2003. *Las ocho relaciones y el memorial de Colhuacan,* edited by Rafael Tena. 2 vols. Cien de México/Conaculta, Mexico City.

Christie, Jessica Joyce (editor). 2003. *Maya Palaces and Elite Residences: An Interdisciplinary Approach.* University of Texas, Austin.

Davies, Nigel. 1977. *The Toltecs Until the Fall of Tula.* University of Oklahoma, Norman.

de Rojas, Gabriel. 1927. Relación de Cholula. *Revista Méxicana de Estudios Históricos* 1:(Apéndice):158-169.

Díaz, Gisele, and Alan Rodgers. 1993. *The Codex Borgia.* Dover Publications, New York.

Dunning, Nicholas P., and Jeff Karl Kowalski. 1994. Lords of the Hills: Classic Maya Settlement Patterns and Political Iconography in the Puuc Region, Mexico. *Ancient Mesoamerica* 5:63-95.

Erosa Peniche, José A. 1948. *Guide Book to the Ruins of Uxmal,* transated by Julio Granados. Yikal Maya Than, Merida.

Evans, Susan T. 2004. Aztec Palaces and Other Elite Residential Architecture. In Evans and Pillsbury 2004:7-58.

Evans, Susan T., and Joanne Pillsbury (editors). 2004. *Palaces of the Ancient New World.* Dumbarton Oaks Research Library and Collection, Washington, D.C.

Fash, William L., and Leonardo López Luján (editors). 2009. *The Art of Urbanism: How Mesoamerican Kingdoms Represented Themselves in Architecture and Imagery.* Dumbarton Oaks Research Library and Collection, Washington, D.C.

Flannery, Kent V., and Joyce Marcus. 1983. Urban Mitla and its Rural Hinterland. In *The Cloud People,* edited by Kent V. Flannery and Joyce Marcus, pp. 295-300. Academic, New York.

Graham, Ian. 1992. *Corpus of Maya Hieroglyphic Inscriptions: Volume 4, Pt. 2, Uxmal.* Peabody Museum of Archaeology and Ethnology, Cambridge.

Graña-Behrens, Daniel. 2002. *Die Maya-Inschriften aus Nordwestyukatan, Mexiko.* Ph.D. Dissertation, Philosophischen Fakultät, Rheinischen Friedrich-Wilhems-Universität zu Bonn, Bonn.

Houston, Stephen D. (editor). 1998. *Function and Meaning in Classic Maya Architecture.* Dumbarton Oaks Research Library and Collection, Washington, D.C.

Inomata, Takeshi, and Stephen D. Houston. 2001. *Royal Courts of the Ancient Maya.* 2 vols. Westview, Boulder.

Kelley, David H. 1982. Notes on Puuc Inscriptions and History. Supplement to Mills 1979.

Konieczna, Barbara, and Pablo Mayer Guala. 1976. Uxmal, Yucatan: informe de la temporada 1973–1974. In *Investigaciones arqueológicas en el sureste,* No. 27, pp. 1-18. Centro Regional del Sureste, Mexico City.

Koontz, Rex. 2009. Social Identity and Cosmology at El Tajin. In Fash and Luján 2009:260-289.

Kowalski, Jeff K. 1987. *The House of the Governor.* University of Oklahoma, Norman.

— 1990. A Preliminary Report on the 1988 Field Season at the Nunnery Quadrangle, Uxmal, Yucatan, Mexico. *Mexicon* 12:27-33.

— 1994. The Puuc as Seen from Uxmal. In *Hidden among the Hills,* edited by Hanns J. Prem, pp. 93-120. Acta Mesoamericana 7. Von Flemming, Möckmühl.

— 2003. Collaboration and Conflict: An Interpretation of the Relationship between Uxmal and Chichén Itzá during the Terminal Classic/Early Postclassic Periods. In Prem 2003:235-272.

— 2007. What's "Toltec" at Uxmal and Chichén Itzá? Merging Maya and Mesoamerican Worldviews and World Systems in Terminal Classic to Early Postclassic Yucatán. In *Twin Tollans: Chichén Itzá, Tula and the Epiclassic to Early Postclassic Mesoamerican World,* edited by Jeff K. Kowalski and Cynthia Kristan-Graham, pp. 250-313. Dumbarton Oaks Research Library and Collection, Washington, D.C.

Kowalski, Jeff K. (editor). 1999. *Mesoamerican Architecture as a Cultural Symbol.* Oxford University, Oxford.

Kowalski, Jeff K., Alfredo Barrera Rubio, Heber Ojeda Más, and José Huchim Herrera. 1996. Archaeological Excavations of a Round Temple at Uxmal: Summary Discussion and Implications for Northern Maya Culture History. In *Eighth Palenque Round Table, 1993*, edited by Martha J. Macri and Jan McHargue, pp. 281-296. Pre-Columbian Art Research Institute, San Francisco.

Kowalski, Jeff K., and Nicholas P. Dunning. 1999. The Architecture of Uxmal: The Symbolics of Statemaking at a Puuc Maya Regional Capital. In Kowalski 1999:274-297.

Kubler, George. 1962. *The Art and Architecture of Ancient America*. Penguin, Baltimore.

Kurjack, Edward B., Rubén Maldonado Cárdenas, and Merle Green Robertson. 1991. Ballcourts of the Northern Maya Lowlands. In *The Mesoamerican Ballgame*, edited by Vernon L. Scarborough and David R. Wilcox, pp. 145-159. University of Arizona, Tucson.

Lamb, Weldon. 1980. The Sun, Moon, and Venus at Uxmal. *American Antiquity* 45:79-86.

Landa, Diego de. 1978. *Relación de las cosas de Yucatán*. Editorial Porrua, Mexico City.

Mills, Lawrence (editor). 1979. *The Puuc: New Perspectives*. Scholarly Studies in the Liberal Arts 1. Central College, Pella.

Mohar Betancourt, Luz María. 2004. *Códice Mapa Quinatzin: Justicia y Derechos Humanos En El México Antiguo*. Centro de Investigaciones y Estudios Superiores en Antropología Social, Mexico City.

Nielsen, Jesper, and Toke Sellner Reunert. 2009. Dante's Heritage: Questioning the Multi-Layered Model of the Mesoamerican Universe. *Antiquity* 83:399-413.

Offner, Jerome A. 1982. *Law and Politics in Aztec Texcoco*. Cambridge University, Cambridge.

Pohl, John M. D. 1999. The Lintel Paintings of Mitla and the Function of the Mitla Palaces. In *Mesoamerican Architecture as a Cultural Symbol*, edited by Jeff K. Kowalski, pp. 176-197. Oxford University, Oxford.

— 2002. Los dinteles pintados de Mitla. *Arqueología Mexicana* 10(55): 64-67.

— 2005. The Arroyo Group Lintel Painting at Mitla, Oaxaca. In *Painted Books and Indigenous Knowledge in Mesoamerica: Manuscript Studies in Honor of Mary Elizabeth Smith*, edited by Elizabeth H. Boone, pp. 109-128. Publication 69. Middle American Research Institute, Tulane University, New Orleans.

Pollock, Harry E. D. 1980. *The Puuc*. Memoirs of the Peabody Museum 19. Peabody Museum of Archaeology and Ethnology, Harvard University, Cambridge.

Prem, Hanns J. (editor). 2003. *Escondido en la selva*. Universidad de Bonn/Instituto Nacional de Antropología e Historia, Bonn and Mexico City.

Rhyne, Charles S. 2008a. *Architecture, Restoration, and Imaging of the Maya Cities of Uxmal, Kabah, Sayil, and Labná*. Online: http://academic.reed.edu/uxmal/.

— 2008b. Annotated Bibliography. *Architecture, Restoration, and Imaging of the Maya Cities of Uxmal, Kabah, Sayil, and Labná*. Online: http://academic.reed.edu/uxmal/bibliography.html.

Ringle, William M. 2003. Feathered Serpents and the League of Mayapan. Paper presented at the symposium "Cities & Towns of the Ancient Maya North in Classic Times," Second Annual Tulane Maya Symposium and Workshop, Tulane University, New Orleans.

— 2004. On the Political Organization of Chichen Itza. *Ancient Mesoamerica* 15:167-218.

— 2009. The Art of War: Imagery of the Upper Temple of the Jaguars, Chichen Itza. *Ancient Mesoamerica* 20:15-44.

Ringle, William M., and George J. Bey III. 2001. Post-Classic and Terminal Classic Courts of the Northern Maya Lowlands. In *Royal Courts of the Ancient Maya: Volume 2, Data and Case Studies*, edited by Takeshi Inomata and Stephen D. Houston, pp. 266-307. Westview, Boulder.

— 2008. Preparing for Visitors: Political Dynamics on the Northern Plains of Yucatan. Paper presented at the VI Mesa Redonda de Palenque, Palenque.

— 2009. The Face of the Itzas. In Fash and Luján 2009:329-383.

Ringle, Willliam M., Ramon Carrillo Sánchez, and Julieta Ramos Pacheco. 2005. La organización de las zonas urbanas en la zona de Bolonchén durante el Clásico Tardío-Terminal. Paper presented at the Segunda Congreso Internacional de Cultura Maya, Merida.

Ringle, William M., Tomás Gallareta Negrón, and George J. Bey, III. 1998. The Return of Quetzalcoatl: Evidence for the Spread of a World Religion during the Epiclassic Period. *Ancient Mesoamerica* 9:183-232.

Ruz Lhuillier, Alberto. 1954. Uxmal: temporada de trabajos 1951–1952. *Anales del Instituto Nacional de Antropología e Historia* 6:49-67.

— 1957. *Trabajos de restauración en Uxmal: temporada de 1956*. Unpublished report on file, Centro de Yucatán, Instituto Nacional de Antropología e Historia, Merida.

— 1958. El juego de pelota de Uxmal. In *Proceedings of the International Congress of Americanists* (31st session, Mexico, 1954), vol. 1, pp. 635-665. Mexico City.

Schele, Linda. 1998. The Iconography of Maya Architectural Façades during the Late Classic Period. In Houston 1998:479-518.

Schele, Linda, and Peter Mathews. 1998. *The Code of Kings*. Scribner, New York.

Seler, Eduard G. 1904. The Wall Paintings of Mitla. In *Mexican and Central American Antiquities, Calendar Systems, and History*, edited by Charles P. Bowditch, pp. 243-324. Bulletin 28, Bureau of American Ethnology, Washington, D.C.

— 1917. *Die Ruinen Von Uxmal*. Abhandlungen der Königlich Preussischen Akademie der Wissenschaften Philosophisch-Historische Klasse 3. Verlag der Königl. Akademie der Wissenschaften, Berlin.

Smith, Robert E. 1971. *The Pottery of Mayapan*. 2 vols. Papers of the Peabody Museum of Archaeology and Ethnology 66. Harvard University, Cambridge, Mass.

Stanton, Travis W., and Tomás Gallareta Negrón. 2001. Warfare, Ceramic Economy, and the Itza: A Reconsideration of the Itza Polity in Ancient Yucatan. *Ancient Mesoamerica* 12:229-245.

Stephens, John L. 1963. *Incidents of Travel in Yucatan* [1843]. 2 vols. Dover, New York.

Sugiyama, Saburo. 1989. Iconographic Interpretations of the Temple of Quetzalcoatl at Teotihuacan. *Mexicon* 11:68-74.

Taube, Karl A. 1992. The Temple of Quetzalcoatl and the Cult of Sacred War at Teotihuacan. *RES* 21:53-87.

— 2001. The Breath of Life: The Symbolism of Wind in Mesoamerica. In *The Road to Aztlan: Art from a Mythic Homeland*, edited by Virginia M. Fields and Victor Zamudio-Taylor, pp. 102-123. Los Angeles County Museum of Art, Los Angeles.

— 2004. Flower Mountain: Concepts of Life, Beauty, and Paradise among the Classic Maya. *RES* 45:69-98.

Thompson, J. Eric S. 1941. A Coordination of the History of Chichen Itza with Ceramic Sequences in Central Mexico. *Revista Méxicana de Estudios Históricos* 5:97-112.

Vallo, Michael. 2003. Xkipché Ceramics. On Current Data, Methods, Results and Problems. In Prem 2003:309-338.

von Winning, Hasso. 1987. *La Iconografía de Teotihuacán; los Dioses y los Signos*. Estudios y Fuentes del Arte en Mexicano 47. Universidad Nacional Autónoma de México, Mexico City.

Waldeck, Frédéric de. 1838. *Voyage pittoresque et archéologique dan la province d'Yucatan (Amérique Centrale), pendant les années 1834 et 1836*. Bellizard Dufou, Paris.

Zantwijk, Rudolf A. M. Van. 1963. Principios organizasadores de los mexicas, una introducción al estudio del sistema interno del regimen azteca. *Estudios de cultura náhuatl* 4:187-222.

Zapata Alonzo, Gualberto. 1983. *Guide to Puuc Region: Uxmal, Kabah, Xlaapaak, Sayil, Labná*. Produccíon Editorial Dante, Merida.

9 In the Shadow of the Pyramid

Excavations of the Great Platform of Chichen Itza

Geoffrey E. Braswell and Nancy Peniche May

Abstract

The largest monumental construction at Chichen Itza is the Great Platform, a leveled surface so large that it dwarfs the Castillo, the Temple of the Warriors, the Group of 1000 Columns, and all the other structures that stand upon it. Yet the construction history of this platform has been poorly understood. Archaeological investigations conducted in 2009 reveal at least ten major construction episodes for the Great Platform, and serve to link the construction sequences of many of the buildings that the platform supports. This long history indicates that the basic orientation and planning of the Great Platform was established at an early date, and that the center of Chichen Itza was not built all at once—by "Toltec" invaders or by "Mexicanized" Maya—but instead slowly evolved. Moreover, the "International" style of art and architecture that dominates the final stages of construction in the heart of Chichen Itza also developed gradually over time, revealing a pattern of adoption, innovation, and adaptation. In sum, the rulers, architects, and artists of Chichen Itza were not the passive recipients of foreign influence, but instead were active participants in the creation of the International style.

Chichen Itza is justly famous for its beautiful architecture, carved lintels, hieroglyphic texts, stone sculpture, and even painted murals (Figures 1.1, 9.1, and 10.1). For this reason, Chichen Itza has become the most visited archaeological site in southern Mexico and Central America. Each day, an average of 5,000 tourists visit the ancient city, and during the equinoxes the number can be more than 40,000. Tourists are no longer allowed to climb any of the major structures, but they still come to see the Great Ballcourt, the Castillo, the Temple of the Warriors, the Group of 1000 Columns, and other great structures built on the Great Platform (Figure 9.2). Very few are aware that the huge space (roughly 600 by 400 meters) on which they walk is artificial and, in fact, the largest construction at Chichen Itza. The main road connecting Merida to Valladolid once passed over the Great Platform, and the remains of a small modern settlement built on it are still clearly visible. Sewage conduits, electrical lines, and irrigation pipes run in, on, and beneath the Great Platform. The surface of the immense plaza has even been scraped and leveled for better acoustics during musical performances. Thus, the Great Platform often has been treated as negative space between structures instead of as the greatest of all monuments at Chichen Itza.

Figure 9.1. Carved lintel, Akab' Tz'ib' (Structure 4D1), Chichen Itza (Braswell et al. 2009:Figura 1.3).

Why Study the Great Platform?

The construction histories of the Great Platform and the structures built on it are central to debates concerning the chronology and external connections of Chichen Itza. In what can be considered the traditional chronology of Chichen Itza, the Great Platform and its structures are referred to as "New Chichen," and are considered to be built in a style called "Maya-Toltec" (Tozzer 1957). The implication is that this portion of the site was built significantly later than "Old Chichen," the location of the Caracol, the Nunnery, the Initial Series Group, the Principal Group of the Southwest, and many other important groups and structures. These are all south of the Great Platform (Figure 9.3). Another implication of this traditional interpretation is that "Maya-Toltec" Chichen Itza would have been built relatively quickly—over the period of roughly A.D. 1050 to 1200—while earlier portions of the site could have developed more slowly, beginning about A.D. 800. In this scenario, it might even be that the entire Great Platform was built in a single construction episode or in a very limited number of phases.

Related to the traditional model of two sequential architectural styles—one "Chichen Maya," one "Toltec-Maya"—is the notion that the two periods during which the structures were built were characterized by distinct ceramic complexes: Cehpech and Sotuta (Chapter 1; Smith 1971; see also Brainerd 1958 for clear ceramic descriptions but a different nomenclature). Cehpech pottery was therefore considered to be earlier, associated with "Chichen Maya" architecture (i.e., related to the Puuc style), and Maya in character. In contrast, Sotuta pottery was considered to be later, associated with International-style architecture at Chichen Itza, and used by the Toltec-Mayas. Since the late 1970s, however, many scholars have questioned this model. Joseph Ball (1979) summarized an important discussion among scholars concerning a chronological "overlap" between what was viewed as purely Maya pottery (i.e., Cehpech) and what had been considered to be a hybrid of Maya and foreign types and modes (i.e., Sotuta). Charles Lincoln (1986, 1990), in fact, argued that the overlap between the two ceramic complexes was total. Today, most ceramicists favor a partial overlap model in which Cehpech has an earlier origin than Sotuta (Braswell et al. 2011; Robles Castellanos 2000; Varela Torrecilla 1998). At Chichen Itza, there is still some disagreement as to whether there was a Cehpech phase before Sotuta (Cobos 2003; Peréz de Heredia Puente 2005; Schmidt 2007), but it is clear that virtually all visible structures were built during a time when Sotuta pottery was dominant at Chichen Itza and minor amounts of Cehpech pottery were consumed at the site. The ceramic overlap model—either partial or full—has very important architectural implications, including that the Great Platform could be at least partially contemporaneous in construction and use with "Old Chichen."

More recently, many scholars have sought to push back the chronology of Chichen Itza so that most of its standing architecture dates to the Terminal Classic and Early Postclassic periods, or about A.D. 850–1050/1100 (especially Ringle et al. 1998; see also Bey and Ringle 2007; Braswell 2003; Braswell and Glascock 2003; Braswell et al. 2011; Cobos 2003; Kowalski 2007). We view regionally produced Cehpech and Sotuta ceramics (as opposed to imported pottery within each complex) as belonging to the same general tradition. The distinctions between Cehpech and Sotuta are therefore relatively minor, and based as much on local and regional differences in clay resources and participation in distinct foreign exchange networks as they are on chronology. In arguing that Sotuta and Cehpech are similar, we are also explicitly denying the possibility that most Sotuta types are derived from pottery made by the Toltecs or other central Mexicans. Although there is still discussion about the relative chronologies of the Great Platform and "Old Chichen" (Cobos 2003; Lincoln 1986; Ringle et al. 1998; Schele and Mathews 1998), the distinction between the International-style architecture of the former and the more Puuc-related architecture of the latter has to do with the public nature of the Great Platform as a center for pilgrims arriving from all over Mesoamerica (Ringle 2004; Ringle et al. 1998). In contrast, "Old Chichen" was the regal residential and administrative zone of the city, connected with local and regional affairs (see Grube and Krochock [2007] for analyses of texts from south of the Great Platform).

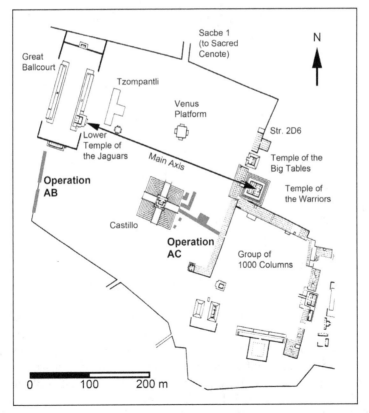

Figure 9.2. Great Platform of Chichen Itza, showing locations of excavations east of the Castillo (Operation AC) and at the wall (Operation AB). Structures discussed in the text are labeled, and the main axis of the Great Platform is shown (after Ruppert 1943:Figure 1).

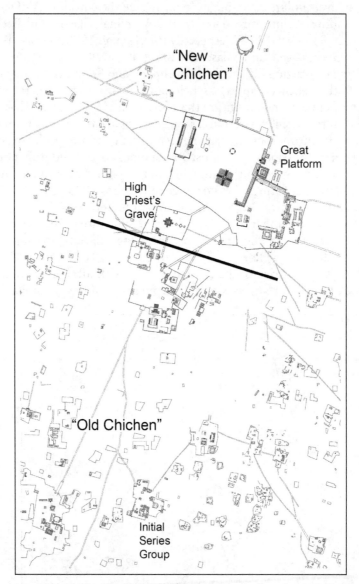

Figure 9.3. "Old Chichen" and "New Chichen" (Braswell et al. 2009:Figura 1.5).

Scientific work in the Great Platform can help answer these old questions regarding chronology, affiliation, and interaction, as well as other basic questions concerning the growth and expansion of the city. Some questions that we had before beginning our research include: (1) Was the Great Platform built all at once?; (2) Did it expand slowly in one or more directions as buildings were added?; (3) Did it coalesce as existing, smaller platforms expanded towards each other and merged?; (4) What is the construction sequence of the important buildings on the Great Platform, and what does this tell us about its design?; and (5) Was the basic "International" plan of the Great Platform established from the start, or was it imposed upon some earlier conception of space and architecture?

In 2008, Braswell was invited by Rafael Cobos Palma, director of the archaeological project *Chichén Itzá: estudio de la cominidad del Clásico Tardío* and professor at the Universidad Autónoma de Yucatán (UADY), to form a team of advanced graduate students from the University of California, San Diego (UCSD) in order to conduct research alongside students and professors as part of the UADY project. Four graduate students from UCSD worked on the Great Platform under the direct supervision of Braswell. Two more UCSD students conducted survey as part of the UADY team directed by Cobos. In order to begin to answer the questions outlined above, our research in 2009 focused on two areas (Figure 9.2): the east side of the Castillo (Operation AC) and a portion of the wall that surmounts the Great Platform south of the Great Ballcourt (Operation AB, described in Chapter 10). First Braswell and then Peniche directed excavations east of the pyramid from April until late July 2009. Upon conclusion of our work, our northern test pits were expanded by Mauricio Germon of UADY under the direction of Cobos. This chapter and our report to Cobos (Peniche et al. 2009) describe research conducted by the UCSD team, but do not include descriptions of later work by UADY scholars.

Our work to the east of the pyramid was designed specifically to link floors associated with that platform with those of the West Colonnade of the Group of 1000 Columns, that is, to understand how the construction episodes of these structures relate and also to find now buried structures in between them. In order to accomplish this, we dug a 77.5-meter trench connecting the steps of the pyramid to the entrance of the West Colonnade, and also dug many test pits to the north and south in order to further expose features discovered in our trench. In the case of the wall, we were interested in understanding when it was built and in how many phases, as well as linking it to the construction of the Great Ballcourt and the Castillo. Here, our conclusions are somewhat more preliminary because we did not excavate a trench directly connecting the wall to the pyramid. Nevertheless, the results we have suggest a rather strong hypothesis for growth on the west side of the Great Platform. As a result of our work in these two places we now have a rough construction sequence for the Great Platform.

Previous Investigations of the Great Platform

Research conducted by UCSD scholars and later by the UADY team on the Great Platform builds upon more than one hundred years of previous investigation. It is necessary to acknowledge the importance of this work. The first to dig on the Great Platform and report about it were Alice and Augustus Le Plongeon. During their excavations of the Venus Platform in 1875, the Le Plongeons dug below the plaza level and into the Great Platform itself. A section drawing of this excavation reveals that they encountered three floors: one at ground level and two red-painted plaster floors below the final level of the plaza (Desmond 2001, 2008). In other words, the section suggests that the Platform of Venus was built on top or flush with the final floor (i.e., what we call plaster floor Feature AC6).

Members of the Carnegie Institution also investigated the Great Platform (Morris et al. 1931:1:167, Figure 106; for a useful summary, see Bey and Ringle 2007:409-411). They were the first to establish a stratigraphic link between the Castillo, the West Colonnade, and the Temple of the Warriors. In sum, they concluded that the West Colonnade is the earliest of these constructions, followed by the Castillo, which was followed in turn by the Temple of the Warriors. Our research directly supports their conclusions regarding the West Colonnade and Castillo, and indirectly supports their conclusion regarding the Temple of the Warriors.

The Carnegie excavators placed six test-pits in three general locations: the West Colonnade, the Great Platform itself, and at the base of the low terrace abutting the Castillo (Figure 9.4) In all three places, they found three floors, referred to here as Carnegie Floor 1 (lowest), Carnegie Floor 2, and Carnegie Floor 3 (the uppermost and latest). Because their test pits were not connected and many were spaced quite far apart, it cannot be demonstrated from their work alone that these are the same floors throughout all their excavations. In order to do this, it is necessary to trace connections between floors and across the test pits. Thus, it is possible that some of the Carnegie floors could be the surfaces of different platforms rather than three continuous surfaces. In fact, there are places on the Great Platform where at least five floors are known. Moreover, the depth beneath the ground surface at which a floor is found is often assumed to be constant. Put another way, floors are generally thought to be flat. Nevertheless, drainage is an important problem with any open-air floor, and plazas as large as the Great Platform must be sloped to drain water away from the center (see González de la Mata et al. 2005). Our excavations demonstrate that the various floors of the Great Platform were built with a one-percent grade. Over 77.5 meters (the distance from the Castillo to the West Colonnade) this implies a drop of three quarters of a meter. Therefore, a second problem in interpreting the Carnegie excavations is that a single continuous floor should be found at very different levels depending on where their test pits were dug.

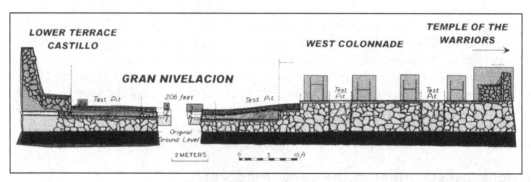

Figure 9.4. Profile and floors of the Great Platform (Morris et al. 1931:1:167, Figure 106).

At the West Colonnade, the Carnegie team discovered that the lowest floor, Carnegie Floor 1, lips up onto a low platform in front of the West Colonnade. This clearly corresponds with our plaster floor Feature AC2 (see Figure 9.4). This platform was later covered flush to its top by Carnegie Floor 2, which corresponds to our plaster floor Feature AC1. Carnegie Floor 3 is later, and nearly flush with the level of the floor of the colonnade itself. Here we found the subfloor ballast of Feature AC6, the final floor of the Great Platform east of the Castillo, but the plaster from the final floor disappeared long ago.

Correspondences between the floors that we excavated and the three Carnegie floors are much less clear at the base of the Castillo than at the West Colonnade. We do not know the exact location of the Carnegie test pit at the base of the pyramid, which complicates matters because our own excavations revealed a total of five floors near the eastern edge of the Castillo rather than the three discussed by the Carnegie. These floors (from top to bottom: Feature AC6, an unnamed floor, Feature AC1, Feature AC2, and Feature AC3) are discussed in the next section. Erosa Peniche (1948) in his excavations noted the presence of five floors in front of the Castillo-sub, so it seems likely that the Carnegie test pit was placed in an area where the construction history of the Great Platform is less complex.

At the Castillo, the Carnegie team excavated at the foot of the low platform at the base of the pyramid. The Carnegie team observed that this platform rests on Carnegie Floor 2, and a re-plastering event (Carnegie Floor 2A) lips up on the platform. It is not clear from their report if the base of the first body of the Castillo also rests on Carnegie Floor 2. If the low platform is a slightly later construction, Carnegie Floor 2 may lip up onto the first body beneath and behind the low platform. Carnegie Floor 2 could be either our plaster floor Feature AC1 or an unnamed plaster floor (found only in Test Pits 128 and 154). The latter identification seems more plausible, because we have clear evidence in front of the eastern stair that plaster floor Feature AC1 actually passes a significant distance below the Castillo, which rests on ballast placed on top of plaster floor Feature AC1. Nonetheless, our poorly preserved and unnamed floor also is at a level that should pass beneath the Castillo.

Carnegie Floor 3 dates to some time after the construction of the Castillo and the low platform (but perhaps was part of the same general construction phase), and Carnegie Floor 1 predates the great pyramid. At the Castillo, Carnegie Floor 3 most likely corresponds with floor Feature AC6. All that is preserved of this final floor at the centerline of the stair is its underlying ballast and a thin lip of plaster on the first row of stones. We think, therefore, that the Castillo was built roughly at the same time as floor Feature AC6, and not significantly before it. This is because all the other floors we uncovered pass beneath the base level of the pyramid. At the Castillo, Carnegie Floor 1 is either our plaster floor Feature AC1 or the more deeply buried plaster floor Feature AC2. Put another way, we are not sure if Carnegie Floor 1 refers to the same surface at the Castillo as it does at the West Colonnade. Measurements taken within the Castillo by Rudolfo Canto in aid of our research imply that our plaster floor Feature AC2 corresponds with the floor that lips up onto the Castillo-sub.

In more recent years, Agustín Peña of the Instituto Nacional de Antropología (INAH) excavated and consolidated the West Colonnade. During this work, he excavated the entrance to the Group of 1000 Columns, adjacent to the eastern end of our principal trench. Deeply buried within the entrance were contexts containing Late Classic pottery. Peter Schmidt of INAH excavated a very significant and important series of pits for the installation of light fixtures for the sound and light show. One of our workmen on the Great Platform participated in Schmidt's excavations near the Venus Platform, and indicated that a floor and possible structure were exposed there. Desmond (2008) recalls visiting these excavations and seeing a red-painted plaster floor. Working with Schmidt on the *Proyecto Chichén Itzá*, Rocío González de la Mata (personal communication to Braswell 1995) also dug test pits for the cables leading to the lightning rods on top of the Castillo. She discovered traces of four red-painted floors beneath the current destroyed surface of the last floor. Our excavations merged with hers in Test Pit 128 and support her conclusions. Finally, Victor Castillo Borges (1998; Schmidt 2007:163-165) cleared and consolidated the Temple of the Big Tables to the north of the Temple of the Warriors, and revealed a substructure built—like the Lower Temple of the Jaguars—at plaza level. The artistic program of this substructure clearly ties it to this other building, as well as to the Temple of the Chacmool and the Castillo-sub. For this reason, Castillo Borges (1998:192) considers all four structures to be roughly contemporary. The results of these previous excavations of the *Proyecto Chichén Itzá* are extremely important, and they shed much light on our interpretations and clarify some of our own doubts.

The wall surrounding the Great Platform also has a long history of exploration. Ruz Lhuillier (1948) excavated an important structure, the Western Gate, between the northern and southern sections of the wall that were excavated by the UCSD team (Chapter 10). This was one of 13 entrances to the Great Platform, and one of only two on its western side (Peréz

Ruiz 2005). The Western Gate was destroyed by the construction of the highway that was the principal road between Merida and Valladolid from about 1950 until the 1970s. This road is still the major entrance for merchants and site custodians.

More recently, our friends and colleagues from Schmidt's *Proyecto Chichen Itzá* conducted extensive excavation and consolidation operations of the wall. Eduardo Peréz de Heredia Puente (1994) excavated and consolidated Access 1 and Structure 2D13, where Sacbe 1 joins the Great Platform. Other members of the team studied Access 10 (behind the Northeast Colonnade), Access 9 (leading to Sacbe 6 southeast of the Steambath), Accesses 7 and 8 (south of the Market), Access 6 (used today as the hotel entrance), Access 13 (at the Temple of Xtoloc), Access 5 (between the Temple of Xtoloc and the ballcourt in the Group of 1000 Columns), and—most recently—Access 4 (south of the Castillo at the pedestrian walkway to the High Priest's Grave). Schmidt's team also consolidated those portions of the wall immediately north and south of Ruz Lhuiller's (1948) excavations, that is, in the center of the 94-meter long portion of the wall excavated by the UCSD team. Peréz de Heredia Puente (2005:cuadro 14) analyzed 52 sherds from Schmidt's excavations, and concludes that the western wall was built during the late-to-terminal facet of the Sotuta phase, which he dates to A.D. 1100–1200. We acknowledge that this construction is late, but prefer to shift this 50 to 100 years earlier in time.

Peréz Ruiz (2005) summarizes much of this work, and reaches an interesting conclusion. Many of the accesses in the wall studied by Peréz Ruiz were blocked by hastily added walls, step-fret-shaped parapets, or even stacked column stones. An implication is that when the wall was first built, defense from attack may not have been its primary purpose. Peréz Ruiz (2005: 921) concludes that at some point during the history of Chichen Itza, it became necessary to block or reinforce entrances in the existing wall in order to shore up defenses. Our own work (Chapter 10) strongly supports Peréz Ruiz's conclusion, and suggests that the wall proper was strengthened with a thick buttress wall made of stones scavenged from existing structures.

One final recent discovery of the *Proyecto Chichén Itzá* well to the south of the Great Platform is relevant to work conducted by the UCSD team. While excavating the Temple of the Initial Series, José Osorio León (2004, 2005) discovered a fourth and earliest substructure, called Structure 5C4-I. Schmidt (2007:157, 182) suggests that the pottery associated with the substructure is pre-Sotuta in date (ca. A.D. 600–800/850) and pertains to a "Proto-Slateware horizon" of the Late Classic period. Osorio León (2005) and Peréz de Heredia Puente (2001) refer to this complex as Yabnal/Motul. Braswell has examined the small sample (N=13) of obsidian recovered from the substructure and the fill that later covered it. The obsidian was visually sourced to El Chayal (N=7), Ixtepeque (N=4), and Ucareo or Zaragoza (N=2). This is a remarkably high percentage of obsidian from Maya sources for Chichen Itza (cf. Braswell and Glascock 2003:Table 3.1; Braswell et al. 2011:Table 2), and the procurement pattern is generally more consistent with a Late Classic date than with a Terminal Classic one. But the presence of some Mexican-source obsidian (especially if it comes from the Ucareo source) might suggest mixing with materials that date to after A.D. 800/850. Perhaps these two artifacts are from later fill that covered the substructure. From the perspective of excavations conducted by UCSD staff on the Great Platform, what is most important is that this early substructure of the Temple of the Initial Series is constructed of roughly cut stones covered with a thick layer of stucco retaining traces of paint. In these respects, it is similar to architecture that we excavated on the Great Platform dating to Stage IA and Stage IIA. Nonetheless, we prefer a date of A.D. 800–850 for our earliest architecture, and perhaps—but not necessarily—for the earliest known substructure of the Temple of the Initial Series.

Absolute Chronology of the Great Platform

Absolute dates for the Great Platform specifically and "New Chichen" in general are very few in number. There are just two inscriptions with hieroglyphic dates from "New Chichen," and both are controversial. The first inscription is from a hemispherical stone object framed by a flat halo containing 24 hieroglyphs (Wren et al. 1989). The "Great Ballcourt stone," as it is known, was recovered in 1923 by Miguel Angel Fernández in the southern end of the ballcourt (Lizardi Ramos 1936, 1937). Figurative carving on the hemisphere is rendered in the International style, and closely echoes the theme of decapitation seen on the panels of the Great Ballcourt. Glyphs 6 and 7 contain the calendar round date of 11 Cimi 14 Pax. Wren (1986, cited in Wren et al. 1989) prefers a reconstructed Long Count date of 10.1.15.3.6 (A.D. 864) for this calendar round. The best argument for this equivalency is that it is close to the range A.D. 869–889, the very limited time frame in which most of the dated hieroglyphic texts at Chichen Itza fall. Later reconstructions would place the Great Ballcourt stone more than a decade later than any other date for an inscription at Chichen Itza that was accepted in 1989 (see Ringle et al. 1998:Table 2). A reconstruction of A.D. 864, however, implies that the Great Ballcourt stone is actually one of the oldest texts—if not the oldest dated text—known from the site. Moreover, the implication of an early reconstruction is that there is a substantial (and perhaps total) overlap of both the "Chichen-Maya" style architecture of "Old Chichen" and the "Toltec-Maya" style art and architecture of "New Chichen" (Wren et al. 1989:27). It is not surprising that Schele and Mathews (1998) accept this chronology—which happens to support their very early dating for Chichen Itza—and argue that the Great Ballcourt was dedicated on this date, fully 14 years before the Temple of the Initial Series in "Old Chichen." But other later Long Count reconstructions are also possible: 10.4.7.16.6 (A.D. 916), 10.7.0.11.6 (A.D. 968), 10.9.13.6.6 (A.D. 1020), or even later. For reasons to be discussed below, we consider A.D. 968 or 1020 to be the most likely dates for the monument, assuming it really does dedicate the Great Ballcourt.

Two more hieroglyphic dates are found on an inscription at the High Priest's Grave (Figure 9.3). Although not located on the Great Platform, this text is relevant because it is on a carved warrior column (Lincoln 1986:162): a hallmark of the International style. Thus column is located on a radial pyramid containing serpent balustrades and other attributes of the full International style. Unlike the Great Ballcourt stone, the High Priest's Grave text begins with a calendar round date and ends with a full Short Count date corresponding to 10.8.10.6.4 (Thompson 1937:185; for a full history of the decipherment and recent confirmation of these dates, see Graña-Behrens et al. 1999; Wagner 1995). Thus, these two dates correlate to A.D. 998, considerably later than any other generally accepted date for a text at Chichen Itza (see Ringle et al. 1998:Table 2). There have been some attempts to suggest that the High Priest's Grave is older than the Castillo and dates to the late ninth or early tenth century (Cobos Palma 2007:330; see also Sharer with Traxler 2006:563). Nonetheless, we consider A.D. 998—as well as the argument presented by Graña-Behrens et al. (1999) for it—to be a completely reasonable date for the construction of the High Priest's Grave, and concur with Schmidt (2007:161, 194) that this structure and the complex in which it is found actually post-dates the Castillo, Venus Platform, and Sacbe 1 on the Great Platform. The pyramidal structure of the Castillo is rather plain and unadorned compared to that of the High Priest's Grave, and its superstructure shares much in common with those found in "Old Chichen." Overall, the High Priest's Grave has more elements of the full International style than does the Castillo, elements that are also found on the Temple of the Warriors which it resembles almost as much as the

Castillo. The Temple of the Warriors, as noted above, post-dates the Castillo. The arrangement of the High Priest's Grave, its small Venus Platform, Sacbe 15, and the Cenote of Xtoloc is of course reminiscent of the Castillo, the large Venus Platform, Sacbe 1, and the Sacred Cenote. But the High Priest's Grave and its three altars—as well as the presence of a large shaft tomb in the pyramid—also closely recall Structures Q58, Q59, Q59a, and Q60 at Mayapan. Given the similarities of the High Priest's Grave to both of these architectural arrangements, it is reasonable to consider that the High Priest's Grave dates to a time between the Castillo of Chichen Itza and Structure Q58 of Mayapan. We agree with Schmidt (2007), and consider the High Priest's Grave to be roughly contemporary with the Temple of the Warriors.

The late dates from the High Priest's Grave have three important implications. First, a later correlation for the Great Ballcourt stone—the only other monument to combine a Maya date with International-style artwork—can no longer be considered aberrant. Dates of A.D. 968 or A.D. 1020 for the Great Ballcourt stone are both entirely reasonable, given a date of A.D. 998 for the Osario column. Second, final-stage architecture on the Great Platform that is built in the same full International style as the High Priest's Grave likely dates to the late tenth or early eleventh century, that is, one hundred years or more after the dated structures in "Old Chichen" were built. Thus, although some overlap of use and even construction is clear,[1] it is entirely reasonable to argue that many of the buildings of "Old Chichen" date to the Terminal Classic, and many of those now visible on the Great Platform date to the Early Postclassic period. Third, the Castillo dates to some time earlier than the High Priest's Grave, perhaps the early or middle tenth century (see also Bey and Ringle 2007). Therefore we consider the Castillo to be the oldest known structure now visible on the Great Platform, and date it to the beginning of the Early Postclassic period, probably between A.D. 950 and 1000.

Radiocarbon dates are quite rare for Chichen Itza. A single sample from a beam in the superstructure of the Castillo has twice been subjected to radiometric assay (Andrews and Andrews 1980:Table 4). The two dates are 1160±70 B.P. (Y-626) and 1140±100 B.P. (Y-626-bis). These dates tell us only that it is likely that the tree used to make the beam was cut after about A.D. 780 and before A.D. 969/1000 (the one-sigma ranges for each calibrated date; Ringle et al. 1998:Table 1). These dates indicate only that the Castillo was built during or after the Terminal Classic period. Thus, they are consistent with a construction date for the Castillo of A.D. 950–1000.

Construction Sequence of the Great Platform as Revealed by UCSD Excavations

This section describes the ten construction stages that UCSD investigators have identified for the Great Platform and wall. The first eight of these stages pertain to the Great Platform itself, and the last two to the wall. Another section of this chapter links this sequence to other well-known structures on the Great Platform.

Data obtained from 56 test excavations (Figure 9.5) conducted from April through July 2009 allow us to suggest a preliminary sequence for the different architectural features revealed on the east side of the Castillo. Evidence for the first three construction stages was found close to the Castillo and the fourth stage was identified in the middle of the plaza. The fifth through eighth stages correspond to different plaster floors that formed the Great Plaza. The majority of the features corresponding to each construction stage were first observed in our principal trench (Figure 9.6).

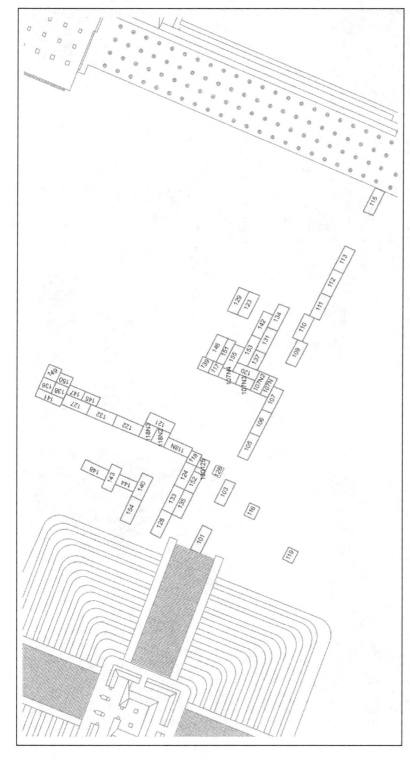

Figure 9.5. Plan of Operation AC, showing principal trench between the Castillo and the West Colonnade of the Group of 1000 Columns, as well as test pits (Braswell et al. 2009:Figura 1.2).

Figure 9.6. Operation AC, excavations east of the Castillo. Test Pits 111-113 and 115 of the principal trench (right of center, near tree line) have already been backfilled. Nancy Peniche is visible striding north, east of Feature AC10 (Peniche et al. 2009:cover photo).

Stage I

The earliest construction stage that we observed in the Great Platform consists of platform Feature AC16 (Figure 9.7). We located the eastern side of this platform in Test Pit AC128 (Figure 9.8). The platform was constructed of crudely faced stones that were covered with thick plaster painted yellow. The length of the eastern face of the platform is unknown, but it cannot extend more than six meters farther to the south. The platform stands 56 centimeters above plaster floor Feature AC17, which was built on bedrock leveled in some areas with *sascab* (marl). One of the most fascinating aspects about platform Feature AC16 is that it was built on the same axis as the Castillo. That is, the orientation of architectural features that characterizes the final version of the Great Platform was already established during its earliest known construction phase.

A second platform, Feature AC21, may also date to Stage I, but we did not expose floors that allow us to link directly this second platform to Feature AC16. All we can say for certain is that platform Feature AC21 dates to sometime before Stage III. For this reason, we assign platform Feature AC16 to Stage IA and platform Feature AC21 to Stage IB/IIB. Platform Feature AC21 is discussed in more detail below, because its style suggests to us that it probably dates to a time after the construction of platform Feature AC16.

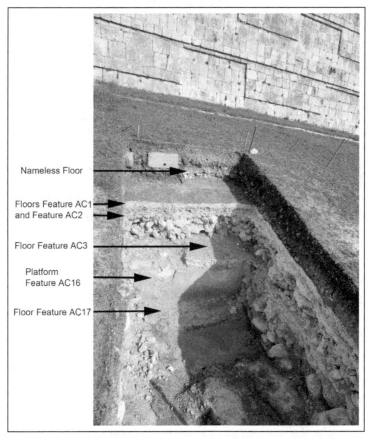

Figure 9.7. Platform Feature AC16, as well as later floors (after Braswell et al. 2009:Figura 1.8).

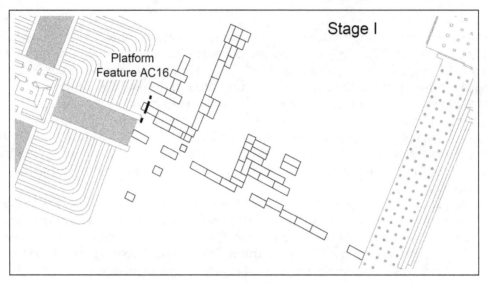

Figure 9.8. Stage I of construction, showing location of platform Feature AC16 (after Braswell et al. 2009:Figura 1.7).

Stage II

The best-preserved—and most beautiful—plaster floor we uncovered is that of platform Feature AC3, constructed during Stage IIA (Figure 9.9–9.10). The construction of platform Feature AC3 signaled a change in the orientation of the Great Platform as well as an eastern extension of it. Platform Feature AC3 was built at the same level as the plaster floor of platform Feature AC16, and completely encompassed that earlier structure. We were able to explore only a portion of the eastern side of platform Feature AC3; for this reason its complete dimensions are not known.

Platform Feature AC3 extends at least 22.5 meters (northeast to southwest). In Test Pit 130, we observed a probable corner. We argue that sharp differences in the color of the floor, along with visibly overlapping plaster, imply that the floor was later extended to cover the Stage III platform Feature AC10. Following this change in the surface of the floor of platform Feature AC3, the platform turns west from the corner and then appears to turn to the north (where the east-facing wall of the platform is called Feature AC20). We located neither the northeastern nor southeastern corner of platform Feature AC3.

The height of the platform above bedrock varies because of considerable irregularities in the ground surface. The platform itself was constructed using cut but undressed stones and covered in its entirety with a thick cap of stucco painted red. This plaster was found in an excellent condition in almost all contexts where Feature AC3 was exposed. The quality and style of the masonry is very similar to that of the earlier Stage IA platform, Feature AC16. It differs considerably from that of platform Feature AC21, which we assign to Stage IB/IIB. Although we lack sufficient stratigraphic evidence to prove this hypothesis, stylistic similarities suggest that platform AC3 was built before platform AC21. Nonetheless, we can affirm that platform Feature AC21 predates the construction of platform Feature AC10, built in Stage III.

Platform Feature AC21 was discovered in Test Pits 127 and 141 (Figure 9.10). We exposed only a portion of this platform, but were able to determine that it was constructed on the same orientation as platform Feature AC16 and all structures dating to Stage III and later. It is not on the same axis as platform Feature AC3. Platform Feature AC21 is rectangular and was constructed using finely dressed stones and was coated with a thin layer of stucco. This distinguishes it from both platforms Feature AC16 and Feature AC3. This is the earliest appearance that we documented of these two characteristics of the International style, found in all structures built during and after Stage III.

Figure 9.9. Platform Feature AC3, Stage IIA (after Braswell et al. 2009:Figura 1.10).

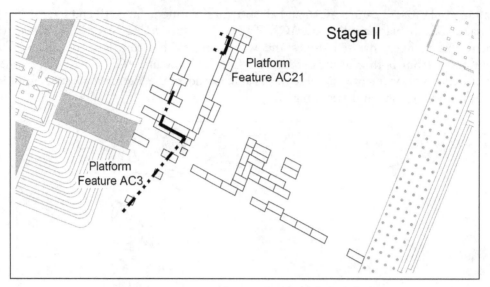

Figure 9.10. Stage II of construction, showing location of platform Feature AC3 and platform Feature AC21 (after Braswell et al. 2009:Figura 1.9).

Stage III

Platform Feature AC10 is the second construction displaying aspects of the International style, consisting of a *talud* surmounted by a projecting cornice and vertical element (Figure 9.11c). The construction of Platform Feature AC10 buried the northeastern portion of platform Feature AC3 as well as the small platform Feature AC21 built during Stage IB/IIB (Figure 9.12). Because platform Feature AC10 was constructed at the same level as platform Feature AC3, we consider it to be an extension of the Stage II platform designed to integrate it with platform Feature AC21.

The orientation and architectural characteristics of platform Feature AC10 are distinct from those of the earlier platform Feature AC3 (Figure 9.13). Platform Feature AC10 was constructed following the same orientation as the earlier platforms Feature AC16 and Feature AC21. The southeast corner of platform Feature AC10 (where it joins the earlier platform Feature AC3) was found, as well as portions of its east and south walls and a stair (Figure 9.14). The stair is probably a later addition. The east wall of Feature AC10 consists of a *talud* built of finely cut and dressed stones and covered with a fine and thin layer of red stucco. The wall is capped with a cornice that was dismantled in some places prior to building a later floor (Feature AC2). In contrast, the south wall of Feature AC10—a feature built against the older platform Feature AC3, and hence, hidden—was built of cut but undressed stones. We found several sections of round columns incorporated into the fill where platform Feature AC10 was built against platform Feature AC3 (Figure 9.11b). Although these were not in situ, we can assume that structures with columns were built at Chichen Itza before Stage III.

Figure 9.11. Platform Feature AC10: (a) view southwest towards Castillo; (b) view north from southeast corner; (c) view south during excavation of stair Feature AC19 (Braswell et al. 2009:Figura 1.12).

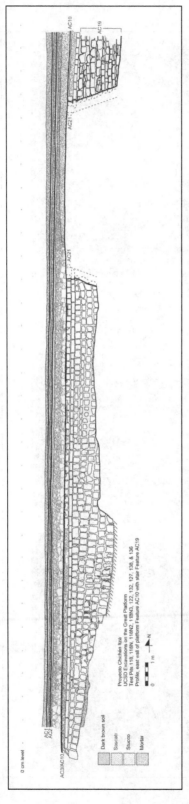

Figure 9.12. Profile of east side of platform Feature AC10 (after Peniche and Braswell 2009:Figura 3.21).

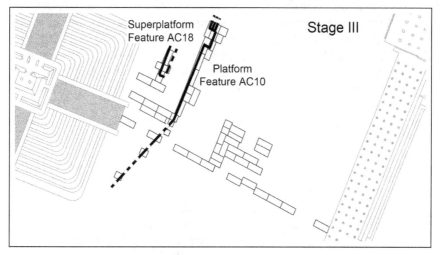

Figure 9.13. Stage III of construction, showing location of platform Feature AC10 and superplatform Feature AC18 (after Braswell et al. 2009:Figura 1.11).

Figure 9.14. Stair Feature AC19 on platform Feature AC10 (after Peniche and Braswell 2009:Figura 3.36).

As discussed, the construction of platform Feature AC10 re-established the original orientation of platforms Feature AC16 and Feature AC21. This orientation continues with later constructions on the Great Platform, with the notable exception of the Venus Platform. We consider it reasonable to describe the large platform created by adding Feature AC10 to the north side of Feature AC3 as the first version of the Great Platform, albeit much smaller than its final form. Our excavations revealed a very small superplatform on top of platform Feature AC10. The walls of this superstructure were dismantled but it was possible to observe their positions because of marks left in the plaster floor. It is interesting to speculate about other structures that may have been built upon this platform. If the Castillo-sub contains beneath it an even earlier structure, it would have been built along with the painted plaster floor that covers the Stage III platform. Although it is only a hypothesis, we suspect that such a structure exists, and that it was in Stage III that the basic plan of the Great Platform—consisting of a large platform built with elements of the International style and supporting a central pyramid—was established.

Stage IV

The fourth stage of construction consists of a major expansion of the Great Platform to the east (plaster floor Feature AC7 and *sascab* floor Feature AC4) and the construction of a patio-gallery structure (Feature AC8) at the eastern end of the extension (Figure 9.15). In order to create more flat space east of the platform formed by Feature AC3 and Feature AC10, fill was placed above *kancab* (red soil) and exposed bedrock. Human remains and stucco fragments painted in vivid colors were placed at the foot of the Feature AC3 platform prior to filling and leveling the ground to the top of the platform (Figure 9.9). We also found worked stones from dismantled structures incorporated into this fill. A *sascab* floor (Feature AC4) was built flush with the top of the platform formed by Feature AC3 and Feature AC10. This *sascab* floor extended out into the middle of what today is the plaza east of the Castillo. Here there is a change to a hard plaster floor (Feature AC7), which supported the patio-gallery structure Feature AC8 (Figure 9.16). The plaster floor continued a few meters behind (east) of the structure, where it turns down to the ground level. This marks the eastern extent of the Great Platform during Stage IV. We tentatively date Stage IV to just before A.D. 900.

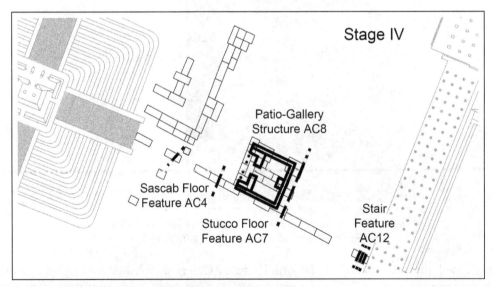

Figure 9.15. Stage IV of construction, showing location of patio-gallery structure Feature AC8, the eastern extent of the Great Platform (plaster floor Feature AC7), and the enigmatic stair Feature AC12 (after Braswell et al. 2009:Figura 1.13).

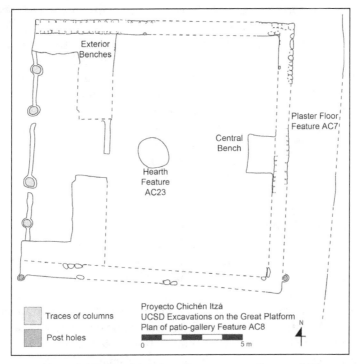

Figure 9.16. Plan of patio-gallery structure Feature AC8
(after Peniche and Braswell 2009:Figura 3.26).

Figure 9.17. Patio-gallery structure Feature AC8: (a) view from northeast corner looking southwest towards Castillo; (b) view looking north showing plaster "speed bump" connecting columns (Braswell et al. 2009:Figures 1.14-1.15).

The patio-gallery structure Feature AC8 is only partially preserved because it was dismantled during the next construction stage (Figure 9.17). We consider this patio-gallery to be the earliest version of the compound known as the Group of 1000 Columns, which—although technically not a patio-gallery itself—contains one and somewhat resembles an extremely large patio-gallery. The Stage IV patio-gallery measures 13 meters on each side. Because it was dismantled in antiquity, we do not know its original height. The data we have suggest that it was completely covered in stucco. Unfortunately, the benches (both interior and exterior) and columns were also dismantled, but traces remain in the plaster floor showing where they once were located. The gallery is fronted by four columns. Each measures 50 centimeters in diameter. The columns are linked by a strange plaster feature that we refer to as a "speed bump" (Figure 9.17b). This feature was added on top of the floor, and we think that its function was to impede water from flowing into the structure. The gallery also had two lateral L-shaped benches to the north and south.

In the interior patio, we discovered the remains of a destroyed bench or altar built against the back (east) wall. Aligned with this central bench and the access to the patio from the gallery, we found a depression filled with ash and burned calcium carbonate. Associated with this were the remains of an incense burner. This is probably a firebox or *tlacuilli*, as such features are known in Nahuatl.

A final feature that we excavated is worthy of mention. This is the stair Feature AC12, which consists of steps. The stair was located in our easternmost unit, just west of the entrance to the West Colonnade and Group of 1000 Columns (Figure 9.15). The stair rises toward the east, but the platform surface that it originally faced was dismantled sometime in the past. We cannot assign the stair to any single construction stage, but it was covered up during Stage V. Thus, we date it to some period before Stage V.

Stage V

During Stage V, the eastern portion of the plaza reached its current size. This was accomplished by dismantling the patio-gallery structure Feature AC8, adding fill on top of it, and building the red-painted plaster floor Feature AC2 (Figure 9.18a). Plaster floor Feature AC2 corresponds with the earliest of the floors observed by the Carnegie project, Carnegie Floor 1. At this time, the West Colonnade and the Castillo-sub were also built. Survey measurements taken inside the Castillo demonstrate that the floor that lips up onto the Castillo-sub is plaster floor Feature AC2. It is likely, then, that the eastern portion of the Great Platform looked very much the same as it does today. At the center was a large pyramid, and to the east was the West Colonnade. We tentatively date Stage V to the first half of the tenth century A.D.

The Great Platform is one of the largest platforms in the Maya world. During the rainy season it acts like a watershed. Draining the platform is a primary consideration. The floors that constitute the Great Platform at different construction phases, therefore, were deliberately sloped. During Stage V, the plaster floor Feature AC2 was sloped at about a one percent grade to the east, that is, toward the West Colonnade, which also was built during Stage V. At this time, however, the entrance to the West Colonnade was elevated and approached by climbing two low terraces. Water would not have flown into the opening of the Group of 1000 Columns because of the elevated nature of the West Colonnade. We assume that water was drained either north or south from the West Colonnade, but lack detailed evidence to support this.

Stage VI

This stage consisted of building the plaster floor Feature AC1 (Figure 9.18b), the uppermost floor that is still well preserved today. The red color of floor Feature AC1 was made by incorporating broken and ground up pottery sherds into the plaster.

Figure 9.18. Stage V, VI, and VIII floors: (a) view looking west of Stage V floor Feature AC2, which corresponds with the Castillo-sub and the West Colonnade; (b) view looking west of floor Feature AC1, which passes beneath the east stair of the Castillo; (c) plaster from Stage VIII floor Feature AC6 lipping up on first step of east stair of Castillo. (Braswell et al. 2009:Figures 1.16-1.18).

At the West Colonnade, the plaster floor Feature AC1 corresponds with Carnegie Floor 2. At its western edge, it raised the level of the Great Platform and buried the lower of two low terraces leading up to the West Colonnade. In effect, then, it lowered the apparent height of the colonnade. This could have created significant problems with the flow of water into the West Colonnade and the Group of 1000 Columns. Floor Feature AC1, however, was constructed not with an eastern cant, but drops to the north with a slope of about one percent. Thus, during Stage VI, water was drained towards the northern side of the Great Platform rather than to its eastern edge. The northern boundary of the Great Platform during Stage VI is not known; however, for reasons discussed below, it could not have been much north of an imaginary east–west line today defined by the Temple of the Big Tables and the Venus Platform.

As described above, we are not completely sure if Carnegie Floor 2 at the West Colonnade is the same as Carnegie Floor 2 at the Castillo. We are certain, however, that plaster floor Feature AC1 predates the Castillo because it passes a significant distance beneath the eastern stair of the pyramid, which is built on ballast fill placed on top of plaster floor Feature AC1.

Stage VII

This construction stage is limited to a modification (without an assigned feature number) to the floor of the Great Platform that we identified in Test Pits 128 and 154 (Figure 9.5). This unnamed plaster floor is poorly preserved, but its stratigraphic position is both above floor Feature AC1 and underneath the level of the Castillo. It was built, therefore, after Stage VI and before the final floor (Feature AC6) and the Castillo. Because this unnamed floor was found in just two test pits, we do not know its extent.

Stage VIII

The Castillo was built during Stage VIII. The plaster surface of the floor that corresponds to this stage, called floor Feature AC6, was not found in any test pit east of the Castillo because it was close to the modern ground surface and has suffered recent destruction. We did find considerable amounts of mortar and small stones—constituting the subfloor ballast—throughout our excavations. Traces of the plaster surface of Feature AC6—perhaps representing the resurfacing of the floor—are preserved on the first step of the eastern stair of the Castillo (Figure 9.18c). We date Stage VIII to the second half of the tenth century A.D.

Although the Stage VIII plaster floor Feature AC6 was not preserved in the eastern portion of the Great Platform, we believe we found it beneath the wall west of the Castillo and south of the Great Ballcourt (Figure 9.2).

Stages IX and X

Chapter 10 discusses excavations of a 94-meter section of the wall, south of the Great Ballcourt and north of the pedestrian entrance leading from the museum to the Castillo. Excavations in the vicinity of the wall reveal a total of three construction phases: (1) a western expansion of the Great Platform; (2) the construction of the wall proper; and (3) the construction of the buttress wall. We argue that these three stages correspond to Stage VIII, Stage IX, and Stage X in our complete construction sequence.

We placed a test pit east of the wall and within the Great Platform, roughly 20 meters south of the Great Ballcourt. The test pit revealed that the only floor of the western portion Great Platform is the final floor. We assume that this is floor Feature AC6, but did not connect the test pit directly to our excavations on the east side of the Castillo, more than 250 meters away. Excavations beneath the wall proper (Feature AB2), beneath the buttress wall (Feature AB5), and within the drains that are incorporated into both reveal that this plaster floor is well preserved and predates the construction of the wall.

Tentative Construction Sequence for Major Structures on the Great Platform

Our data, as well those gathered by previous scholars, allow us to tentatively tie our construction sequence to other structures built on the Great Platform. Figure 9.19 summarizes this construction sequence.

Architecture dating to Stage IA and Stage IIA—built in what we call the Early Great Platform style—differs significantly from later structures on the Great Platform. The only known structure at Chichen Itza built in a similar style is Structure 5C4-I, the earliest substructure of the Temple of the Initial Series (Osorio León 2004, 2005; Schmidt 2007).

Members of the *Proyecto Chichén Itzá* date this structure to the Late Classic period (A.D. 600–850; Schmidt 2007:157) because of the presence of "Proto-Slateware" or Yabnal/Motul pottery. As a tentative hypothesis, we propose that Stage IA and Stage IIA architecture on the Great Platform is roughly contemporary with Structure 5C4-I, and hence, is either Late Classic or early Terminal Classic in date.

The earliest constructions that have elements of the International style are the poorly understood platform Feature AC21 (Stage IB/IIB) and platform Feature AC10 (Stage III). We have evidence that buildings with columns were dismantled during the Stage III expansion of the platform. Column drums were found tossed into the fill between the Feature AC3 and Feature AC10 platforms. These could be from an International-style structure or from a building in a local style. Although columns were an important feature of some International-style structures, they appear in the northern Maya lowlands no later than the Early Classic period (Figure 1.4). In any event, platform Feature AC10 suggests that by the beginning of Stage III, certain aspects of the International style were established in the core of Chichen Itza.

During Stage IV, the Great Platform was expanded to the east and a patio-gallery structure (Feature AC8) was built on top of it. This type of structure is generally considered a hallmark of the International style. It is possible that by this time or even during Stage III, the Great Platform contained an early version of the Castillo, one that still remains buried beneath the Castillo-sub.

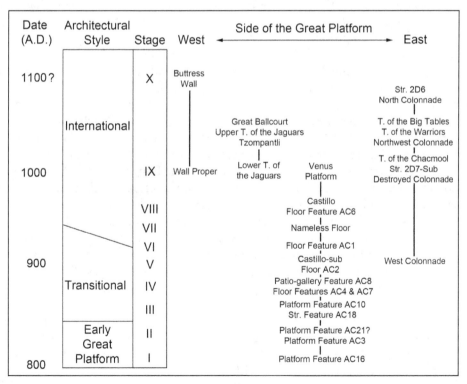

Figure 9.19. Construction sequence of the Great Platform (after Braswell et al. 2009:Figura 1.21).

Stage V is the first of our construction phases to which previously known structures on the Great Platform pertain. At this time, the eastern plaza reached its maximum and current extent, the Castillo-sub was erected, and the West Colonnade was built. Both of these structures contain strong aspects of the International style, but lack many of its final features such as serpent columns, warrior reliefs, and (relevant to the Castillo-sub) radial stairs. Marquina (1952:852) argues that the Castillo-sub is transitional between the "Maya" and the "Toltec" periods, but Bey and Ringle (2007:412) see the Castillo-sub as marking an Epiclassic phase of the cult of Quetzalcoatl that predates Early Postclassic Tula Grande. We agree, and think it also predates Early Postclassic Chichen Itza. In sum, we date the Castillo-sub to the beginning of the tenth century A.D. and suggest it is the second of three pyramids built on this spot.

Our excavations date the Castillo to Stage VIII, that is, after the eastern portion of the Great Platform was raised (plaster floor Feature AC1) and an even higher (and unnamed) floor—still below the Castillo itself—was added close to the northeastern side of the Castillo-sub. We consider our poorly preserved floor Feature AC6 (on the Great Platform we have only ballast fill and pockets of mortar from below the plaster) to be the same as Carnegie Floor 3, and date the construction of the Castillo to this stage, sometime during the late tenth century A.D.

Other structures built on the Great Platform date to even later times. We can assign most of the visible structures to a period after our Stage VIII (Figure 9.19). Moreover, many—if not all—of them were built before our Stage X. Augustus and Alice Le Plongeon's section drawing of the Venus Platform suggests that it was built on top of the Feature AC6 floor, that is, after the Castillo (Desmond 2001, 2008). The Venus Platform, therefore, could be roughly contemporary with the wall proper (Feature AB2) or date to a later time.

According to Morris et al. (1931), the three Carnegie floors (including our final floor Feature AC6) pass beneath the Temple of the Chacmool and the Demolished Colonnade, which were built together. These structures, therefore, postdate the construction of the Castillo itself. Marquina (1952) considers them to be "Toltec," while others argue that they date to a time "at least partially contemporary with Tula Grande" (Bey and Ringle 2007:412). The Temple of the Warriors and the Northwest Colonnade were built at an even later time, but—because of the number of replastering events—probably not that long after the Temple of the Chacmool. Finally, Morris et al. (1931, vol. 1) argue that the North Colonnade of the Group of 1000 Columns was built last. These latest structures, therefore, all date to construction phases after Stage VIII and probably after Stage IX, that is, after the wall proper was built (the reason for this is discussed below). Large-scale horizontal excavations designed to link sections of the wall with these structures could refine and complicate this sequence. In other words, we acknowledge that many of the structures that are shown in Figure 9.19 as roughly contemporaneous with the Stage IX wall might be assigned to their own stages. For example, we cannot at this time determine whether the wall predates or postdates the Temple of the Chacmool.

It is generally thought that the Castillo defines the center of the platform in its current configuration, but in reality the Castillo stands roughly 30 meters south of the main axis of the Great Platform. An equal distance north of the central axis is the Venus Platform, aligned with Sacbe 1 and the Cenote of Sacrifice and not with other buildings on the Great Platform. The construction of the Temple of the Chacmool and its counterpart, the Lower Temple of the Jaguars (which was later incorporated into the Great Ballcourt), established this central axis for the Great Platform. Today, this axis is defined by a clear line of site from the center of the throne in the Temple of the Warriors, over the Chacmool, and to the Jaguar throne in the center of the Lower Temple of the Jaguars (Figure 9.2). It is reasonable to expect that both ends of the axis were built as part of the same plan and at the same time. We argue, therefore, that the Lower Temple of the Jaguars is probably contemporary with the Temple of the Chacmool. Following Castillo Borges (1998:192) and Schmidt (2007:165), we consider the substructure of the Temple of the Big Tables to be roughly contemporary with these other two structures. Moreover, the Venus Platform may also have been built at this time in order to create partial symmetry (albeit at a much smaller scale and on a different orientation) with the Castillo. Although there may be some slight chronological differences, we think it likely that the construction of the wall proper also dates to about this time. In other words, we hypothesize that the wall proper, the Venus Platform, the Lower Temple of the Jaguars, the Temple of the Chacmool, the Demolished Colonnade, and the substructure of the Temple of the Big Tables were all probably constructed at about the same time during Stage IX, shortly after A.D. 1000. Again, we caution that further excavations could refine this chronology and allow it to be subdivided.

Excavations near the wall reveal that there is only one floor to the Great Platform just south of the Great Ballcourt. We assume that this is the plaster floor Feature AC6. We also assume that this same floor corresponds with the Lower Temple of the Jaguars. We were not able to excavate the wall or follow the floor to where they meet the South Temple of the Great Ballcourt because a modern dirt road runs immediately south of that structure. Nonetheless, it seems likely to us that the wall proper passes underneath the Great Ballcourt and behind the Lower Temple of the Jaguars. That is, we argue that the Great Ballcourt was built sometime later than Stage IX constructions including the wall and the Lower Temple of the Jaguars. Moreover, the northern half of the western edge of the Great Platform may have been expanded to the west during the construction of the Great Ballcourt. We assume that the Tzompantli, which forms part of the Great Ballcourt complex, was also built at this time. A reasonable hypothesis for further testing is that the Temple of the Warriors, the Northwest Colonnade, and the Temple of the Tables were built at roughly this time, mirroring the construction of the Great Ballcourt, Upper Temple of the Jaguars, and Tzompantli. The paintings of the Upper Temple of the Jaguars and the Temple of the Warriors are similar enough in style and iconographic content to argue that they are roughly contemporary, and there are many strong artistic and architectural similarities shared by these two buildings and the High Priest's Grave (see Schmidt 2007). We date the Great Ballcourt, Upper Temple of the Jaguars, Temple of the Warriors, Temple of the Big Tables, Northwest Colonnade, and Tzompantli constructions very generally to the early or middle eleventh century, based in part on the calendar round date on the Great Ballcourt stone. Assuming that this sculpture was originally carved for the Great Ballcourt and was not moved there from a different portion of the site, we consider a correlation of A.D. 1020 to be more likely than A.D. 864. Finally, the strong similarities shared by the Upper Temple of the Jaguars, the Temple of the Warriors, and the High Priest's Grave—which dates to A.D. 998—also make it likely that they were all built in the very late tenth to early eleventh centuries, some 50 years or so after the Castillo.

It is entirely possible that the latest construction episodes were not precisely simultaneous. In particular, we wonder if Structure 2D6 was built somewhat after the Temple of the Warriors. One of many questions that requires further research is the northern extent of the Great Platform in earlier times. As mentioned above, three floors pass underneath the Venus Platform and the Temple of the Chacmool, which date them to a time later than Stage VIII. Lilia Fernández Souza and Dylan Clark of the UADY team placed two test pits west of

Structure 2D6 and in the Great Platform. The southernmost of these was about ten meters from the northwest corner of the Temple of the Tables. Both of these test pits reveal that the final floor, again what we presume to be either Feature AC6 or a northern extension that was built flush against it, is the only floor in this portion of the Great Platform. Put another way, plaster floor Feature AC1 (Stage VI) seems to have ended somewhere north of the Temple of the Chacmool but south of Structure 2D6. We infer from the Le Plongeons' section drawing and description that it (and a second plaster floor, perhaps Feature AC2 or our unnamed floor) continue under the Venus Platform, but probably did not go much further north. We do not know precisely when the Great Platform was expanded to the north, but it may have happened after the construction of the Temple of the Chacmool and the Venus Platform, and certainly before the construction of Structure 2D6. Unfortunately, Castillo Borges (1998) does not discuss floors in front of or under the Temple of the Big Tables.

The latest building episode noted by the Carnegie consists of the construction of the North Colonnade, and, by extension, much of the Group of 1000 Columns. At this time, we cannot tie this directly to the Temple of the Tables and Structure 2D6.

Stage X, the construction of the buttress wall, appears to be later in time than the construction of the Great Ballcourt, and contemporary with other modifications to the wall system described by Peréz Ruiz (2005). We argue this because some sculpture found in the buttress wall seems to come from the platform jutting east from the center of the Tzompantli, that is, a part of the ballcourt complex. Given that the buttress wall was built using stones scavenged from other structures, we conclude that it is among the last major constructions on the Great Platform. We are not sure of the precise date it was built, but significant quantities of late ceramics were found around and at the foot of the wall, just off the platform. Stage X may date to after A.D. 1050 and perhaps even to the early twelfth century.

Lithic, Ceramic, and Absolute Chronologies

At the time of writing this chapter, the only materials studied by members of our project are chipped stone artifacts excavated before June 2009, analyzed by Lauren Hahn (2009). In addition to analyzing materials from the wall and the Great Platform, Hahn also had access to the lithic artifacts recovered from Structure 2D6 by members of the UADY team. Two conclusions are particularly noteworthy. First, the density of lithic materials at Chichen Itza is extremely low. The chipped stone to ceramic ratio calculated for the wall is more in line with sites in the "Chert-Free Zone" (Hearth and Fedick 2011) than with sites in those parts of Yucatan where high quality lithic material is naturally found. Despite the great importance of Chichen Itza as a center of trade, relatively little stone suitable for flaked tool industries was imported to the site. Second, obsidian from the wall and Structure 2D6 suggests that these structures were built and used very late in the history of Chichen Itza. The obsidian source that is most commonly represented in these two areas is Ixtepeque (30%). Nevertheless, the most common obsidian source at Chichen Itza as a whole is Ucareo (30%; Braswell et al. 2011:Table 2). Ucareo and the other central Mexican sources are characteristic of the period A.D. 850–1050. In contrast, great quantities of Ixtepeque obsidian are diagnostic of the Postclassic period (Braswell 2003; Braswell et al. 2011; Escamilla Ojeda 2004). The presence of relatively greater quantities of Ixtepeque obsidian mixed with material from central Mexican sources demonstrates that the wall and Structure 2D6 were used—and possibly built—very late in the history of Chichen Itza, perhaps as late as A.D. 1050–1100/1200. Use of these constructions very well might have overlapped with the beginning of significant occupation at Mayapan.

The ceramics collected by our subprojects were not yet analyzed when we left Mexico, but will be studied by Socorro Jimenez of the UADY. Nonetheless, we can make several tentative conclusions based on observations we made in the field. First, ceramics recovered from the wall date to the Terminal Classic and Postclassic periods. In addition to numerous examples of Sotuta pottery, we also recovered some Tases ceramics and possibly a few sherds assigned to the Hocaba complex. Like the obsidian, the pottery found at the wall implies a rather late date for its use. Peréz de Heredia Puente (2005:Cuadro 14), who studied ceramics recovered by Peter Schmidt from the same section of the western wall, proposes that it was built during the late-to-terminal facet of the Sotuta phase, which he dates to about A.D. 1100–1200. We think the twelfth century is too late a date for the wall proper, but it could be consistent with the defensive buttress (Chapter 10).

We recovered very little pottery from primary behavioral contexts in the Great Platform. That is, most of the sherds were recovered from mixed fill and date to a time before or during each construction episode. We have little doubt that we recovered small quantities of Late Classic, Early Classic, and perhaps even Late Preclassic pottery. Such pottery is found in very low amounts in many fill contexts at Chichen Itza (Schmidt 2007). The presence of such old sherds in mixed fill aids little in determining the date of a particular construction. Nevertheless, we made several important observations. First, our field notes from excavations east of the Castillo do not mention any pottery belonging to the Hocaba or Tases complexes. For this reason, we date all features that we exposed within that portion of the Great Platform to a time before about A.D. 1050. Second, we recovered Sotuta ceramics in great numbers from all of our excavations dating to Stage IV or later. In several places, these sherds were found in direct contact with bedrock. It very well may be that the fill of Stage I, Stage II, and especially Stage III constructions also contains large quantities of Sotuta ceramics, but we did not record such observations in the field. Alternatively—and certainly worthy of close attention—structures built during Stages IA and IIA may date, like the earliest substructure of the Temple of the Initial Series, to a Late Classic, pre-Sotuta, "Proto-Slateware" horizon (see Osorio León 2004, 2005; Schmidt 2007:182). The architecture of Stages IA and IIA certainly closely resembles this early substructure more than any other construction known at Chichen Itza.

In any event, we can say unequivocally that construction Stages IV–VIII date to the Sotuta phase, that is, to about A.D. 800/850–1050/1100. For reasons outlined above and having to do with the inscription at the High Priest's Grave—a structure that is later in style than the Castillo and roughly contemporary with the Temple of the Warriors and Upper Temple of the Jaguars—we date the construction of the Stage VIII Castillo to about A.D. 950–998.

We also found noteworthy the amount of Cehpech pottery that we recovered, particularly in Stage IV and earlier contexts. Although we are not ceramic specialists, Thin Slate is particularly easy to identify, and we were surprised how often a Thin Slate sherd came to our attention. This helps us determine a lower date of A.D. 700 for Stage IV, but we strongly suspect that this is at 100 to 200 years too early.

In sum, our very preliminary notes regarding the ceramics collected during our excavations of the Great Platform and wall suggest that, for the most part, construction dates to the Sotuta phase, or roughly A.D. 800/850–1050/1100. It is possible that Stages IA–IIA date to somewhat earlier Late Classic times, but the data currently available to us neither demonstrate nor refute this possibility. Stages IV to VIII are probably within the range of A.D. 850/900–950/1000. Stage IX most likely dates to the middle to late tenth century. Finally, the Stage X buttress wall could date to the late eleventh or even twelfth century A.D.

We are confident that Jimenez' future analysis of the ceramics that we recovered will resolve these questions, particularly the important one concerning the placement of Stage I and IIA structures in the Late Classic period.

Conclusion: The Maya, the Toltecs, and the International Style

The construction history of the Great Platform is complex, but it seems highly unlikely that any of the structures we excavated were built before the Late Classic period. Moreover, only the Stage IA to Stage IIA structures may date to this period, and this still needs to be resolved through ceramic analysis and radiocarbon dating. Conversely, the last construction episode studied by us probably took place between about A.D. 1050 and A.D. 1100/1200. In sum, the entire sequence certainly represents no more than 600 years, and we strongly suspect that it was about 300 years in length.

The traditional history of Chichen Itza divides the period of occupation of the great city into two periods: one called "Chichen Maya" and one "Toltec-Maya." We identify three general architectural periods of construction on the Great Platform, but prefer "International style" to any phrase containing the word "Toltec." We call these the "Early Great Platform," "Transitional," and "International" periods.

The Early Great Platform period is typified by platforms faced with crudely cut rocks forming vertical walls. These walls were covered with thick layers of stucco. This period corresponds to our construction Stages IA and IIA. We tentatively date this style to the early Terminal Classic period, most probably the ninth century A.D. The only other place where this style has been noted before is the earliest substructure of the Temple of the Initial Series, which could be a century older still.

The Transitional period is typified by the adoption of some, but by no means all, of the characteristics of the International style. Over time, more and more traits of the style were added in a gradual fashion. The earliest evidence we have for the Transitional period is platform Feature AC21, which is dated to Stage IB/IIB, that is, some time before the building of platform Feature AC10. We suspect for stylistic reasons that platform Feature AC21 postdates both the Feature AC16 and the Feature AC3 platforms. Unlike these Early Great Platform features, Feature AC21 is made of well-cut stones. We suspect that it may closely resemble the Stage III Feature AC10 platform in which it was later incorporated. This Stage III platform consists of a *talud* and flaring cornice, has curved corners, and is built of very finely cut and faced stones covered with only a thin coat of stucco. The stair Feature AC19 is flanked to the south by a protrusion that forms a large balustrade. The *talud*, cornice, and balustrade are all features of the International style. We consider it probable that Stage III dates to the middle or late ninth century A.D., and most likely was contemporary with many of the dated structures in "Old Chichen."

Later Transitional period (Stage IIB-V) structures that incorporate more aspects of the International style are the patio-gallery structure Feature AC8 (built in Stage IV), the West Colonnade, and the Castillo-sub (both built in Stage V). The first two of these incorporate columns in a manner that probably originated in northwest Mexico. The Castillo-sub, although it somewhat resembles the later Castillo, is not a radial pyramid, lacks serpent columns and balustrades, and has no warrior images. Nevertheless, the Castillo-sub does contain a Chacmool sculpture and has certain iconographic elements on its façade that belong to the International style (Bey and Ringle 2007: 412-413). We tentatively propose a date in the early tenth century for the Castillo-sub, built during Stage V. This, too, overlaps with construction in "Old Chichen."

Stage VI and VII are known to us only from plaster floors (Feature AC1 and an unnamed floor). We cannot say for certain whether it is better to assign them to the Transitional period or to the full-fledged International style. The International period is well represented by the Castillo (Stage VIII, the earliest known structure in the full International style), the Venus Platform, Temple of the Chacmool, Lower Temple of the Jaguars, Demolished Colonnade (all thought to date approximately to Stage IX), Upper Temple of the Jaguars, Great Ballcourt, Tzompantli, Temple of the Warriors, Northwest Colonnade, North Colonnade, Temple of the Tables, High Priest's Grave, and Structure 2D6 (all dating to a time between Stage IX and Stage X).

Bey and Ringle (2007) present a very complete comparative analysis of the chronologies of Chichen Itza and Tula. Based on their work, we suggest that the Transitional period (Stages III–V/VII) is probably contemporary with the Terminal Corral and Early Tollan periods of Tula, that is, A.D. 850–900/950. During this time period, Chichen Itza emerged as one of many important cultic centers dedicated to Quetzalcoatl/Kukulcan. At Chichen Itza, some aspects of the central Mexican cult were adopted and, at the same time, modified for use in a fundamentally Maya context. The Castillo-sub, which faces north to the Sacred Cenote, is the most important temple of this period and its orientation demonstrates a tie to earlier Maya concepts that made the site sacred. We noted that Thin Slate wares (which date to about A.D. 700–900) are not rare in fill contexts dating to this time, suggesting that the Transitional period may be contemporaneous with the early facet of the Sotuta phase. The final period of construction is the International period (Stages VIII–X), which we tentatively date to the period A.D. 900/950–1050/1100 or even later. Most of the important structures were built before Stage X, that is, during the tenth and early eleventh centuries. But the Stage X buttress wall could date to the late eleventh or even twelfth century.

If the ceramics of the Transitional period belong to the early facet of the Sotuta phase, those of the ensuing International period belong to the late facet. The full array of artistic and architectural attributes of the International style appear at Chichen Itza during the International period. This includes the construction of buildings with similar counterparts at Tula Grande. For this reason, perhaps it is best to define the International period as dating to the Early Postclassic and not to the Terminal Classic period.

It is beyond the scope of this chapter to re-evaluate the nature and direction of exchange between central Mexico and Chichen Itza. Nevertheless, we wish to emphasize that our excavations have lengthened and pushed back in time the transition between the "Maya" and "International" styles. The work of the Carnegie Institute and of Erosa Peniche on the Great Platform limited this transition to our Stage V, the construction stage when the Castillo-sub was built. But our research indicates that aspects of the International style emerged in earlier structures dating to Stage IV, Stage III, and even Stage IB/IIB. If the orientation of the Stage IA structure is viewed as critical, the orientation of the Great Platform can even be said to have existed from its earliest inception, implying great continuity throughout the history of construction. The gradual nature of the transition to the full International style—which we see as taking place over the century of A.D. 850–950—is not consistent with the rapid imposition of a foreign religion and artistic sensibility on Chichen Itza. Instead, it implies a long period of in situ development, adoption, and adaptation of architectural and artistic ideas.

Bey and Ringle (2007) argue that during what we call the Transitional period, the flow of ideas from Chichen Itza to sites in central Mexico may have been more dominant than the return flow to the Maya area. What is certain to us is that the International style of architecture at Chichen Itza does not represent a site-unit intrusion. Instead, it represents a gradual transition and transformation that began in the Terminal Classic and continued well into the Early Postclassic period.

Acknowledgments

First and foremost, we thank Rafael Cobos Palma, Director of *Chichén Itzá: estudio de la cominidad del Clásico Tardío,* for his invitation to form a team of graduate students from UCSD and work alongside members of the UADY project. UCSD staff at Chichen Itza included Braswell and Peniche, and also Lauren D. Hahn, Kiri L. Hagerman, Megan R. Pitcavage, Misha Miller-Sisson, and Beniamino P. Volta. We also thank the UADY scholars Lilia Fernández Souza, Mauricio Germon Roche, and Rodolfo Canto Carrillo for their daily colleagueship, as well as Dylan Clark of Harvard University. Kate Jarvis and Oliver Boles of University College London were of great help to Peniche in June and July 2009. We also gratefully acknowledge Elisabeth Flores Torruco, Director of the Archaeological Zone of Chichen Itza, and her staff for their help and assistance. Funding for the greater project was generously awarded by the UADY, INAH (both to Cobos), UCMEXUS-CONACYT, and UCSD (both to Braswell). Funds from all of these sources supported our staff in Piste, Yucatan, and provided for our daily needs. Monies from the last three sources paid for workers on the Great Platform. Braswell would also like to thank his friends and colleagues of the *Proyecto Chichén Itzá*, particularly Peter J. Schmidt, Rocío González de la Mata, José F. Osorio León, Francisco Peréz Ruiz, and Eduardo Peréz de Heredia Puente for many years of support and fruitful collaboration.

Note

1. As our excavations show, there are structures buried within the Great Platform that pre-date the International style and may even be older than the visible "Chichen Maya" structures of "Old Chichen." Moreover, architecture in "Old Chichen" continued to be built and modified well into the "Toltec-Maya" period. The House of the Atlantean Columns, the House of the Snails, and later versions of the Temple of the Initial Series are all examples.

References

Andrews IV, E. Wyllys, and E. Wyllys Andrews V. 1980. *Excavations at Dzibilchaltun, Yucatan, Mexico.* Middle American Research Institute, Publication 48. Tulane University, New Orleans.
Ball, Joseph W. 1979. Ceramics, Culture History, and the Puuc Traditions: Some Alternative Possibilities. In *The Puuc: New Perspectives*, edited by Lawrence Mills, pp. 18-35. Central College, Pella, Iowa.
Bey, George J., III, and William M. Ringle. 2007. From the Bottom Up: The Timing and Nature of the Tula-Chichén Itzá Exchange. In Kowalski and Kristan-Graham 2007:376-427.
Brainerd, George W. 1958. *The Archaeological Ceramics of Yucatan.* Anthropological Records 19. University of California, Berkeley.
Braswell, Geoffrey E. 2003. Obsidian Exchange Spheres. In *The Postclassic Mesoamerican World*, edited by Michael E. Smith and Frances F. Berdan, pp. 131-158. University of Utah, Salt Lake City.

Braswell, Geoffrey E., and Michael D. Glascock. 2003. The Emergence of Market Economies in the Ancient Maya World: Obsidian Exchange in Terminal Classic Yucatán, Mexico. In *Geochemical Evidence for Long-Distance Exchange*, edited by Michael D. Glascock, pp. 33-52. Bergin and Garvey, Westport.

Braswell, Geoffrey E., Iken Paap, and Michael D. Glascock. 2011. The Obsidian and Ceramics of the Puuc Region: Chronology, Lithic Procurement, and Production at Xkipche, Yucatan, Mexico. *Ancient Mesoamerica* 22:125-154.

Braswell, Geoffrey E., Nancy Peniche May, and Lauren D. Hahn. 2009. Excavaciones en la Gran Nivelación de Chichén Itzá llevadas a cabo por cuerpo docente y estudiantes de posgrado de la UCSD: Marzo-julio 2009. In Peniche May, Hahn, and Braswell 2009:1-41.

Castillo Borges, Victor Rogerio. 1998. *Liberación y restauración de la Estructura 2D7 o Templo de Las Grandes Mesas de Chichén Itzá*. Licenciatura thesis, Facultad de Antropología, Universidad de Yucatán, Merida.

Cobos, Rafael. 2003. *The Settlement Patterns of Chichén Itzá, Yucatán, Mexico*. Ph.D. dissertation, Department of Anthropology, Tulane University, New Orleans. University Microfilms, Ann Arbor.

— 2007. Multepal or Centralized Kingship? New Evidence on Governmental Organization at Chichén Itzá. In Kowalski and Kristan-Graham 2007:314-343.

Desmond, Lawrence G. 2001. Augustus Le Plongeon (1826–1908): Early Mayanist, Archaeologist, and Photographer. In *Oxford Encyclopedia of Mesoamerican Cultures*, vol. 2, edited by David Carrasco, pp. 117-118. Oxford University, New York.

— 2008. Excavation of the Platform of Venus, Chichén Itzá, Yucatan, Mexico: The Pioneering Fieldwork of Alice Dixon Le Plongeon and Augustus Le Plongeon. In *Tributo a Jaime Litvak King*, edited by Paul Schmidt Schoenberg, Edith Ortiz Diaz, and Joel Santos Ramirez, pp. 155-166. Instituto de Investigaciones Antropológicas, UNAM, Mexico City.

Escamilla Ojeda, Bárbara del Carmen. 2004. *Los artefactos de obsidiana de Mayapán, Yucatán*. Licenciatura thesis, Facultad de Ciencias Antropológicas, Universidad Autónoma de Yucatán. Merida.

Erosa Peniche, José A. 1948. *Guia para visitar las ruinas de Chichén-Itzá*. Editorial Maya Than, Merida.

González de la Mata, Rocío, José F. Osorio, and Peter J. Schmidt. 2005. El flujo divino: Manejo del agua en Chichen Itza. In Laporte, Arroyo, and Mejía 2005:847-855.

Graña-Behrens, Daniel, Christian Prager, and Elisabeth Wagner. 1999. The Hieroglyphic Inscription of the "High Priest's Grave" at Chichén Itzá, Yucatán, Mexico. *Mexicon* 21:61-66.

Grube, Nikolai, and Ruth J. Krochock. 2007. Reading between the Lines: Hieroglyphic Texts from Chichén Itzá and its Neighbors. In Kowalski and Kristan-Graham 2007:205-249.

Hahn, Lauren D. 2009. Análisis preliminar de los artefactos de piedra tallada recuperados por el Proyecto Chichén Itzá: Marzo-mayo 2009. In Peniche May, Hahn, and Braswell 2009:197-226.

Hearth, Nicholas F., and Scott L. Fedick. 2011. Defining the Chert Paucity Problem in the Northern Maya Lowlands: A First Approximation. In *The Technology of Maya Civilization: Political Economy and Beyond in Lithic Studies*, edited by Zachary X. Hruby, Geoffrey E. Braswell, and Oswaldo Chinchilla Mazariegos, pp. 69-75. Equinox, London.

Kowalski, Jeff Karl. 2007. What's "Toltec" at Uxmal and Chichén Itzá? Merging Maya and Mesoamerican Worldviews and World Systems in Terminal Classic to Early Postclassic Yucatan. In Kowalski and Kristan-Graham 2007:251-313.

Kowalski, Jeff Karl, and Cynthia Kristan-Graham (editors). 2007. *Twin Tollans: Chichén Itzá, Tula, and the Epiclassic to Early Postclassic Mesoamerican World*. Dumbarton Oaks, Washington, D.C.

Laporte, Juan Pedro, Bárbara Arroyo, and Hector Mejía (editors). 2005. *XVIII simposio de investigaciones Arqueológicas en Guatemala, 2004*. Museo Nacional de Arqueología y Etnología, Guatemala.

Lincoln, Charles E. 1986. The Chronology of Chichen Itza: A Review of the Literature. In *Late Maya Lowland Civilization*, edited by Jeremy A. Sabloff and E. Wyllys Andrews V, pp. 141-198. School of American Research/University of New Mexico, Albuquerque.

— 1990. *Ethnicity and Social Organization at Chichen Itza, Yucatan, Mexico*. Ph.D. dissertation, Department of Anthropology, Harvard University, Cambridge, Mass. University Microfilms, Ann Arbor.

Lizardi Ramos, César. 1936. Los secretos de Chichén Itzá. *Excelsior*, 21 December. Mexico City.

— 1937. New Discoveries of Maya Culture at Chichén Itzá. *Illustrated London News*, 3 July, pp. 12-15. London.

Marquina, Ignacio. 1952. *Arquitectura prehispánica*. Instituto Nacional de Antropología e Historia, Secretaría de Educación Pública, Mexico City.

Morris, Earl H., Jean Charlot, and Ann A. Morris. 1931. *The Temple of the Warriors at Chichén Itzá, Yucatán*. 2 vols. Publication 406, Parts 1 and 2. Carnegie Institute of Washington, Washington, D.C.

Osorio León, José F. 2004. *La Estructura 5C4 (Templo de la Serie Inicial): Un edificio clave para la cronología de Chichén Itzá*. Licenciatura thesis, Facultad de Antropología, Universidad de Yucatán, Merida.

— 2005. La Sub-estructura de los Estucos (5C-4-I): Un ejemplo de arquitectura temprana en Chichen Itza. In Laporte, Arroyo, and Mejía 2005:836-846.

Peniche May, Nancy, and Geoffrey E. Braswell. 2009. Operación AC: Exploración de la sección este de la Gran Nivelación durante el lapso del 21 de abril al 24 de julio. In Peniche May, Hahn, and Braswell 2009:109-196.

Peniche May, Nancy, Lauren D. Hahn, and Geoffrey E. Braswell. 2009. *Excavaciones de la UCSD en Chichén Itzá: Informe de la temporada de campo 2009 al Proyecto Chichén Itzá*. Unpublished report on file at the Universidad Autónoma de Yucatán, Merida, and at the University of California, San Diego. Online: http://www.anthro.ucsd.edu/files/Informe%20Chichen%20Itza%202009%20UCSD.pdf.

Peréz de Heredia Puente, Eduardo. 1994. Informe de excavaciones en el Sacbé 1. Manuscript, Proyecto Chichén Itzá Instituto Nacional de Antropología e Historia, Merida.

— 2001. La arquitectura y la cerámica del Clásico Tardío en Chichén Itzá. Excavaciones en el Edificio de la Serie Inicial (5C4). Paper presented at the X Encuentro de Investigadores de la Cultura Maya, Universidad Autónoma de Campeche, Campeche.

— 2005. La secuencia ceramica de Chichén Itzá. In *Los investigadores de la cultura maya* 13, pp. 445-466. Universidad Autónoma de Campeche, Campeche.

Peréz Ruiz, Francisco. 2005. Recintos amurallados: una interpretación sobre el sistema defensivo de Chichén Itzá, Yucatán. In Laporte, Arroyo, and Mejía 2005:917-926.

Ringle, William M. 2004. On the Political Organization of Chichen Itza. *Ancient Mesoamerica* 15:167-218.

Ringle, William M., Tomás Gallareta Negrón, and George J. Bey. 1998. The Return of Quetzalcoatl: Evidence for the Spread of a World Religion during the Epiclassic Period. *Ancient Mesoamerica* 9:183-232.

Robles Castellanos, J. Fernando. 2000. Review of *El clásico medio en el noroccidente de Yucatán: La fase Oxkintok Regional en Oxkintok (Yucatán) como paradigma* by Carmen Varela Torrecilla. *Latin American Antiquity* 11:206-207.

Ruppert, Karl. 1943. *The Mercado, Chichen Itza, Yucatan*. Contributions to American Anthropology and History 43. Publication 546. Carnegie Institution of Washington, Washington, D.C.

Ruz Lhuillier, Alberto. 1948. *Puerta Occidental de la Muralla de Chichén-Itzá*. Instituto Nacional de Antropología e Historia S. E. P., Dirección de Monumentos Prehispánicos, Zona Maya, Merida.

Schele, Linda, and Peter Mathews. 1998. *The Code of Kings: The Language of Seven Sacred Maya Temples and Tombs*. Scribner, New York.

Schmidt, Peter J. 2007. Birds, Ceramics, and Cacao: New Excavations at Chichén Itzá. In Kowalski and Kristan-Graham 2007:150-203.

Sharer, Robert J., with Loa P. Traxler. 2006. *The Ancient Maya*. 6th edn. Stanford University, Stanford.

Smith, Robert E. 1971. *The Pottery of Mayapan: Including Studies of Ceramic Material from Uxmal, Kabah, and Chichen Itza*. 2 vols. Papers of the Peabody Museum of Archaeology and Ethnology 66. Harvard University, Cambridge, Mass.

Thompson, J. Eric S. 1937. *A New Method of Deciphering Yucatecan Dates with Special Reference to Chichen Itza*. Contributions to American Archaeology and Ethnology 22. Publication 483. Carnegie Institute of Washington, Washington, D.C.

Tozzer, Alfred M. 1957. *Chichén Itzá and its Cenote of Sacrifice: A Comparative Study of Contemporaneous Maya and Toltec*. 2 vols. Memoirs of the Peabody Museum of Archaeology and Ethnology 11 and 12. Harvard University, Cambridge, Mass.

Varela Torrecilla, Carmen. 1998. *El clásico medio en el noroccidente de Yucatán: La fase Oxkintok Regional en Oxkintok (Yucatán) como paradigma*. BAR International Series 739. British Archaeological Reports, Oxford.

Wagner, Elisabeth. 1995. The Dates of the High Priest Grave ("Osario") Inscription, Chichen Itzá, Yucatán. *Mexicon* 17:10-13.

Wren, Linnea. 1986. The Great Ball Court Stone of Chichén Itzá. Paper presented at the Sixth Palenque Roundtable, Palenque.

Wren, Linnea, Peter Schmidt, and Ruth Krochock. 1989. The Great Ball Court Stone of Chichén Itzá. *Research Reports on Ancient Maya Writing* 25:23-27. Center for Maya Research, Washington, D.C.

10 Divide and Rule

Interpreting Site Perimeter Walls in the Northern Maya Lowlands and Beyond

Lauren D. Hahn and Geoffrey E. Braswell

Abstract

Walls surrounding all or part of a site center have long been recognized as important archaeological features, but often little consideration is given to their function beyond their apparent defensive use. Recent investigations of the site wall at Chichen Itza in the northern lowlands highlight the need for a strong framework within which to interpret wall features, as well as the importance of viewing wall structures as dynamic systems that may have served multiple functions simultaneously or over time. Such a framework will allow researchers to understand site walls as part of larger systems of social control in addition to providing insight into the practice of warfare among the ancient Maya. In the case of Chichen Itza, the wall that surrounds a large part of the ceremonial center appears to have been built originally as a symbolic structure, part of an elite program of separating the ceremonial precinct from its mundane surroundings. In contrast, late additions to the wall indicate the possibility of an increased need for defense in the site center.

In 1976, E. Wyllys Andrews V and Edward Kurjack published one of the earliest reports on walled sites in the Maya area, a discussion of the sites and site walls at Ake, Cuca, and Muna in the northern lowlands (Figure 1.1). In this work, which was based on ground survey and aerial reconnaissance, Andrews and Kurjack recognized the usefulness of site perimeter walls in understanding patterns of political organization, boundary creation, and warfare among the ancient Maya. Nevertheless, 35 years after the publication of this pioneering study, site walls are still underappreciated and poorly understood.

A number of sites throughout the Maya area, and especially in the northern lowlands, contain walls that surround all or part of the site center. These features appear as integral components of the programs of monumental architecture, yet their importance is often overlooked. Walls are often assumed to be defensive structures, an interpretation based solely on their existence, without any consideration of alternative or additional functions. Several scholars have called for a more nuanced or holistic approach to the interpretation of site perimeter walls, but a strong framework for such an approach has yet to be proposed (Rice and Rice 1981; Ringle et al. 2004). In this paper, we discuss this problem of interpretation, as well as the possible implications of investigating wall features as dynamic, multifunctional, and important components of Maya sites. Based upon excavations carried out in 2009 at the northern lowland Maya site of Chichen Itza, this chapter offers an example of the potential utility of walls in understanding processes of warfare and power through social and ideological control.

Interpretation of Site Perimeter Walls

The investigation of site walls may be key to understanding the nature of warfare for the northern lowlands, the Maya area, and perhaps even for archaic states in general. This is because the presence and characteristics of defensive fortifications, which often include walls, indicate the arenas within which conflict occurred as well as the strategies and tactics employed in war (Webster 1993:420-422).

Webster (1993:435-441) has proposed a model of Maya warfare in which Maya elites of the Classic period "devised ideological charters which…defused the terror of war, making it a special and noncompetitive royal display." Such warfare was intended to maintain the balance of power and to legitimize rulership. According to Webster, increasing environmental and political stresses and the inflexibility of this ideological framework led to "warfare [that] was more frequent, more intense, more lethal, and less constrained by political/ideological conventions during the Terminal Classic/Early Postclassic than it had ever been before" (Webster 1993:439). In addition to being practiced in a more destructive manner, warfare during this period may have shifted from peripheral arenas and second-tier sites along frontiers, such as those described by Connell and Silverstein (2006) during the Late Classic, to central places including major political centers. Such pervasive violent conflict may in turn have been an important contributing factor in the restructuring of the Maya world during the Postclassic period, accompanying and contributing to the political decentralization that took place at that time.

Importantly, the presence of defensive fortifications at sites away from frontiers often signifies "a weakness or absence of central authority" (Keegan 1993:145) in archaic societies. Thus, if a model of escalating warfare accompanied by the breakdown of social and political institutions in the Terminal Classic to Early Postclassic periods is accurate, fortifications may have been built at sites that were political central places.

It is tempting to view site perimeter walls as direct indicators of warfare in the archaeological record, and these structures can certainly provide insight into conflict in the ancient Maya world. Nevertheless, simply identifying site walls with warfare both understates the complexity of wall systems and misrepresents the scale and nature of warfare among the Maya. Dahlin (2000:294) correctly states that "perimeter walls are probably not a good indicator of the frequency or severity of warfare" because they may represent only that the "threat of siege tactics" existed. Some sites actually may have perimeter walls that were built without any defensive purpose in mind. Instead of merely equating the presence of site walls with the need for defense, care should be taken in identifying the attributes of such walls that indicate their function (Webster 1993:419).

An inherent quality of any wall is that it creates a physical boundary on the landscape. Walls are useful to the archaeologist, because they are features that "represent emic expressions of the prehistoric functional definition of space" (Webster 1980:835). In some cases, perimeter walls may be intended to form barriers against the outside world, built to protect against threats from without. In other instances, walls may be manifestations of ideological barriers—for instance, the boundary between sacred ritual space and areas of mundane daily activity. In fact, site walls in the Maya area may have performed many functions simultaneously:

> As boundary features, wall or ditch/embankment systems may have functioned to define and protect social space, to delineate sacred space symbolically, to control human traffic and commerce, or to restrict access to elite and/or administrative zones. These functions, of course, are not mutually exclusive. In addition it should be noted that any of these possible uses may [sic] also have had a defensive aspect as well (Rice and Rice 1981:272).

Although the functions of ancient walls may have been multiple and concurrent, most interpretations of walls, and especially those found in the Maya area, consider that they served one of three major functions: defense, water management, or the delineation of social space.

Three Hypotheses for Wall Function

To reiterate, the three major functions proposed for site perimeter walls should not be viewed as mutually exclusive, nor should they be thought of as the only possible purposes that wall structures could have served in the prehistoric world. Instead, they highlight the principal functions of perimeter walls so that the relative importance of secondary or additional functions might be accurately interpreted. Moreover, site walls share basic morphological and functional traits, including the fact that they create physical boundaries or barriers on the landscape. Thus there are no unambiguous wall "types" associated with each of the three functional hypotheses.

Walls Built for Defense

The defensive potential of site walls is the most commonly discussed function of such features found in the northern Maya lowlands. Of the eleven northern lowland sites with walls surrounding all or part of the site center, a defensive interpretation has been posited for ten: Ake, Cuca, Chacchob, Chunchucmil, Dzonot Ake, Ek Balam, Mayapan, Muna, Uxmal, and Yaxuna (Dahlin 2000; Kurjack and Andrews 1976:323; Ringle et al. 2004:507-509; Suhler et al. 2004:471-473; Webster 1978). The existence of large-scale warfare among the ancient Maya has been thoroughly documented through iconographic evidence as well as excavation. There is no question that militarism was both a threat to and an investment undertaken by Maya elites, especially in the Late and Terminal Classic eras. We do not dispute the interpretation of the walls at these ten sites as defensive constructions, but it is necessary to define the features that support this interpretation.

In order to understand the defensive function of site perimeter walls in the Maya area, we follow Dahlin's (2000) distinction between "fortified towns" and "barricaded sites." According to him, walls surrounding fortified towns are more formal in style, and represent greater investments in time and labor than barricades. Northern lowland sites with fortification-type perimeter walls include Cuca and Muna (Kurjack and Andrews 1976), as well as Chacchob and possibly Ek Balam. The walls at these fortified towns are built with formal masonry techniques, which may include vertical, plastered façades, the use of dressed facing stones, and the integration of formal gateways into the original construction (Dahlin 2000:291-292). In many places they are designed to "take strategic advantage of local topographic variations to enhance [their] effective height" (Webster 1978:378), and the walls may incorporate stylistic elements drawn from other major architectural features of the site. Portions of the walls at some fortified towns were built atop previous *sacbe* or road constructions, supporting Kurjack and Andrews' (1976:323) argument that they are derived from earlier boundary markers. Additional defensive features reported in association with walls at fortified towns include concentric rings of fortifications with baffled gateways and the use of narrow "killing alleys" through which invaders would have to pass (Demarest et al. 1997:231; Ringle et al. 2004).

In contrast to the wall systems at fortified towns, barricade walls are low constructions, typically about 1.5 meters high, which were hastily built often using dry-laid masonry techniques and scavenged materials. These barricades represent "last ditch efforts" (Dahlin 2000:294) at defending sites from invading forces. Where they are recovered intact, barricades may signify that the defenders were overrun. This is because barricades would likely have been dismantled if defense was successful (Dahlin 2000:296).

The site walls at Ake and Chunchucmil in the northern lowlands are examples of the barricade type of wall. These walls are ovoid or irregularly rounded in plan, and designed to enclose earlier constructions, in some cases passing within meters of structures or incorporating the structures into the walls (Dahlin 2000; Kurjack and Andrews 1976:322). It is possible that some of these barricades may have been topped with wooden palisades, as Demarest et al. (1997) describe for several sites in the Petexbatun region. Other archaeological indicators of barricades include *ad hoc* reutilization of stones and other materials scavenged from nearby structures, the lack of other associated features such as benches, stairs, or gates, and the lack of concern for aesthetics or permanence (i.e., such walls are often built without the use of stabilizing materials or plaster facing; Dahlin 2000:286-287). Overall, barricade-type walls are distinctly informal in comparison to the highly formal architecture of fortification walls, and are often found with other evidence indicating invasion, battle, and siege. Such evidence may include extensive burning at the time of abandonment, ritual termination of structures, and rapid depopulation due to abandonment or annihilation (Dahlin 2000:294-296). Barricade walls undeniably represent defensive constructions, because their style and locations indicate that they were not part of the construction plan of the centers where they are found. Instead they were rapidly built in response to threats of attack.

Recognizing the distinction between barricade- and fortification-type walls is critical because it allows us to see a difference in function even among walls built for defensive purposes. Although barricade walls represent responses to imminent warfare, fortification walls are more indicative of the potential of attack or the representation of power. Formally built fortification walls must be understood in relation to other monumental constructions, and especially as structures with multiple possible functions.

Walls Built for Water Management

A second possible primary function of site perimeter walls is their use in systems of water management. This possibility is not nearly as commonly invoked as the defensive hypothesis, and it merits discussion here in part because this function has been largely absent from the literature on site walls in the northern lowlands, despite the fact that the region generally lacks available surface water and often suffers from drought. It is possible that water management played a larger part in the planning and construction of site walls than previously recognized.

The control of water by Maya elites has been well documented. Kunen (2006), Lucero (2006), and Scarborough (2006) have identified access to or control over this limited resource as one way that Mesoamerican elites gained, legitimized, and maintained their position. The growth of a mutually dependent relationship between rural farmers and the central authority was formalized and justified by incorporating water ritual and imagery into activities controlled and performed by elites (Kunen 2006:101-115). Many different types of water-management features have been documented throughout the Maya area, but most relevant to this chapter are the large "convex watershed" systems created by sloping plazas, ditches, and reservoirs that came into use during the Classic period (Scarborough 2006:229-230).

The availability of water was a major concern for Maya elites, especially in areas lacking reliable year-round water sources. Thus it is perhaps not surprising that water-management features, including walls and drainage systems, should be integrated into the design strategies of large centers. One important example of this type of feature may be the Great Earthwork at the site of Tikal. Silverstein et al. (2009) reinterpret this ditch and embankment system, and refute its original interpretation as a defensive feature. When originally documented in the 1960s, the Great Earthwork was described as a massive "defensive barrier and hinterland boundary" (Silverstein et al. 2009:45). Nevertheless, the earthwork has many features that are inconsistent with a defensive interpretation, such as a discontinuous perimeter. These factors, combined with a more detailed understanding of karst limestone and soil drainage patterns, have led Silverstein and colleagues to hypothesize that the Tikal earthwork was designed to channel water into reservoirs for storage. In light of this new information, it is necessary to consider the possibility of water-management functions as important aspects of walls at other sites throughout the Maya area, especially where walls are integrated into convex watershed-type architectural complexes—such as large, elevated plazas or platforms—and catchment systems.

Walls Built to Delineate Social Space

The final hypothesis for the major function of site walls involves the delineation of social space. By underlining "social boundaries [and creating] categories of 'insider' and 'outsider,'" walls may represent symbols of authority (Arkush and Stanish 2005:6). Especially where they are integrated into complexes of monumental architecture, walls can be seen as "part of a general construction trend formalizing the relationship between center and periphery" (Ringle et al. 2004:510). Site walls create a formal boundary, which may strengthen the perception of architectural centers as powerful, sacred, or separate from the outside world. As Ringle et al. (2004:510) argue, walls may "have been designed to present the image of a powerful center, a type of construction permitted only the most powerful of regional centers." Additionally, site walls may have performed a psychological function, increasing the impressiveness of already formidable monumental architecture by "obscur[ing] the impressive expanse of the main plaza until passage of the final barrier," often a formal gateway or entry structure (Ringle et al. 2004:510).

It is equally possible that such site walls were intended to be defensible, but at the same time so intimidating that they never had to be manned. That is, psychological and social functions may indeed be auxiliary roles of all defensive walls. As Arkush and Stanish (2005:6) state, "fortification walls send powerful messages: of fierceness, numbers, and impregnability to outsiders and of solidarity and fear and possibly the need for leadership to insiders." In other words, monumental walls may assert the power of elites over prospective enemies as well as their own populations.

Three categories of features identify a site perimeter wall as a structure primarily intended to demarcate sacred or elite space. First, any wall features that imply a defensive function, such as ditches along its outside, extreme size, or the fortification and baffling of entrances, should be absent or should represent a minimal investment in labor, materials, and other resources. Second, walls designed primarily for the purpose of defining social space should be stylistically similar to other structures at the site that are believed to have ritual or social significance. Such walls may be integrated into the stylistic program of the site center through adornment, including plaster facing and the use of iconic imagery that reinforces the sacred or powerful nature of the area within the wall. Finally, consideration should be given to the structures or area that the wall encloses. Although many perimeter walls enclose most or all of a site core, patterns in the use of space may be visible through comparison of the structures within and outside of the walls. For example, walls designed to delineate social space might contain only major temples and palaces. They generally do not create seemingly arbitrary boundaries between structures of similar size and function. Such walls might enclose one or more specific architectural complex within the site core. They should not enclose large numbers of commoner households.

Applying these criteria may help archaeologists move beyond the view of walls as static constructions intended only to defend sites. By recognizing these and other possible functions of perimeter walls, these interesting structures can be seen as part of the larger design strategy of the sites where they appear, allowing researchers to understand better processes of social control and conflict.

Warfare and the Destruction of Chichen Itza

The site of Chichen Itza in the northern Maya lowlands is famous for its massive pyramids, expansive plazas, beautiful artwork, and for its political prominence during the Terminal Classic and Early Postclassic periods (ca. A.D. 800/850–1050/1100). Chichen Itza is also well known for the militaristic focus of its iconographic program, as well as for the role that warfare may have played in its rise to power and its interaction with neighboring polities (Kowalski and Kristan-Graham 2007a). Painted murals in the Upper Temple of the Jaguars (Figure 10.1; Miller 1978) depict battle scenes, as do other murals from Room 22 of Las Monjas (Bolles 1977). Murals in the Temple of the Warriors depict warriors and the taking of captives, although no clear battle scene is shown (Morris et al. 1931; see also Martínez de Luna 2005). Carved and painted scenes of individuals dressed as warriors are found associated with many of the largest structures on the Great Platform of Chichen Itza, and also in other parts of the site. Frequently, such warriors appear on columns (most famously in front of the Temple of the Warriors) or on doorjambs (e.g., at the entrances to the temple atop the Castillo pyramid). Low relief images show processions of warriors (e.g., in the Lower Temple of the Jaguars) or even mythical battles or scenes depicting the training of warriors (i.e., the north and south panels of the Temple of the Wall Panels; Baudez and Latsanopoulos 2010; Wren et al. 2001). Although warfare and warriors are not the only themes presented in the artistic corpus of Chichen Itza, they certainly are the most common.

Most depictions of warfare at the site are thought to show events that took place before the founding of Chichen Itza or during its rise to power. Not surprisingly, there are no images at Chichen Itza that are thought to depict the fall of the great city. Moreover, despite more than a century of extensive archaeological investigation, the particulars of the decline and abandonment of Chichen Itza are not well understood. In fact, the fall of the Itza is known better from ethnohistorical sources than from archaeology.

Figure 10.1. Detail of the reconstructed and repainted mural located southwest of the doorway, Upper Temple of the Jaguars, Chichen Itza (Braswell et al. 2009:Figura 1.4).

Hunac Ceel and the Fall of the Itza

The most important sources concerning the destruction of Chichen Itza are the *Chilam Balam of Mani* (which forms a part of the *Codex Pérez*; Craine and Reindorp 1979), the *Chilam Balam of Chumayel* (Edmonson 1986; Roys 1967), and the *Chilam Balam of Tizimin* (Edmonson 1982). These three texts, which depict the history of later periods from two very different perspectives, appear to agree to a remarkable extent concerning the events leading up to the destruction of the Itza. Unfortunately, the episode is described in only the barest of outlines and in a confusing order. Moreover, the basic chronology of the events—which implies that Uxmal, Chichen Itza, and Mayapan were contemporary sites—is not in accord with archaeological data (see Chapter 8). In all three versions, the destruction of the Itza is described as taking place during K'atun 8 Ajaw, a period of particularly ill portent. But to which K'atun 8 Ajaw do these sources refer? Assuming that this date is relatively accurate and does not merely attempt to fit most major disasters in the history of Yucatan into either K'atun 8 Ajaw or K'atun 13 Ajaw—from our point of view, probably a poor assumption—there are three possibilities. These are the periods that began in A.D. 948, A.D. 1204, and A.D. 1461. From an archaeological perspective, the first is too early for both the destruction of Chichen Itza and the rise of Mayapan as an important capital. Many scholars have favored the second date, which certainly makes sense for a period when Mayapan was an important city. But this date now appears, admittedly on the grounds of negative evidence (see Schmidt 2007), to be a century or more too late for the end of Chichen Itza and perhaps 250 years after the collapse of Uxmal. Finally, the third date is far too late for the decline of Chichen Itza, but instead seems reasonable for the collapse of Mayapan. This last possibility is important, however, because Edmonson (1982) argues that what is described in the *Chilam Balam of Tizimin* is not, in fact, the destruction of Chichen Itza. Instead, for him, the text describes the expulsion of the Itza nobility from Mayapan as a prelude to the destruction of the Late Postclassic city. The *Chilam Balam of Mani* seems to support this final interpretation by placing the life of Hunac Ceel,[1] a central player in this drama, close to the time of the Spanish conquest (Craine and Reindorp 1979:127).

The actions that the three documents discuss focus on the betrayal by *u keban than* ("the sinful words" [Edmonson 1982:8] or "the treachery or plot" [Roys 1967:137, 177]) of Hunac Ceel, the lord of Mayapan. It is not clear in any of the sources what that treachery was. One reconstruction begins with an event in the *Chilam Balam of Mani*. An unnamed individual is said to have *tumenel zipci Ah Ulil ti chuplal yatan yet-ahaulil* ("sinned against Ah Ulil, the ruler [of Izamal], against the wife of his fellow-ruler"; Roys 1967:179). Roys (1967:177, 179) interprets this as the kidnapping of the bride of the king of Izamal by Chac Xib Chac, lord of the Itza. Craine and Reindorp (1979:122) translate (from a free Spanish translation by Solís Alcalá [1949]) a phrase as "war was declared and took place in the sixteenth year of the katún [8 Ajaw] by mandate of the sacred Itzam Caan," but Roys (1967:178) views this as taking place in the tenth year of the *k'atun*.

How the fall of the Itza lords is brought about is described in more than one source. Hunac Ceel, the lord of Mayapan, plotted with the lord of Izamal and seven other individuals against the Itza at a banquet. The names of these seven individuals are of particular interest. Both the *Chilam Balam of Tizimin* and the *Chilam Balam of Mani* (in order) name them as Ah Sinteyut Chan/Ah Zinteyut Chan (Cinteotl Chan), Tzum Tecum/Tzuntecum (Tzontecome), Taxcal (Tlaxcalli/Tlaxcallan), Pantemit (Pantemitl), Xuch Ueut/Xuchueuet (Xochihuehuetl), Ytzcoat/Itzcuat (Itzcoatl), and Kakalcat/Kakaltecat (Cacalacatl/Cacaltecatl; Craine and Reindorp 1979:139; Edmonson 1982:9). These names are all derived from Nahuatl, and perhaps refer to central Mexican mercenaries brought to Mayapan (see Chapter 12). They could be among the Ah Canul referred to in the *Chilam Balam of Mani* and elsewhere, even though both halves of that double lineage name are Mayan and well-known at Chichen Itza, Izamal, and elsewhere. The *Chilam Balam of Chumayel* (Roys 1967:137) describes the final event of the banquet as the giving of the "questionnaire." This is assumed to be the "interrogation of the chiefs" or riddles in the language of Zuyua given to nobles (Roys 1967:25-31, 88-98). The *Chilam Balam of Tizimin* seems to imply that the Itza "were destroyed by Hunac Ceel because of the giving away of their knowledge" (Edmonson 1982:9), which could be a reference as well to a failure in answering the riddles.

The short "Second Chronicle" of the *Chilam Balam Chumayel* briefly discusses what happens to the Itza after these events. In this section, it is said that the treachery of Hunac Ceel came after 13 *k'atuns* of rule (i.e., 256 solar years and 98 days). *Ca paxi u cabob ca biniob tan yol che Tan-xuluc-mul u kaba* ("Their town was abandoned and they went into the heart of the forest to Tan-xuluc-mul, as it is called" [Roys 1967:50, 140]). Tan-xuluc-mul may be a lake near Lake Peten Itza, so perhaps this is a reference to a movement of some of the Itza to Tayasal after the incident involving Hunac Ceel (Means 1917:128, cited in Roys 1967:140).

Despite the rather close agreement of the three books of *Chilam Balam*—Mani, Chumayel, and Tizimin—the events surrounding the actions of Hunac Ceel are not as clear as we could wish. First, the precise reasons why a lord of Mayapan would take it on himself to exact revenge for a slight against the lord of Izamal are unknown. Second, the nature of his trickery or treachery is unclear. Third, and quite problematic from an archaeological perspective, is the fact that the central events seem to take place at Mayapan, that is, at a time after the decline of Chichen Itza. Fourth, it is not entirely clear where the lords of the Itza were living when they were cast out of the League of Mayapan—were they still based in Chichen Itza, or did they live in Mayapan itself? Fifth, although most interpretations argue that the Hunac Ceel events precede the destruction and abandonment of Chichen Itza in K'atun 8 Ajaw, Edmonson (1982) argues that the events take place later in time and are related to the destruction of Mayapan in a later K'atun 8 Ajaw. Thus it seems most likely that the books of *Chilam Balam* are both conflating and expanding different events and individuals in order to make them fit into different epochs. Sixth, although many interpretations seem to imply or assume that the Itza were driven out of Chichen Itza during a military action—perhaps overseen by individuals with Nahuatl-derived names who served as mercenaries—unambiguous references to a battle are few. The clearest mentions of the physical destruction of Chichen Itza are found in a song in the *Chilam Balam of Chumayel* (Roys 1967:38, 114-116), which cites twice that "the town is lost" and asks "who burned it?" (Knowlton 2010:256).

Excavations of the Wall at Chichen Itza in 2009

Although there is ample iconographic evidence of Itza warfare and ethnohistorical accounts that describe the fall of the Itza, actual occurrences of conflict at the site itself are not unambiguously documented in either of these sources of data or by archaeological investigation. One clear place to look for such evidence is the wall that surrounds the Great Platform.[2] It is reasonable to ask if the wall was built or later modified for defensive purposes. The vague and difficult to interpret descriptions of the fall of the Itza that are found in the books of *Chilam Balam* do not allow us to answer this question. Moreover, the wall is also an important and integral part of the monumental core of the site, so could have served purposes other than defense. For all these reasons, the wall at Chichen Itza provides an important opportunity to test the interpretive framework described in this chapter.

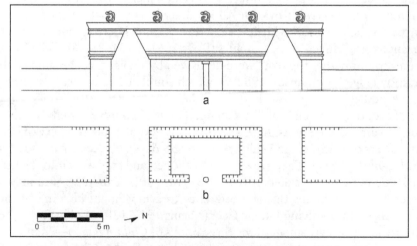

Figure 10.2. Hypothetical reconstruction of Str. 2C12, Chichen Itza:
(a) profile, (b) plan (after Ruz Lhuillier 1948).

During our spring 2009 field season, the authors directed excavations along a 94-meter stretch of the wall surrounding the great platform, on which a large portion of the site center is built (Figure 9.2). Other project members from the University of California, San Diego who helped excavate the wall include Megan Pitcavage and Kiri Hagerman. Because of time constraints, we were unable to expose a wide area outside (west of) the wall or to oversee its final consolidation. These important tasks were accomplished by students from the Universidad Autónoma de Yucatán working under the supervision of Rafael Cobos Palma, Director of the project *Chichén Itzá: Estudio de la comunidad del Clásico Tardío*.

The portion of the wall excavated during the 2009 field season lies between the southern end of the Great Ballcourt and the southwestern corner of the Great Platform. The latter is now beneath the modern causeway built as the principal tourist entrance to the archaeological zone. This stretch of the wall is broken approximately 40 meters south of the Great Ballcourt by an access road that leads into the site (the old Merida–Valladolid highway), which is flanked on both sides by short portions of the wall that were recently consolidated by members of the *Proyecto Chichén Itzá*, directed by Peter Schmidt. The road itself passes through a section of the wall where a structure and entrance to the Great Platform once stood (Figure 10.2). These were excavated by Ruz Lhuillier (1948) before construction of the road destroyed these features.

Figure 10.3. Northern excavated section of the wall during preparation for consolidation, looking northwards towards the Great Ballcourt. The sloping edge of the Great Platform (Feature AB1) is the lower visible feature, the upper one is the buttress wall (Feature AB5).

The primary goals of our excavations, called Operation AB, were to: (1) describe the architectural features of the wall; (2) establish the construction sequence of the Great Platform in this area; and (3) determine why the wall was built and what its functions were. This section of the wall was also chosen for excavation in order to catalogue and preserve its remaining intact architectural features before they became even more damaged as a result of heavy foot traffic.

The major construction features of the wall were all built in the core-veneer style typical of monumental construction at Chichen Itza, with rectangular, cut facing stones mounted into a core of unworked cobble-stone fill. Essentially, the wall consists of a thin, double-faced construction that is buttressed on its western side by a thick addition. These are built directly atop the Great Platform, the edge of which is defined by a sloped *talud* that runs along a significant portion of the excavated length of the wall (Figure 10.3, lower masonry feature).

In describing and interpreting the construction of this portion of the wall, one major fact is clear: the wall was built in two stages. The first stage included the construction of the thin eastern wall, Feature AB2/AB15, which we refer to as the "wall proper" (Figure 10.4). This was built on top of the already existing Great Platform. Most of the edge of the Great Platform is marked by a sloping wall, Feature AB1/AB12. We refer to this as the "*talud* wall."

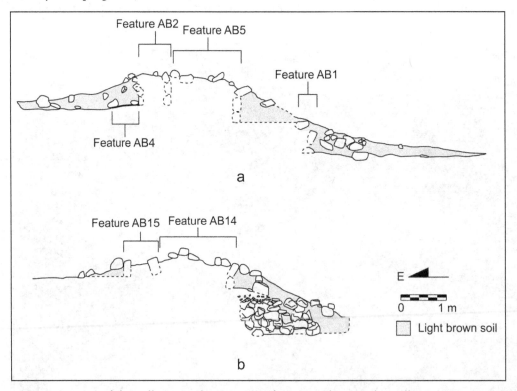

Figure 10.4. Sections of the wall: (a) northern excavated portion, showing the wall proper (Feature AB2), buttress wall (Feature AB5), the remains of the sloping edge of the Great Platform (Feature AB1), and remains of the plaster floor that probably correspond with Great Platform Stage VIII (Feature AB4); (b) southern excavated portion, showing the wall proper (Feature AB15) and the buttress wall (Feature AB14). In this area the sloping edge of the platform was encountered only as fill stones.

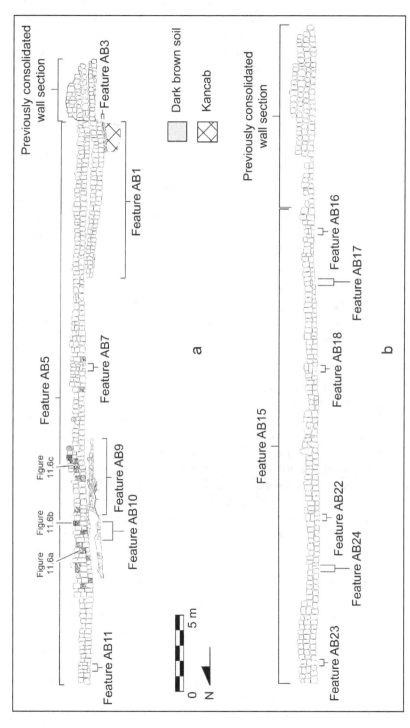

Figure 10.5. Profiles of the wall: (a) northern excavated portion, western (exterior) face showing location of architectural sculpture incorporated randomly into the buttress wall (Feature AB5), drains (Features AB7 and AB11), and sloping edge of the Great Platform (Features AB1, AB9, and AB10); (b) southern excavated portion, eastern (interior) face showing the wall proper (Feature AB15) and six drains (Features AB16-18, 22-24). Drains are much more numerous near the southwestern corner of the Great Platform than in the northern excavated section, suggesting that water was diverted in this direction. Three pieces of sculpture in the buttress wall are labeled Figure 11.6a-c. Larger images of these pieces appear in Figure 11.6.

The plaster facing and floors found in numerous areas show that the wall proper and edge of the Great Platform were, although not built at the same time, in simultaneous use. This is because plaster on the wall proper lips down onto and seamlessly blends with the final surface of the Great Platform. At some time after the construction of the wall proper, a thicker western wall, Feature AB5/AB14, was added. We refer to this as the "buttress wall." It is built on top of the Great Platform but outside of the wall proper. Just south of the Great Ballcourt, the buttress wall was built on top of three layers of plaster floors, implying that it was a later addition built against the wall proper. That the buttress wall has no western face, but instead consists of fill laid directly against the wall proper, supports this conclusion.

With the exception of the *talud*, which is missing in places where the ground level rises naturally and next to a *sascabera*, these major features are present along the entire excavated portion of the wall, and analogues to them are visible on the surface in unexcavated portions of the north and south edges of the Great Platform. On the basis of clear differences in construction style, we discuss these two feature sets as representative of two phases in the history of the construction of the wall. These correspond to Stages IX and X of the entire construction sequence of the Great Platform (Chapter 9).

Initial Function of the Wall Proper

In the first stage of construction, the wall was built on top of the Great Platform. It was set back from the *talud* wall that defines the edge of the platform. At this time, the wall proper does not seem to have functioned primarily as a defensive construction.

Perhaps the most important trait indicating that the Stage IX wall was not originally planned as a defensive structure is its thickness. Defensive barriers at sites such as Dzonot Ake, Cuca, Ake, and Chacchob are typically between two and five meters thick (Dahlin 2000:289-292). Thick walls can be stood on by defenders, a strategic advantage against attacking forces. In contrast, the Stage IX wall proper is just 55-60 centimeters thick, which would prohibit the ability of defenders to move around freely on top of it. Additionally, because the wall is so thin it is unstable. It could have been broached easily by attacking forces. Moreover, features associated with walls built to guard against potential attackers are mostly absent from the wall proper of the Great Platform. Several structures associated with entrances have benches, but these do not provide defensible positions along a significant portion of the wall. No fully baffled gateways or "killing alleys" are present, but partially baffled entrances exist elsewhere on the wall (Pérez Ruiz 2005). It is important to note that these baffles were not part of the original construction of the wall, but are later additions.

It is unlikely that the entire Great Platform and wall proper functioned as a water-collecting system. On the contrary, the design of both indicates that the removal of water from the western portion of the Great Platform was a concern. We excavated nine drains in the wall that are integral to the Stage IX construction (Figure 10.5). These served to prevent the accumulation of water on the Great Platform and behind the wall. Channels or underground diversion systems, such as those reported by Gonzáles de la Mata et al. (2005) elsewhere at Chichen Itza, would have been more effective in dealing with water control.

Because of the poor state of preservation of the plaster surface of the Great Platform, the precise slope of the final surface—in fact, the only platform floor near our excavations of the wall—is unknown (see Chapter 9 for a discussion of earlier floors excavated east of the Castillo). It is certain, however, that the surface was intentionally sloped towards its edges in order to prevent flooding and to channel rainwater off the Great Platform. It seems likely that during Stage IX, a great deal of the water on the western side of the Great Platform was diverted towards its southwestern corner. Drains in the southern half of our excavations, that is, near the corner, are placed closer together than in the northern half (Figure 10.5b). This suggests that the now destroyed final surface of the southwestern portion of the Great Platform sloped in this direction.

The height of the wall proper (which we estimate to have been between 1.5 and 2.0 meters) is far greater than what would have been needed to divert rainwater to specific drains. Most importantly, we did not identify any water catchment features either on top of the Great Platform or off of it, below the drains. The lack of reservoirs, *chultuns*, and other water-storage devices indicates that directing water to such collection features was not a function of this portion of the wall. Thus, the wall must have been built for a reason other than the diversion of water, and the drains were a solution to a water-management problem caused by the construction of the wall.

Because defensive potential and water management were not likely the primary purpose for the initial construction of the wall proper during Stage IX, it is probable that the wall was built principally to aid in defining the monumental core of Chichen Itza as sacred or elite space. The wall proper would have served as a boundary between the center of the site and the outside world. This symbolic barrier enhanced the formal and awe-inspiring effect of the monumental architecture enclosed within it. We argue that the wall proper of Stage IX, although undecorated, served a purpose not unlike that of the *coatepantli*-like wall north of Pyramid B at Tula.

The Stage IX wall proper was built in the core-veneer masonry style typical of other constructions on the Great Platform. It also was covered with plaster. Together, these suggest that the wall proper was an integrated part of the design of the Great Platform. The formal construction of the wall proper enhanced its impressiveness, which in turn increased the grandeur and powerful appearance of the site center.

The structures built on the Great Platform and enclosed by the wall were monumental constructions with ritual or cosmological significance. No residential structures have been found within the wall, and almost all of the structures on the Great Platform are decorated with images that reinforce concepts of elite political legitimacy. The wall forms a boundary between this sacred space and the world outside.

The wall proper articulated with Structure 2C12, the double archway described by Ruz Lhuillier (1948). This gateway was undoubtedly a symbolic structure (Figure 10.2), because of its size and decoration (Ruz Lhuillier 1948:3-4). Together with the wall itself, Structure 2C12 served both a symbolic and a practical function. It allowed the inhabitants of Chichen Itza to observe and authorize all movement into or out of the site center in this area.

Later Function of the Wall Proper and Buttress Wall

Although it is unlikely that the wall proper was originally intended as a defensive structure, later additions added during Stage X would have enhanced the defensive potential of the wall. The addition of the buttress wall outside (west) of the wall proper tripled its total thickness. It is likely that the increased thickness during Stage X reflects an anticipated need for a wall that could better withstand an attack. Because we excavated no place where both the wall proper and buttress were preserved to their full height, it is unclear if the addition of the buttress wall would have allowed the wall proper to function as a parapet. Nonetheless, the increased stability supplied by the buttress wall would certainly have been an advantage to defenders.

The most striking aspect of the outer addition is its seemingly hasty construction. Although it is built in core-veneer style, in contrast to hastily built rubble or stacked-stone barricades described at other sites, the workmanship of this feature is of notably poorer quality than the Stage IX wall proper. The Stage X addition incorporates many stones scavenged from other structures. Among these are 64 sculptured pieces (Figure 10.6) and four *metates*. It is obvious from their random locations and orientations within the buttress wall that the symbolic content of the sculpture was not important to the builders of this feature. This *ad hoc* use of material from nearby structures recalls Dahlin's (2000) description of the Chunchucmil barricade. Although traces of original paint were observed adhering to several of the sculpted stones, the surface of the buttress wall itself was not plastered. This represents a departure from previous building conventions, and implies that the function of the Stage X buttress, rather than its appearance, was of paramount importance.

Figure 10.6. Pieces of architectural sculpture incorporated into the buttress wall Feature AB5: (a) MN25, (b) MN16, (c) MN49, and (d) MS64, recovered from excavations in the southern excavated section of the wall. The sculptural blocks are oriented as found in the wall, and the locations of (a)-(c) are shown in Figure 11.5.

We argue that the Stage X addition to the wall was a response to conflict. Several of the features of the buttress wall—most notably its hasty construction, the reuse of scavenged materials, and a lack of concern with aesthetics—suggest that it was a barricade hurriedly constructed in response to the threat of attack. This feature might be contemporary with other additions that close off or limit access to the Great Platform, including a crude wall that narrows the entranceway at the southern end of Sacbe 1 and the C-shaped parapets limiting access from Sacbes 2 and 74 (Pérez Ruiz 2005:887-890). It therefore seems probable that defense became a major concern during the later days of occupation of the site.

Conclusions

Our 2009 excavations of a 94-meter section of the western wall of the Great Platform at Chichen Itza suggest that it is unlikely that the wall was originally intended primarily as either a water-management feature or as a defensive fortification. Instead, it most likely served as a symbolic construction. Nevertheless, it seems likely that changes in regional politics—perhaps including events described in the books of *Chilam Balam*—and the practice of warfare, made defense of the site a concern towards the end of its occupation.

The Chichen Itza wall is unique in the northern Maya lowlands in that its two construction phases reflect two very different primary concerns. In its earlier form, the Great Platform wall most closely resembles the wall at Uxmal. That wall encloses and defines the ceremonial center of Uxmal, but has numerous gaps and wide entranceways. For this reason, it most likely was not constructed as a defensive fortification (Dahlin 2000:293). The Stage X buttress-wall addition at Chichen Itza, however, has numerous elements in common with hastily built fortifications of the barricade type, and in this way most closely resembles the acropolis fortification of nearby Yaxuna. There, an *ad hoc* wall was speedily constructed around part of the center of the site in a "last-ditch effort" at defense (Freidel 2007; Suhler et al. 2004). Nevertheless, no major burning events or ritual terminations that scar significant portions of the landscape have been discovered at Chichen Itza, and the exact process of abandonment is not clearly observable in the archaeological record. Further investigation into the factors that contributed to the decline of Chichen Itza is needed.

The three functional hypotheses outlined in this chapter provide a solid basis for investigating wall systems. As a major category of site walls, defensive fortifications may have played an active part in redefining the conduct of warfare in the Maya area. Allen and Arkush (2006:7) note that "fortification may have had the potential to alter regional political landscapes dramatically" in archaic societies. More generally, the role of defensive and non-defensive walls is an avenue of significant promise for archaeologists wishing to investigate political interaction, particularly during times of duress and social change. It is important to stress that the Chichen Itza wall—or any other wall system—need not serve a single function. On the contrary, modifications to wall systems, which reflect changes in present or anticipated needs and concerns, imply changes in function over time. It is clear that wall systems, as components of warfare, ideology, and political interaction, reflect major social transformations.

Acknowledgments

The authors of this chapter recapitulate the thanks expressed in Chapter 9 to each and every member of the team from the Universidad Autónoma de Yucatán, and also gratefully acknowledge support from the same sources. We also especially thank Megan R. Pitcavage and Kiri L. Hagerman for their assistance during excavations in the field, and Timothy Knowlton for sharing his knowledge of the books of *Chilam Balam*.

Notes

1. Our assumption in this section is that all references to Hunac Ceel are to the same individual. If this was a hereditary title or there were more than one individual with this name, interpreting the chronologies of the books of *Chilam Balam* becomes even more difficult.

2. Many—if not most—of the largest architectural groups at Chichen Itza are surrounded by walls, with formal entrances built at *sacbe* termini. In this sense, the wall surrounding the Great Platform is not a unique construction at the site.

References

Allen, Mark W., and Elizabeth N. Arkush. 2006. Introduction: Archaeology and the Study of War. In Arkush and Allen 2006:1-19.

Arkush, Elizabeth N., and Mark W. Allen (editors). 2006. *The Archaeology of Warfare: Prehistories of Raiding and Conquest*. University Press of Florida, Gainsville.

Arkush, Elizabeth N., and Charles Stanish. 2005. Interpreting Conflict in the Ancient Andes: Implications for the Archaeology of Warfare. *Current Anthropology* 46:3-28.

Baudez, Claude-François, and Nicolas Latsanopoulos. 2010. Political Structure, Military Training, and Ideology at Chichen Itza. *Ancient Mesoamerica* 21:1-20.

Bolles, John S. 1977. *Las Monjas, A Major Pre-Mexican Architectural Complex at Chichen Itza*. University of Oklahoma, Norman.

Connell, Samuel V., and Jay E. Silverstein. 2006. From Laos to Mesoamerica: Battlegrounds between Superpowers. In Arkush and Allen 2006:394-433.

Craine, Eugene R., and Reginald C. Reindorp. 1979. *The Codex Pérez and the Book of Chilam Balam of Maní*. University of Oklahoma, Norman.

Dahlin, Bruce H. 2000. The Barricade and Abandonment of Chunchucmil: Implications for Northern Maya Warfare. *Latin American Antiquity* 11:283-298.

Demarest, Arthur A., Matt O'Mansky, Claudia Wolley, Dirk Van Tuerenhout, Takeshi Inomata, Joel Palka, and Héctor Escobedo. 1997. Classic Maya Defensive Systems and Warfare in the Petexbatun Region. *Ancient Mesoamerica* 8:229-253.

Demarest, Arthur A., Prudence M. Rice, and Don S. Rice (editors). 2004. *The Terminal Classic in the Maya Lowlands: Collapse, Transition, and Transformation*. University Press of Colorado, Boulder.

Edmonson, Munro S. 1982. *The Ancient Future of the Itza: The Book of Chilam Balam of Tizimin*. University of Texas, Austin.

— 1986. *Heaven Born Merida and Its Destiny: The Book of Chilam Balam of Chumayel*. University of Texas, Austin.

Freidel, David. 2007. War and Statecraft in the Northern Maya Lowlands: Yaxuná and Chichén Itzá. In *Twin Tollans: Chichén Itzá, Tula, and the Epiclassic to Early Postclassic Mesoamerican World*, edited by Jeff Karl Kowalski & Cynthia Kristan-Graham, pp. 345-375. Dumbarton Oaks, Washington, D.C.

González de la Mata, Rocio, José F. Osorio, and Peter J. Schmidt. 2005. The Divine Flow: Water Management at Chichén Itzá. In LaPorte, Arroyo, and Mejía 2005:847-855.

Keegan, John. 1993. *A History of Warfare*. Alfred A. Knopf, New York.

Knowlton, Timothy. 2010. Nahua Vocables in a Maya Song of the Fall of Chichén Itzá: Music and Social Memory in the Construction of Yucatecan Ethnicities. In *Astronomers, Scribes, and Priests: Intellectual Exchange between the Northern Maya Lowlands and Highland Mexico in the Late Postclassic Period*, edited by Gabrielle Vail and Christine Hernández, pp. 241-259. Dumbarton Oaks, Washington, D.C.

Kowalski, Jeff Karl, and Cynthia Kristan-Graham. 2007a. Chichén Itzá, Tula, and Tollan: Changing Perspectives on a Recurring Problem in Mesoamerican Archaeology and Art History. In Kowalski and Kristan-Graham 2007b:13-83.

— (editors). 2007b. *Twin Tollans: Chichén Itzá, Tula, and the Epiclassic to Early Postclassic Mesoamerican World*. Dumbarton Oaks, Washington, D.C.

Kunen, Julie L. 2006. Water Management, Ritual, and Community in Tropical Complex Societies. In Lucero and Fash 2006:100-115.

Kurjack, Edward B., and E. Wyllys Andrews, V. 1976. Early Boundary Maintenance in Northwest Yucatán, Mexico. *American Antiquity* 41:318-325.

Laporte, Juan Pedro, Bárbara Arroyo, and Héctor E. Mejía. (editors). 2005. *XVIII Simposio de Investigaciones Arqueológicas en Guatemala, 2004*. Museo Nacional de Arqueología e Historia, Guatemala.

Lucero, Lisa J. 2006. The Political and Sacred Power of Water in Classic Maya Society. In Lucero and Fash 2006:116-128.

Lucero, Lisa J., and Barbara Fash (editors). 2006. *Precolumbian Water Management: Ideology, Ritual, and Power*. University of Arizona, Tucson.

Martínez de Luna, Lucha Aztzin. 2005. *Murals and the Development of Merchant Activity at Chichen Itza*. Unpublished M.A. thesis, Department of Anthropology, Brigham Young University. Provo.

Means, Philip A. 1917. *History of the Spanish Conquest of Yucatan and of the Itzas*. Papers of the Peabody Museum 7. Harvard University, Cambridge, Mass.

Miller, Arthur G. 1977. Captains of the Itza: Unpublished Mural Evidence from Chichén Itzá. In *Social Process in Maya Prehistory: Studies in Honor of Sir Eric Thompson*, edited by Norman Hammond, pp. 197-225. Academic Press, New York.

— 1978. Capitanes del Itza: Evidencia mural inedita de Chichén Itzá. *Estudios de Cultura Maya* 11:121-154.

Morris, Early H. Jean Charlot, and Ann Axtell Morris. 1931. *The Temple of the Warriors at Chichen Itza, Yucatan*. 2 vols. Carnegie Institute of Washington, Washington, D.C.

Pérez Ruiz, Francisco. 2005. Recintos Amurallados: Una Interpretación Sobre el Sistema Defensivo de Chichen Itza, Yucatán. In LaPorte, Arroyo, and Mejía 2005:881-890.

Rice, Don S., and Prudence M. Rice. 1981. Muralla de Leon: A Lowland Maya Fortification. *Journal of Field Archaeology* 8:271-288.

Ringle, William M., George J. Bey III, Tara Bond Freeman, Craig A. Hanson, Charles W. Houck, and J. Gregory Smith. 2004. The Decline of the East: The Classic to Postclassic Transition at Ek Balam, Yucatán. In Demarest, Rice, and Rice 2004:485-516.

Roys, Ralph L. 1967. *The Book of Chilam Balam of Chumayel*. University of Oklahoma, Norman.

Ruz Lhuillier, Alberto. 1948. *Puerta Occidental de la Muralla de Chichen-Itza*. Report to the Instituto Nacional de Antropologia e Historia, Dirección de Monumentos Prehispanicos, Zona Maya, Mérida.

Scarborough, Vernon. 2006. An Overview of Mesoamerican Water Systems. In Lucero and Fash 2006:22 3-235.

Schmidt, Peter J. 2007. Birds, Ceramics, and Cacao: New Excavations at Chichén Itzá. In Kowalski and Kristan-Graham 2007b:150-203.

Silverstein, Jay E., David Webster, Horacio Martinez, and Alvaro Soto. 2009. Rethinking the Great Earthwork of Tikal: A Hydraulic Hypothesis for the Classic Maya Polity. *Ancient Mesoamerica* 20:45-58.

Solís Alcalá, Ermilo. 1949. *Códice Pérez. Traducción libre del maya al castellano por el Dr. E Solís Alcalá*. Imprenta Oriente, Merida, Mexico.

Suhler, Charles, Traci Ardren, David Freidel, and David Johnstone. 2004. The Rise and Fall of Terminal Classic Yaxuna, Yucatán, Mexico. In Demarest, Rice, and Rice 2004:450-484.

Webster, David. 1978. Three Walled Sites of the Northern Maya Lowlands. *Journal of Field Archaeology* 5:375-390.

— 1980. Spatial Bounding and Settlement History at Three Walled Northern Maya Centers. *American Antiquity* 45:834-844.

— 1993. The Study of Maya Warfare: What it Tells Us about the Maya and What it Tells Us about Maya Archaeology. In *Lowland Maya Civilization in the Eighth Century A.D.*, edited by Jeremy A. Sabloff and John S. Henderson, pp. 415-444. Dumbarton Oaks, Washington, D.C.

Wren, Linnea, Kaylee Spencer, and Krysta Hochstetler. 2001. Political Rhetoric and the Unification of Natural Geography, Cosmic Space and Gender Spheres. In *Landscape and Power in Ancient Mesoamerica*, edited by Rex Koontz, Kathryn Reese-Taylor, and Annabeth Headrick, pp. 257-277. Westview, Boulder.

Part IV

THE LATE POSTCLASSIC TO HISTORICAL PERIODS

11 Rain and Fertility Rituals in Postclassic Yucatan Featuring Chaak and Chak Chel

Gabrielle Vail and Christine Hernández

Abstract

Data from Maya codices and murals provide important information for interpreting artifacts excavated from cave and *cenote* contexts throughout the Maya area. The assemblage of artifacts recovered from the chambers of Balankanche Cave in Yucatan, believed to date to the same time period as nearby Chichen Itza, includes ceramic vessels in a variety of forms (including a number with modeled effigies of the Mexican rain god Tlaloc), miniature manos and metates, spindle whorls, and a variety of other objects that had both utilitarian and ritual functions. An analysis of this material indicates that these artifacts may be linked specifically to two Yucatecan deities known for their associations with creation, fertility, and rain and water—the male rain god Chaak and the female creator deity Chak Chel. This chapter examines scenes from the Maya codices and Postclassic mural art to propose a scenario by which the Balankanche assemblage might have been created.

The study of codices, mural art, and archaeological assemblages that we report on in this chapter is an outgrowth of our ongoing research of Precolumbian Maya codices that E. Wyllys Andrews V supported and encouraged over a period of many years as a mentor to both of us in his role as director of the Middle American Research Institute at Tulane University. Studies of the Maya codices indicate that they were complex documents created by an intellectual elite class of scribes in northern Yucatan who were fluent not only in their own regional script, iconography, mythology, and astronomy, but also in that of the wider Maya world and of contemporary cultures living in the central highlands and Gulf Coast regions of Mesoamerica (Vail and Aveni 2004, Part III; Vail and Hernández 2010). Our work builds on earlier understandings of these complex interrelationships to which many scholars, including Will, have contributed (Andrews 1979).

The extant Maya screenfolds—the Dresden, Madrid, and Paris codices—date to the century or so preceding Spanish contact, although they contain material originally composed during several different time periods.[1] They consist of compilations of calendrical and hieroglyphic instruments called almanacs that include copies of earlier (Classic period) devices, revised and updated versions of almanacs from this earlier time period, and still others relevant to the

Postclassic milieu during which the codices were painted and intended to be used. In this chapter and in Will's honor, we turn our newly found understanding of codical dating, themes, and iconography to the material record of northern Yucatan, specifically that of Balankanche Cave. Our goal is to reconsider previous interpretations of artifact assemblages consisting primarily of ceramic and stone vessels believed to be the result of rainmaking rituals.

Balankanche Cave

The cavern of Balankanche lies approximately four kilometers west of Chichen Itza in an area characterized by several Terminal Classic to Early Postclassic platforms (A.D. 800–1050/1100, also called the "Florescent period"). Long known to local inhabitants, as well as to biologists and explorers, the cave was not believed to contain significant archaeological remains until explorations in 1959 by José Humberto Gómez revealed the presence of a masonry wall that blocked access to an extensive area of the cavern. Scientific excavations directed by E. Wyllys Andrews IV and conducted by William Folan, George Stuart, Victoria Segovia, and others revealed six groupings of artifactual remains within the chambers sealed by the wall (Andrews 1970:5-7).

Work within the cave environment was hampered by several factors. At the time the sealed chambers were first accessed, the passageways were extremely dangerous and navigable only with difficulty. Moreover, the hazardous conditions were exacerbated by complete darkness, lack of ventilation, and humidity. It seems clear that such conditions would have been an issue for the ancient Maya who utilized the cavern as well (Andrews 1970:6).

Andrews and the Mexican archaeologists in charge of the project determined that, rather than excavating and removing all of the artifacts, they would leave a number of them *in situ* and create a museum within the cavern. With this in mind, they devoted a considerable effort to enlarging the passageways and improving conditions within the cave. Archaeological work included: (1) mapping the caverns; (2) making detailed drawings of each of the individual groups of offerings, totaling more than 500 artifacts; (3) numbering and cataloging the material as it was exposed; and (4) photographing the large effigy censers and other artifacts left *in situ*. Smaller items were taken to the lab, where they were photographed, drawn, and catalogued.

The unsealed portion of the cave was used primarily as a source of potable water from the Preclassic period until shortly before the Spanish conquest. Andrews (1970:7) notes that at least four of the passages in that part of the cavern lead to underground pools of water. Artifacts recovered from these passages include a wide range of pottery types (although not predominantly water jars), indicating a long period of use. Other categories of artifacts were recovered from contexts deeper within the cave. These include spindle whorls and beads, which Andrews believed to be dedicatory offerings, and large potsherds apparently used to excavate clay and mineral beds to provide materials for making pottery.

A total of three walls were found within the cave, all constructed during the prehispanic period. The first is at the entrance and consists of a circular stonewall that is two meters thick, roughly two meters high, and approximately 35 meters in diameter. It was not excavated, so its age remains unknown. The second wall, 30 meters into the cave along the principal passage, was fashioned of crude stone laid in thick mud, presumably from the cave floor (Andrews 1970:7-8). Most of the 86 potsherds recovered from excavating the wall are described as "Formative monochromes," with a small sample (18 potsherds) from incised dichrome jars that Brainerd dated to the Formative to Early period transition. In terms used today, this indicates a date spanning the Late Preclassic to Early Classic period for this feature. The presence of the wall "establishes that, for at least the second half of this long span, from approximately 0 A.D., the cave was used for more than merely a source of water" (Andrews 1970:8).

It is to this possible ceremonial function of the cave that we next turn. For reasons that remain unclear, the areas where the artifacts were deposited were sealed off by the prehispanic users. Calibrated radiocarbon dates from deposits within the sealed portion of the cave suggest a date range of A.D. 968 to 1009 (Andrews et al. 2003:152), indicating that its period of most intense use corresponded with that of nearby Chichen Itza.

Table 11.1. Number of artifacts recovered from offering assemblages in Groups I-VI at Balankanche Cave grouped according to artifact type.

Artifact Category	Count
Effigy censers w/modeled features of Mexican Tlaloc	36
Other Tlaloc representations	5
Studded biconical censers	34
Carved stone censers	20
Miniature plates and jars	33
Spindle whorls	25
Miniature manos and metates	252
Miscellaneous offerings	88

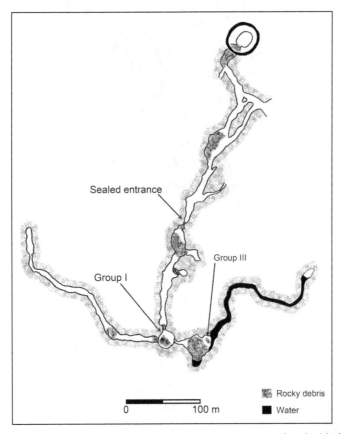

Figure 11.1. A plan of the Balankanche Cave complex with Groups I and III highlighted (redrawn by Christine Hernández from an original drawing by George E. Stuart in Andrews 1970:Figure 2).

Most of the artifacts (77 percent) recovered from the six named groups of offerings at Balankanche consist of pottery and stone vessels and miniatures of various kinds, including plates, jars, *manos*, and *metates* (Table 11.1). The remaining artifacts include spindle whorls and miscellaneous pottery vessels, beads of various materials, mosaic pieces, and a few chipped stone artifacts. Andrews (1970:9-10) observed a patterned distribution of artifact types across the six groups identified within the cavern, suggesting that the assemblage reflects complex ritual behavior taking place in those areas of the cave.

Our discussion focuses on the artifacts from two of the six groups—Group I, the "Throne of the Balam," and Group III, the "Water Chamber" (Figure 11.1). The first of these is the most dramatic in appearance because it is characterized by a stone column formed by one or more stalactites and stalagmites growing together. In drawings and photographs, it appears almost treelike in form (see frontispiece to Andrews 1970). It features two handprints in red ochre, similar to others that were found on the roof of the tunnel leading to Group II. Andrea Stone (1989) notes that red-painted handprints like those found on the pillar in Group I are the most common form of art found associated with cave features.

Twenty-nine large censers of clay and stone were arranged in the area in front of the pillar; most were placed in cavities, but others were sometimes simply left on the floor (Figure 11.2).

Figure 11.2. Group I artifacts *in situ* in the central chamber of the sealed portion of Balankanche Cave. Note the placement of Tlaloc effigy censers and miniature *manos* and *metates* in cavities carved out around the column. Image from the Merle Greene Robertson Collection, courtesy of the Latin American Library, Tulane University.

At least a dozen of the censers had been smashed before being deposited. The types of censers found include 12 Tlaloc effigy censers, 13 studded biconical censers, and four carved stone censers. Also recovered were three miniature pottery vessels (plates and jars), four miniature *manos* and *metates*, and 15 other objects, including pottery and jewelry (Andrews 1970:10-11).

Figure 11.3. Detail of Group III artifacts *in situ* in the "Water" Chamber of Balankanche Cave, including Tlaloc effigy censers, more than 200 miniature *manos* and *metates*, and all 25 of the spindle whorls recovered from the cave. Image courtesy of the Middle American Research Institute, Tulane University.

Group III, to the east of Group I, is located on a ledge above an underground lake. It consists of the largest number of offerings in the cave (Figure 11.3). Group III includes 15 large censers (six Tlaloc effigies, seven studded biconical censers, and two made of carved stone), 232 *manos* and *metates* piled together on the floor, 17 miniature vessels, 25 spindle whorls, and 15 miscellaneous objects. Among this last class of artifacts are bolster-rim basins, plates made of Chichen Slate ware, a miniature Tlaloc effigy jar, and a vessel cover in the form of a jaguar head (Andrews 1970:11).

Previous interpretations of the artifactual assemblages have focused on the probability that they were used in rainmaking or *ch'a-chaak* rituals (Andrews IV 1970; Thompson 1975). The presence of the Tlaloc effigy censers in conjunction with an underground water source makes this a viable interpretation, as do the water jars found in several contexts. Nevertheless, the occurrence of large concentrations of objects (such as the *manos*, *metates*, and spindle whorls) associated with female deities in Maya art and with female activity areas and the burials of women at a number of prehispanic sites remains to be explained (Bell 2002; Dacus 2006; Kowalski and Miller 2006; Vail and Stone 2002).

Several other objects and features found in the cave's passageways and chambers are also relevant to our understanding of the rituals that may have been performed in these spaces. In addition to those previously described, Andrews and his team discovered a large number of hearths and firepits in the sealed chambers of the cave and also found a fragment of a wooden drum (*tunk'ul*) that had been reworked in the passageway between Groups I and IV (Andrews 1970:15, 63).

Regeneration and Renewal Rituals Focused on Chaak and Chak Chel

In order to understand better the types of rituals that were performed in underground spaces such as caves and *cenotes*, we turn now to the Late Postclassic iconographic and epigraphic record. In the Maya codices, caves and *cenotes* are associated almost exclusively with the rain god Chaak (Vail and Hernández n.d.). Chaak is a quadripartite deity who was believed to dwell in watery underground places like caves, *cenotes*, and springs during the dry season and to emerge from these locations in May to initiate the rainy season (Redfield and Villa Rojas 1934; Sosa 1989; Thompson 1970:251-253, 256; Vail and Hernández n.d.).

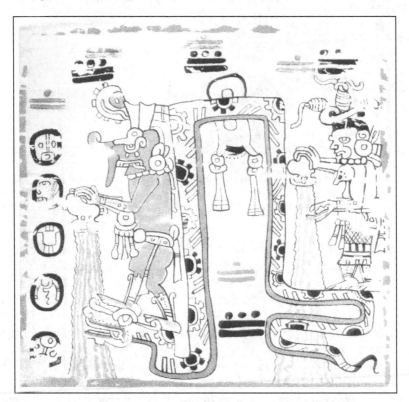

Figure 11.4. The almanac on page 30a of the Madrid Codex (after Brasseur de Bourbourg 1869–70:Plate 27).

Chaak has a number of attributes in common with the Mexican deity Tlaloc, who is also a quadripartite rain god believed to dwell on the tops of mountains. This aspect of Tlaloc is most vividly described by Durán (1971:156) in his account of a rainmaking ceremony conducted during the *Huey Tozontontli* festival (corresponding to the month of April) by Aztec nobility at a sanctuary that scholars believe to be associated with the remains of a structure resting atop Cerro Tlaloc, east of Mexico City (Aveni et al. 1988; Iwaniszewski 1994; López 1997;

Morante 1997; Townsend 1991). Garibay's (1965:26) recounting of the *Historia de los mexicanos* reveals the mythological underpinnings of this mountaintop ceremony

Chaak shared the role of rainmaker with an elderly deity named Chak Chel, who is pictured on a number of occasions in the Maya codices emptying her jar of water to provide rains for the earth. In one particularly revealing scene, Chaak and Chak Chel are both standing on the body of a serpent, engaged in this activity (Figure 11.4). The serpent (*kàan*) may here be serving as a rebus for the sky (*ká'an*). Chaak is painted blue, the color of water (and hence of fertility). Chak Chel wears a figure-eight headdress (a symbolic serpent) in her hair, as well as three spindles wound with cotton thread. Chak Chel is one of a complex of Maya goddesses who are linked to the generative acts of spinning and weaving and to the giving of life. She is also the patron of midwives and the female member of the creator couple (Taube 1992:101). She has a counterpart in the deity Yaxper of the Tz'utujil Maya living on Lake Atitlán in highland Guatemala, who likewise wears a twisted cloth headdress symbolic of a serpent, which is said to be an umbilical cord connecting her to the sky (Christenson 2001:95, 97).

Figure 11.5. Chaak and Chak Chel seated on a *kab' ch'e'en* collocation in the middle frame of Dresden page 42b (after Förstemann 1880).

Chak Chel is associated with the bringing of both life-giving and destructive water. In both roles, she is paired almost invariably with Chaak. She is also shown with Chaak on several occasions in scenes with a hieroglyphic collocation reading *kab' ch'e'en* ("earth cave") (Figure 11.5). We have argued elsewhere that this expression refers to the primordial cave of creation for the Maya, from which the various items necessary for human life derived, including rain, maize, and cacao.[2] A mural from Structure 16 at Tulum, clearly Postclassic in date, portrays what we believe to be this creation place (Figure 11.6). Issuing from the gaping jaws of an earth monster (indicating that the scene takes place within the earth), intertwined serpents frame a layered series of scenes that focus on Chaak and an elderly female deity who can be identified as one of the manifestations of Chak Chel. In the lowermost register, Chaak and Chak Chel appear together holding serpent scepters, commonly identified as lightning and the source of Chaak's generative power; it is believed to be what causes the rains to fall and the seeds to germinate (Martin 2006). This germination appears to be one of the major themes of the bottom register. In the next level, Chaak sits astride a jaguar throne,[3] Chak Chel holds an effigy of Chaak, and a miniature version of the maize god appears, with his hand raised to his face in a gesture that signifies his impending death. This may refer to the mythological period when maize was not available to those living on the surface of the earth, as described in the colonial Yucatec text known as the Book of Chilam Balam of Chumayel (Knowlton 2010:61-62).

Figure 11.6. Reconstruction of Mural 2 of Tulum Structure 16 showing flowering vegetation growing out of a *cenote*. After a painting by F. Dávalos in Miller (1982:Plate 37).

Figure 11.7. Detail from the upper façade portion of Mural 2 in Tulum Structure 16 showing Chak Chel grinding maize. Original artwork by Christine Hernández.

The upper two registers are outside of the area enclosed by the mouth of the earth monster, suggesting that they may refer to an ascent to the surface of the earth. In the lower of these two registers, the maize god appears again, this time representing a healthy maize plant. Chaak and Chak Chel are also pictured. In the uppermost register, gaping serpent mouths give birth to glyphs representing sprouting maize. To the right, Chak Chel, wearing a Mexican-style *quechquemitl* (upper garment), kneels in front of a *metate* with serpent feet (Figure 11.7). If this scene is analogous to mythologies related in the highlands of Guatemala and in central Mexico, she may here be pictured in the act of grinding the maize kernels (corresponding to bones in central Mexican sources) that were used to form humans. Chaak stands in front of her, perhaps as the source of the water that is mixed with the maize to create the first humans.

The mythological scene portrayed on the Tulum mural has a number of parallels with a ritual that is re-enacted on a yearly basis in the Tz'utujil community of Santiago Atitlán during the week before Easter (Christenson 2001:91-101). This involves the construction of a *monumento* to symbolize the mountain shrine and cave (*Paq'alib'al*) that is home to the Tz'utujil ancestors and the earth lord, as well as being the birthplace of the rains and sustenance. A female elder of the community, who represents the creator Yaxper, plays a key role in the construction of the *monumento*, decorating it with fruit and flowers (Christenson 2001:Figures 4.15 and 4.16). The figures of central importance to the ritual and its surrounding mythology, then, involve creator deities associated with rain and fertility who are comparable to Chaak and Chak Chel among the prehispanic Yucatec Maya. Additionally, one of the principal features of the *monumento* is a framework made of twisted cords (Christenson 2001:Figure 4.13), similar to those seen in the Tulum mural.

The Tz'utujil ceremony concludes with the resurrection of the maize god (who is also believed to represent Jesus Christ). This calls to mind the "birth" of the maize from the open-mouthed serpents in the Tulum mural. Christenson notes that this yearly ritual can be described as a world renewal ceremony and that its focus is agricultural fertility. As we have shown, this also is the central theme of Mural 2 from Tulum Structure 16. The sprouting vegetation portrayed in the mural is matched by the hanging of greenery and fruits on the contemporary *monumento* to symbolize fecundity and rebirth. In both the Tz'utujil ceremony and the Tulum mural, acts of world renewal and creation are associated with paired male and female deities or deity impersonators.

The pairing of Chaak and Chak Chel in the Tulum mural is of particular interest to us given evidence from various sources, including Balankanche and the Maya codices, of shared ideology between the cultures of central Mexico and the northern Maya area during the Late Classic to Postclassic periods. In the next section, we consider several examples of cultural sharing and the importance of this deity pair in the worldview of the Postclassic Maya.

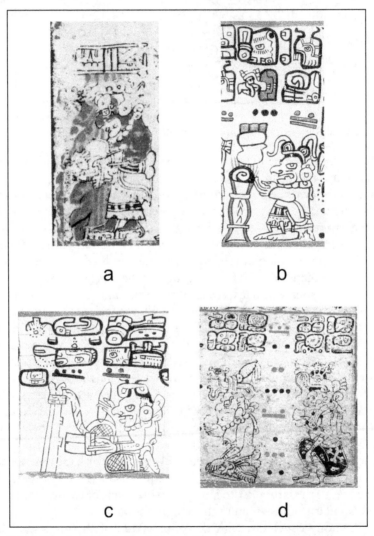

Figure 11.8. Elderly female deities in the Maya codices: (a) Chak Chel (Dresden page 67a); (b) the earth goddess Sak Ix Kab' (Madrid page 107b); (c) a conflation of Chak Chel and the earth goddess, labeled Ix Kab' Chel (Madrid page 102d); (d) female versions of the creator Itzamna and the death god Kimil (Dresden page 9c). After Brasseur de Bourbourg (1869–70:Plates VI and XI) and Förstemann (1880:Plates IX, LXVII).

In the narrative related in the *Popol Vuh* (Christenson 2003), the male creator is analogous to the Yucatecan creator deity Itzamna, who is paired with Chak Chel on several occasions in the Maya codices, although less frequently than Chaak is. Because we are missing hieroglyphic captions for many of the scenes in the codices that picture elderly female goddesses, it is sometimes difficult to identify them. There are two distinctive named deities that fit this category: Chak Chel (Figure 11.8a; see also Dresden page 72; Madrid 10b) and Sak Ix Kab' (Figure 11.8b; see also Madrid pages 102c and 108c). Deities with composites of both names also occur (Figure 11.8c; see also Dresden page 2b), as do elderly female figures that take the names and attributes of Itzamna and of the death god Kimil (Figure 11.8d). The former would undoubtedly be identified as Chak Chel in the absence of Itzamna's name in the hieroglyphic caption. The two are commonly identified as male and female aspects of the same underlying creative principle (Vail and Stone 2002).

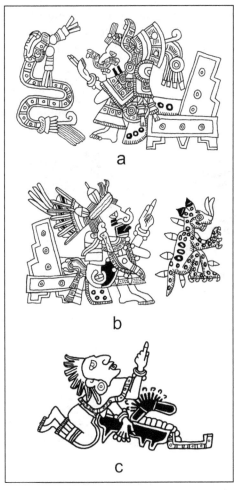

Figure 11.9. Representations of highland Mexican goddesses: (a) Chalchiuhtlicue and her day sign Serpent; (b) Tlazolteotl and her day sign Jaguar; (c) Omecihuatl grinding maize on a metate (after Codex Borgia 1976:11-12). Original artwork by Christine Hernández.

This situation seems to us comparable in several respects to that in central Mexico during the same time period, where there are a number of deities who can be related to Chak Chel and her various aspects. For example, she can be compared to the Mexican goddess Chalchiuhtlicue ("Jade Her Skirt"), the goddess of lakes, rivers, and springs, whose flooding of the earth led to the end of the fourth creation (Figure 11.9a). Chalchiuhtlicue has been identified as the wife of Tlaloc and may be cognate with the aspect of Chak Chel who appears with Chaak in the codices (Figure 11.10a). Moreover, like Chak Chel, Chalchiuhtlicue is associated with serpents; she is the patron of the day Serpent (*Chicchan* in the Maya calendar) and sometimes wears a double-headed serpent nose ornament.

Another Mexican goddess who shares attributes with the Chak Chel complex is Tlazolteotl (Figure 11.9b), who is the goddess of childbirth, the patron of weavers, and the "absorber of sins," from which she derives her name ("Filth Goddess"; Boone 2007:43). Her day sign is Jaguar (*Ix* in the Maya calendar), which provides an interesting parallel to Chak Chel in that one of this deity's manifestations is as a jaguar goddess (Figure 11.10b). Additionally, Tlazolteotl wears ear ornaments of unspun cotton and often appears with spindles in her headdress.

A third deity worth mentioning is Omecihuatl, who is the elderly female half of the highland Mexican creator couple. A representation on page 9 of the Borgia Codex depicts Omecihuatl grinding on a *metate* in a fashion very similar to the portrayal of Chak Chel in Mural 2 at Tulum (Figure 11.7). In the Borgia example, she is shown as associated with the twentieth day sign Flower and the goddess of flowers Xochiquetzal (Figure 11.9c).

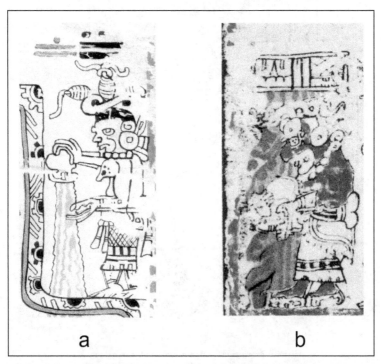

Figure 11.10. Aspects of Chak Chel likened to Mexican goddesses: (a) beneficent Chak Chel (Madrid page 32a); (b) destructive jaguar aspect of Chak Chel (Dresden page 67a). After Brasseur de Bourbourg (1869–70:Plate XXVII) and Förstemann (1880:Plate LXVII).

Figure 11.11. Center panel from Madrid pages 75-76.
Original artwork by Christine Hernández.

The comparison with Omecihuatl highlights another important example of elderly female goddesses in the codices. A figure commonly identified as Chak Chel is pictured on pages 75-76 of the Madrid Codex, seated opposite the creator Itzamna beneath what has been described as the central world tree (Figure 11.11). Here, she is believed to represent the female half of the creator couple. She and Itzamna are both associated with glyph T503, which is the day *Ik'* ("wind, breath, and life") and is also used in the Madrid Codex to represent a maize seed (Macri and Vail 2009; Vail and Hernández 2002–2010). We have previously suggested that this imagery refers to the creation of humans from maize (Vail and Hernández 2009), much as the scene showing Chak Chel grinding seems to have this association in Mural 2 from Tulum.

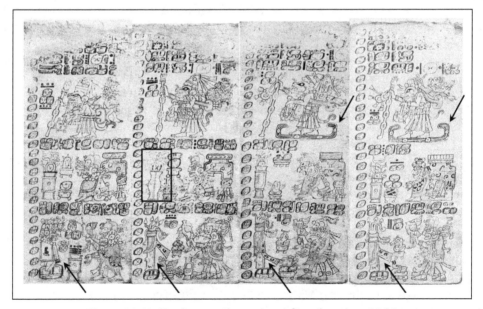

Figure 11.12. Yearbearer ceremonies on Dresden pages 25-28
(after Förstemann 1880:Plates XXV-XXVIII).

Although there is nothing in the iconography of Madrid pages 75-76 to suggest that this scene takes place in a cave, we are struck by the resemblance of the central element, or what may be the world tree, to the pillar occurring in the main chamber of Balankanche Cave, which Barrera Vásquez (1970:72) compares to a ceiba tree. During rituals associated with the yearbearer ceremonies (occurring during the five days marking the transition from one year to the next), incense of various types, including sap from the copal and rubber trees, was burned in censers similar to those in the cave with biconical projections or "spikes" (Figure 11.12, highlighted section on Dresden page 26). On the Dresden yearbearer pages, we see this ritual being performed in front of a tree or column set up to mark the start of a new year (Figure 11.12, lower register of each page). It is also of interest that two of the four Dresden yearbearer pages (27 and 28) picture *cenotes* in the context of rituals associated with this period of time (Figure 11.12, upper register), suggesting another possible link to the Balankanche assemblage.

There is good evidence, as these and other data (discussed below) suggest, to link the artifacts deposited at Balankanche with New Year rituals and those performed in the early spring in preparation for the agricultural season. We believe that, in addition to the ceremonies documented by Landa (Tozzer 1941) and the other chroniclers, these included activities associated with renewing the world and replicating the acts performed by the deities Chaak and Chak Chel in primordial times, such as are portrayed in painted murals and codices from the Postclassic period and re-enacted in rituals performed today in the highlands of Guatemala. Acts of world creation and generation that are indicated by the Balankanche artifacts include: (1) the pouring of water from jars (an activity performed by both Chaak and Chak Chel in the Maya codices); (2) the use of spindle whorls to make cotton, an act associated with the creation of rain clouds by the daughters of the earth lords in highland Chiapas today (Morris 2000); and (3) the symbolic grinding of maize to form humans (another act performed by Chak Chel in creation narratives). The jaguar lid to the pottery vessel found in Group III may also suggest an association with Chak Chel, or perhaps more generally with dark underground spaces beyond the secular, civilized environs of villages and towns. This stems from the association of jaguars with darkness, night, and caves in Mesoamerican thought (Miller and Taube 1993:102-103; Seler 1963, 1:75-76).[4]

Other features from the cave may also be associated with renewal rituals such as those performed at the start of a new year. We call attention particularly to the lighting of fires, an activity performed during various ceremonies, but which had special significance at the beginning of the new year, when a new fire (*suhuy k'aak'*) was drilled as part of the rituals that initiated the month *Pop* (Gates 1978:70-71). Given the poor ventilation occurring in the chambers of the cave, it seems likely that fires would have been lit for ceremonial reasons at Balankanche, rather than to provide light for the ritual participants. If this were the case, then a yearbearer association would provide a good explanation for the fires and hearths in the cave. Additionally, the burning of incense, suggested by the numerous censers, may be related to the contemporary Maya practice of creating black smoke to call the rain-laden clouds (Thompson 1970:166). Among the Tz'utujil Maya of Santiago Atitlan, smoke from burning incense is said to symbolize "rain clouds which are born inside sacred mountains" (Christenson 2001:153). Such a meaning would fit the Balankanche censers especially well, both because they were used within a cave context and because they commonly portray the rain deity Tlaloc. That this was also one of the functions of the yearbearer ceremonies is suggested by the emphasis placed on the burning of copal incense in the Dresden almanac on pages 25-28, which portrays the renewal rituals performed at the start of the new year.

The playing of drums and other musical instruments was also an important component of the New Year ceremonies occurring at the beginning of the month *Pop* (seen, for example, on Madrid page 37a). Drums were associated particularly with the sound of thunder and were meant to call forth the rains (Thompson 1970:266, 268). In this regard, it is of interest to note that a fragment of a *tunk'ul* was found in the cave.

The deposition of each of the items described above (with the exception of the materials that depict Xipe Totec, discussed below) can be explained quite satisfactorily as the result of yearly ceremonies of renewal and regeneration that focused on replicating the primordial acts of Chak Chel and Chaak. Rather than focusing specifically on *ch'a-chaak* rituals, we would like to emphasize that the artifactual assemblage points quite clearly to the performance of ceremonies that emphasize the creator deity Chak Chel, as well as on Chaak.

Spindle whorls, in addition to *manos* and *metates*, have been found in assemblages from other caves in the Maya area, as well as from deposits in other ritual locales such as rock shelters and caches (Brady 1989; 1995:34; William Ringle, personal communication 2010; Robinson 2008; Stone 1995:41), indicating that the data from Balankanche are not unique but fit into a ritual pattern that extends from northern Yucatan, through the southern lowlands, and into highland Guatemala. On the basis of these examples, it is clear that both male and female gendered activities were performed in cave contexts during the Classic and Terminal Classic periods.

The question of whether women participated in these cave rituals or whether Chak Chel impersonators were men is one that remains to be discussed. Although most ethnohistoric and ethnographic sources agree that women were prohibited from rituals performed within caves (e.g., Barrera Vásquez 1970:73), there are indications that there were certain exceptions. Among the Tojolab'al in highland Guatemala, for example, men and women participate in dances (and sometimes fertility rituals) in caves (Vogt and Stuart 2005:174). This theme may also be illustrated on a Classic-period pottery vessel from the site of Los Naranjos, Honduras, which has been interpreted as showing the primordial human couple having sexual intercourse in a cave (Nielsen and Brady 2006). Similar activities may have taken place in the cave of Naj Tunich as well, judging from an image of an embracing couple painted on the wall (Drawing 18), although Stone (1995:196) is not certain if the second participant is female or a male taking on a female role. Bassie-Sweet (1991:84) notes that the word *ch'en* "cave" also refers, among the Tzotzil Maya, to the vagina (Laughlin 1975:132). This suggests that rain was produced by a symbolic sexual act within cave environments. It is of interest in this regard that what appears to be rain issues from the genitals and armpits of a figure who can be identified as Chak Chel in the Madrid Codex (on pages 30b and 32b). We also know from sources such as Landa (Tozzer 1941:145, 147) that elderly women (presumably meaning women past menopause) could participate in certain ceremonies, and there is strong evidence from the ethnographic material discussed above suggesting that elderly women played key roles in rituals associated with acts of world renewal. Whether they had a similar role at Balankanche remains unknown.

There is some precedent in the art of nearby Chichen Itza for inferring that men took on female roles in certain ritual contexts. Andrea Stone (1999) notes that a number of the representations of Chak Chel and other female deities on architectural columns at the site lack breasts, suggesting to her that they may have been men dressed in the guise of female deities. Additionally, some of the male warriors portrayed at the site wear an upper garment that is commonly associated with women, known as a *quechquemitl*. This may serve to link them to the generative power of this creator goddess (Kowalski and Miller 2006:163). Similarly, male rulers in Classic period contexts took on the attributes of the moon goddess at times as a means of harnessing her powers (Looper 2002). It is certainly possible that the same practice may have taken place at Balankanche, although we believe that it is just as likely that an elderly woman was chosen to reenact the role played by Chak Chel at creation, as suggested by Mural 2 from Tulum and contemporary practices of the Tz'utujil Maya.

Although this question cannot be answered with the data available to us, what is clear from ethnohistoric and ethnographic contexts is the importance of male and female (or dual sexed) primordial ancestors or creator deities (Christenson 2003). Within this framework, it makes perfect sense for the artifactual assemblage from Balankanche to represent both male and female activities and for them to be focused on the things most important for human existence—rain and water and the life-giving sustenance of maize.

Other Renewal Rituals

New Year rituals described by Landa and other sources focus on regeneration and renewal (Taube 1988; Tozzer 1941). The artifacts from the cave, as well as the presence of effigies or representations of central Mexican deities linked to rain (Tlaloc), fit well with this theme and are of special interest because they may correspond to iconographic elements in the International style found at nearby Chichen Itza during this same period (Boone and Smith 2003). Other aspects of the Balankanche materials that show connections with central Mexican pantheons and the theme of regeneration are the stone effigy censers with attributes of Xipe Totec (Figure 11.13). Of the 20 carved stone censers recorded, 14 have faces or figures carved onto them. Eight of the full-sized figures appear to wear flayed human skin and carry the accoutrement of warriors. Three additional censers portray Tlaloc, but with the addition of details that suggest a conflation with Xipe Totec.

The appearance of Xipe Totec iconography on vessels left as offerings at Balankanche is especially interesting considering descriptions by colonial-period chroniclers of the public rituals known as *Tlacaxipehualiztli* celebrated in January through March by Aztec people (Durán 1971:180-183, 416; Sahagún 1981, II:47-58). The climax of the three-month ceremony had a strong military component: Jaguar and Eagle warriors wounded captives in mock gladiatorial fights, the hearts of captives were removed, their bodies were flayed and dismembered for ritual cannibalism and trophies, and their skins were worn and paraded by elite individuals. In contrast, the denouement of the festival in early to mid-March celebrated themes of regeneration and fecundity. The acts performed included begging for food alms, blessing the first flowers of spring, and depositing flayed skins in mountain shrines, caves, or symbolic caves at the base of temples dedicated to Xipe Totec. Seler's (1963, 1:127-135) analysis of a song venerating Xipe Totec and *Tlacaxipehualiztli* rites (especially the offerings of hearts and blood from war captives and the wearing and casting off of flayed human skins) led him to describe Xipe Totec as a distinctly male deity responsible for the regeneration and fecundity of the earth.

In the central highlands, the end of *Tlacaxipehualiztli* heralded the early spring season when farmers began the process of preparing and blessing fields prior to planting. The propitiations made to Xipe Totec at this time were designed to ensure agricultural success.[5] The timely commencement of the rainy season was a significant concern during the months preceding planting, leading local priests to decorate idols and representations of Tlaloc and deposit them in temples, mountains, and caves during *Tlacaxipehualiztli*:

...[the priests] now melted the rubber and painted stripes with it upon the paper. Once the stripes had been painted, the papers were taken to the hills, where the caves, shrines, places of sacrifice, and temples were filled with little stone and clay idols. These were then dressed in the striped paper, which was placed upon them like a scapular... (Durán 1971:416)

In light of colonial-period accounts and Seler's analysis, perhaps the Xipe Totec vessels and some of the Tlaloc effigy censers painted with black spots and stripes—as well as black trickle ceramics encountered in the Balankanche deposits—represent a Terminal Classic Maya version of widely shared beliefs and ritual practices conducted by ancient Mesoamericans to ensure the success of the rains and the growth of food crops prior to the planting season (Figure 11.14).

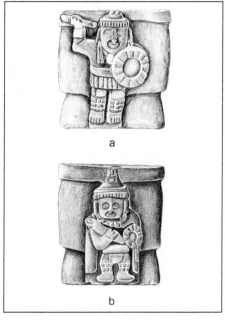

Figure 11.13. Examples of carved stone censers portraying figures wearing flayed skins (after drawings by Hipólito Sánchez in Andrews 1970:Figure 22a, c). Image courtesy of the Middle American Research Institute, Tulane University.

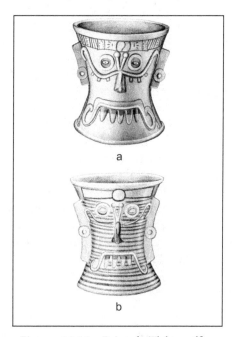

Figure 11.14. Painted Tlaloc effigy vessels from Balankanche Cave (after drawings by George E. Stuart and Hipólito Sánchez in Andrews 1970: Figures 8a and 9d). Image courtesy of the Middle American Research Institute, Tulane University.

Conclusion

The artifacts from Balankanche suggest that several different rituals and depositional activities occurred within the cave. These involved regeneration and renewal events that may have been performed at different times during the yearly ceremonial cycle. We believe that the majority of the artifacts from Balankanche are likely the result of rituals performed over a period of many years associated with renewing the world and replicating the acts performed by the deities Chaak and Chak Chel in primordial times. These include the pouring of water from jars, the use of spindle whorls to make cotton, and the symbolic grinding of maize to form humans. Whether these rituals were performed by women deity impersonators or by men is a question that cannot be answered at present.

The presence of Xipe Totec effigy vessels in the Balankanche deposits is intriguing. Did they contain the cast-off skins of flayed sacrificial victims, as was described for the Aztec *Tlacaxipehualiztli* rites of early spring? Although we cannot say one way or the other from the data at hand, we put forth the following suggestions concerning the Balankanche ritual assemblage. First, the occurrence of Tlaloc effigy censers, especially those painted with black spots and stripes, as well as pottery vessels related to water gathering (either functionally or symbolically, as in the case of black trickle ceramics), and effigies of figures wearing flayed skins represent rituals directed at propitiating deities for both rain and agricultural foodstuffs. We know from ethnohistorical and ethnographic sources that such rituals could take place during the inauguration of a new year, in the months prior to the planting and rainy season, during a later time if there were a delay in the start of the rains, and possibly in the early half of the growing cycle when the harvesting of the "first fruits" was celebrated. Second, it seems clear that the complex of ritual practices and beliefs concerning caves, rain, and agricultural fertility and renewal so vividly described and portrayed for the Late Postclassic Maya had deep temporal roots in Yucatan. In fact, ceramics recently dated by Michael Smyth (2000:Table 1) in architectural deposits adjoining the Gruta de Chac suggest a ritual use of that cave to petition rain from the Early to Middle Classic period (A.D. 500–700). A similar trajectory of increasingly elaborate rainmaking and sustenance rituals performed in caves has also been proposed for the Late to Terminal Classic period in Belize (Moyes et al. 2009).

Previous reconstructions of the rituals performed at Balankanche have lacked convincing explanations for the presence of several hundred artifacts associated with female activity spheres and foreign deities. By linking them with rituals invoking Chaak and Chak Chel, on the one hand, and Tlaloc and Xipe Totec on the other, they can be explained quite satisfactorily.

Notes

1. The three Maya codices known to be of prehispanic origin are named after the European cities where they are currently housed. The authenticity of a fourth codex, called the Grolier Codex, continues to be debated (Baudez 2002; Boone and Smith 2003; Carlson 1983; Coe 1973; Milbrath 2002).

2. The prehispanic Maya did not necessarily believe that one particular cave was the source of all life; rather, this would have varied from region to region and tradition to tradition. A reference to *kab' ch'e'en* occurs in an important text (Stela C) from Classic-period Quirigua in the southern Maya lowlands, dating to the eighth century. In the Quirigua text, three stones are set up at the start of the present era (13.0.0.0.0 4 Ahaw 8 Kumk'u, in August 3114 B.C.); the middle stone, in the form of a serpent, was placed at *kab' che'en*. The serpent stone located at *kab' ch'e'en* is pictured and named on Dresden page 31b-35b, in a scene that we interpret as the gift of the rains (*chaak*) to the earthly realm. Additionally, there are several references in Postclassic Maya painted texts to *wuk ha' nal* ("Seven Water Place") that we believe refers to a concept similar to that of Chicomoztoc ("Seven Chambered Cave") referenced in central Mexican origin stories (Vail 2008; Vail and Hernández n.d.).

3. The jaguar throne pictured in this scene may be compared with that shown in the Vase of the Seven Gods (illustrated in Reents-Budet 1994:318-319), where it is associated with God L of the Underworld. We find it of interest that, in the Tulum mural, there are indications of spikes on the tail of the jaguar, suggesting a conflation with Itzam Kab' Ayin, the crocodilian earth monster named in the books of *Chilam Balam*. This creature appears in the register above God L in the vase scene.

4. According to Seler (1963, 1:75-76), the jaguar is the animal aspect of the Mexican deity Tepeyollotl, whose name ("heart of the mountain") refers to caves. Jaguars were associated with the

earth and with darkness, especially darkness that devours, like that seen in the apparition of the earth swallowing the sun at dusk, or its shadow covering the sun during a solar eclipse. In the painted books of the Borgia Group from highland Mexico, the third day of the Mexican calendar, House, is represented in part by a jaguar. In the Maya calendar, the third day is *Ak'b'al*, signifying "darkness."

   5. Seler (1963, 1:130-131) goes further, proposing a relationship between Xipe Totec and Tlazolteotl, specifically the lunar aspect of the latter. Both deities have connections to sacrifice, the beverage *pulque*, and to the earth. The monthly celebrations (*Tlacaxipehualiztli* and *Ochpaniztli*) for the two deities frame the agricultural season and have certain rites in common, notably the sacrifice of deity impersonators.

References

Andrews, E. Wyllys IV. 1970. *Balankanché, Throne of the Tiger Priest*. Middle American Research Institute Publication 32. Tulane University, New Orleans.
Andrews, E. Wyllys V. 1979. Early Central Mexican Architectural Traits at Dzibilchaltun, Yucatan. In *Proceedings of the International Congress of Americanists (42nd session, Paris, 1976)*, vol. 8, pp. 237-249. Paris.
Andrews, Anthony P., E. Wyllys Andrews, and Fernando Robles Castellanos. 2003. The Northern Maya Collapse and its Aftermath. *Ancient Mesoamerica* 14:151-156.
Ardren, Traci (editor). 2002. *Ancient Maya Women*. Alta Mira, Walnut Creek.
Aveni, Anthony F., Edward Calnek, and Horst Hartung. 1988. Myth, Environment, and the Orientation of the Templo Mayor of Tenochtitlan. *American Antiquity* 53:287-309.
Barrera Vásquez, Alfredo. 1970. The Ceremony of *Tsikul T'an Ti' Yuntsiloob* at Balankanché. In Andrews IV 1970:72-78.
Bassie-Sweet, Karen. 1991. *From the Mouth of the Dark Cave: Commemorative Sculpture of the Late Classic Maya*. University of Oklahoma, Norman.
Baudez, Claude-François. 2002. Venus y el Códice Grolier. *Arqueología Mexicana* X (55):70-79.
Bell, Ellen. 2002. Engendering a Dynasty: A Royal Woman in the Margarita Tomb, Copan. In Ardren 2002:89-104.
Boone, Elizabeth. 2007. *Cycles of Time and Meaning in the Mexican Books of Fate*. University of Texas, Austin.
Boone, Elizabeth, and Michael E. Smith. 2003. Postclassic International Styles and Symbol Sets. In *The Postclassic Mesoamerican World*, edited by Michael E. Smith and Francis F. Berdan, pp. 186-193. University of Utah, Salt Lake City.
Brady, James E. 1989. *An Investigation of Maya Ritual Cave Use with Special Reference to Naj Tunich, Petén, Guatemala*. Ph.D. dissertation, Department of Anthropology, University of California, Los Angeles. University Microfilms, Ann Arbor.
— 1995. A Reassessment of the Chronology and Function of Gordon's Cave #3, Copan, Honduras. *Ancient Mesoamerica* 6:29-38.
Brasseur de Bourbourg, Charles E. 1869–1870. *Manuscrit Troano: Etudes sur le système graphique et la langue des Mayas*. Imprimerie Impériale, Paris.
Carlson, John B. 1983. The Grolier Codex: A Preliminary Report on the Content and Authenticity of a Thirteenth-Century Maya Venus Almanac. In *Calendars in Mesoamerica and Peru: Native American Computations of Time*, edited by Anthony F. Aveni and Gordo Brotherson, pp. 27-57. BAR International Series 174. British Archaeological Reports, Oxford.
Christenson, Allen J. 2001. *Art and Society in a Highland Maya Community: The Altarpiece of Santiago Atitlan*. University of Texas Press, Austin.
— 2003. *Popol Vuh: The Sacred Book of the Maya*. O Books, New York.
Coe, Michael D. 1973. *The Maya Scribe and his World*. The Grolier Club, New York.
Durán, Fray Diego. 1971. *The Book of the Gods and Rites and the Ancient Calendar*. University of Oklahoma, Norman.

Dacus, Chelsea. 2006. Weaving the Past: An Examination of Bones Buried with an Elite Maya Women. Report submitted to the Foundation for the Advancement of Mesoamerican Studies, Inc. Online: www.famsi.org/research/dacus/index.htm.

Förstemann, Ernst. 1880. *Die Maya Handschrift der königlichen öffentlichen Bibliothek zu Dresden*. Verlag der A. Naumann'schen Lichtdruckerei, Leipzig.

Garibay Kintana, Ángel María. 1965. *Teogonía e Historia de los Mexicanos*. Editorial Porrua, Mexico.

Gates, William. 1978. *Yucatan before and after the Conquest*. Dover, New York.

Hanks, William F., and Don S. Rice (editors). 1989. *Word and Image in Maya Culture: Explorations in Language, Writing, and Representation*. University of Utah, Salt Lake City.

Iwaniszewski, Stanislaw. 1994. Archaeology and Archaeoastronomy of Mount Tlaloc, Mexico: A Reconsideration. *Latin American Antiquity* 5:158-176.

Kowalski, Jeff K., and Virginia E. Miller. 2006. Textile Designs in the Sculptured Facades of Northern Maya Architecture: Women's Production, Cloth, Tribute, and Political Power. In *Sacred Bundles: Ritual Acts of Wrapping and Binding in Mesoamerica*, edited by Julia Guernsey and F. Kent Reilly, pp. 145-174. Boundary End Archaeology Research Center, Barnardsville.

Knowlton, Timothy. 2010. *Maya Creation Myths: Words and Worlds of the Chilam Balam*. University Press of Colorado, Boulder.

Laughlin, Robert M. 1975. *The Great Tzotzil Dictionary of San Lorenzo Zinacantan*. Smithsonian Contributions to Anthropology 19. Smithsonian Institution, Washington, D.C.

Looper, Matthew. 2002. Women-Men (and Men-Women): Classic Maya Rulers and the Third Gender. In Ardren 2002:171-202.

Macri, Martha, and Gabrielle Vail. 2009. *The New Catalog of Maya Hieroglyphs. Volume 2: The Codical Texts*. University of Oklahoma, Norman.

Martin, Simon. 2006. Cacao in Ancient Maya Religion: First Fruit from the Maize Tree and Other Tales from the Underworld. *In Chocolate in Mesoamerica: A Cultural History of Cacao*, edited by Cameron L. McNeil, pp. 154-183. University Press of Florida, Gainesville.

Milbrath, Susan. 2002. New Questions Concerning the Authenticity of the Grolier Codex. *Latin American Indian Literatures Journal* 18:50-83.

Miller, Arthur G. 1982. *On the Edge of the Sea: Mural Painting at Tancah-Tulum, Quintana Roo, Mexico*. Dumbarton Oaks, Washington, D.C.

Miller, Mary E., and Karl A. Taube. 1993. *The Gods and Symbols of Ancient Mexico and the Maya: An Illustrated Dictionary of Mesoamerican Religion*. Thames & Hudson, New York and London.

Morante López, Rubén B. 1997. El Monte Tlaloc y el calendario mexica. In *Graniceros: Cosmovisión y meteorología indígenas de Mesoamérica*, edited by Beatriz Albores and Johanna Broda, pp. 109-139. Universidad Nacional Autónoma de México, Mexico City.

Morris, Walter F. 2000. *The Living Maya*. Harry N. Abrams, New York.

Moyes, Holley, Jaime J. Awe, George A. Brook, and James W. Webster. 2009. The Ancient Maya Drought Cult: Late Classic Cave Use in Belize. *Latin American Antiquity* 20:175-206.

Nielsen, Jesper, and James E. Brady. 2006. The Couple in the Cave: Origin Iconography on a Ceramic Vessel from Los Naranjos, Honduras. *Ancient Mesoamerica* 17:203-217.

Redfield, Robert. and Alfonso Villa Rojas. 1934. *Chan Kom, A Maya Village*. Publication 248. Carnegie Institution of Washington, Washington, D.C.

Reents-Budet, Dorie. 1994. *Painting the Maya Universe: Royal Ceramics of the Classic Period*. Duke University, Durham and London.

Robinson, Eugenia. 2008. Memoried Sacredness and International Elite Identities: The Late Postclassic at La Casa de las Golondrinas, Guatemala. In *Archaeologies of Art: Time, Place and Identity*, edited by Ines Domingo, Danae Fiore, and Sally K. May, pp. 131-170. Left Coast, Walnut Creek.

Sahagún, Fr. Bernardino de. 1981. *Florentine Codex: General History of the Things of New Spain*, Book 2. Translated by Arthur J. O. Anderson and Charles E. Dibble. Monographs of the School of American Research 14 (III). School of American Research, Santa Fe.

Seler, Eduard. 1963. *Commentarios al códice Borgia*, vol. 1. Fondo de Cultural Económica, Mexico City.

Smyth, Michael. 2000. A New Study of the Gruta de Chac, Yucatán, México. Report submitted to the Foundation for the Advancement of Mesoamerican Studies, Inc. Online: www.famsi.org/reports/97011.

Sosa, John R. 1989. Cosmological, Symbolic and Cultural Complexity among the Contemporary Maya of Yucatan. In *World Archaeoastronomy*, edited by Anthony F. Aveni, pp. 130-142. Cambridge University, Cambridge.

Stone, Andrea J. 1989. Painted Walls of Xibalba: Maya Cave Painting as Evidence of Cave Ritual. In Hanks and Rice 1989:319-335.

— 1995. *Images from the Underworld: Naj Tunich and the Tradition of Maya Cave Painting*. University of Texas, Austin.

— 1999. Architectural Innovation in the Temple of the Warriors at Chichen Itza. In *Mesoamerican Architecture as a Cultural Symbol*, edited by Jeff K. Kowalski, pp. 289-319. Oxford University, New York.

Taube, Karl. 1988. *The Ancient Yucatec New Year Festival: The Liminal Period in Maya Ritual and Cosmology*. Ph.D. dissertation, Department of Anthropology, Yale University. University Microfilms, Ann Arbor.

— 1992. *The Major Gods of Ancient Yucatan*. Studies in Pre-Columbian Art and Archaeology 32. Dumbarton Oaks, Washington, D.C.

Thompson, J. Eric S. 1970. *Maya History and Religion*. University of Oklahoma, Norman.

— 1975. Introduction to the Reprint Edition. In *The Hill Caves of Yucatan* by Henry C. Mercer, pp. vii-xliv. 2nd edn. Zephyrus and University of Oklahoma, Teaneck and Norman.

Townsend, Richard F. 1991. The Mt. Tlaloc Project. In *To Change Place: Aztec Ceremonial Landscapes*, edited by David Carrasco, pp. 26-30. University Press of Colorado, Niwot.

Tozzer, Alfred M. 1941. *Landa's Relación de las cosas de Yucatan*. Papers of the Peabody Museum of American Archaeology and Anthropology 18. Harvard University, Cambridge, Mass.

Vail, Gabrielle. 2008. El tema del sacrificio en el arte y los textos mayas del Posclásico Tardío. *Temas Antropológicos* 30(2):5-31.

Vail, Gabrielle, and Anthony F. Aveni. 2004. Research Methodologies and New Approaches to Interpreting the Madrid Codex. In *The Madrid Codex: New Approaches to Understanding an Ancient Maya Manuscript*, edited by Gabrielle Vail and Anthony F. Aveni, pp. 1-30. University Press of Colorado, Boulder.

Vail, Gabrielle, and Christine Hernández. 2002–2010. *The Maya Codices Database, Version 3.0*. Online website and database, www.mayacodices.org.

— 2009. Cords and Crocodilians: Creation Mythology in Late Postclassic Maya Iconography and Texts. In *The Maya and their Sacred Narratives: Text and Context in Maya Mythologies*, edited by Geneviève Le Fort, Raphaël Gardiol, Sebastian Matteo, and Christophe Helmke, pp. 89-107. Acta Mesoamericana 20. Anton Saurwein, Markt Schwaben.

— (editors) 2010. *Astronomers, Scribes, and Priests: Intellectual Interchange between the Northern Maya Lowlands and Highland Mexico during the Late Postclassic Period*. Dumbarton Oaks, Washington, D.C.

— n.d. The Role of Caves and Cenotes in Late Postclassic Maya Ritual and Worldview. Submitted for publication in *Acta Americana*.

Vail, Gabrielle, and Andrea Stone. 2002. Representations of Women in Postclassic and Colonial Maya Literature and Art. In Ardren 2002:203-228.

Vogt, Evon Z., and Stuart David. 2005. Some Notes on Ritual Caves among the Ancient and Modern Maya. In *In the Maw of the Earth Monster*, edited by James E. Brady and Keith M. Prufer, pp. 155-185. University of Texas, Austin.

12 Poor Mayapan

Clifford T. Brown, April A. Watson, Ashley Gravlin-Beman, and Larry S. Liebovitch

Abstract

The material culture of Mayapan (ca. A.D. 1250–1400), the last great capital city of the northern Maya lowlands, has often been described as "decadent." Such descriptions, however, are highly subjective. In this chapter, we consider poverty and wealth at Mayapan from a perspective based in modern economics. We find that, as in modern societies, wealth (as measured by house size) at Mayapan fits a Pareto distribution. Nevertheless, compared to two Classic-period sites in Mexico—Palenque and Sayil—the distribution of wealth was more equal at Mayapan, suggesting that economic inequality was less extreme at the Postclassic city. One cause for the decadent material culture of Mayapan, therefore, was that the city was impoverished when compared to its Classic predecessors.

In this essay we analyze the magnitude and distribution of wealth at Mayapan and explore the implications of our findings for the general interpretation of the economy, society, and culture of that city. Mayapan, Yucatan, Mexico, is the largest and most important Maya archaeological site dating to the Late Postclassic period, and therefore inspires a lot of curiosity among archaeologists. Their interest is piqued because, founded by the legendary Kukulcan, Mayapan was the political capital of the largest and most powerful Maya state of its period. Because of its size and power, Mayapan also served as the social and cultural capital of the northern lowlands at the same time. Because it was a late prehistoric site, Mayapan was discussed in many historical chronicles from the early colonial period, and so we possess unusually detailed information about it. As an archaeological site, Mayapan is exceptionally well preserved, and it has been excavated more extensively than most sites; as a result, we have an unusually large body of data from it. For all these reasons, Mayapan plays a central role in the scholarship of the Late Postclassic period. We ought, therefore, to understand Mayapan society rather well, but this does not seem to be true.

We pay a price for our ignorance. Mayapan culture is a vital link between the historic period and the Classic period (A.D. 250–900). If we cannot understand Mayapan society—given the bright, historical portraits we have of Hunac Ceel (Chapter 10), of the Xiu and the Cocom, the Chel and the Canul—what can we claim about our comprehension of the Maya of the Classic period?

POOR MAYAPAN 307

Figure 12.1. Detail from map of Mayapan
(redrawn and edited from revised map in Pollock et al. 1962).

Views of Mayapan

Our understanding of Mayapan has evolved over the decades, influenced inevitably by both intellectual trends in archaeological theory—which are in turn molded by their social and cultural milieus—and also by the growing body of archaeological data produced by archaeological investigations. Over the past few decades, our views of Mayapan have changed significantly (Aldana 2003; Aveni et al. 2004; Brown 1999, 2005, 2006; Brown and Witschey 2003; Milbrath and Peraza Lope 2003; Peraza Lope et al. 2006; Pugh 2001, 2003; Rathje 1975; Russell and Dahlin 2007). Here, we limit our discussion to two of the most prevalent perspectives: the traditional view that Mayapan was "decadent" and the newer idea that the economy of the polity used cost-control measures to develop efficiencies.

Late Postclassic Decadence

In the middle decades of the twentieth century, Mayapan and its regional culture were considered decadent by archaeologists. Even as late as 1984 (Freidel and Sabloff 1984), archaeologists continued to call the Late Postclassic the "Decadent" period. This view arose for at least three reasons. First, as expressed by the most influential Mayanist of the pre-War years, "the archaeological importance of Mayapan…appeared to be far less than its political preeminence in the thirteenth, fourteenth, and fifteenth centuries…would have demanded" (Morley 1938:141). In other words, Morley thought the ruins *called* Mayapan seemed too small to really be *the* Mayapan of chronicles and histories. Morley revised his opinion, however, after Ralph T. Patton conducted a preliminary survey of the site in 1938, partly at his own expense, but under the auspices of the Carnegie Institution (Figure 12.1).

Patton's survey followed the great wall in its circuit around the site and also included the ceremonial center. He traced the course of the great wall and briefly described its construction. He showed that the masonry consists of large irregular blocks laid without mortar. It measures about nine kilometers in circumference, is three to four meters thick, and stands about two meters high when viewed from the exterior. Patton identified the parapet along the outer edge, the interior stairways, and nine of the portals or entryways. The survey of the ceremonial center revealed large colonnades and four round structures, both rare forms of architecture in the Maya canon. Patton also located a number of stelae with short-count dates (Morley 1938:142). It is apparent from other evidence that Patton located and mapped the main *sacbe* at the site and the large residential groups associated with it. Thus, a modified perspective on the city emerged:

> although Mayapan reached a position of first importance only at the close of Maya history when architectural decadence was well under way, its size satisfactorily agrees with the political preeminence ascribed to it by both the native and the Spanish chroniclers (Morley 1938:142).

Another reason why earlier archaeologists considered Mayapan culture to be decadent was that the art, architecture, and material culture displayed strong influences from central Mexico, from the widespread International art style (also called "Mixteca-Puebla"). This is not surprising given: (1) the broad geographical distribution of the International style during this period; and (2) the presence of Aztec mercenaries brought to Mayapan from Tabasco by the Cocom rulers. The International style is manifest particularly in the mural paintings, whereas more generic central Mexican influence can be seen in the extensive use of columns, beam-and-mortar roofs, the frequency of round temples and serpent temples, the presence of double temples, the use of arrowheads, the famous Chen Mul effigy incense-burners depicting Mexican gods (Taube 1992; Thompson 1957), and many other attributes.

To call Mayapan decadent, therefore, is to call the International style and central Mexican culture decadent. This reflects a prejudice that judged the culture of the Maya to be superior to that of their central Mexican counterparts. This chauvinism was particularly pronounced among North Americans who saw Maya writing, astronomy, and mathematics as evidence of cultural superiority (Proskouriakoff 1955; Thompson 1966). They contrasted the supposedly peaceful Maya with the sanguinary and militaristic Aztecs and found the latter lacking (Pollock et al. 1962; Thompson 1966). Archaeologists extended this view to art and architecture too, calling Classic Maya art a high art style and thereby denigrating the other Mesoamerican aesthetic traditions by comparison. Obviously, these kinds of aesthetic judgments are by their very nature subjective.

The third reason why Mayapan culture was considered to be decadent was the apparent low quality of the material culture, which seems shabby and impermanent. We think of this as "expedient" architecture, by analogy to expedient stone tools, which are casually made by the most convenient and cost-effective method. Mayapan masonry, for example, is poor when compared to that of Chichen Itza or the Puuc sites (Smith 1962). Stones are rarely squared, and many of those that are dressed—particularly in the ceremonial center—appear to have been scavenged from earlier Puuc-style sites. Not only is the masonry at Mayapan generally made of rough stones, but also it is poorly mortared. The bonding in Classic buildings can be irregular but is, typically, better than that of the Mayapan-style constructions. The Puuc-style masonry that immediately precedes Mayapan-style masonry in the northern lowlands does not usually have true bonding because the veneer masonry is not load bearing. As a result of the low-quality masonry, Mayapan-style architecture is uneven and irregular and was therefore commonly covered with thick layers of stucco. Mayapan-style buildings also collapsed faster than those built in earlier styles. Even the dry-laid stone houselot walls (*albarradas*) at Mayapan were built using less labor-intensive techniques than in earlier times (Brown 1999:126-127).

Mayapan ceramics are equally expedient in that they are coarse, soft, and friable compared to most Late and Terminal Classic pottery. One can characterize the lithic assemblage as dominated by expedient tools (Brown 1999:450-451, 455-456). Formal tools are rare, particularly in residential areas. Thus, the view of Mayapan as decadent was in part a reflection of the perceived quality of many aspects of the material culture.

Efficiency and Economy

William Rathje (1975) provided an alternative economic explanation for the expediency of Mayapan culture. In this work, "The Last Tango at Mayapán," Rathje applied General Systems Theory to the economic system of Late Postclassic Period Maya society. The kind of systems theory he employed is now outdated, but it earned him a few paragraphs in the history of archaeological theory (Trigger 1989:324-325). In contrast to the transience of systems theory, his economic reinterpretation of Mayapan culture successfully displaced the traditional decadent view.

Rejecting the frankly prejudiced view that Mayapan represented a decadent culture in decline, he argued that the expedient quality of Late Postclassic material culture was a consequence of greater efficiencies that evolved in the context of a rapidly expanding mercantile trading system.

> In the Classic/Postclassic transition, the role of material culture seems to have changed in relation to population integration. Over a period of time, the cost-control trajectory is proposed to have led to lower production costs per item and greater resource dispersion over social and geographical space. By the Postclassic, these trends in material culture production-distribution may have fostered interdependence among populations through an expanding social and economic (rather than ideological) order..., while at the same time they produced variety in response to local information-processing and -deciding needs... Thus, while Classic populations were to a large extent integrated through the costly maintenance of an elite minority, Postclassic populations were most probably integrated through a rising standard of living locked into large scale population participation in a commerce which emphasized economic efficiency and mass consumption (Rathje 1975:435-436).

Rathje's (1975) article remains a landmark because it successfully shifted the terms of the debate about Late Postclassic culture from the frankly subjective and poorly defined discussion of decadence to the economic arena where it belongs—at least in part. This was a major change that has had a far-reaching influence on the study of the Maya Postclassic.

An Alternative Perspective on Mayapan: Poverty and the Distribution of Wealth

Unpersuaded that the shoddy material culture of Mayapan is the inevitable result of a universal systems trajectory, we decided to explore a more specific historical explanation that nonetheless carries broad implications. Calling the material culture of Mayapan "expedient" is merely a polite, technical way of saying that it was *cheap*. We think that the expedient quality of the artifacts and architecture of Mayapan reflect an inability to purchase expensive items, and therefore indicate that poverty was widespread. Our position, therefore, contrasts with Rathje's view of a "rising standard of living" during the Late Postclassic.

The issues of poverty and inequality are interrelated. For example, in the modern world much poverty is not the result of an overall absence of wealth or resources but rather of their extremely unequal distribution within society. Poverty and inequality are large topics in many fields, such as sociology, economics, anthropology, and development. Poverty can be difficult to define, is not exclusively economic, and any definition should include cultural and psychological factors. We are concerned with both total wealth and its distribution because the lack of the first and great inequality in the second can produce widespread poverty.

In the large literature on these topics, we find many measures of poverty and inequality (Cowell 2000). Each provides a different summary of the characteristics of the phenomenon. We have chosen three approaches to the study of the distribution of wealth: (1) fitting Pareto and exponential distributions to our empirical data; (2) calculating Gini coefficients; and (3) using absolute measures of wealth that contrast with the first two approaches, which both measure relative distributions. We describe these below.

Pareto and Exponential Distributions

Wealth and income are most often modeled as following a type of power-law called the Pareto distribution, named after a sociologist who first applied it in his study of income (Pareto 1897, 1971). Pareto recognized that income was not distributed in society in accordance with a "bell curve" or normal distribution. If it were, then there would be a few rich, a few poor, and a large number of middle class citizens. In modern economies, there are only a very few truly rich people, and ever-increasing numbers of people in ever-lower income classes. The poor actually outnumber the middle class, even in the United States where almost everyone likes to define themselves as middle class.

Pareto observed that the distribution of income forms a power-law. Simple power-law distributions take the form

$$y = kx^{-c}$$

where y is the probability of observing a particular value of x, k is constant, x is the variable (income or wealth in our case), and c is a parameter defining the distribution. Power-law distributions are extremely skewed—most of the data cluster with low values of x—and they have a long right tail, meaning a few extreme outliers with very high values of x—the superrich. This skew means that income and wealth are distributed very unequally. Economists have studied why this should be and particularly why the statistical distributions of wealth and income take the form they do (e.g., Champernowne 1953; Davies and Shorrocks 2000; Mandelbrot 1960, 1961; Sargan 1957; Stiglitz 1969; Yakovenko and Silva 2005).

Recent studies, however, show that modern distributions of wealth and income may not all be strict power laws, but rather form more complex curves. For example, Drăgulscu and Yakovenko (2001) show that although the right tail of the income and wealth curves in the United States and Britain do match power laws, the portion of the curve with low incomes is actually best modeled as an exponential distribution or perhaps even as a lognormal distribution (e.g., Clementi and Gallegati 2005). Exponential distributions are also skewed, but much less so than power laws, so that a society with an exponential distribution of wealth is somewhat more egalitarian than one with a power law distribution. The consensus is that the wealth (and income) of the rich is distributed as a power law, but the functional form of the lower end of the curve may be more ambiguous (Davies and Shorrocks 2000).

In our study of Mayapan and other sites, presented here, we evaluated the functional form of empirical wealth distributions by using the multihistogram method developed by Liebovitch. This method is particularly effective in determining the precise form of skew functions (power-laws, exponentials, etc.) and also in estimating their parameters (Brown and Liebovitch 2010:26-39).

Gini Coefficient

The Gini coefficient is the index most widely used to describe the degree of inequality in the distribution of resources, most often wealth or income. The Gini coefficient describes how much the cumulative distribution of wealth in a population diverges from a distribution in which everyone possesses equal wealth. The index varies from 0 to 1 (or 0 to 100 as used throughout this chapter), with low values indicating a more equal distribution of wealth and high values reflecting a more unequal distribution. The Gini coefficient can be estimated from empirical data in various ways. We use the formula:

$$G = \frac{\sum_{i=1}^{n}(2i-n-1)x'_i}{n^2\mu}$$

where i is the rank order of an individual, n is the number of total individuals, x'_i is the variable value of the individual, and μ is the population average (Damgaard and Weiner 2000:1139).

Absolute Measures of Wealth

By "absolute measures," we mean the use of descriptive statistics such as the arithmetic mean, median, mode, and sum of wealth for a particular population. Such measures contrast with those described above, which characterize the distribution rather than the magnitude of wealth.

Measurements of Wealth and Inequality in Archaeology and Anthropology

The differences between these three measures of wealth and its distribution are significant. The purpose of studying the type of distribution—Pareto, exponential, or otherwise—is to determine the generic form of the function that describes the overall patterning of the data. This can give us insight into the process that produced the phenomenon. For example, exponential, Poisson, and normal distributions are all produced by simple random processes. In contrast, Pareto distributions are typically generated by complex processes that spontaneously self-organize to produce power law distributions. For example, preferential attachment models (Barabasí and Albert 1999), which in our case would translate to a "rich get richer" process, produce power law distributions. On the other hand, if the probability of an individual being rich or getting richer were a simple random function, then a power-law distribution of wealth would not emerge. Thus, the functional form of the distribution helps us infer how it emerged.

Despite its utility and potential, this approach has not seen much use in archaeology. The only study of the Pareto distribution in prehistory we are aware of is Abul-Magd's (2002) analysis of house sizes at Akhetaten, the New Kingdom capital established by the Pharaoh Akhenaten at what is today Tell el-Amarna. Using data from Kemp (1989), Abul-Magd examined the distribution of house sizes and found a Pareto distribution. Taking house size as a proxy for household wealth, he concluded that the distribution of wealth was similar to that in modern societies. The functional forms of many other archaeological data sets could be profitably studied.

The Gini coefficient has been used in archaeology, which is not surprising given its ubiquity in economics. The advantage of the Gini coefficient is that it simply summarizes the total deviation from equality. But its simplicity and generality may obscure the pattern or structure of that deviation. Therefore, the same Gini coefficient can be derived from substantially different distributions of wealth. For this reason, detailed investigation of inequality usually requires multiple methods.

Anthropologists have used the Gini coefficient to study inequality in different types of societies, with interesting results. Among a sample of hunter-gatherer societies, the distribution of material wealth yields modest Gini coefficients, ranging from less than 10 to above 40, with a mean of 25 (Smith et al. 2010). These relatively low values imply a relatively equitable distribution of wealth. Horticulturalists have a similar range, with Gini coefficients running from near 0 to about 60, with a mean of 26.5 (Gurven et al. 2010). In contrast, both pastoralists and agriculturalists have markedly higher Gini coefficients. For pastoralists, the figures run from 20 to 69 (the mean is 42), a range almost identical to that of modern nations (Borgerhoff Mulder et al. 2010). The inequality in material wealth of a sample of agricultural societies produces the highest Gini coefficients, which vary from 45 to 70.8 with a mean of 57 (Shenk et al. 2010). Economic historians have also reported Gini coefficients for a number of societies around the world, from China to Latin America (Milanovic et al. 2007). The range of coefficients and their means are strikingly close to their modern analogs.

Several archaeologists have also employed Gini coefficients to summarize wealth distributions inferred from archaeological data. Randall McGuire (1983; estimates amended in

McGuire 2001) calculated Gini coefficients using structure sizes as a proxy for Paquime (Casas Grandes) and several Hohokam sites. He found a range of values that span most of the modern spectrum and discussed how they changed over time. He has also used the Gini index to estimate inequality in grave lots (McGuire 2001). Morris (1987:141-143) also used grave lots to estimate inequality using the Gini coefficient, in his case for pre-Classic Greek interments from Athens. Schulting (1995) has used the Gini coefficient to examine inequality in house sizes, and by implication wealth or status, from several sites in the interior of British Columbia. Ames (2008) has discussed the use of the Gini index in archaeology to study social ranking and stratification.

In sum, economists and anthropologists have used these measures to study and evaluate inequality in a variety of (mostly) contemporary societies, while archaeologists have employed both house sizes and burial furniture as proxies to measure inequality.

Measuring the Distribution of Wealth at Maya Sites

In archaeology, we often try to measure or evaluate social phenomena that are difficult to detect directly. Fortunately, wealth is different. Three sources of data—residential architecture, household goods, and burial practices—are commonly used by archaeologists to study wealth and stratification. In this chapter, we consider the size of residential architecture as a proxy variable for wealth because architecture "is probably the strongest and most consistent expression of wealth levels in agrarian states... Such societies exhibit a great range of variation in the size and quality of housing, and these factors related directly to the level of a household's access to goods and services..." (Smith 1987:301). We chose residential architecture as a measure of wealth because houses are common. We can estimate the sizes of many houses because we have extensive and accurate maps of Maya sites. In contrast, we have reliable samples of household artifacts for only the tiny proportion of households that have been excavated. Excavated burials also form a much smaller and biased data set. Thus, house sizes comprise the best set of data for studying the distribution of wealth. Ideally, we would develop a careful estimate of the labor investment represented by each residential building (Abrams 1994), but that would be difficult because of a lack of existing data, and so instead we have collected data on house sizes from published maps and tables.

We evaluate the distributions of house sizes for three Maya sites: Mayapan, Palenque, and Sayil. We expected that we would find: (1) that Mayapan was poorer than Palenque and Sayil; and (2) that the distribution of wealth at Mayapan was more unequal than at the other sites. The second expectation may seem contradictory, but there often is a correlation between absolute poverty and the unequal distribution of wealth. In the modern world, countries with high Gini indices (e.g., Namibia, Botswana, Haiti, Angola, Columbia, and Bolivia) also exhibit extreme, chronic, and institutionalized poverty (Central Intelligence Agency 2011; United Nations Development Programme 2009).

Mayapan

There are more than 4,000 structures within the great wall at Mayapan. Most are residential in function. We know this because the archaeologists of the Carnegie Institution of Washington identified and defined the "Mayapan house type" (Ruppert and Smith 1952, 1957; Smith 1962:217), and noted that it resembled in detail the typical house described by Landa (Tozzer 1941:180). The dwellings are rectangular, wider than they are deep, and usually rest upon a platform or substructure (Figure 12.2). In the wide, open front of the house are two or more low benches with one or more passages leading between them to the back room of the house. The long, narrow back room usually runs the full width of the building, although in some cases there is evidence of a transverse wall subdividing the room into two segments. Occasionally, the back room is a bit lower than the front room, requiring a step down into what Landa said were sleeping quarters (Tozzer 1941: 85-86). Sometimes small altars were constructed against the back wall of the rear room on the central axis of the building. There is much variation in the floor plans of dwellings, but many conform in detail to these specifications. At Mayapan, the functions of dwellings are securely supported by direct ethnohistorical evidence (Smith 1962:217). The ascription of residential function to these buildings can, therefore, be made with a level of confidence unmatched at many Classic-period sites, where "the principle of abundance" (Thompson 1892) and the presence of grinding stones and utilitarian ceramics are often used to infer structure function.

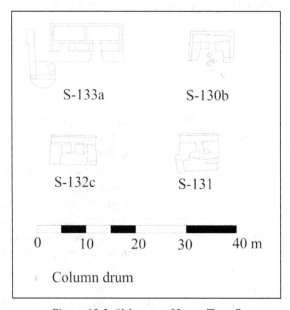

Figure 12.2. "Mayapan House Type."

We selected a random sample of residences from the map of Mayapan and measured their areas. New field measurements might have been preferable, but recent field projects have generally found the Carnegie map to be quite accurate and complete (Brown 1999). Karl Ruppert and A. Ledyard Smith apparently made scale drawings of nearly all the structures on the Carnegie map (Smith 1962:172), but these drawings, which would be of great value, have been lost. To take the random sample, we first tabulated all of the structure numbers. We found a few structures on the map that were not numbered, and we numbered them ourselves using the Carnegie system. We used a random number generator to select our sample, and then we measured the areas of the structures using calipers on an original copy of the map. Finally, we excluded structures that did not appear to be residential. Among these are buildings that are considered to be temples, altars, *oratorios*, kitchens, terraces, and other special constructions. We also excluded structures measuring less than 20 square meters in area as non-residential. This size has been proposed as part of the definition of the "minimum residential unit" in the

Maya lowlands (Ashmore 1981:47), and its applicability to the residential architecture of Mayapan seems clear. The remaining 1,214 structures in our sample all appear to be residential.

Palenque

We wished to compare the distribution of wealth at Mayapan to that from a Classic-period site, and we chose Palenque, Chiapas, because of the availability of Edwin Barnhart's (2001) superb map and accompanying data (Figure 12.3). We extracted the dimensions of all the structures listed in Appendix A of that work, and then excluded those structures that appeared to be non-residential by taking into account his descriptions and comments in the text and their appearance on the map. Because the structures at Palenque often lack obvious surface features, such as the walls, benches, and columns that are so common at Mayapan, it was often difficult to distinguish residences from other types of buildings. The lack of surface features is probably partly attributable to the high rate of colluviation at the site, which has partially buried many of the structures. Again, we excluded structures smaller than 20 square meters in area from consideration. Our final sample consists of 1,135 structures.

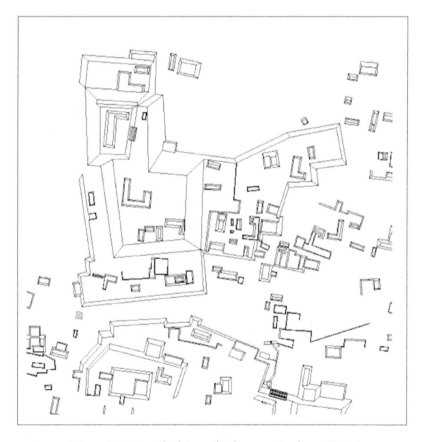

Figure 12.3. Detail of map of Palenque (Barnhart 2001).

Sayil

Sayil is a major Puuc site in the hill country of southern Yucatan that dates to the Late and Terminal Classic periods. The site was partially mapped by Jeremy Sabloff and Gair Tourtellot (1991). To obtain our data on residence sizes, we used their map and the electronic database included on the disc distributed with the publication (Figure 12.4). We reviewed the data, which includes the inferred function of the mapped structures. As at the other sites, we excluded structures smaller than 20 square meters in area. Our sample size for Sayil is 767 domestic structures.

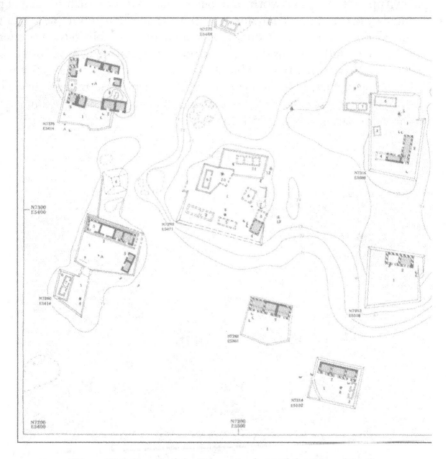

Figure 12.4. Detail of the Demetrio sheet of the map of Sayil (Sabloff and Tourtellot 1991).

Results

For each of our three data sets we: (1) calculated descriptive statistics; (2) studied the functional form of the distribution, paying particular attention to its right tail; (3) calculated the characteristic parameter of the distribution; and (4) calculated the Gini coefficient. We review the results below.

Mayapan

The distribution of residential structure sizes at Mayapan clearly shows a power-law or Pareto distribution. On a double logarithmic plot, a power-law is a straight line (Figure 12.5a). The exponent of the power law, which is the essential parameter of the distribution, is 3.02. The Gini coefficient is approximately 32, which is modest and indicates a rather low level of inequality in the distribution of wealth. This value is comparable to those of the European Union and some underdeveloped nations such as Mongolia (Central Intelligence Agency 2011). Descriptive statistics for the Mayapan sample are shown in Table 12.1. The median house size of about 48 square meters is close to Jones' (1952) estimate of the average size of the houses at Mayapan, (50 square meters), and it is even closer to the mean size (46.7 square-meters) of the 40 houses mapped by Brown (1999:131). The range (573) is, as we will see, modest compared to that at the other sites. The skew is high, as is expected for this kind of distribution.

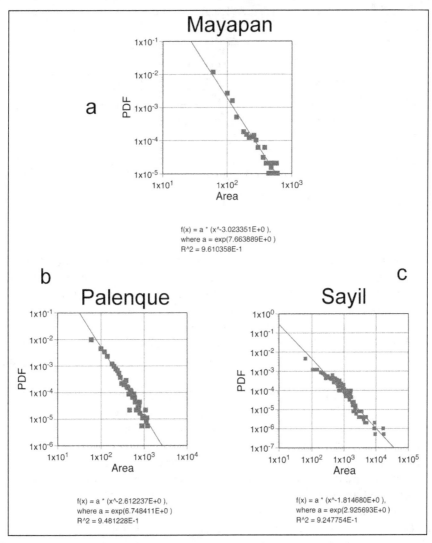

Figure 12.5. Pareto distribution of house sizes at: (a) Mayapan; (b) Palenque; and (c) Sayil.

Palenque

The Palenque data reveal a distribution similar in functional form to that of Mayapan and modern examples (Figure 12.5b). The distribution is a power law with an exponent of approximately 2.61. The Gini coefficient for this data set is approximately 44, which indicates greater inequality than we saw at Mayapan and on par with the United States in 2007 (Central Intelligence Agency 2011). The descriptive statistics for the Palenque house sizes are summarized in Table 12.1. The median house size, 70 square-meters, is much larger than at Mayapan by almost 47 percent. The range at Palenque is also larger, by 93 percent, all of which represents an increase in the top brackets because in both cases the lower end of the distribution began at 20 square-meters.

Table 12.1. Descriptive statistics for houses at Mayapan, Palenque, and Sayil.

House Area (m^2)	Mayapan	Palenque	Sayil
Mean	57	104	291
Standard Error	1	3	28
Median	48	70	65
Mode	38	60	20
Standard Deviation	45	113	777
Sample Variance	2030	12850	604305
Kurtosis	40	22	207
Skew	5.0	4.0	12.1
Range	573	1108	15377
Minimum	20	20	20
Maximum	593	1128	15397
Sum	69070	118090	223234
Count	1214	1135	767

Sayil

As at the other two sites, the distribution of house sizes, and presumably wealth, is a power-law (Figure 12.5c). In this case, the exponent is 1.81, lower than either Mayapan or Palenque. The Gini coefficient for the same data set is 71, much higher than at either of the other sites and comparable in the modern world only with Namibia (Central Intelligence Agency 2011). The descriptive statistics are presented in Table 12.1. At Sayil, the median house size is 65 square meters, slightly lower than at Palenque and significantly higher than at Mayapan. The range in sizes is far greater than even at Palenque, exceeding that of Mayapan by an order of magnitude.

Distribution of Wealth and Poverty at Mayapan, Palenque, and Sayil

First and most fundamentally, it is very interesting that the house sizes at all three sites are distributed approximately as power laws. If we use these dwelling sizes as a proxy for wealth, then all the sites exhibit distributions of wealth that are mathematically similar to those from modern societies; that is, they are modeled by the Pareto distribution. The exponents of the power laws decrease dramatically from Mayapan to Palenque to Sayil, indicating progressively greater inequality The Gini coefficients are in agreement with the power law exponents. The coefficients indicate that the distribution of wealth was more equal at Mayapan, less so at Palenque, and extremely unequal at Sayil. Nevertheless, Mayapan was clearly the poorest site. The descriptive statistics show that houses at Mayapan were smaller with a much lower median area. The difference is statistically significant. Comparing the house sizes at Mayapan and Palenque using a Mann-Whitney U test yields a probability value that is extremely small, meaning that the difference between medians of the two data sets is highly significant and not due to chance alone. In addition, given the more expedient masonry, lower substructure platforms, and other architectural features, the Mayapan houses probably represent a lower investment of labor per square meter than those at Palenque. The same is true when comparing the Mayapan houses to those at Sayil. Therefore, we conclude that poverty was more severe at Mayapan, which helps explain the expedient nature of the material culture there.

It is reasonable to ask if factors other than wealth might account for the differing house sizes at these sites. They are, after all, found in different environments. Mayapan is a fortress city whose battlements look out on a hot, dry plain. Palenque occupies a narrow mountain shelf that overlooks the alluvial plains of Tabasco in one of the wettest parts of the Maya lowlands. Sayil fills the center of a valley in the low karst hills of the Puuc region, an area much drier than Palenque but a little wetter than Mayapan. The architecture, engineering, and masonry of the buildings at all three sites also differ, but those differences do not seem to correlate well with environmental or topographical variables. For example, settlement within the great wall at Mayapan is much denser than at most Classic-period sites, but in fact the area within the wall is not filled. The northern half of the site and especially the northeast corner are sparsely settled. It therefore seems unlikely that lack of space within the defenses drove people to build smaller houses.

Mayapan, with its Mediterranean climate, is friendly to outdoor activities. Palenque, in contrast, with all its rain, may have demanded more roofed area in households. Roofing, whether vaulted or thatched, is expensive, and the houses of Palenque *should be* smaller in area as a result. They are also densely packed, filling the mountain bench where the site is located. Nevertheless, the median house size at Palenque is the largest of all three sites. Sayil, although circumscribed by hills, does not fill its valley. It seems unlikely that house sizes there were inhibited by the topography or climate. Therefore, we believe that the variation in house sizes that we have documented is attributable primarily to economic and cultural forces, rather than to differences in geography and weather patterns.

Conclusion

The discovery of Pareto distributions of wealth at ancient Maya cities is significant. The Pareto distributions are important because they share a generic form, a particular type of mathematical function called a power law, which describes a surprising number of phenomena. Pareto distributions of wealth have been documented in modern nations around the world for over a century, in ancient Egypt (Abul-Magd 2002), and now in both Classic and Postclassic Maya cities. Although their changing parameters are historically interesting in the Maya case, what is arguably more important is their widespread presence in remarkably different societies. The economies of these diverse societies could not possibly be very similar. Therefore, the distribution of wealth has a certain general pattern despite significant differences in underlying economic systems. In physics, categories of dynamic systems that exhibit generic behavior despite differences in their details are called "universality classes," and their universality is often described by power-law relations (Kadanoff 1971; see Deift [2007] for a broader definition). The most plausible explanation for the existence of Pareto distributions of wealth in ancient Maya society is that the dynamics of the economies of complex societies must share certain fundamental properties despite their many differences.

The fact that ancient and modern economies share important characteristics does not mean that the formalist, neoclassical model of economics is true and that the substantivists are wrong. It says nothing, for example, about the ubiquity of rational or maximizing economic behavior. In fact, take it to be self-evident that each economy is embedded in its culture. But this does not mean that specific kinds of economies cannot share significant traits. As Stuart Plattner remarked, "*All* generalizations across different societies cannot be invalid" (1989:13, emphasis in original). Our finding is only one of a number of structural similarities that have been detected between ancient state economies and modern capitalist ones. These discoveries do, however, contradict the primitivist belief that ancient economies are categorically and inevitably different from modern ones (Smith 2004:74-76). Our task now is to identify the specific dynamic processes of economies that generate Pareto distributions of wealth in ancient societies. This will be more difficult than it may sound because economists do not agree on the causes of Pareto distributions.

In recent years, econophysicists have explained Pareto distributions of wealth primarily in terms of exchange processes (e.g., Bagrow et al. 2008; Ispolatov et al. 1998), although factors such as inheritance are also relevant (Smith et al. 2010; Stiglitz 1969). One of the best-known dynamic models is Bouchaud and Mézard's (2000) model of wealth condensation, which predicts that exchange tends to reduce inequality. An agent-based archaeological version of this model has been elaborated by Bentley et al. (2005), who found the same effect. Initially trade produces extreme inequalities in wealth in the form of a power-law distribution, but beyond a certain threshold, further increases in trade tend to reduce inequality. The pattern documented in the present study matches that evolutionary pattern. The intensive trade of the Late Postclassic period may have induced greater equality at Mayapan than that seen at the earlier Classic-period sites.

A different theory for the development of Pareto distributions of wealth has been proffered by Manus Midlarsky, a well-known political scientist. In his book *The Evolution of Inequality* (1999), he argues that the scarcity of land in agricultural societies can lead, by several mechanisms, to a Pareto distribution of wealth. This argument is relevant to our case because Midlarsky (1999:49) asserts that: (1) growing populations increase the scarcity of a finite resource such as land, thus creating greater inequality; and (2) population loss can have an ameliorating effect on inequality. This was the case in the Maya lowlands. Numerous archaeological surveys (e.g., Culbert and Rice 1990) have shown that during the Late Classic period, populations—including those in rural areas—reached peak densities that were surprisingly high and probably unsustainable. The succeeding catastrophic decline in population is called the "Classic Maya Collapse."

In the Puuc region, where Sayil is located, maximum population density was reached during the Terminal Classic period (Dunning 1992). In the Mayapan region of central Yucatan, we have surprisingly few data concerning the distribution of Late Postclassic population outside of the city itself. What information we have, however, indicates that people were scattered in small, nucleated rural settlements, and that the total population was much less and lower in density than during the Late Classic period (Brown et al. 2006). In fact, we argue that population density in the Mayapan region was much lower during the Late Postclassic period than in the Puuc during the Terminal Classic period or in the Palenque region during the Late Classic period. According to Midlarksy's scenario, the decline in population during the Postclassic period could account for the greater equality seen at Mayapan than at earlier Classic-period Palenque and Sayil.

The research reported in this chapter can be expanded. The distribution of wealth at other sites can be explored. The use of labor investment for the construction of houses would be an improvement over the use of house size. It is not difficult to estimate labor investment, but collecting the necessary data in the field would itself be labor intensive. One could also use household goods and grave lots to produce an alternative estimate of wealth. We are particularly interested in the evolution of the Pareto distribution of wealth from a different kind of distribution that seems to have reigned in earlier societies, a change that seems to be associated with the transition to state-level society. More generally, we advocate the use of approaches derived from econophysics and complex systems. We find them fruitful, as we hope our chapter illustrates.

References

Abrams, Elliot M. 1994. *How the Maya Built their World: Energetics and Ancient Architecture*. University of Texas, Austin.

Abul-Magd, Adel Y. 2002. Wealth Distribution in an Ancient Egyptian Society. *Physical Review E*, 66: 057104.

Aldana, Gerardo. 2003. K'uk'ulkan at Mayapán: Venus and Postclassic Maya Statecraft. *Journal for the History of Astronomy* 34(114):33-51.

Ames, Kenneth M. 2008. The Archaeology of Rank. In *Handbook of Archaeological Theories*, edited by R. Alexander Bentley, Herbert D. G. Maschner, and Christopher Chippindale, pp. 487-513. Altamira, Lanham.

Ashmore, Wendy. 1981. Some Issues of Method and Theory in Lowland Maya Settlement Archaeology. In *Lowland Maya Settlement Patterns*, edited by Wendy Ashmore, pp. 37-69. University of New Mexico, Albuquerque.

Atkinson, Anthony B., and Francios Bourguignon (editors). 2000. *Handbook of Income Distribution*, vol. 1. Elsevier, Amsterdam.

Aveni, Anthony F., Susan Milbrath, and Carlos Peraza Lope. 2004. Chichén Itzá's Legacy in the Astronomically Oriented Architecture of Mayapán. *RES: Anthropology and Aesthetics* 45:123-143.

Bagrow, James P., Jie Sun, and Daniel ben-Avraham. 2008. Phase Transition in the Rich-Get-Richer Mechanism due to Finite-Size Effects. *Journal of Physics A: Mathematical and Theoretical* 41:1-8.

Barabasí, Albert-Lázló, and Réka Albert. 1999. Emergence of Scaling in Random Networks. *Science* 286: 509-512.

Barnhart, Edwin L. 2001. *The Palenque Mapping Project: Settlement and Urbanism at an Ancient Maya City*. Ph.D. dissertation, Department of Anthropology, University of Texas, Austin. University Microfilms, Ann Arbor.

Bentley, R. Alexander, Mark W. Lake, and Stephen J. Shennan. 2005. Specialisation and Wealth Inequality in a Model of a Clustered Economic Network. *Journal of Archaeological Science* 32:1346-1356.

Borgerhoff Mulder, Monique, Ila Fazzio, William Irons, Richard L. McElreath, Samuel Bowles, Adrian Bell, Tom Hertz, and Leela Hazzah. 2010. Pastoralism and Wealth Inequality. *Current Anthropology* 51:35-48.

Bouchaud, Jean-Philippe, and Marc Mézard. 2000. Wealth Condensation in a Simple Model of Economy. *Physica A, Statistical Mechanics and its Applications* 282:536-545.

Brown, Clifford T. 1999. *Mayapán Society and Ancient Maya Social Organization*. Ph.D. dissertation, Department of Anthropology, Tulane University. University Microfilms, Ann Arbor.

— 2005. Caves, Karst, and Settlement at Mayapán, Yucatán. In *In the Maw of the Earth Monster: Mesoamerican Ritual Cave Use*, edited by James E. Brady and Keith M. Prufer, pp. 373-402. University of Texas, Austin.

— 2006. Water Sources at Mayapán, Yucatán, México. In *Precolumbian Water Management: Ideology, Ritual, and Power*, edited by Lisa Lucero and Barbara Fash, pp. 171-188. University of Arizona, Tucson.

Brown, Clifford T., and Larry S. Liebovitch. 2010. *Fractal Analysis*. Quantitative Applications in the Social Sciences 165. Sage, Thousand Oaks.

Brown, Clifford T., Carlos Peraza Lope, Walter R. T. Witschey, and Rhianna Rogers. 2006. Results of Survey in Central Yucatan. Paper presented at the 71st Annual Meeting of the Society for American Archaeology, San Juan, Puerto Rico.

Brown, Clifford T., and Walter R. T. Witschey. 2003. The Fractal Geometry of Ancient Maya Settlement. *Journal of Archaeological Science* 30:1619-1632.

Central Intelligence Agency. 2011. Distribution of Household Income—Gini Index. C.I.A. World Factbook online edition. Online: https://www.cia.gov/library/publications/the-world-factbook/rankorder/rawdata_2172.text.

Champernowne, David G. 1953. A Model of Income Distribution. *The Economic Journal* 63:318-351.

Chatterjee, Arnad, Sudhakar Yarlagadda, and Bikas K. Chakrabarti (editors). 2005. *Econophysics of Wealth Distributions*. Springer Italia, Milan.

Clementi, Fabio, and Mauro Gallegati. 2005. Pareto's Law of Income Distribution: Evidence for Germany, the United Kingdom, and the United States. In Chatterjee, Yarlagadda, and Chakrabarti 2005:3-14.

Cowell, Frank A. 2000. Measurement of Inequality. In Atkinson and Bourguignon 2000:87-166.

Culbert, T. Patrick, and Don S. Rice (editors). 1990. *Precolumbian Population History in the Maya Lowlands*. University of New Mexico, Albuquerque.

Damgaard, Christian, and Jacob Weiner. 2000. Describing Inequality in Plant Size or Fecundity. *Ecology* 81:1139-1142.

Davies, James B., and Anthony F. Shorrocks. 2000. The Distribution of Wealth. In Atkinson and Bourguignon 2000:605-75.

Deift, Percy. 2007. Universality for Mathematical and Physical Systems. *Proceedings of the International Congress of Mathematicians, Madrid, Spain, 2006*, pp. 125-152. Online: http://www.icm2006.org/proceedings/vol1.html.

Drăgulscu, Adrian, and Victor M. Yakovenko. 2001. Exponential and Power-law Probability Distributions of Wealth and Income in the United Kingdom and United States. *Physica A* 299: 213-221.

Dunning, Nicholas P. 1992. *Lords of the Hills: Ancient Maya Settlement in the Puuc Region, Yucatán, Mexico*. Prehistory Press, Madison.

Freidel, David A., and Jeremy A. Sabloff. 1984. *Cozumal: Late Maya Settlement Patterns*. Academic, Orlando.

Gurven, Michael, Monique Borgerhoff Mulder, Paul L. Hooper, Hillard Kaplan, Robert Quinlan, Rebecca Sear, Eric Schniter, Christopher von Rueden, Samuel Bowles, Tom Hertz, and Adrian Bell. 2010. Domestication Alone Does Not Lead to Inequality. *Current Anthropology* 51:49-64.

Ispolatov, Slava, Paul L. Krapivsky, and Sidney Redner. 1998. Wealth Distributions in Asset Exchange Models. *The European Physical Journal B* 2:267-276.

Jones, Morris. 1952. Map of the Ruins of Mayapan, Yucatan, Mexico. Current Reports 1. Carnegie Institution of Washington, Washington, D.C.

Kadanoff, Leo P. 1971. Critical Behavior. Universality and Scaling. In *Critical Phenomena: Proceedings of the International School of Physics 'Enrico Fermi'*, pp. 100-117. Academic, New York.

Kemp, Barry. 1989. *Ancient Egypt: Anatomy of a Civilisation*. Routledge, London.

Mandelbrot, Benoit B. 1960. The Pareto-Lévy Law and the Distribution of Income. *International Economic Review* 1(2):79-106.

— 1961. Stable Paretian Random Functions and the Multiplicative Variation of Income. *Econometrica* 29:517-543.

McGuire, Randall H. 1983. Breaking Down Cultural Complexity: Inequality and Heterogeneity. *Advances in Archaeological Method and Theory* 6:91-142.

— 2001. Ideologies of Death and Power in the Hohokam Community of La Ciudad. In *Ancient Burial Practice in the American Southwest: Archaeology, Physical Anthropology, and Native American Perspectives*, edited by Douglas R. Mitchell and Judy L. Brunson-Hadley, pp. 27-44. University of New Mexico, Albuquerque.

Midlarsky, Manus I. 1999. *The Evolution of Inequality: War, State Survival, and Democracy in Comparative Perspective*. Stanford University, Stanford.

Milanovic, Branko, Peter H. Lindert, and Jeffrey G. Williamson. 2007. *Measuring Ancient Inequality*. Policy Research Working Paper 4412. The World Bank Development Research Group Poverty Team. Online: http://elibrary.worldbank.org/docserver/download/4412.pdf?expires=1295217620&id=id&accname=guest&checksum=69AED1229C92EA793DF8A571A932AD3.

Milbrath, Susan, and Carlos Peraza Lope. 2003. Revisiting Mayapán: Mexico's Last Maya Capital. *Ancient Mesoamerica* 14:1-46.

Morley, Sylvanus G. 1938. Chichen Itza. In *Year Book* No. 37, pp. 141-143. Carnegie Institution of Washington, Washington, D.C.

Morris, Ian. (1987). *Burial and Ancient Society: The Rise of the Greek City-State*. Cambridge University Press, Cambridge.

Pareto, Vilfredo. 1897. The New Theories of Economics. *The Journal of Political Economy* 5:485-502.

— 1971. *Manual of Political Economy*. Augustus M. Kelley, New York.

Peraza Lope, Carlos, Marilyn A. Masson, Timothy S. Hare, and Pedro Candelario Delgado Kú. 2006. The Chronology of Mayapán: New Radiocarbon Evidence. *Ancient Mesoamerica* 17:153-175.

Pollock, Harry E. D., Ralph Roys, Tatiana Proskouriakoff, and A. L. Smith. (1962). *Mayapan, Yucatan, Mexico*. Carnegie Institution of Washington. Publication 619. Washington, D.C.

Plattner, Stuart. 1989. Introduction. In *Economic Anthropology*, edited by Stuart Plattner, pp. 1-20. Stanford University, Stanford.

Proskouriakoff, Tatiana. 1955. The Death of a Civilization. *Scientific American* 192: 82-88.

Pugh, Timothy W. 2001. Flood Reptiles, Serpent Temples, and the Quadripartite Universe: The Imago Mundi of Late Postclassic Mayapán. *Ancient Mesoamerica* 12:247-258.

— 2003. A Cluster and Spatial Analysis of Ceremonial Architecture at Late Postclassic Mayapán. *Journal of Archaeological Science* 30:941-953.

Rathje, William L. 1975. The Last Tango in Mayapán: A Tentative Trajectory of Production-Distribution Systems. In *Ancient Civilization and Trade*, edited by Jeremy A. Sabloff and Carl C. Lamberg-Karlovsky, pp. 409-448. University of New Mexico, Albuquerque.

Ruppert, Karl, and A. Ledyard Smith. 1952. Excavations in House Mounds at Mayapan. Current Reports 4. Carnegie Institution of Washington, Washington D.C.

— *House Types in the Environs of Mayapan and at Uxmal, Kabah, Sayil, Chichen Itza, and Chacchob*. Current Reports 39. Carnegie Institution of Washington, Washington, D.C.

Russell, Bradley W., and Bruce H. Dahlin. 2007. Traditional Burnt-Lime Production at Mayapán, Mexico. *Journal of Field Archaeology* 32:407-423.

Sabloff, Jeremy A., and Gair Tourtellot. 1991. *The Ancient Maya City of Sayil: The Mapping of a Puuc Region Center*. Publication 60. Middle American Research Institute, Tulane University, New Orleans.

Sargan, John D. 1957. The Distribution of Wealth. *Econometrica* 25:568-590.

Schulting, Rick J. 1995. *Mortuary Variability and Status Differentiation on the Columbia-Fraser Plateau*. Archaeology Press, Simon Fraser University, Burnaby.

Shenk, Mary K., Monique Borgerhoff Mulder, Jan Beise, Gregory Clark, William Irons, Donna Leonetti, Bobbi S. Low, Samuel Bowles, Tom Hertz, Adrian Bell, and Patrizio Piraino. 2010. Intergenerational Wealth Transmission among Agriculturalists. *Current Anthropology* 51:65-83.

Smith, A. Ledyard. 1962. Residential and Associated Structures at Mayapan. In Pollock et al. 1962:165-319.

Smith, Eric Alden, Monique Borgerhoff Mulder, Samuel Bowles, Michael Gurven, Tom Hertz, and Mary K. Shenk. 2010. Production Systems, Inheritance, and Inequality in Premodern Societies. *Current Anthropology* 51:85-94.

Smith, Eric Alden, Kim Hill, Frank W. Marlowe, David Nolin, Polly Wiessner, Michael Gurven, Samuel Bowles, Monique Borgerhoff Mulder, Tom Hertz, and Adrian Bell. 2010. Wealth Transmission and Inequality among Hunter-Gatherers. *Current Anthropology* 51:19-34.

Smith, Michael E. 1987. Household Possessions and Wealth in Agrarian States: Implications for Archaeology. *Journal of Anthropological Archaeology* 6: 297-335.

— 2004. The Archaeology of Ancient State Economies. *Annual Review of Anthropology* 33:73-102.

Stiglitz, Joseph E. 1969. Distribution of Wealth and Income among Individuals. *Econometrica* 37:382-397.

Taube, Karl A. 1992. *The Major Gods of Ancient Yucatán*. Studies in Pre-Columbian Art and Archaeology 32. Dumbarton Oaks, Washington, D.C.

Thompson, Edward H. 1892. The Ancient Structures of Yucatan Not Communal Dwellings. *Proceedings of the American Antiquarian Society* 8:262-269.

Thompson, J. Eric S. 1957. Deities Portrayed on Censers at Mayapan. Current Reports 40. Carnegie Institution of Washington, Washington, D.C.

— 1966. *The Rise and Fall of Maya Civilization*. Rev. edn. University of Oklahoma, Norman.

Tozzer, Alfred M. 1941. *Landa's Relación de las Cosas de Yucatan*. Papers of the Peabody Museum of Archaeology and Ethnology 18. Harvard University, Cambridge, Mass.

Trigger, Bruce G. 1989. *A History of Archaeological Thought*. Cambridge University, Cambridge.

United Nations Development Programme. 2009. *Human Development Report 2009: Overcoming Barriers*. United Nations, New York. Online version at http://hdrstats.undp.org/en/indicators/161.html.

Yakovenko, Victor M., and A. Christian Silva. 2005. Two-class Structure of Income Distribution in the USA: Exponential Bulk and Power-Law Tail. In Chatterjee, Yarlagadda, and Chakrabarti 2005:15-23.

13 Maya Collapse or Resilience?

Lessons from the Spanish Conquest and the Caste War of Yucatan

Rani T. Alexander

Abstract

Recent calls to extricate the Maya from the stereotype of collapse have singled out cultural resilience as the viable new brand for the political present. In this paper I examine two episodes of Maya collapse and reorganization in Yucatan: the Spanish invasion (A.D. 1511–1546) and the Caste War (A.D. 1847–1901). Using the framework of resilience theory, I explore archaeological evidence of settlement aggregation and dispersal, reorganization of the built environment, and household production to reveal how strategies enacted before each catastrophe compare with those of their aftermaths. My evidence suggests that some native communities pursued consistent strategies that maintained or increased resilience of historic-period socioecological systems, whereas others suffered losses of autonomy under the Spanish colonial and post-independence regimes.

Will Andrews' approach to the Classic Maya collapse always has been to assemble empirical archaeological evidence to explain variations in social transformations (Andrews et al. 2003; Sabloff and Andrews 1986; see also Andrews 1990). Viewing the Classic-period collapse of the central and southern lowlands as the apocalyptic endgame of a great tradition just does not work well for archaeologists who work in Yucatan. The consensus reached by contributors to a recent volume on the Terminal Classic in the Maya Lowlands is that Andrews is right (Demarest et al. 2004). The evidence does not support a pan-Maya catastrophe. New data have muddied the waters, failing to reveal a neat, chronologically uniform decline in population and political institutions. Many scholars who sift through the range of variation between A.D.750–1000 are now asking "What Maya Collapse?" (Aimers 2007).

Some point out that we should be looking at the other side of the coin (McAnany and Yoffee 2010a:10; Pyburn 2006; Scarborough 2009; Scarborough and Burnside 2010); that the real story is cultural resilience—the remarkable suite of adaptations to a tropical environment that allowed the Maya to produce surpluses that supplied great urban centers for over 2,000 years. They revive an old idea that the collapse was just one of several shifts from maximization to resilience that occurred in the Maya area as macroregional systems underwent waves of economic prosperity and depression (Marcus 1993, 1998; Scarborough 1998, 2000; see also Adams 1974, 1978; Lattimore 1951:531, 547; 1962; Sanders and Webster 1978; Skinner 1985:288). I submit that the question Maya scholars should be asking is not "What Maya Collapse?" but "Which Maya Collapse?" and, further, "What do we mean by resilience?"

In this paper I explore historic examples of reorganization of Maya socioecological systems on the Yucatan peninsula using the framework of resilience theory, known as Panarchy (Gunderson and Holling 2002; Redman 2005). In addition to the collapse of the eighth through tenth centuries A.D., the Maya experienced at least two later episodes of reorganization that rarely receive attention in collapse research: the Spanish conquest of the sixteenth century and the Caste War of nineteenth-century Yucatan. Here, I marshal documentary and archaeological evidence to illuminate the reorganization of not-so-ancient Maya society.

Historic examples of Maya reorganization offer several important perspectives to collapse research. First, they provide alternatives to the standard cases used for cross-cultural comparison, which usually contrast well-known ancient civilizations from the Old and New Worlds. Moreover, they facilitate appraisal of differences in the duration, scale, and extent of structural change caused by internal and external factors (see Kolata 2007). Further, they can be used to build bridging arguments between the processes of reorganization and patterning in the archaeological record. Finally, study of the ninth-, sixteenth-, and nineteenth-century reorganizations on the Yucatan peninsula enables comparison of sequential developmental cycles over the *longue durée* (Redman and Kinzig 2003).

Resilience Theory and Collapse

Resilience theory is an interdisciplinary framework for explaining adaptive change in complex ecological and social systems (Holling and Gunderson 2002). Panarchists envision adaptive cycles unfolding in four stages: exploitation, conservation, release, and reorganization (Figure 13.1). In this framework resilience is a dynamic concept, measured by the magnitude of disturbance that can be absorbed before the system changes its structure (Holling and Gunderson 2002:28). Of particular interest to collapse researchers are the release and reorganization phases of the adaptive cycle. Release, or collapse, is defined by low ecosystem resilience, where impacts of external forces on structural vulnerabilities provoke crisis and transformation. The succeeding reorganization stage is characterized by high ecosystem resilience, where the release of capital and resources permit wide latitude among actors to form new and unexpected structural associations.

Resilience theorists focus on three properties that shape trajectories of change in ecosystems and organizations: potential, connectedness, and resilience. Potential is a system-specific measure of accumulated resources, productivity, knowledge, or biomass and nutrients. It sets limits on available options for change and determines the number of future alternatives. Connectedness is the degree of internal control that a system exerts over external variability. Changes between internal and external interconnections cause shifts in system stability. High connectedness means that the system can control its own destiny. Ecosystem resilience is the capacity of the system to weather unexpected disturbances; it determines how vulnerable the system is to unexpected shocks. Levels of resilience shift as the system moves through the four stages of the adaptive cycle.

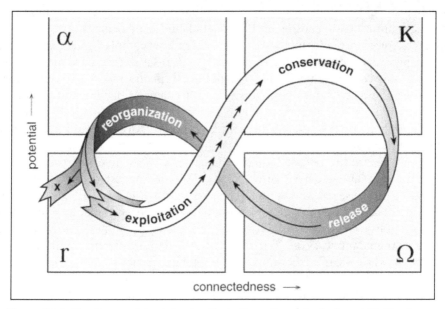

Figure 13.1. The Stages of the Adaptive Cycle (from *Panarchy* by Lance H. Gunderson and C.S. Holling. Copyright © 2002 Island Press. Reproduced by permission of Island Press)

Resilience theorists generally predict greater homogeneity and connectedness among social and ecological units before collapse, whereas diversity and looser connections among socioecological units prevail in the succeeding reorganization stage (Folke et al. 2002). Diversity is a strategy that improves the availability of raw materials and buffers against future change. It promotes resilience because it guards potential for creating new structural combinations of resources and opportunities for innovation. Further, as social and ecological units become more tightly connected in the conservation stage of the adaptive cycle, organizational structures sometimes become inflexible, which can lead to drastic collapse and regional scale transformation.

In looking at how cultural systems rebound, archaeologists face the challenge of integrating specific and historically contingent trajectories with more general cross-cultural regularities (Schwartz and Nichols 2007). In the Maya lowlands, Scarborough (2009; Scarborough and Burnside 2010, see also Dunning et al. 2009) has argued that heterarchical connectedness, which fostered interdependence among self-organizing, resource-specialized communities, characterized reorganization and growth stages of adaptive cycles that followed on the heels of local and regional collapses. In addition, these heterarchical organizations managed the tropical environment by means of an economic logic known as labortasking, which enhanced potential and promoted long-term resilience by intensively managing wetlands through highly skilled labor pools. Highly skilled agriculturalists that practice labor-intensive agriculture on their own land and rely on intergenerational transmission of ecological knowledge are also known as smallholders (Netting 1993; Pyburn 1998). By contrast, during the conservation and release stages, Maya political leaders imposed a rigidly connected, top-down political economic structure. They accelerated exploitation of the wetlands by investment in new technology and labor organization, an economic logic known as technotasking (Scarborough 2003:13-16).

Political factionalism and conflict ensued, which inhibited the slow and steady monitoring of smallholders' agricultural base, causing anthropogenic landscape degradation.

Although archaeology provides numerous examples of how complex systems move through stages of the adaptive cycle, three problems plague applications of resilience theory in archaeology. First, potential, connectedness, and resilience are difficult to measure archaeologically. As Margaret Nelson and colleagues discovered, measurement of decline and increase in the diversity of social and ecological units relies on variables that are difficult to operationalize (Nelson et al. 2006). In their study of the twelfth-century reorganization of the Mimbres region of the American Southwest, they expected the archaeological record would reveal a decline in diversity before the release (collapse) stage, and subsequent increases in diversity during reorganization phase. Analysis of the data, however, suggested that inter-household diversity, measured by house size and configurations of features and activity areas, was greater before the collapse than during the reorganization phase. Diversity in resource use, measured by relative proportions of wild and domestic cultigens and fauna remains, showed no change between stages of the adaptive cycle. Yet, expectations for residential stability matched the model. Settlements were occupied continuously for longer periods before the collapse than during the reorganization stage. Nelson and colleagues concluded that tradeoffs in the advantages and costs of diversity must be weighed for specific cultural-ecological situations.

Second, as Redman (2005; Redman et al. 2004) has pointed out, explanations for the growth or collapse of complex socioecological systems suffer from contradictory propositions about cause and effect. One of the most common archaeological collapse narratives is that increasing populations and the push by central authorities to maximize production placed unsustainable pressures on the productive landscape, leading to overexploitation, irreversible land degradation, and ultimately to the breakdown of the sociopolitical system (e.g., Adams 1978; Culbert 1988). Nevertheless, archaeologists also have proposed collapse narratives where this causal chain is reversed. For example, high populations and complex political economies fostered investment of labor and capital in hydraulically engineered landscapes. When the central authority failed, the population declined and it became impossible to maintain sophisticated agrarian infrastructure. For this reason, deterioration and environmental degradation ensued (e.g., Fisher 2005, 2009).

Finally, archaeologists often assume that the survival or replacement of social practices is rooted in prior systems, and some practices demonstrate long-term continuities. In the Maya case, the multiple local and regional collapses produced by dynamic cycling of the political economy arguably were followed by a return to highly resilient heterarchical political structures and labortasked wetland management systems (Scarborough and Burnside 2010). Nonetheless, for most complex systems, similarities and differences among sequential adaptive cycles are not subject to rigorous scrutiny. Both small-scale, local change and macroscale external stimuli create system feedback and may cause release. Consequently, it is difficult to predict patterns of regeneration based on how previous systems fell apart.

Are the Maya resilient over the long term? According to the definition of resilience offered by Panarchists, the answer is no. Maya history is characterized by numerous peaks of political centralization and valleys of decentralization (Marcus 1993, 1998). Cycles of growth and decline occurred in both the prehispanic and the historic periods. The frequency, amplitude, and spatial extent of Maya collapses set them apart from similar phenomena observed for other civilizations. The largest and most centralized polities proved extremely vulnerable to droughts, political competition and instability, and macroregional economic shifts. Additional investigation is needed to determine if sequential reorganizations in the Maya lowlands were predicated on consistent sets of resilient strategies, as Scarborough has argued. Nevertheless, Mayanists also have studied numerous sites and regions that did not collapse during the ninth century A.D., especially on the Yucatan peninsula. These were less impacted by external forces because production was highly diversified and people followed risk-averse strategies. They maintained high potential and connectedness over long time periods, that is, they practiced resilience (Aimers 2007; Alexander 2005; McAnany and Gallareta Negrón 2010; Pyburn 1998, 2008).

Were the same strategies of the Classic Maya collapse and Terminal Classic reorganization in play following the Spanish Conquest and the Caste War? The advantages and costs of agricultural intensification based on investment in labor (labortasking) or investment in technology (technotasking) shifted with population decline and recovery, but some variables are consistent. Political factionalism, for example, is important both at the local and regional level for all instances of collapse, but local leaders pursued disparate tactics of accommodation and resistance in the face of hegemonic expansion.

In conservation stages, changes in the built environment, evident in construction of civil and religious architecture, suggest heightened connectedness. Alienation of land from native communities also characterizes the conservation stages before collapse, but the replacement of smallholder agricultural management systems with technology-based production was not absolute. Some groups of smallholders maintained and rebuilt traditional ecological knowledge throughout release episodes. Some forms of technology-based commodity production were compatible with the largely labortasked agricultural sector. Moreover, as was the case in the Terminal Classic period, some architecturally elaborate, resource-specialized sites were abandoned during release stages, whereas others demonstrated continued occupation.

As with the twelfth-century Mimbres reorganization in the American Southwest, the evidence from Yucatan suggests inter-household diversity was greater before collapse than during subsequent reorganization phases. By contrast, patterns of settlement aggregation and residential stability in Yucatan run contrary to those described by Nelson and colleagues and resilience theorists (Nelson et al. 2006). In Yucatan, aggregation and residential stability characterized the release and reorganization stages, whereas dispersal and residential mobility (indicative of agricultural intensification and diversification) distinguished the growth and conservation stages of historic adaptive cycles.

Historic-Period Collapse in Yucatan

I turn here to questions of Maya reorganization using examples of historic-period collapse in Yucatan. My specific archaeological and documentary data come from two projects conducted in central Yucatan (Figure 13.2). Since the mid-1980s I have investigated historic-period settlement and household change in Yaxcaba, Yucatan, and most recently I expanded the investigation to the rural areas to the south and west of Valladolid, including Ebtun (Alexander 2004, 2006, 2008a, 2008b; Alexander et al. 2008). In both areas I conducted archival research, extensive archaeological surveys, and mapping of colonial and post-independence period sites.

Table 13.1 lays out the adaptive cycles for Yucatan after A.D. 1450. The historic period is characterized by two cases of Maya collapse. Stages of release and reorganization occurred in the sixteenth through seventeenth centuries and again in the mid-nineteenth through mid-twentieth centuries. Both episodes were marked by severe demographic decline, comparable in scale to that of the ninth-century Classic Maya collapse. Warfare and violence were commonplace. These phases were political and ideological battlegrounds as well, and the documentary record reveals diverse political strategies ranging from accommodation to active and passive resistance during these phases (Scott 1990). From the historical narrative it is possible to tease apart strategies indicating shifts in potential, connectedness, and resilience for historic-period systems.

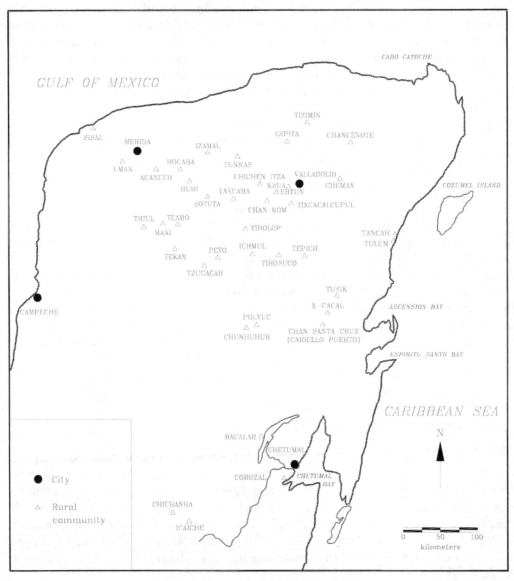

Figure 13.2. Map of nineteenth-century Yucatan.

Table 13.1. Adaptive cycles in Historic-period Yucatan.

DATE	ADAPTIVE CYCLE STAGE	EVENTS	TRENDS IN RURAL YUCATAN
1450–1560	**Release**	Drought, collapse of Mayapan, Spanish invasion, Great Revolt	Political fragmentation, drastic population decline, warfare and violence, extirpation of 'idolatry'
1560–1700	**Reorganization**	*Congregación, repartimiento,* Religious conversion, famines and epidemics	Continued population decline (nadir), migration and flight. Spread of Spanish administration and Christianity, new technology
1700–1780	Exploitation	Bourbon Political Reforms	Population growth, increased trade, hacienda expansion
1780–1847	Conservation	Mexican Independence	Population growth, expansion of agribusiness
1847–1910	**Release**	Caste War, Porfiriato, Mexican Revolution	Population decline, warfare and violence, migration, latifundismo, new *cruzob* religion
1910–1946	**Reorganization**	Cardenist Agrarian reform	Dispersal, colonization and redistribution of new lands, spread of socialist ideology
1946–1991	Exploitation	Roll back Agrarian reform, colonization law, nationalization of foreign enterprise	Neolatifundismo
1991–present	Conservation	Salinas neoliberal reforms, NAFTA	Sale of ejido lands, foreign investment, increased trade, migration, urbanization

The sixteenth-century Maya collapse, often attributed to the Spanish conquest and the disastrous introduction of foreign pathogens, arguably began in the late fifteenth century with a severe drought and the political disintegration of Mayapan (Hodell et al. 2005). As Yucatan became enmeshed in Spain's overseas empire during the sixteenth and seventeenth centuries, potential and connectedness declined severely. Native populations experienced drastic and protracted demographic decline, tribute was demanded of indigenous communities under the *encomienda* system, settlements were forcibly aggregated and relocated, and inhabitants were subjected to compulsory religious conversion (Bricker and Hill 2009; Quezada 1993; Restall 1997). Historians' projections indicate a 95 percent population decline between A.D. 1500 and 1550 (Farriss 1984; Restall 1997). By contrast, archaeological evidence suggests regional variability in rates of decline. That is, the demographic slide was less precipitous in some regions (cf. Andrews and Robles Castellanos 2009; Kepecs 1999).

Forced resettlement (*congregación*) severely altered connectedness. Attempts to salvage relationships between native communities and places on the landscape are evident in Maya-language documentary records. *Congregación* involved measuring and delineating the lands of native city-states, a process called *conformación de los montes*. Several sets of Mayan-language documents related to this process survive: the Xiu papers for the polity of Mani (Quezada and Okoshi Harada 2001), the *Titles of Ebtun* for allied Cupul towns (Roys 1939), and the *Documentos de Tierras de Sotuta* (Codice Perez, ca. 1837) for the polity of Sotuta (Roys 1939). The famous wheel maps of Yucatan also were produced during this process (Roys 1943). According to Roys (1939), Maya farmers still retained rights to cultivate their lands, which after resettlement were often very distant from their places of residence. Land incursions and boundary problems were common. Disputing native parties measured their lands, established boundaries, transferred property, and renegotiated agreements over a period of three centuries. The Maya inhabitants of Cupul retained private and municipal ownership of their lands, which largely corresponded to the early colonial-period boundaries of the native polity, into the twentieth century. For the inhabitants of Sotuta (especially Yaxcaba) and Mani, however, land use history has played out differently.

In the late sixteenth and seventeenth centuries, Spanish authorities extracted resources via the *repartimiento de efectos*. Spaniards advanced money and materials to native villagers and in return collected cloth, honey, and wax. Garcia Bernal's (2005:240-260) data indicate that agents of the governor regularly demanded burdensome quantities of cotton cloth and wax from Yaxcaba, Ebtun, and related communities, which required inhabitants to strip the landscape of resources. Although both *encomiendas* and *repartimientos* exemplify the accelerated resource extraction implemented by hegemonic states, the documentary and archaeological records offer little evidence that production of tributary and *repartimiento* goods was based on the introduction of new technologies controlled by Spaniards. Land ownership has emerged as a critical variable that underwrote landscape change, agrarian strategies and intensification, and transmission of local ecological knowledge (Netting 1993; Pyburn 1998). By pursuing a litigious strategy that allowed the residents of Ebtun and related communities to hold onto their ancestral lands, Maya maintained and increased potential, connectedness, and resilience during the reorganization stage of the sixteenth to seventeenth centuries and thereafter.

During the subsequent exploitation stage, climatic variation produced famines and other agricultural disasters, which in addition to epidemics, retarded demographic recovery. These misfortunes are detectable in elevated mortality rates seen in wills and parish death records in Yucatan. Victoria Bricker and Rebecca Hill's (2009) analysis provides a glimpse of how famines caused by multiyear droughts, hurricanes, and locusts affected rural mortality patterns in seventeenth- and eighteenth-century Yucatan. The highest frequencies of deaths correspond to years in which multiple disasters occurred.

High mortality took enormous tolls on households and communities, and severely disrupted the transmission of traditional ecological knowledge, local political authority, and religious practice. Nonetheless, the documentary evidence also reveals several coping strategies (Bricker and Hill 2009:252), which increased system resilience and potential. Death of a spouse severely upset the division of labor in agrarian households, and remarriages peaked following severe famines and epidemics. In addition, children who lost both parents were adopted or fostered, and in some cases received bequests of property from adoptive parents. At the community level, municipal administration and leadership, as well as administration of religious confraternities, was often disrupted. Yet, deaths of established local leaders afforded opportunities to younger community members and individuals from non-elite families to assume office (Quezada 1985).

In the late eighteenth and early nineteenth centuries, rural populations rebounded through the succeeding conservation stage of the adaptive cycle. The Bourbon political reforms, the constitutional reforms of the Cortes de Cadiz, and the progressive agenda implemented by a newly independent Mexico raised expectations among rural people for social justice and equitable participation in the political process (Dumond 1997; Guemez Pineda 1994). In practice, however, the growth and redistribution of population in rural areas, accompanied by expansion of the hacienda economy that produced cattle, sugar, and henequen, deepened socioeconomic disparities. Alienation of native land increased during this phase, resulting in a loss of potential for native communities. In several cases, the easiest way to resolve a land dispute between towns was to sell the land to an outsider (Roys 1939:18). Maya officials manipulated land sales along the boundary surveyed between Cupul and Sotuta to remedy trespass and uncomfortable usufruct arrangements. In central Yucatan, land for the earliest and largest haciendas was sold in the eighteenth century. Nevertheless, native communities devised strategies to prevent land alienation and their success varied from region to region. In some cases (notably for Ebtun) native communities were able to restrict cattle-raising activities as a condition of sale, or repurchased land that had been sold to outsiders.

Under the 1812 Constitution of Cadiz, town councils (*ayuntamientos*) were elected in all sizeable towns, and Spanish Creoles moved quickly to monopolize local politics to the exclusion of native leaders (Dumond 1997:52-54; Guemez Pineda 2005; Rugeley 1997, 2009). After independence in 1821, rural populations grew apace. As Spanish Creoles flooded the countryside, post-independence legislation and policies allowed them to gain the upper hand in almost every instance. Disruptions to native leadership were more severe in some regions than others (Rugeley 1997). Socioeconomic disparities were exacerbated in the years immediately before the Caste War as Creoles claimed and purchased sizeable tracts of *terrenos baldíos*, enlarging existing haciendas. Nevertheless, this process also varied regionally. In the Ebtun region, although Creoles established numerous small haciendas, claims of *terreno baldío* were uncommon. The farmers of Ebtun pursued litigious tactics that preserved land ownership and therefore maintained potential, whereas the inhabitants of Yaxcaba did not. Overall, the evidence suggests Yaxcaba's system was more vulnerable to external variables. Resources and capital were accumulated and stored by elites in the form of large, architecturally elaborate haciendas, and political and economic policy encouraged the growth of the cattle industry.

By the mid-nineteenth century, the socioecological system was primed for a new release stage of the adaptive cycle. The invasiveness of the Yucatecan post-independence progressive agenda radically constrained community decision-making and ignited the Caste War of Yucatan, a revitalization movement that resulted in a new religion with its own priesthood and ritual practices (Bricker 1981; Cline 1947; Reed 2001; Rugeley 1997). The protracted conflict resulted in a demographic decline of 40 percent for the peninsula (Dumond 1997:238). Nevertheless, documentary data show substantial subregional variability. The population in the Yaxcaba region declined by 90 percent between 1841 and 1862, and the population in the Ebtun region declined by 72 percent between 1841 and 1883 (Alexander 2004:47, 65; 2008a). In the succeeding reorganization stage after the Mexican Revolution of 1910, the redistribution of land to new and existing farming communities sparked widespread changes, and agrarian reform fused with a new *campesino* social identity (Eiss 2008b; Wells and Joseph 1996). This heightened both potential and connectedness. With the neoliberal reforms of the 1990s, Yucatecan farmers yet again face the latest challenges posed by global change. Land increasingly is alienated from native communities, and the population is moving to urban centers. Political-economic policies encourage accelerated exploitation of new resources by means of capital and technological investment, particularly around Ebtun. Local political factionalism is rife. Wealth is accumulated and concentrated in the hands of a few. These changes are increasing system vulnerability and decreasing resilience.

Archaeological Consequences of the Panarchic Cycle

One of the advantages of studying historical cases of Maya collapse is that archaeological patterning can be matched to specific historical processes. Here, I examine variability in three sets of archaeological data. I look at oscillations of settlement aggregation and dispersal, the development of the built environment among different kinds of sites, and archaeological site structure of residential units.

Settlement Aggregation and Dispersal

Maya settlement patterns are a sensitive indicator of how successive stages of adaptive cycles have unfolded over the last 500 years. Sites recorded from my archaeological surveys fall into six categories, which roughly correspond to settlement categories defined by historians: *cabeceras* (large towns, civil-religious administrative centers), *pueblos* (auxiliary towns), *haciendas* (landed estates), privately owned *ranchos* (small agricultural and animal husbandry operations), independent *ranchos* (unofficial farming settlements), and land parcels that possess important geomorphological features, such as *cenotes* (natural water sources) or *rejolladas* (sinkholes). All sites are multicomponent and usually contain material from multiple prehispanic periods, as well as the colonial, postcolonial, and modern eras.

Variation in Maya settlement patterns are related to the long-term exercise of a distinct mobility strategy whose component tactics—dispersal, drift, and flight—allowed farmers to maintain productivity on fragile tropical soils and to resist the worst exigencies of the colonial and nationalist regimes (Farriss 1978; 1984:199-214; Patch 1993:62-66; Redfield and Villa Rojas 1934:34; Robinson and McGovern 1980). *Dispersal* is a temporary shift in residence from town to outlying agricultural plots during seasons of peak agricultural activity. It promotes agricultural intensification by moving labor closer to production locales, increasing crop oversight, and reducing travel time. *Drift* is short-distance migration in which individuals or households move between towns or to new settlements for greater periods of time, sometimes "leapfrogging" among towns surrounding major urban centers. *Flight*, by contrast, is permanent long-distance migration beyond the boundaries of political authority that often occurs in response to factionalism, polity fragmentation, and political unrest. These mobility patterns were serious impediments to attempts by the Spanish colonial regime to control the flow of labor and resources. Dispersal, drift, and flight decrease connectedness and foil hierarchical resource extraction strategies. Householders' decisions to disperse, to move to another community, or to flee, were made in the context of changing population densities and political and economic policies that encouraged overexploitation. Mobility was the primary strategy by which householders adjusted potential, connectedness, and resilience at the local level.

In Yucatan long-term patterns of dispersal, drift, and flight have structured the archaeological record to create two kinds of places that show differences in intensity of use, residential stability, and sequences of occupation (Alexander 2004, 2006, 2008a, 2008b). *Cabeceras* and *pueblos* are places used for permanent residence. Consequently they are characterized by the presence of monumental civil and religious architecture, developed water sources (wells and *norias*), and houselots. Household series (the sequence of households that occupy a residential location for more than one generation) span several hundred years, reflecting a full range of residential activities associated with tropical agriculture and animal husbandry.

Ranchos, haciendas, and land parcels, on the other hand, are places used for special-purpose production. These places have natural features, such as *cenotes*, caves, and *rejolladas*, as well as modifications to those features, such as wells, corrals, water troughs, and shrines. Farmers move their residences to these places either permanently or temporarily in order to increase labor efficiency in production. These sites demonstrate short household series of less than one hundred years, reuse of existing site furniture, and intensive production in the houselot. Residential episodes are interspersed with lengthy periods of extensive use for agricultural production and animal husbandry.

Table 13.2. Distribution of population in the Ebtun Region among settlement classes in 1841 (during a conservation stage) and 1883 (during a release stage).

YEAR	SETTLEMENT CLASS	N	POP MEAN	POP SUM	% POP	DECLINE 1841–1883
1841	*cabecera*	2	1211.5	2423	14.2%	
	pueblo	8	1302	10419	61%	
	rancho	21	215	1360	8.0%	
	hacienda	29	94	2734	16%	
	sitio	8	15	122	.7%	
Total		68	251	17058		
1883	*cabecera*	2	678	1356	28.6%	44%
	pueblo	8	342	2742	57.8%	74%
	rancho	20	11	229	4.8%	83%
	hacienda	10	39.5	395	8.3%	86%
	sitio	3	7.3	22	.46%	82%
Total		43	110	4744		72%

Sources: **Archivo General del Estado de Yucatan (AGEY)**
Fondo Municipios, Libros Valladolid, Padron General de todos los habitantes de este Municipio 1883.
Poder Ejecutivo, Censos y Padrones, vol. 2 Exp. 17, 1841 Ebtun. Padron general de habitantes del pueblo de Ebtun, partido de Valladolid, con expresion de sexos, edades y ocupaciones, 17 f., caja 1.
Poder Ejecutivo, Censos y Padrones, vol. 3, Exp. 25, 1841 Pueblo de Kahua (Kaua). Padron general de habitantes del pueblo de Kahua y su comarca de haciendas, sitios y ranchos del partido de Valladolid, con expresion de sexos, edades y ocupaciones. Kahua, Abril 24, de 1841. folios 12, caja 2.
Poder Ejecutivo, Censos y Padrones, vol. 1, Exp. 6 Pueblo de Cuncunul. Padron general de habitantes del pueblo de Cuncunul del partido de Valladolid, con expresion de sexos edades y ocupaciones, Cuncunul, Mayo 1 de 1841, fjs. 10, caja 1.
Poder Ejecutivo, Censos y Padrones, vol. 1, Exp. 10. Pueblo de Chichimila. Padron general del pueblo de Chichimila y su comprension, partido de Valladolid, con expresion de sexos, edades, y ocupaciones. Chichimila, agosto 25 de 1841. fjs. 42 caja 1
Poder Ejecutivo, Censos y Padrones, vol. 5, Exp. 70. Pueblo de Tixcacalcupul. Padron general de habitantes del pueblo de Tixcacalcupul y su comprension de haciendas, sitios, y ranchos del partido de Valladolid, con expresion de sexos edades y ocupaciones. Tixcacalcupul mayo 5 de 1841, fjs 41 caja 2-BIS
Poder Ejecutivo, Censos y Padrones, vol. 6, Exp. 73. Pueblo de Uayma. Padron general de habitantes del pueblo de Uayma y su comarca de haciendas, sitios y ranchos del partido de Valladolid, con expresion de sexos, edades y ocupaciones, Uayma, mayo 14 de 1841. fjs 11. caja 2-BIS
Poder ejecutivo, Censos y Padrones, vol. 7, Exp. 59. Pueblo de Tekom. Padron general de habitantes del pueblo de Tekom y su comarca, partido de Valladolid, con expresión de sexos, edades, y ocupaciones. Tekom mayo 4 de 1841 fjs 15.

Over the last 500 years, settlement systems underwent cycles of aggregation and dispersal. Census data from the Ebtun region before and after the Caste War illustrate the dramatic shifts in the distribution of population among different kinds of settlements between the release stage (1883) and the preceding conservation stage (1841; Table 13.2). During the release stage, people lived predominantly in the *cabeceras* and the *pueblos*. *Ranchos*, *haciendas*, and land parcels were used extensively or occupied temporarily. Settlement aggregation occurred during both historic-period collapses. It was encouraged under resettlement policy after the conquest (Gerhard 1993) and following the violence of the nineteenth-century Caste War (Dumond 1997).

By contrast, during stages of exploitation and conservation people lived permanently on distant land parcels, *ranchos*, and *haciendas*, as well as in the *pueblos* and *cabeceras*. Settlement dispersal coincided with economic expansion and population growth. It raises potential by enhancing agricultural intensification and diversification. In central Yucatan, however, land pressure was not the underlying condition that prompted people to move permanently to rural settlements (Alexander 2004, 2006). It is likely that farmers were quick to respond to economic opportunities, agrarian reform, and better access to markets through agricultural intensification, especially of locations possessing hydrological resources such as *cenotes* and *rejolladas* (see Netting 1993). Dispersal had the added benefit of distancing household production and activities from the supervision of authorities.

The Built Environment

The creation and destruction of the built environment, often measured by the size or volume of masonry architecture, corresponds to different stages of historic adaptive cycles in Yucatan. The scale of civil, religious, and residential masonry architecture varies by site type and time period, but allows archaeologists to gauge changes in connectedness. Spanish policies of the sixteenth century initiated drastic transformation of the built environment of rural Maya communities. Authorities imposed internal settlement reorganization. Religious architecture, initially the *ramada* chapel, was constructed on a plaza usually containing a water source. *Solares* and streets were aligned along a grid plan, and surrounding dispersed populations were brought to join the original inhabitants (Alexander 2004; Andrews 1991; García Targa 2000; Millet and Burgos 1994; Millet et al. 1993). The town or *cah* became the focus of community identity and the center of religious practice. Entrances to the town along roads were marked by wooden crosses erected atop *mojoneras* (stone boundary markers).

Permanently occupied *cabeceras* and *pueblos* have substantially greater amounts of masonry construction than do *ranchos* or other sites that demonstrate discontinuous occupations. Ambitious construction projects that expanded and remodeled civic and religious architecture correspond to stages of exploitation and conservation in the adaptive cycle. For example, churches were expanded and remodeled in the eighteenth century (Figure 13.3; Alexander 2004; Bretos 1992; see Taylor 1996). Spanish Creoles expanded *ayuntamientos* in the early nineteenth century, which prompted the replacement of perishable *audiencia* buildings with masonry *palacios municipales* (Figure 13.4). These colonial-style masonry buildings usually have *portales* (a front porch with columns) and a row of enclosed back rooms with multiple doorways. Churches and *palacios municipales* offer obvious and graphic expressions of prevailing ideology and historical memory (Alexander et al. 2008).

Figure 13.3. The church in Yaxcaba. The final phase of construction dates to 1757 (photo by Jeanne Randall, 1999).

Figure 13.4. The *palacio municipal* of Ebtun.

Figure 13.5. The *casa principal* of Hacienda Cetelac.

Masonry residential constructions that convey increasing class differences were built in *cabeceras* and *pueblos* during the conservation stages of the late eighteenth and early nineteenth centuries, and again in the late twentieth century (see Alexander and Andrade 2007). The elaboration of masonry infrastructure on *haciendas* corresponds to stages of economic expansion and consolidation, but varied subregionally (Figure 13.5). The destruction of *hacienda* architecture during the Caste War also varied regionally (see Strickon 1965). The most elaborate *haciendas* date to the Porfiriato era (1876–1911) and are mostly located in the henequen-producing areas of northwest Yucatan that were least affected by the Caste War. By contrast, in central Yucatan most haciendas were used for cattle production and remain in ruins today (Alexander 2003). Twentieth-century constructions at these locations reflect shifts in community identity and connectedness. If a new municipality was founded at the location of a *hacienda* destroyed during the Caste War, the religious and residential architecture associated with the *hacienda* remains unused or is reused for ordinary domestic purposes. New churches were constructed for the town, and the materials of the *casa principal* of the hacienda were recycled for new buildings.

Finally, after the Mexican Revolution, local political identities were reformulated, and this process is visible in the construction of civic architecture. Some *ranchos* and land parcels became independent municipalities during this reorganization stage. Civic and religious architecture was constructed in distinctive post-revolutionary style (Figure 13.6). Municipalities formed after the Mexican revolution often symbolized their legitimacy and political autonomy by building large and elaborate civic structures. In the *pueblos*, the *palacio municipal* is never larger than the church. In municipalities established after the revolution, however, the municipal building dwarfs the religious architecture and dominates the plaza. Connectedness among rural villages in Yucatan, evidenced by the construction of civil and religious masonry architecture, increased dramatically in the early nineteenth century and again in the mid- to late twentieth century, at the outset of conservation stages of the adaptive cycle.

Figure 13.6. The *comisaria municipal* of Xanla.

Today, the built environments of town centers form canvasses that display a representation of the past shared by the community, and current attitudes are tangibly expressed on commemorative monuments and masonry buildings. Often stones bearing dates are carefully preserved and reset over lintels, doorways, and gates, which evoke the temporal depth, legitimacy, and permanence of the community. Many churches and shrines also incorporate Precolumbian carved stones into the façade as decoration, evoking links to the prehispanic era. Some examples may be interpreted as syncretic or resistant expressions. Contemporary material evidence further reflects shifting relationships between identity and place. It is an indicator not only of political connectedness but also of ties between the community and its past (Alexander 2012). Community attitudes about the Caste War, for example, are visible in the distribution of dressed crosses across the landscape (Dumond 1985). In some *pueblos* of central Yucatan, notably Tixcacalcupul and Tekom, the crosses that form boundary markers are consistently dressed and adorned with embroidered *huipiles* (Figure 13.7). By contrast, other *pueblos*, exemplified by Ebtun, Cuncunul, and Kaua, pointedly leave all crosses bare.

Figure 13.7. Shrine with dressed cross at Tzaab, a *rancho* affiliated with Tixcacalcupul. The shrine is oriented and placed atop a prehispanic structure.

Household Production

In the Yaxcaba region, the archaeological investigation went a step further to describe the range of spatial variation among residential units—houselots or *solares*—within three kinds of settlements, a *pueblo*, an independent *rancho*, and a *hacienda*. These data offer a glimpse of variation in household production for a conservation stage of the adaptive cycle, in the nineteenth century before the onset of the Caste War (Alexander 2004). The results show that differences in population growth, access to land, tax status, and distance from authority prompted different responses among Maya householders in different settlements. Because the conservation stage is marked by accumulation and storage of capital resources, increasing economic stratification, competition, and a push for the extraction of resources by central authorities, different groups of farmers practiced varied risk-mitigation strategies depending on threats to land ownership and propensity for crop failure. Diversification of production within the residential lot was a common response to increased risk of crop failure on distant agricultural fields, particularly if cattle were likely to invade agricultural plots.

Variation in houselot size and the numbers and kinds of dwellings and features that constituted residential space suggest differences in agricultural production, labor organization, and the structure of patron–client relationships among Maya living in the Yaxcaba region. Differences in mean houselot size were statistically significant among the three settlements. The settlement with the lowest rate of population growth and least threat of land pressure, the *hacienda*, had the largest lots, whereas the settlement with the greatest rate of population growth and greatest threat of land pressure, the independent *rancho*, had the smallest houselots. Because *hacienda* workers owned no land and shared outlying fields with the cattle of the estate, cultivation of foodstuffs within the houselot garden was the most secure component of the agricultural system. Cultivation of distant cornfields carried greater risk of crop failure. By contrast in the *rancho*, milpa was cultivated on land near the settlement, because outfield land was threatened by cattle. Consequently, houselots were divided as the population grew, because extending the area of settlement would have infringed on arable land that was in short supply.

Differences in the mean number of ancillary features (animal pens, gardening features, water storage, and *chich* piles [stone rubble foundations for small perishable structures]) per lot are also statistically significant among the three sites. The *pueblo* had notably fewer animal pens and other features than did the *rancho* or the *hacienda*. Intensified production and diversification within the settlement zone was most evident in the independent *rancho*, whose access to agricultural land was severely restricted. Distance from civil and ecclesiastical authority made it difficult to collect taxes from the inhabitants, and probably made animal husbandry an attractive option for augmenting household income in the *rancho*.

At the *hacienda*, garden areas within the houselot were critical for maintaining household subsistence, because outlying milpa plots would have been at risk of destruction by cattle. The solution was to expand the size of the garden zone of the houselot, such that the lot itself replaced infield milpa plots. Also, because the taxes of *hacienda* workers were paid by the estate owner and recorded as debts, raising pigs within the houselot could be performed "on credit" and became an important supplement to household subsistence. Inhabitants who raised pigs and poultry at the *pueblo*, however, would have incurred civil and religious taxes. In the *pueblo* garden zones within the houselots were substantial, but were used less intensively than at the other two settlements.

According to resilience theorists, diversity of household production strategies is expected to characterize the reorganization stage of adaptive cycles, as resources and innovations are combined in new ways. In early nineteenth-century Yucatan, however, archaeological evidence for household diversity is greatest in the conservation stage, before the Caste War collapse. Diversified production within the houselot supplied alternatives for people who had lost land or who had limited access to arable land. Inter-household diversity in this cultural-ecological context raised potential for both smallholders and shareholders (agriculturalists who do not own land and who negotiate share or wage labor contracts in exchange for access to land) and buffered them from system-wide declines in resilience.

Conclusion

This investigation of periods of historic collapse and reorganization on the Yucatan peninsula offers several lessons for the study of the Classic Maya collapse. First, the magnitude of the demographic decline in the historic cases is comparable to (or exceeds) the Maya collapse of the eighth through tenth centuries. The ancient Maya collapse is not unique. Furthermore, when viewed from the long-term perspective, even the relatively recent socioecological systems of the nineteenth and twentieth centuries are quite vulnerable to external forces that decrease resilience.

Second, the results indicate wide-ranging variability in residential stability and the lengths of occupations of different sites. Most *cabeceras* and *pueblos* are examples of sites that did not collapse, and have been continuously occupied for over 500 years. These communities often maintain historical memory of places of origin via colonial land titles. Consequently, *ranchos* and land parcels were temporarily abandoned, but not forgotten, as people fled to larger centers during release stages. Other places, most notably *haciendas*, were short lived. The architecturally elaborate estates originated as the government of Yucatan began a push to accelerate production and extraction of resources that could be lucratively exported on the world market during the conservation stage of the adaptive cycle. *Haciendas* are examples of sites that did collapse.

Third, some communities practiced radically divergent political agendas in the face of collapse, intended to preserve autonomous leadership. The Xiu of Mani engaged in strategies of accommodation to manage political continuity and guard connectedness through the stages of reorganization (Quezada and Okoshi Harada 2001). By contrast, the Cocoms of Sotuta and their allies in the eastern provinces rose in revolt against the Spaniards (Chamberlain 1948). Active resistance in the eastern part of the peninsula and pacific accommodation in the west were later repeated during the Caste War (Dumond 1997).

Further, several communities developed tactics for preserving land ownership. The litigious strategy of Ebtun of measuring and micromanaging the sale, inheritance, transfer, and recovery of land guarded potential for agricultural intensification and the preservation of traditional ecological knowledge (Roys 1939). Mobility strategies of dispersal, drift, and flight provided new opportunities and heightened potential for many communities during reorganization stages (Alexander 2006). Reconfiguration of the built environment raised connectedness, solidified community identity, and expressed new or prevailing ideologies.

Finally, variation in the archaeological site structure of residential space suggests that even in conservation stages when central authorities pushed for accelerated production and extraction of resources and the socioecological system was most vulnerable, many householders pursued diversified strategies and proved adept at agricultural risk management. Although these sites later collapsed during the Caste War, a pattern of dispersed settlement resumed after the Mexican revolution, renewing the cycle of colonization and growth in the mid-twentieth century.

Many trends and processes of the historic-period release and reorganization stages resonate with those noted for the Maya collapse of the late eighth through tenth centuries. Some evidence suggests that they are consistent over the *longue durée*, yet people adapted strategies to specific cultural ecological challenges. Although documentary and archaeological evidence indicate wide variability in community-level responses to historic-period collapse, native communities engaged in tactics that preserved potential and avoided overly rigid connectedness, which ultimately enhanced resilience.

Currently, native communities in Ebtun and Yaxcaba are experiencing another conservation stage of the adaptive cycle. State-sponsored resource extraction via a technotasking economic logic is increasingly evident on the rural landscape. Community lands are expropriated by big business and tourism. The *cenotes* of Ebtun have been seized for the production of thermoelectric energy by the Felipe Carrillo Puerto plant. Kaua has an international airport that serves the Chichen Itza archaeological zone. Few young people follow their parents into agricultural production and instead migrate to the cities. The government builds schools, health centers, parks, and promotes cooperative stores and small businesses in rural communities which alter the built environment. Government projects intended to improve housing, water, and electrical utilities have heightened connectedness and changed the face of rural life. Yet, in some cases these activities have provoked political factionalism and conflict. If past collapses are any indication, however, Maya communities will come up with new strategies to maintain and improve resilience in the twenty-first century.

References

Adams, Robert McC. 1974. The Mesopotamian Social Landscape: A View from the Frontier. In *Reconstructing Complex Societies: An Archaeological Colloquium*, edited by C. B. Moore, pp. 1-20. Supplement to the Bulletin of the American Schools of Oriental Research 20. Henry N. Sawyer Company, New York.
— 1978. Strategies of Maximization, Stability, and Resilience in Mesopotamian Society, Settlement, and Agriculture. *Proceedings of the American Philosophical Society* 122:329-335.
Aimers, James J. 2007. What Maya Collapse? Terminal Classic Variation in the Maya Lowlands. *Journal of Archaeological Research* 15:329-337.
Alexander, Rani T. 2003. Architecture, Haciendas, and Economic Change in Yaxcabá, Yucatán, Mexico. *Ethnohistory* 50:191-220.
— 2004. *Yaxcabá and the Caste War of Yucatán: An Archaeological Perspective*. University of New Mexico, Albuquerque.
— 2005. Isla Cilvituk and the Difficulties of Spanish Colonization in Southwestern Campeche. In *The Postclassic to Spanish-Era Transition in Mesoamerica: Archaeological Perspectives*, edited by Susan Kepecs and Rani T. Alexander, pp. 161-183. University of New Mexico Press, Albuquerque.
— 2006. Maya Settlement Shifts and Agrarian Ecology in Yucatán, 1800–2000. *Journal of Anthropological Research* 62:449-470.
— 2008a. From the Caste War to the Revolution: Demography, Settlement and Identity in Ebtun, Yucatán. Paper presented at the 41st Annual Conference on Historical and Underwater Archaeology, Albuquerque.

— 2008b. The Secondary Products Revolution Comes to Yucatán. Paper presented at the 73rd Annual Meeting of the Society for American Archaeology, Vancouver.
— 2012. Prohibido Tocar este Cenote: The Archaeological Basis for the Titles of Ebtun. *International Journal of Historical Archaeology* 6(1). In press.
Alexander, Rani T., and Sandra A. Andrade. 2007. Frontier Migration and the Built Environment in Campeche. *Estudios de Cultura Maya* 30:175-196.
Alexander, Rani T., with contributions by José Díaz Cruz, Adam Kaeding, Ruth Martínez Cervantes, Matthew Punke, and Susan Kepecs. 2008. *La Arqueología Histórica en los Pueblos de Ebtun, Cuncunul, Kaua, Tekom, y Tixcacalcupul, Yucatán, México*. Report to the Consejo de Arqueología, Instituto Nacional de Antropología e Historia, Mexico City.
Andrews, Anthony P. 1990. The Fall of Chichen Itza: A Preliminary Hypothesis. *Latin American Antiquity* 1:258-267.
— 1991. The Rural Chapels and Churches of Early Colonial Yucatan and Belize: An Archaeological Perspective. In *The Spanish Borderlands in Pan-American Perspective*, edited by David H. Thomas, pp. 355-374. Columbian Consequences 3. Smithsonian Institution, Washington, D.C.
Andrews, Anthony P., E. Wyllys Andrews, and Fernando Robles Castellanos. 2003. The Northern Maya Collapse and its Aftermath. *Ancient Mesoamerica* 14:151-156.
Andrews, Anthony P., and Fernando Robles Castellanos. 2009. La Arqueología Histórica del Noroeste de Yucatán. In *Arqueología Colonial Latinoamericano, modelos de estudio*, edited by Patricia Fournier García and Juan García Targa, pp. 115-131. BAR International Series 1988. British Archaeological Reports, Oxford.
Bretos, Miguel. 1992. *Iglesias de Yucatán*. Producción Editorial Dante, Merida.
Bricker, Victoria R. 1981. *The Indian Christ, the Indian King*. University of Texas, Austin.
Bricker, Victoria R., and Rebecca Hill. 2009. Climatic Signatures in Yucatecan Wills and Death Records. *Ethnohistory* 56:227-268.
Chamberlain, Robert S. 1948. *The Conquest and Colonization of Yucatan 1517–1550*. Carnegie Institution of Washington Publication 582, Washington, D.C.
Cline, Howard F. 1947. Related Studies in Early Nineteenth Century Yucatecan Social History. In *Microfilm Collection of Manuscripts on Middle American Cultural Anthropology*. University of Chicago Library, Chicago.
Culbert, T. Patrick. 1988. The Collapse of Classic Maya Civilization. In *The Collapse of Ancient States and Civilizations*, edited by Norman Yoffee and George L. Cowgill, pp. 69-101. University of Arizona, Tucson.
Demarest, Arthur A., Prudence M. Rice, and Don S. Rice (editors). 2004. *The Terminal Classic in the Maya Lowlands: Collapse, Transition, and Transformation*. University Press of Colorado, Boulder.
Dumond, Don E. 1985. The Talking Crosses of Yucatan: A New Look at their History. *Ethnohistory* 32:291-308.
— 1997. *The Machete and the Cross: Campesino Rebellion in Yucatan*. University of Nebraska, Lincoln.
Dunning, Nicholas P., Timothy Beach, Sheryl Luzzadder-Beach, and John G. Jones. 2009. Creating a Stable Landscape: Soil Conservation and Adaptation among the Ancient Maya. In Fisher, Hill, and Feinman 2009:85-105.
Eiss, Paul K. 2008a. Constructing the Maya. *Ethnohistory* 55:503-508.
— 2008b. El Pueblo Mestizo: Modernity, Tradition and Statecraft in Yucatán, 1870–1907. *Ethnohistory* 55:525-552.
Farriss, Nancy M. 1978. Nucleation versus Dispersal: They Dynamics of Population Movement in Colonial Yucatan. *Hispanic American Historical Review* 58:187-216.
— 1984. *Maya Society Under Colonial Rule: The Collective Enterprise of Survival*. Princeton University, Princeton.
Fisher, Christopher T. 2005. Demographic and Landscape Change in the Lake Pátzcuaro Basin, Mexico: Abandoning the Garden. *American Anthropologist* 107:87-95.

— 2009. Abandoning the Garden: The Population/Land Degradation Fallacy as Applied to the Lake Pátzcuaro Basin in Mexico. In Fisher, Hill, and Feinman 2009:209-231.
Fisher, Christopher T., J. Brett Hill, and Gary M. Feinman (editors). 2009. *The Archaeology of Environmental Change: Socionatural Legacies of Degradation and Resilience*. University of Arizona, Tucson.
Folke, Carl, Steve Carpenter, Thomas Elmqvist, Lance H. Gunderson, C. S. Holling, and Brian Walker. 2002. Resilience and Sustainable Development: Building Adaptive Capacity in a World of Transformations. *Ambio* 31:437-440.
García Bernal, Manuela Cristina. 2005. El Gobernador de Yucatan Rodrigo Flores de Aldana. In *Economía, Política, y Sociedad en el Yucatán colonial*, edited by Manuela Cristina García Bernal, pp. 141-260. Ediciones de la Universidad Autónoma de Yucatán, Merida.
García Targa, Juan. 2000. Análisis histórico y arqueológico del asentamiento colonial de Tecoh [Estado de Yucatán, México], siglo XVI. *Ancient Mesoamerica* 11:231-243.
Gerhard, Peter. 1993. *The Southeast Frontier of New Spain*. University of Oklahoma, Norman.
Guemez Pineda, Arturo. 1994. *Liberalismo en Tierras del Caminante, Yucatan, 1812–1840*. Colegio de Michoacan, Zamora.
— 2005. *Mayas: Gobierno y Tierras frente a la Acometida Liberal en Yucatán, 1812–1847*. El colegio de Michoacán, Universidad Autónoma de Yucatán, Zamora and Merida.
Gunderson, Lance H., and C. S. Holling (editors). 2002. *Panarchy: Understanding Transformations in Human and Natural Systems*. Island Press, Washington, D.C.
Hodell, David A., Mark Brenner, Jason H. Curtis, Enrique Medina-Gonzalez, Idelfonso Chan-Can, Alma Albornaz-Pat and Thomas P. Guilderson. 2005. Climate Change on the Yucatan Peninsula during the Little Ice Age. *Quaternary Research* 63:109-121.
Holling, C.S. and Lance H. Gunderson. 2002. Resilience and Adaptive Cycles. In Gunderson and Holling 2002:25-62.
Kepecs, Susan M. 1999. *The Political Economy of Chikinchel, Yucatán, Mexico: A Diachronic Analysis from the Prehispanic Era through the Age of Spanish Administration*. Ph.D. dissertation, Department of Anthropology, University of Wisconsin-Madison. University Microfilms, Ann Arbor.
Kolata, Alan L. 2007. Before and After Collapse: Reflections on the Regeneration of Social Complexity. In Schwartz and Nichols 2007:208-221.
Lattimore, Owen. 1951 [1940]. *Inner Asian Frontiers of China*. Beacon, Boston.
— 1962. An Inner Asian Approach to the Historical Geography of China. In *Studies in Frontier History: Collected Papers 1928–1958*, pp. 492-500. Oxford University, London.
Marcus, Joyce. 1993. Ancient Maya Political Organization. In *Lowland Maya Civilization in the Eighth Century AD*, edited by Jeremy A. Sabloff and John S. Henderson, pp. 111-183. Dumbarton Oaks, Washington, D.C.
— 1998. The Peaks and Valleys of Ancient States: An Extension of the Dynamic Model. In *Archaic States*, edited by Gary M. Feinman and Joyce Marcus, pp. 59-94. School of American Research, Santa Fe.
McAnany, Patricia A., and Tomás Gallareta Negrón. 2010. Bellicose Rulers and Climatological Peril? Retrofitting Twenty-First-Century Woes on Eighth-Century Maya Society. In McAnany and Yoffee 2010b:142-175.
McAnany, Patricia A. and Norman Yoffee. 2010a. Why We Question Collapse and Study Human Resilience, Ecological Vulnerability, and the Aftermath of Empire. In McAnany and Yoffee 2010b:1-17.
McAnany, Patricia A., and Norman Yoffee (editors). 2010b. *Questioning Collapse: Human Resilience, Ecological Vulnerability, and the Aftermath of Empire*. Cambridge University, Cambridge.
Millet Cámara, Luis M., and Rafael Burgos Villanueva. 1994. La Guardianía de Izamal y sus construcciones religiosas en el siglo XVI. *Cuadernos de Arquitectura Virrenal* 14:3-13. Facultad de Arquitectura, Universidad Nacional Autónoma de México.

Millet Cámara, Luis, Heber Ojeda Mas, and Vicente Suárez Aguilar. 1993. Tecoh, Izamal: Nobleza Indígena y Conquista Española. *Latin American Antiquity* 4:48-58.

Nelson, Margaret C., Michelle Hegmon, Stephanie Kulow, and Karen Gust Schollmeyer. 2006. Archaeological and Ecological Perspectives on Reorganization: A Case Study from the Mimbres Region of the U.S. Southwest. *American Antiquity* 71:403-432.

Netting, Robert McC. 1993. *Smallholders, Householders: Farm Families and the Ecology of Intensive Sustainable Agriculture*. Stanford University, Stanford.

Patch, Robert W. 1993. *Maya and Spaniard in Yucatan*. Stanford University Press, Stanford.

Pyburn, K. Anne. 1998. Smallholders in the Maya Lowlands: Homage to a Garden Variety Ethnographer. *Human Ecology* 26:267-286.

— 2006. The Politics of Collapse. *Archaeologies* 2:3-7.

— 2008. Pomp and Circumstance before Belize: Ancient Maya Commerce and the New River Conurbation. In *The Ancient City: New Perspectives on Urbanism in the Old and New World*, edited by Joyce Marcus and Jeremy A. Sabloff, pp. 247-272. SAR Press, Santa Fe.

Quezada, Sergio. 1985. Encomienda, Cabildo y Gubernatura Indigena en Yucatan, 1541–1583. *Historia Mexicana* 34:662-684.

— 1993. *Pueblos y Caciques Yucatecos, 1550–1580*. El Colegio de Mexico, Mexico.

Quezada, Sergio, and Tsubasa Okoshi Harada. 2001. *Papeles de los Xiu de Yaxá, Yucatan*. Universidad Nacional Autonoma de Mexico, Mexico, D.F.

Redfield, Robert, and Alfonso Villa Rojas. 1934. *Chan Kom: A Maya Village*. Publication 448. Carnegie Institution of Washington, Washington, D.C.

Redman, Charles L. 2005. Resilience Theory in Archaeology. *American Anthropologist* 107:70-77.

Redman, Charles L., Steven R. James, Paul R. Fish, and J. Daniel Rogers. 2004. Introduction: Human Impacts on Past Environments. In *The Archaeology of Global Change*, edited by Charles L. Redman, Steven R. James, Paul R. Fish, and J. Daniel Rogers, pp. 1-8. Smithsonian Books, Washington, D.C.

Redman, Charles L., and Ann P. Kinzig. 2003. Resilience of Past Landscapes: Resilience Theory, Society, and the Longue Durée. *Conservation Ecology* 7:14.

Reed, Nelson. 2001. *The Caste War of Yucatan*. Rev. edn. Stanford University, Stanford.

Restall, Matthew. 1997. *The Maya World: Yucatec Culture and Society 1550–1850*. Stanford University, Stanford.

Robinson, David J., and Carolyn G. McGovern. 1980. La migración regional yucateca en la época colonial: el caso de San Francisco de Umán. *Historia Mexicana* 30:99-125.

Roys, Ralph L. 1939. *The Titles of Ebtun*. Publication 505. Carnegie Institute of Washington, Washington, D.C.

— 1943. *The Indian Background of Colonial Yucatan*. Publication No. 548. Carnegie Institution of Washington, Washington, D.C.

Rugeley, Terry. 1997. *Yucatan's Maya Peasantry and the Origins of the Caste War*. University of Texas, Austin.

— 2009. *Rebellion Now and Forever: Mayas, Hispanics and Caste War Violence in Yucatán, 1800–1880*. Stanford University, Stanford.

Sabloff, Jeremy A., and E. Wyllys Andrews V (editors). 1986. *Late Lowland Maya Civilization: Classic to Postclassic*. School of American Research and the University of New Mexico, Albuquerque.

Sanders, William T., and David Webster. 1978. Unilinealism, Multilinealism, and the Evolution of Complex Societies. In *Social Archaeology, Beyond Subsistence and Dating*, edited by Charles L. Redman, M. J. Berman, E. V. Curtin, W. T. Langhorne, Jr., Nina M. Versaggi, and J. C. Wanser, pp. 249-302. Academic, New York.

Scarborough, Vernon L. 1998. Ecology and Ritual: Water Management and the Maya. *Latin American Antiquity* 9:135-159.

— 2000. Resilience, Resource Use, and Socioeconomic Organization: A Mesoamerican Pathway. In *Environmental Disaster and the Archaeology of Human Response*, edited by Garth Bawden and Richard M. Reycraft. Anthropological Papers, Maxwell Museum of Anthropology 7. University of New Mexico, Albuquerque.

— 2003. *The Flow of Power: Ancient Water Systems and Landscapes*. School of American Research, Santa Fe.

— 2009. Beyond Sustainability: Managed Wetlands and Water Harvesting in Ancient Mesoamerica. In Fisher, Hill, and Feinman 2009:62-82.

Scarborough, Vernon L., and William R. Burnside. 2010. Complexity and Sustainability: Perspectives from the Ancient Maya and the Modern Balinese. *American Antiquity* 75:327-363.

Schwartz, Glenn M., and John J. Nichols (editors). 2007. *After Collapse: The Regeneration of Complex Societies*. University of Arizona, Tucson.

Scott, James C. 1990. *Domination and the Arts of Resistance: Hidden Transcripts*. Yale University, New Haven.

Skinner, G. William. 1985. Presidential Address: The Structure of Chinese History. *Journal of Asian Studies* 44:271-292.

Strickon, Arnold. 1965. Hacienda and Plantation in Yucatan: An Historical-Ecological consideration of the Folk–Urban Continuum in Yucatan. *América Indígena* 25:35-65.

Taylor, William B. 1996. *Magistrates of the Sacred: Priests and Parishioners in Eighteenth-Century Mexico*. Stanford University, Stanford.

Wells, Alan, and Gilbert M. Joseph. 1996. *Summer of Discontent, Seasons of Upheaval: Elite Politics and Rural Insurgency in Yucatan, 1876–1915*. Stanford University, Stanford.

Part V

CONCLUSIONS

14 Yucatan at the Crossroads

Joyce Marcus

Inspired by a flurry of new fieldwork in Yucatan, by the chapters in this book, and by Geoff Braswell's request that I write about the directions Maya archaeology might take, I will review what we have learned and suggest how we might move forward.

The Yucatan Peninsula is divided among three Mexican states: Yucatan, Campeche, and Quintana Roo. It comprises almost 200,000 square kilometers, or two-thirds of the Maya region. Yucatan, however, receives neither two-thirds of all funding nor two-thirds of the attention of Maya archaeologists. For these and other reasons, mentioned below, it is not surprising that the story of the northern Maya lowlands is less well documented than that of the southern lowlands.

Indeed, when the term "Maya" is mentioned, most people immediately think of the southern lowlands, with its myriad cities, giant temples, and white roof-combs poking up through the green rainforest, and its thousands of hieroglyphic texts providing the names, deeds, and rites of Maya kings and queens. Many young archaeologists arrive in the southern lowlands, fall in love with it, and cannot imagine leaving it for another region. Still others begin in the northern lowlands, grow tired of the dense secondary growth and the *acahuales*, and end up going to the southern lowlands.

Now, however, the northern lowlands seems to have a hard core of excellent archaeologists who look as if they will stay and continue to conduct long-term excavations and surveys (e.g., Anderson 2003, 2009; Ardren 1997; Ardren et al. 2003; Bey et al. 1998; Bey and May Ciau 2005; Bond-Freeman et al. 1998; Burgos et al. 2003; Gallareta Negrón et al. 2003, 2004; Glover and Amador 2005; Glover et al. 2005; Hutson et al. 2004; Johnstone 2001; Magnoni et al. 2008; Mathews 2001, 2003; Mathews and Morrison 2006; Morrison 2000; Rissolo et al. 2005; Shaw and Mathews 2005; Sierra Sosa 1999, 2001; Smith 2000; Smyth 2006, 2008, 2009; Smyth and Rogart 2004; Stanton 2000; Stanton and Ardren 2005; Stanton et al. 2010; Uriarte Torres 2004, 2007; Varela Torrecilla 1998; and the authors of the papers in this volume).

One reason the contributions of the northern lowlands have never been fully appreciated relates to the image of the region: it is still perceived as the poor country cousin of the southern lowlands. This view persists despite the fact that it was interregional interaction that set in motion many of the developments seen in the northern lowlands, southern lowlands, and Guatemalan highlands. All three areas were inextricably linked by language, history, the exchange of craft goods and raw materials, and a wide range of co-occurring processes that united the Maya world. Each area contributed key elements to the emergence of new social and political institutions (Marcus 2008).

Without this interaction, none of the apogees and collapses seen in these regions can be understood. Large numbers of people moved between regions. Without economic competition and political conflict, some of their political institutions would not have emerged. Collapses seem less mysterious when one can document refugees moving from one region to another. To be sure, our increasingly fine-grained chronologies suggest that one region occasionally had a headstart on another, but even these may be the apparent products of where one excavates and what is preserved there.

If we continue to downplay our data from the northern lowlands, we will lack essential pieces of the Maya puzzle. Giving those data their due will make it easier to explain the dynamic cycles so characteristic of Maya societies (Marcus 1992, 1993, 1998; Sharer with Traxler 2006).

Features of the Northern Lowlands

What were the distinctive features of the northern lowlands that played a role in both local and regional developments? What might the northern lowlands have contributed to making Maya civilization what it was?

Let us begin with the fact that the Yucatan Peninsula has no rivers, and includes some of the driest zones within the Maya area. In the northwestern corner of the Yucatan Peninsula, for example, some places receive no rain during the dry season; and even during the rainy season, when they receive about 50 centimeters, they experience very high rates of evapotranspiration.

Much of the northern lowlands has thin or poor soils, and more than 25% has been characterized as having virtually no soil at all (Beach 1998; Isphording and Wilson 1973; Luzzadder-Beach 2000; Perry et al. 1995, 2002, 2003). Bedrock is exposed in these deflated zones. Although having no soil in some locales was a negative for ancient Maya farmers, it can be a positive for archaeologists. Exposed bedrock can allow archaeologists to locate the remains of Paleoindian and Archaic sites on the surface. In other words, a systematic and comprehensive survey of areas with exposed bedrock should yield important data on early periods.

The poor soils of the northern lowlands, in tandem with low rainfall and high evapotranspiration rates, posed formidable challenges to the support of large concentrations of people. It would have been particularly difficult during the long dry season for thousands of people to meet their daily water needs (Houck Jr. 2006). In spite of these difficulties, the ancient Maya clearly made a successful living, as exemplified by the particularly arid area where the site of Chunchucmil is located.

Chunchucmil lies 68 kilometers southwest of Merida and 55 kilometers northwest of Uxmal. Fortunately, it is less than 20 kilometers from a swampy estuary, which could be navigated with canoes to gain access to the Gulf of Mexico. By A.D. 500 it had become an urban center with walled residential groups, streets, and a possible marketplace. Chunchucmil apparently specialized in maritime trade, and met the needs of its population by importing basic subsistence items, all the while exhibiting a brand of urbanism that seems distinct from that seen in the southern lowlands (Ardren et al. 2003; Dahlin 2009; Dahlin et al. 2005, 2007; Stanton et al. 2000, 2010). Given its thin soils and its location, Chunchucmil evidently relied much less on maize and more on estuary and marine foods than was the case with other sites on the peninsula (Mansell et al. 2006).

In the 20 square-kilometer urban area that includes Chunchucmil, archaeologists estimate a population of more than 40,000 people from A.D. 400 to 550. Chunchucmil was in fact so urban that its density of structures was the highest of any Maya site during this era (Dahlin 2009; Dahlin et al. 2005, 2007; Magnoni et al. 2008; Vlcek et al. 1978). One of the key natural features that allowed this population concentration was a double ring of *cenotes*, or natural wells, that appeared along bedrock faults associated with a 65 million-year-old crater (Pope et al. 1996). That unusual configuration influenced groundwater, serving to accelerate and channel its flow along the ring of *cenotes*. This ring of natural wells continues to provide ready access to drinking water today (Luzzadder-Beach 2000). We will return to the Chunchucmil site later in this chapter.

In addition to its aridity, the Yucatan Peninsula differs from the rest of the Maya region in that only one language, Yukatek, was spoken there. Such monolingualism is noteworthy, especially compared to the Guatemalan highlands, where many mutually unintelligible Mayan languages were spoken.

Another feature that sets the northern lowlands apart is the fact that, as a peninsula, it has access to marine resources along three coastlines. Although known as "The Land of the Turkey and the Deer," the Yucatan Peninsula could just as well have been called "The Land of Marine Resources." With its thousands of kilometers of ocean frontage, Yucatan provided access to stingray spines, marine shells, manatees, salt deposits, sea sponges, turtles, and all kinds of fish and marine mammals (Andrews 1969; Hamblin 1984; Lange 1971; McKillop and Healy 1989).

The demand for such marine products throughout Maya prehistory is evident from the archaeological record. That demand, however, manifested itself differently from site to site and from time period to time period. In some eras there was greater emphasis on the use of marine items for personal adornment or burial offerings. Other sites show greater use of marine products in the enactment and performance of rituals, such as funerals, inaugurations, *k'atun*-ending (20-year) celebrations, or building dedication rites.

Following the emergence of hierarchical societies in the Middle Preclassic, there were secular and sacred rites that required stingray spines, marine sponges, marine animals, or shells. From Preclassic times onward, there was an increase in societal complexity and a concomitant increase in the demand for marine products. The populations of the Yucatan Peninsula were well situated to procure marine products and insert them into local, regional, and interregional exchange networks, plugging them into the southern lowland and Guatemalan highland networks.

These exchange networks have been of great interest to Maya archaeologists for decades, but much more would be known if we had quantified data from a range of houses, neighborhoods, and sites (Marcus 2009). We have abundant data from middens, caches, and burials, but lack information on family-to-family variation. By excavating a large number of houses in their entirety, we could see what products were used and imported by every household, and which were used and imported by a select few.

One important future task will be to determine what items the northern lowlands were exporting. We can begin thinking about this topic by looking at sixteenth-century documents, which can be an appropriate starting place even though we always need to remind ourselves that sixteenth-century A.D. exports may not be the same as the Preclassic exports.

Complicating our effort to quantify the exports of the northern lowlands is the fact that many may have been perishable. The exports might have included honey, shrimp, cotton, cloth, tobacco, salt, and feathers; perhaps in the future we can confirm some of these through residue analysis or the excavation of waterlogged cave and *cenote* deposits.

Looking Backward

For decades a handful of northern lowland sites, including Mayapan, Chichen Itza, Uxmal, and Tulum, dominated our discussions of the area. Since all were regarded as very late sites, archaeologists began to think that the major role of the northern lowlands was to absorb immigrants who fled northward from the collapsing cities of the southern lowlands.

That scenario has been substantially revised during the last two decades. We now know that many southern lowland cities were not abandoned; that many southern lowland residents did not flee to the northern lowlands; that many northern lowland sites had earlier occupations than expected; and perhaps most significantly, that the northern lowlands were responsible for many innovations once credited to the south (e.g., Andrews and Robles Castellanos 2004; Andrews and Sabloff 1986; Chase and Rice 1985; Demarest et al. 2004; Fash et al. 2004; Rice 1988).

Three recent themes that have emerged are: (1) the pace, tempo, and rhythm of the developments in each region; (2) the nature of their co-evolution; and (3) the causes and mechanisms that delayed, stimulated, or accelerated their developments.

Paleoindian and Archaic Eras

The last few decades of survey and excavation have revealed a long sequence of occupation and substantial evidence for nucleated, dense populations on the Yucatan Peninsula. For the earliest eras, however, few sites have been extensively excavated. The number of known Paleoindian and Archaic sites is small, in spite of recent efforts (e.g., Andrews and Robles Castellanos 2004; González González et al. 2008, 2010; Lohse 2010). The potential is there, however, to (1) document the transition from a nomadic existence to a sedentary way of life and (2) identify an Early Preclassic period for Yucatan.

The Preclassic Era

Our knowledge of the Middle Preclassic (800–300 B.C.) and Late Preclassic (300 B.C.–A.D. 250) has grown enormously in recent years. Most of the new studies build on the substantial foundation made by E. Wyllys Andrews IV, E. Wyllys Andrews V, and Anthony P. Andrews, and as each year goes by, we appreciate and increasingly value their pioneering survey and excavation projects (e.g., Andrews and Andrews 1980; Andrews 1979b, 1981, 1988, 1990, 2003; Andrews et al. 1980, 1984, 2008; Andrews and Ringle 1992; Ringle and Andrews 1988, 1990).

For the Preclassic I think we will always use the reports on Komchen and Dzibilchaltun as our solid foundation, and we will use the ongoing regional surveys as guides to designing future excavation projects. One key survey, conducted by Anthony Andrews and Fernando Robles Castellanos (2004), covered an area of about 2200 square kilometers, extending from the coastal ports of Progreso and Celestun to the city of Merida. The survey was designed to obtain new data for the files of the Atlas Arqueológico del Estado de Yucatán (Garza Tarazona de González and Kurjack 1980), and it did so by discovering 249 prehispanic sites, 140 of them dating to the Preclassic.

The variety and complexity of sites during the Middle Preclassic (Anderson 2009; Andrews and Robles Castellanos 2004:8; Andrews 1986; Ball 1977; Boucher and Palomo Carrillo 2005; Peraza Lope et al. 2002) suggest a three-tiered hierarchy of settlements, from hamlets with scattered mounds at Tier 3 of the hierarchy, to Tier 2 sites with substantial pyramids arranged around formal plazas with ballcourts, to at least one Tier 1 site that covers two square-kilometers and has a ballcourt, pyramids, causeways (*sacbeob*), and a well-defined plaza.

The largest of the Tier 1 sites is Xtobo, southwest of Dzibilchaltun, where David S. Anderson has been working. Anderson's mapping and excavations at Xtobo have revealed Middle Preclassic monumental architecture and five causeways that radiate out from a well-defined central plaza (Anderson 2003, 2009). Immediately to the south of the plaza is a ballcourt.

During Middle Preclassic times, ballcourts seem more common at sites in northwestern Yucatan than anywhere else. The Andrews–Robles Castellanos survey discovered that 23 of the Middle Preclassic sites had ballcourts, that they were always located near the center of the settlements, had a north–south alignment between 345 and 25 degrees, measured between 10–15 meters in length and five-eight meters in width, and enclosed a playing surface roughly six-to-seven meters wide (Anderson 2003, 2009; Andrews and Robles Castellanos 2004; Medina Castillo 2003, 2005).

In the Puuc region, one of the few known Middle Preclassic ballcourts was found at Paso del Macho (Gallareta Negrón and Ringle 2004). At the northern edge of the Puuc zone is Xocnaceh, a site with a huge Middle Preclassic Acropolis 8.5 meters high and 150 meters by 150 meters at the base (Gallareta Negrón and Ringle 2004; Gallareta Negrón et al. 2005).

Anderson's work at Xtobo resulted in the creation of detailed topographic maps of 67 hectares of continuous settlement and the mapping of 387 structures. Anderson estimates that Xtobo had a population of about 1,500 people. Interregional exchange is documented by the fact that the obsidian at Xtobo comes from San Martín Jilotepeque and El Chayal, two of the major quarries in the Guatemalan highlands.

The density of structures at Xtobo (5.78 per hectare) is comparable to the density of structures at Komchen, meaning that these two Preclassic sites have a greater density than that found at many Late Classic (A.D. 550–900) centers in the southern lowlands (Anderson 2009; Ringle and Andrews 1990). The strategy of concentrating a lot of people into settlements in the driest sector of Yucatan, beginning sometime in the Preclassic, sets the stage for later developments, such as the Early Classic urbanism at Chunchucmil.

Let us look at a few other Preclassic sites in Yucatan. North and east of Xtobo is Caucel, a site with 1,500 structures in an 8 square-kilometer area; 90 percent of the structures are considered to be Preclassic in date (Hernández Hernández 2008; Uriarte Torres 2007). Further north and east in Quintana Roo, the Yalahau survey discovered many Middle Preclassic sites (Glover et al. 2005; Rissolo et al. 2005). Other large Middle Preclassic sites on the Yucatan Peninsula include Poxila (Robles Castellanos et al. 2006), Xocnaceh (Gallareta Negrón and Ringle 2004; Gallareta Negrón et al. 2005), Ake (Roys and Shook 1966), Dzibanche (Nalda 2004), and of course, Calakmul, at the southern end of the Yucatan Peninsula (Carrasco Vargas and Colón González 2005; Folan et al. 1995a, 1995b; Marcus and Folan 1994; Pincemin et al. 1998).

Although the number of extensively excavated Preclassic sites is still small, progress is being made. More Preclassic sites need to be the focus of multi-year horizontal excavations, especially those sites where Classic-period overburden is not present. This lack of overburden is unfortunately not the case at Calakmul, a city that went on to become one of the most monumental capitals in the Maya area (Folan et al. 1995b; Grube 2004; Marcus 1987, 2004; Martin and Grube 2008).

Given the number of Middle Preclassic sites, we can infer both that Yucatan had a large population in that era, and that additional extensive surveys are likely to yield even more Middle Preclassic sites. If future large-scale surveys use the same methods employed by Andrews and Robles Castellanos (2004), the task of comparing and contrasting the results from region to region would be greatly facilitated.

Such surveys might even make Yucatan an epicenter of Preclassic studies. That would perhaps help to remove the perception that the north was a poor country cousin of the south.

What we still lack are very extensive excavations of Preclassic buildings and neighborhoods, along the lines of what Andrews IV and Andrews V accomplished at Dzibilchaltun and Komchen. Such excavation would probably reveal more about Preclassic social rank from burials, household inventories, comparisons of building plans, and so forth. There are hints that the northern lowlands were experiencing the same evolutionary developments and innovations that occurred to the south, and in some instances were even more precocious for their time.

More extensive excavations at Preclassic centers in the north would complement what we know from southern sites like Barton Ramie (Willey et al. 1965; Hohmann 2002), Blackman Eddy (M. K. Brown and Garber 2003; Garber et al. 1998), Cahal Pech (Aimers et al. 2000; Awe 1992; Powis 1996), Cuello (Andrews and Hammond 1990; Hammond 1991; Robin 1989), Cerros (Freidel 1978; Scarborough 1991), El Mirador (Dahlin 1984; Forsyth 1989; Hansen 1984, 1990, 1994; Matheny 1980, 1986, 1987); Nakbe (Forsyth 1993; Hansen 2002, Hansen et al. 1991), and Pacbitun (Healy and Awe 1999; White et al. 1993).

Perhaps most importantly, we need to find the Early Preclassic that must be there given the large number of Middle Preclassic sites that have been found everywhere that archaeologists look.

Given the size and number of Middle Preclassic settlements in the northernmost corners of the Yucatan Peninsula, it is clear that local populations and in situ developments have been seriously underestimated. It is time to stop arguing that immigrants from the south were responsible for advances made in the north. Regional exchange of all kinds probably connected much of the Maya lowlands, and we need not invoke population movements to explain the interregional similarities (Stanton 2000). In fact, surveys in several parts of the northern lowlands suggest that well over half the sites found were occupied in the Late Preclassic (Anderson 2009; Andrews and Robles Castellanos 2004; Gallareta Negrón et al. 2003, 2004; Mathews and Maldonado Cárdenas 2006; Morrison 2000; Stanton 2000).

The Classic Era

The Early Classic (A.D. 250–550) has been the focus of several recent projects in the northern lowlands. We have learned much more about Yaxuna (Ardren 1997; Johnstone 2001; Stanton 2000; Stanton et al. 2010), Ichmul (Shaw 2008), Yo'okop (Shaw 2008), as well as relations between Yo'okop and Calakmul in southern Campeche. This Early Classic tie between Yo'okop and Calakmul is one example of interregional interaction between the northern and southern lowlands (Shaw 2008). One of the few hieroglyphic texts known from Yo'okop mentions the ruler named Sky Witness, a man who ruled Calakmul at ca. A.D. 560; unfortunately, the text gives few details.

One hopes that the work at Yaxuna will inspire more excavation at Early Classic sites such as Actun Toh, Ake, El Naranjal, Huntichmul, Ikil, Izamal, Kantunilkin, Ox Mul, Siho, Tres Lagunas, Uci, Victoria, and Xcambo (Burgos et al. 2003; Ceballos Gallareta 2003, Jiménez Álvarez 2002; Mathews 1998; Mathews and Maldonado Cárdenas 2006; Quiñones Cetina 2006; Roys and Shook 1966; Sierra Sosa 1999, 2001).

Two of the key Early Classic sites in the Puuc region were Chac (Smyth 2006, 2008, 2009; Smyth and Ortegón Zapata 2006) and Oxkintok (López Vázquez and Fernández Marquínez 1987; Rivera Dorado 1988, 1989, 1990, 1992; Varela Torrecilla 1998). Oxkintok, which lay at the edge of the Puuc ridge, has produced Teotihuacan-style cylindrical tripod vessels, as well as a number of buildings displaying *talud-tablero* architecture (Rivera Dorado 1988, 1989; Varela Torrecilla 1998; Varela Torrecilla and Braswell 2003). Both the pottery and architecture at Oxkintok, which date to ca. A.D. 500–600, seem to be variants or copies of Gulf Coast and highland Mexican forms (Ortiz and Santley 1998).

Michael Smyth's (2008) work at Chac, a site near Sayil, has been of particular interest because it has raised a whole series of questions about relationships between Yucatan and Teotihuacan (Stanton 2005). Smyth has found cylindrical tripod vessels, *candeleros*, *floreros*, green Pachuca obsidian, round burial cists, *talud-tablero* architecture, and other apparent non-local elements. Speaking about the site of Chac, Smyth (2008:402) notes, "While no one material category by itself is convincingly diagnostic of Teotihuacan contact, the presence of multiple categories and the convergence of the evidence are compelling." To Smyth, these items suggest direct interaction with Teotihuacan, but we should not rule out the possibility that some of them passed through the hands of intervening groups and some were local imitations.

Perhaps the strongest evidence at Chac for direct foreign interaction with Teotihuacan is a series of residential structures and a number of round burial cists constructed in a Teotihuacan style. Such cists are similar to those known from Teotihuacan. One cist at Chac included a tripod plate with the image of Tlaloc, and a *candelero*. The non-elite residential structures at Chac had rooms arranged around patios, oriented about 15 degrees east of cardinal north. One of these structures contained a rectangular altar in the center of the patio, and the residential group was surrounded by a large masonry wall. Since such compounds are supposedly unusual for the northern lowlands, Smyth thinks that they may have housed Teotihuacanos. If several skeletons from these cists at Chac had been shown to be Teotihuacanos, the argument would have been much more compelling. Additional evidence includes a cylindrical vase with coffee-bean appliques, found beneath the stucco floor of Structure E-III in the Chac Pyramid Plaza (Smyth 2006:126). Some tripod vessels look to be local imitations, while others look to be made on Fine Buff, a ware apparently produced at Matacapan. One vessel at Chac had non-local motifs and the hollow round supports typical of Gulf Coast ceramics. Unfortunately, however, pots are not people. In reassessing the data for Chac, Travis Stanton (2005:31) concludes that "…none of this evidence proves that Teotihuacan men were permanently living in the northern Maya lowlands."

In sum, there is growing evidence suggesting that the Maya were active agents in adapting and modifying foreign styles to fit their own needs, and this process of adoption, emulation, and modification is still poorly understood (e.g., Braswell 2003a, 2003b; Marcus 2003; Varela Torrecilla and Braswell 2003).

At Chac and at Oxkintok we see local imitations of Teotihuacan-style artifacts mixed with objects whose style had already been modified by people who lived between Teotihuacan and the Puuc area. The mediated interaction of Yucatan with highland Mexico, the Gulf Coast lowlands, Chiapas, and the highlands and lowlands of Guatemala is rarely emphasized. There has been a tendency to see interaction as direct and the response of the Maya as passive.

The Teotihuacan–Maya picture is fascinating, yet we should avoid simplistic interpretations. Influence is unlikely to have been one-way. Evidence continues to mount that Teotihuacan borrowed and modified Maya features for its own use (e.g., Braswell 2003a, 2003b; Marcus 2003; Taube 2003; Varela Torrecilla and Braswell 2003). The number of intervening societies that lived between the Maya area and Teotihuacan is so great that we will need: (1) a type of network analysis that connects all the nodes, gateways, trade routes, and pathways; and (2) a careful evaluation of each kind of commodity.

Another of the interesting Early Classic discoveries is just how urban Chunchucmil was. From A.D. 400 to 550 it covered perhaps 25 square kilometers, featuring three times as many people in its nine-square-kilometer central zone than did Tikal. The residential groups of Chunchucmil, bounded by walls and *albarradas*, make it an early forerunner of the urban centers that we see later in the Yucatan Peninsula. The number of mapped residential groups at Chunchucmil has now reached 1,000, with more than 400 being of the bounded houselot type. We should look forward to seeing many of those houselots fully excavated, and their features and artifact inventories published (e.g., Hutson et al. 2006).

The data emerging from the Chunchucmil project suggest that that site was actively participating in maritime trade, using canoes to exploit the estuary, coastal salt flats, and ocean resources. At the same time, the residents of Chunchucmil evidently had to import many essential products (including food and wood) to the site. This raises a series of questions: Was there a road or canal that connected Chunchucmil to the coast, only 27 kilometers away? Were there intermediate sites along the way, with storage for transshipment of the items brought to and from the coast?

One reason the political complexity of the Early Classic northern lowlands has been underestimated is its relative lack of hieroglyphic texts. Even when we do have texts for the northern lowlands, they are most often integral building components such as lintels, capstones, jambs, and walls, rather than free-standing stelae (an excellent Late Classic example would be that at Sisila; see Benavides Castillo 2003 and Pollock 1980).

We need to remind ourselves that the presence or absence of writing is not the key criterion for political complexity or social stratification. As George Bey (2006:36) aptly states, "The Early Classic Maya in the north were not country bumpkins living in the backwaters of the Maya world but instead a culturally distinct group that took a different trajectory to some extent from that of the south. The limited number of texts and polychromes in the north is not a result of the area being culturally backward but the result of an indigenous and not-fully-understood regional cultural tradition." One northern city with hieroglyphic texts is Chichen Itza (e.g., Graña-Behrens 2006; Graña-Behrens et al. 1999; Krochock 1988, 1998, 2002). In this volume, Geoffrey Braswell and his students report on their recent excavations there.

In addition, there have been recent excavations in the Initial Series Group, a complex of buildings that may have housed the most important lineages at Chichen Itza (Schmidt 2005). The site of Chichen Itza has a long occupation, with its occupants choosing styles and motifs eclectically. Contrasting styles were selected by groups occupying various building clusters, connected one to another by intra-site causeways. It now appears that, rather than being the passive recipient of foreign styles brought to Yucatan by highland Mexicans, the northern lowlands borrowed elements from several different areas (see Braswell and Peniche May, this volume). Our assessment has now changed from seeing the northern Maya as passive recipients to viewing them as active agents (Cobos 2006; Braswell and Peniche May, this volume).

The epigraphic record at Chichen Itza (and other Yucatec sites) has been variously interpreted as evidence of: (1) a monarchy with a divine ruler and his support staff of priests and officeholders; or (2) a kind of *multepal*, or joint rule, in which several lineages co-ruled the city and its subject territory. The pendulum continues to swing back and forth between these positions. Recently, however, the monarchical model has come to the fore, putting the government of Chichen Itza more closely in line with those of the southern lowlands (e.g., Plank 2004; Ringle 2004; Zender 2004). In this view it would have been the political collapse of Chichen Itza that created the conditions for joint rule, the kind of administration that came to characterize the Postclassic Maya at Mayapan.

In addition to Chichen Itza, key sites with hieroglyphic texts include Oxkintok (Rivera Dorado 1988, 1989, 1990, 1992), Xcalumkin (Pollock 1980), Edzna (Benavides Castillo 1997; Forsyth 1983; Matheny 1987), Uxmal (Kowalski 1985; Ruppert and Smith 1957), Coba (Folan et al. 1983; Ruppert and Denison 1943), and Ek' Balam (Lacadena García-Gallo 2005; Vargas de la Peña and Castillo Borges 2005). Of all these, perhaps the most spectacular masterpieces of hieroglyphic writing are the texts painted on the walls and capstones at Ek' Balam—especially in the palace and court of the ruler, which lay inside concentric walls.

The Ek' Balam palace, known as Structure 1 or the Acropolis, was 162 meters long, 68 meters wide, and more than 32 meters high. Here archaeologists Leticia Vargas de la Peña and Víctor Castillo Borges have so far exposed 72 rooms. Elsewhere inside the walled precinct were plazas, temples, residential quarters, a sweatbath, altars and shrines, stelae, and painted walls with hieroglyphic texts. One *sacbe* on the west led to the outer wall of the precinct, while two others led to the front (or south) side.

The Mural of the 96 Glyphs, found on the wall of Room 29-sub inside the Acropolis, reports the A.D. 770 arrival of a man associated with the prestigious title, "*kalo'mte* of the north." Apparently under his auspices, a new ruler named Ukit Kan Lek Tok' took the throne of Ek' Balam and administered the Kingdom of Talol. This new king is said to have come from Man, a place we have yet to identify but which may be linked to Mani.

Alfonso Lacadena García-Gallo (2005) has concluded that because this ruler was the founder of the royal dynasty at Ek' Balam, he went on to become the most-often-mentioned ruler in the texts of Ek' Balam. A spectacularly preserved structure, with a stucco façade modeled in the form of an earth monster, was the final resting place of Ukit Kan Lek Tok'. That structure, found on the fourth level of the west wing of the Acropolis, was called by the ancient Maya *sak xok naah*, "the White House of Reading." Ukit Kan Lek Tok', in some ways, was treated like the Copan ruler Yax K'uk' Mo'o, since both were regarded as dynastic founders. Their final resting places were shrines and their royal successors referred to these founders with great reverence. Among the Ek' Balam rulers who referred back to the dynastic founder were K'an B'ohb' Tok', Ukit Jol Ahkul, and K'inich Junpik Tok'.

Prior to the discovery of these texts at Ek' Balam, archaeologists had underestimated the nature of divine kingship in the northern lowlands. Although divine kingship exists in societies that lack writing, it is more difficult to demonstrate. To be sure, the evidence for scribes and the carvers of stelae is much earlier in the southern lowlands, the Guatemalan highlands, and the Pacific piedmont than in the northern lowlands (e.g., Marcus 1976; Mora-Marín 2008; Saturno et al. 2006).

The finds by the Jaina Archaeological Project, however, are making investigators reconsider whether or not Late Preclassic writing existed in the northern lowlands (see Benavides Castillo and Grube 2002 to compare Jaina's Panel 3 with Stela 10 at Kaminaljuyu and with Monument 60 at Izapa). Will future excavations in the northern lowlands uncover additional examples of early Maya writing? After all, less than a decade has passed since William Saturno discovered a column of hieroglyphs painted on a wall at San Bartolo, a site northeast of Tikal. That was a significant find because it put writing in the southern lowlands closer in time to its appearance in the Guatemalan highlands (Saturno et al. 2006). Until Saturno's discovery, the Guatemalan highlands and Pacific piedmont had laid claim to the oldest writing within the Maya region. Now the discoveries at Jaina, Oxkintok, Ek' Balam, and elsewhere suggest that, despite the greater numbers of stelae with hieroglyphs in the southern lowlands, the north may have had its own long tradition of writing.

Our views are also being changed by new discoveries at Calakmul in Campeche, near the geographic transition between the northern and southern lowlands. One discovery is the spectacular Late Preclassic façade of Substructure IIc; others include Early Classic murals and stelae (Carrasco Vargas and Colón González 2005; Pincemin et al. 1998). Before the discovery of Stela 114 at Calakmul, the northernmost site with a fifth-century date (8.19.15.12.13 or A.D. 431) was Balakbal (Marcus and Folan 1994; Ruppert and Denison 1943). Stela 114 has added a century of time depth to the Calakmul dynasty (Pincemin et al. 1998) and future discoveries could add more.

Ivan Šprajc's (2004, 2008) systematic survey in southeastern Campeche has raised our estimates of Early Classic occupation in that area. Many of these key sites were in the social and political web of Calakmul. Our understanding of the Early Classic is further enriched by new survey and excavation data from southern Quintana Roo (Nalda 2004; Esparza Olguín and Pérez Gutiérrez 2009). In particular, the excavations at Dzibanche and nearby sites have been key to our current understanding of Early Classic politics, especially the relationship of the Quintana Roo sites to the Kaan Polity later administered by Calakmul. The fact that the Kaan (or snake head) emblem glyph appears in texts at Dzibanche, El Resbalon, and Pol Box even before that emblem appears at Calakmul has piqued interest in the role of southern Quintana Roo in the founding of the Calakmul dynasty (Carrasco Vargas and Boucher 1987; Esparza Olguín and Pérez Gutiérrez 2009; Marcus, this volume; Šprajc et al. 2005; Velásquez García 2004, 2005).

The snake head was used by Calakmul as its emblem glyph from A.D. 636 to 736 (Grube 2004; Marcus 2004; Martin 2005). Before A.D. 636, and again after A.D. 736, Calakmul seems to have used a bat as its polity name. If future research upholds this sequence—use of the bat emblem, then the snake-head emblem, and then re-use of the bat emblem—we may have evidence for political cycling that will be difficult to equal with data from any other Maya region. To be sure, it is ironic that we are now learning so much about Calakmul from distant sites whose monuments are in a better state of preservation (Marcus 1987, 2004). Like so many Yucatan Peninsula sites, Calakmul carved its monuments on poor-quality soft limestone, leaving its once-legible hieroglyphic texts highly weathered, eroded, and illegible.

The Postclassic Era

The Yucatan Peninsula, of course, abounds with Postclassic and colonial sites. Among the most celebrated are Mayapan, Tulum, Dzibilchaltun, Becan, Coba, Edzna, and Chichen Itza, and the sites of Cozumel Island (Anderson 1998; Andrews and Robles Castellanos 1985; Andrews et al.

2003; Andrews and Sabloff 1986; Benavides Castillo 1997; Folan et al. 1983; Freidel 1981; Freidel and Sabloff 1984; Lothrop 1924; Masson and Peraza Lope 2008; Milbrath and Peraza Lope 2003).

The full story of Mayapan is becoming better known as archaeologists return there to augment the work conducted by the Carnegie Institution of Washington (Pollock et al. 1962). This work uses sixteenth-century documents to complement the excavations of this walled city, which encloses more than 4,000 structures in a 4.2 square-kilometer area (Brown 1999; Jones 1962; Marcus and Sabloff 2008; Masson and Peraza Lope 2008; Pollock et al. 1962). We now know that residential settlement extended outside these walls despite the fact that defense and personal safety were major concerns. The original founding of Mayapan is still shrouded in mystery.

Ethnohistoric documents indicate that a Mayapan ruler named Hunac Ceel conquered Chichen Itza. From A.D. 1100 to 1300, according to sixteenth-century documents, a Triple Alliance called the League of Mayapan was co-administered by Chichen Itza, Uxmal, and Mayapan. Later, with the collapse of the governments at Uxmal and Chichen Itza, Mayapan came to be governed by a *multepal* or joint rule. That alliance involved the Kokoom, the ruling lineage at Chichen Itza, the Xiw, the ruling lineage at Uxmal, and a few other groups.

By A.D. 1400 the Xiw had been expelled from Mayapan, leaving the Kokoom to dominate that polity (Tozzer 1941). Remnants of the Xiw faction, however, became angry and revolted against the Kokoom. Diego de Landa reports that all the members of the Kokoom royal house in Mayapan were killed during the Xiw revolt. That statement has been reinforced by excavations at Mayapan, which show the burning of buildings and widespread destruction.

Mayapan was a city modeled after the Classic metropolis of Chichen Itza. The Temple of Kukulcan at Mayapan was a smaller version of Chichen Itza's Castillo; its Round Temple was a smaller version of the Caracol of Chichen Itza. When the Round Temple at Mayapan was excavated in the 1990s, archaeologists found the four doorways described in the sixteenth century by Diego de Landa (see Tozzer 1941).

The sixteenth-century documents also shed light on the colonial archaeology of Yucatan (e.g., Andrews 1984; Alexander 1999, 2004). When the Spaniards arrived they found the peninsula divided into autonomous provinces called *kuchkabaloob*. These provinces represented the polities formerly united by the *multepal* at Mayapan, an alliance that succeeded for a time in centralizing the administration of Yucatan. All those autonomous provinces had resurfaced when the centralized administration at Mayapan collapsed.

Looking Ahead

What might the future hold for archaeologists working in Yucatan? To begin with, some periods are so poorly known that they are in great need of attention. Two very important contributions would be to document: (1) the transition from the Archaic to the Early Preclassic period; and (2) the transition from the Early Preclassic to the Middle Preclassic. Without such research the very high density of Middle Preclassic sites cannot be understood.

Conducting household archaeology at a site of any period would also be a contribution. The northern lowlands is particularly suitable for household archaeology since (in contrast to the Peten) many stone alignments, small structures, and even entire house groups can be detected right on the surface. Many more houses could probably be excavated per season than in the southern lowlands. Huge sums of money would not be needed to dig such houses, unlike the expenses involved when excavating huge temple pyramids.

We should consider increasing the amount of fieldwork being conducted at Preclassic sites in Yucatan. This work should include documenting the variety of house types, village plans, storage and other features, tool kits, mortuary settings, neighborhoods, and sociopolitical networks.

Mayanists speak often of daily activities, household rituals, and the lives of commoners, and yet few are actually digging large numbers of Maya households and piece-plotting everything they find. We need many such studies before we can compare household-to-household activities, and even more before we can compare whole villages. In some parts of the northern lowlands, the soil is so thin that whole barrios could be exposed with minimal earth removal.

I frequently ask my students to describe their chosen archaeological site without referring to its pottery. This makes them aware of the unrealistic burden we place on ceramics in our effort to explain the past. Work in the northern lowlands shows us that the links between ceramic spheres and political control are neither simple nor direct. One community can be under the control of another for a few years and not have its ceramics affected. One community can be autonomous, but use the same ceramic assemblage as another. A case in point is the much-discussed relationship, distribution, and dating of Sotuta and Cehpech ceramics in the northern lowlands.

Sotuta pottery dominated at Chichen Itza, but the nearby site of Yaxuna (only 19 kilometers away) had no Sotuta ceramics until Period IVb. At this point, Sotuta pottery appeared for the first time in association with the deliberate destruction of buildings (Shaw and Johnstone 2006:151-152). The lack of Sotuta pottery at Yaxuna during Period IVa (and before) has been interpreted as evidence that Yaxuna was autonomous, and that "a powerful barrier prohibiting the free exchange of goods" existed. At the site of Ek' Balam, less than .01 percent of the assemblage consisted of Sotuta sherds, leading archaeologists to regard that site as autonomous. At the site of Ichmul de Morley, Sotuta ceramics constituted 10.6 percent of all the sherds, leading archaeologists to conclude that Ichmul de Morley was not wholly influenced by either Chichen Itza or Ek' Balam (Smith et al. 2006). The site of Yula, just five kilometers south of Chichen Itza, provides a contrast; 97 percent of its ceramics were Sotuta in style (Anderson 1998). In addition, two lintels at Yula were very similar to those at Chichen Itza.

It is likely that the percentage of Sotuta sherds at each of these sites will continue to be used to infer political control or autonomy, but we may be placing too large an explanatory burden on ceramics. A site can lose or gain its independence multiple times during a single century, and pottery does not aid us in such instances, since our 300-year ceramic periods tend to mask short-term political oscillations.

Hieroglyphic texts sometimes allow us to detect short-term oscillations between autonomy and subordination, but without such texts and the dates they provide, the task can be formidable. Many short-term episodes of control or autonomy can be documented in the southern lowlands, because we have so many well-preserved texts from so many more sites.

The Pace and Tempo of Developments in the Highlands and Lowlands

Future research in Yucatan could take many directions, but if I had to isolate one interesting problem, it would be to look beyond the local details and compare the pace of developments in the three major regions of the Maya world. Now that we know that the northern lowlands were not simply the recipients of influence from the south, we need to know which innovations we can attribute to Yucatan and which occurred simultaneously in both the north and south.

Having scrapped the notion of an active south and a passive north, we should consider the possibility that one of the engines driving Maya civilization was the competitive interaction among regions. The Yucatan Peninsula, at least as early as the Middle Preclassic, would have been one of the regions driving both local and pan-Maya developments. Had there been no such interaction—no exchanges, no alliances, no competition, and no conflict—one of the major catalysts of social evolution would have been missing. And as we have seen, there is growing evidence that the northern lowlands, too often treated like a passive recipient of ideas, was an innovator in many cases.

The Impact of E. Wyllys Andrews V

If you are to raise the archaeology of Yucatan to its rightful position, it is appropriate that you dedicate this volume to E. Wyllys Andrews V. No noble lineage—not even the Kokoom and Xiw lineages of Mayapan—has made a greater contribution to Yucatan than the lineage founded by E. Wyllys Andrews IV.

The collective attention of this family to the Yucatec environment, to careful stratigraphy, to empirical detail, and to maintaining high standards has set the bar very high. Their presentation of hard-won field data and their efforts to quantify and explain their datasets in meaningful ways will endure forever.

I close by mentioning some of the contributions of "Will" Andrews V. We can see in his long series of publications not simply a desire to rework the datasets of a previous generation (as so many archaeologists do) but to generate his own. His goal was to understand how the Maya lived, changed, and evolved through time by contributing primary data on all time periods, and he did it by directing original project after original project.

Figure 14.1. Will Andrews (right) engages in high-level modeling and problem solving while the author (center) holds the stadia rod at Structure 10L-29, Copan, March 1991.

Will generated new data on the residences of commoners and kings, and on the activities of both low-status and royal families. His interests have included cities and villages such as Dzibilchaltun and Komchen; the earliest ceramics of the northern and southern lowlands; the architecture of Puuc centers like Sayil and Labna; the demise of a Maya king and his palace at Copan; and the southeastern periphery of the Maya region at Quelepa. His fieldwork has given him a unique perspective on the peopling of the Maya area, its early villagers, the nature of collapse and abandonment, and much more (Andrews 1979a, 1979b, 1981, 1990, 2003).

Because Will has contributed in so many ways to our understanding of the Maya—from northernmost Yucatan to eastern El Salvador—he now deserves to sit back and relax while we toast him with an appropriate beverage.

I once visited Will while he and Bill Fash, Bob Sharer, Ricardo Agurcia, and Geoff Braswell were conducting excavations at Copan (Figure 14.1). Over the years I had visited a lot of fine archaeological projects; but when I returned from my trip to Copan, I sat down, removed one site from my list of "Top 10 All-Time Projects," and put the Copan Project into its vacated slot. The work being conducted there was that impressive.

I venture to say that the contributions of Will Andrews will stand the test of time, and I hope that his work will encourage future archaeologists to build on his firm foundation—to map entire sites, excavate whole public buildings, expose scores of houses and patios, and piece-plot every object on every ancient floor.

References

Aimers, James J., Terry G. Powis, and Jaime J. Awe. 2000. Preclassic Round Structures of the Upper Belize River Valley. *Latin American Antiquity* 11:71-86.

Alexander, Rani T. 1999. Mesoamerican Houselots and Archaeological Site Structure: Problems of Interference in Yaxcaba, Mexico, 1750–1847. In *The Archaeology of Household Activities*, edited by Penelope Allison, pp. 87-100. Routledge, London.

— 2004. *Yaxcabá and the Caste War of Yucatán: An Archaeological Perspective*. University of New Mexico, Albuquerque.

Anderson, David S. 2003. So Much More Than Ballcourts: Preclassic Settlement in Northwest Yucatan. Paper presented at the 68th Annual Meeting of the Society for American Archaeology, Milwaukee.

— 2009. Xtobo and the Emergent Preclassic of Northwest Yucatan, Mexico. Paper presented at the 74th Annual Meeting of the Society for American Archaeology, Atlanta.

Anderson, Patricia K. 1998. *Yula, Yucatán, Mexico: Terminal Classic Maya Settlement and Political Organization in the Chichen Itza Polity*. Ph.D. dissertation, Department of Anthropology, University of Chicago. University Microfilms, Ann Arbor.

Andrews, Anthony P. 1984. The Political Geography of the Sixteenth Century Yucatan Maya: Comments and Revisions. *Journal of Anthropological Research* 40:589-596.

Andrews, Anthony P., E. Wyllys Andrews V, and Fernando Robles Castellanos. 2003. The Northern Maya Collapse and its Aftermath. *Ancient Mesoamerica* 14:151-156.

Andrews, Anthony P., and Fernando Robles Castellanos. 1985. Chichen Itza and Coba: An Itza-Maya Standoff in Early Postclasssic Yucatan. In Chase and Rice 1985:62-72.

— 2004. An Archaeological Survey of Northwest Yucatan, Mexico. *Mexicon* 26:7-14.

Andrews IV, E. Wyllys. 1969. *Archaeological Use and Distribution of Mollusca in the Maya Lowlands*. Middle American Research Institute, Publication 34. Tulane University, New Orleans.

Andrews IV, E. Wyllys, and E. Wyllys Andrews V. 1980. *Excavations at Dzibilchaltun, Yucatan, Mexico*. Middle American Research Institute, Publication 48. Tulane University, New Orleans.

Andrews V, E. Wyllys. 1979a. Some Comments on Puuc Architecture of the Northern Yucatan Peninsula. In *The Puuc: New Perspectives*, edited by Lawrence Mills, pp. 1-17. Scholarly Studies in the Liberal Arts Publication 1. Central College, Pella, Iowa.

— 1979b. Early Central Mexican Architectural Traits at Dzibilchaltun, Yucatan. *Proceedings of the 42nd International Congress of Americanists* 8:237-249. The International Society of Americanists of Paris, Paris.

— 1981. Dzibilchaltun. In *Supplement to the Handbook of Middle American Indians*, vol. 1, edited by Jeremy A. Sabloff, pp. 313-341. University of Texas, Austin.

— 1986. Olmec Jades from Chacsinkin, Yucatan and Maya Ceramics from La Venta, Tabasco. In *Research and Reflections in Archaeology and History: Essays in Honor of Doris Stone*, edited by E. Wyllys Andrews V, pp. 11-49. Middle American Research Institute Publication 57. Tulane University, New Orleans.

— 1988. Ceramic Units from Komchen, Yucatan, Mexico. *Cerámica de Cultura Maya* 15:51-64.

— 1990. The Early Ceramic History of the Lowland Maya. In *Vision and Revision in Maya Studies*, edited by Flora S. Clancy and Peter D. Harrison, pp. 1-19. University of New Mexico, Albuquerque.

— 2003. New Thoughts on Komchen and the Late Middle Preclassic. Paper presented at the Second Annual Tulane Maya Symposium, New Orleans.

Andrews V, E. Wyllys, George J. Bey III, and Christopher Gunn. 2008. Rethinking the Early Ceramic History of the Northern Maya Lowlands: New Evidence and Interpretations. Paper presented at the 73rd Annual Meeting of the Society for American Archaeology, Vancouver.

Andrews V, E. Wyllys, and Norman Hammond. 1990. Redefinition of the Swasey Phase at Cuello, Belize. *American Antiquity* 55:570-584.

Andrews V, E. Wyllys, Norberto González Crespo, and William M. Ringle. 1980. *Map of the Ruins of Komchen, Yucatan, Mexico*. Middle American Research Institute, Tulane University, New Orleans.

Andrews V, E. Wyllys, and William M. Ringle. 1992. Los mayas tempranos en Yucatán: Investigaciones arqueológicas en Komchén. *Mayab* 8:5-17.

Andrews V, E. Wyllys, William M. Ringle, P. J. Barnes, Alfredo Barrera Rubio, and Tomás Gallareta Negrón. 1984. Komchen, an Early Maya Community in Northwest Yucatán. In *Investigaciones Recientes en el Área Maya: XVII Mesa Redonda*, Tomo I, pp. 73-92. Sociedad Mexicana de Antropología, Mexico City.

Andrews V, E. Wyllys, and Jeremy A. Sabloff. 1986. Classic to Postclassic: A Summary Discussion. In *Late Lowland Maya Civilization*, edited by Jeremy A. Sabloff and E. Wyllys Andrews V, pp. 433-456. University of New Mexico, Albuquerque.

Ardren, Traci A. 1997. *The Politics of Place: Architecture and Cultural Change at the Xkanha Group, Yaxuná, Yucatán, Mexico*. Ph.D. dissertation, Department of Anthropology, Yale University. University Microfilms, Ann Arbor.

Ardren, Traci A., Aline Magnoni, and David Hixson. 2003. The Nature of Urbanism at Ancient Chunchucmil. Paper presented at the Second Annual Tulane Maya Symposium, New Orleans.

Awe, Jaime J. 1992. *Dawn in the Land Between the Rivers: Formative Occupation at Cahal Pech, Belize and its Implications for Preclassic Development in the Maya Lowlands*. Ph.D. dissertation, Institute of Archaeology, University of London, London.

Ball, Joseph W. 1977. The Rise of the Northern Maya Chiefdoms: A Socioprocessual Analysis. In *The Origins of Maya Civilization*, edited by Richard E. W. Adams, pp. 101-132. University of New Mexico, Albuquerque.

Beach, Timothy. 1998. Soil Constraints on Northwest Yucatan, Mexico: Pedoarchaeology and Maya Subsistence at Chunchucmil. *Geoarchaeology* 13:759-791.

Benavides Castillo, Antonio. 1997. *Edzná: Una Ciudad Prehispánica de Campeche*. Instituto Nacional de Antropología e Historia, Mexico City.

— 2003. Labores de conservación arquitectónica en Sisilá, Campeche. *Mexicon* 25:161-164.

Benavides Castillo, Antonio, and Nikolai Grube. 2002. Dos monolitos tempranos de Jaina, Campeche, México. *Mexicon* 24:95-97.

Bey III, George J. 2006. Changing Archaeological Perspectives on the Northern Maya Lowlands. In Mathews and Morrison 2006:13-37.

Bey III, George J., Tara M. Bond, William M. Ringle, Craig A. Hanson, Charles W. Houck, and Carlos Peraza Lope. 1998. The Ceramic Chronology of Ek Balam, Yucatan, Mexico. *Ancient Mesoamerica* 9:101-120.

Bey III, George J., and Rossana May Ciau. 2005. Los orígenes preclásicos de un centro Puuc en el Distrito de Bolonchen: Las evidencias de Kiuic. Paper presented at the Segundo Congreso Internacional de Cultura Maya, Merida.

Bond-Freeman, Tara M., George J. Bey III, Charles W. Houck, and William M. Ringle. 1998. Ceramic Evidence from the Middle Preclassic Period at Ek Balam and Xuilub, Yucatán, Mexico. Paper presented at the 97th Annual Meeting of the American Anthropological Association, Philadelphia.

Boucher, Sylviane and Yoly Palomo Carrillo. 2005. Cerámica del Preclásico Medio y Tardío en depósitos sellados del sitio de Tzubil, Yucatán. *Temas Antropológicos* 27:153-188.

Braswell, Geoffrey E. 2003a. Introduction: Reinterpreting Early Classic Interaction. In Braswell 2003c:1-43.

— 2003b. Understanding Early Classic Interaction between Kaminaljuyu and Central Mexico. In Braswell 2003c:105-142.

Braswell, Geoffrey E. (editor). 2003c. *The Maya and Teotihuacan: Reinterpreting Early Classic Interaction*. University of Texas, Austin.

Brown, Clifford T. 1999. *Mayapán Society and Ancient Maya Social Organization*. Ph.D. dissertation, Department of Anthropology, Tulane University. University Microfilms, Ann Arbor.

Brown, M. Kathryn, and James F. Garber. 2003. Evidence of Conflict During the Middle Formative in the Maya Lowlands: A View from Blackman Eddy, Belize. In *Ancient Mesoamerican Warfare*, edited by M. Kathryn Brown and Travis W. Stanton, pp. 91-108. AltaMira, Walnut Creek.

Burgos, Rafael, José Estrada, and Juan García. 2003. Una aproximación al patrón de asentamiento del sitio de Izamal, Yucatán. *Los Investigadores de la Cultura Maya* 11:313-324. Universidad Autónoma de Campeche, Campeche.

Carrasco Vargas, Ramón, and Marinés Colón González. 2005. El reino de Kaan y la antigua ciudad maya de Calakmul. *Arqueología Mexicana* 13(75):40-47.

Carrasco Vargas, Ramón, and Sylviane Boucher. 1987. Las escaleras jeroglíficas del Resbalón, Quintana Roo. In *Primer Simposio Mundial sobre Epigrafía Maya 1986*, pp. 1-21. Ministerio de Cultura y Deportes, Instituto de Antropología e Historia y Asociación Tikal, Guatemala.

Ceballos Gallareta, Teresa. 2003. *La cronología cerámica del Puerto Maya de Xcambó, Costa Norte de Yucatán: Complejo Xtampú*. Tesis profesional, Licenciado en Ciencias Antropológicas en la Especialidad de Arqueología, Universidad Autónoma de Yucatán, Merida.

Chase, Arlen F., and Prudence M. Rice (editors). 1985. *The Lowland Maya Postclassic*. University of Texas, Austin.

Cobos, Rafael. 2006. The Relationship between Tula and Chichén Itzá: Influences or Interactions? In Mathews and Morrison 2006:173-183.

Dahlin, Bruce H. 1984. A Colossus in Guatemala: The Preclassic City of El Mirador. *Archaeology* 37(5):18-25.

— 2009. Ahead of its Time? The Remarkable Early Classic Economy of Chunchucmil. *Journal of Social Anthropology* 9:341-367.

Dahlin, Bruce H., T. Beach, S. Luzzadder-Beach, D. Hixson, S. Hutson, A. Magnoni, E. Mansell, and D.E. Mazeau. 2005. Constructing the Subsistence Economy at Chunchucmil, Yucatan, Mexico: A Case for a Convergence of Evidence Argument. *Ancient Mesoamerica* 16:229-247.

Dahlin, Bruce H., C. T. Jensen, R. E. Terry, D. R. Wright, Timothy Beach, and Aline Magnoni. 2007. In Search of an Ancient Maya Market. *Latin American Antiquity* 18:363-384.

Demarest, Arthur A., Prudence M. Rice, and Don S. Rice (editors). 2004. *The Terminal Classic in the Maya Lowlands*. University Press of Colorado, Boulder.

Esparza Olguín, Octavio Q., and Vania E. Pérez Gutiérrez. 2009. Archaeological and Epigraphic Studies in Pol Box, Quintana Roo. *The PARI Journal* 9(3):1-16.

Fash, William L., E. Wyllys Andrews, and T. Kam Manahan. 2004. Political Decentralization, Dynastic Collapse, and the Early Postclassic in the Urban Center of Copan, Honduras. In Demarest, Rice, and Rice 2004:260-287.

Folan, William J., Ellen R. Kintz, and Laraine A. Fletcher. 1983. *Coba: A Classic Maya Metropolis*. Academic, New York.

Folan, William J., Joyce Marcus, and W. Frank Miller. 1995a. Verification of a Maya Settlement Model through Remote Sensing. *Cambridge Archaeological Journal* 5:277-283.

Folan, William J., J. Marcus, S. Pincemin, M. del R. Domínguez Carrasco, L. Fletcher, and A. Morales López. 1995b. Calakmul: New Data from an Ancient Maya Capital in Campeche, Mexico. *Latin American Antiquity* 6:310-334.

Forsyth, Donald W. 1983. *Investigations at Edzná, Campeche, Mexico: Volume 2, Ceramics*. Papers of the New World Archaeological Foundation 46. Brigham Young University, Provo.

— 1989. *The Ceramics of El Mirador, Petén, Guatemala*. El Mirador Series, Part 4. Papers of the New World Archaeological Foundation 63. Brigham Young University, Provo.

— 1993. The Ceramic Sequence at Nakbé. *Ancient Mesoamerica* 4:31-53.

Freidel, David A. 1978. Maritime Adaptation and the Rise of Maya Civilization: A View from Cerros, Belize. In *Prehistoric Coastal Adaptations: The Economy and Ecology of Maritime Middle America*, edited by Barbara L. Stark and Barbara Voorhies, pp. 239-265. Academic, New York.

— 1981. Continuity and Disjunction: Late Postclassic Settlement Patterns in Northern Yucatan. In *Lowland Maya Settlement Patterns*, edited by Wendy Ashmore, pp. 311-332. University of New Mexico, Albuquerque.

Freidel, David A., and Jeremy A. Sabloff. 1984. *Cozumel: Late Maya Settlement Patterns*. Academic, New York.

Gallareta Negrón, Tomás, George J. Bey III, and William M. Ringle. 2003. *Investigaciones arqueológicas en las ruinas de Kiuic y la zona Labná-Kiuic, Distrito de Bolonchén, Yucatán, México, temporada 2002*. Report prepared for the Consejo de Arqueología del Instituto Nacional de Antropología e Historia, Mexico City.

— 2004. *Investigaciones arqueológicas en las ruinas de Kiuic y la zona Labná-Kiuic, Distrito de Bolonchén, Yucatán, México, temporada 2003*. Report prepared for the Consejo de Arqueología del Instituto Nacional de Antropología e Historia, Mexico City.

Gallareta Negrón, Tomás, and William M. Ringle. 2004. *The Earliest Occupation of the Puuc Region, Yucatan, Mexico: New Perspectives from Xocnaceh and Paso del Macho*. Paper presented at the 103rd Annual Meeting of the American Anthropological Association, Atlanta.

Gallareta Negrón, Tomás, William M. Ringle, Rossana May C., Julieta Ramos P., and Ramón Carillo Sánchez. 2005. Evidencias de ocupación durante el período preclásico en el Puuc: Xocnaceh y Paso del Macho. Paper presented at the Segundo Congreso Internacional de Cultura Maya, Merida.

Garber, James F., W. David Driver, Lauren A. Sullivan, and David M. Glassman. 1998. Bloody Bowls and Broken Pots: The Life, Death, and Rebirth of a Maya House. In *The Sowing and the Dawning: Termination, Dedication, and Transformation in the Archaeological and Ethnographic Record of Mesoamerica*, edited by Shirley B. Mock, pp. 125-133. University of New Mexico, Albuquerque.

Garza Tarazona de González, Silvia, and Edward B. Kurjack. 1980. *Atlas Arqueológico del Estado de Yucatán*. 2 vols. Instituto Nacional de Antropología e Historia, Mexico City.

Glover, Jeffrey B., and Fabio Esteban Amador. 2005. Recent Research in the Yalahau Region of Quintana Roo: Methodological Concerns and Preliminary Results of a Regional Survey. In Shaw and Mathews 2005:51-65.

Glover, Jeffrey B., Dominique Rissolo, and Fabio Esteban Amador. 2005. The Yalahau Preclassic: Reflections on Initial Survey and Ceramic Data. *Mono y Conejo* 3:23-31.

González González, Arturo H., Carmen Rojas S., Alejandro Terrazas M., Martha Benavente S., Wolfgang Stinnesbeck, Jerónimo Avilés, O. del Río L., and Eugenio Acevez N. 2008. The Arrival of Humans on the Yucatan Peninsula: Evidence from Submerged Caves in the State of Quintana Roo, Mexico. *Current Research in the Pleistocene* 25:1-24.

González González, Arturo H., Alejandro Terrazas M., Martha Benavente, Jerónimo Avilés, Eugenio Aceves, and Wolfgang Stinnesbeck. 2010. La arqueología subacuática y el poblamiento de América. *Arqueología Mexicana* 18(105):53-57.

Graña-Behrens, Daniel. 2006. Emblem Glyphs and Political Organization in Northwestern Yucatan in the Classic Period (A.D. 300–1000). *Ancient Mesoamerica* 17:105-123.

Graña-Behrens, Daniel, Christian Prager, and Elisabeth Wagner. 1999. The Hieroglyphic Inscription of the 'High Priest's Grave' at Chichén Itzá, Yucatán, Mexico. *Mexicon* 21:61-66.

Grube, Nikolai. 2004. El origen de la dinastía Kaan. In *Los Cautivos de Dzibanché*, edited by Enrique Nalda, pp. 114-131. Instituto Nacional de Antropología e Historia, México.

Hamblin, Nancy L. 1984. *Animal Use by the Cozumel Maya*. University of Arizona, Tucson.

Hammond, Norman. 1991. *Cuello*. Cambridge University, Cambridge.

Hansen, Richard D. 1984. *Excavations on Structure 34 and the Tigre Area, El Mirador, El Petén, Guatemala: A New Look at the Preclassic Lowland Maya*. M.A. thesis, Department of Anthropology, Brigham Young University, Provo.

— 1990. *Excavations in the Tigre Complex, El Mirador, Petén, Guatemala*, El Mirador Series, Part 3. Papers of the New World Archaeological Foundation, no. 62. Brigham Young University, Provo.

— 1994. Investigaciones Arqueológicas en el Norte del Petén, Guatemala: Una Mirada Diacrónica de los Orígenes Mayas. In *Campeche Maya Colonial*, edited by William J. Folan, pp. 14-54. Universidad Autónoma de Campeche, Campeche.

— 2002. The Architectural Development of an Early Maya Structure at Nakbé, Petén, Guatemala. www.famsi.org.

Hansen, Richard D., Ronald L. Bishop, and Federico Fahsen. 1991. Notes on Maya Codex-Style Ceramics from Nakbe, Peten, Guatemala. *Ancient Mesoamerica* 2:225-243.

Healy, Paul F., and Jaime J. Awe (editors). 1999. *Belize Valley Preclassic Maya Project: Report on the 1996 and 1997 Field Season*. Occasional Papers in Anthropology 13. Department of Anthropology, Trent University, Peterborough.

Hernández Hernández, Concepción. 2008. Trabajo de salvamento arqueológico en Caucel, capital de la provincia de Chakan en el siglo XVI. *Los Investigadores de la Cultura Maya* 9:295-319.

Hohmann, Bobbi M. 2002. *Preclassic Maya Shell Ornament Production in the Belize Valley, Belize*. Ph.D. dissertation, Department of Anthropology, University of New Mexico, Albuquerque. University Microfilms, Ann Arbor.

Houck Jr., Charles W. 2006. Cenotes, Wetlands, and Hinterland Settlement. In Mathews and Morrison 2006:56-76.

Hutson, Scott R., Aline Magnoni, and Travis W. Stanton. 2004. House Rules? The Practice of Social Organization in Classic Period Chunchucmil, Yucatán, Mexico. *Ancient Mesoamerica* 15:75-92.

Hutson, Scott R., Aline Magnoni, Daniel E. Mazeau, and Travis W. Stanton. 2006. The Archaeology of Urban Houselots at Chunchucmil, Yucatán. In Mathews and Morrison 2006:77-92.

Isphording, W. C., and E. M. Wilson. 1973. Weathering Processes and Physical Subdivisions of Northern Yucatán. *Proceedings of the Association of American Geographers* 5:117-121.

Jiménez Álvarez, Socorro del Pilar. 2002. *La cronología cerámica del puerto Maya de Xcambó, Costa Norte de Yucatán: Complejo Cerámico Xcambó y Complejo Cerámico Cayalac*. Tesis profesional, Licenciado en Ciencias Antropológicas en la Especialidad de Arqueología. Universidad Autónoma de Yucatán, Merida.

Johnstone, Dave. 2001. *The Ceramics of Yaxuná, Yucatán*. Ph.D. dissertation, Department of Anthropology, Southern Methodist University. University Microfilms, Ann Arbor.

Jones, Morris. 1962. Map of Mayapan. In Pollock et al. 1962.

Kowalski, Jeff Karl. 1985. The Historical Interpretation of the Inscriptions of Uxmal. In *Fourth Palenque Round Table*, edited by Elizabeth P. Benson, pp. 235-247. Pre-Columbian Art Research Institute, San Francisco.

Krochock, Ruth. 1988. *The Hieroglyphic Inscriptions and Iconography of the Temple of the Four Lintels and Related Monuments, Chichén Itzá, Yucatán, Mexico*. M.A. thesis, University of Texas, Austin.

— 1998. *The Development of Political Rhetoric at Chichén Itzá, Yucatán, Mexico*. Ph.D. dissertation, Department of Anthropology, Southern Methodist University. University Microfilms, Ann Arbor.

— 2002. Women in the Hieroglyphic Inscriptions of Chichén Itzá. In *Ancient Maya Women*, edited by Traci Ardren, pp. 152-170. AltaMira, Walnut Creek.

Lacadena García-Gallo, Alfonso. 2005. Los jeroglíficos de Ek' Balam. *Arqueología Mexicana* 13(76):64-69.

Lange, Frederick W. 1971. Marine Resources: A Viable Subsistence Alternative for the Prehistoric Lowland Maya. *American Anthropologist* 73:619-636.

Lohse, Jon C. 2010. Archaic Origins of the Lowland Maya. *Latin American Antiquity* 21:312-352.

López Vázquez, Miguel, and Yolanda Fernández Marquínez. 1987. Excavaciones en el Grupo May. Estudio de la Arquitectura. In Dorado 1987:31-43.

Lothrop, Samuel K. 1924. *Tulum: An Archaeological Study of the East Coast of Yucatan*. Carnegie Institution of Washington, Publication 335. Washington, D.C.

Luzzadder-Beach, Sheryl. 2000. Water Resources of the Chunchucmil Maya. *Geographical Review* 90:493-510.

Magnoni, Aline, Scott R. Hutson, and Travis W. Stanton. 2008. Landscape Transformations and Changing Perceptions at Chunchucmil, Yucatán. In *Ruins of the Past: The Use and Perception of Abandoned Structures in the Maya Lowlands*, edited by Travis W. Stanton and Aline Magnoni, pp. 193-222. University Press of Colorado, Boulder.

Mansell, Eugenia Brown, Robert H. Tykot, David A. Freidel, Bruce H. Dahlin, and Traci Ardren. 2006. Early to Terminal Classic Maya Diet in the Northern Lowlands of the Yucatán (Mexico). In *Histories of Maize*, edited by J. E. Staller, R. H. Tykot, and B. F. Benz, pp. 173-185. Academic, New York.

Manzanilla, Linda R., and Claude Chapdelaine (editors). 2009. *Domestic Life in Prehispanic Capitals: A Study of Specialization, Hierarchy, and Ethnicity*. Memoirs of the Museum of Anthropology, University of Michigan, Ann Arbor.

Marcus, Joyce. 1976. The Origins of Mesoamerican Writing. *Annual Review of Anthropology* 5:35-67.

— 1987. *The Inscriptions of Calakmul: Royal Marriage at a Maya City in Campeche, Mexico*. Technical Report of the Museum of Anthropology, University of Michigan 21. Ann Arbor.

— 1992. Dynamic Cycles of Mesoamerican States. *National Geographic Research & Exploration* 8:392-411.

— 1993. Ancient Maya Political Organization. In *Lowland Maya Civilization in the Eighth Century A.D.*, edited by Jeremy A. Sabloff and John S. Henderson, pp. 111-183. Dumbarton Oaks Research Library and Collections, Washington, D.C.

— 1998. The Peaks and Valleys of Ancient States: An Extension of the Dynamic Model. In *Archaic States*, edited by Gary M. Feinman and Joyce Marcus, pp. 59-94. SAR, Santa Fe.

— 2003. The Maya and Teotihuacan. In Braswell 2003c:337-356.

— 2004. Calakmul y su papel en el origen del estado maya. *Los Investigadores de la Cultura Maya* 12:14-31.

— 2008. The Archaeological Evidence for Social Evolution. *Annual Review of Anthropology* 37:251-266.

— 2009. Understanding Houses, Compounds, and Neighborhoods. In Manzanilla and Chapdelaine 2009:257-266.

Marcus, Joyce and William J. Folan. 1994. Una estela más del siglo V y nueva información sobre Pata de Jaguar, gobernante de Calakmul, Campeche en el siglo VII. *Gaceta Universitaria* IV (15-16):21-26. Universidad Autónoma de Campeche, Campeche.

Marcus, Joyce and Jeremy A. Sabloff. 2008. Cities and Urbanism: Central Themes and Future Directions. In *The Ancient City*, edited by Joyce Marcus and Jeremy A. Sabloff, pp. 323-336. School for Advanced Research, Santa Fe.

Martin, Simon. 2005. Of Snakes and Bats: Shifting Identities at Calakmul. *The PARI Journal* 6(2):5-15.

Martin, Simon, and Nikolai Grube. 2008. *Chronicle of the Maya Kings and Queens: Deciphering the Dynasties of the Ancient Maya*. 2nd edn. Thames & Hudson, London.

Masson, Marilyn A., and Carlos Peraza Lope. 2008. Animal Use at the Postclassic Maya Center of Mayapán. *Quaternary International* 191:170-183.

Matheny, Raymond T. 1980. *El Mirador, Petén, Guatemala, An Interim Report*. Papers of the New World Archaeological Foundation 45. Brigham Young University, Provo.
— 1986. Investigations at El Mirador, Petén, Guatemala. *National Geographic Research* 2:332-353.
— 1987. Early States in the Maya Lowlands during the Late Preclassic Period: Edzna and El Mirador. In *City States of the Maya: Art and Architecture*, edited by Elizabeth P. Benson, pp. 1-44. Rocky Mountain Institute for Pre-Columbian Studies, Denver.
Mathews, Jennifer P. 1998. *The Ties That Bind: The Ancient Maya Interaction Spheres of the Late Preclassic and Early Classic Periods in the Northern Yucatan Peninsula*. Ph.D. dissertation, University of California, Riverside. University Microfilms, Ann Arbor.
— 2001. Radiocarbon Dating of Mortar and Charcoal Intrusions in Architectural Mortar: A Case Study in the Maya Region, Quintana Roo, Mexico. *Journal of Field Archaeology* 28:395-400.
— 2003. Megalithic Architecture at the Site of Victoria, Quintana Roo. *Mexicon* 25:74-77.
Mathews, Jennifer P., and Rubén Maldonado Cárdenas. 2006. In Mathews and Morrison 2006:95-118.
Mathews, Jennifer P., and Bethany A. Morrison (editors). 2006. *Lifeways in the Northern Maya Lowlands: New Approaches to Archaeology in the Yucatán Peninsula*. University of Arizona, Tucson.
McKillop, Heather, and Paul F. Healy (editors). 1989. *Coastal Maya Trade*. Occasional Papers in Anhtropology 8. Trent University, Peterborough.
Medina Castillo, Edgar. 2003. Los juegos de pelota de la región noroeste de Yucatán. In *Proyecto Costa Maya: Reporte Interino, Temporada 2002*, edited by Fernando Robles Castellanos and Anthony P. Andrews, pp. 62-87. Instituto Nacional de Antropología e Historia, Centro Yucatán, Merida.
— 2005. *El juego de pelota del preclásico medio en el noroeste de Yucatán, México*. Universidad Autónoma de Yucatán, Merida.
Milbrath, Susan, and Carlos Peraza Lope. 2003. Revisiting Mayapan: Mexico's Last Maya Capital. *Ancient Mesoamerica* 13:1-46.
Mora-Marín, David. 2008. Análisis epigráfico y lingüístico de la escritura maya del periodo preclásico tardío: implicaciones para la historia sociolingüística de la región. In *XXI Simposio de Investigaciones Arqueológicas en Guatemala, 2007*, edited by Juan Pedro Laporte, Bárbara Arroyo, and Héctor E. Mejía, pp. 853-876. Ministerio de Cultura y Deportes, Guatemala.
Morrison, Bethany A. 2000. *Ancient Maya Settlement of the Yalahau Region: An Example from the El Edén Wetland*. Ph.D. dissertation, Department of Anthropology, University of California, Riverside. University Microfilms, Ann Arbor.
Nalda, Enrique (editor). 2004. *Los Cautivos de Dzibanché*. Instituto Nacional de Antropología e Historia, Mexico City.
Ortiz, Ponciano, and Robert S. Santley. 1998. Matacapan: un ejemplo de enclave teotihuacano en la costa del golfo. In *Los Ritmos de Cambio en Teotihuacan: Reflexiones y Discusiones de su Cronología*, edited by R. Brambila and Rubén Cabrera, pp. 377-460. Instituto Nacional de Antropología e Historia, Mexico City.
Peraza Lope, Carlos, Pedro Delgado, and Barbara Escamilla. 2002. Investigaciones de un edificio del preclásico medio en Tipikal, Yucatán. *Los Investigadores de la Cultura Maya* 10:263-276.
Perry, Eugene, Luis E. Marin, J. McClain, and Guadalupe Velázquez. 1995. The Ring of Cenotes (Sinkholes), Northwest Yucatan, Mexico: Its Hydrogeologic Characteristics and Association with the Chicxulub Impact Crater. *Geology* 23:17-20.
Perry, Eugene, Guadalupe Velázquez-Olimán, and Luis Marín. 2002. The Hydrochemistry of the Karst Aquifer System of the Northern Yucatan Peninsula, Mexico. *International Geology Review* 44:191-221.
Perry, Eugene, Guadalupe Velázquez-Olimán, and R. A. Socki. 2003. The Hydrogeology of the Yucatan Peninsula. In *The Lowland Maya Area: Three Millennia at the Human-Wildland Interface*, edited by Arturo Gómez Pompa, Melinda F. Allen, Scott L. Fedick, and J. J. Jiménez-Osornio, pp. 115-138. Food Products, New York.
Pincemin, Sophia, J. Marcus, L. Florey Folan, W. J. Folan, M. del R. Domínguez Carrasco, and A. Morales López. 1998. Extending the Calakmul Dynasty Back in Time: A New Stela from a Maya Capital in Campeche, Mexico. *Latin American Antiquity* 9:310-327.

Plank, Shannon E. 2004. *Maya Dwellings in Hieroglyphs and Archaeology: An Integrative Approach to Ancient Architecture and Spatial Cognition*. BAR International Series 1324. John and Erica Hedges, Oxford.

Pollock, Harry E. D. 1980. *The Puuc: An Architectural Survey of the Hill Country of Yucatan and Northern Campeche*. Memoirs of the Peabody Museum of Archaeology and Ethnology 19. Harvard University, Cambridge, Mass.

Pollock, Harry E. D., Ralph L. Roys, Tatiana Proskouriakoff, and A. Ledyard Smith. 1962. *Mayapan, Yucatan, Mexico*. Publication 619. Carnegie Institution of Washington, Washington, D.C.

Pope, K. O., S. C. Ocampo, G. L. Kinsland, and R. Smith. 1996. Surface Expression of the Chicxulub Crater. *Geology* 24:527-530.

Powis, Terry G. 1996. *Excavations of Middle Formative Period Round Structures at the Tolok Group, Cahal Pech, Belize*. M.A. thesis, Trent University, Peterborough, Ont.

Quiñones Cetina, Lucía. 2006. Del preclásico medio al clásico temprano: una propuesta de fechamiento para el área de Izamal, Yucatán. *Estudios de Cultura Maya* 28:51-66.

Rice, Don S. 1988. Classic to Postclassic Maya Household Transitions in the Central Peten, Guatemala. In *Household and Community in the Mesoamerican Past*, edited by Richard R. Wilk and Wendy Ashmore, pp. 227-248. University of New Mexico, Albuquerque.

Ringle, William M. 2004. On the Political Organization of Chichén Itzá. *Ancient Mesoamerica* 15:167-218.

Ringle, William M., and E. Wyllys Andrews V. 1988. Formative Residences at Komchen, Yucatan, Mexico. In *Household and Community in the Mesoamerican Past*, edited by Richard R. Wilk and Wendy Ashmore, pp. 171-197. University of New Mexico, Albuquerque.

— 1990. The Demography of Komchen, An Early Maya Town in Northern Yucatan. In *Precolumbian Population History in the Maya Lowlands*, edited by T. Patrick Culbert and Don S. Rice, pp. 215-243. University of New Mexico, Albuquerque.

Rissolo, Dominique, José Manuel Ochoa Rodríguez, and Joseph W. Ball. 2005. A Reassessment of the Middle Preclassic in Northern Quintana Roo. In Shaw and Mathews 2005:66-76.

Rivera Dorado, Miguel (editor). 1988. *Oxkintok 1*. Misión Arqueológica de España en México, Madrid.

— 1989. *Oxkintok 2*. Misión Arqueológica de España en México, Madrid.

— 1990. *Oxkintok 3*. Misión Arqueológica de España en México, Madrid.

— 1992. *Oxkintok 4*. Misión Arqueológica de España en México, Madrid.

Robin, Cynthia. 1989. *Preclassic Maya Burials at Cuello, Belize*. BAR International Series 480. British Archaeological Reports, Oxford.

Robles Castellanos, Fernando, Angeles Cantero Aguilar, and Antonio Benavides Rosales. 2006. *Proyecto arqueológico Poxilá, municipio Umán, Yucatán. Temporada de campo 2005: Informe para el Consejo Nacional de Antropología de México*. Centro INAH Yucatán, Merida.

Roys, Lawrence, and Edwin M. Shook. 1966. Preliminary Report on the Ruins of Ake, Yucatan. *Memoirs of the Society for American Archaeology* 20. Salt Lake City, Utah.

Ruppert, Karl, and John H. Denison, Jr. 1943. *Archaeological Reconnaissance in Campeche, Quintana Roo, and Peten*. Publication 543. Carnegie Institution of Washington, Washington, D.C.

Ruppert, Karl, and A. Ledyard Smith. 1957. *House Types in the Environs of Mayapan and at Uxmal, Kabah, Sayil, Chichen Itza, and Chacchob*. Current Reports 39. Carnegie Institution of Washington, Washington, D.C.

Saturno, William A., David Stuart, and Boris Beltrán. 2006. Early Maya Writing at San Bartolo, Guatemala. *Science* 311:1281-1283.

Scarborough, Vernon L. 1991. *Archaeology at Cerros, Belize, Central America: Volume 3, The Settlement System in a Late Preclassic Maya Community*. Southern Methodist University, Dallas.

Schmidt, Peter J. 2005. Nuevos hallazgos en Chichén Itzá. *Arqueología Mexicana* 13(76):48-55.

Sharer, Robert J., with Loa P. Traxler. 2006. *The Ancient Maya*. 6th edn. Stanford University, Stanford.

Shaw, Justine M. 2008. *White Roads of the Yucatán*. University of Arizona, Tucson.

Shaw, Justine, and Dave Johnstone. 2006. Classic Politics in the Northern Maya Lowlands. In Mathews and Morrison 2006:142-154.

Shaw, Justine M., and Jennifer P. Mathews (editors). 2005. *Quintana Roo Archaeology*. University of Arizona, Tucson.
Sierra Sosa, Thelma Noemí. 1999. Xcambó: Codiciado enclave económico del Clásico Maya. *Arqueología Mexicana* 7(37):40-47.
— 2001. Xcambó. *Mexicon* 23:27.
Smith, J. Gregory. 2000. *The Chichén Itzá-Ek Balam Transect Project: An Intersite Perspective on the Political Organization of the Ancient Maya*. Ph.D. dissertation, Department of Anthropology, University of Pittsburgh. University Microfilms, Ann Arbor.
Smith, J. Gregory, William M. Ringle, and Tara M. Bond-Freeman. 2006. Ichmul de Morley and Northern Maya Political Dynamics. In Mathews and Morrison 2006:155-172.
Smyth, Michael P. 2006. Architecture, Caching, and Foreign Contacts at Chac (II), Yucatan, Mexico. *Latin American Antiquity* 17:123-149.
— 2008. Beyond Economic Imperialism: The Teotihuacan Factor in Northern Yucatan. *Journal of Anthropological Research* 64:395-409.
— 2009. Beyond Capitals and Kings: Domestic Organization and Ethnic Dynamics at Chac-Sayil, Yucatan. In Manzanilla and Chapdelaine 2009:131-149.
Smyth, Michael P., and David Ortegón Zapata. 2006. Foreign Lords and Early Classic Interaction at Chac II, Yucatan. In *Lifeways in the Northern Maya Lowlands: New Approaches to Archaeology in the Yucatán Peninsula,* edited by Jennifer P. Mathews and Bethany A. Morrison, pp. 119-141. University of Arizona, Tucson.
Smyth, Michael P., and Daniel Rogart. 2004. A Teotihuacan Presence at Chac II, Yucatan, Mexico. *Ancient Mesoamerica* 15:17-47.
Šprajc, Ivan. 2004. Maya Sites and Monuments in SE Campeche, Mexico. *Journal of Field Archaeology* 29:385-407.
— 2008. *Reconocimiento arqueológico en el sureste del estado de Campeche, México: 1996–2005*. BAR International Series 1742. Paris Monographs in American Archaeology 19. Oxford: Archaeopress.
Šprajc, Ivan, William J. Folan, and Raymundo González Heredia. 2005. Las Ruinas de Oxpemul, Campeche: su redescubrimiento después de 70 años de olvido. *Los Investigadores de la Cultura Maya* 13:19-27.
Stanton, Travis W. 2000. *Heterarchy, Hierarchy, and the Emergence of the Northern Lowland Maya: A Study of Complexity at Yaxuna, Yucatan, Mexico (400 B.C.–A.D. 600)*. Ph.D. dissertation, Department of Anthropology, Southern Methodist University. University Microfilms, Ann Arbor.
— 2005. Taluds, Tripods, and Teotihuacanos: A Critique of Central Mexican Influence in Classic Period Yucatan. *Mayab* 18:17-35.
Stanton, Travis W., and Traci Ardren. 2005. The Middle Formative of Yucatan in Context: The View from Yaxuna. *Ancient Mesoamerica* 16:213-228.
Stanton, Travis W., Traci Ardren, and Tara M. Bond. 2000. Chunchucmil as a Specialized Trade Center in Western Yucatán. Paper presented at the 65th Annual Meeting of the Society for American Archaeology, Philadelphia.
Stanton, Travis W., David A. Freidel, Charles K. Suhler, Traci Ardren, James N. Ambrosino, Justine M. Shaw, and Sharon Bennett. 2010. *Archaeological Investigations at Yaxuná, 1986–1996: Results of the Selz Foundation Yaxuna Project*. BAR International Series 2056. Archaeopress, Publishers of British Archaeological Reports, Hadrian Books, Oxford.
Taube, Karl A. 2003. Tetitla and the Maya Presence at Teotihuacan. In Braswell 2003c:273-314.
Tozzer, Alfred M. 1941. *Landa's Relación de las Cosas de Yucatán: A Translation*. Papers of the Peabody Museum of American Archaeology and Ethnology 18. Harvard University, Cambridge, Mass.
Uriarte Torres, Alejandro. 2004. El Preclásico en Dzibilchaltun: Perspectiva del Sacbe 2. *Los Investigadores de la Cultura Maya* 12:349-363.
— 2007. Aproximación al estudio de los patrones de asentamiento preclásicos de Caucel, Yucatán. Paper presented at the Séptimo Congreso Internacional de Mayistas, Merida.

Varela Torrecilla, Carmen. 1998. *El Clásico Medio en el Noroccidente de Yucatán. La Fase Oxkintok Regional en Oxkintok (Yucatán) como Paradigma.* BAR International Series 739. British Archaeological Reports, Oxford.

Varela Torrecilla, Carmen, and Geoffrey Braswell. 2003. Teotihuacan and Oxkintok: New Perspectives from Yucatan. In Braswell 2003c:249-272.

Vargas de la Peña, Leticia, and Víctor R. Castillo Borges. 2005. Hallazgos Recientes en Ek' Balam. *Arqueología Mexicana* 13(76):56-63.

Velásquez García, Erik. 2004. Los escalones jeroglíficos de Dzibanché. In Nalda 2004:79-103.

— 2005. The Captives of Dzibanche. *The PARI Journal* 6(2):1-4.

Vlcek, David T., Silvia Garza Tarazona, and Edward B. Kurjack. 1978. Contemporary Farming and Ancient Maya Settlements: Some Disconcerting Evidence. In *Pre-Hispanic Maya Agriculture*, edited by Peter D. Harrison and B. L. Turner II, pp. 211-223. University of New Mexico, Albuquerque.

White, Christine B., Paul F. Healy, and Henry P. Schwarcz. 1993. Intensive Agriculture, Social Status, and Maya Diet at Pacbitun, Belize. *Journal of Anthropological Research* 49:347-375.

Willey, Gordon R., William R. Bullard, Jr., John B. Glass, and James C. Gifford. 1965. *Prehistoric Maya Settlement in the Belize Valley.* Papers of the Peabody Museum of Archaeology and Ethnology 54. Harvard University, Cambridge, Mass.

Zender, Marc. 2004. *A Study of Classic Maya Priesthood.* Ph.D. dissertation, University of Calgary, Calgary. University Microfilms, Ann Arbor.

Index

absolute dates 21; *see also* radiocarbon dating
Acanceh 6, 13, 128
    Structure 1 11
accelerator mass spectrometry 127
accession 97, 108
activity areas 289, 328
Actun Toh 355
adaptive cycle 326–9, 332–4, 336, 338, 340–42
Adivino-Pajaros complex 192
administration 68, 72, 223, 357, 359
    hierarchy 88–91
agrarian reform 333, 336
agricultural intensification 329, 334, 336, 341
agriculturalists 6, 312, 327, 341
agriculture 3, 5, 94, 133, 159–61, 327, 334
Agua Potable complex 153, 157, 162
Aguateca 69, 78
Ah Kin Chel 120–21, 129
Ake 6, 10, 13, 122, 127–8, 131, 264, 266–7, 276, 353, 355
    Structure 1 11
Akhenaten 312
Akhetaten 312
albarradas 122, 309, 356
alliance 68, 70, 91, 108, 359
almanac 290
analogy 221, 309
ancestor worship 68
Andes 65
Andrews, Anthony 2, 20–21, 26–8, 44–5, 48, 59, 155, 157, 161–2, 175–8, 224, 325, 331, 336, 352–4, 358–9
Andrews, E. Wyllys IV 12–14, 19, 52, 170, 230, 286–90, 301, 351–4, 358–9, 361
Andrews, E. Wyllys V 2, 5, 12–16, 21, 26–7, 29, 52, 88, 124, 138, 144, 161–2, 170, 180, 238, 264, 285, 287, 325, 352, 354, 361
Andrews, George 202–3, 219, 224
antechamber 72
apron corbel 127
apsidal house 44
ArcGIS 174
archaeological evidence 45, 88, 325, 326, 331, 341, 342
archaic states 9, 68, 265

architectural core 75, 79, 81, 83, 84
architectural decadence 308
architectural feature 67, 68, 75, 77, 83, 238, 266; *see also* ballcourts; Chichen Itza; floor; Great Platform; Mayapan house
architectural traits 29, 191, 193
architecture 2, 5, 8, 10, 13, 16–19, 28–9, 43, 45, 47, 50, 66–7, 73, 82, 126, 128, 133, 137, 147, 152, 191, 225, 238, 257, 277, 308–9, 319, 329, 334, 336, 362
    ballcourts 43, 46, 48, 54, 56
    Chenes style 17
    Chichen Itza 229, 231
    Chichen Maya 230
    Chichen Maya style 237
    chiefdom 70, 79
    Chunchucmil 137
    civic 338
    expedient 309
    folk 131
    fortification walls 267
    Great Platform 241, 253
    hacienda 338
    International style 20, 24, 27, 229–32, 237, 238, 243, 244, 248, 253, 254, 258, 259, 260, 300, 308, 309
    Mayapan 308, 310
    megalithic 127, 128, 129, 131
    megalithic style 8, 10, 11, 120, 127, 130, 131, 133, 137, 146
    monumental 13, 95, 96, 122, 133, 134, 150, 264, 268, 353
    Old Chichen 260
    palaces 68
    power 65, 67, 70, 73, 81
    Preclassic 84
    prehispanic 152
    Proto-Puuc 134
    public 9, 13, 25, 67, 71, 129, 149, 152, 225
    Puuc 18
    Puuc style 16, 18, 24, 29, 131, 191, 230
    regional 119
    residential 15, 54, 70, 83, 313, 315, 338
    talud-tablero 14, 355
    Uxmal 222

art 1–3, 19, 24, 28, 47, 68, 229, 237, 285, 288–9, 299, 308–9
assemblage 158, 288, 360; *see also* Balankanche; caves; ceramics; Mayapan
of artifacts 82, 152, 160, 286, 299, 300, 302
Atlas Arqueológico del Estado de Yucatán 175, 352
authority 191, 193, 265, 267, 268, 328, 332, 340
autonomy 29, 90, 108, 325, 360
autosacrifice 207, 213
axis mundi 197
Aztecs 2, 213, 290, 300, 302, 308–9
documents 24

Bajo Laberinto 100
Balakbal 97, 101, 358
Balankanche Cave 21, 26, 285–9, 288, 294. 298–302
Ball, Joseph 6, 10, 12, 15, 20–21, 52, 60, 68, 144–5, 153, 155, 161, 163, 230, 353
ballcourt 3, 8, 43–52, 54, 56–60, 72–3, 78, 94, 96, 122, 149, 194, 198, 202–3, 219–20, 223–5, 236–7, 256, 353
features 50, 56; *see also* architecture
Lazero Cardenas 52
marker stones 46
Paso de la Amada 44
ring 46
San Jeronimo 54
Sinab 52
Sinantoh 52
sites 50, 51, 52, 54
Ulila 52
Uxmal 199, 206, 220
walls 46, 48, 50, 73
Xanila 50
Xtobo 54
ballgame 25, 43–5, 47–8, 57–9, 73, 220, 225
belts 58
helmets 48
iconography 48
balls, rubber 44–5
Baluartes phase 12
Barnhart, Edwin 315
barricades 266–7, 278
Barton Ramie 354
Bat Polity 97, 100–102, 108
battle 267, 269, 272
Becan 358
Belize 1, 5–7, 13, 30, 73, 80, 92, 106, 176, 182, 302
Belize River 92
benches 46, 48, 57, 220–21, 250, 267, 276, 314–15
blade-production 125
bladerunning 137

Blom, Frans 3, 43, 45, 172, 176
Bocas de Dzilam 155, 162
Bolonchen District 203
Bourbon political reforms 332
Braswell, Geoffrey 19–20, 22–3, 28, 84, 106, 132–5, 162–3, 230, 231–3, 235–6, 239, 241–9, 251, 253, 256, 260, 270, 349, 355–6, 362
built environment 66, 131, 191, 325, 329, 334, 336, 339, 341–2
built form 66
burial 15, 58, 68, 71, 73, 82, 92, 289, 313, 351, 354–5
offerings 351
practices 313

Cahal Pech 354
Cahokia 130
Calakmul 3, 8, 10, 13–15, 19–20, 22, 88, 92, 94, 96–108, 110–11, 122, 353–4, 358
Campanillo 56–8
Campeche 1–3, 13, 15, 19, 88, 93–4, 100, 104, 108, 143–5, 153, 156, 161, 163, 171, 175, 349, 354, 358
Canbalam ceramic sphere 153–4, 162
candeleros 134, 355
Candzibaantun 97
cannibalism 300
Cansahcab Regional Integration Project 119, 129, 131
Canul 271, 306
captives 68, 98, 269, 300
cardinal directions, five 197
Carnegie Institution 170, 171, 176, 233, 308, 313, 359
carving, miniature 219
Casas Grandes 313
Caste War 28–9, 325–6, 329, 333, 336, 338–42
archaeology 28
Castilla elastica 48
Castillo 8, 16–17, 20, 26, 43–4, 152, 229, 231, 233–41, 245, 248–59, 269, 276, 353, 356–9
Castillo Borges, Victor 16–17, 235, 255–6, 357
Castillo-sub 234–35, 248, 250–51, 253–4, 258–9
cathedral cities 24
Catherwood, Frederic 13, 172
cattle 333, 338, 340
Caucel 44, 59, 74, 78, 84, 353
causeway 93, 95–6, 122, 131, 273
cave 4, 15, 132, 285–9, 292–3, 298–302, 352
assemblage 3
rituals 299
Cehpech sphere 16, 21, 153, 156, 157
Celestun 352
cenote 180, 285, 292, 352

Cenote of Xtoloc 238
censers
    biconical 289, 298
    carved stone 289, 300, 301, 339
    clay 288
    effigy 206, 286, 288, 289, 292, 300, 301, 302
    stone 288
ceramic assemblage 155, 156, 157, 360
ceramic figurine 47, 58
ceramic group 10, 21, 26, 77, 156, 157
    Achote 21
    Altar Fine Orange 21, 155
    Balancan Fine Orange 21
    Chum Unslipped 21
    Chunhinta 10
    Holactun Cream 21
    Joventud 10, 77
    Joventud Red 10
    Maquina Red 21
    Muna Slate 16, 21
    Teabo Red 21
    Ticul Thin Slate 21, 156, 157
    Tipikal 9, 60, 77
    Unto 60
    Vista Alegre 21
    Xanaba 77
    Zupulche 21
ceramic overlap model 230
ceramic seriation 51
ceramic traditions 21, 158
ceramics; *see also* pottery
    black trickle 301, 302
    Cehpech 20, 21, 198, 360
    Chichen Itza-style 20
    Chicanel sphere 148
    Early Nabanche 9
    hard-fired 22
    hard-paste 15
ceremonial bars 47
ceremonial function 82, 287
Cerro Tlaloc 290
Cerros 354
Chaak 18, 223, 285, 290–96, 298–9, 301–2
    mask 205
Chac II 6, 15, 120, 132–4, 137
Chac Mool 215
Chacchob 6, 266, 276
Chacsinkin 9
Chak Chel 285, 290–302
Chakanputun 143–5, 147, 152, 159, 163
Chalcatzingo 56–7, 82
Chalchiuhtlicue 295–6
Champoton 10, 28, 143–63, 175
Champoton Regional Settlement Survey 28, 143, 146, 148, 151, 163
Chan Pich 130

Chel 120, 293–6, 299, 306
Chen Mul effigy incense-burners 309
chert 78, 159
Chetumal 1
Chiapas 1, 5, 7, 44, 56–7, 171, 17–6, 298, 315, 356
Chicacotra 91
Chichen Itza 1, 3, 19–27, 29, 31, 47, 175, 191, 193–4, 202, 205–7, 209–10, 213–16, 220–25, 229–31, 236–8, 244, 252–60, 265, 269–72, 274, 276–7, 279–80, 285, 287, 299–300, 309, 342, 352, 356–60; *see also* Great Ballcourt; Great Platform
    abandonment 19, 269, 272, 279
    architectural features 274
    collapse 26, 270, 357
    government 25
    wall
Chichen Maya 24, 230, 237, 258
Chiconauhtla 222
Chicxulub crater 179–80
chiefdoms 3, 9, 65–7, 70–73, 79, 80–84, 90
    competition 90
    cycling 91
    group-oriented 71
    housing 70, 71
    individualizing 65–6, 71, 81–3
    Near East 70
Chiik Nahb 100, 102, 105, 108
Chilam Balam, Books of 13, 24, 26–7, 163, 224, 270–72, 279, 292, 302
    Chumayel 270–72, 292
    Mani 27, 224, 270–71
    Tizimin 270–71
children 71, 92, 185, 332
Chimbote 158
chipped stone 288
    artifacts 256
Cholula 24
Chontal Maya 144
Chuncan 152
Chunchucmil 13–15, 119–20, 122, 124–6, 132–8, 266–7, 278, 350–51, 353, 356
Chunhinta 52, 77
cinnabar 77, 134
circular house 92
circumscription 12
cities 13–14, 19–20, 24–5, 29, 96, 99, 105, 108, 119–20, 124–5, 151, 161, 194, 220, 222, 224, 302, 319, 342, 349, 362
    abandonment 19, 159, 161, 225, 269, 272, 279, 352
    collapse 102, 352
city-states 144, 181, 331
Clark, Dylan 43, 48, 56, 57, 58, 125, 175, 255, 260
Classic Maya Collapse 20, 29, 320

Classic period 7, 8, 10, 12, 13, 15, 16, 19, 20, 22, 26, 30, 47, 48, 60, 74, 77, 78, 81, 119, 120, 122, 127, 133, 134, 137, 145, 149, 151, 157, 253, 265, 268, 285, 287, 300, 302, 306, 320
Classic Period 150
Classic to Postclassic transition 145, 147, 161
clay 231, 286
clay idols 301
climate 185, 319
climate, Yucatan 4
climatic change 161
cloud signs 203
coastal communities 20, 160, 161
coastal network 157
coastal settlement 13, 145, 152, 159
coastal trade 133, 145, 159, 162
coastal trade routes 158, 159, 162
coastal trading communities 15
coastal zones 143, 145, 151, 152, 158, 161, 162
coatepantli 277
Coatimundi Aguada 100
Coba 1, 6, 13, 16, 19, 20, 21, 25, 27, 122, 124, 126, 357, 358
Cocom 27, 29, 306, 308
codex 47, 105, 108, 302
Codex Borgia 212, 295
Codex Mendoza 195, 196, 222
Codex-style vessels 105
codices 3, 285, 290, 291, 294, 295, 296, 297, 298, 302
Cofitachequi 91
Colhuacan 222
collapse 19, 20, 25, 28–9, 96, 144, 224, 325, 327–9, 334, 341, 362
    Caste War 341
    political 19
    research 326
colonial archaeology 359
colonial period 16, 224, 306
Columns Group 222
Comalcalco 144
commercialism 162
commoner 28, 70, 71, 73, 208
    households 269
complex system 321, 328
concentric zones 123, 124
configurational approach 125
conjuring 68, 214
connectedness 327–34, 336, 338–9, 341–2
    heterarchical 327
    property of change 326
conquest 28–9, 104, 193, 223–4, 336
conservation 29, 326–7, 329, 332, 335–6, 338, 340–42
construction, monumental 21, 229, 274

construction phases 75, 80, 250, 252, 254, 279
contextual approach 125
Copan 3, 17–18, 20, 22, 30, 135–6, 357, 361–2
    Structure 10L-22 17–18
Copan Acropolis 18
core-veneer masonry 16, 277
corporate strategies 71, 82
cosmology 43
cotton 69, 291, 298, 301, 332, 351
    ornaments 296
council 191, 193, 195, 219, 221–3
council hall 195, 221–3
council of war 222
court 191, 195, 221, 357
Cozumel Island 358
craft 68, 79, 125, 133, 349
creator couple 291, 296–7
creator deity 295, 299–300
Cuca 6, 264, 266, 276
Cui 158
Culhuacan 224, 225
cult
    pan-Mesoamerican 24
    of Quetzalcoatl 25
    of sacrifice 205
cultural behavior 66
cultural resilience 325
cultural traits 14, 43, 144
Cupul 224, 331, 333
cylinder tripod vessels 134

dance platform 72
decadence 2, 28, 308–10
decoration see jaguar; serpent
defensive fortifications 92, 265, 268, 279
deities 220, 223, 285, 289, 290, 291, 292, 294, 295, 296, 298, 300, 301, 302, 303
    creator 285, 293
    feathered serpent 24
    female 285, 299
    female creator 285
    fertility 3
    rain 3, 302
deity impersonator 302–3
demographic decline 3, 12, 13, 19, 330, 331, 333, 341
demographic movement 155, 159, 162
depopulation 19, 267
diachronic processes 153
Diego Duran 43, 44
dispersal 325, 329, 334, 336, 341
distributional approach 125, 137
diversification 161, 329, 336, 340
Documentos de Tierras de Sotuta 331
domestic activities 67, 68, 71, 78

domestic platform 75, 79, 84, 120, 129, 130, 131
doors, Uxmal 213, 214, 217
drains 252, 275, 276, 277
Dresden almanac 298
drift 334, 341
drought 3, 20, 21, 29, 161, 267, 331
    Terminal Classic 21
drum 213, 290
Duran, Fray Diego de 43
dynamic cycling 3, 328
dynamic model 320
dynastic capital 16
Dzibanche 97, 98, 99, 102, 103, 104, 106, 107, 108, 353, 358
Dzibiac Red 21
Dzibilchaltun 6, 12, 14, 16, 19, 20, 21, 25, 122, 124, 127, 170, 177, 220, 352, 353, 354, 358, 362
Dzitas Slate 21
Dzonot Ake 6, 266, 276
Dzudzuquil 77

E Group 96
EAAMS 170, 174, 176, 177, 180, 182, 183, 184
Early Classic sites 14, 136, 355
Early Formative 5, 30
Early Great Platform 252, 258
Early Great Platform style, definition 258
Early Nabanche complex 9, 77
Early Postclassic 19–28, 147, 159, 231, 238, 254, 259–60, 265, 269, 286
Early Preclassic 5, 30, 44, 57–9, 352, 354, 359
Early Tollan 259
earth monster 18, 292, 293, 302, 357
Ebtun 329, 332, 333, 335, 336, 337, 339, 341, 342
ecclesiastical authority 340
economic change 148
economic inequality 306, 310, 312–13, 318
economic stratification 340
economics 306, 310, 312, 320
econophysics 321
ecotones 159
Edzna 6, 12, 15–16, 19, 25, 133, 151, 153, 156–59, 162, 357–8
Ehecatl serpent 212
Ek Balam 6, 16–17, 19–20, 25, 30, 175, 220, 266
El Baul 95
El Macayal 56
El Manati 58
El Meco 6, 27
El Mirador 8, 92–3, 95–7, 101–2, 104, 106–8, 120, 127, 354
El Naranjal 127–31, 355
El Opeño 58

El Resbalon 97–8, 102–3, 358
El Tajin 24, 220
El Tigre pyramid 92
El Vergel 56
El Zapote 147, 159
elites 15, 22, 59, 66, 68, 70, 72, 81–2, 92, 130–31, 158, 221, 265–8, 333
    activities 68
    control 158
    culture 43
    tombs 134
emblem glyph 16, 88–9, 97, 99, 101, 104–5, 108, 181, 358
emulation 131, 355
enclave 15, 134
encomienda 331
Epiclassic 23, 145, 162, 191, 193–4, 214, 220, 254
Epiclassic period 145, 162, 194
Erosa Peniche 198, 234, 259
esoteric knowledge 158
estates 25, 191, 197, 219, 221, 223, 334, 341
"Eve" of Naharon 4
evolution 12, 321, 352, 361
exotic goods 81, 82, 159, 162
exploitation 326, 327, 332, 333, 336
    marine resources 160

family ritual 97
farmers 20, 125, 130, 267, 300, 331, 333, 334, 336, 340, 350
farming cities 125, 136
feasting 72, 223
Feathered Serpent Pyramid 210, 213
Fernández Souza, Lilia 23, 255, 260
Fernández, Miguel Ángel 23, 90, 91, 237, 255, 260, 355
figurine 57
Finca Acapulco 56
Fine Orange ware 22, 157
fine paste 154, 156, 157, 158, 162
fishing lines 160
flayed skin 300, 301, 302
flight 174, 334, 341
floors 80, 233–5, 241, 250, 255, 259, 276; see also Great Platform
    Carnegie 254
    earth 94
    Feature AC1, 234
    Feature AC6, 233
    Great Platform 234, 250, 251
    Great Plaza 238
    lime-plastered 80
    red-painted 235
    stucco 77, 355
floreros 134, 355
food refuse 68
foraging 5

formal audiences 68
fortification 20, 266, 267
frontiers 265
fusion of culture 7

game 43–4, 47, 58–9, 73; *see also* ballcourt; ballgame
garden city 122, 124
garden plots 94
Garibay 291
gateway, baffled 267, 276
gateway community 13, 133
General Systems Theory 309
Gini coefficient 310–12, 316–8
GIS 170, 175, 181–3
Google Earth 170, 176, 181, 183–5
gourds 5
governance 191, 194, 221
government 44, 57, 97, 171, 177, 197, 341, 342, 357
    centralized 108
Grande 147, 155, 160
Great Ballcourt 47, 229, 233, 237–8, 252, 254–6, 259, 273, 276
    stone 237, 238, 255
Great Platform 31, 202, 229–38, 241–2, 247–8, 250–60, 269, 272–80
    Access 1 236
    Access 4 236
    Access 5 236
    Access 6 236
    Access 9 236
    Access 10 236
    Access 13 236
    architectural features 241
    Carnegie Floor 1 234–5, 250
    Carnegie Floor 2 234–5, 251
    Carnegie Floor 3 234–5, 254
    Feature AC1 234–5, 240–48, 250–54, 256, 258–9
    Feature AC2 234–5, 241–4, 247, 250–51, 253, 256, 258
    Feature AC3 234, 242–4, 247–8, 253, 258
    Feature AC6 234–5, 251–2, 254–6
    Feature AC7 248
    Feature AC10 244, 245
    Feature AC16 241
    Feature AC19 247
    Feature AC21 241, 242
    Sacbe 1 236, 237, 254, 278
    Sacbe 6 236
    Sacbe 15 238
    Structure 2D13 236
    Structure 2D6 255, 256, 259
    Structure 5C4-I 236, 252
greenstone 9
Grijalva River Valley 56
groundstone weights 160

Group of 1000 Columns 229, 233, 235–6, 239, 250–51, 254, 256
Gruta de Chac 15, 302
Guararé 91
Guatemala 18, 28, 31, 56, 88, 93–4, 132, 134, 171, 176, 183, 209, 291, 293, 298–9, 356
Gulf Coast 24, 133, 137, 143–5, 154–7, 161, 285, 355–6
Gulf of Mexico 162, 350

Habuc structure 121
hacienda 152, 333, 338, 340
Hall of Columns 222
headband 217
    flowered 209–10, 213
headdress 57, 111, 207, 210–11, 213, 291, 296
    feathered 205, 211, 215
hearths 4, 68, 79, 289, 298
helmet 214
hereditary rank 90
hierarchy 3, 65, 73, 83, 92, 104, 137, 151, 205, 221, 353
    political 161
hieroglyphs 89, 90, 95, 100, 199, 237, 357–8, 360
Hocaba 26, 225, 257
    ceramic complex 26, 198, 257
honey 332, 351
House of the Governor 194–5, 198, 202–5, 210, 217, 223, 225
household 68, 71, 144, 321, 329, 335–6, 340–41, 351, 354
    activities 71, 360
    archaeology 359
    goods 313
    income 340
    production 325
    rituals 360
    series 335
    wealth 312
houselot 122, 126, 309, 335, 340–41, 356
Huey Tozontontli 290
human remains 4, 248
Hunac Ceel 270–71, 279, 306, 359
hunter-gatherer 91, 312
Huntichmul 355
hunting 5

Ichmul de Morley 6, 23, 360
iconography 47, 73, 191, 193, 196–7, 208, 285–6, 298, 300
    feathered serpent 199
ideology 72, 279, 294, 336
Ikil 355
incense 48, 58, 298
    burner 250
inequality 92, 311, 317, 320
Initial Series Group 31, 230, 356

inland trade routes 161
institutionalization 84
Instituto Nacional de Antropología e Historia 1, 163
International style 20, 24, 27, 229, 237–8, 243–4, 248, 253–4, 258–60, 300, 308–9
    artwork 238
internationalism 14, 24, 132, 137
interregional exchange 78, 82, 143, 159, 162, 351
interregional interaction 119, 132, 349, 354
investiture 25, 191, 193, 206, 211, 213–14, 220, 224
    ceremonies 25
Isla Cerritos 6, 22, 23, 26
Itzam Nah 205, 223
Itzamatul structure 121
Itzamkanac 144
Itzamna 294, 295, 297
Itzmal Chen group 27
Ixtepeque obsidian 256
Ixtlilxochitl 195, 221, 222
Izamal 10, 13, 16, 19, 23, 119–22, 124, 127–33, 136–7, 185, 271–2, 355

jade 9, 22, 57, 92, 132, 134, 213
jaguar 69, 203, 206, 219, 296
    deity 302
    god of the underworld 206
    goddess 296
    lid 289, 298
    seat 203
    throne 292, 302
Jaina 6, 161, 358
jars 286, 288, 289
Jenney Creek 7
Joventud 10, 52, 77

Kaan Polity 89, 97–8, 103–6, 108, 358
Kaminaljuyu 5, 22, 77, 95, 135–6, 358
Kancab 6, 131
Kantunil 6, 120, 122
Kantunilkin 6, 127, 355
Kaymuch 147
killing alley 267, 276
Kimil 294–5
Kinich Kak Moo pyramid 120, 131
Kinichna 97, 107
Kinil 183
kneepads 47
Komchen 2, 6–10, 12, 29, 52, 56, 88, 352–4, 362
Kukulcan 24–5, 259, 306, 359

La Danta Group 96
La Florida 92
La Libertad 56
La Milpa 124–5, 136
La Muralla 92
La Venta 9, 47, 56–8, 82
La Venta Stela 2, 47, 57
labor 68, 70, 90, 92, 95–6, 122, 125–6, 266, 269, 309, 313, 319, 321, 327–9, 334–5, 340–41
    force 101
    collective 71, 82
    tasking 327, 329
Lake Peten Itza 271
Lamanai 92
land degradation 328
LANDSAT 170, 174, 176, 184
Las Monjas 269
Late Classic period 9, 12, 15–16, 18, 23, 69, 149–50, 158–9, 161, 236, 253, 258, 320
Late Postclassic Period 26–8, 145, 159, 222, 224, 271, 290, 306, 308–10, 320
Lazero Cardenas 52
League of Mayapan 224, 272, 359
Le Plongeon, Alice 199, 254
Le Plongeon, Augustus 199, 202, 233
limestone 4, 48, 74, 101, 126, 130, 160, 268, 358
Lincoln, Charles 230
lineages 80, 108, 356, 357, 361
literacy 120
lithic debitage 158
lithic tools 159
Loltun Cave 4
long-distance exchange 132, 156, 159, 162
looting 75
Lord Chaak 223
Los Alacranes 103, 108
Lower Temple of the Jaguars 206, 215, 235, 254–5, 259, 269
luxury goods 71

maize 5, 214, 292–3, 295, 297–8, 300–301, 350
    god 293
Mamom 8, 10, 52, 148
Man of El Templo 4
manos and *metates* 285, 288, 289, 299
Mapa Quinatzin 195, 215, 221, 222
mapping 3, 122, 126, 147, 150, 170, 176, 181, 286, 329, 353
Margarita tomb 135
marine extraction zones 159
marine resources 152, 159, 161, 351
market 13, 15, 28, 125–6, 132, 341
    center 15, 126, 137
    economies 13
    economy 119
    system 23
marketing 19, 125–6, 132, 137

marketing model of distribution 126
marketplace 122, 125, 350
    exchange 125
Marquina, Ignacio 254
marriage 82, 91, 108
mask 18, 205–6, 212–14, 217, 223
    corner 18
    deity 214
    monster 18
    Nunnery 223
    serpent 206
    stack 192, 197, 203, 205, 207–10, 214–15, 217–19
    stucco 10–11, 13, 92, 96
    Tlaloc 192, 203
mass grave 27, 92
mat motif 95
Matacapan 135–6, 355
material record 286
materiality 131
Maya
    calendar 296, 303
    codices 298
    collapse 325, 326, 329, 331, 341, 342
    lowlands 1–10, 12–23, 25–6, 28–31, 52, 65–6, 77, 83–4, 96, 106, 119, 120, 143–5, 153, 158, 161, 253, 266, 269, 279, 302, 306, 315, 319–20, 327, 329, 349, 354–5
    reorganization 325
    state 88, 97, 98, 104, 108, 306
Maya–International style transition 259
Mayapan 3, 26–8, 170, 177, 224, 238, 256, 266, 270–71, 306, 308–11, 313–15, 317–20, 331, 352, 357–9, 361
    assemblage 309
    culture 309
    house 319
    map 307
McGuire, Randall 312
megalithic platform 10, 128, 129, 130, 131
megalithic polity 128
Mercado 213
mercantilism 19, 144, 159, 162
Merida 2, 3, 10, 16, 66, 73, 74, 229, 236, 273, 350, 352
Mesoamerica 3, 5, 23, 43–4, 46–8, 50, 56–9, 65, 67, 70, 72, 79, 91–2, 108, 145, 162, 212, 224, 231, 285
metates 278, 288–9, 293, 295–6
Metepec phase 135
Mexican Revolution 333, 338
Mexico 3, 15, 22–3, 27, 44, 47, 56–8, 66, 82, 88, 93, 119, 134, 143–5, 171–2, 177, 224, 229, 257–60, 290, 293–4, 296, 303, 306, 308, 332, 356
Middle American Research Institute 2–3, 12, 59, 170, 172–3, 285, 289, 301

Middle Preclassic period 2–3, 5–10, 12, 16, 29–30, 43–5, 48, 52, 56–9, 65–6, 73–5, 77–8, 81–3, 95, 100, 127, 145, 148, 150, 351–4, 359, 361
migration 4, 29, 334
    models 7
    routes 24
militarism 208, 266
    competition 98
    conquest 144
    control 20
    expansion 20
    prowess 90, 91
miniatures 288, 289
Mirador Basin 88–93, 97, 102, 105–8
Mississippi Valley 130
Mitla 194, 216, 222–3, 225
Mixteca-Puebla 27, 308
Monte Alban 25
monumentality 8, 90, 92, 108; *see also* architecture; construction; sculpture; staircase
Moquel 152, 155
Morley, Sylvanus G. 176, 199–200, 308, 360
Morris 233–4, 254, 269, 298, 313
mosaic goggles 206
mosaics 203, 205
mound construction 91
multepal 25, 357, 359
Muna 6, 16, 21, 157, 264, 266
municipal administration 332
Muralla complex 156–7
murals 3, 27, 47, 215, 225, 229, 269–70, 285, 292–3, 298, 302, 308, 358

Naachtun 92, 101
Nacxit 213
Nakbe 8, 56, 92–7, 105–8, 354
Nakum 18
Natá 90
net weight 160
nets 5, 160
network 24
    analysis 356
    strategies 65–6, 71, 81–3
    trans-isthmian 144
New Chichen 230, 232, 237
New River 92
New World 1, 4, 326
Nezahualcoyotl 195, 221
Nezahualpilli 195
Niop 147, 151–3, 155, 157, 159–60, 162
nobles 68, 205, 217, 221, 223, 271
North Colonnade 254, 256, 259
Northeast Colonnade 236
Northern Lowlands 350
Northwest Colonnade 254, 255, 259

notched ceramic sherds 160
Nunnery 193–9, 202–6, 208–12, 214–15, 219–22, 224, 230
Nunnery complex 199
    Building Y 199
Nunnery Quadrangle of Uxmal 191–3, 195–8, 200, 202, 206, 209, 211–13, 215–16, 218, 221–3

Oaxaca 222
obsidian 19, 22–4, 28, 78, 125–6, 132–4, 137, 159, 162, 236, 256–7, 353
occupational specialization 125
Ocute 91
offerings 58, 67, 72, 213, 286, 288–9, 300, 351
officials 69, 72, 205, 208, 222, 333
Old Chichen 230–32, 237–8, 258–60
Olmec 9, 29, 44, 48, 56, 58
    colossal heads 48
    culture 44
Omecihuatl 295–7
oracles 222
Osario 25, 238
    pyramid 25
Osorio León 31, 236, 252, 257, 260
Otompan 224
Otumba 22
owl 205, 207
Ox Mul 355
Oxkintok 6, 13–15, 23, 25, 120, 128, 132–7, 355, 357–8
Oxpemul 101

Pacaya 92
Pacbitun 354
Pachuca 22–3, 132, 134, 355
    obsidian 355
Pacific Coast and Piedmont 5
Pakbeh Regional Economy Program 119
palace 19, 31, 67–70, 73, 78–9, 83–4, 96–7, 105, 124, 131, 170, 194–5, 203, 205, 221–3, 269, 357, 362
    features 68
    Motecuhzoma's 222
    Moteuczoma's 196
    presentation 69, 79
    scenic 69, 79, 83
    structure 31
    Texcocoan 195
palacio municipal 337, 338
Palaeoindian period 3, 5
Palenque 69, 104, 108, 211, 213, 306, 313, 315, 317–20
Paleoclimatic studies 161
Palmar 158
Panama 90–91
Paquime 313
Paredon 22

Pareto distribution 306, 310, 312, 317–21
Parita 90–91
Pascual de Andagoya 91
Paso de la Amada 44, 57, 80–82
Paso del Macho 7, 56, 353
pastes, Early Nabanche 7
pastoralists 312
patios 126, 355, 362
performance 299, 351
    platform 80, 81
    structures 73
peripheral region 65
periphery 1, 120, 123–4, 143, 203, 268, 362
    Gulf Coast 161
perishable roof 75
Peten 6–7, 9, 10, 12–13, 22, 30, 104, 132, 144, 153, 171, 176, 359
Pico de Orizaba 22
picota 197
Pitaya 48, 49
plano-relief vessels 135
plaster smoothers 77
Platform of Venus 233
plazas 19, 68, 75, 96, 149–50, 234, 268–9, 353, 357
Plumbate 198
Pol Box 93, 98, 102, 108, 358
political
    actor 71, 81–3
    authority 95, 224, 334
    autonomy 338
    boundary 158, 181
    complexity 12, 65–6, 72–3, 108, 356
    cycling 88–9, 99, 358
    ideology 194, 219
    institution 59, 265, 325, 350
    integration 65–6, 71, 81
    landscape 144, 148, 151, 159, 224, 279
    organization 9, 65–6, 70, 73, 83–4, 88, 124, 149, 194, 205, 264
    reorganization 149
    ritual 191, 193
    status 80
politics 43, 120, 131, 279, 333, 358
polyadic redistribution 28
Popol Vuh 295
population
    density 13, 320
    levels 5, 12, 16, 20
Porvenir 92
Postclassic period 1, 3, 13, 19–20, 22, 25–9, 43, 52, 120, 143–5, 147, 149, 152, 156–7, 159, 162–3, 212, 220, 222, 224, 238, 254–7, 265, 271, 285–6, 290, 292, 294, 298, 302, 306, 308–10, 319–20, 357–8
potential 277, 279, 327–34, 336, 341–2, 352
    property of change 326
Potonchan 144

pottery 2, 5, 7–10, 15–16, 21–3, 26, 28–30, 51, 121, 133–5, 137, 157–8, 198, 230–31, 235–6, 251, 253, 257, 286, 288–9, 298–9, 355, 360; *see also* ceramics
   and status 158, 162
   Bah-phase 7
   Cehpech 21, 26, 230, 257
   Dzudzuquil 52
   Early Nabanche 7
   Ek-phase 7
   groups 52
   imported 158
   Mamom 10
   miniature 289
   Nabanche 10
   polychrome 2, 13, 15, 22, 69, 81, 107, 158, 162
   Sotuta 21, 22, 26, 230, 257, 360
   Tipikal 52
   Tipikal/Unto 52
   vessels 288, 302
poverty 28, 306, 310, 313, 319
power 44, 66–71, 73, 77, 80–84, 97, 106, 108, 124, 133, 152, 223–4, 265, 267–9, 306, 310–12, 318, 320
   Chichen Itza 269
   coercion 67
   consent 67
   shared 71
power law 310–12, 317–20
Poxila 6, 8, 9, 66, 78, 81, 353
Preceramic period 5
Preclassic period 10, 12, 30, 52, 56, 58, 65–6, 75, 77, 81, 83–4, 148–52, 209, 286
preferential attachment 312
PREP 119, 122, 125, 138
priesthood 211, 214, 222–3, 333
Principal Group of the Southwest 230
processions 68, 81, 215, 269
Progreso 352
projectile point 160
Proto-Slateware horizon 236
Provincia Plano relief 198
Proyecto Champoton 145, 146, 152, 153
Proyecto Costa Maya 44, 45, 59, 157
public architecture 8, 65, 67, 69–73, 79–83, 92, 96, 101, 170, 362
public space 47, 68, 70, 79, 81–2
public works 90
pueblo 340
Puuc
   florescence 20
   hills 1, 56, 132, 156, 225
   masonry 16
   region 7, 10, 15–16, 18–21, 29, 83, 132, 144, 171, 202, 224, 319–20, 353, 355
   sites, abandonment 225

pyramids 54, 92, 101, 126, 131, 233, 254, 269, 353, 360
   Peten-style 10–11
   temple 8

quadrangles 192, 225
quechquemitl 293, 299
Quelepa, El Salvador 3
Quetzalcoatl 24–5, 208, 213–14, 225, 254, 259
quevís 90
Quintana Roo 1–2, 4, 10, 19, 27–8, 88, 94, 100, 104, 108, 121, 127, 175, 349, 353, 358
   cave systems 4

radiocarbon dating 51, 199, 200, 238, 258
rain 21, 292–3, 298–300, 302, 319, 350
   god 285, 290
rainfall 350
rainmaking 289–91, 302
   ritual 286
rainy season 250, 290, 300, 302, 350
rancho 339, 340
Rancho Potrero Grande 152
Rathje, William 28, 162, 308–10
reciprocity 125
recreation 43
recycling flakes 159
redistribution 72, 125, 333
regional centers 52, 56, 177, 268
regional network 162
regional settlement patterns 52, 73, 83–4
regionalism 12
   ceramic 10
Relación de Cholula 214
release 29, 326–9, 333, 335–6, 341–2
religion 24, 259, 333
renewal
   ceremony 293, 299
   ritual 298–302
reorganization 28, 144, 326–9, 332–3, 336, 338, 341–2
   Yucatan 341
repartimiento 332
residential core 122, 123–4
residential periphery 122–4
residential platforms 79, 81, 152
resilience 28–9, 326–30, 332–4, 341–2
   strategies 3
   theory 28, 325–8, 341
Rio Coatzacoalcos 155
Rio Copilco 144
ritual 43–4, 47–8, 59, 67–68, 70–73, 78–9, 81–2, 92, 126, 196–7, 224, 266–7, 277, 279, 288, 293, 298–302, 333
   caves 4
   creation 21
   fertility 21

function 67, 72, 285
institution 43
renewal 3, 21
significance of walls 269
termination 81, 267, 279
water 268
riverine food resources 160
road system 96, 101
Round Temple group 27
rounded corner 75, 77, 127, 130
royal court 68, 69, 191
royal residential quarter 195
rubber 48, 56–8, 301
Ruinas de San Angel 27
rulers 9, 25, 47, 98, 102–5, 108, 213, 215, 229, 300, 308, 357
   Calakmul 104
   joint 25
   Palenque 104
ruling class 43

Sacala Sur 122
sacbes 8, 13, 69, 75, 78–81, 121–2, 149–50, 267, 278, 280, 308, 357; *see also* Great Platform
Sacred Cenote 238, 259
sacred offerings 21
sacrifice 44, 103, 301–3
sak xok naah 357
Salama Valley 5
salt 12–13, 132, 351–2, 356
San Andres 9
San Bartolo 209, 358
San Dimas 6, 147, 149–53, 155, 157–62
San Francisco barrio 122
San Jeronimo 54–5
San Lorenzo 56, 58, 82, 130
San Lorenzo Monument 34, 58
San Mateo 56
San Roman 130
Sangana 91
Santee-Wateree drainage 91
Savannah River 91
Saxche 158
Sayil 16, 25, 224, 306, 313, 316–20, 355, 362
Schmidt, Peter 31, 230, 235–7, 252, 255, 257, 260, 270, 273, 356
sculpture 17, 197, 202–3, 229, 255–6, 258, 275, 278
   monumental 58
secondary clients 191, 193
sedentism 5
serpent 202–3, 205, 208, 210–11, 213–14, 219, 224, 291, 293, 302, 308
   balustrades 237
   bars 203
   bicephalic 219
   columns 254, 258

feathered 24, 194, 199, 202–3, 205, 208–11, 213, 215, 219–20, 223, 225
   nose ornament 296
   scepter 292
   temples 205, 224, 308
serrated motif 214
settlement
   aggregation 325, 329, 334
   ecology 161
   hierarchies 9, 73, 75, 79, 82–3, 130–31
   pattern 54, 65, 75, 78, 97, 125, 143, 149, 151–2, 159–61, 177, 180, 334
shells 159, 160
shrine
   private 68
   radial 203
siege tactics 265
Siho 6, 23, 355
Silho Fine Orange 21, 198
Sinantoh 54
site abandonment 91, 267
Sky Witness 103, 108, 354
Skyraiser 105
slaves 90
sleeping benches 68, 79
smallholders 327, 329, 341
Smith, A. Ledyard 21, 23, 26–7, 52, 60, 128, 162–3, 175, 183, 198, 230, 300, 302, 309, 312–14, 320, 349, 357, 360
Snake Head king 103, 108
Snake Head Polity 94, 97, 100, 102–5, 107–8
social complexity 65, 67, 72, 119
social distance 68
social institution 191, 193
social relations, asymmetrical 65–6, 73
social space 266, 268–9
social stratification 44, 54
sociocultural anthropology 44
socioecological systems 325–6, 328, 341
sociopolitical system 44, 328
   complexity 4, 71–2
   hierarchy 91
   power 82
   stratification 54, 59
Soconusco 80
soil cores 5
solar eclipse 303
solar macaws 220
solar market system 162
Sotuta 21–2, 26, 198, 223, 225, 230–31, 236, 257, 259, 333, 341, 360
   ceramics 23, 198, 223, 225, 231, 257, 360
   complex 21, 198, 225
South Temple of the Great Ballcourt 255
Spanish conquest 3, 21, 27–8, 195, 271, 286, 326, 331
specialized gathering 160
spindle whorls 285–6, 288–9, 298, 301

spindles 291, 296
sport 43–4
SRTM DEM 182
staircase
    monumental 150
    radial 254
stalactites 4, 288
stalagmites 4, 288
states 13, 65–6, 70, 73, 83, 96, 104, 143, 161, 224, 332, 349
    agrarian 313
    formation 108
status 22, 44, 54, 66, 68, 70–72, 90, 158, 197, 313, 340, 362
    difference 44, 126
    distinctions 126
    emulation 130
    hierarchy 125
stemmed blades 160
Stephens, John Lloyd 13, 127, 172, 198, 203, 208, 210, 220
stone *see also* chipped stone
    carved 103
    huts 192, 205, 208, 210, 212, 214–15, 217
    platforms 8, 94, 96, 126
    structures, public 9
storage of information 72
strategic marriages 71
stratification 313, 356
Stripe Eye 212
Structure 1714 (Xaman Susula) 65–6, 73, 75–84
stucco 75, 236, 242, 243, 244, 248, 250, 258, 309; *see also* floor; mask; walls
    bench 77
    decoration 135
    facade 357
subfloor caches 73
subsistence systems 144, 161
Suema 91
supernatural 44
surface collection 51, 121, 145–6, 148, 150, 153
surface water 4, 267
symbols of rulership 95
synonyms 182

Tabasco 9, 13, 144–5, 155–6, 158, 161–2, 171, 176, 308, 319
talud wall 274, 276
talud-tablero 14, 134, 355
Tamarindito 69, 78
Tases complex 26, 257
tattoos 90
Tayasal 271
technotasking 327, 329, 342
Temple of the Big Tables 235, 251, 255–6

Temple of the Initial Series 236–7, 252, 257–8, 260
Temple of the Tables 255–6, 259
Temple of the Wall Panels 269
Temple of the Warriors 229, 233, 235, 237, 254–5, 257, 259, 269
Temple of Xtoloc 236
temples 19, 72, 80, 92, 96, 124, 126, 132, 149–50, 170, 269, 300–301, 308, 314, 349, 357
Tenayuca 222
Teopantecuanitlan 56
Teotihuacan 14–15, 23–4, 29, 47, 120, 130, 132, 134–5, 137, 194, 205–7, 210, 213, 221, 355–6
Teotihuacan-style artifacts 355
Terminal Archaic period 5
Terminal Classic period 1, 3, 15–16, 18–24, 26–9, 74, 119, 121–2, 131, 143–5, 149–53, 156–62, 191, 225, 231, 236, 238, 253, 257–60, 265–6, 269, 286, 299, 301–2, 316, 320, 325, 329
test pits 51, 122, 126, 134, 137, 145, 233–5, 239, 252, 255
Tetitla 205
Texcoco 194–5, 208, 221, 22–5
Thin Slate 257, 259
Thompson, J. Eric S. 13, 24–5, 144, 199, 237, 289–90, 298–99, 309, 314
throne 65, 68–9, 75, 77–82, 84, 97, 108, 202, 213, 219, 221–2, 254, 292, 302, 357
    room 3, 8, 82–4
    structure 69, 79
Ticopo-2, 129
Tiho 192
Tikal 10, 12–14, 20, 30, 69, 79, 89, 92, 95–6, 103–4, 108, 122, 124, 136, 170, 180, 268, 356, 358
    Lost World Group 69
Tintal 92
Tinum 21
Titles of Ebtun 331
Título de Totonicapan 213
Tixmeauc 183
Tlacaxipehualiztli 300, 302–3
Tlacopan 224
Tlaloc 197, 203, 285, 288–90, 296, 298, 300–302, 355
Tlapacoya 58
Tlatilco 58
Tlazolteotl 295, 296, 303
tobacco 352
Tohil Plumbate 21–2, 198
Tollan 194
Toltecs 2, 3, 21, 23–4, 191, 194, 197, 206, 208, 212–15, 219–25, 229–31, 237, 254, 258

Tolteca-Chichimeca 222
Toltec-Maya 24, 260
tourism 29, 342
trade 9, 13–14, 19, 22–4, 28, 54, 71–2, 92, 120, 133, 153, 157, 159, 162, 320, 350
    alliances 90
    center 13, 134, 256
    imported goods 9, 27
    international 158
    interregional 158
    long-distance 159
    maritime 356
    maritime networks 144
    maritime routes 144, 154
    networks 143, 144, 156, 159, 161
    prestige goods 9, 71, 82, 84, 92
    route 20, 132, 137, 144, 356
trading post 15
Transitional period 258–60
tree
    ceiba 197, 298
    rubber 298
Tres Lagunas 6, 10, 127, 355
Tres Zapotes 9
triadic structure, double 10
Triple Alliance 222, 359
T-shaped platform 75
Tula 3, 23–4, 194, 220, 222, 224, 254, 259, 277
Tula Grande 254, 259
Tulane University 2, 59, 172–3, 285, 288–9, 301
Tulum 1, 6, 27, 292–4, 296–7, 300, 302, 352, 358
Tulum mural 293–4
Tulum-Tancah 27
turquoise 22, 24
twisted cord 293
Type-Variety classification 51, 153
Tzompantli 255, 256, 259
Tzotzil 299

U K'it Kan Le'k Tok' 16–18, 30
Uaxactun 77, 96
Uaymil 6, 23, 161
Ucareo 22, 236, 256
Uci 10, 13, 119, 129–31, 355
UCRIP 119, 129, 130, 138
Ulila 54
Ulumal 6, 147, 149–53, 155, 157, 159–62
umbilical cord 291
underworld 196–7, 220
Uneh Chan 104, 108
universality 319
Upper Temple of the Jaguars 213, 255, 257, 259, 269, 270

upperworld 196–7, 219
urban centers 119, 124, 132, 137, 325, 333–4, 356
urbanism 15, 119, 122, 124–6, 132, 137, 191, 350, 353
U-shaped throne 205
Usumacinta region 156, 162
Uxmal 1, 3, 18–19, 23–5, 69, 191–4, 196–9, 201–2, 205–8, 210–13, 215, 217, 219–25, 266, 270, 279, 350, 352, 357, 359
    collapse 19, 25
Uxul 101

Valladolid 229, 236, 273, 329
Valley of Mexico 9
Valley of Oaxaca 9, 25, 72, 80, 82, 92
Venus Platform 233, 235, 237, 247, 251, 254–5, 259
Veracruz 9, 22, 58, 135, 144–5, 155–6, 158, 161–2, 214
Victoria 6, 127, 128, 355
Villa Madero 152
villages 5, 56, 75, 90, 92, 298, 338, 360, 362
    autonomy 90
    life 5, 7, 29
    satellite 91
visions 68
V-shaped motifs 205, 208

waist belts 47
Wakna 92, 96
Waldeck 215
wall 75, 220, 244, 264, 315, 356, 357
    Ake 264
    barricade 267
    bench 46
    boundary 122, 280, 356, 359
    buttress 236, 252, 256–7, 259, 273–8
    cave 286
    Chichen Itza 236, 264
    defensive 3, 276–7, 279
    defining sacred space 3
    Early Great Platform 258
    garden plot 94
    Great Platform 248
    houselot 126, 130, 309
    load-bearing 16
    perimeter 265
    retaining wall 127, 129
    site perimeter 265–8
    social control 264
    social space 269
    stone 122, 126
    stucco 258
    trenches 130
    water management 268
    wattle-and-daub 80

war 47, 71–2, 90, 97, 205–8, 210, 213, 221–2, 265, 271, 300
    council house 221–2
    captives 300
    council 205, 208, 221
    prisoners 90
    serpent 207
warfare 70, 208, 210, 264–7, 269, 272, 279
    endemic 20
warriors 91, 108, 207–8, 211, 213, 215, 221–2, 269, 299–300
    professional 90
water jars 286, 289, 298, 301
water management 266–7, 277
water storage 340
wealth 28, 68, 71, 80, 82, 126, 306, 310–13, 318–21
    distribution 315, 317; see economic inequality
weaving 291
West Colonnade 233–5, 239, 250–51, 254, 258
Western Gate 235
wetlands 327
Woman of Hoyo Negro 4
Woman of Las Palmas 4
world creation 298
world religion 19, 24

Xaman Susula, collapse 82
Xanila 48, 50–51, 78
Xaya 183
Xcalumkin 6, 25, 175, 357
Xcambo 6, 13–14, 120, 132–3, 135–7, 153, 157, 355

Xelha 6, 27–8
Xicalango 144
Xipe Totec 299–303
Xiu 27, 29, 224, 306, 331, 341
Xkipche 20
Xocaneh 8
Xochicalco 24, 210, 220
Xocnaceh 6–9, 66, 78, 81, 353
Xolalpan phase 135
Xtobo 8, 10, 52, 54–5, 59, 66, 73, 75, 77, 79, 81–3, 353
Xtukil 184
Xulnal 92

Yalahau 10, 12, 30, 127, 175, 353
Yalahau region 10, 12, 30, 127
Yaxcaba 329, 332–3, 337, 340, 342
Yaxchilan Lintel 24, 203
Yaxcopoil 6, 128
Yaxper 291, 293
Yaxuna 6, 8, 10, 12, 19–20, 25, 133, 135–6, 266, 279, 354–5, 360
yearbearer 298
Young Man of Hol Chan 4
Yucatan peninsula 1, 144–5, 155, 157, 161, 326, 329, 341
Yula 6, 360

Zacualtipan 22
Zapotecs 222, 225
Zaragoza 22, 236

CPSIA information can be obtained
at www.ICGtesting.com
Printed in the USA
JSHW021034271219
3113JS00002BB/144